Witness to the Young Republic

Benjamin Brown French at about sixty-five, from an original painting by Constantino Brumidi. (Courtesy Peter S. French)

BENJAMIN BROWN FRENCH

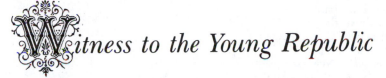

Witness to the Young Republic

A Yankee's Journal, 1828–1870

Edited by

Donald B. Cole and John J. McDonough

University Press of New England

Hanover and London

UNIVERSITY PRESS OF NEW ENGLAND
Brandeis University
Brown University
Clark University
University of Connecticut
Dartmouth College
University of New Hampshire
University of Rhode Island
Tufts University
University of Vermont

Printed in the United States of America

Designed and produced by Christopher Harris/Summer Hill Books
Perkinsville, Vermont

∞

Library of Congress Cataloging-in-Publication Data

French, Benjamin B. (Benjamin Brown), 1800–1870.
 [Diaries. Selections]
 Witness to the young republic : a yankee's journal, 1828–1870 /
Benjamin Brown French ; Donald B. Cole and John J. McDonough,
editors.
 p. cm.
 Bibliography: p.
 Includes index.
 ISBN 0-87451-467-3
 1. United States—Politics and government—1815–1861. 2. United States—
History—Civil War, 1861–1865—Personal narratives. 3. Washington (D.C.)—
History—Civil War, 1861–1865—Personal narratives. 4. French, Benjamin B.
(Benjamin Brown) 1800–1870—Diaries. 5. Politicians—United States—
Diaries. I. Cole, Donald B. II. McDonough, John J. (John Joseph),
1926–   . III. Title.
E338.F74 1989
973.6—dc19   88-39145
                                                        CIP

5 4 3 2 1

For my sister Constance
Donald B. Cole

For my wife Dorothy and
my mother Madrienne
John J. McDonough

Contents

Maps and Illustrations

Preface

The journal of Benjamin Brown French opens a window on the world of an upper-class Northern public servant whose career spanned the years from the Age of Jackson through the Civil War and Reconstruction. The view from this window is wide since French traveled throughout the North, and his interests included law, journalism, literature, the writing of poetry, farming, Freemasonry, politics, government, and telegraphy. As a young politician in New Hampshire and later as a quintessential man-about-Washington, French made it his business to know important people and to write about them in his journal. He was indeed a witness to the young republic. Since he cared deeply about his family, his journal also presents an intimate picture of family life at the time.

The journal is a long one. Between the first entry in 1828 and the last in 1870, French found time to write over 3,700 pages, of which about a third have been selected for this edition. In making these selections we have chosen passages on the basis of their interest and historical value. We have included, for example, all references to prominent men and women, as well as French's many character sketches. Most of the material relating to politics, Andrew Jackson, Abraham Lincoln, slavery, and the Civil War has been retained, as well as much valuable social and economic information. Enough detail concerning French and his family and friends has been preserved to tell the vivid human story. We have used ellipsis points to show where entries have been abbreviated, and we have included a calendar of the complete journal so that the reader will know which entries have been entirely omitted. Scholars may consult the missing passages in the complete microfilm edition of French's journal and other papers at the Library of Congress.

Our intent throughout has been to present the text as French wrote it; the words are all his except for the few that have been bracketed. In the interests of consistency and clarity, however, we have made a few changes in punctuation and spelling. Some of the commas and dashes, which French used much too liberally, have been removed or replaced silently by other marks of punctuation. To avoid incomplete or run-on sentences we have occasionally created new ones, and sentences without periods have had them added, in each case without mention. Otherwise, when marks of punctuation have been added, brackets have been used. The punctuation of dates and addresses has been regularized silently, and the datelines at the start of each entry have been made uniform in style. The place at which an entry was written is cited only when it differs from the previous entry.

French spelled well, and we have generally left his spelling as it is. We have not tried to improve on nineteenth-century spelling or usage; "eat," for example, meaning "ate," stands unchanged. Capitalization or the lack of it is also retained. Thus, the word "Negro" is left uncapitalized. On occasion, however, we have corrected careless spelling errors without notice. In the case of proper names we have used French's spelling for the first reference, corrected it if necessary in the footnote, and used the correct spelling thereafter. A consistent policy has been established for the use of italics or quotation marks when referring to books, plays, poems, paintings, and names of ships.

We have tried to identify each person when first mentioned in the text. In the interest of brevity we have restricted our notes to birth and death dates (when available) and essential information pertinent to the context. For congressmen and senators we have included party affiliation and dates of service.

Historians have been aware of the existence of the French journal for many years. In 1904 Amos Tuck French, a grandson, edited a 136-page volume, *From the Diary and Correspondence of Benjamin Brown French,* but had only a few copies printed for private circulation. French's family correspondence was acquired by the Library of Congress in 1922 and 1936. The journal, however, was not acquired until 1970, when Stuyvesant Leroy French, the son of Amos Tuck French, added it to the papers of Benjamin Brown French at the Library. Our edition of the journal is designed to introduce French to the American public.

D. B. C.
December 1988   J. J. McD.

Acknowledgments

While on the trail of the generous, good-natured Benjamin Brown French we found many equally generous, good-natured people who helped make this book possible. Among the many assisting us at the Library of Congress we wish to mention Gillian Anderson, Patrick Dempsey, Mary Anne Ferrarese, James Gilreath, John Knowlton, Oliver Orr, Ford Peatross, John R. Sellers, Norman Shaffer, Richard Stephenson, John Wolter, and Virginia Wood. The staff at the New Hampshire Historical Society was uniformly affable and efficient. Jacquelyn H. Thomas and her staff at the Phillips Exeter Academy Library provided their usual friendly encouragement and professional skill.

Others who helped along the way were Inge Baum at the Library of the Scottish Rite of Freemasonry, Washington, D.C.; Ellen Clark of the Mount Vernon Ladies Association; Sister Mada-anne Gell, VHM, of Georgetown Visitation Preparatory School; Abby L. Gilbert of the Treasury Department; John F. Hackett of the Office of the Architect of the Capitol; Kathleen C. McDonough, New Hampshire State Library; Myriam Marshall, Georgetown University Archives; Betty Claire Monkman, Office of the Curator of the White House; Alan Virta, Boise State University; and Donna Wells, Gallaudet College.

We are thankful to Courtney Stewart Delaney and to John J. McDonough III for preparing our maps. Krista Anderson, Dorothy M. McDonough, and Courtenay Thomas did a superb job of typing directly from a photocopy of the handwritten manuscript. Dorothy also prepared the calendar; she was really a third editor. Susan A. Cole and Richard F. Niebling helped prepare the manuscript for the publisher.

Much of the financial burden of the project was borne by the National Historical Publications and Records Commission (NHPRC), which provided three generous grants, and by Phillips Exeter Academy, which served as the co-sponsoring institution. We are grateful to Charles C. McLaughlin, Harold D. Moser, and Robert V. Remini for helping us persuade the NHPRC that the project deserved support. At the NHPRC we are particularly indebted to Frank G. Burke, Sandra Anderson, Roger Bruns, Mary Giunta, and Sarah Jackson. At Exeter, James A. Del Buono and his business staff helped the project run smoothly. Additional support came from former principal Stephen G. Kurtz and the trustees of Phillips Exeter, who granted one of us a sabbatical leave, and from the Lillian Radford Trust of Houston, which provided the same editor with a generous research grant.

The editors appreciate that at the University Press of New England Director Thomas L. McFarland, Managing Editor Mary Crittendon, and Charles Backus, now director of Syracuse University Press, were almost as excited about the project as we were. Above all, we wish to thank Peter and Katherine French for their interest and many kindnesses, and particularly for their willingness to let us have copies made of family photographs and paintings. They share our delight in making the journal of Peter's great-great-grandfather available to the public.

Benjamin and Elizabeth French were part of large, loving families and so are we. Dorothy, Tootie, and the many children and grandchildren have kept us going.

D. B. C.

J. J. McD.

December 1988

Chronology of Benjamin Brown French

1800	Born in Chester, N.H.
1811, 1815–1817	At North Yarmouth, Maine
1819	Serves briefly in army
1819–1824	Studies law under father
1825	Marries Elizabeth Richardson
1825	Starts law practice in Sutton, N.H.
1827	Moves to Newport, N.H.; clerk of courts, Sullivan County
1828–1830	Assistant clerk, N.H. Senate
1829–1833	Editor and proprietor, *New Hampshire Spectator*
1831–1833	Represents Newport in N.H. House of Representatives
1833	Serves on committee to meet Andrew Jackson in Boston
1833	Moves to Washington
1833–1845	Works in Clerk's office, U.S. House of Representatives
1837	Son Francis born
1842	Moves into house at 37 East Capitol St.
1843	Son Benjamin born
1845–1847	Clerk of House of Representatives
1847–1853, 1868	Grand Master, District of Columbia Masons
1847–1850	President, Magnetic Telegraph Company
1853–1855	Commissioner of Public Buildings
1855	Elected treasurer of U.S. Agricultural Society
1856	Moves from Democratic to Republican party
1859–1865	Grand Master of the Knights Templar of the U.S.
1860–1861	Clerk of the committee of claims of the House of Representatives

1861	Chief marshal for inaugural parade of President Lincoln
1861	Elizabeth French dies
1861–1867	Commissioner of Public Buildings
1862	Marries Mary Ellen Brady
1865–1870	Trustee, Columbia Institution for the Deaf and Dumb
1867	Takes clerkship in Treasury Department
1870	Dies in Washington

Witness to the Young Republic

Introduction

One January evening in 1825 a solidly built young man of twenty-four and a slight, brown-eyed woman of nineteen slipped out of their homes in Chester, New Hampshire, met with a minister down a country lane, and were secretly married. In later years this unconventional act, which was kept hidden for six months, seemed out of character for the rather proper Benjamin Brown French, though not so for the outspoken, strong-minded Elizabeth Richardson French. At the time, however, it was only one in a series of acts in which the young French rebelled against tradition and authority.

Benjamin's father, Daniel French, had moved to Chester in 1799 to take over a law practice and had married Mercy Brown, daughter of Benjamin Brown, the town's leading merchant. Perched on a ridge half-way between the Atlantic seacoast and the Merrimack River valley, Chester had begun to produce a long list of politicians, judges, attorneys, clergymen, editors, and businessmen. Daniel French ranked among these, for he rose to be the Federalist state attorney general during the War of 1812 and became renowned as the mentor of many law students who went on to establish their own reputations. By 1825 Daniel had built the largest house in Chester and was the town's principal taxpayer.

Mercy Brown French gave birth to Benjamin Brown French on September 4, 1800, and then died eighteen months later, leaving her husband with an infant to raise. Daniel French married twice more—first Betsey Flagg, the granddaughter of Ebenezer Flagg, who had preached in Chester for nearly sixty years; and when Betsey died in 1812, her sister, the widow Sarah Flagg Bell, became his third wife. When Benjamin married Elizabeth Richardson in secret in 1825, he was the eldest in a family of four sons and seven daughters.

Never at ease with his father, Benjamin was twice sent off to North Yarmouth, Maine, where he studied under his uncle Francis Brown and at the local academy. Brown, a Federalist Congregational clergyman,

1

later became president of Dartmouth College during the struggle between the college and the state of New Hampshire that culminated in
the Dartmouth College Supreme Court case. After studying law with his
father for two years, in 1819 French ran away to an island in Boston
Harbor and enlisted in the U.S. Army under Lieutenant Benjamin Louis
E. de Bonneville, later made famous by Washington Irving's stories of
his adventures in the fur trade. Tracked down by his family two months
later, Benjamin was brought back to resume his studies.

Elizabeth Richardson moved to Chester at this time, when her father,
Chief Justice William M. Richardson of the New Hampshire Superior
Court, took his family there from Portsmouth. He was a stern, imposing
man, who had stood up to President Brown in the Dartmouth College
case, and Benjamin found him so intimidating that he dared not ask
him for Elizabeth's hand. When the two lovers finally revealed that they
were married, they found both families unsympathetic because Benjamin
had no job and no income. His grandmother declared that he had disgraced the family.

Despite this inauspicious start, French moved rapidly into a career in
law, politics, and journalism, but he continued his unorthodox ways by
moving to Sutton, New Hampshire. Forty miles to the northwest, nestled
between Mount Kearsarge and Lake Sunapee, Sutton was far more rustic
than Chester. Settled after the Revolution, it had few of the stately homes,
business establishments, and stagecoach lines that Chester could boast.
It was Baptist rather than Congregational, Republican-Democratic rather
than Federalist-Whig, and it looked west to Newport and Claremont in
the Connecticut Valley rather than east to Exeter and Portsmouth on the
seacoast. The young couple spent two happy years in Sutton—Benjamin
practicing law, hunting, and serving in the militia, and Elizabeth, or
"Bess" as she was called, taking in boarders to help pay the rent.

In 1827 they moved to Newport, where Benjamin—now a major in
the militia and called "Major" ever after—soon took over management
of the *New Hampshire Spectator*. Still rebellious, he deserted his family's
party and served as a Jacksonian Democrat in the state's lower house
from 1831 to 1833. His career paralleled that of Franklin Pierce, who
was admitted to the bar in 1827, elected to the House in 1829, and
named speaker in 1831. He and French became good friends, and one
of the early entries in French's journal describes a wrestling match in
which the twenty-six-year-old Pierce pinned the thirty-one-year-old
French three or four times. Both enjoyed good fellowship and merry-
making and were drawn to attractive women; in his journal French reports Pierce in *"raptures"* over Fanny Kemble on seeing her on the stage.[1]

In 1833 French was on a committee that traveled to Boston to invite Andrew Jackson to visit Concord during his tour of the northeast. Jackson agreed and made Concord his last stop before returning to Washington. The journal for June 1833 contains a vivid description of the scene in Boston when Jackson arrived, with French declaring that the crowd was so tightly packed that "a person could have walked upon the heads and shoulders of the multitude."[2]

Pierce and French moved to Washington late in 1833, Pierce a congressman and French an assistant clerk in the House of Representatives. Leaving Elizabeth in Chester, French boarded with Pierce and other Democrats near the Capitol building. Though complaining that he was lonely for Elizabeth and New Hampshire, French enjoyed himself in the nation's capital, working long hours in the House, making dozens of new friends, going about the city in the evening, and watching political giants such as Henry Clay and Thomas Hart Benton battle over the Bank of the United States and other national issues.

As an assistant clerk French had to conform to the calendar of the Congress, which met the first Monday of every December and remained in session until March on odd-numbered years and until midsummer on even-numbered years. While Congress was in session, he was extremely busy reading and recording bills, tabulating votes, and in general helping to keep the House running smoothly. Like the members of Congress, he was able to take a long vacation in the summer and early fall, and he used this time to travel back to New Hampshire. Since French's move to Washington coincided with the advent of the railroad, he was able to use this new form of transportation almost from its start. In November 1835, for example, while returning to Washington, he traveled by train from Lowell, Massachusetts, to Providence, Rhode Island, boarded a steamboat for New York City, crossed New Jersey by train to the Delaware River, proceeded downstream by steamer to Philadelphia and New Castle, took a train to the head of Chesapeake Bay, embarked once again on a steamer to Baltimore, and then came on by train to Washington. This trip took four days but was later cut to three.

When Elizabeth joined him in Washington, the couple first stayed at a boardinghouse, but after the birth of their first son, Francis, in 1837, a small house was rented on Capitol Hill. In a few years they were able to build a house of their own on a large lot at 37 East Capitol Street, later part of the site for the Library of Congress. Here their second and last child, Benjamin, was born in 1845, and here they stayed until they died. Life was active at 37 East Capitol because the Frenches frequently had relatives or other guests staying overnight or for weeks at a time.

Since French kept a careful record of what his family and visitors said and did, a detailed sketch of life in a busy, well-to-do Washington home during the middle of the nineteenth century emerges in the journal.

Benjamin and Elizabeth were not the only Frenches and Richardsons living in Washington. Simon Brown, the husband of Benjamin's oldest sister, Ann, was librarian for the House of Representatives before moving to Concord, Massachusetts, and becoming editor of the *New England Farmer.* Benjamin managed to find a government job for his youngest brother, Edmund, who married Margaret Brady in 1848 and began to raise a large family on a small salary. He also arranged a position for the Reverend Charles P. Russell, who had married Elizabeth's youngest sister, Louisa. By the outbreak of the Civil War, Benjamin and Elizabeth had almost a dozen nieces and nephews in Washington.

On their trips north the Frenches frequently stopped in Brooklyn with either Benjamin's sister Catharine, who was married to Dr. P. P. Wells, or with another sister, Ariana, who had married Charles Soule. In Massachusetts they could stay in Concord with the Browns or on Rainsford Island in Boston Harbor with Elizabeth's oldest sister, Sarah, and her husband, Dr. Lemuel Barker. North of Concord, in Lancaster, Massachusetts, they occasionally visited Elizabeth's sister Mary and her husband, John S. J. Vose.

Other Frenches had remained in New Hampshire—unmarried sisters Harriette, Elizabeth, and Helen in Chester, and brother Henry Flagg French in Exeter. Even though Henry was eleven years his junior, Benjamin felt close to him, especially when Henry married Elizabeth's sister Anne in 1838. Henry stayed in Chester as his father's law partner until the old man's death in 1840, then moved to Exeter, where he advanced from county solicitor to judge of the court of common pleas. Henry and Anne had four children, the youngest of whom, Daniel Chester French, became one of America's most famous sculptors, known especially for his statue of Abraham Lincoln in the Lincoln Memorial.

After the death of Daniel French, the family home was maintained by Benjamin's stepmother, Sarah Flagg French, until her own death in 1878. The three-story mansion, considered by some the handsomest house in Chester, was as much a family focal point as 37 East Capitol. Chester always remained a haven for Benjamin and stirred his heart—the familiar old house, the tree on which he and his brothers and sisters had carved their names, the lane where he and Elizabeth had been married, the graveyard where his mother was buried, the woods in which he had hunted, and Lake Massabesic, where he had fished and where the family continued to have picnics.

The elaborate family structure, with one focus in Chester and another in Washington, enhances the value of French's journal as family history. Details of marriage customs and attitudes appear from the time of the Frenches' secret marriage to the time late in the journal when Benjamin chose not to attend the marriage of his younger son, from whom he had become somewhat estranged. The most traditional marriage occurred when his first son, Francis Ormond French, married Ellen Tuck, the daughter of prominent Exeter attorney and former congressman, Amos Tuck, uniting two of the leading families in New Hampshire. Unfortunately, the event took place under a cloud, coming as it did on March 5, 1861, one month before the outbreak of the Civil War and two months before the death of Elizabeth from cancer. After her death Benjamin soon fell in love with his brother Edmund's sister-in-law, Mary Ellen Brady, who had nursed Elizabeth throughout her illness and then stayed on to manage Benjamin's household. Only a few family members appear to have criticized this arrangement or the marriage that followed.

The journal also offers glimpses of nineteenth-century child rearing. Francis Ormond French caused his parents scarcely a moment of worry as he moved smoothly from Phillips Exeter Academy to Harvard and finally to law school. He was an outstanding success in law and banking. His brother, Benjamin, on the other hand, rather like his father, fought authority, refused to study, failed at Exeter, drank too much, stayed up all hours of the night chasing fire engines, and then slept until eleven in the morning. But unlike his father, young Benjamin did not change his ways after marriage, and he shamed his father by failing to provide for his wife and child. The journal offers little evidence that fathers exercised harsh or even firm control over their children.

Nor did they rule their wives. Elizabeth French, who had shown a rebellious streak by marrying without her parents' consent, was rarely cowed by Benjamin. She good-naturedly made fun of his letters, nagged him about staying out too late, warned him of the evils of drink, and generally ordered his life. Elizabeth's mother also proved to be full of spirit when Benjamin tried to interfere in settling her husband's estate. Since none of the French or Richardson women was employed outside the home, the journal reinforces the concept that nineteenth-century men and women occupied separate spheres, but within their sphere the women were not dominated by men.

These women did not live easy lives. The many pregnancies and the high percentage of children dying at birth give ample evidence of the way that women suffered. Margaret Brady French bore fourteen children and saw six die before becoming adults. Daniel French had eleven children by three wives, of whom two wives and three children died early in life. Benjamin Brown French's maternal grandparents, Benjamin and

Prudence Brown, had six children, of whom four died before reaching thirty.

Illness and death were common. French suffered increasingly from headaches, dizziness, and finally from gallstones. He also endured frequent toothaches, usually without going to the dentist because extractions were so crude and painful. Once he paced back and forth for over an hour in front of the dentist's office, finally losing his nerve and going home to daub creosote on the offending tooth. Elizabeth, after several years of dizziness, headaches, and pain, sought advice from doctors in New York before finally discovering that she had breast cancer. She underwent a mastectomy with the assistance of anesthesia in November 1860 and lived barely long enough to see Francis married and the Civil War begin. A number of young people—Benjamin's sisters Harriette and Elizabeth and Mary Ellen's sister Sarita—were ill throughout most of their short lives.

In spite of the hazards, French and those around him appear to have led happy, often festive lives. Since French was a convivial man who enjoyed people and parties, we are treated to a succession of intimate descriptions of recreation among the prosperous. Hunting or fishing in the early mornings, billiards or bowling for an idle noontime hour, baseball in the afternoon, and croquet at teatime helped the days pass easily. Pleasant excursions down the Potomac and charming picnics at Lake Massabesic or along the Concord River could occupy an entire day. More ambitious events included a week-long tour of the White Mountains; a sailing trip from Boston Harbor to Gloucester, Marblehead, and Salem; and a cruise to the Isles of Shoals off the coast of New Hampshire. Menus for these affairs often defy description, but an eight-pound lobster featured at one deserves special mention.

On a typical evening a group of French's friends and relations would drop by for several hours of conversation or games—perhaps euchre, whist, or cribbage. Usually the parlor was filled with people, some playing cards, others chatting or writing letters. There is a fascinating description of an evening in Concord when some of the young people (including Daniel Chester French, who was already experimenting with artistic expression) put on a show in which they projected silhouettes on a screen by shining a light behind objects of various shapes. On more than one evening French reports reading John Greenleaf Whittier's *Snow-Bound* aloud to a group of his brothers and sisters and their children. Family letters were also read aloud, as well as articles and stories from current periodicals. There was much eating and drinking—cakes, ice cream, lemonade, whiskey punch—more than Benjamin and several of his stout sisters needed. The evenings generally ended by ten-thirty or eleven.

French describes his work as much as his play. As a Democrat, his fortunes at first depended on the political success of the Jacksonians. He advanced from assistant clerk to chief clerk in the House of Representatives during Martin Van Buren's presidency and finally to Clerk of the House following James K. Polk's election; but when the Whigs took control of the House in 1847, French was dismissed from office. In his journal he explains in detail the political maneuverings that swirled around the Clerk's office.

French's dismissal coincided, fortunately, with his growing involvement in telegraphy. Thanks to pressure from his former boardinghouse messmate, Francis O. J. Smith, and Amos Kendall, business manager for Samuel F. B. Morse's telegraph, French had invested in the business. This soon led to his election as a director and eventually as president of the Magnetic Telegraph Company. Even though he was later eased out of the presidency, he remained involved in the company.

French had other sources of income as well. In 1847 he had investments in western land, Washington real estate, railroads, bank stock, and other stocks and bonds. Later he spread out into insurance companies and stone quarries. The business experience acquired from these enterprises and his familiarity with Washington made French a natural agent and lobbyist. Seeking additional income in 1850, he set up an agency to assist clients in collecting claims from the government.

In spite of these many interests, French was eager to regain a place in the U.S. government following Franklin Pierce's election as President in 1852. French was given the office of commissioner of public buildings but was removed two years later because of his association with the Know-Nothing party. This dalliance with the Know-Nothings was the first step in French's transition from the Democratic party to the Republican party. In 1861 Abraham Lincoln reappointed French commissioner of public buildings.

Since French was particularly attentive to his journal during these years, it is of considerable value for its commentary on Lincoln, whom he saw often, and on the atmosphere of wartime Washington. As an old militia officer the Major felt qualified to remark on military strategy and did so freely. His description of events surrounding the first Battle of Bull Run provides an exceptionally vivid portrayal of conditions in the nation's capital at that painful time.

One of French's more pleasant duties was presenting visitors to Mary Lincoln at her many receptions. When Willie Lincoln died, however, French had the less pleasant task of making the funeral arrangements. After Lincoln's assassination French again had to make plans for the funeral and later had to answer charges that Mary Lincoln had misappropriated public belongings when she left the White House. French stayed on as commissioner for two more years, under Andrew Johnson, and then was pushed out of his job by radical Republicans when he supported the President during the battle over Reconstruction.

French's performance as clerk and commissioner does not constitute his complete record, nor does it provide the full measure of the man. His amiability, common sense, and skill in speaking and writing led to dozens of other positions. He served on a committee to observe the anniversary of the burning of Washington by the British and on another to raise funds for soldiers' families. He was trustee of the Columbia Institution for the Deaf and Dumb. In addition, he helped govern the District of Columbia as a member of the water board, the committee on streets, the common council, and the board of aldermen. A leading Republican, he was a natural selection as chief marshal for Lincoln's first inauguration and as a member of the second inaugural ball committee.

Two positions that broadened his outlook by taking him out of Washington were grand master in the order of Freemasonry and treasurer of the U.S. Agricultural Society. From the death of George Washington to the Civil War those charged with laying the cornerstones of new buildings in the District of Columbia used the services of the grand masters of the Washington Lodge, including French, who would don the mason's apron and wield the trowel that had passed down from Washington himself. When President Millard Fillmore, who owed his rise to the Anti-Masons, was unwilling to ask the Masons to take part in dedicating the extension of the Capitol building in 1851, the outcry was such that he had to back down and invite French and the Masons to perform. One of French's great moments as a Mason took place in 1867, when he accompanied Andrew Johnson to Boston for a national meeting of the Masonic Knights Templar, of which French had also been grand master.

French had always been interested in farming. He loved his own garden, and he enjoyed discussing agriculture with Simon Brown and with Henry Flagg French, who was briefly president of the Massachusetts College of Agriculture. In one entry he describes a happy afternoon helping Brown prune his apple trees. French's role as treasurer of the U.S. Agricultural Society took him on several tours of the West, including trips to Lexington and Louisville, Kentucky. His position also brought him close to the society's president, the eccentric Ben Perley Poore, a difficult man with whom even the good-natured French had trouble working.

French's delight in meeting people, his skill in sizing them up, and his ability to record his impressions in pithy prose made him an excellent "journalist," to use his own term. Not only did he tell a story well, but he rarely failed to give his opinion. Not as strong as he would like to have been but invariably stronger than he realized, he was adept at detecting strength and weakness in others. Although he worried more than was necessary and felt too often that others were taking advantage of him, he developed a philosophy that carried him through life. When his fortunes were at a low ebb, he was comforted by the belief that the pendulum would eventually swing back in his direction. A favorite expression was "I bide my time," and he never used it more aptly than in 1869 when he learned that Elizabeth's nephew, William A. Richardson, was to become Assistant Secretary of the Treasury and would be able to help him.

Philosophic as he was, French could still be petty and self-righteous, quick to make unkind observations about those who treated him badly. But he had too much love for humankind and he was too sentimental to remain angry for long; he almost always recanted and strove to make amends. After ridiculing Ben Perley Poore, for example, French atoned by citing his friend's better qualities.

French's love of politics makes his journal a storehouse of political information. One of the first entries after his arrival in Washington contains his opinions of Andrew Jackson, Henry Clay, and Amos Kendall; and one of the last, thirty-seven years later, makes a bitter comparison of Attorney General Ebenezer R. Hoar and Secretary of the Treasury George S. Boutwell. Every President from John Quincy Adams to Ulysses S. Grant came under French's not always friendly scrutiny. Adams he called a troublemaker over the question of slavery, Martin Van Buren was "cold as an icicle,"[3] William Henry Harrison a "broken-down old man,"[4] John Tyler "vacillating,"[5] and James K. Polk, who sat with French on the Jackson statue committee, too cautious. Zachary Taylor, whom he accompanied on a trip to Richmond, was considered incompetent; Millard Fillmore was ridiculed because of his Anti-Masonry; Franklin Pierce became two-faced and ungrateful; James Buchanan was a "weak old man";[6] Andrew Johnson was naive; and Grant was unwilling to take advice. Only Jackson and Lincoln came off unscathed. But French's innate kindness usually won out, and in the end most of the Presidents received a more favorable assessment. In 1868 French, who had held a grudge against Pierce for years, finally paid a friendly visit at the former President's summer home overlooking the ocean at Little Boar's Head, New Hampshire. Within two years both men were dead.

French observed lesser figures with equal keenness. Among those from northern New England, congressman and telegraph entrepreneur Francis O. J. Smith of Maine was his favorite. Family ties made him the confidant of Amos Tuck, a founder of the Republican party in New

Hampshire, and John S. Keyes, the powerful sheriff of Middlesex County, Massachusetts. Aside from Lincoln the man he most admired in politics was Joshua R. Giddings, the antislavery congressman from Ohio.

It is worth noting that of these all but Smith were Whigs and thus French's political opponents. French was never so committed to a political party that he made enemies in the other camp. When the party system underwent a major transformation in the 1850s, French shifted from the Democrats to the Republicans. But like many Democrats who switched he was never wholly Republican in his views, and when the Civil War was over he found himself closer to Andrew Johnson, also a former Democrat, than to the radical Republicans. He supported Democrat Horatio Seymour in 1868, and had he lived until 1876, he would undoubtedly have backed the Democratic candidate, Samuel J. Tilden, another old Jacksonian, who was as conservative, literate, and interested in sound investments as was French.

Like many white Northerners, French wavered on the issue of slavery during the era of the Civil War. True to his conservative nature and his Democratic politics, French entered the 1850s in sympathy with the slaveowners. After visiting Michael B. Carroll's large Maryland plantation in 1851, French reported that the slaves were happy and well clad—the women, he insisted, better dressed than farm wives in New Hampshire. He emphatically disagreed with a visiting minister who favored abolishing slavery, and he was in many respects a typical doughface, or Northern Democrat with Southern principles.

Later, frightened by Southern expansionism and influenced by antislavery congressmen such as Giddings and Tuck, he began to have doubts. He bitterly attacked Pierce and Stephen A. Douglas for the Kansas-Nebraska Act in 1854, noting that he wanted slavery abolished—not at once, to be sure, but "gradually."[7] John Brown's raid in 1859 alarmed him and checked his abolitionism. On the eve of the Civil War, French was a moderate Republican opposed to the spread of slavery but also opposed to "hotheads,"[8] both Northern and Southern, who endangered the Union.

After emancipation French disapproved of giving blacks equal rights. He wrote on one occasion that the freedmen were aggressive and hard to get along with. When one black woman sued for the right to ride on a railroad car reserved for whites, French accused her of trying to create an issue.

In the summer of 1870 French spent his last months in familiar ways. Always a capable handyman, he renewed the oilcloth and the floor in his dining room in June. Always a patriot and still with an unruly streak, he fired his Colt revolver out the window on the Fourth of July. As one of the "Oldest Inhabitants" of the city, he took part in a ceremony presenting a handsome block of marble to those in charge of constructing the Washington Monument. Still fond of food, he devoted part of one entry to an account of buying ice cream. On July 27 he took a final excursion down the Potomac, this one sponsored by Henry D. Cooke, the wealthy banker and brother of Jay Cooke. The invitation was appropriate because in that same year Francis Ormond French began a decade-long business association with the Cookes. Reminiscing on July 23, French described the old days when he was studying with his father and courting Elizabeth Richardson.

Assistant Secretary of the Treasury William A. Richardson was boarding with the Frenches at the end of July when Benjamin first mentioned that he was suffering from shortness of breath. On August 8, feeling ill, he decided to put down his pen when Mary Ellen, calling from downstairs, told him to rest. "*I obey,*"[9] he wrote and never picked up his pen again. He died at 1:00 A.M. on August 12.

Several years earlier French had watched the solemn funeral procession for Abraham Lincoln and the great review for the Union army in Washington. He had also enjoyed elaborate Masonic parades in Chicago, St. Louis, Baltimore, Washington, and elsewhere. It was, therefore, unfortunate that he was not able to record his impressions of the enormous funeral procession staged by the Masons in honor of their late grand master, Benjamin Brown French, on August 14, 1870—the greatest event, according to his niece, Mary French, ever put on for a private citizen in the nation's capital. It was the sort of event that French would have appreciated.

All footnotes for this introduction and for the introductions to each chapter refer to entries in the journal unless otherwise indicated.

1. Jan. 14, 1834.
2. July 20, 1833.
3. June 19, 1840.
4. April 1, 1841.
5. June 11, 1843.

6. Jan. 1, 1861.
7. April 25, 1857.
8. Nov. 4, 1860.
9. Aug. 8, 1870.

ONE

The New Hampshire Years

1828–1835

orn in 1800, Benjamin Brown French moved through much of the nineteenth century in step with the events of those times. As a diarist, he commences briskly, and with only a few false starts soon finds his style and hits his stride. Neither was to desert him for the next forty-two years.

In August 1828 French and his wife Bess were living in Newport, New Hampshire, a small town on the Sugar River, fifteen miles east of Claremont and ten miles west of Sunapee Lake. While here, French was employed as county clerk of courts, proprietor and editor of the *New Hampshire Spectator,* and assistant clerk of the New Hampshire senate. He was later a member of the lower house for three years. At Concord it was possible to know most of the principals involved in state affairs, and French clearly found enjoyment and satisfaction in mingling with them and sharing in their deliberations and activities. This and other character traits quickly emerge in French's journal and remain on display throughout his life. His patriotism, his deep sense of family and the pleasure he took in company, his heartiness as well as his tendency to become melancholy, his curiosity and openness to new impressions (but not always new ideas), his tenderheartedness and sentimentality are among these qualities, as well as the pride he took in himself as a hunter and fisherman. In matters of religion French reveals himself to be a free, but not profound, thinker. He was respectful toward religion but remained suspicious and distrustful of the demands of orthodoxy.

French also seems to have had a gift for being in the right place at the right time. In only the second entry in his journal, made while visiting Nantasket Beach, south of Boston, he spotted President John Quincy Adams and described him, deftly and unforgettably, as dressed in "a black coat, yellow nankin pantaloons & a blue cloth cap."[1] In the summer of 1834, while traveling by stage and ship from Washington to New Hampshire, French was at various times in the company of Nicholas

Biddle, John Quincy Adams, Achille Murat (the one-time crown prince of Naples) and an unnamed gentleman from whom he received a lecture on Swedenborgianism. Such chance encounters were to occur again and again in French's life, whether with the notable, the interesting, or the merely curious. An early demonstration of braille was quickly comprehended and fully appreciated; Halley's Comet was watched in October 1835, "blazing among the constellations";[2] his boardinghouse messmates in Washington were unhesitatingly sketched; and he always loved to count the crowd.

Franklin Pierce, who was to have a significant influence upon French for more than twenty-five years, makes his earliest appearance in the journal in May 1831, when he and French fell in together along a country road while on their way to serve in the New Hampshire legislature. In 1833–1834, when both were in Washington for the first time, French characterized Pierce as "my long tried & most highly esteemed friend."[3] Andrew Jackson could not be considered in terms of such intimacy, but French saw the Old Hero on a number of occasions. As in New Hampshire, it was also relatively easy in nineteenth-century Washington to come before, and gain the attention of, powerful people. French's on-the-scene description of the presidential visit to Boston in June 1833 is memorable, not only for its detail but for the riveting sense of Jackson's personality that it conveys. Even at such a time, however, French's native curiosity and abounding energy also led him to visit the Athenaeum, witness an exhibition of automata, attend the theater, go to a fire, and wander the streets of Boston.

French's thoughts on his wife throughout his journal are invariably affectionate, playful, and tender, leading to the conviction that the life they shared was mutually fulfilling. Bess was clearly a source of strength, and Benjamin was very dependent upon her. Whenever they were separated, if only for a few days, he missed her sorely, for he could not bear to be alone. Steadfast faithfulness to Bess, however, did not preclude frequent expressions of appreciation for other women, whether for their beauty or for other qualities.

The circumstances surrounding French's swift transition in December 1833 from New Hampshire to Washington, a move that transformed his domestic and public life, are not taken up in his journal. The surprising announcement that he would be leaving to become a clerk in the U.S. House of Representatives is made only in a letter of December 12 to Henry Flagg French. Financial strains were mentioned in an earlier letter and again later in the journal but were probably not the only reason.[4]

French's views on keeping a journal are given in several places in this first chapter. After all but abandoning it for twenty-seven months, between 1829 and 1831, he resumed writing simply because he wished to remember what had taken place. Following a second lengthy interruption the reasons for keeping to the task were more subtle. He felt that without the journal he had been "living without a motive" and that his mind had become "like a building without a tenant" and was "falling into ruin."[5] Finally, after completing the first of what was eventually to be an eleven-volume journal, French reviewed the entire volume and concluded that it was "not only of interest but of *use*"[6] to him. The Yankee requirement had been fulfilled.

1. Aug. 21, 1828.
2. Oct. 24, 1835.
3. Feb. 17, 1834.
4. Benjamin B. French to Henry F. French, Dec. 4 and Dec. 12, 1833. Benjamin Brown French Papers, Library of Congress. Journal, Dec. 21, 1833.
5. Sept. 10, 1835.
6. Oct. 18, 1835.

Journal

Chester, N.H., Wednesday, August 13.[1] Set out for Boston with Mrs. French;[2] went to Nashua the first day, took breakfast at Daniel Richardson's[3] in Tyngsboro the next morning, & arrived at Boston at 3 o'clock P.M.[;] arrived at Hingham the next day at 10 A.M.[,] went to the railroad in Quincy[4] that afternoon & saw the Rifle Rangers, a company from Boston encamped near that place. While on my visit at H. went to *Nantasket beach,* Cohasset & Weymouth.

1. French appears to have prepared a retrospective account of the events of August 13–29, 1828, while visiting in Chester, a practice he followed frequently throughout his forty-two years of keeping a journal.
2. Elizabeth French (1805–1861) was now twenty-three years old.
3. Daniel Richardson (1783–1843), Elizabeth's uncle, who was a lawyer, was postmaster of Tyngsborough, Mass., for thirty-five years.
4. The railroad in Quincy, Mass., was the first to be chartered in the United States. Three miles long, it used horses to haul stone from granite quarries in Quincy for the Bunker Hill Monument.

Thursday, August 21. Visited Nantasket Beach a second time, & near the Hotel saw John Quincy Adams[,][1] President of the U.S.; he was returning from a fishing excursion, his dress was a black coat, yellow nankin pantaloons & a blue cloth cap; the same evening saw him as he passed through Hingham on his return to Quincy; he was on horseback & wore the same dress.

1. John Quincy Adams (1767–1848), in the final year of his presidency, had left Washington on August 5 for his home in Quincy.

Friday, August 22. Started from Hingham[,] passed through Boston & arrived at Tyngsboro about 8 o'clock P.M. where we spent the night.

Saturday, August 23. Went to Chester, passed over the Bridge at Nashua, and arrived at C. about sunset.

Thursday, August 28. Went to Portsmouth with Mrs. F. & Miss M. W. Richardson.[1] Saw my beloved & ever to be remembered Grandma,[2] found her in good health & spirits. At the age of 75 she appears to enjoy her faculties and is as lively as she ever was since my recollection.

1. Mary W. Richardson (b. 1808), Mrs. French's sister.
2. Mary Lunt Brown (1753–1838) was the second wife of Benjamin Brown (d. 1818), French's maternal grandfather.

Friday, August 29. Visited the Navy yard, went on board a ship of the line & a frigate of the first class both on the stocks & nearly ready to be launched. Never had been on board such ships before & had formed no correct idea of their immense bulk. May they waft my Country's thunder to the remotest seas in safety, & when such ships are viewed by men of foreign nations our flag *must* be respected. If ever I felt proud of my Country it was when I stood on the deck of one of her first-rate men-of-war & thought that a few years since our Navy was but a flotilla of gunboats that hardly dared venture out of sight of land, while at that moment our flag was flying at the mastheads of many a gallant ship that owned no superior on the oceans.

Newport, N.H., Monday, September 15. Politicks at the present time are the all-engrossing topic of discourse. Wherever a person may chance to be in company, he will hear nothing but politicks discussed. In the ballroom, or at the dinner table, in the Stagecoach & in the tavern; even the social chitchat of the tea table must yield to the everlasting subject.

How many friendships are broken up! With what rancor the political war is carried on between the editorial corps! To what meanness[,] vulgarity & abuse is that champion of liberty, in proper hands, the press prostituted! With what lies and scandal does [sic] the columns of almost every political paper abound! I blush for my country when I see such things, & I often tremble with apprehension that our Constitution will not long withstand the current which threatens to overwhelm it. Our government is so based that an *honest* difference between American citizens must always exist. But the rancorous excitement which now threatens our civil liberties and a dissolution of this Union does not emanate from an *honest* difference of opinion, but from a determination of an unholy league to trample down an Administration, be it ever so pure, & be its acts ever so just. It must not be. There is a kind Providence that overlooks the destinies of this Nation who will not suffer it to be overthrown by a party of aspiring office seekers & political demagogues. . . .

Sunday, October 5. Extract from a letter which I this day wrote to my good friend D. Currier, Jr., Esq.[1]

I have become intolerably lazy of late as far as regards my friendly correspondence. It is a melancholy fact that, as we arrive at mature age and plunge into the vortex of business, *old* friends (that is to say the friends of our youth) and youthful associations are forgotten. The cold-hearted *world* is our all in all, and how to make two cents of one is the great, the momentous desideratum that engrosses all minds from the age of 21 to 75. *Then,* Alas, man discovers that "all these things are *vanity."* I acknowledge, for one, that the love of "filthy lucre" increases with me as I advance in life, but, as yet, I keep a little corner in my heart which is uncontaminated by the *base stuff,* where I turn once in a while—and memory rambles with delight through scenes of bygone days. . . .

1. David Currier, Jr. (1800–1875), was at various times town moderator of Chester and a selectman. He also served several terms as a state representative.

Monday, October 18. On the 16th inst. I went to Charlestown, N.H., with Mr. Geo. L. Avery,[1] & returned yesterday in the Stage. At C. I saw my friends Misses Mary M. & Frances R. G. Kent.[2] Took tea with them at Mrs. West's[3] & passed a very pleasant evening at whist. . . .

A few moments before we sat down to tea at Mrs. West's an old gentleman from Connecticut called . . . upon business. He was invited to take a seat at the table, with which invitation he readily complied, by seating himself within about two feet of the table and stooping forward far enough to reach his plate, etc. He entered without ceremony into conversation, wished to know how soon N.H. voted for a "King." "A president you mean[,]" said Mr. Gordon.[4] "No[,] I call them Kings. I know no difference between King George & the King of the United States. Who do you vote for in this State[,] for King Adams or Jackson?"[5] "We expect Adams will obtain the most votes." "Well I hope Adams will get it, for they turned his father out before his time, & I always thought he did well, and I don't see but what his son has done as well as anybody could do & I hope he will be King four years more. I am upwards of eighty years old & was out in the revolution." The old gentleman was then asked if he would take another cup of tea. "Yes," said he, and passed his cup to Mrs. W.[,] "I never allows myself to be beat by any woman in drinking tea, though it was the principal cause of the revolutionary war." Then followed the whole story of the destruction of tea in Boston Harbor. . . . After tea we had hoped to have no more of his company, but alas, we reckoned without our host. He had entered into the spirit of '76, or more properly speaking, the spirit of '76 had entered into him, a chord had been touched which probably would have vibrated until this time, could he have found listners. He was eloquent in his way & after talking of Washington, & Lafayette, of Trenton, Stillwater, Saratoga & Bennington, of Stark & Gates, of the traitor Arnold, & forty others, after exhausting the patience of his audience again & again, he regretted exceedingly that he had left his horse on the other side of the river, *otherwise he would have spent the night with Mr. Gordon!*[6] . . .

1. Most likely George Avery (1798–1889), of Plainfield, N.H., near French's home in Newport. Avery later moved to Vermont and Kansas.
2. Mary M. and Frances R. G. Kent were members of one of the prominent families in Chester. Another Kent, Abigail, later served as companion to Mrs. Franklin Pierce while she was in the White House.
3. Frances West was the second wife of Benjamin West (d. 1817), who had been a well-known attorney in Charlestown.
4. Probably Winthrop Gordon (1776–1862) of Brentwood, N.H.
5. The discussion concerned the upcoming presidential election of November 1828, in which John Quincy Adams, although defeated by Andrew Jackson, received all of New Hampshire's electoral votes. In all of New England, Jackson received only one electoral vote—from Maine.
6. John Stark (1728–1822), Horatio Gates (1728?–1806), and Benedict Arnold (1741–1801), Revolutionary soldiers, were all involved in the campaign that led to the surrender of John Burgoyne at Saratoga, October 17, 1777. Stark, a New Hampshireman in command of New Hampshire troops, was especially revered in his home state.

Friday, November 12. Set off from Newport a[t] 4 o'clock P.M. with Mrs. French & my Brother Henry Flagg French[1] (who came to Newport to visit me on the 21 of Octr. last) in the Stagecoach, arrived at Concord at ½ past eleven P.M.[,] started from Concord Nov. 13 at 4 A.M. & arrived at Chester at 10. Oh these Stagecoaches.

1. Henry Flagg French (1813–1885) was the son of Daniel French and Sarah Flagg Bell French (1782–1878), Daniel's third wife. The rich correspondence that passed between Benjamin and Henry for nearly forty years forms a part of the Benjamin Brown French Papers in the Manuscript Division, Library of Congress.

Monday, January 5. Returned to Newport this day after having spent eight weeks at Concord, at one of the most laborious sessions of the Legislature I have ever attended.

Tuesday, January 20. Mrs. French returned to Newport from Chester.

[No entries for 1830 have been included. The next entry is in 1831.]

Concord, N.H., Sunday, May 1. I have for a long time been thinking that I would keep a daily journal. I forget many things which transpire which might be remembered if I had a journal to refer to. Therefore I commence this, but God only knows how long this *fit* will last. I may journalize this once & never more, & I may continue it years. This morning at ½ past five I set out from Newport, came to Hopkinton in Company with J. Breck, Esq.,[1] & brought a little daughter of his (Mary). His horse injured by heat. Found F. Pierce[2] at Hopkinton, dined with him, came on to this place in company with him. He was on horseback. This day Miss Merinda Preston[3] died at 3 A.M. Went to the dancing school with her last winter. She was sick only a week. She was a good girl. . . .

I saw Merinda a fortnight since last Sabbath in all the glow of youthful loveliness, just as I came from a *graveyard,* and some light remark was made. *Now* she is lying *in the grave.*

I like to ramble among the tombs; it is a melancholy pleasure, but I like it. It reminds me that I am mortal. . . .

1. James Breck, a native of Boston, was a leading figure in business and politics, first in Croyden and then in Newport.
2. Franklin Pierce (1804–1869), of Hillsborough, N.H., lawyer, U.S. congressman and senator, general in the Mexican War, and President of the United States from 1853 to 1857. At this time he was serving as a member of New Hampshire's lower house, to which he was elected speaker in 1831 at age twenty-six.
3. Marinda Preston, the daughter of Benjamin Preston of Newport, was sixteen years old at the time of her death.

Thursday, June 2. Have spent this day, or the day just passed, rather pleasantly. Pierce told me a devlish good remark that Barnes[1] made of the Atty. Gen. Sullivan,[2] but I can't stop to write it now for I am sleepy. Do it after I get up in the morning.

June 2d[,] ½ past 9 evening. The anecdote above alluded to is this.

Barnes has a very exalted opinion of Sullivan. In conversation with Pierce he said[,] "Sullivan, it is true, does not shine much in a common case because his mind is engaged in literary matters, but take him in a case of importance & he shines; he is the most powerful man I ever saw, why he's—a lion; in a great case he *will lash his tail* and *growl terribly*." That is what I should call a climax not to be *overtopped*. This day was the one generally appropriated to the parade of the "Election."[3] Much discussion took place in the House upon the policy of wasting time & money for the sake of showing off the Legislature. It was at length concluded to have the parade *this year*, but dispense with it hereafter. I prophecy it will not be dispensed with; the majority of mankind like a display, & though they should be assured of melting together in one mass, or be suffocated with dust, they would still travel off up to the meeting house behind the *trainers*,[4] to the rub-a-dub of

> the spirit stirring drum
> And the vile squeaking of the wrynecked fife.

Breck called on me this evening. Barton[5] came in, they did not speak to each other. Thank God I cannot harbor malice so. I do really believe I could not retain malice against the worst scoundrel that ever existed over half an hour. Went to ride with Pierce this morning. Was in at the State Temperance meeting, took the chair as Vice President, came home and drank a glass of rum by mistake, thought it was wine, & poured it into a tumbler full of Lemonade. Pierce quizzed me for it very much. Never mind, I shall pay him one day. Temperance is a glorious affair— if it be not *intemperately* followed. There are men in the world who never ought to have been unclouted[6]—they are children in years. One of this class made a motion that *foreign* wines should be *debarred* access to those throats which were so often stretched in the cause of temperance. How very ridiculous; those very wines, if they could be generally used in the community would do more to promote the cause of Temperance than 10,000,000 speeches from grown-up babies. I wish the Temperance cause *well* with all my heart, but I fear the imprudence of the *Reverend* Clergy will upset it all—they are the most imprudent class in the whole community, the orthodox clergy I mean, they think everything must be driven—not so—men may be *coaxed* but not driven. I fear I am getting to be a heretic. Is there a hereafter? I believe there *must be*; it cannot be that we are to end when this tenement of clay becomes uninhabited. If so what *motive* could have caused our existence. But on this serious matter I grow sleepy, & it's after 10. I am for bed.

1. Isaac O. Barnes (1798–1864), brother-in-law of Levi Woodbury. At this time he was serving in the state legislature as a representative from Barnstead, Strafford County. He

was an ardent supporter of Franklin Pierce in 1852 but turned to James Buchanan in 1856.

2. George Sullivan (1771–1838), son of Gen. John Sullivan, was twice attorney general of New Hampshire, 1805–1806 and 1815–1835, as well as a state and U.S. representative.

3. "Election" week, the first week of the legislative session in New Hampshire, was the occasion of Concord's most gala season.

4. Militiamen.

5. Cyrus Barton (1795–1855), editor of the Concord *New-Hampshire Patriot*. He died at Loudon while making a political speech, falling into the arms of his opponent.

6. Taken out of swaddling clothes.

Friday, June 3. Arose at 5 this morning, rode horseback, attended a session of the House, was appointed one of a Committee to wait on his Excellency the Governor-elect[1] & inform him of his election, went to Hopkinton through all the dust & heat of 90 degrees weather with a horseback escort in front[,] thought I should roast, waited on Gen. Dinsmoor[,][2] then took dinner—returned to Concord[,] arrived at ½ past 4, went into the house[,] made one motion—"Out of order[,]" said Mr. Speaker,[3]—never—never move that a report be accepted except something to be acted upon by the body reported to is embraced in it. Waited on the Gov.-elect into the Capital & he was sworn into office. Read the *Concord Register*[,] saw "Mr. French moved" rather too many times for a new Member; must be careful in future—it becomes young men to be modest & retiring. I am naturally diffident, but a desire to do everything that I happen to think should be done at the moment the thought occurs has led me into more embarrassing situations than I ever mean to be placed in in future. Pierce makes a devlish fine Speaker & everybody likes him, but if ever he places me on a Committee with a certain gentleman from Coos[4] again, I rebel; this man was on the Committee to wait on the Gov.-elect today and acted like a fool. "Want of *decency* is want of sense." Governor's message—good. Have a great hole through my stocking which lets my big toe out—very uncomfortable[,] so I'll pull it off & sleep, "perchance to dream."

1. John Bell (1765–1836) served as governor of New Hampshire, 1828–1829. Although born in Londonderry, N.H., he was a longtime resident of Chester.

2. Samuel Dinsmoor (1766–1835), a Keene lawyer, served as U.S. congressman, 1811–1813, and as governor of New Hampshire, 1831–1833. His title of General resulted from service in the state militia.

3. Franklin Pierce.

4. The representatives from Coos County in 1831 were B. Burbank, Benjamin Drew, William Holkins, Clovis Lowe, and Ranson Twitchell.

Tuesday, June 7. Hav'nt journalized any since Friday. Must bring up matters to this date. Saturday went to Chester with Mr. Speaker Pierce.

Saw all my good friends, & my wife's portrait. The last made me feel melancholy; it is a most admirable *likeness,* but the countenance was finished when she had the sick headache & looked sober. The painter hit it exactly. My thoughts naturally were with the original, and I almost wept to think the time might come when I should have nought but the picture to remind me that all I loved was gone. I can't think of it—Who can bear the idea that "Tis *nothing* that they loved so well." . . .

Wednesday, June 8. What a melancholy mood I left off in last night. Many who imagine that I am gay & happy at all times are much deceived; I am often melancholy, but seldom except when alone.

Saturday was at Chester, walked over to the "great rock" Sabbath evening with D. Currier, Jr., Mary W. R.[,] F. Pierce, Anne R.[1] and *Louise*[2] (I like that way of spelling it & pronouncing it much better than Lo-i-sa, I absolutely hate the latter way). . . .

. . . Returned to Concord Monday morning. Pierce was well pleased with his visit, we talked all the way from Chester to this place & never did twenty-three miles appear shorter to me. We elected my good friend Ralph Metcalf[3] Secretary of State yesterday. It gave me more satisfaction than almost anything else that has taken place this session.

1. Anne Richardson (1811–1856), a younger sister of French's wife.
2. Louisa Richardson (1814–1906), another younger sister of French's wife.
3. Ralph Metcalf (1798–1858), of Concord, was New Hampshire's secretary of state, 1831–1836; clerk in the U.S. Treasury Department, 1838–1840; and Know-Nothing governor of New Hampshire, 1855–1857.

Friday, June 10. . . . Wilson[1] said he should go to Chester today; wish I was going with him. Went to ride with Maj. Gibson[,][2] who is another good fellow; there are five or six with whom I have become intimately acquainted this session, men every inch of them, & whose acquaintance I hope may, if it has not already, ripen into a friendship which death— no not even death—can alone destroy. I take pleasure in here making a record of the best of them—Pierce, Carroll, Farrington, Freese, Gibson, & Curtis.[3] These are men for whom I would do any honorable thing— for the two first I have a very special liking. Gove[4] of Goffstown is a good fellow too & many others with whom I have made acquaintance will not soon be forgotten. Williams[5] of Lancaster is one. He is too diffident. Give me a man who is hand and glove with you, who can sit up 'til midnight[,] tell a good story & not flinch when a bottle of good old Maderia [sic] is set before him, who can smoke a cigar & laugh at the gay world—or who can pay to the tale of woe the tribute of a tear. It is not unmanly to weep, but to *cry* is; let me see the tear stand in the eye of a stern unyielding man, & I will venture to prophecy that the lives[,] the liberties[,] the *fortunes* of his fellow men are safe in that man's hands. . . .

1. James Wilson (1797–1881), a representative from Keene, was the leader of the opposition to the Democrats in the New Hampshire legislature. He served in the state militia, 1820–1840, rising to the rank of major general, and served as a Whig in the U.S. Congress, 1847–1850.

2. John Gibson was a representative from Francestown.

3. Arlond Carroll was a representative from Pittsfield. He roomed with Franklin Pierce during this session of the legislature. James Farrington (1791–1859) represented Rochester, Andrew Freese (b. 1804) represented Deerfield, and Nathaniel Curtis represented Hopkinton.

4. Charles F. Gove (1793–1859) was a representative from Goffstown.

5. Jared Williams (1796–1864), a native of Connecticut, opened a law practice in Lancaster, Coos County, N.H. He was a state representative in 1830 and 1831. He later served as a U.S. congressman, 1837–1841; governor of New Hampshire, 1847–1849; and U.S. senator, 1853–1854.

Wednesday, June 15. . . . Went to a party at Horatio Hill's[1] last evening; it was pleasant, there was fine music on the piano, & some tolerably good singing. There were handsome girls there too, but what are handsome girls to me? "*One* good heart's enough." Atherton[2] & Pierce were quite "smashed" by a pair of bright eyes, & a beautiful face, but for my own part I would as soon think of falling in love with an elegant piece of statuary, a face cut in alabaster—give me eyes that can pierce the very soul, & a countenance that bespeaks a mind within. Was invited today to a party at Mr. I. Hill's[3] tomorrow evening, think I shall go. Must prepare a speech for tomorrow[,] can do it best in bed[,] so good night to my journal. . . .

1. Horatio Hill purchased the *New-Hampshire Patriot* from his brother, Isaac Hill, in 1829.

2. Charles Gordon Atherton (1804–1853), lawyer and politician of Amherst, N.H., served as a representative in the New Hampshire legislature in 1830, and as speaker, 1833–1835. He later was a U.S. congressman, 1837–1843, and senator, 1843–1849.

3. Isaac Hill (1788–1851) was for many years editor of Concord's influential *New-Hampshire Patriot*. Following service in the New Hampshire legislature and as second comptroller of the U.S. Treasury, he was elected to the U.S. Senate and served from 1831 to 1836. He was governor of New Hampshire from 1836 to 1839.

Saturday, June 18. . . . Thursday made a short speech in the House. The first time I have attempted anything like a set speech, was not embarrassed after I had commenced. I believe it took pretty well; at any rate the vote of the House upon the question was full in favor of the measure advocated. In the evening attended a party at Hon. Isaac Hill's, a very pleasant one, a jam though, saw my old acquaintance Mrs. Susan Rebecca Barnes.[1] She has lost none of her animation, but is the same lively[,] good-natured woman she was when I knew her years ago. I enjoyed her company very much; she is literary & can converse as sensibly as any woman with whom I ever was acquainted. Came home & had quite a trial of strength in Pierce's room. He is the most powerful man of his size I know of; he laid me on a bed three or four times notwithstanding I used every exertion to prevent him. Went to bed about two o'clock.

Arose yesterday morning at 6. Wrote a speech on the militia, attended the session of the House, Committee met at 2 P.M.[,] drew a short Bill, attended the afternoon session. A long debate took place upon the passage of a bill to incorporate the Francestown Bank. Gove of Goffstown & Col. Lane opposed it, & Wilson, Farley, Kitteridge, & Gibson advocated its passage.[2] Farley is a man of strong mind & great keenness of perception; I like his speeches. Wilson talks well, his manner is admirable, but I do not think he reasons so closely as Farley. I voted in favor of the Bank & was accused by C. F. Gove of voting against my party. It was not a party question in my view, & even if it had been I should not have sacrificed my conscience at the shrine of party; if any of my own party expect to *drive* me to vote contrary to my own convictions, if they suppose I came here to violate my oath, they will find themselves somewhat mistaken. I never act upon anything as a legislator until I am convinced I am acting for the interest of the public & so I shall ever act fearless of all consequences. Was up last night until one o'clock, & arose this morning at 6. "Palm be civil" yet runs in my head. Have not played cards before this session. Lost about a dollar, fine business for a member of the "Onerabble" the House as an old gentleman used to call it. These late hours do not affect me, or if they do the effect is favorable. I feel very much better with six hours sound sleep than with more, & I do believe were I to accustom myself to that quantity at all times I should be freer from the dreadful headaches I am so often afflicted with.[3]

1. Susan Rebecca Barnes, wife of Isaac O. Barnes, sister of Levi Woodbury, and Isaac Hill's sister-in-law. She later gained some renown for her poetry.

2. Charles Lane (1799–1876) was a representative from Sanbornton. George F. Farley (1793–1855) was a representative from New Ipswich. Jacob Kittredge (1794–1831) was a representative from Dover.

3. Mention of severe, sometimes incapacitating headaches occurs throughout French's journal.

Thursday, June 21. Went to Chester on Saturday, Metcalf went with me. All well at C.[,] returned yesterday morning. . . .

It has been said I am sentimental. I am—and it disgusts me to witness the coarseness of mankind at times. I have seen those who have sworn at the altar to love & protect, who I believe would, without the least hesitation[,] violate their marriage vows. I cannot respect such, and I can but wonder at the depravity of man's heart. I was up last night till one and I blush & feel ashamed of myself when I think that of a company of men who *ought* to be chaste [and] modest[,] what they are not, I made one—I was vulgar among *gentlemen* who ought not to be vulgar, & I now forswear any more of it. I *will* restrain myself. It is improper, unjustifiable, disgusting, degrading—my conscience reproaches me—I am done. . . .

Newport, Tuesday, August 14. . . . This day I have been hunting after pigeons, but found none. Went to the top of Blueberry Hill in Wendell.[1] It is considerable of an eminence, & from the top the prospect is beautiful. As I stood upon the bare rock & viewed the beautiful Sunapee winding away among its islands like a vast river, & glittering with the reflections of a bright sun, as I heard the afternoon breeze breathing through the bright green forest beneath me & felt its cooling influence upon my burning brow, as I beheld the blue hills of my own New Hampshire stretching around and forming a horizon, among which Kearsarge reared its bare & cragged summit toward the Heavens, . . . as I stood there this day I felt as if I could write poetry that would bear reading more than once, & felt that my soul was kindled into a new existence.[2] . . .

1. Wendell was renamed Sunapee in 1850. It is a town on the western shore of Sunapee Lake.
2. French wrote poetry throughout his life. His best known examples probably are *Fitz Clarence*, published in 1844, and the hymn sung by the Baltimore Glee Club immediately before Lincoln's Gettysburg Address. Since he was prompt and reliable as a versifier, French's talent was often called upon on dedicatory, celebratory, or funereal occasions. Mount Kearsarge is a solitary peak of nearly 3,000 feet near New London.

Sunday, March 3. . . . Extracts from a letter, written this day, to John P. Hale, Esq.,[1] of Dover.

Oh Politics—Politics—how I pity the poor devil who worships at your shrine. He must discard conscience—bid farewell to truth—say adieu to virtue—and swear by all that's holy that he & his party are right and everybody else is wrong. He must submit his character to, that worse than firey ordeal, the publick press. He must be always unhappy—always in a fever—his pulse never less than 120, and he can never hope to *rest* his head upon the pillow, for his *throbbing temples* forbid it. There is only one consolation attending the politician; in the coldest weather there is no danger of his freezing, for he, himself, is "a perpetual thaw." . . .

1. John P. Hale (1806–1873), a Dover lawyer, was a representative in the New Hampshire legislature in 1832. He was later a U.S. congressman, 1843–1845; senator, 1847–1853 and 1855–1865; and candidate for the presidency of the United States on the Free-Soil ticket in 1852. He served as minister to Spain from 1865 to 1869.

Sunday, June 2. Almost *two months* since I have written a single word in this Journal! Well I believe I must give up journalizing. But I have been very much engaged. There has been a term of the Court of Common Pleas since, immediately after which I went to Boston. Met Atherton[,] Dinsmoor, J. W. Prentiss, Judge Parker, Chamberlain, and many others with whom I am well acquainted there.[1] Attended the Theatre three nights; saw Charles Kemble & his daughter Fanny play in *The Gamester, The Stranger,* and *Much Ado about Nothing.*[2] Thought Kemble's acting *good* & Fanny Kemble as Mrs. Haller excellent, but not so good, as a whole, in the other characters in which I saw her. Attended the May fair at Faneuil Hall; it was as splendid as any scene I ever saw, except some of Nature's own, which man cannot approach. Spent three as pleasant days in the city as I ever spent in my life. Returned in the Stage, & never was so crowded, and never rode with such unpleasant passengers. From Nashua to Amherst there were *24* persons in, and upon, the Stage.

The wind blew as "twould blown" its last,

And the dust came into our faces in such clouds as I never saw before, and which would have done honor to an Arabian desert. The inside of the Stage was filled with females & children. I rode on top, & there was at least a *Stage load* of baggage. We arrived at Amherst—a fat old woman would not get out herself or let anyone else. Two ladies, who were under my protection, could not easily squeeze by her, & though I scorn to bandy words with a woman, I could not but tell her that she behaved like, what she appeared to be, a vulgar old fool, & if she would permit the other passengers to get out she might stay there to all eternity. She got out at last, & I was really vexed when I ascertained that the old harridan was to be a passenger in the same Stage with me. We came on to Henniker with the said woman[,] a man & his wife & three children, one of whom, an infant, *yelled* nearly all the way. At 4 the next morning got under way for Newport. Cold[,] chilly morning, I was shut up in a close Stage with said man & family, & other passengers sufficient to fill all *vacancies,* & oh—if ever a poor mortal came nearer suffocation than I did I pity him from the bottom of my heart. Arrived at Newport about 9 A.M. and never did I return more fervent thanks to Heaven than when I left that Stage at my own door.

Since I returned I have been very much employed in writing (I mean copying) for July Term of the Superior Court. Have, however, found time to build a boat & navigate Sugar river a little. Yesterday Mrs. French was *very sick,* sicker than I ever saw her before. She is much better today. Expect to go to Concord tomorrow to attend a session of the General Court. Father & Mother were here last week.

1. John Prentiss (1778–1873) was the founder of the *New Hampshire Sentinel* in Keene in 1799. Judge Edmund Parker (1783–1856) was an Amherst lawyer, in whose office Franklin Pierce had completed his legal studies. Chamberlain was perhaps Levi Chamberlain (1788–1868) of Fitzwilliam, solicitor for Cheshire County.

2. Charles Kemble (1775–1854), Welsh actor who played in the larger cities of the United States during the course of a tour, 1832–1834. Frances Anne Kemble (1809–1893), actress daughter of Charles, accompanied her father and in 1835 published *Journal of a Residence in America,* relating to that tour. *The Gamester* was written in 1633 by the English dramatist James Shirley (1596–1666), and *The Stranger* was an adaptation of *Menschenhass und Reue* (1789), a play by the German author and dramatist August Friedrich Ferdinand von Kotzebue (1761–1819).

Concord, N.H., Wednesday, June 5. . . . We set off from Bradford[1] at a little before five in the Stage—10 passengers on board. I rode with the driver. The horses were—two *colts* upon the pole, that never before were harnessed to the stage, an old cross mare & a *blind* horse for leaders— none of us knew, except the driver[,] *the nature* of the team. We proceeded one mile & found a small bridge up. All got out, the horses were driven through the mud, water, etc., upon one side of the bridge. After a long consultation, which was peculiarly interesting to us passengers, who were somewhat impatient, a yoke of oxen was placed upon the pole & the coach drawn through. We then set off again & had proceeded perhaps half a mile when, in descending a hill, the colts refused to hold back, the leaders turned around & commenced kicking, & the coach ran into a deep gutter. I jumped off, in the expectation that it would upset, but it did not. The passengers again dismounted, the coach was dragged into the highway & we once more got under way. Within half a mile, in descending another hill we once more had a kicking-up frolic. The passengers again got out, & the horses were shifted, the old mare being placed upon the pole, & one of the colts with the other leader. I made up my mind that we should be upset before we arrived in Concord. However it was neck or nothing. So on we went again. One passenger remarked that he thought none of us should get *killed* without we met with *a real* accident. We passed on quite comfortably about three miles further when the forward axeltree [sic] broke off in the middle, the coach dropped upon the wheel horses & the old mare kicked merrily; she *stove* the footboard to pieces, & came very near *barking* the shins of the driver & one of the outside passengers. This seemed to be something very near *a real* accident, but no one was killed, or even hurt. Another desertion of the coach took place, the passengers concluded to walk on[,] which we did until the Ladies, of whom there were two, became fatigued, when a horse & chaise was procured. We walked three miles to Warner, the driver went back to Bradford with two of the horses & returned with another coach; he arrived at Warner about nine o'clock in the evening, from whence we set off as soon as possible & were landed safe at the Columbian in this town at one A.M. yesterday morning.

I should have said that after our second *whirling about,* & the shifting of the horses, I commenced an enquiry of the driver as to his horses when he told me that two of them were colts that never ran in the stage before. I soon noticed that the off leader tripped against everything which happened to lie in the road, & that he was governed entirely by the other horse and the reins. I had the curiosity to enquire the reason. "O[,]" said the driver, with perfect *nonchalance*[,] "he is blind." "What[,] perfectly blind?" said I in some astonishment! "Yes[,]" said he, "but I shall get a good summer's work out of him & then sell him." . . .

1. A small town approximately ten miles east of Newport and twenty miles west of Concord.

Thursday, June 6. The House organized yesterday morning at about ½ past eleven, C. G. Atherton, Speaker. . . .

Monday, June 10. Saturday at about noon set off with Mr. Speaker Atherton for Dunstable in a chaise. At Amoskeag we stopped to dine. After dinner Atherton was taken exceedingly sick at the stomach, was very faint, and I was considerably alarmed; however, after washing his temples in camphor, etc., he revived, and in a short time became able to pursue his journey. We arrived at his house in Dunstable at about 6 o'clock evening. Mrs. Atherton,[1] who is a special favorite of mine, was absent at Amherst, and I felt quite disappointed at not seeing her. We found plenty to eat & drink, which, in this gluttinous [sic] world, is the main chance, and I enjoyed myself well. . . . After dinner we went to Chester, and arrived there at four o'clock, almost frozen. . . .

Found all the folks at Chester well. My wife, whom I love with all the affection that Petrarch ever loved his Laura, notwithstanding we have been married since Jany. 11, 1825, welcomed me as affectionately as— let me see—as what—I cannot find a comparison—but not half as affectionately as she usually does, and all because I went to Nashua instead of going directly to Chester. However, it was only an assumed want of affection as I do verily believe.

Enjoyed my visit at Chester well. Came away at 8 this morning, cold and comfortless weather again. Arrived here safe at ½ past 12. And here I am at 9 o'clock writing in my chamber. . . . Recd. a letter from Newport today. All well there. Parson Nye[2] has been abusing me shamefully in his last paper. I care not. He & his paper are far beneath the contempt of anyone. He is a weakminded old *office seeker,* and as truly despicable as any man I ever knew—at least his course is so. I was angry when I first saw the *Advocate,*[3] & if he had been in this town I should assuredly have inflicted personal chastisement upon him. He was not[,] however, and I saved myself the disgrace. . . .

    1. Ann Clark Atherton, wife of Charles G. Atherton.
    2. Jonathan Nye (1781–1843), Unitarian minister in Claremont, N.H.
    3. The *Farmers Advocate and Political Adventurer,* a weekly, was published in Newport from 1831 to 1832.

Monday, June 17. *Almost* a week since I have reported myself here. Well, a dull and businesslike week it has been to me. Never was so free from all excitement in my life as I have been since this session commenced. Retire at about 10 & *sleep well.* The Legislature has done nothing of importance this week. A committee, of which I am one[,] is to repair to Boston & invite the President of the U.S. to visit the Legislature. We contemplate starting on Wednesday next, and I anticipate a pleasant time.

Dr. Howe[1] (the Greek historian)[,] with several of the pupils of the Asylum for the Blind at Boston, gave a publick exhibition at the Representatives Hall on Thursday afternoon last. It was exceedingly interesting. The books used for the blind were exhibited, and the blind *read* from them with considerable facility. They are made by impressing the type through the paper so that the letters may be felt. They write by pricking through paper with some sharp pointed instrument. A sentence was written by Gov. Dinsmoor, Dr. Howe whispered it to one of the pupils, who immediately wrote it & it was read aloud to the audience by another. They were adepts in musick. A *piano*forte was present[,] & they played & sung admirably. One of them, a boy 6 years of age, answered many questions in mathematics readily & gave the process by which he came to his conclusions. . . .

The exhibition was witnessed by a very large audience, who appeared to be deeply interested. Such exhibitions always affect my feelings very much. . . .

Yesterday I went, in company with Atherton, Gove & Peaslee,[2] to visit the Shakers at Canterbury.[3] Found Mr. I. Hill, & many members of the House there. I have before attended a Shaker Meeting at Enfield, &

therefore there was nothing new to be seen. Their worship is curious, but no doubt sincere, & therefore acceptable to the most High.

Their religion is one which must be "pure and undefiled" if they live in accordance with its precepts, but I doubt; knowing as much as I do of the world, I cannot believe they are so very ascetic as they profess to be. We took dinner at the Shaker Village and returned about 4 o'clock to Concord. I spent the day as pleasantly, and *I* believe with as much *piety*[,] as many and many an one who sought the *Worldly* sanctuaries devoted to the Almighty. What Bigots this world is composed of!!

Mr. Hill introduced me to the venerable Francis Winckly.[4] Who, that has purchased a paper of garden seeds for the past twenty years, does not well remember the almost talismanic initials F. W. And who does not as well know that they are the initials of this venerable & worthy man, who is now, I believe, at the head of the Shakers of N.H. if not of New England. He is a robust[,] hearty-looking man, and appears as if Time had dealt very kindly with him. He appeared very conversant with the politics & occurrences of the day. I talked freely upon them. Mr. Hill promised to introduce him to the President if he would come to Concord while the President is here. He expressed quite a desire to see the old Hero.

1. Samuel Gridley Howe (1801–1876), of Boston, served as a surgeon in the Greek war for independence from Turkey, 1824–1830, and published *Historical Sketch of the Greek Revolution* in 1828. Thereafter he was head of the Perkins Institution for the Blind. His wife was Julia Ward Howe, composer of "The Battle Hymn of the Republic."

2. Charles H. Peaslee (1804–1866) was a representative from Concord.

3. Canterbury, on the Merrimack River just north of Concord, is the site of one of the earliest Shaker settlements in America, established in 1792.

4. Francis Winkley (1759–1847) was one of the signers of the covenant for the Shaker community in Canterbury in 1796. The community raised its own garden seeds and sold the surplus.

Newport, Saturday, July 20. Although but little more than a month has elapsed since I wrote any in my journal it seems to me at least *a year.* The scenes which have been presented in my life's drama have been full of interest, and more has been crowded into one little month than has often passed before me in a year. On the 19th of June at five o'clock P.M. Col. Barton, C. F. Gove, Esq., Leonard Wilcox, Esq.,[1] & myself set off from Concord, as a Committee of the Legislature to wait on Andrew Jackson, President of the United States, and extend to him an invitation to visit Concord while the Legislature was in session. We went as far as Chester the first night, and the next day arrived in Boston at about

6 P.M. We all took lodgings at the Tremont House, which we found crowded with boarders. All the conversation was upon the visit of the President[,] who was expected at 4 o'clock the next day.

Friday morning [June 21] came and with it all the bustle & confusion which upon the occasion might be expected. I called, with my associates, upon Charles Gordon Green, Esq.,[2] the Editor of the *Boston Statesman & Morning Post,* &, by the way, a man of talents & one whose friendship I value. Soon after my friends concluded to walk out & visit Bunker Hill, they left me[,] and I wended my way to the Athenaeum gallery of paintings,[3] where I passed the time until two o'clock in examining some of the most beautiful paintings I had ever seen and I never passed a few hours more to my mind. After dinner I took my station at a window of the Tremont House, and saw all the troops & cavalcade pass out to escort in the President. Much of it was splendid. I never before saw the Boston Truckmen[4] mounted & in their white frocks; it was a sight worth going to Boston to see. They appeared as though they were the real bone and muscle of the city, and as they passed I could not but imagine what sturdy cavalry they would make.

Soon after four a flag was run up upon the flagstaff at the top of the dome of the State House, which was the signal that the President was within the city, a salute was fired and all the city bells commenced ringing. Tremont Street was crowded with the populace all pushing toward the Common. I left my station at the window & passed up to the Common with the multitude, where I found all the Engine Companies paraded in two lines & the Scholars of the schools of the city within them, also in two ranks, leaving a passageway between for the President & his suite to pass through. I remained on the Common until it was announced that the President was about entering the lines, when I returned to the Tremont, & resumed my station. In a few moments it was said[,] "He has gone down Washington Street"; the tide turned[,] and the crowd, like a vast river, came rolling back through Tremont Street. Nothing but one solid mass of heads could be seen as far as the eye could reach either way, and between the Tremont House and the Theatre I really believe a person could have walked upon the heads and shoulders of the multitude. The Independent Cadets were formed in the lower part of the Theatre, and as soon as the President came into the lower end of Tremont Street they formed directly across from the Theatre to the door of the Tremont House, where the President was to lodge while in the city. It was very much like throwing a dam across a river. The crowd became a jamb, the soldiery kept their posts, coaches[,] equestrians, pedestrians, boys[,] girls, whites & negroes were wedged into one common mass, & no one could say this arm is mine without a very particular examination, so dense was the crowd. As soon as those composing the rear of the jamb ascertained what was the matter they turned down another street, & passing round came up by the King's Chapel into Tremont Street. However, by this time the escort troops began to arrive and form in ranks upon each side of the Street, and soon after the uncovered head of the President, distinguished by its thick white hair, was seen advancing, and the air was rent with cheers. He was in a barouche, drawn by 4 elegant greys, accompanied by the Mayor of the city.[5] His suite followed, they all drove up to the door and alighted at about 6 o'clock, amid the most hearty cheering that I ever heard.

I immediately went, in company with my companions, to the President's drawing room—we were introduced by Secretary Woodbury,[6] & Col. Barton delivered the Message of invitation. We then passed about the room & were introduced to Vice President Van Buren[7] & others. The President appeared soon after upon the balcony in front of his lodgings, & the Multitude testified their gratification by again welcoming him with cheers. We soon recd. an answer in writing to our invitation, & Col. Barton & myself retired to our room to write letters, etc. We were invited to dine with the President, but did not, as we had promised to write various letters, which could not be done at any other time. At 7 o'clock Saturday morning Col. Barton left in the Stage for Concord.

At ten the President walked to the State House accompanied by his suite and a large concourse of citizens. I made one of the little fishes which followed in the wake of the Leviathan. We repaired to the Representatives' Hall where the President was addressed by His Excellency Levi Lincoln,[8] Gov. of Massachusetts, in a very neat and appropriate manner, after which there was a continual stream of citizens passing through for two or three hours, to everyone of whom the President bowed. He became so much fatigued that it was thought advisable to close the doors, or Heaven only knows how long they would have kept him bowing. At about 2 such as had tickets repaired to the Senate Chamber, where a sumptuous collation was spread upon two rows of tables extending quite around the Hall, one within the other. After partaking I went to my lodgings. At 4 P.M. the President reviewed the Boston Brigade[9] on the Common. I was present, and I should suppose there were nearly a hundred thousand people present. The Mall, from one end to the other, presented one solid mass of human heads—indeed the whole common as far as one could see from about its centre, except so much as was set apart for the troops, presented nothing but a crowd of spectators. I could not but reflect how small *one* man was among all that multitude, & yet *one* man had caused its assemblage and on one alone every eye rested.

At about 6, in company with Isaac O. Barnes, Esq., I strolled off down into Sea Street; hardly a soul was to be seen, that part of the city was deserted, and silence enjoyed undisputed sway. I felt relieved when I escaped the noise. We passed over Fort Hill (I believe) and into Broad Street and up into State Street & from there to the Tremont, where all was bustle again. At ½ past 7 the bells began to ring for fire. Having a curiosity to see the Boston Fire Department *in operation,* I walked down very leisurely to where the fire was *trying to be.* It was in a *wool* storehouse, & could not *get out.* I stayed until I began to find myself somewhat too closely jammed, when I *cleared out* for my boardinghouse again.

I went to see Maetrel's[10] exhibition of automata in the evening, and was amused and surprized. No one can comprehend it. The exhibition of the burning of Moscow is truly wonderful. It seems as if it must be governed by something other than the art of man, & is evidence of what man *can* do.

I saw Master Burke[11] in Sir Peter Fearle, in *The School for Scandal,* on Thursday Evening [June 20]. He did not come up to my expectations. I could not get rid of the idea that he was a mere boy, & it spoiled all the effect of the play. His style of playing the violin was excellent, & I thought much more of it than of his acting.

On Sunday morning Gove, Wilcox & I left Boston for Concord, passed through Lowell & Derry to Chester, where we spent the night. Set off early the next morning and arrived at Concord at ten A.M. [June 24]. Legislation went on very well until Friday, notwithstanding the arrival of the escort troops on Wednesday. The President arrived in Concord at about three o'clock Friday afternoon [June 28], and was received with all the cordiality which could be bestowed. I never saw people so happy as all appeared. There were some croakers who kept themselves hidden until all was over, & then commenced finding fault. The President remained in Concord until Monday morning. But I need not here record all which was done to render his visit pleasant—is it not recorded in the publick newspapers of the day? It is enough for me to say that everything was done which could be[,] & I believe he left us truly gratified with his visit. I was present when he left & I know he left his blessing behind him.

Mr. Van Buren dined with us at Mr. Lincoln's[12] on Saturday [June 29]. Hon. G. P. Osgood, Hon. F. Pierce, H. Hubbard, Mr. Sibley, Marshall of Massachusetts, & R. Metcalf, Secy. of State, were present, and we had a most capital time.[13] I must not omit to record here that Mrs. Atherton, the Speaker's Lady, came up with the Presidential cavalcade from Nashua, & remained with us until the close of the Session. She *is* an elegant woman. Mrs. French came to Concord Sabbath eve and remained until Wednesday morning, & we had an exceedingly pleasant family. No one seemed to enjoy himself, after the Ladies came, better than my friend Gove. After the President left, the Legislature pursued the even tenor of their ways until Friday, on which day the devil seemed to possess some of the members, & it was the most stormy *last Friday* of the Session I have ever known. The yeas and nays were called ever so many times, & at four P.M. a call of the House was moved & ordered, & all who did not answer, being 42, were entered upon the payroll for two days less pay than they otherwise would have received. The session closed at 10 A.M. Saturday, and I came to Newport in company with Governor Dinsmoor[,] who I found one of the most sociable, pleasant, companionable men with whom I have ever travelled. He was a member of the long Congress of 1811–12 when war was declared against Great Britain, and he gave me an account of all the interesting proceedings of that very interesting session. He was "a war hawk," and of course was abused by the federal party.

I found Judge Richardson[14] at my House. The Superior Court held a session here this week, commencing on Tuesday & closing on Thursday. Present the whole court. They all boarded with me, as also did Col. [James] Wilson[,] Mr. Henderson & Mr. Gilchrist.[15] As it was a law term there were very few people in town. Judge Richardson is still here, & will probably leave on Monday. He has said much since he has been here of the literature of the present day. He is an admirer of Cicero, Horace, Homer, Milton & Shakespeare[,] thinks *Tom Jones* & *Don Quixote* two as good novels as were ever written. He does not admit much of the poetry of this age as being above mediocrity. Rogers he thinks the best poet, Moore writes the best songs, Byron sometimes writes very well, but there is too much low stuff about his writings.[16] He publishes as if he did not care what he wrote, and as if he held the opinion of the world in contempt. In speaking of the poetry of Keats he remarked, after reading a stanza, "Who would undertake to ascertain what he means—it is a very simple matter clothed in a great redundancy of words. The character of poetry now is to get together all the beautiful figures possible, & apply them at random—they are like fireflies in a swamp, you see them glitter but what they are after you cannot ascertain."

1. Leonard Wilcox (1799–1850) was a representative from Orford. He was appointed to the U.S. Senate in March 1842 to take the seat vacated by the resignation of Franklin Pierce.

2. Charles Gordon Greene (1804–1886) became a political confidant of Franklin Pierce and wrote a campaign biography of him in 1852. President Pierce appointed Greene to the position of naval officer of the Port of Boston.

3. The Boston Athenaeum has been described by the late Walter Muir Whitehill, its

longtime director and librarian, as "a proprietary library founded in 1807 that promotes in its own curious way the functions of research and pleasant general reading. . . ."

4. The Boston Truckmen, a body of several hundred mounted horsemen, wearing white frocks and black hats, were a leading feature of the city's public ceremonies and processions.

5. Charles Wells (1786–1866) was a National Republican and mayor of Boston in 1832 and 1833.

6. Levi Woodbury (1789–1851), of Francestown and Portsmouth, N.H., had a full career as jurist and statesman. He was a governor of New Hampshire, 1823–1824; a state legislator, 1825, serving as speaker; U.S. senator, 1825–1831 and 1841–1845; U.S. Secretary of the Navy, 1831–1834; U.S. Secretary of the Treasury, 1834–1841; and Associate Justice of the U.S. Supreme Court, 1845–1851.

7. Martin Van Buren (1782–1862), eighth President of the United States, was serving as Vice President at the time of Jackson's tour of the northeast in June and July 1833.

8. Levi Lincoln (1782–1868) was first elected governor of Massachusetts in 1825 and was reelected annually until 1834. Thereafter he served as a U.S. congressman from Massachusetts, 1834–1841.

9. The Boston Brigade, as reviewed by Jackson, was made up of the officers of the Third Brigade, mounted, and eight light infantry companies, under the command of Brigadier General Tyler.

10. Johann Nepomuk Maelzel (1772–1838), German musician and mechanician, was exhibiting "The Conflagration of Moscow" and "The Automaton Chess-Player" at Boston's Concert Hall. Edgar Allan Poe was intrigued by the latter and wrote about it in the *Southern Literary Messenger* in 1836.

11. Charles St. Thomas Burke (1822–1854), American actor and dramatist, began his career on the stage in his infancy. French meant "as" Sir Peter Fearle, not "in."

12. Zebina Lincoln, of Concord, N.H., was part owner of a dry goods establishment. In 1834 he became proprietor of the Eagle Coffee House.

13. Gayton Pickman Osgood (1797–1861) was a U.S. congressman from Massachusetts, 1833–1835. Henry Hubbard (1784–1857), of Charlestown, N.H., was at this time serving as a U.S. congressman. He was later elected as a Democrat to the U.S. Senate, 1835–1841, and was governor of New Hampshire, 1841–1843. Jonas L. Sibley was the U.S. district marshal in Boston.

14. Judge William M. Richardson (1774–1838), Elizabeth French's father, was chief justice of the New Hampshire Superior Court, 1816–1838.

15. Either Samuel H. Henderson or William M. Henderson, cousins. Both were businessmen in Dover, N.H. John James Gilchrist (1809–1858) became chief justice of New Hampshire and was made chief justice of the newly established court of claims by President Franklin Pierce.

16. Samuel Rogers (1763–1855), English poet, wrote *The Pleasures of Memory.* Thomas Moore (1779–1852), Irish poet, wrote *Lalla Rookh.* George Gordon, Lord Byron (1788–1824), English Romantic poet.

Washington, Saturday, December 21. At ½ past 1 o'clock this morning I arrived in this city. It is to me next to impossible to keep a daily journal. I have attempted it many times but cannot. I am now here and I came here to earn money, not to spend it. I have left behind me all I love on this earth—my dear wife—and nothing but a hope and a wish that I may here earn enough to pay my debts would ever have tempted me to leave my happy home. I started from Newport one week ago this day at a little past eleven A.M. with as sad a heart as ever *man* possessed, and I left as sad a one to regret my absence, but though distance separate us, thought, which knows no bounds, can pass from one to the other in a single second, and I can record here such ideas as hereafter *we* can both read and live over again *together* the time that was passed in separation.

It seems to me as if I never commenced a winter so happily as I did this one, and had it not been for my own extravagance in time past I might have still been passing it with the same happiness in which it was commenced, but *duty* called me here, and I hope and trust, that performed, I shall be enabled to return to my happy home and spend many joyful years with her whom a kinder fate than I deserve has appointed that I shall pass, *I hope,* my life.

I have been about the City today with Col. Pierce & Judge Hubbard, who have each of them shown themselves my *true* friends by their exertions in my behalf. I was this day introduced to Amos Kendall[1] for the first time; his is a name which will be connected with the history of this Union and which, I believe, will hereafter assume an importance which many dream not of. He is, undoubtedly, the best political writer in the Country, and however much Gen. Jackson's enemies may affect to despise him, they fear him. He is a great man, & will be a greater, or I do not judge him aright. I entered the Capitol today, for the first time, and I viewed it with thoughts and emotions which I cannot express—*will it always be the capitol of my happy country?* I fear the seeds are already sown whose fruit will be disunion, but God forbid it!

1. Amos Kendall (1789–1869), born in Massachusetts and a graduate of Dartmouth College, moved to Kentucky where he became a tutor in the household of Henry Clay. He then edited *The Argus of Western America* in Frankfort for a number of years but gave it up to serve in Washington as Andrew Jackson's fourth auditor of the Treasury. One of the most influential of Jackson's "Kitchen Cabinet," he eventually became Postmaster General and remained in that post under Martin Van Buren. He later became a business associate of S. F. B. Morse and of Benjamin Brown French in the operation of the Magnetic Telegraph Company.

Monday, December 30. On Saturday Decr. 28th I entered upon the duties of engrossing Clerk, and if the House of Representatives does not take an extraordinary course in regard to the appointment of Clerk, I may hope that I am, for a time at least, settled down as a citizen of this city.[1] I have been strangely driven about the world since my youth, but I have always found warm friends wherever I have happened to be located, friends from whom it has been hard to part, and in leaving Newport I shall feel as if I was going away from *home*. Since I arrived here I have heard many of the great men of the land debate. Mr. Clay, Mr. Webster, Mr. Benton, Mr. Forsyth, Mr. M'Duffie, Mr. Polk & others.[2] Of Clay I have not that exalted opinion which I once had. I believe him to be heartless, and selfish; he is eloquent, but he lacks judgment very much.

Polk is quite an eloquent man. M'Duffie I do not like, and of the others I have not seen enough to make up a judgment.

I spent Saturday evening at Secretary Woodbury's, and spent it very pleasantly. There was a small party.

I have called at Mr. Webber's[3] twice since I have been in the City, and he has called on me often—he is [as] good-hearted pleasant [a] man as I ever wish to meet with, and I believe he is a true friend to me. I have not yet called either upon the President or Vice President.

1. French described his daily routine in a letter to Henry Flagg French, Washington, January 11, 1834. "I live as much like a hermit here as ever I did in New England. My course of life is this. I arise at about ½ past 7 (just as soon as there is a fire built in my room), wash, shave and dress, and then read the morning paper till 9, when the breakfast bell rings, eat breakfast & go immediately to the Capitol, where I either read or write, till 12, when both Houses commence their session, if they make any business for me I do it, if not I go into either the Senate or House and hear the debates. At a little past 3 the Senate & House usually adjourn, I remain at my office till I find there is nothing wanted of me, then go to my boardinghouse and dine at 4. After dinner go to my chamber & either read or talk with Pierce till 6, when the supper bell rings, take *two cups* of tea, & repair to my chamber and read or write letters till ten, eleven, or twelve, just as the fit takes me, & then go to bed. If there is a party, and I am invited, I go, & usually return by ½ past 10. So pass my days one after another."

2. Henry Clay (1777–1852), of Kentucky, had been elected to the U.S. Senate in 1831. Daniel Webster (1782–1852) had just been reelected as a U.S. senator from Massachusetts. Thomas Hart Benton (1782–1858), of Missouri, was reelected to the U.S. Senate in 1829. John Forsyth (1780–1841), of Georgia, was elected to the U.S. Senate in 1829. George McDuffie (1790–1851), of South Carolina, served as a congressman from 1821 to 1834. James K. Polk (1795–1849), who was to become the eleventh President of the United States, was serving as a congressman from Tennessee in 1833.

3. John A. Webber was a clerk in the appointments division of the Post Office Department.

Saturday, January 4. . . . The first day of January I attended, *with all creation beside* I should imagine, at least with a very great crowd, the President's drawing room, but I have written two accounts of it—one to the *Patriot*[1] & one to my wife, and I shall not write another here.

1. Isaac Hill's *New-Hampshire Patriot.*

Tuesday, January 14. Have this moment returned from the Theatre where I saw Charles Kemble & Fanny in *The Hunchback.*[1] Fanny, as Julia, was superb; it seems to me as if she played very much better than she did when I saw her in May, at Boston, except as Mrs. Haller in *The Stranger,* where she *is perfect.* The House was full tonight, and the audience very respectable. Pierce has come home *in raptures* with Miss Fanny.

1. A play by the Irish preacher and author, James Sheridan Knowles (1784–1862).

Monday, February 17. Since I wrote in this book last my dear wife arrived here in good health. My brother Henry came with her and right glad and happy was I to see them. They arrived Thursday, January 23d, at half past 2 P.M.[,] having been about a week on the way, and Henry left this City last Wednesday morning for N.H. There are feelings which cannot be described and such were mine upon the arrival of the dearest being to me on earth, "my own my cherished wife."

Ever since I arrived here the two Houses of Congress have been engaged in the consideration of the question in relation to the removal of the public deposits from the Bank of the United States to the local banks. The question has agitated the whole Country, and petitions and memorials are poured in upon Congress, & upon the presentation of each a discussion arises. On Tuesday last, Feby. 11, one of the most heartrending occurrences took place in the house. Hon. Thomas T. Bouldin[1] arose to speak about half past one P.M.[;] he had proceeded but a few sentences when he fell into the arms of a gentleman next him, and in a few moments expired. Mrs. Bouldin was in the gallery. She came down, and upon being told that her husband was dead her shrieks were truly heartrending. I was present during most of the awful scene, and I never saw men so agitated. I never saw so many pale countenances. Truly "in the midst of life we are in death." The funeral was attended at the House of Representatives on Thursday, & the scene was solemn and impressive.

It has been my fortune to board, very often, during my life with a large family of publick men—such as members of the Legislature, etc., & I find that I soon forget their names and characters. I am now boarding in a mess of members of Congress &˙their ladies. As a matter of reference hereafter, and as a matter of amusement at the present time[,] I will endeavour with perfect impartiality to note their characters & appearance here. And first,

Hon. Ether Shepley, Senator from Maine, residence ————.[2] Mr. Shepley is apparently about 50 years of age, small in stature, with a countenance which does not indicate much talent. He is a benevolent-looking man, and one would know, from his appearance[,] that he was religiously inclined. He possesses considerable talent, notwithstanding the index I have above alluded to, and has already made a very excellent speech in the Senate this session. He is possessed of a strong mind & reasons very correctly upon every subject on which he attempts to converse. He is somewhat peculiar in his manners, and I have heard him say things which led me to believe that he was naturally pure & simple-minded. He is a valuable man.

Hon. Isaac Hill, Senator from New Hampshire, residence Concord. I have been acquainted with Mr. Hill many years, and he is emphatically a political man. His whole soul is devoted to this one subject. Mr. Hill's personal appearance is not prepossessing. He is about 43 years of age, is perhaps 5 feet 10 inches in height, and is considerably lame, one leg being shorter than the other. His countenance is cadaverous, but is strongly marked with the lines of care & vexation; of the latter, he has had enough to kill a man of weak nerves. His eye is jet black and bright & piercing, and indicates excitability. He is a man of undoubted talents but has, most unfortunately for himself, a hesitancy of utterance which renders it almost impossible for him to speak with fluency; still he is an excellent reader and reads without the least hesitation; hence he never undertakes to address any assembly until he has written at length what he intends to say, after which he reads it. Mr. Hill will hardly admit that any man whose political views are different from his own can possess any political honesty. No man is more ready than he is to extend the hand of charity where he knows the object is a worthy one, & as a citizen he is highly esteemed, as well by his political enemies as his friends. But when he becomes prejudiced against anyone he is as bitter as any man I ever knew; I have seen him when excited against a man, when his eyes flashed fire, almost, and when I could not but be reminded of Byron's description of the Corsair,

There was a laughing devil in his sneer.[3]

He is a bitter enemy to the gentlemen of the bar, and often abuses them very unreasonably. Every gentleman who boards at this house, except him, is a lawyer.

Hon. Samuel Beardsley,[4] Representative from New York. The most perfect gentleman in his appearance that I have seen in Washington, a modest, unassuming man, but possessed of good talents, a handsome debater and close reasoner. His speech upon the Bank question made at this session, does him much credit. In stature Mr. B. is about 6 feet in height, well proportioned, & I call him *handsome*. His age I should judge from his appearance is about 45.

Hon. Rufus McIntire,[5] Representative from Maine, and during the last war a Capt. in the U.S. Army, where he proved himself a brave man. A man of most sterling merit. Perfectly unassuming in his manners, and gentlemanly in his deportment, possessing good talents. I have never heard him address the House and I doubt whether he ever speaks except to make motions, reports, etc. But would to Heaven the world was filled with such men as Cap. McIntire. He is, as a friend of his very justly remarked of him, "pure gold." His age is about 50.

Hon. Sherman Page,[6] Representative from New York—residence, Unadilla. How shall I do justice to thee my warm-hearted, blunt, honest and witty friend? Mr. Page is a man of great information, and, I suspect, possessed of a very retentive memory. With a countenance sober and solemn enough for the gravest person that ever existed, he will give birth to some witty or shrewd remark which "sets the table in a roar." He seems to fathom the character of every man he looks at at a single glance, and he seldom speaks without saying something original. He is a good judge of Human nature, and possesses a feeling heart. Although perfectly plain in his manner of speech, & sometimes almost blunt, he never intentionally wounds the feelings of anyone, as I believe. His talents are of a rare order, and such as must always render him a favorite wherever he happens to be. He is an old hunter, & can tell the crack of a rifle from the round[,] full explosion of a musket, I'll venture to predict, for many is the stately buck that has fallen beneath his aim. He is known in New York as the grand Sachem of the Unadilla Hunt. In stature Mr. Page is not over five feet 8 inches, is considerably portly and appears as if he had eat a great many good dinners in his day. He is, take him all in all, a sociable, merry, upright, well-disposed man, and one whom I value quite highly as a friend. His age is not far from 50 I should think.

March 21.[7] Next to Mr. Page at the table sits Hon. Franklin Pierce, of New Hampshire, my long tried & most highly esteemed friend. At the age of 27 he can boast—no he *cannot*—for boasting is not in his nature— but I can boast for him, that he has been Speaker of the House of Representatives of N.H., the duties of which office he sustained with high honor to himself & with credit to the State, and is now a member of the 23d Congress, and has already distinguished himself on the floor of the House in one of the neatest & best delivered speeches that I have heard this session. A more honorable[,] upright & generous-hearted man than Franklin Pierce does not exist.

Hon. Aaron Vanderpoel[8] of New York. Residence Kinderhook. I should think about 35 years of age. About 6 feet in height, well proportioned and very muscular in his appearance. He has made one set speech & spoken a number of times in the House. He is quite a good Speaker, but is not possessed of that logical mind which must always be the great requisite to finished argument. Vanderpoel can talk—and does talk loud & almost incessantly—but he seldom *argues*. He is vain & blustering, he courts the acquaintance of great men, drinks wine in large quantities, & boasts of it, is exceedingly annoying to the servants, whom he often denominates, to their faces[,] *"My sweet scented friend."* He professes a great deal of democracy while his practice shews that he would delight in nothing so much as to be hand and glove with an Aristocracy. He is at times very imprudent in his remarks, as a politician. Still I think I can see, through all this, a good heart & honorable feelings, & take Aaron

Vanderpoel aside from the bustle that attends high life, and I have no doubt he would be found to be a good companion, and possessed of a disposition to render those about him happy.

Hon. Francis O. J. Smith,[9] Representative from Maine. Residence, Portland. About 30 years of age. About 5 feet 7 inches in height, well proportioned, & possessed of a very good physiognomy. One of the most industrious men I ever knew—and in perseverance, to effect any object he undertakes, I never met with his equal. He is possessed of fine talents, & speaks well, & always to the purpose. Indeed, if life & health are spared him I am of opinion he will stand high in the ranks of public men a few years hence. He is very amiable I should think, with the exception (if it may be called an exception) that he never suffers one who has wantonly injured him or his friends to go unpunished, if he can, by any honest means, bring about their punishment; and, on the other hand, his friends may always rely upon all his exertions in their behalf upon any occasion when they are called for.

Hon. Philemon Dickerson,[10] Representative from New Jersey. Six feet 6 inches in height and very straight, & not very fleshy. I have never heard him speak in the House, & he seldom converses much, but, judging from what little I have heard him say, & what I have heard of him I should judge that he is a talented & very amiable man. He is about 50, I should think.

Hon. Noadiah Johnson,[11] Representative from New York. Apparently about forty. A middling-sized, well-built, athletic man. Very sensible, amiable and well informed. He is one, among the few, whom I like.

Hon. Abijah Mann, Jr.,[12] Representative from New York. Between forty & forty-five years of age. His personal appearance is not very prepossessing, but he improves very fast upon acquaintance. He is entirely unstudied, both as regards dress, manners, and conversation, but makes as many shrewd remarks as any one of the mess, excepting perhaps Mr. Page. They are entirely different in their manners & way of saying things, & still, taken as a whole, there is more resemblance between them than between any other two of the mess. Mr. Mann often speaks in the House, & in repartee & bitter irony few are his equals—indeed he never speaks but to the purpose anywhere, & his every remark contains something worth remembering. He *wastes* no words, although he talks considerable. He uses an illustration for almost everything, some of which are *very original & full of point.*

Hon. Joel Turrell[13] of New York, a Representative. About 35 years of age, 6 feet in height, & exceedingly well proportioned. Very fair complexion, &, in my estimation, a handsome man. He says but very little, but when he does converse it is with sense & to the purpose. I should, from what I have now seen of him, set him down for a good-natured, ease-loving, careless sort of a man, who placed but little value upon his money, & with whom an acquaintance would be worth having.

Hon. William Wilkins,[14] Senator of Pennsylvania, boarded here the first of the session, & I had the opportunity of forming some acquaintance with him. He is about 60 years of age, I should judge, is about 5 feet 10 inches in height, very spare, & without color in his face. He is a very jovial & good-natured, and in manner a polished gentleman. He is very gallant to the ladies, & has the character of being quite a beau. Of his talents I have only to say they cannot be otherwise than good or he never would have received the entire vote of Pennsylvania for the Vice-Presidency. And his late speech in the Senate upon the removal of the deposits is also evidence of his superior talents.

Hon. Hugh L. White,[15] President *pro tem* of the Senate, of Tennessee, also boards here, but he does not eat at the mess table, & therefore I have seen him but seldom. In stature he is about 6 feet, very spare, and judging from appearance he is over 60 years of age. His face is as thin as that of any man I ever saw, in health, & I believe he enjoys very good health. As to his talents or character I cannot judge. From what I have seen of him, however, I should pronounce him very amiable & gentlemanly. . . .

1. Thomas T. Bouldin (1781–1834) was a congressman from Virginia. He had served in the 21st and 22d Congresses, 1829–1833, but had been defeated when running for the 23d. Following the death of John Randolph, Bouldin was elected to his seat in the 23d Congress and occupied it from December 2, 1833, until his own death on February 11, 1834.

2. Ether Shepley (1789–1877) was a resident of Saco while serving as a Democrat in the U.S. Senate, 1833–1836. He resigned to become a justice of the Maine supreme court. French had left the place of Shepley's residence blank in his journal.

3. Lord Byron wrote *The Corsair* in 1813. It became immensely popular and thousands of copies were sold. The line quoted by French, describing Conrad, the corsair, is in the ninth stanza of the first canto.

4. Samuel Beardsley (1790–1860), of Utica, served in Congress as a Democrat from 1831 to 1836 and from 1843 to 1844. In 1844 he was appointed to the New York supreme court.

5. Rufus McIntire (1784–1866), of Parsonfield, served in Congress as a Democrat, 1827–1835.

6. Sherman Page (1779–1853), Democratic congressman, 1833–1837.

7. French resumed his entry of February 17 on March 21, before making a separate entry for March 21.

8. Aaron Vanderpoel (1799–1870), Democratic congressman, 1833–1837.

9. Francis Ormond Jonathan Smith (1806–1876) was born in Brentwood, N.H., and had attended Phillips Exeter Academy. He served in Congress as a Democrat from Maine, 1833–1839. While still a congressman, he became involved in a partnership with S. F. B. Morse for the promotion of the telegraph. Smith and French became very close friends and business associates. French named his first son after him—Francis Ormond French.

10. Philemon Dickerson (1788–1862), Democratic congressman, 1833–1836 and 1839–1841.

11. Noadiah Johnson (1795–1839), Democratic congressman, 1833–1835.

12. Abijah Mann, Jr. (1793–1868), Democratic congressman, 1833–1837.

13. Joel Turrill (1794–1859), Democratic congressman, 1833–1837. He was U.S. consul in the Sandwich Islands, 1845–1850.

14. William Wilkins (1779–1865), Democratic and Anti-Masonic senator, 1831–1834. He was U.S. minister to Russia, 1834–1835; Democratic congressman, 1843–1844; and Secretary of War, 1844–1845.

15. Hugh Lawson White (1773–1840) was elected to fill the Senate seat vacated by Andrew Jackson's resignation in 1825. He served until 1840. After breaking with Jackson over Van Buren's candidacy for the presidency, White himself ran for the office in 1836.

Friday, March 21. This day, was placed in the centre of the Rotunda, at the Capitol[,] a bronze statue of Thomas Jefferson. From descriptions of the man and from portraits I have seen of him, I should think it was a very good likeness, and certainly the bust is admirably executed, but I will take another time, after I have examined it more closely, to describe it. The bust was presented to Americans by Lieut. Levy[1] of the U.S. Navy. . . .

1. Uriah Phillips Levy (1792–1862) had a long and controversial career as a sailor and naval officer.

Friday, May 23. This day Mrs. French & myself have been to Mount Vernon. We went in company with Mr. & Mrs. Smith, Mrs. Olney, Mr. & Mrs. [Henry] Hubbard, Mrs. Polk, Mrs. Grundy, Mrs. Henry King, & Mr. Hubbard's little son Aaron.[1] We went to both the tombs (the old one which is much dilapidated and contains nothing except old rubbish, & the new one in which the remains of Washington & his wife are deposited)[,] to the garden[,] which is a splendid one, & is now filled with all sorts of hothouse plants & beautiful flowers. We also went into the house & passed through the rooms which the father of his Country so often passed through. The furniture, pictures, etc., which were in the House in the lifetime of its former illustrious owner are, save a single picture, removed. In the room occupied by Washington, as his office, hangs an engraved portrait of Louis Six[teenth][2] which was there in Washington's lifetime, & which now hangs in the same place in which it then hung. In the hall, in a glass case, hangs the key of the French Bastille sent to Washington by Napoleon Bonaparte, and in the parlour, which is a very large, airy & elegant room, is a marble firepiece presented to Washington by Lafayette. It is most beautifully and elaborately chizzelled in relief, the figures all representing something relative to Agriculture & rustic life. There is a plough, a boy just about mounting a horse or a mule, a child with fat cheeks, its apron gathered up in one hand, apparently filled with something, etc. The figures are well proportioned and beautifully grouped.

Everything except the garden & interior of the house appears to be going to ruin. The old tomb is fast crumbling away, & over the door is an aperture through which I looked. It contains old boxes (probably the outside coffins, in which the remains of those who have heretofore been placed in the tomb were enclosed) broken to pieces, & thrown in a pile at the farther part. The new tomb is built in a spot selected by Washington himself, and of brick burned by him for the purpose previous to his decease. It is roughly built, the front shewing rough brickwork, in the centre of which is a small iron door, hung in a stone doorcase. Directly over this door is a stone tablet on which is that part of the burial service commencing "I am the resurrection and the life," etc. At the top, above the tablet[,] is inscribed on stone, "The Washington Family." The tomb is built upon inclining ground, it is covered with earth, & there is a quantity of *old brush* thrown onto it, through which all manner of weeds are making their way. From it I plucked a sprig of evergreen & a weed. The garden[,] containing several acres, is kept in excellent order, & is filled with greenhouse plants, Lemons, oranges, etc., & the walks are beautifully arranged & bordered with box. The greenhouse was empty, the plants having been yesterday all taken out & placed about the garden. An old servant, who went about with us, called the garden "the West Indies." He pointed out to us the windows of the chamber in which Washington died. He was not one of the General's slaves, but a slave of his brother[3] who resided in Alexandria, & he used to be at Mount Vernon almost daily & was well acquainted with the General.

Our visit was very pleasant, and as I passed about the grounds & stood before the tomb, I thought how many illustrious individuals had passed in the very footpaths I was traversing & had stood where I then was, & paid to the shade of the mighty man whose remains were there deposited the tribute of gratitude for a Free & Independent Country. I thought of the good Lafayette, of Jefferson[,] Madison & Monroe, & I doubted whether ever another man would live, in America, whose memory would be so dearly cherished as was that of George Washington.

1. Mrs. Olney, perhaps the wife of G. W. Olney, who was seeking to become postmaster of Portland, Maine. He was a friend of F. O. J. Smith. Sarah Childress Polk, wife of James K. Polk. Ann Rodgers Grundy, whose husband, Felix Grundy (1777–1840), was a Democratic senator from Tennessee. Mrs. Henry King, wife of the Democratic congressman from Pennsylvania, 1831–1835.

2. French wrote "Six" but crossed out "teenth." The portrait is of Louis XVI (1754–1793), King of France. It still hangs in the large dining room at Mount Vernon.

3. John Augustine Washington (1736–1787).

Chester, Thursday, July 24. . . . On Thursday, July 10th[,] at 6 o'clock P.M. myself & wife started from the City of Washington for this State, and after a pleasant Journey of four days we arrived here at 3 o'clock P.M. on Monday July 14th. From Washington to Baltimore we were in Company with Col. Achille Murat,[1] son of Murat, formerly King of Naples, & nephew of Napoleon Bonaparte. He possesses all the vivacity natural to the French. He appeared to be very well informed upon every subject upon which he conversed, and I was very much pleased with him. Some allusion was made to his being a Prince—"True," said he, "I was born a Prince but now I am more than a Prince, I am an American Citizen."

Mr. A. W. Paine, better known as the *Reis Effendi*[2] of the Boston *Morning Post*, for which he has been a constant correspondent for the last 8 months, came as far as New York in company with us. He is a very sensitive genius. He & Col. Murat had much conversation together, to which I listened with much pleasure. There was also in the stage, from Washington to Baltimore, a Pennsylvania farmer, who said[,] "The Germans in that State were very ignorant, they did not know anymore than *oxes*." From Bordentown, where we spent the second night of our journey, to Newport, R.I., we had in our company Nicholas Biddle[3] and John Q. Adams. Mr. Adams accompanied us to Providence, Mr. Biddle stopped at Newport. I had no opportunity to hear the latter converse, but his personal appearance is very much in his favor. I knew him as soon as I cast my eyes on to him from a caricature I had seen of him in company with Jackson in some print relating to the U.S. Bank. Nothing uncommon occurred on our journey. The sea was rather rough as we came round Point Judith, & many of the passengers were seasick. I was not sick, although I felt no particular desire to eat breakfast. . . . From Providence to Boston the ride was very tedious, as we were more than seven hours travelling about 40 miles. There was a gentleman in the Stage, however, who some interested us by giving us a regular lecture upon Swedenbourgeanism,[4] he being a convert to that faith. . . .

1. Achille Murat (1801–1847), son of Joachim Murat, marshal of France under Napoleon and King of Naples. Achille, crown prince of Naples, emigrated to the United States in 1823 and resided in Florida for much of the time thereafter.
2. Turkish words for a respected gentleman of authority.
3. Nicholas Biddle (1786–1844), of Philadelphia, was the president of the Second Bank of the United States from 1823 to 1839.
4. Swedenborgianism is the system of philosophy and theology attributable to the Swedish mystic Emanuel Swedenborg (1688–1772).

Thursday, September 10. What a break in my journal! More than thirteen months have elapsed since I have written a word by way of journalizing. . . .

One . . . motive which induces me again to commence a journal is—it has for sometime past seemed to me as if I was living without a motive, and as if my mind was becoming a mere chaos—as if, like a building without a tenant, it was falling into ruin. . . .

But, before commencing upon a regular journal of *the present*, I must fill the hiatus that now forms *the stride* in my journal from July 24th, 1834, to Sep. 10, 1835; and, to use one of Tom Cringle's[1] nauticalities, I will now commence—

Bringing up the leeway.

After the record of July 24th, 1834, I spent the time until the latter part of October in N.H. I visited Newport twice during the time, I was also at Exeter, Hampton Beach, Portsmouth, Dover, Great Falls, etc. . . . Upon one of the last days of October, my wife & myself started for the City of Washington. . . . Arrived in Boston that evening & remained there until the next day noon, then took the stage for Providence, where we arrived in the evening. Early the next morning I went to the Steam-boat & secured a stateroom, returned to the hotel, & with my wife visited a picture by—I forget who—*The Opening of the Sixth Seal*. It was in a bad light, & undoubtedly appeared to great disadvantage, & neither of us were at all gratified with the visit. At noon went on board the boat, had a fine passage through the Sound, but the tide was so strong that it was with much difficulty that we got through Hell Gate. As the boat passed round to the Battery we saw the Philadelphia boat just under way; she was hailed by the Captain & all the Philadelphia passengers transferred on board her in a small boat. Bess & myself were among them, & on we went. Arrived in Philadelphia that evening, remained there until the next morning[,] then took the boat for Baltimore, where we arrived the same afternoon. The next morning we took the Stage for Washington where we arrived at two o'clock P.M. and right happy was I when I once more found myself safely deposited in *our* little parlor up three pair of stairs, at Mrs. S. A. Hill's.[2]

. . . The first Monday in December Congress commenced its session. I will not undertake to detail here the events of the winter connected with my observation. Suffice it to say, that Warren R. Davis,[3] a member of the House from S. Carolina, died, and while attending his funeral a crazy fellow named Lawrence[4] attempted to assassinate the President; he snapped two pistols at his breast, both of which missed fire, though the percussion caps exploded—this, of course, caused a great excitement for a time. A short time before the close of the session, Mr. Ewing,[5] a member of the House, was attacked, & somewhat disfigured, by Lieut. Lane[6] of the Army, while passing from the Capitol to his (Ewing's) boardinghouse.

I saw part of the affray. This also was the subject of a three-day's talk, and was deemed of sufficient importance to be made a matter of enquiry by the House of Representatives. It, however, resulted in the making of a few speeches & nothing more. At length the 3d of March came, & with it one of the stormiest closings of a Congress, it is said, that ever was known. The House did not adjourn until about 3 o'clock A.M. of the 4th. I was present at the Clerk's table during nearly the whole evening & night, & can well imagine that a more *uproarious* ending could not well have been made. After a night of vain attempts to transact business, at three, the Speaker after a few remarks declared the House adjourned *sine die*. Many important bills were lost, & the General Appropriation bill was but just saved.

. . . On the 20th of May was holden the great democratic convention at Baltimore. The gathering together of so many from all sections of the Union, in the immediate vicinity of Washington, brought many visitors to that city, and among them many of my old and tried friends from New Hampshire. . . .

On the 31st day of May at 2 o'clock P.M. we started from Washington for New Hampshire. In the Stage were Gen. M'Neil, Mr. Thornton, S. D. Fletcher, Mrs. Webber & 3 children, a Mr. Wright formerly of this town (Chester), & a Scotch lady.[7] After one of the most dusty & fatigueing rides I ever remember to have taken, we arrived at Baltimore; the following morning we left in the boat, & as fast as steam & Stages could carry us we came on to this place, where we arrived without the occurrence of any particular incident or accident, on Thursday the 4th day of June, my brother having met me at Derry with a carriage. We found all well here.

After remaining here a few days I went to Concord where the Legislature being in session, I met hundreds of old acquaintances. I spent a few days at Concord, then went to Newport, where I remained 5 weeks, then returned here. . . . Since I returned from Newport I have visited Maine. At Portland I spent a day very pleasantly in company with Hon. F. O. J. Smith, Carroll[8] of Concord, S. Brown,[9] etc. The two latter were there attending to land speculation. I also met Hon. Jos. Hall[10] of Camden, at Portland, and was highly gratified to see him. From Portland I went to N. Yarmouth, where I found my good old grandmother—now more than 82 years of age—in good health & retaining all her faculties. . . . With North Yarmouth, and its Academy, there are many associations in my mind of entirely opposite kinds—pleasure & pain, happiness and melancholy are there—but I will not specify. . . . From N. Yarmouth I went to Bath, where I spent 4 days with my friends, returned to Portland in the Steamboat *McDonough,* remained in Portland one day & then came

on in the Stage, through Dover, to this place, where I have been ever
since. . . . Yesterday I read the *Yemassee*, "A Romance of Carolina" by the
author of *Guy Rivers*[,] *Martin Faber*, etc. The author's name[,] I have been
told, is Simms.[11] The book is rather interesting.

1. Michael Scott (1789–1835), Scottish author and businessman, published *Tom Cringle's Log* in installments in *Blackwood's Magazine*, 1829–1833. It first appeared in book form
in 1834.
2. Mrs. Silas A. Hill ran the boardinghouse on Pennsylvania Avenue where French
lived during his first two years in Washington.
3. Warren Ransom Davis (1793–1835), Democratic congressman, 1827–1835.
4. Richard Lawrence was a thirty-year-old unemployed housepainter. He was seized
immediately and on April 11, 1835, was found not guilty because of insanity and was
committed to an asylum.
5. John Ewing (1789–1858), Whig congressman from Indiana, 1833–1835 and 1837–
1839.
6. John F. Lane (d. 1836) accosted Ewing on January 26, 1835, in front of the Botanic
Garden. He struck Ewing with an iron cane, while Ewing drew a sword from his cane.
The incident arose from a controversy between Ewing and Lane's father, Congressman
Amos Lane (1778–1849), in the House of Representatives.
7. John McNeil (1784–1850), of Hillsborough, N.H., was Franklin Pierce's brother-
in-law. McNeil was decorated for his actions in the War of 1812. James B. Thornton (1800–
1838), grandson of Matthew Thornton, signer of the Declaration of Independence, was
speaker of the New Hampshire House of Representatives, 1829 and 1830. After serving
as second comptroller of the U.S. Treasury, 1830–1836, he was chargé d'affaires to Peru,
where he died in 1838. Sherman D. Fletcher (b. 1810) of Westford, Mass., was later treasurer of that town, 1853–1882. Mrs. Webber was the wife of French's friend John A.
Webber.
8. Probably Henry H. Carroll (d. 1846), who had been a law student in the office of
Franklin Pierce and thereafter was an editor of the *New-Hampshire Patriot*. In 1844 he was
secretary of the Democratic convention at Baltimore.
9. Simon Brown (1802–1873) married French's half-sister Ann (b. 1808) in 1828.
10. Joseph Hall (1793–1859), Democratic congressman from Maine, 1833–1837. He
was an unsuccessful candidate for mayor of Boston in 1849.
11. William Gilmore Simms (1806–1870), South Carolina novelist and poet. The works
cited by French were published, respectively, in 1833, 1834, and 1835.

Monday, September 14. When I arose yesterday morning I intended to
attend church and hear my pattern of an Orthodox parson, Mr. Clement,[1] hold forth, but circumstances changed my determination. . . .

. . . Parson Clement . . . is my pattern of an Orthodox parson—I take
pleasure in his company & in hearing his discourses. He does not appear
to deem it derogatory to his holiness to wear a face dressed in smiles,
upon all proper occasions; he can enjoy a good story and laugh with
those that laugh upon the relation of it. He does not deem it necessary
to make the constant burden of his sermons, what most orthodox ministers of my acquaintance do theirs—viz.[,] "You are totally depraved
from your birth, you must repent or go to hell. The human mind is
naturally a ruin, and must be entirely rebuilt ere you can have any hope

of happiness hereafter." Which, in my opinion, is tantamount to saying—
God has created you imperfect, it is your duty *to remedy his imperfections*!

Instead of harping forever on points of doctrinal belief, the majority
of Mr. C.'s sermons are moral and practical. He tells his hearers what
they must do to be happy here—how they ought to live to keep their
consciences void of offence toward one another, & to prepare themselves
by correct lives here to enjoy an eternity of perfection. This is what a
truly good minister should do. He should be the father of his flock—
they should love him & feel that under his protection they are safe from
the wolves of the intellectual world. The course Mr. Clement has pursued
since he was ordained here has done more to moralize, aye, *to christianize,*
the inhabitants of Chester, than could be done by a bigoted, long-faced,
zealot in three quarters of a century—indeed such an one never could
bring about what Mr. C. has. I esteem—I love the man. May he be long
preserved as the Spiritual Shepherd of the people of my native parish.

1. Rev. Jonathan Clement, D.D., was the pastor of Chester's Congregational Church
from 1831 to 1845, years "favored by a continued religious interest and progress in temperance work." John Carroll Chase, *History of Old Chester* (1926), p. 79.

Friday, September 18. How still it seems! The company is gone, and *we*
have been making such a racket—the Frenches, the Flaggs, Madame
Russell[1] & the Richardsons—how we did laugh & talk, sing & dance,
write crambo[2] and phrenologise! And now the ticking of the timepiece
& the scratching of my steel pen are the only *noises* that fall upon my
ear, though Anne and Louise sit at my elbow, one *immersed* in Mrs. Opie,[3]
the other diligently engaged in a sort of a *literary* ramble through *Flora's
Interpreter.*[4] Well, such a frolick does one good at times. I have enjoyed
this day right well. . . . Oh Chester! . . . I do love this town, with which
all—ay *all*—of my early associations are connected. Its hills & vallies, its
lakes & streamlets are familiar to me, and in its forests I am perfectly at
home. I have looked forth in a morn of Spring and seen the Ocean, like
a thread of silver, glittering in the horizon.[5] I have gazed *into* the western
sky upon a summer's evening, when the last rays of the departed sun
were streaming upward toward the zenith & bordering the tiny clouds
with fringes of golden light, till imagination had formed a vast sea, check-
ered with its shining islands—'twas glorious!

1. Madame Russell, undoubtedly the mother of Charles P. Russell, minister of the Congregational Church in nearby Candia, who later married Elizabeth's sister Louisa.
2. Crambo is a rhyming game in which a word or line chosen by one side must be
matched by the other side with another word or line rhyming with it.
3. Amelia Opie (1769–1853), English novelist and poet, who ceased writing after becoming a Quaker in 1825.

4. *Flora's Interpreter: or, The American Book of Flowers and Sentiments,* by Sarah Josepha Buell Hale (1788–1879), was published in 1832. Mrs. Hale was born in Newport, N.H., and resided there until 1828, when she moved to Boston to edit the *Ladies' Magazine.*

5. The opening sentences of Chase's *History of Chester* are "From the top of 'Walnut Hill' in Chester by the aid of a glass the ocean and ships passing along the coast may be seen and in the evening Portsmouth lights can be plainly distinguished. The Isles of Shoals also come into view on a clear day."

Sunday, September 27. . . . The Judge returned from Amherst yesterday and Father & mother came up in the evening to eat fruit. After they left, the Judge played ever so many old tunes that I love to hear, and then I went to bed & dreamed *horrible* dreams & waked & was glad they *were* dreams. . . . Walked after breakfast with Henry. Went to the graveyard & stood at the head of my mother's grave—she died at 24! Nothing but a *broken slate stone* marks her grave! It shall not always be so, if I live. I am her *only* child, and at some future day I will erect a stone to mark the spot where her remains sleep, worthy of the virtue & goodness of herself and of the affection of her only son.[1]

1. French did this. See November 18, 1843.

Gilford, N.H., Tuesday, September 29. At 8 o'clock yesterday morning, Bess, Anne & Louise & myself started from Chester in a Carryall, with a span of the very laziest horses that I ever saw. We proceeded on for the first 30 miles very comfortably, at the rate of 4 miles an hour. It was then 3 o'clock & we had 17 miles to travel to arrive here. After stopping half an hour to "*bate,*" we again got under way, horses duller than ever, and with all the strength of this good right arm, with a tough walnut stick and a good lash at the end of it, I could not get along 3 miles an hour. It became dark and we could no longer gaze out upon the party-colored forests, . . . & we became somewhat impatient to arrive at our journey's end, but the horses were lashed & pounded in vain; they had taken their jog & like a pair of obstinate mules, they were determined not to be beaten out of their own notions of a befitting pace after nightfall—but, with singing, talking, laughing, telling stories, and as far as myself was concerned, some scolding & swearing, at ½ past nine we arrived at Doctor Barker's,[1] where we met with a "highland welcome," & where we now are. This forenoon I have been looking about at the factories,[2] etc., have seen them cast plough irons at the furnace. I never before saw any iron cast, &, of course, it was a curiosity to me.

1. Dr. Lemuel M. Barker was the husband of Sarah Richardson (b. 1800), Elizabeth French's oldest sister. The Barkers later moved to Washington and then to Rainsford Island in Boston Harbor.

2. The Gilmanton Iron Works took advantage of the bog iron in the area to produce nails, horseshoes, and tools from 1780 until after World War II.

Chester, Monday, October 5. . . . Tomorrow is to be muster day, & the mighty preparation for militia display is going on. I just heard the "clinking of hammers," but somewhat doubt whether it was "the armorers closing rivets up." I am certain "the sun has *not* made a golden set tonight," neither doth it "promise a goodly day tomorrow."[1] I should like to see the old 17th paraded once more; for many a year I made one among its invincibles, as a member of the Chester Light Infantry, & for old acquaintance sake I hope for a pleasant day.

1. French is borrowing from Shakespeare's *Henry V*, Act iv, Prologue, for his hammers, armorers, and rivets, and from *Richard III*, Act v, scene 3, lines 19–21, for the sun's "golden set" and the promise of "a goodly day."

Wednesday, October 7. Yesterday was *almost* a lost day to me. Head ached all day, & oh how it rained. The Militia began to assemble at Orcutt's[1] at a little after daylight, & there they remained all day. One *heroic* captain,[2] warmed by military ardor, paraded his company at ½ past 6 A.M. while it was raining in torrents—they stood it like heroes, till they were drenched to the very skin—and undoubtedly felt as proud of having accomplished so glorious an achievement, as ever the troops of Napoleon did after devoting a Marengo or an Austerlitz[3] to the care of Madame Fame. . . . A little before dark, the barroom, stable and horse shed were evacuated, & the soldiery dispersed, somewhat crestfallen to be sure, for their plumes, which stood so erect at morning, had assumed somewhat the appearance of a dunghill cock's tail after a day's rain has reduced it, apparently, to a single semicircular feather. . . .

1. Ephraim Orcutt's tavern, across the street from the home of Daniel French, was a stopping point for the Boston-Concord stage. The house is now owned by Peter S. French, great-great-grandson of Benjamin Brown French.
2. Benjamin Pillsbury, postmaster of Chester, 1822–1833.
3. Marengo in Italy and Austerlitz in Moravia were the sites, respectively, of victories by Napoleon over the Austrians, June 14, 1800, and over combined forces of Russia and Austria, December 2, 1805.

Thursday, October 8. At 10 o'clock yesterday morning Henry, Edmund,[1] Mr. Currier & myself started for the forest after squirrels. We were absent nearly all day, & the *spoils* amounted to 13 grey squirrels. H. killed 8, Ed. 3, Currier 1 and myself 1—rather small for me who did *once* profess to be quite a sportsman in the squirrel line. I had the pleasure

of roaming the old woods, where I have roamed a thousand times—
perhaps not *quite a thousand*—say a hundred times—before. . . .

Presented John S. Brown, Esqr.'s son Francis a portrait of President
Brown, he having been named for him.[2] Who knows but the mere presentation of the portrait of so truly great and good a man may have a
good effect upon the future life of the donee. He will be told that he
was named *for* that man; the history of him will be impressed upon the
child's mind; his virtues & his piety will be a theme upon which his
worthy parents will delight to converse to their child, & he will naturally
come to the determination that he will preserve the name in its purity. . . .

1. Edmund French (1818–1901), Benjamin's youngest half-brother, later moved to
Washington and lived out his life there.
2. Francis Brown (1784–1821), Benjamin's uncle, was president of Dartmouth College,
1815–1820. John S. Brown, brother of Simon Brown, was active in the affairs of Chester
as a sheriff, coroner, and innkeeper.

Wednesday, October 14. . . . The comet has been visible for four or five
evenings to the naked eye.[1] It appeared the most brilliant last Sabbath
evening. Through a small spyglass it appears very like the moon when
partially obscured by a hazy atmosphere. . . .

1. Halley's Comet.

Saturday, October 18. Yesterday, wrote a letter to F. O. J. Smith. Bess
has concluded to accompany him & his lady to Washington in their private carriage, & I am to go alone, & shall be there 3 or 4 weeks before
she arrives. I once thought that I never would be in Washington again
without her while she lived, but Mr. & Mrs. S.[1] have succeeded in persuading me to revoke my determination. . . .

Today I went with Father to the "Moon place," where he intended to
discharge a tenant, & we went prepared for war, but it ended in a very
peaceable excursion indeed, for the good-natured looking Irishman soon
succeeded in convincing the old gentleman that he (the Irishman) was a
tolerably clever fellow, & "instead of biting he was bit," for the squire
suffered him to remain longer & gave him 150 cents! . . .

Got very foolishly vexed after dinner because Bess would not shew me
a piece of Louisa's poetry. Afterwards she handed it to me but I refused
to read it—a pretty specimen of my want of government over my temper
to end this book with, but nevertheless a *fact* that I cannot in conscience
fail to record for my own edification. . . .

Sabbath evening, Octr. 18th. . . . Upon the whole, by far the greater
proportion of the matter contained in my journal, thus far, is not only

of interest but of *use* to me, and instead of giving up the determination to keep a general record of the events of my life, I am induced to go on with increased interest & care, & have here to record a sincere regret that I have not kept a regular journal ever since I commenced in this very book in Aug. 1828. There is something in everyone's life, let it be ever so monotonous, that will be interesting to himself & his friends, & if he keeps a faithful journal it must be necessarily a transcript of his life.

1. Junia Bartlett Smith, born in Kingston, N.H., was a second cousin of S. F. B. Morse's wife.

Saturday, October 24. . . . The weather has changed and it is quite cold. The stars are shining out from a clear blue heaven, the new moon has just disappeared below the horizon, & the comet is blazing among the constellations—and here I am writing, in the sitting room, while the Ch. Jus. & my father are talking, the latter with his usual earnestness[,] about an application for a road from Derry to—somewhere—to the making of which the Chesterites are greatly opposed. The Judge says, when he tries a case he always tries it on general principles, & pays but little attention to *the blarney* the lawyers put into it. . . .

Sunday, October 25. . . . The Judge has been nearly all day endeavoring to solve, satisfactorily to himself, the following passage in Milton

> They pass the planets seven, and pass the fixed,
> And that chrystalline sphere whose balance weighs
> The trepidation talked, and that first moved. . . .

I wish I had half the Judge's perseverance in hunting any such matter that I cannot understand at a single reading, but I have not a tithe of his learning if I had the disposition.

Friday, October 30. . . . After tea we all *dressed up,* & went to Capt. Benjamin Fitz, Jr.'s[1] wedding. It was in his new house, and the bride *was* Miss Climena Green[2] of Deerfield—she is about 21 years of age, he not far from 35. I was very much interested in this wedding, and was very happy to have an opportunity to attend it. The bridegroom is about 6 months my junior. We were born within a very short distance of each other, we were *brought up* together, and during childhood were almost inseparable companions. We went chestnutting & plumming together,

we climbed apple trees & slid down hill together, & we did everything
that boys do together, not omitting fighting underneath the seats at
school, & until we were 15 the intimacy between us existed. Then I left
Chester for a season of years, and on my return my friend had united
himself to the orthodox church. I was somewhat of too wild a nature to
associate with *the elect,* & from that time our companionship seems to
have been broken off; still I have felt a deep interest in the Captain's
welfare, as I do in the welfare of all those who were young with me, &
it rejoiced my heart to see him stand up, with his young fair bride, before
the sacred priest, & resign his bachellorship forever. . . .

1. Benjamin Fitz (1800–1854).
2. Climena Green (1814–1875).

TWO

A Democratic Clerk in Washington

1835–1841

When French accepted his position in Washington, his interests, like those of many other Americans at the time, shifted from his narrow, local world to the great expanding nation that lay outside New Hampshire. During the next half dozen years his attention shifted from Jacksonian Democracy in the Granite State to national party battles and from the small financial ventures of a rural state to the investment possibilities in a national economy. Short horseback and stage-coach rides from one small town to another were replaced by journeys of hundreds of miles by steamboat and railroad to cities such as New York, Philadelphia, and Baltimore. In 1830 French was thirty years old, married with no children, eking out a living from government, law, and journalism in the country town of Newport. By 1840 he was forty, living with his wife and child on Capitol Hill, relishing his position as chief clerk, writing to his brother about investments in land and railroads, and visiting family members who had moved to Boston, New York, and beyond. He was part of the revolution that was changing the lives of many in the United States.

French's journal does not immediately reflect the dramatic alteration in his life. During his first two years in the Clerk's office Benjamin spent at least half of his time in New Hampshire, and Elizabeth almost all of hers. When in Washington, he was so busy at work, so beguiled by the pleasures of the city, and so unsure of how long he would stay that few entries were made in the journal. But as he settled into his job and after Elizabeth came to live with him, trips to New Hampshire became visits rather than homecomings, and his journal began to fill with descriptions of city life. After November 1835 the journal of Benjamin Brown French becomes a national rather than a New Hampshire story.

French and his friends were enthralled by the technological changes that were taking place. When the patent office burned in 1836 and the models of hundreds of inventions were destroyed, Congressman Andrew

54

Beaumont of Pennsylvania told French not to worry because Americans were so inventive that they could replace the office with "a building as large as the President's House & the Yankees [would] fill it with models in two years."[1] Anxiety soon tempered this enthusiasm. On learning that the steamboat *Pulaski* had gone down with two hundred on board, an alarmed French wrote: "Such losses are dreadful. . . . Something must be done, or steam navigation had better never have been discovered—it will prove, to the human race rather a curse than a blessing."[2]

French nevertheless welcomed the opportunities for new investments, which he frequently discussed in his letters to Henry Flagg French. Intrigued by the opportunities that lay in the West, he listened eagerly to the tales of Lieutenant Benjamin L. E. de Bonneville, who had just returned from hunting fur in the West, and to those of a land speculator from Detroit. It is obvious in this chapter that French shared the mania for western speculation that gripped Americans before the Panic of 1837.

French was even more interested in politics than business. On his arrival in Washington he was introduced to the boardinghouse system, the breeding ground of party politics, and showed his party commitment by moving into good Democratic establishments. He first boarded at S. A. Hill's on Pennsylvania Avenue with Franklin Pierce and other Democrats from New England and New York. After Elizabeth came to stay, the couple roomed first at Masi's and then returned to Hill's, where the clientele had widened to include Democrats from Virginia and Alabama as well as the North—part of what Martin Van Buren called the alliance of "the planters of the South and the plain republicans of the North."[3]

But with a father and a father-in-law highly placed on the bench and bar of New Hampshire, French was not a "plain republican." Somewhat self-consciously he pointed out the contradictions in Jacksonian Democracy. "I am acquainted," he wrote, "with many who pride themselves upon their *democracy*—but whose every action shows that they think themselves too good to associate with any save the *nabobs* of the land. . . ." French claimed that he "despis[ed]" such people, but it is clear that he had some of their qualities himself. He admitted that he was not "certain that it [was] possible to have a government without an aristocracy."[4]

He was also scornful of the rougher side of the new democratic system of government—the spoils system, corruption, violence, and frequent waste of time. After one particularly graphic description of an all-night session of Congress in which many members fell asleep, he proclaimed that he had "seldom known any beneficial result from a night session."[5] French never missed an opportunity to describe the numerous fights that broke out on the floor of the House, and he was outraged by the senseless duel in which Congressman William J. Graves of Kentucky shot and killed Congressman Jonathan Cilley of Maine.

This ambivalence about democracy was applied also to the administration of Martin Van Buren. French was initially enthusiastic about Van Buren, remarking that the President-elect was "one of the most perfect gentlemen [he had] ever seen,"[6] but four years later he had changed his mind, describing Van Buren as a "coldhearted[,] *calculating* man."[7] For a Democratic officeholder he was strangely objective about the campaign of 1840. After traveling out to Bladensburg, Maryland, for a Democratic rally, he commented that the speakers were trying to "tickle the ear and stir up the feelings of the multitude. . . ."[8]

The chapter that follows serves as one man's description of the political and economic changes of the 1830s.

1. Dec. 15, 1836.
2. June 21, 1838.
3. Martin Van Buren to Thomas Ritchie, Jan 13, 1827, Van Buren Papers, Library of Congress.
4. Nov. 28, 1836.
5. April 2, 1837.
6. Dec. 2, 1836.
7. Nov. 10, 1840.
8. June 23, 1840.

Journal

Providence, R.I., Wednesday, November 4. On board steamer *Benj. Franklin* at the wharf. Here I am, after a pleasant passage from Chester, from which place I started at half past 8 o'clock yesterday morning. This parting with friends—dear friends—how it makes one feel. A sickness at the heart always comes over me at such partings, but they must take place and we must learn to bear them. We cannot live always, nor can friends always reside together. I have left behind me *one heart* that is so blended with my own that even distance has not its usual power to separate—the light of distant stars will mingle & form one atmosphere of light, & though the Atlantic—or even the entire hemisphere—separate two beings, their hearts may still beat on in unison, & the affections still remain unbroken, like a chain of living light. How happy have I been for the past 5 months and Hope whispers, I shall again be so. But I must proceed with plain matter of fact.

Henry brought me as far as Derry in a wagon, from thence I came to Lowell in the Stage—*only* 15 passengers (24 is the usual number) & perhaps half a ton of baggage. Oh how I *do hate* stagecoaches as they are managed here—the rule is never to run an extra, if it can be possibly avoided, & *never* to refuse a passenger. Thanks to the genius of Fulton for the glorious discovery of the application of steam to the purpose of locomotion! Dined in Lowell, and at 2 o'clock—off we were whirled upon the railroad, at the rate of a mile in less than 2 minutes, toward Boston. I never traveled so fast before, though I have traveled on the same road. We were but one hour—*excluding* a stop of 10 minutes—in passing from Lowell to Boston (24 miles). Took lodgings at the Bromfield House, where I met my old & dear friend D. Currier, Jr., Esq. Walked up to the State House and gazed at the statue of Washington a while—the thought struck me that it was rather a *cold* way of holding our friends in remembrance, this turning them into marble. . . . At nine o'clock this morning started from Boston, in the cars, for this place and arrived here at eleven. The road from Boston here is excellent & quite romantic in its location. At Canton there is a superb viaduct across the river, in passing which the village & factories are below you. At East Brattlebrough, the road passes through the middle of a graveyard, and there stand the monuments on either hand as *memento moris,*[1] to the living who chance to pass that way. . . .

1. Reminders of mortality.

Delaware River, Thursday, November 5. Steamer *New-Philadelphia.* Noon. When I concluded my notes of yesterday, the boat was under weigh, & we had a lovely night to pass through the sound. The sky was cloudless, & hardly a breath of air was in motion—the full moon shone in all her glory. I paced the deck & watched the sparks from the chimnies for a long time, streaming away over our stern & falling upon the waters, where their bright souls were extinguished and their little *black bodies* were left to float uncared for upon the deep, while countless millions kept pouring forth to fill their places. How like human life it was! . . . Arrived at N. York a few minutes past 5 this morning. The city was sleeping, and in darkness, except that the moon threw her light from the western sky, over roof & steeple, and a few white sails were to be seen scattered over the harbor. Not one of the ten thousand souls of busy day was to be heard—it was like the city of the dead. We passed up round the battery & the boat hauled in at the wharf. I shook hands with Col. Force[1] of Washington, who came on from Providence, handed him my letters to place in the P.O.[,] bid him good-by & went on board the

Swan, and between 6 & 7 we were off for South Amboy. Not a single passenger on board the boat that I ever saw before. Arrived at Amboy about 9—passed across to the Delaware on the Railroad—never traveled on a railroad so slow before. Got on board this boat a little before 12, and now at 15 minutes past we are steaming it onward for Philadelphia at a good round rate. No one here that I know—all—all strange faces!

1. Peter Force (1790–1868), mayor of Washington, D.C., 1836–1840, collected and published source materials on early American history.

Friday, November 6. At about 3 o'clock yesterday Afternoon we arrived at Philadelphia. I stopped at the U.S. Hotel. . . . Attended the Theatre— Mme. Celeste[1] played. She always plays in dumb parts. . . . Celeste has a *penchant* for performing male characters. I dislike it, I would never see a female upon the stage in male attire, could I avoid it, and it is only pardonable under circumstances where in actual life such disguise would seem to be necessary—but a female in breeches, through play after play, and character after character, though it shocks not *my delicacy,* for I never carry any with me to a Theatre—still it lowers the female character in my estimation, especially when I see the most respectable female audiences gazing on with much apparent satisfaction. It ought not to be tolerated by the respectable of the female sex. Celeste is handsome & dances elegantly.

Retired at ½ past 11, pretty much exhausted with the fatigue of the day. Arose at 6 this morning, came immediately on board the Steamer *Robert Morris,* and here I am on the Delaware, *boiling* on toward New Castle, where we are to take the cars for Frenchtown. It has rained a little this morning, but the weather is very calm, and thus far my passage on has been as smooth and exciteless as need be. I have read all the newspapers I could get, *thoroughly.* Have read several Temperance publications. . . .

1. Mme. Celeste (1815–1882), French actress who visited America, 1834–1835.

Washington, Sunday, November 8. From the *Morris,* I passed across to Frenchtown in the cars, & at a little before 12 [Friday, November 6] found myself under weigh on the Chesapeake for Baltimore, on board the fastest steamer in the Union—The *George Washington.* At quarter past 3 we were at the wharf at Baltimore! Went immediately to the railroad depot, & took a ticket for this place. At ½ past 5 we started, and at 8 we landed on Pa. Avenue in this Metropolis. Came immediately to Mr. S. Masi's,[1] & took up my residence for the winter. Yesterday went to the Capitol in the morning & shook all my fellow *officials* by the hand, & was glad—aye very glad to meet them. They are all good fellows—never, among so few were there more generous hearts, & *entire* souls, associated. God bless them, from Col. Franklin[2] down, God bless every one of them.

Was nearly all day arranging my room. Attended the Theatre in the evening. The House is very much improved in appearance, but the smell & the smoke of cookery is still there, and the noise is enough to craze one who cares anything about the play. . . .

1. Masi kept a boardinghouse on C Street.
2. Walter S. Franklin of Pennsylvania was Clerk of the House from 1833 until his death in 1838.

Monday, November 9. . . . An enormous caravan of *living animals*, and *dead* wax figures, came into the city today. They paraded through Pa. Avenue twice, with music playing & banners flying. There were between 30 & 40 carriages drawn by 130 horses. Three elephants and two camels accompanied the train, and taken all together it made quite an imposing spectacle.

Tuesday, November 10. Mrs. Masi had a little party last evening. I dreaded it, for I thought it would be so stupid where there would be so few that I am acquainted with. Went down at about 8, & was introduced by Mr. Webber. Soon became acquainted & began to feel at home—music commenced & I listened & enjoyed. Then dancing was proposed & even I danced. Then there was some fine song singing by those who understood how to sing. . . .

Thursday, November 12. After writing in my journal day before yesterday, Thornton, Fletcher,[1] Pease, Marr[2] & myself went shooting. We rambled off a mile or two into the woods, & killed 5 sparrows!! one each. It was glorious sport! Fletcher's gun would not go off, & so he touched *it off* with a piece of lighted tow,[3] which was lighted by a flash from Thornton's gun. I did not arrive home until after dark, & then the skin was worn off my toes & I was tired enough. Slept all the better for the sport! Yesterday nothing occurred worth recording, before tea. Had a new carpet put down in my room here, & wrote a letter to Mrs. French. While at tea, recd. a note from Webber asking me to call at his house, as Capt. Bonneville[4] was there. I went up immediately after tea & stayed till nine, then B., W.[5] & I called at the Washington Coffee House & eat[6] 3 small plates stewed oysters. Capt. Bonneville was a lieutenant of the

8th Regt. U.S. Infantry, in 1819, & when I was a sergeant of a detachment of recruits of that Regt. at Fort Warren, Boston Harbour, Lieut. B.
commanded the detachment for a short time. He was young, generous
& honorable, & a great favorite of mine. I obtained liberty to provide a
substitute, and in procuring one I expended the last cent of money I
had on earth. I had no means to get away from the Island and in this
emergency I went to Lieut. Bonneville & stated my difficulty, & he, without a moment's hesitation, handed me five dollars. It was to me, then,
equal to unbounded wealth, for it answered all my purpose, and from
that day to this I have never thought of Bonneville but with feelings of
respect & gratitude. From the day I left Ft. Warren until last evening I
have not seen him and this morning I have enclosed to him 10 dollars
with a note expressive of my thanks for his kindness. Since I saw him he
has been stationed at the South & West, until nearly 4 years since, when
he obtained a furlough & went off into the region of the Rocky Mountains trading & hunting. He was so long absent that he was supposed to
be dead, & was dropped from the Army list. He has very recently returned and is now here to get reinstated in his rank. May Fortune favor
him. He gave us a very interesting account of his western tour, last evening, and some very amusing anecdotes in relation to the mode of catching beaver, killing bears, wolves, etc. The interview, to me, was very
pleasant & very interesting indeed. . . .

1. Thornton and Fletcher had been with French on the stage the previous May heading
for New England.
2. James H. Marr was a clerk in the Post Office Department.
3. Tow is broken flax or hemp fiber.
4. Benjamin L. E. de Bonneville (1796–1878) had just returned from the fur-hunting
expedition that Washington Irving described in his *Adventures of Captain Bonneville.*
5. John A. Webber.
6. Archaic form of "ate," often used by French.

Sunday, November 15. . . . A letter came this morning from my brother
(the entire contents of which related to the Chester P.O. & was for the
P.M. Gen.) enclosed to Col. Franklin. The sharp-eyed fellows at the City
Post Office ascertained by *peeping,* that the enclosure was for me, and
erased the word "Free" & charged 50 cts. I went to the City P.O. on
receiving it[,] shewed the Clerk the enclosure, & claimed a deduction. He
could not make it, but referred me to the P.M. Gen. I am not yet so far
gone in miserly propensities, as to run after the *Post Master General of the
United States of America,* to get a deduction in my Post Office account of
the paltry sum of 50 cents—neither do I consider it very *dignified* in any
officer to exercise that *espionage,* over the correspondence of a free citizen
of this republic, that shall enable him or his myrmydons,[1] to ascertain,

by the miserable business of *peeping* into letters, what their contents are. Well, I have this to console me—the revenues of my country are increased 50 cents today, by the sponging of that sum from my pocket to pay for business exclusively relating to the General P. Office!! . . .

1. Myrmidons, faithful followers who carry out orders without question.

Tuesday, November 17. Just as I had finished the foregoing last evening Mr. Whitney[1] came in, just from attending a lecture on Phrenology, & quite warmed up with the subject. We conversed upon that, and other subjects until about 11—then he left & I retired. Today called, with Col. Burch,[2] upon the President of the U.S. The old Hero looks in good health. While there, Govs. Cass[3] & Forsyth came in, & we met Gov. Woodbury at the door, so I had the pleasure of seeing a majority of the men who rule the nation today. I have seen none of them except Gov. Woodbury since last spring. They all appear as if the world went smoothly with them—the same good natured smile lurks about the corners of Forsyth's mouth as when he used to stand as the champion of the Democratic party in the Senate. He is the best looking man of the Cabinet. . . .

1. Whitney was a mechanic who boarded at Masi's.
2. Samuel Burch was chief clerk in the office of Clerk of the House.
3. Lewis Cass (1782–1866) was governor of the Michigan Territory, 1813–1831; Secretary of War, 1831–1836; and unsuccessful candidate for President in 1848.

Monday, November 23. . . . This morning went, as usual, to the Capitol, & Sherman [Fletcher] brought me a letter from my beloved Elizabeth. Was very much pleased to receive it. Wrote a while, then walked over & viewed the improvements in the Senate Chamber. It is very much improved in some respects. The Reporters' desks are moved down upon the floor, & the circular gallery is prepared for the ladies, &, it is said, they are not to be admitted on the floor of the Senate. This is all proper, for with such crowds as used to jam in last winter and winter before last to hear Clay & Webster, it was nearly impossible to get about the chamber at all, & with such a buzzing as was continually going on directly at the backs of the Honorable Senators, in the shape of whispering & laughing, it must have been with much effort that they could attend to the matters before the Senate—I know it was very annoying. . . .

Tuesday, November 24. Today, I suppose my wife left Chester, for Kingston, where she is to meet Mr. & Mrs. Smith,[1] & tomorrow they are to

start for this city. Oh what an anxious weary week will the next be to
me. If she could imagine how I passed the time before when I knew she
was on the way here[,] she never would have consented to accompany
Mr. & Mrs. Smith, and I—oh what a simpleton I was to consent. But it
is too late to repent. All I can say now is—May she be protected from
all harm, & may the weather prove propitious till she arrives here in
safety. This has been quite a cold, winter-like day, and it rains this evening. It does not promise well for the starting upon a long journey tomorrow.

1. Congressman Francis O. J. Smith of Maine,.

Saturday, November 28. . . . Have been cherishing a pair of whiskers for
two months past, but they came out in all the colors of the rainbow—*red*
predominating—and they looked so *piggy* that I made a sacrifice of them
today. I know my wife will be glad of that.

Monday, November 30. . . . I certainly expected a letter from Chester
this morning which should give me some information about my wife, but
none came. Oh how disappointed I was. I never felt more so in my life.
I learn from gentlemen who have arrived from the North that it is good
sleighing there now. Will Mr. Smith come in his carriage! It must be
horrid to himself & the ladies, if he does. I hope he will so far depart
from his usual manner as to forego once in his life, a favorite project. I
have done little else all day than calculate the chances that Mr. S. would
or would not take his carriage—and I have reckoned up when he would
arrive here[,] let him start how & when he may, provided the rivers
remain open. I cannot think, even if he takes his carriage that he will
come all the way by land. Anxiety & uncertainty mingled, make me very
restless, sensitive & unhappy, but a few days more & it will be gone. I
shall, I trust[,] see Bess, before this week is gone, in health & happiness. . . .

Wednesday, December 2. I recd. a letter from Harriette[1] this morning.
I was glad to receive it for it gave me assurance that Mrs. French had
left Chester. This was better than entire uncertainty—but why does not
Smith write, if but a line to tell me how they get along? . . .
   . . . I have procured *The Mayor of Windgap*[2] to read. If I can but get
interested in that, I may get rid of a portion of time without constantly
thinking of my wife & making myself unhappy by imagining how un-

pleasantly she must be situated, riding in an open Barouche, day after day, in this horrid cold weather. Smith could not have selected a worse time, and with a carriage too, through the snow! I can't think of it with any patience. . . .

1. Harriette French (1815–1841), Benjamin's half-sister.
2. Michael Banim (1796–1874), *The Mayor of Windgap* (London, 1835). One of the *O'Hara Tales,* stories of Ireland modeled on the Waverly Tales of Sir Walter Scott.

Thursday, December 3. . . . There is, boarding with me here, a young man by the name of Whitney[1] whom I *"cotton to"* considerably. He is a gentleman of taste & refinement, & when I say he is a mechanic I say it not in disparagement, but as highly honorable to him, for he is a living evidence that an accomplished mind may as readily be formed at the mechanic's bench, as over Blackstone, Galen, or John Henry.[2] Mr. Whitney is well educated, I should judge from his appearance & conversation, apparently of a very amiable disposition, & well educated in the school of politeness.

Last evening & today I have read *The May[or] of Windgap.* It is quite interesting, though there is a little too much Irish about it for my taste. . . .

1. Marginalia: Poor Whitney—he afterwards died in Philadelphia of smallpox.
2. Authors of learned treatises.

Saturday, December 5. Two days more are among *the past* since I wrote here—two *anxious weary* days, but I have been very much employed at the office & the time has not seemed so long. Col. Hall arrived last evening & Pierce today at noon. Both gave me information of my wife's being at Philadelphia, and this evening Judge Hubbard and family came. They left Mrs. French in Baltimore & she will be here tomorrow! Wrote a letter today to Mrs. Richardson.[1] This evening Hall, Pierce, Thornton, Paine,[2] Webber & Hubbard have been at my room & we have passed the evening very pleasantly. Discussed politics & political men, gunnery, speculation, etc., drank a couple of bottles of wine & smoked sundry cigars. Mr. Paine has a rare faculty of amusing by odd comparisons, remarks, etc., & has really contributed *very much* to my amusement this evening. I was even pleased with him. Thornton remarked that Daniel Webster was the greatest orator God ever made—aye the greatest he ever could make! Paine said, "What will you bet of that!" . . .

1. Betsey Smith Richardson (1774–1841), mother of Elizabeth French.
2. Orris S. Paine was later clerk in the land office.

Wednesday, December 9. Well, "just as I expected," days have gone since I wrote any in my journal. At 5 o'clock Sabbath evening my dear wife arrived in health, and *how* glad I was to see her. . . .

Congress commenced its session on Monday. It took some little more than the ordinary time to organise on account of a motion by Mr. Patton[1] of Va. to choose a Speaker by a *viva voce* vote instead of by ballot. The question was debated some time, Col. Franklin, the Clerk, presiding. Mr. Polk was elected Speaker at the first Ballot. The sudden death of Hon. Senator Smith[2] of Conn. on Sabbath morning had delayed business some. He is to be buried today. Called upon the President evening before last. Found him in excellent spirits—the proceedings in the opening of the Session pleased him very much. . . .

1. John Mercer Patton (1797–1858), Democratic congressman, 1830–1838.
2. Nathan Smith (1770–1835), Whig senator, 1833–1835.

Tuesday, December 15. . . . Yesterday Mr. Smith took me into his carriage & we went out calling & leaving cards. The first time I have entered a carriage drawn by horses, since I was in Boston! Attended the National Theatre once last week; it is handsome inside, but the *saloon* is nothing under heaven but a common *grog shop.* If Heaven should be located here in Washington there would certainly be a grog shop in one corner! Everything here seems to be contaminated by haunts of dissipation—even the Capitol itself has not escaped. . . .

Sunday, March 20. It being the first day of *dust.* Once more, after a lapse of more than 3 months, I am journalising. . . . I have repaired to the Capitol at 9 o'clock every morning, except Sundays, and *headache* days, which have not been many, & returned about 4, dined & visited, or had company, or attended the Theatre. . . .

Sunday, April 10. . . . We had quite a scene in the House of Representatives a fortnight ago last night [March 27]. The House was in session until ½ past 4 on Sabbath morning. Messrs. Wise[1] & Bynum[2] had quite a war; at about 2 o'clock A.M. called each other "damned rascal" & "damned Scoundrel," & came very near having a personal collision *pistol in hand*! but were prevented by their friends, and the matter was settled between them by the intervention of the House. It was, in my opinion, a most disgraceful scene. I was at the Clerk's table all night—Franklin being sick, & Johnston[3] tired out. . . .

1. Henry A. Wise (1806–1876), congressman from Virginia, 1833–1844, shifted from Democrat to Whig over the Bank question.

2. Jesse A. Bynum (1797–1868), Democratic congressman from North Carolina, 1833–1841.

3. Robert N. Johnston (d. 1845), assistant clerk of the House.

Sunday, November 27. . . . I remained in the city until the Thursday morning succeeding the 4th of July, at ½ past 2 o'clock, when with my "better half" I started for the North. The weather was excessively hot, and the boats were crowded. We arrived in Philadelphia that afternoon. Col. Pierce & Lady[1] & Mr. Jarvis[2] & Lady were in company with us. We all took private lodgings in Philadelphia. . . . Friday morning we left Phila. & at about 3 P.M. found ourselves on board the steamer *Massachusetts,* bound for Providence, at the wharf in N.Y. At 5 we were under way & without incident or accident worthy of note we arrived in Providence the next day afternoon—having been detained 5 hours in the sound by fog. At 3 P.M. we arrived in Boston, and the first person who presented himself as we got out of the cars was my good brother-in-law Dr. Wells.[3] We remained at his house until Wednesday morning, and then, in company with Mrs. Wells we took the cars for Lowell, and at 1 o'clock P.M. arrived safely at Chester, where we were cordially welcomed by those we love.

I passed the principal part of the time while absent from this City at Chester, a great portion of which was occupied in recording the reports of the Committee of Claims of the H.R. made at the preceeding session. This, in my opinion[,] is an entirely useless labor, as the record is made up from *the printed report,* but custom has made it the duty of the Clerk of the House to have it done, & "that tyraness of fools" still calls on him to keep up the manuscript records. In the infancy of the Government, when there were few reports, & not the half of that few were printed, it was well enough to record them, but now, when the *printed reports* of a single Committee form a royal octavo volume, 2 inches thick, & all the reports of any importance are printed, it does seem to me an utter waste of time to copy these printed reports into a large record book. But it is done, & my past summer has nearly all been spent in doing it. I visited Newport, N.H., saw my friends & *enemies,* & enjoyed my visit. Went to Merrimack to see Thornton (who left the Country last month as chargé de affaires to Peru) three times. Visited Concord twice, Tyngsborough, Westford, Windham, etc. Fished & hunted some & with various success. When I arrived in Chester I found my brother Henry quite interested in the science of *Taxidermy*—or, in plain English, skinning & preserving

birds. I, at once, joined him & we collected and "put up" about 50 specimens—some of them very elegant—in the course of the summer.

I stayed in Chester until Monday, Octr. 17. At 10 A.M. on that day we
bade adieu to our kith & kin and took the Stage for Boston. At Andover
got on board the railroad cars & arrived in Boston about 4 P.M. Took an
Omnibus for Roxbury, where we arrived before dark. We staid with my
good brother and sister, Mr. & Mrs. Wells, until Wednesday morning,
when we bade them good-by and went to the Depot of the Boston &
Providence railroad. . . . When we arrived in Providence the wind was
blowing very fresh from the South. We went on board the *Providence*, &
at 2 were off. At dark we were off Point Judith, the wind blowing a gale,
almost everybody seasick. The gale continued through the night, and we
did not get into New York until 4 P.M. on Thursday. The Captain of the
boat said it was the roughest sea he ever experienced in the Sound. We
took lodgings at a Mrs. Mavers'[4] in John Street, and were very well taken
care of. At 6 the next morning we were under way for Philadelphia, &
without further adventure worthy of note, we arrived in this city about
8 o'clock Saturday evening [November 26]. We came to this house, Mrs.
S. A. Hill's, where we are very comfortably situated, and where we expect
to spend the winter, and where I intend to journalize a little once in a
while. . . .

1. Jane Means Appleton Pierce (1806–1863).
2. Leonard Jarvis (1781–1854), Democratic congressman from Maine, 1829–1837.
3. Dr. P. P. Wells, husband of French's half-sister Catharine (b. 1810), later moved to
Brooklyn.
4. Rebecca Maver ran a boardinghouse at 13 John St.

Monday, November 28. I attempted yesterday to bring up my journal,
but found it rather a tiresome business, & left many matters unnoticed
that I intended to have touched upon. I feel dreadful dull this evening,
as if I had rather "go to bed" than anything else, & I even resorted to
my journal as a sort of a refuge from *ennui*. By the way—I read *The
Diary of a Dèsennuyée*[1] last week, & was much amused with it. It gives a
description of a fashionable season in London and I doubt not the picture
is drawn to the life. How *like* many of the scenes are to our fashionable
winters here! Notwithstanding our boast of republicanism we are the
aristocracy. I am acquainted with many who pride themselves upon their
democracy—but whose every action shows that they think themselves too
good to associate with any save the *nabobs* of the land—who would go
farther to get a nod from an English *attaché* than I would to shake the
hand of King William himself. I am not certain that it is possible to have
a government without an aristocracy. Make it as democratic as you will,

there must be rulers, & if they themselves are not aristocratic there will always be a parcel of hangers-on about them who will set themselves up as being a little better than the common people—and who will turn up their noses at anyone beneath the grade of a Member of Congress, or General in the army, or Captain in the Navy. For my own part I utterly despise a man in whom I see indications of such feelings. The dignity of human nature, & the pride of place, should always be kept up—it is both proper and right that they should be, but neither of these forbid one to treat all his well behaved fellow beings with respect & kindness— & they do forbid anyone, bearing the form of man, to cringe & fawn in the presence of those he deems a little superior to himself; his doing so is evidence that he is not endowed with a proper spirit to do credit to any office in a democratic Government. —But where is this digression leading me?

Today I have been to the Capitol as usual &, as usual, returned, eat my dinner, called upon Mr.& Mrs. Morse, who are boarding here, spent an hour very pleasantly. Mr. Morse was here when I first came to this city in 1833, on his way to St. Augustine. He then resided in New York. He has since moved to Detroit, & is in raptures with that portion of our country. One would suppose, to hear him converse, that fortunes were as plenty as prairie wolves in the West. He is not singular, however, in his opinions. All Western men talk in the same manner, & I have been half inclined, many times, to seek my fortune in the Western world. Mr. & Mrs. M. came in after tea & spent an hour with us. Then Bess & I played backgammon[,] then I wrote in this journal, & now I will go to rest. It has snowed nearly all day. Winter seems to be coming in earnest.

1. *The Diary of an Ennuyée,* by the Irish writer Anna Murphy Jameson, published in 1826.

Friday, December 2. Members of Congress are coming into the city hourly, almost. My good friend Hon. F. O. J. Smith of Maine arrived on Tuesday evening. No N.H. members yet. Last evening Mr. Smith & I called upon Mr. Speaker Polk, and he amused us very much in describing to us the late Presidential electioneering campaign in Tennessee. His health appears to be in a miserable state, still he is in excellent spirits, which will overcome his ill health if anything can. James K. Polk is a man after my own heart. There is about him none of that starched appearance that high station sometimes gives a man. He is urbane & gentlemanly in his manners, communicative & even jocose, he is a man calculated to please everybody. He possesses great energy of disposition, and firmness of purpose. And he sustained himself as well as any man could have done, through the last long, laborious, fatiguing and stormy session. And notwithstanding the furious attacks upon him, even while presiding as Speaker, notwithstanding an evident league of a certain cabal to break him down by embarrassing him with question after question of order, his equanimity was never disturbed[,] and at the close of the session those who placed him in the station which he so highly honors could say with sincerity[,] "Well done thou good & faithful servant." From the first moment I became acquainted with Col. Polk, to this time, I have held him in great esteem & admiration. He shall have my vote for President if he is ever nominated for that office. . . .

Evening. Called on Mr. Van Buren today, in company with Mr. Morse. Found him ever so agreeable. I have always remarked that men as they attain toward the upper round of fortune's ladder, grow less and less haughty, & seem to lose much of that peculiar manner which says[,] "I am better than you." How apt the world are to imagine great men as surrounded by "a glory" or in some way superior in appearance to their fellow men. A child of a friend of mine was taken by his father to see President Jackson. When he returned his mother asked him how he liked the President. He answered[,] "Why, he is nothing but an old grey-headed man!" This is so perfectly characteristic of mankind. Though they do not think Napoleon, or Alexander, or Washington or Jefferson were really lions with long shaggy manes and fiery eyes, they imagine them, in personal appearance, to have been something more than mere men. Until I have been in the habit of seeing our great men daily, I confess I felt a sort of awe in the presence of men who stood high on our roll of fame. But I find them men & some of them, in some things, rather weak men. Mr. Van Buren is one of the most perfect gentlemen I have ever seen.

We called at the President's. He is too sick to see company, though recovering his health it is said. He has been dangerously sick. . . .

Wednesday, December 7. Yesterday at 12 o'clock the President sent his annual message to both Houses of Congress. I had a severe headache and did not stay to hear it read but procured a copy, came home & read it. It [is] the last *annual* message he will ever deliver, and I shall not be surprised if it is *the last,* for the President's health is said to be very feeble. This one page does not strike me as being so great a state paper as the preceding ones. It is a plain, business like, and dignified document, however, and will, hereafter rank among the best American State Papers. . . .

Friday, December 9. . . . . I was somewhat amused yesterday at hearing a member of the House relate one of John Quincy Adams's comparisons. He (Mr. A.) said that that part of the President's late message relative to the U.S. Bank reminded him of the story of the woman who called her husband "crack-louse." He undertook to chastise her for it, but the more he punished the more she persisted in calling him "crack-louse." At last he concluded to duck her, but as soon as her head appeared above the water she would repeat the annoying term, and when he had held her under so long that she despaired of ever coming again to the surface, she raised her hands above her head & made the motion of cracking a louse with her nails. "So," said Mr. A., "it is with the President, he has said all he could against the Bank, he has put it down, he is not yet contented, but just as he is about to retire from office, and while he is on a bed of sickness, he gives his parting anathema to the Bank—he thrusts up his hand above the waves & makes the 'crack-louse' motion!" I record this here that I may turn to it, in after days—when both the President & ex-President are in their graves—should I survive them— and read what one great man can be led by his feelings to say publickly of another.

Tuesday, December 13. . . . . The President counts the days that must elapse before he can return to the Hermitage. He longs for the time to arrive. How natural. And what a comment upon human greatness. Here is a man whom a Nation has delighted to honor. He has been the right arm of his country's defence—the bravest of her brave. He has been in her counsels as a Senator—he has been for nearly eight years the supreme head of the Nation—and he now, in his old age, is tired of public life and longs for the time to come when he can once more settle down in the quiet of the Hermitage & live out the remainder of life allotted to his portion as the plain unostentatious citizen—the farmer of Tennessee. I much doubt whether he ever sees his beloved Hermitage again, though I hope that happiness may still be in store for him.

Mr. Bouldin,[1] one of the boarders here, attended the Theatre last evening & saw *Pocahontas*[,] a play written by Mr. G. W. P. Custis.[2] He remarked, at the breakfast table this morning, that it was *most perfect in its kind,* for it was the most supremely ridiculous play he ever saw performed!

1. James W. Bouldin (1792–1854), Democratic congressman from Virginia, 1834– 1839, had replaced his brother.
2. George Washington Parke Custis (1781–1857), son of George Washington's stepson John P. Custis.

Thursday, December 15. Yesterday was a day not particularly to be remembered by me, but I shall not soon forget the events of this. At about ½ past 3 this morning Mr. Smith awoke me by informing me that there was a fire he believed at the Post Office. I immediately arose & went into his room & stood at the window some time, but could see no indications of fire, and only heard the distant cry, such as I have heard in this city many times before & paid no heed to. I thought it was a false alarm & retired again to rest. In about 15 minutes Mr. S. again knocked at my door and assured me it was the Post Office. I dressed myself & sallied out. When I arrived at the P.O. the flames were just bursting out at one window of the city office. In a very short time the entire end of the building occupied as the city P.O. & Patent office was enveloped in a sheet of flame. Not a single article was saved from either of those offices. The General P.O. end of the building remained untouched by the flames for a long time—so that nearly everything of value was saved from it. The building was completely destroyed by 7 o'clock. It was one of the most magnificent fires I ever beheld. Not a breath of air was stirring, & the combustible matter in the building caused the flames to mount high above the roof. The pieces of burning paper which were whirled into the air by the flames, the *storm* of sparks which were showered around, the thousands of people collected around, making a sea of human heads, the clattering of the engines, & the bawling of rough voices all conspired to make the scene exciting & interesting. But never was there anything more inefficient than the fire department of this city. They were there— *after the building was past saving*—and they worked tolerably well in keeping the buildings in the vicinity wet—but all seemed to be Captains, & at times, of the immense crowd present enough could not be procured to man the hydraulion! All stood wonder stricken, except the officers of the General P.O. with their efficient head—Mr. Kendall—they labored as became *men* to save the Government property, & they did save it. Were I an incendiary commend to me the Washington City Fire Department— I could burn the whole city for aught they would do to prevent me.

All the talk today has been about *the fire.* I was some amused at our breakfast table, when upon the subject being mentioned one of the gentlemen asked[,] "What fire?" To which inquiry there was a general response—"The Post Office & Patent Office has been burned this morning." The questioner for a moment appeared perfectly incredulous. At length he asked, if anything was saved. "Nothing from the City P.O. or Patent office," was the reply, "No," said Mr. Beaumont,[1] "there is not even the model of a mouse trap left." Some one regretted the loss of the models. "Oh[,]" said Mr. B.[,] "build a building as large as the President's House & the Yankees will fill it with models in two years." It seems the gentleman who was so much surprised, had slept through the whole alarm.

Mr. Bailey Peyton[2] of Tennessee, made a flaming speech today, following in the track his friend Wise had marked out for him. It was a rigmarole of abuse of the President, & among other things he told an anecdote said to be made by Judge R.[3] at my expense. Mr. P. laid the *venue* in R.I.—probably mistaking Newport, N.H., for Newport, R.I.

1. Andrew Beaumont (1790–1853), Democratic congressman from Pennsylvania, 1833–1837.
2. Balie Peyton (1803–1878), Whig congressman from Tennessee, 1833–1837.
3. Judge William M. Richardson, French's father-in-law.

Sunday, January 8. . . . On Wednesday evening [January 4] attended a party at Mr. Forsyth's. It was as usual a jam, but very brilliant & gay. Yesterday Col. Franklin invited a few friends to dine here with him, & nearly all our mess were invited to dine at Mr. Blair's.[1] I dined at home, & with Col. F. & his friends. We had enjoyed ourselves until about 9, when the gentlemen returned from Blair's. All seemed to be in *excellent spirits,* & the advent of the 8th of January was celebrated with as much hilarity by our mess, I suspect, as it ever was by any company of individuals. . . .

1. Francis P. Blair (1791–1876) was editor of the Democratic administration newspaper, the Washington *Globe,* 1830–1845.

Chester, Sunday, April 2. Well—here I am in the same back chamber where I passed a goodly portion of my infancy. How well do I remember, when a mere child, of being put to bed in this very chamber, as soon as it "was dark under the table," and when the house maid, in her wisdom *and kindness,* used to promise that if any bears or ghosts came after me, she would come up with the great fire shovel, and drive them away! And then how I used [to] lie and listen to the beating of my own heart and conjecture, in vain, what it could be that kept up *such a pounding.* . . .

From about the 10th of February, until the close of the session, on account of the trial of R. M. Whitney,[1] first, & then on account of the sickness of Mr. Johnston—Mr. Franklin's assistant in the House—I was under the necessity of doing duty constantly at the Clerk's table, and as there were a number of night sessions, my duties were excessively arduous. As all night sessions are very nearly alike I will endeavour to sketch one here.

The vast Hall of the House of Representatives is lighted by astral lamps and candles, and I should judge the light, when fully lighted for an evening session, is equal to that of at least 1,000 candles. The beautifully painted roof, the vast pillars, the red drapery about the Speaker's chair & between the columns, all appear richer, if possible, by artificial light than by the light of day, as it is introduced into that Hall. The galleries are usually crowded during an evening session—the Ladies' gallery particularly—with all the gentility of Washington in the Session—for Washington in the Session, & not in the Session, is hardly the same place. The members are nearly all in their places, and, as the Senate is not often in session, the "potent, grave & reverend Signors," may be seen scattered about the Hall. If the House happens to be *in good humor,* & some interesting subject is under debate, I know of no more imposing spectacle than an evening session. But when eleven or twelve o'clock arrives, the spectators begin to thin off, & the members drop away one after another. Those who remain become tired and sleepy. By one, the debaters grow angry, motions are made to adjourn & negatived, noise & confusion frequently occurs, the Speaker calls "order—order" at the top of his voice, members may be seen sleeping in their seats or stretched upon the sofas & chairs, & even upon the carpet in the esplanade, or back of the Speaker's chair. At 2 o'clock, or thereabout, someone will move a call of the House, & if it is agreed to & persisted in, by about 5 A.M. the Sergt. at arms begins to report members, who have been arrested by him, as, in attendance, they come into the Hall wrapped in their cloaks or overcoats, with their toilets unattended to, looking as little like "the first gentlemen in" America as possible. Their names are called as they appear & their excuses taken—some are fined, some excused, just as the caprice of the House happens to dictate. By daybreak a quorum is in attendance, & after wasting a night, a little after sunrise the House in its wisdom adjourns! I have witnessed this farce many times & have seldom known any beneficial result from a night session. I have known the House to sit until about 11 the day following the evening, & adjourn to the next day, & I have known a number of night sessions, when the House adjourned about daybreak—or perhaps not until sunrise—& met again at 10, 11 or 12 o'clock—the members & officers as unfit as possible to do business.

1. Reuben M. Whitney (b. 1791), once a director of the Bank of the United States, went over to the Jackson side and played a part in the attack on the Bank in 1832–1833. Here he is being questioned about his role in the removal of the deposits from the Bank.

Washington, Tuesday, September 19. During the month of May the President issued his proclamation calling an extra session of Congress, to meet on the 4th of this month. This call necessarily *called* all the Clerks to their posts & myself among the rest; so on the 6th day of June I left N.H. and came to this City. Boarded on Capitol Hill at Mrs. Sprigg's—where I am now boarding. I remained in this City until the 20th of July, & then returned to N.H. where I tarried until the last day of August, & then in company with F. O. J. Smith returned to this city & came immediately to Mrs. Sprigg's. Yesterday the news reached me that unto me a son was born on Tuesday the 12th of Septr. at 8 o'clock P.M. His name is Francis Ormond.[1] This news was, to me, the most joyful of any I ever received, for I have felt, ever since I ascertained that my wife was likely to add another being to the mass that inhabit this globe, that it might deprive me of her whom I hold so dear—but she has survived & is well & I am happy. . . .

1. Young Francis was named for Francis Ormond J. Smith.

Tuesday, December 26. . . . Well, from Sep. 19th to Octr. 16th the House of Representatives kept its officers, if not hard at work, very constantly in attendance. Circumstances placed me at the Clerk's table in the Hall, & kept me there night after night, until I was very nearly worn out. On Sunday morning Octr. 14th[1] by leave of Col. Franklin, I left this City in the cars for Baltimore at which place I located at the Eutaw House, where I slept away the afternoon & night of Sunday, & the next morning took the cars, with many members of Congress, for Wilmington, where we arrived all safe about 11 o'clock. We then took the boat for Philadelphia and arrived there about 2 o'clock. In short at 6 o'clock Wednesday evening I was at Haverhill, Ms., where I hired a horse and chaise & arrived at Chester at 10 o'clock that evening, where I found my wife & child well, & was happy. I spent the time among my kith & kin, very pleasantly indeed until the 14th day of Nov. when, with Bess & little Frank, I took the Stage—a regular northeast snow storm being in progress—and by stage & railroad and omnibus arrived at Dr. Wells's in Roxbury, at 8 o'clock P.M. Our good brother & sister were not a little surprised at seeing us, not expecting us at all in consequence of the storm. We were right glad to reach the end of that day's journey. At noon on Thursday we again got under way from Boston, and on Saturday evening, Nov. 18, arrived safe & sound & without accident at this city, & took up our abode at Mr. S. Masi's[2] in C street. . . .

1. Sunday was the 15th.
2. Francis O. J. Smith also boarded at Masi's that session.

Tuesday, January 9. The troubles on our Canadian frontier, growing out of the attempt in that Colony of the revolutionists to *republicanize* that

Government, are making much excitement. Yesterday in the Ho. Reps. a great part of the session was occupied in a discussion of this subject. Yesterday wrote a letter to Sister Harriette. Am doing duty in the Hall daily, now, Mr. Johnston being sick.

Monday, January 22. All is still, here, in relation to the Canada war. Messrs. Wise & Gholson[1] had a regular bout of blackguardism, in the House last Tuesday. They applied to each other epithets which no *gentleman* can suffer to be applied to himself with impunity—& no apology or explanation was made. A week has passed, & still nothing *belligerent* has taken place between them, as everyone supposed there must, for they are, professedly, honorable & fearless men. . . .

Am reading Lockhart's life of Scott.[2] Finished the 5th part last evening. What a glorious man Scott was. He was a model for mankind, but alas, alas, the World "will never look upon his like again." So kind, so brave, so gentlemanly, so honorable, so *"unspotted"* from the adulations of an admiring & wondering world! I would willingly have surrendered one half my life to have been the intimate friend of Walter Scott, the other half. I envy J. G. Lockhart the place he held. Stars, garters, & knightly belts, political honors and literary fame, what are they, or what would they be in comparison with the high satisfaction of having been the friend & acquaintance of Walter Scott? I have always admired him since I first read his *Lady of the Lake*. . . . Last evening I took up the 2d Vol. of Davis's life of Aaron Burr & *galloped* through the account of his duel with Hamilton & his subsequent letters, etc. I think it shows one of the coldest & most calculating hearts imaginable. I think Burr possessed all the attributes of a gentleman—he was a scholar, was brave & gentlemanly, but was governed by no moral principle. He was not that subtle, *contriving* double dealing man, that I have heard him represented to be, but judging from what I have read of him he was an odd compound of mortality. In regard to the duel I think Hamilton was as much in the wrong as Burr, & they were both unnecessarily punctilious. Hamilton, no doubt, had abused Burr, but if an honest explanation could have been made, the duel might have been avoided. Burr's letters to his daughter are the *strangest* letters for a father to write to a daughter that I ever read. They are an anomaly in letter writing. He loved her—oh how well, & she seemed to be the only object he could *love*, & in her bosom he placed *all* his confidence & it was not misplaced. The man who can read her husband's letters—after the terrible catastrophe that had befallen her began to impress itself upon his mind & until impression became reality—& not weep—aye who will not shut the book with the feeling that some terrible misfortune has *just* happened to himself—must profess a heart as hard as adamant. I read that portion of the book sometime since, & last evening I again ran over it. But I will never read it again *in the evening,* for it haunted me worse than ever the Flying Dutchman did the poor sailor, nearly all night.[3]

Yesterday, for the first time, our dear little Frank sat up on the floor alone, & stood in the corner. He is getting more & more interesting, daily. He is his mother's pet & his father's darling. . . .

1. Samuel J. Gholson (1808–1883), congressman from Mississippi, 1836–1838.
2. John G. Lockhart (1794–1854), Scottish novelist and biographer, published this well-regarded biography in 1837–1838, shortly after Scott's death (1832).
3. Matthew L. Davis, *Memoirs of Aaron Burr* (1836–1837). Burr's daughter Theodosia married Joseph Alston (later governor of South Carolina) in 1801.

Wednesday, February 21. . . . Saw one of the hardest fights between two dogs this morning that I have ever seen—how much like *men* they acted—obstinate & surly, & the one that was beaten would not surrender. Dogs are like men in many particulars but unlike in one—*"dogs are honest."*

Wednesday, February 28. Since I wrote last herein an event has occurred which has caused more general gloom & general excitement than any one I have ever known in this city. I refer to the death of Hon. Jonathan Cilley,[1] a Representative in Congress from Maine, who fell, on Saturday last, in a duel with Hon. Wm. J. Graves[2] a Representative in Congress from Ky. This is the first fatal Congressional duel that has ever occurred since the organization of this Government, and the *cause*—which was, in fact, *no cause for a duel*—the manner & the fatal termination have excited the public mind exceedingly. Yesterday, the funeral was attended by an immense concourse of people & a more solemn assembly it has never been my lot to witness. The funeral service was read by Mr. Slicer,[3] Chaplain of the Senate, & the sermon—a very eloquent & appropriate one—was preached by Mr. Reese,[4] Chaplain of the House of Representatives.

I was well acquainted with Mr. Cilley. He was about 35 years of age, of middling stature, rather spare in his person, gentlemanly in his bearing, & honorable in his feelings & actions, so far as they ever came under my observation. He was a man of fine talents & a ready & able debater. He was a native of N. Hampshire—& his ancestors were brave, patriotic & honorable. . . .

1. Jonathan Cilley (1802–1838), Democratic congressman, 1837–1838.
2. William J. Graves (1805–1848), Whig congressman, 1835–1841.

3. Henry Slicer, Methodist.
4. L. R. Reese, Methodist.

Saturday, March 10. Engagements & laziness combined have caused ten days to pass without a word here. The excitement all over the Union caused by the death of Mr. Cilley, is immense. The press of New England & New York is exceedingly severe upon all concerned in the duel, but the vials of their wrath are poured particularly upon the head of Mr. Wise—he is denounced as the cause of Cilley's death. Had he possessed a spark of honor—true chivalric honor such as pervades the bosom of every *gentleman*—he would have refused to be an actor in the tragedy.[1] On the 12th of February he & Mr. Cilley had a misunderstanding in the House, & enough was then said to lead everyone to suppose that Wise would challenge him, for Cilley crouched not beneath the attack, & stood his ground manfully. And with hatred for Cilley rankling in his bosom, he had the meanness to act as second to Mr. Graves, &, I have been told, when Graves was out the day previous to the duel[2] practising, Wise clapped him on the shoulder & remarked[,] "Graves, you must kill that damned Yankee." A person at the Arsenal has asserted publickly that he heard Wise use this language—& too well did the pupil follow the commands of the demon.

My friends at Chester write me now every mail. Judge Richardson is very sick—he cannot live many years for no constitution can stand against such severe attacks as he has. He may recover from this attack, but my mind is prepared to hear of his decease at any time. My father is also, somewhat indisposed, but no danger is now apprehended in his case. Had a long and very amusing letter from Henry today. He expresses himself fully upon the subject of revivals of religion & protracted meetings. He ridicules the idea of dragooning people into religion in a single day—and his sentiments agree with mine exactly. . . .

1. Marginalia: 1847. My opinion is entirely changed in regard to this matter.
2. Marginalia: It was the day on which the duel was fought.

Monday, March 12. After I wrote the foregoing on Saturday, Mr. Bynum's statement to the Committee of examination upon the duel was brought into the office to be copied. It is a clear & precise statement, & will raise him in the public estimation exceed[ing]ly—for it shows that he did *all* that a man could do to prevent the fatal issue of the combat—while it also bears evidence that Mr. Wise urged it on with a fiend-like thirst for blood. Let him bear the public scorn & detestation he so richly merits with an unshrinking front if he can. If he is human his bosom

must be a hell. He has been a member of Congress since the commencement of the 23d Congress—he was elected as supporter of Gen. Jackson's
administration. He soon deserted both his friends & his principles. During that Congress he shot his former friend, Coke,[1] through the arm, in
a duel. His wife and brother have died, his house has been burned, he
has been either a principal, or second, in three duels, in each of which
blood has been shed; he has avowed, on the floor of the House, his
determination to have murdered a man if he had but moved a hand
which happened to be in his pocket, & which Wise supposed contained
a weapon; besides having a dozen brawls in the House, in which he
seemed to seek a fight—all since he commenced his Congressional career! What can his heart be made of!?[2]. . .

1. Richard Coke, Jr. (1790–1851), a plantation owner from Virginia, was a Democratic
congressman, 1829–1833.
2. Marginalia: 1847. An outpouring of malice which I regret, and take back!

Thursday, March 29. Since I wrote in this journal last my mind has been
burdened by sad news—I have been afflicted, deeply & sorely afflicted.
On Saturday evening last I received a letter from Uncle Mitchell[1] of
North Yarmouth [Maine] giving me information that Grandmother
Brown was dead, & on Tuesday evening came, the not unexpected, but
nonetheless melancholy, intelligence that Judge Richardson had departed from the cares & troubles of this world. Though neither of these
persons were relations, *by blood*, to me, circumstances have rendered them
as dear as if they had actually stood in that relation. Mrs. Brown was the
second wife of my Grandfather, & was married to him previous to the
marriage of my Father & Mother. She was the only Grandmother, & I
may say the only *mother*, my infancy knew, for she reared me with all the
care & indulgence that she could have extended to an only & beloved
child—& the love that she gave me in my infancy remained unchanged
to her death. . . .

To Judge Richardson the ties of gratitude alone would have bound me
with a strength that death alone could sever, but when to those the relationship of father to my wife—of grandfather to my dear boy—are
added I may say that when the intelligence of his death came I felt as if
my cup of affliction was indeed full.

His virtues, his honesty of purpose, his uniform kindness of disposition, his faithfulness as a public servant, & his stern integrity, were well
known to me—but they will be hereafter a portion of the history which
will attach to him when N. Hampshire's worthiest sons shall be com-
memorated. He was a great & a good man, & in his death he gave the

best evidence that his conscience was void of offence, & that he feared not to meet his God. He died on Friday morning March 23d. My Grandmother died on Tuesday morning March 13th.

> Spring may bloom, but *they* we loved
> Ne'er shall taste its sweetness.

But they will enjoy a more glorious spring in those "Sweet fields beyond the swelling flood" that "Stand dressed in living green."

These bereavements ought, & I trust will, impress upon my mind more strongly than ever the lesson that in life we ought to prepare for death. And while I mourn that my friends have passed away I ought to rejoice that they were so well prepared for death, & I am bound to be thankful that they were so long spared to me.

Francis was vaccinated last Monday, & the disease is just coming upon him. Rev. T. Gilman Brown,[2] son of my uncle, the late Rev. Francis Brown[,] is now in this city. I was very happy to meet him. He has the reputation of possessing talents of a high order. My wife & little Frank are to leave this city for N.H. the last of next week, or week after, & I shall not, probably, see them again till August. How I dread the separation. . . .

1. Jacob Mitchell, husband of French's aunt Hannah Brown (b. 1780).
2. French was referring to S. (Samuel) Gilman Brown (1813–1885), who had just graduated from Andover Theological Seminary and was later president of Hamilton College.

Wednesday, April 4. . . . On Sunday last S. D. Fletcher & myself rode out, in the morning, to the spot where the duel between Graves & Cilley was fought. Stakes are driven down at the spots where each of the parties stood—they were between 90 & 100 yards from each other. One of Cilley's bullets struck a rail in the fence directly behind Graves—it must have passed within a very few inches of him. It perforated the rail near its lower edge, about an inch & a half & then passed out on the lower side, and apparently went farther. I have seen it stated in some newspapers, "that probably Cilley's rifle did not contain any bullet!!" I have also heard it said that his rifle was of so small calibre that if the bullet should strike a man at that distance it would not enter him!! The evidence before my eyes proved the fallacy of both assertions. But *I* wanted not even *that* evidence. I am personally *well* acquainted with General Jones,[1] and a more honorable upright man does not live, & the idea that he would suffer his friend's rifle to be charged improperly is preposterous. I know enough also about rifle shooting to know that there never yet was a rifle constructed with so small a calibre that it would not, with a proper quantity of powder, force a bullet through a man at twice the distance at which these gentlemen fired. The calibre of Cilley's rifle was small, too small for accuracy except upon a perfectly calm day, at 100 yards, but at 60 yards it would have been equal to any good rifle of any calibre. I do not know what the size of Graves's rifle was,[2] but if it was of larger bore than Cilley's, Mr. Wise obtained an advantage over Gen. Jones in pacing the distance. And in obtaining, by lot, the choice of position he obtained a still greater advantage, for Cilley must have had the wind directly in his face, while Graves was entirely sheltered by the woods. Much has been said about the advantage *locally* which Graves had, on the ground that the woods & a fence were behind him while Cilley was in the open field, presenting a fair mark. The fact is, the ground rises directly behind where Cilley stood, so that he was as much covered by the ground as Graves was by the woods. I stood in each position & viewed a man standing in the other, & am convinced in this respect there was no advantage.[3] . . .

1. George W. Jones (1804–1896), delegate to Congress from the Wisconsin Territory, 1836–1839.
2. Marginalia: Note—Nov. 20, 1840. Since I wrote this page I have seen, & closely examined the rifle used by Graves. It is a long heavy gun, carrying a bullet of the size of about 35 or 40 to the pound, and one with which I think I could hit a 4 inch ring five times in six, at the distance at which Cilley & Graves were from each other—It has a fine hair trigger & is called a first rate rifle.
3. French's sketch of the site of the duel follows.

Friday, April 27. A pleasant morning at last. The sun is shining out in all his glory, after the storm, & vegetation looks green[,] fresh & spring-like. The trees are putting forth their leaves, & many of the flowers are in full bloom in the Capitol grounds. Speaking of flowers reminds me of a fact that was related to me yesterday, which illustrates very aptly the truism of Shakespeare, that

> Man—proud man—(dressed) (clothed) in a little brief authority
> Plays such fantastic tricks, etc.[1]

An honorable member of the House of Reps. (J. B—d—)[2] was walking the Capitol grounds with some ladies, a few evenings since, & contrary to the rules, commenced plucking flowers & presenting them to his companions. One of the police stepped up to him & informed him he was transgressing the rules, and asked him to desist, when the *Honorable* member said[,] "I am a member of Congress, & I'll let you know I shall do just what I please," & "suiting the action to the word[,]" he commenced pulling up the flowers by the roots & strewing them about, & after amusing himself in that way until he was satisfied, he said to the person who accosted him, "There, damn you, there is some work for you tomorrow morning to set those roots out again."

Yesterday, as soon as the Journal was read in the House, upon the call of Henry A. Wise the clerk commenced reading the testimony taken by the Committee, in relation to the late duel, making, perhaps, 150 printed pages. Col. Franklin & myself read until we were both nearly exhausted. At about ½ past 3, as I was reading, seeing the House manifest much impatience, & observing that no one seemed to be listening with much attention, I began to read very rapidly—as rapidly as I could articulate distinctly. When I had got *through* Dr. Duncan's[3] testimony, & commenced reading that of Dr. Foltz,[4] Henry A. Wise rose in his place & demanded that the Speaker should preserve order, the House being in great confusion. He then said, "I demand that that testimony should be read so that *I* can hear it, & not *mumbled* over as it is by the Clerk who is now reading." From a *gentleman,* or a man of *honorable* feelings[,] I should not have expected such an insult, but coming from Mr. Wise in his present excited state of feeling, it did not surprise me, & this morning I am happy to ascertain that the *general* opinion among *all* who heard the remark is that it was a base, vulgar, blackguard insult to my feelings, and many have said to me[,] "Keep cool, it will injure him more than it will you."[5] . . .

1. French was adapting the following:

> . . . but man, proud man,
> Drest in a little brief authority,
> Most ignorant of what he's most assured,
> His glassy essence, like an angry ape,
> Plays such fantastic tricks before high heaven
> As make the angels weep. . . .
> —*Measure for Measure,* Act II, Scene 2

2. John C. Brodhead (1780–1859), Democratic congressman from New York, 1831–1833 and 1837–1839.
3. Alexander Duncan (1788–1853) practiced medicine in New Jersey and Ohio and served in the U.S. House of Representatives, 1837–1841 and 1843–1845.
4. Dr. Jonathan M. Foltz (1810–1877), naval surgeon, who served in Washington, 1835–1838.
5. Marginalia: 1847. Forgiven & forgotten. F.

Monday, May 7. Had a letter from Henry, Friday evening, informing me that my dear ones had arrived safely at Chester. He also informed me that he & Anne Richardson, my wife's sister, were engaged. I am rejoiced at this, for I think they will make a most excellent match, & live happily together. The House adjourned over, from last Thursday to this day, in order to have the Hall ventilated, cleaned & purified. The races were going on & of course everybody went to see them. I went out on Thurs-

day, but not on Friday, as it rained, & I did not feel very well. I not only
saw the races on Thursday but attended one of those rascally, low and
vulgar and cruel exhibitions, a cock fight. What pleasure one can feel in
witnessing such a scene I cannot imagine. I felt disgust alone. The *modus
operandi,* is thus. A circular enclosure of about 3 rods in diameter is
fenced in with a close board fence, say 10 feet high, with seats all around
the inside, & in the centre is a level spot about 2 feet lower than the
platform upon which the seats are erected, which is called "the pit." Into
this come two men with each a cock under his arm. They are weighed,
& if found to be nearly of a weight, are judged to be a proper match by
the judges, who are seated in chairs upon one side of the pit. Each man
places his bird upon opposite sides of the pit, within a circle marked
around on the earth, facing each other, & they are liberated. They meet
about the centre, & the fight commences with great vigor. Each cock is
armed with steel spurs, or "gaffs" about 2 inches long, & exceedingly
sharp. If the cocks get out of the circle, or get entangled, or one stops
fighting for a stated time—say ½ a minute—the owners pick them up,
& place them as at first, & the fight goes on again. The first fight I saw
lasted nearly ½ an hour. The other 3 not half as long each. In one of
them one of the cocks was killed in 3 minutes, the other one striking the
spur or gaff through his head. One custom of the owners was disgusting
enough to me. Whenever the cocks were taken up, the owners *licked* the
blood from their combs, heads, & eyes, with their tongues, & *sucked* the
blood out of their throats—pah. It almost made me sick, to see them.
Bets were made very freely & much excitement was manifested. I do not
believe any other *animal* in existence shows so much bravery as a game-
cock—those I saw fought to the last moment, & seemed loath to stop
even when they were so exhausted they could not stand. . . .

Thursday, May 10. . . . On our walk home [Monday evening, May 7]
Mr. Johnston & I conversed about the performance & the perfect fit of
Cline's[1] dress, & this led to a conversation about the old style of dress in
smallclothes[2] & silk stockings— the good old times of white top boots &
cocked hats. He remarked, very truly in my opinion, that the change to
the present fashion of pants, threw this country back a hundred years,
in polish & genteel deportment, & enforced his remark by saying, that
in those times no man could attend a ball or party except in the full
dress of those days—viz. breeches[,] silk stockings & pumps—consequently every gentleman must dress particularly for the place he was to
visit. Now, a gentleman may leave his dinner table in pantaloons & boots,
go to the tavern & spree it till evening, & then go to the party or ball in

all the glory of an after-dinner frolic, without any evening preparation. And then a man does not feel the responsibility of behaving like a gentleman, when he has on the dress of a blackguard. Dress is of great importance, & the first lesson a young man should learn, when of age to appear at all in society, is to always dress neatly. Polonius's advice to his son on this point is as good as could be given—

> Costly thy habit as thy purse can buy,
> But not expressed in fancy; rich, not gaudy;
> For the apparel oft proclaims the man.

1. French and Johnston had attended a performance by Herr Cline, a tightrope walker.
2. Smallclothes were close-fitting knee breeches worn in the eighteenth century.

Friday, May 11. Company, engagements, dissipation *almost,* are now the order of the day with me. How glad I shall be when this session is over, & I am again settled down soberly & steadily with my dear ones. . . . At about 3 this morning, nearly all the dogs in Washington, I should think, assembled just back of my boardinghouse, & spent an hour barking, and at some cows—such an infernal noise as they made I have seldom heard. I arose and looked out & had more than ½ a mind to shoot at them. . . .

Was excessively annoyed for an hour or two yesterday by information from Franklin that a member of the House had been to him & informed him that I had written letters to the *Chicago Democrat* abusing Daniel Webster. The letters I acknowledged, the abuse I promptly denied, & took all the measures in my power to convince Col. F. & his informant that I was innocent, & I believe succeeded. Last evening I looked over every letter I have ever written to that paper & find I have never mentioned Mr. Webster's name but once, & then without censure. The truth is I honor Mr. Webster's talents too much—I feel too proud of being a native of the same state with him to abuse him—however much I may disapprove of some of his political projects. I have praised him in a public address & in the newspaper of which I was formerly editor even although that newspaper was bitterly opposed to him politically, & I here say that I consider him one of the greatest men in this Union. . . .

Saturday, May 12. Yesterday, kept about all day though I felt rather the worse for wear. After the House adjourned played 3 games of Billiards with Crabb.[1] No letter from Chester last evening. Was *a little* disappointed. Heard of the death of Hon. James B. Thornton, & it made me sad. He died at Callao, of dysentery, having left Lima to take passage for this Country for home—poor fellow, that home he is never again to see—and then to meet death in a foreign land, and among strangers—the idea to me, is horrible. . . .

1. Horatio N. Crabb was an assistant clerk in the Clerk's office.

Sunday, May 13. . . . Pierce was in here this morning, & we conversed upon the melancholy subject of the foregoing page. He feels such things as sensibly as any man I ever saw, & were I about to leave this world I would have Frank Pierce at my dying pillow sooner than any other man I ever knew in whose veins flowed none of my own blood. I never—no never, shall forget his kind attentions to me when I was sick once in this city. Pierce gave me some of the particulars of Thornton's sickness & death. He died of dysentery & inflammation of the stomach, & was deranged much of the time while he was sick. . . .

Tuesday, May 15. . . . I went to bed, & had the toothache, & got up & put some kreosote into my tooth—cured it at the expense of some of the skin on the inside of my cheek—and so ended yesterday.

Today shaved & went to the Capitol—smoked a cigar on my way there. Wrote letters & marked box covers till 12 o'clock—then Brown & I walked down to the Navy yard to see the U.S. steam battery *Fulton,*[1] which came round from New York last week. She is an ugly looking craft outside, but looks better when one gets on board, though she appears about as inconvenient for all on board as possible. Her cabin is a mere nutshell, & I could hardly imagine that she could stow away all I saw on board of her, who were attached to her, with any comfort. While there several members of the House came, & a number, among the rest Mr. Crockett[2]—Col. Crockett's son—walked back with us. Crockett & I talked about rifle shooting nearly all the way. I found that he understood all about the science. He is a very clever little fellow, & no more like his father than Jackson is like Van Buren, & I cannot imagine two men more dissimilar. . . .

1. The first steam-driven war vessel, the *Fulton,* was built in 1815 and accidentally destroyed in 1829. The second such vessel, also called the *Fulton,* was launched in 1837.
2. John W. Crockett (1807–1852), Whig congressman from Tennessee, 1837–1841. His father, Davy Crockett (1786–1836), congressman from Tennessee, 1827–1831 and 1833–1835, was killed at the Alamo in 1836.

Wednesday, May 16. . . . Recd. a letter from my wife & a confidential one from Henry last evening. The former gave me much pleasure[;] the latter gave me some information that fretted me some, & evidences to me very plainly that it is never best to offer advice to widows even with the best intentions & wishes for their good. In all the advice I have given relative to the settlement of the estate of Judge R. it was with a single view to the widow's benefit. I thought not of myself & those who are dear to me, & would most willingly have surrendered the last farthing to Mrs. Richardson's comfort, and yet I learn, through that best of mortals, Mary W. R. that Mrs. R. was "very much provoked that I should advise anything about the estate." Good God what is the heart of woman made of—we are not only "fearfully & wonderfully" but very curiously made. Very well—if this is the game, it will be found I can be as miserly, as mean & as grasping as anyone, though I do believe, if I know anything about myself, that it is utterly foreign to my nature to be so. "Something too much of this." . . .

Thursday, May 17. It *was* a hot day yesterday. Was at the Capitol till 10 o'clock last night, House being in session till that time. Came home to tea, however, and experienced an hour of toothache. Went to the dentist's to have it out; he was not to be found. Thought I would certainly have it out today, but there is no pain to stimulate my courage[,] but *if* it aches again as it did last evening it must come out. Wrote to my wife yesterday—letter was a little tinged with a feeling caused by Henry's letter, which she will hardly comprehend. Tis not my talent to conceal my thoughts & carry smiles & sunshine in my face when discontent sits heavy at my heart. Got another pair of new boots this morning. Have only 6 pairs now! Hope these, being buckskin, will be easy to my feet for I have been tormented sufficiently. Henry A. Wise made a great display in the House yesterday with an old Continental bill, a Treasury note & a caricature. He explained & expounded equal to a ranting Methodist & cried up the old continental, while he ran down the Treasury note. He talked like a ranting[,] raving fool, as he is, & the Country will find it out one of these days, as I have long ago. I used to think he was brave & fearless, but am now of a different opinion. He is an "Ancient Pistol"[1] of *modern* times. Franklin thinks I am "no soldier" because I dare not have a tooth drawn. I own "the soft impeachment," & if he had had, as I once had, his jaw & mouth torn to pieces, by the drawing of a tooth, so as not to get over the effects of it for a year[,] he would think "the better part of " *courage* was—or is—to bear the "ache." I shall not, however, much longer if the extraction tears my head off. . . .

    1. Pistol, a swaggering bully, Falstaff 's companion in *Henry IV*, part 2, and *Henry V.*

Saturday, May 19. . . . Awoke at 4 this morning with a confounded toothache—got up & filled it with kreosote but it *insisted* upon aching—bore it with as much patience as possible till sunrise, then got up, dressed, & went down to Maynard's,[1] the Dentist, rang his bell & walked the pavement[,] "being in torment," for 15 or 20 minutes, & never longed for anything more than to see him. At last he appeared. I went in & he performed the operation of extraction very scientifically, and with as little pain to me, I suppose, as possible, but there is no fun, after all, in having a tooth extracted. Paid him a dollar & came home, washed, shaved, & dressed—read the 7th Chapter of Matthew & then wrote this. Rather think I shall have a letter today from someone. Hope whispers[,] "It will be from Bess." . . .

Read the 8th Chapter of Matthew this morning & my old disposition to criticise, & a great want of faith came over me. I would that someone would explain to me *clearly* the meaning of 11th & 12th verses of that chapter. The idea, to my mind, is that the children of the kingdom of heaven shall be cast into outer darkness; of course, without we are taught very erroneously, this cannot be the idea intended. And the story of the devils that were in those men beseeching the Savior to send them into the herd of swine—his granting the request—the herd, *devils & all*, running into the sea and perishing. All this is hard to believe, & yet it *is* or *is not* true. Would that I were endowed with a little more Faith! Would that I could be a Christian! I know I must die—when & how I do not know, but I do know that so far as my observation has extended, the Christian religion has been, at the trying hour, the sheet anchor upon which many a soul, that in health thought little of these things, has placed its entire reliance. But I suppose Mahometamism has carried many a follower of the Prophet, with equal *certainty* to the Heaven which he has promised to his disciples. How I doubt! And "he that doubts is damned." But my head aches too bad to write more now.

1. Edward Maynard, Pennsylvania Avenue.

Thursday, May 24. . . . Came home at a little past 9 & read *De L'Orme*[1] till nearly 11, then went to bed & to sleep. First was waked in the night by the barking of a dog—got up to shoot at him with my pistol, but it was so dark I could not see him, shut my window & went to bed again. The next thing I knew was awaked out of a sound sleep by a tremendous crash—jumped out of bed & ascertained that it was the falling of the plastering in the next chamber. It fell on the bed in which the boys sleep, & had they slept, as usual, it would have fallen directly on their heads, & hurt them very much to say the least, but, providentially, Mrs. Masi went into their room after they had gone to bed, & made them turn their heads to the other end of the bed, thinking that the tremendous rain might start the plastering. It was a lucky escape for them, for the mortar was laid on with no sparing hand—it is at least an inch thick. Cloudy, cold & rainy this morning. House commenced meeting at 10 yesterday. A project is on foot[,] I understand, to adjourn the 2d of July & meet again the 1st of November. To the former I would most willingly agree, but I hope the latter will not take place. I wish the whole people of this Union knew as much as I do about these sessions of Congress. They would *try* to reform their representation. How much we hear about want of time to perform the public business—& I do aver that time enough is *wasted* every session to do all—aye every whit—of the business before Congress, & it is rascally that it should be left, from year to year, as it is. But the people of this country have been, are, and will be, for all time to come, I believe[,] most outrageously humbugged by their representatives. The entire object of more than a majority of each House seems to be to ascertain how much can be taken from the public crib with impunity, & every art is tried to *bleed* the treasury in some shape. I have been astonished that the people would submit tamely to some of the impositions practised upon them—especially by members furnishing themselves with books. . . .

1. Novel by Victor Hugo (1802–1885) about a seventeenth-century French courtesan.

Sunday, June 3. My last week's work was a hard one. Was at the Capitol early & late, & found only time to make the above brief record in my journal. Day before yesterday there occurred in the House one of those disgraceful scenes which occasionally mar the harmony of that body & show what the evil passions in the human breast will lead men to do. Hon. John Bell[1] was addressing the Committee of the whole, & called his colleague, Hon. Hopkins L. Turney,[2] "the tool of tools." Mr. T. sat directly in front of Mr. B. & in the next seat. He immediately rose, turned round so as to face Mr. B. & said[,] "Tis false—tis false." Mr. B. struck at him with his fist, & Mr. T. returned the blow, quite a "scuffle" ensued, the House was in great excitement & disorder. The Speaker took the chair without any ceremony & called to order, members interfered, & the House came to order. The belligerents sat down—as I thought, looking rather ashamed of what they had done. After several motions, a resolution was passed requiring them to apologize to the House for the indignity they had been guilty of, which they did, & so the matter ended—at least for the present. Whether the *gentlemanly code* will be resorted to, to settle the matter between the *Honorable* members remains to be seen. . . .

1. John Bell (1797–1869) of Tennessee, congressman, 1827–1841, and senator, 1847–

1859, had shifted from Democrat to Whig. He ran for President in 1860 on the Constitutional Union ticket.

2. Hopkins L. Turney (1797–1857), Democratic congressman from Tennessee, 1837–1843, and senator, 1845–1851.

Tuesday, June 12. A devlish dog & some cursed cats annoyed me excessively last night with their noise—it was bow-wow-wow & catterwaul half the night. I arose in my wrath & left off a pistol at the dog, but it did not seem to make much impression on him. I have got my gun charged for a shot at him if he troubles me any more.

. . . I had an errand at the Gen. P.O.[,] saw the Hon. Amos Kendall[,] P.M. Gen. He looks more thin and cadaverous than ever, it seems to me. He said he intended to write a notice of Hon. William M. Richardson. I hope he will for he knew him well and is *well* qualified to write a sketch worthy of the memory of the talented & lamented Chief Justice. Came home to dinner, then went again to the Capitol, staid till the House adjourned, & came home & read in the 7th vol. of Lockhart's life of Scott, till a short time since, and now it being bed time will go to bed. Brown came in, & we went to Hubbard's room together but only staid a few moments. No letter from Bess this evening!

Monday, June 18. . . . To return to Scott's life—which I have just finished. Never in my life have I read a book so interesting, in the whole[,] & the 7th vol. is painfully so; during the last hundred pages the tears rushed into my eyes again & again. To trace such a mind from its infancy to its meridian, with the constant recollection of how its emanations have amused, edified and interested you, to contemplate its meridian splendor, & wonder at its power, & then to follow it in its decline till it is released from earth, is one of the most interesting lessons man can study. . . . The world will never look upon his like again.

Thursday, June 21. This has been to me, a dull, heavy, uninteresting day. Mr. S. S. Prentiss[1] of Mississippi has been belaboring the Sub Treasury project most unmercifully. He commenced yesterday evening & closed at about 6 this evening, having spoken at least 8 hours in all. He is a little lame Yankee, apparently not over 30 years of age, and almost diminutive in stature, but he has a gigantic mind well stored with classic lore, & joined with these requisites for an orator is an uncommon command of language. He is a man of first-rate talents, but I should think lacking something in judgment. He is said to be exceedingly "given to revel and ungodly glee," but there is no appearance of this in his actions or manner. . . .

As I came out of the Capitol to dinner today I passed Judge Grundy in conversation with a gentleman, who said just as I was abreast of them[,] "Has the Senate adjourned, Judge?"—to which the Judge replied[,] "No, but as old Niles[2] is reading an address to his constituents I thought I would not stay!" This is a fair specimen of political *friendship*. These worthy Senators are warm political friends—and were Judge G. to have occasion to allude to Judge Niles's speech, on the floor of the Senate, he would doubtless applaud it as the able & convincing argument, of his clearheaded & soundhearted friend from Connecticut, to which he had listened with the greatest pleasure and satisfaction! . . . I think I know much—very much—about politics & politicians. I have been mingling with them from my boyhood, & I have been one among them, & I declare I do not believe there is any such thing as political honesty between man & man. On making this remark I do not mean to be understood that *no* politician is honest in his purposes. For there are some to whom the general term politician will apply, who attach themselves to no party, & who believe they are really honest & whose hearts are engaged for their country's good. I do believe John Quincy Adams believes himself such a man. Though I do not agree with him in all his views, he is much more often right than wrong even to any politically prejudiced mind. So much for politics.

The trainers have been training all day & I have looked at them through a spy glass. Today the news was recd. of the loss of the *Pulaski* steamer, on her passage from Charleston to Baltimore, & of more than 200 persons on board her only 15 are saved! Her loss was occasioned by the bursting of her boiler, which caused her to sink. The Southern members, who had friends on board her look sad and solemn. Gov. Hamilton & his two sons, it is said were on board of her.[3] Such losses are dreadful. The Nation must shake off its apathy about steam navigation and arouse itself; legislation must be had on the subject or nobody's life will be safe who travels. Only last October the *Home* was lost with many valuable lives—recently the *Moselle* was blown up & hundreds of human beings hurried into eternity in a moment—the paper of today contains the account of the burning of the *Washington* on Lake Erie & the loss of more than 50 lives! Something must be done, or steam navigation had better never have been discovered—it will prove, to the human race rather a curse than a blessing. . . .

1. Seargent S. Prentiss (1808–1850), a Democrat born in Maine, had just won a contested election. He served in the House, 1838–1839.

2. John M. Niles (1787–1856), Democratic senator from Connecticut, 1835–1839 and 1843–1849.

3. James Hamilton, Jr. (1786–1857), governor of South Carolina, 1830–1832, did not die on the *Pulaski* but did drown between New Orleans and Galveston, Texas, in 1857.

Saturday, June 23. Yesterday passed like many a day before it. Nothing of importance passed relating to me. Went to the Theatre in the evening & saw Ellen Tree[1] as Jon. Her acting was most capital. I never was better pleased with any acting I ever saw, & I never saw any character played from the opening to the close wherein the actor *looked,* throughout, the character represented. Miss Tree is not beautiful, but the expression of her countenance is sweet, & her eyes are perfect.

Mrs. Masi called on Daniel Webster yesterday to request his aid to that most worthy of all worthy objects, the rearing of orphan children, and he[,] "the Godlike[,]" "the immortal[,]" treated her like a boor & refused to give her a cent. She asked him to look at her book. "No," said he[,] "I don't want to see your book, and would not give a cent in charity without I knew it would prevent a person from starvation." This is not the first time I have heard of Daniel Webster's incivilities. When Hiram Powers,[2] the talented sculptor, came here from the west, I have been told this same great man treated him very uncivilly. Well, thank God, I have no favors to ask of him! . . .

1. Ellen Tree (1805–1880) was an English actress who played in America, 1836–1839 and 1845–1847.

2. Hiram Powers (1805–1873) worked in Washington, D.C., 1834–1837, making busts of Andrew Jackson, Daniel Webster, and others. In 1837 he removed to Italy and was considered one of the leading sculptors in the world.

Tuesday, June 26. . . . Monday—called the ayes & noes more times than I ever did before, & got very tired. The "sub Treasury bill" was defeated in the House by 14 majority! I am not exactly sorry for I have had my doubts as to the policy of the measure ever since its first agitation—and I have got heartily sick of the whole subject. . . .

Wednesday, July 11. . . . I was annoyed very much a few hours yesterday by some information given me by Col. Franklin—viz. that Dixon H. Lewis[1] was bitterly my enemy *because I used my influence to get Follansbee[2] elected Doorkeeper*! & he said to Franklin that were it not for the respect he had for him he (Lewis) would have given me the scoring up I deserved for my interference! And so it has come to this, that a free citizen of this republic is not to urge the election of his friend to an office, without

running the risk of being abused on the floor of the House of Representatives by "the fat baby of the House!" A pretty pass, truly, we are
coming to, but, thank God I am not dependent upon Dixon for a live-
lihood. I ask of him no favors, I want not his friendship, & the company
of a hog weighing about 600 would be far preferable to his. I once
boarded with him a week & *know* his habits & customs. . . .

1. Dixon H. Lewis (1802–1848), Democratic congressman, 1829–1844, and senator,
1844–1848, from Alabama, was noted for his size and his state-rights views.
2. Joseph Follansbee of Massachusetts.

Thursday, July 12. . . . *A scene in the House of Representatives.* . . .
Things went on pretty orderly till about 2 o'clock A.M. though the
Speaker, at times, had much difficulty in preserving order. At about this
time a resolution was introduced to give extra compensation to the pages
and messengers—upon the passage of this resolution the yeas & nays
were called for and ordered, & no quorum voted. A call of the House
was then ordered, on motion of Henry A. Wise, & he & D. H. Lewis,
were loudest in their expressions against suspension of the call or an
adjournment. The roll was called through by Franklin & myself—sleepy
& tired as we were—and it was ascertained that 107 members had answered to their names. The doors of the Hall were then closed & the
Sergeant at arms was sent after the absentees. He brought them in one
by one. . . . During all the process of the call, the sending of members,
the taking and giving of excuses, etc., Henry A. Wise was doing his
best to raise some sort of a riot. At a little before sunrise, I walked round
into the loggia where several members were sitting asleep, & there was
Wise, like a great boy, tickling the noses of the sleepers with a twist of
paper! Dignified & pretty for a member of Congress, upon a Sabbath
morning, thought I. The exhausted members lay about on sofas—or sat
in chairs asleep—while the Speaker, with a seriousness & dignity which
well became him, went through the unpleasant task of stating to each
member as he was brought to the bar, that he had been absent without
leave & contrary to the rules of the House, and asked what excuse he
had to render. After a very useless expenditure of 6 hours, a quorum
was found to be in attendance, *& then the House adjourned*! Wise is getting
to be a perfect nuisance in the House. However well he may behave
during the day, as soon as darkness comes over the earth, like the owl
he commences his hootings, & if his lungs were equal to his impudence,
sunrise alone would stop him. . . .

Chester, Tuesday, July 24. "Rob Roy is on his native hills again." At ½
past 4 P.M. on the 18 inst. in company with my friend S. D. Fletcher, I

took the cars at Washington, & we came on as fast as steam could convey us to Boston, where we arrived on the morning of the 20th at 9 o'clock. At eleven took the cars for Lowell, where I dined & then Geo. Kittredge[1] brought me to this place in a chaise. The journey was so fast that I had no time to tarry on the way, & nothing occurred worthy of note. I found all the folks well here, & all apparently glad to see me. My boy did not know me, & was afraid of me, but I will soon teach him to love me I hope. . . .

1. George Kittredge (b. 1814), son of Dr. Benjamin Kittredge of Chester, died soon after.

Sunday, July 29. Yesterday was a hot day at 5 P.M., thermometer 90 in the shade, & last night was uncomfortably hot. Finished reading *Alice* night before last—sat up till ½ past 12 to finish it. Very interesting. Bulwer[1] possesses a very great mind & understands human nature, but I do not believe the *unnatural* marriage between Templeton & Alice can be justified by a single fact on record since Adam & Eve's days of innocence in Eden. The book is filled with deep thought, & shrewd remark, & is a book to be studied, as are all Bulwer's works, that I have read, & I believe I have read all except *Falkland*. . . .

My wife's Grandmother—Mrs. R.[2]—is now about 90 years of age. . . . How strange are the decrees of Providence! While she lives on at the age of 90, she laments the death of her "dear—her beloved son" (my wife's honored & lamented father), who, at the age of 64, was cut off in the midst of his usefulness! The poor old lady grieved for him with a grief that almost refused to be comforted. She took her bed immediately upon receiving the news of his death, and refused to leave it for two or three weeks.

On the 17th of this month I attended the Quoit club at Washington. Our club ground is in full view of the Capitol, & at sunset the reflection was such as to give that splendid edifice the appearance of being beautifully colored a bright & glowing pink. . . . I could not but reflect how like was that scene to the action of collateral circumstances upon mankind. How often do we see men who, but for the reflection from some source which gives them *the color of greatness*, would be mere pigmies in the scale of human nature. If it would not be *heresey* [sic] *even here* to say it, I would instance Martin Van Buren, the present President of the U.S. The reflection of a political sun made him what he is, in the eyes of this Nation—let that sun set, & he will stand *as colorless,* as mere a mass of *unvivified* humanity as one would wish to behold. *He is not a great man!* I have said it. . . .

1. Edward Bulwer-Lytton (1803–1873) had written over a dozen novels by 1838, including *The Last Days of Pompeii* (1834) and *Alice.*
2. Sarah Merchant Richardson (b. 1748), mother of William M. Richardson, died in 1841.

Tuesday, July 31. . . . In the evening came Mr. & Mrs. Russell.[1] They were married within the past year, &, of course, all is yet romance with them. . . .

1. Louisa Richardson in 1837 married Reverend Charles P. Russell, clergyman in Candia, N.H., 1833–1841.

Sunday, August 12. On the afternoon of last Sabbath (the 5th inst.) Ned[1] and I started in *our* Buggy, with a stout sorrel horse, made on purpose for journeying, to visit Mr. & Mrs. S. L. Chase[2] at Woodstock, Vt. . . . When within about two miles of Goffstown "the rain descended," we pushed forward, Ned holding the umbrella & I craking up[3] the steed. At about ½ past 5 we arrived at the hotel, tolerably well wet, & put up for the night. We found the tavern filled with a certain class of individuals, who, *in true sabbath evening style,* had met, probably to drink grog, discuss politicks & the weather, & counsel together about the various subjects worthy of village gossip, without which no village ever existed. . . .

At ½ past 4 [Monday] we were stirring and at 5 were again on our way. The weather was variable—cool & hot—cloudy & clear. At 9 we were at Henniker where we got a most excellent breakfast, & then pushed on for Newport. While passing along the shores of the Sunapee lake, the rain came again, & I think I never saw it rain faster than it did for 15 or 20 minutes, but as there was no wind our umbrella protected us. At about 2 P.M. arrived at Newport. Put up at Emmons's hotel. Called on many of my friends & acquaintances, & on Tuesday morning at about ½ past 4 or 5 left for Woodstock. Went over the mountain & found a tolerable road. From the summit level to Cornish bridge it is 8 miles, & the road is all the way descending, so we passed over it at a rapid rate, & arrived in Windsor [Vermont]. . . . We pushed on to Hartland, & there breakfasted at *"The Pavilion House!!!"* so was it called in great letters upon the front of the *extended* piazza. We drove up to the door & a boy apparently about 10 years of age took our horse. Of him we bespoke breakfast, & in about an hour the dingling of a bell announced that it was ready. We were ushered into a back room, where we found a tolerably decent meal upon the table, overlooked by 8 portraits painted on boards, and hung against the wall, contiguous to each other, by strings, giving each figure the appearance of being suspended by the neck—& *such paintings*—no, daubs—the eye of man never saw elsewhere intending to give the similitude of the human form divine. The father & mother graced the centre of the *group*, the former appearing like a full moon, with a right jolly rubicund nose, the latter a pale old lady who took snuff & wore a cap that answered for both night & day. . . .

At about 11 o'clock we arrived at Woodstock, one of the prettiest villages I ever saw. After tea Chase, Ned & myself perambulated the streets & saw "the lions," & in the evening I attended an oratorio given by the Claremont Sacred Music Society. . . .

At about 8 Thursday morning we started for Newport, dined at old Mr. Chase's[4] in Cornish, & arrived at Newport at about 5 P.M. having rode nearly all the time in the rain. Spent Friday at Newport. Called on many of my old friends, & was glad to see the old familiar faces once more. At 6 P.M. started again & came to Warner, where we spent the night at my old friend Walker's[.] The next morning came to Concord, saw Col. Pierce there, purchased some books, dined & came here, where we arrived at 5 o'clock after having spent a week very agreeably indeed.

As I am getting economical & careful I will keep a record of *my* expenses during this journey.

Toll at Bedford	.08	Gin	.06
Expenses at Goffstown	1.08	Washing buggy	.20
Breakfast at Henniker &		Toll home	.38
horse bathing	.50	Lodging & breakfast	
Newport, going &		at Warner, etc.	1.08
returning	3.09	Expenses at Concord	.62½
Toll at Cornish bridge	.10	Hostlers	.50
At Hartland	.12	Horse hire	6.00
Breakfast at Hartland	.25		15.56
Horse keeping at			
Woodstock	1.50		

1. French's youngest half-brother, Edmund, was twenty at the time.
2. French's half-sister Sarah (b. 1811) and her husband, Samuel L. Chase.
3. I.e., shouting harshly at.
4. Jonathan Chase (1771–1843), innkeeper in Cornish, was the uncle of Salmon P. Chase, later Chief Justice of the United States.

Saturday, August 18. . . . When I wrote the foregoing[1] my dwelling was a little cottage-like house, directly in front of which, & within 40 rods,

spread a beautiful sheet of water called "Kezar's pond," & within a short
distance in the rear Kearsarge mountain reared his bald summit toward
the sky. "The eternal forest" nearly surrounded the little village in which
I commenced my vocation as an Attorney at law, & take it all in all a
more romantic situation could hardly have been selected. A more honest,
upright, unsophisticated set of beings never lived than the inhabitants
of Sutton. I resided among them 2 years & did as much business as a
young lawyer could have expected, & left them only when I received the
appointment of Clerk of the Judicial Courts in Sullivan County. . . .

1. Earlier in this entry French had included some poetry he had written while he was
living in Sutton, N.H., 1825–1826.

Wednesday, August 22. . . . Yesterday morning I walked down to the
office & thought I saw Henry sitting at the window of the back room. I
went to the Postoffice door which was fastened on the inside, I pounded
against it & bawled out "Hallo, come along and open this door—you are
better able to come & open it than I am to go round to the other door."
It was opened forthwith, but instead of Henry behold it was my venerable
Father that I had been thus unceremoniously addressing. I felt somewhat
mortified, & apologized as I was in my duty bound to do. . . .

Saturday, September 1. . . . Tuesday Gen. Richardson[1] came up. Spent
two or three hours with him, in arranging about a division of the estate,
etc. . . .

Wednesday rose at 5 & went to the stand—no pigeons flew. Read *Jo.
Grimaldi*[2] & the newspaper nearly all day. Watched an hour for the Nashua balloon,[3] in the P.M. but did not see it. . . .

Today Judge Parker has been here & we have labored the entire day
in the office selecting such papers as he deems necessary to *the doing of
justice* "promptly & without delay." Since tea we have walked between 2
& 3 miles together.

Mrs. Smith made us a very pleasant visit of a week & left Wednesday
evening. During the week I have at times been examining the papers in
the office, & have observed with perfect admiration the complete system
to which Judge R. had reduced all his transactions. Every paper he has
ever had which could possibly be of any importance is preserved. All his
expenses from day to day are carefully noted down, receipts are on file
for everything he has ever purchased, I should judge, and every thought
worthy of being recalled seems to be noted. I knew he did nothing without system, but had no idea he had followed it so long & never swerved

from it, & I did not suppose that it entered into all the little operations of business—but it is the way to live—would that I could follow his example!

1. Samuel M. Richardson (1777–1858) of Pelham, N.H., brother of William M. Richardson, was a major in the War of 1812 and afterward a brigadier general in the New Hampshire militia.

2. *Memoirs of Joseph Grimaldi*, English pantomimist, written by Boz (Charles Dickens). Dickens (1812–1870) published *Pickwick Papers* in 1836–1837.

3. The first balloon ascension was in France in 1783; the first in America, in 1793.

Tuesday, September 4. . . . After breakfast Mrs. F.[,] little Frank & I went to Candia & spent the day with Mr. & Mrs. Russell. We had a very pleasant time & returned within the last hour. Saw Ruth Russell[1] for the first time today, was much pleased with her appearance. At a little past noon Mr. R. & I went to *his* new meetinghouse, which is now in the process of being finished & promises to be a very pretty house. . . .

1. Newly born daughter of Louisa and Charles Russell.

Saturday, September 8. Yesterday was a hot day, at noon mercury at 84 above zero, & at 9 o'clock last evening 74—not a breath of air & the weather *weakning* enough. I felt as if it was impossible to stir. Read some in *Twice Told Tales* and a story of Ned Flagg's,[1] in manuscript in the forenoon. The latter had some romantic title—*Gabrielle de Vergi,* I believe—& was—as all wishy washy novels now are—connected with the reign of Philip Augustus.[2] In my opinion it is of no credit to him as a writer. . . . In the afternoon copied the inventory of Judge R.'s law library to send to Cambridge. Charles Clement[3] came, talked with him some—& after tea walked with Anne R. over to the beech tree in the Kittredge[4] pasture, whereon are cut various names of my acquaintance—the living & the dead. That old record of the past calls up associations that are both pleasant and sad in my mind. . . .

1. Edmund Flagg (1815–1890), later a well-known author, was son of Sarah Flagg French's brother Edmund (1787–1815).

2. Philip II, King of France, 1180–1223.

3. Son or brother of Jonathan Clement.

4. Dr. Benjamin Kittredge.

Wednesday, September 19. . . . I am now reading, in the proofs, *The Far West,* which is publish[ed] by the Harper's, & was written by Edmund Flagg, Esq., nephew of my mother-in-law.[1] He is here & the proofs are sent to him. It is, as far as I have read[,] very interesting & very well written.

1. French meant "stepmother."

Sunday, September 22. Thursday morning at 8 o'clock my Father & myself started in *our* buggy for Concord, where we arrived about 12 & remained there until after dinner yesterday, when we returned to this town. I had a very pleasant visit & enjoyed most of the time during my absence. Saw many of my old friends, among them Metcalf, Atherton, Pierce, Stevens,[1] Barton, Judge Parker & Gov. Hill. Was in the Court House nearly all Friday forenoon & heard the arguments of S. D. Bell[2] and I. Bartlett[3] in a case *Walker vs. Derry Turnpike*. They both acquitted themselves very handsomely but the jury did not agree. Had one of my worst headaches, & after dinner laid down & slept—awoke at ½ past 3 & sat at my chamber window at Gass's, which overlooked the amphitheatre where a balloon was in process of inflation by Mr. Lauriat. The rain was falling in torrents, but Yankee curiosity can encounter anything, & there were more than 200 people, very many of whom were ladies, within the enclosure, & the roofs, piazzas & windows of the houses in the vicinity were covered & filled with people. The belfry of the Methodist church was full, & I observed a number astride of the ridgepoles of the buildings enduring the "peltings of the pitiless storm," as unconcerned as if the roof instead of being under, had been over them. One woman, with a child about two years old, took her position on a platform directly beneath my window, which was built on a shed for a clothesyard, where, seated on a box, with an umbrella over her head, she sat & patiently awaited the ascension. At 10 minutes before 5 all the preparations having been made, the balloon was disengaged, & arose majestically into the atmosphere—Mr. L. waving an epitome of the American flag from the car. Its course was northwest, & in less than 5 minutes it disappeared in the clouds. We heard, before I left Concord yesterday, that Mr. L. came down at the Shaker Village at Canterbury where he remained a few moments & again ascended, nothing further was heard from him when I left.[4]

. . . After the balloon rose I again laid down—arose at 6 & went with Atherton to Gov. Hill's—took tea & remained there till 8 o'clock—head ached dreadfully—came home in the rain & mud & went to bed. . . .

1. Simeon Stevens had commanded a regiment in the same militia brigade for which French was quartermaster.
2. Samuel Dana Bell (1798–1863) practiced law in Chester and Exeter and was chief justice of the New Hampshire Superior Court, 1859–1864.

3. Ichabod Bartlett (1786–1853), a leading New Hampshire lawyer, was a National Republican congressman, 1823–1829.

4. L. A. Lauriat, the balloonist, concluded his flight at Northfield, N.H., sixteen miles from Concord, at 6:30 P.M.

Wednesday, September 26. This day I received information, by a letter from Washington, of the death of my esteemed friend & master, Col. Walter S. Franklin. . . .

Monday, October 1. As soon as I heard of the decease of poor Franklin I came to the conclusion to start for Washington tomorrow, & in consequence thereof have done little else than prepare for, and *think over* my departure. Thursday, Friday & Saturday were rainy days, & had nothing interfered I should have been fishing—for it was about the first fishing weather we have had since I came here—but I did not feel like enjoying amusement of any kind. I have been anticipating the pleasure of attending the wedding of my brother Henry & Anne R. and of seeing them settled down in their *new* house—or rather in their old house made "as good as new," wherein I have spent many hours for the past two months in assisting Henry paint[,] paper[,] repair, etc. But I must surrender all my pleasant anticipations on this head & go where duty calls. . . .

Washington, Sunday, November 4. Almost ever since we returned from N.H. I have been preparing to go to housekeeping, and on Tuesday last 30th Octbr. at 10 o'clock A.M. Mrs. French & I came to this house, where we have been laboring like a couple of slaves. We have got things in good order below stairs, but the chambers are yet rather in a state of confusion. Now I look forward to some more comfort.

Thursday, December 6. . . . Congress assembled, as usual, on the 1st Monday of December—being last Monday—and the 1st business that was transacted was the choice of a Clerk, and on the 3d vote, *viva voce*, Hugh A. Garland, Esq.,[1] of Virginia was elected. Thus far I am pleased with the man. He is a gentleman & apparently possesses a disposition to make himself popular with the office. He is reputed to be a very literary man & has been a professor in some college. He is the very opposite in personal appearance, in manners & apparently in habit to my lamented friend Franklin. The latter was free & easy in his manners & habits, liked mirth & fun & good eating & drinking better than any man I ever knew and enjoyed life. The latter is apparently staid, but courteous, retiring in his habits, & I should judge abstemious in his living. He strikes me as being a man of great firmness of purpose & a person who will *work* when necessity requires that he should. I think I shall like him *as a Clerk* better than I did Franklin, but a[s] friend and companion F. could not be surpassed.

1. Hugh A. Garland (1805–1854) was Clerk of the House from 1838 to 1841.

Sunday, May 19. . . . On Friday morning, May 10th, a party of gentlemen, of whom I was one, embarked on board the steamer *Columbia,* on a pleasure excursion to Piney Point,[1] about 100 miles down the Potomac. We went by invitation of Col. Seaton,[2] who is one of the proprietors of the "Pavilion"—a resort of pleasure at that place. . . . Saturday was a most lovely day. We walked about the point, took a view of the beautiful scenery—almost an ocean scene at that place, the river is so wide—played billiards, bowled, played cards, & enjoyed the day. At ½ past 4 sat down to a dinner of many good things & fared sumptuously. Wine & wit flowed abundantly, & we prolonged our sitting till nearly sunset—then all walked out on the beach. Spent the evening at cards. Arose at sunrise on Sunday morning & took a *cold* bath in the Potomac. . . .

1. Piney Point is on the north bank of the Potomac River, not far from where it enters Chesapeake Bay. In the nineteenth century it was a resort that served as a summer social center of Washington dignitaries.
2. William W. Seaton (1785–1866) and Joseph Gales (1786–1860) were proprietors of the *National Intelligencer* in Washington and publishers of the debates of Congress and the *American State Papers.* Seaton was a civic leader in the city and served as mayor, 1840–1850.

Tuesday, May 21. . . . Saturday evening last promised to myself that I would not drink wine or Ardent of any kind till 4th of July. Have had some awkward twinges in my right great toe—rather ominous. I see in my glass of the future an old gentleman bearing a great resemblance to myself, sitting in an easy chair, his feet in flannels, resting upon another chair, & his face bearing evidence that all is *not* peace with him. Let me take heed that this is nothing but a picture. . . .

Sunday, June 9. . . . Thursday[,] Sherman & I went to Georgetown in the carryall. As we were returning, & when descending the pitch to go upon Rock Creek bridge, a nut came of[f] the bolt that attaches the shafts to the axletree & the carryall came against the horse's heels, when he commenced kicking and plunging at a great rate. I dashed through the oilcloth curtain behind, & caught him by the head, & we saved any further accident than the splitting of the whiffletree & crossbars. We unharnessed, hired a man to lead the horse home, left the carryall, & rode home in an omnibus. . . .

Sunday, June 16. . . . Yesterday Messrs. Crabb, Brown, Fletcher & myself went up to the Little Falls of the Potomac, fishing. Our luck was nothing to boast of. We carried plenty of provisions & drink with us, & had a right merry time. The scenery about the falls is quite romantic—the chain bridge 50 or 60 feet from the water, the rocky banks, the old ruins of what once were well built stone flour mills, the mountainous appearance of the west bank of the river above the bridge, the continual passing up & down the stream of fishing boats, all together gave the place, to my eye, quite a touch of the romantic. . . .

Chester, Wednesday, August 14. . . . On Monday evening the 12th past at ½ past seven Mr. John Samuel Sprague Vose[1] was married to Miss Mary Woodbury Richardson & *we* had a wedding that seemed like old times. There were between 70 & 80 people at Mrs. Richardson's and at ½ past 8 the large kitchen was opened & the people all assembled therein around a table richly spread with such delicacies as becometh a wedding feast. Lemonade flowed in abundance but no wine was there. These *ultra* temperance times perhaps justified the fair bride in the omission. . . .

1. Vose was the grandson of John Sprague, chief justice of the Worcester County Court of Common Pleas in Massachusetts, 1798–1800. The couple settled in Lancaster, Mass.

Sunday, September 29. . . . Friday [September 27]. Henry & I went to Amoskeag,[1] & there we saw about a hundred buildings—some finished & some in process of finishing, some elegant, some ugly—all situated as unpleasantly as possible, in the midst of a sand bank. This is the germ of a city, and years hence Amoskeag, or whatever name the present "New Village" may assume, will be a place of note, & *one* of the largest Manufacturing towns in New England. The wind blew, and such a dust as we passed through while there never was encountered except on the Arabian deserts. Our eyes & mouths were well *sprinkled* with it. . . .

At ½ past 10 Bess came home & informed me that unto Henry & his wife Anne, a daughter[2] was born at ¼ past 9 o'clock. Mother as comfortable as could be expected—child healthy, with a full head of dark hair, & a little chubby foot. I am very thankful that all is so well, & my very best wishes will accompany the little daughter on her way to womanhood. . . .

1. The Amoskeag textile mills were started at Amoskeag Falls on the Merrimack River in Manchester, N.H., in 1838.
2. Harriette French.

Washington, Sunday, October 20. On Thursday the 3d inst. Bess, Frank and self left Chester at ½ past 10 A.M. in the Stage. Arrived at Haverhill at 1—took cars—arrived in Roxbury at 4 P.M. Staid at Roxbury till Saturday evening at 5 o'clock. Then went on board the steamboat *Portland* & had a beautiful run to Portland, where we arrived at about ½ past 5 A.M. on Sunday the 6th. Monday, 7th[,] went to North Yarmouth in a chaise—found Uncle & Aunt Mitchell well. On Tuesday afternoon, 8th, returned to Portland, and had a very pleasant visit at Hon. F. O. J. Smith's—remained there until Friday evening, 11th, then took steamer *Portland* at 9 o'clock, & arrived in Boston at 8 A.M. next morning. . . .

Monday, February 3. . . . The first committee ever elected by a *viva voce* vote in the Ho. Reps. U.S. was voted for all at a time (5 members) on Friday last. We were between three & four hours taking one vote, & the moment the role was called through[,] the House adjd. over till today. The tellers & Crabb & I worked nearly all day Saturday arranging the lists to ascertain who was elected, & found after a careful comparison of the tally lists that three members were chosen. Today, I suppose, we shall take another vote & elect the other two. I dread the job. It is now 8 o'clock.

Friday, June 19. . . . We have had considerable company, and I always enjoy company, *if it is of my own choosing,* as well as any person can. Ned remained with us until April, I think. In May Mr. Daniel Richardson & his son Daniel[1] came to the young men's Harrison[2] Convention at Baltimore, and paid us a visit of two or three days, & though I did not approve of the object of their journey, I was exceedingly happy to see them, & enjoyed their visit very much. . . .

The Independent Treasury bill is now, has been since May 27th & will be for a week to come, under consideration in this House. The subject has come to be dull enough. The political world is running mad—both parties are sure of success next fall, & every movement in Congress receives its impulse from some political operation. For my own part I do not doubt that Van Buren will be re-elected. I have supported him steadily from the time he was first brought forward as a candidate for the Presidency, and even long before I ever heard him named for that office, I announced my determination to support him. I have rejoiced in his success & shall still rejoice in it, for his principles I approve & sustain, but I despise the man, for he is cold as an icicle & has no heart or soul.

1. Daniel Richardson (b. 1816), son of William M. Richardson's brother Daniel.
2. William Henry Harrison (1773–1841) had been nominated for President by the Whig party in 1839.

Saturday, June 20. The House adjd. last evening at ½ past 8. Mr. Tilling-hast[1] of R.I. spoke 4 & ½ hours yesterday, & said but little. In the course of his remarks he said, "Sir, this Administration have sent to Cuba for bloodhounds to run down the Indians."[2] A member who sat at my side added, in an undertone, "and to Rhode Island for *puppies* to run down the Administration.". . .

1. Joseph L. Tillinghast (1791–1844) was a Whig congressman, 1837–1843.
2. Tillinghast was referring to the use of bloodhounds to capture Seminole Indians in Florida.

Tuesday, June 23. . . . On Saturday P.M. went to Bladensburg to see how they manage political meetings in this part of the Union. Mr. Brown, Mr. Crabb, Mr. Phillips[1] & myself went in Mr. B.'s carryall. We found about 200 people assembled in a grove—the American ensign was hoisted near the assemblage upon a staff *about 30 feet in length*! and the flag was one of the House of Representative's flags, & a very large one. If it had not been blown out by the breeze it would have trailed upon the ground! To me, who have always seen either a liberty pole a hundred feet in length or a flagstaff upon the top of a signpost upon such occasions supporting the stripes & stars, it looked oddly enough. Well, at the base of two large oaks was a sort of platform upon which sat the *managers* of the meeting, & from which the speakers addressed the assembled multitude. When I arrived Hon. Albert G. Brown[2] of the Ho. Reps. was addressing the meeting with much eloquence. He had been preceded by the Vice President (Col. R. M. Johnson)[,] Mr. Hopkins of the House[,] Mr. J. W. Davis of the Ho. & I believe, some others.[3] Hon. H. M. Watterson[4] of Te[nn]. followed him, & Hon. A. Duncan followed Mr. W. We staid till about ½ past 5 & then came away—leaving Dr. Duncan upon the rostrum. The speaking was good & of that sort calculated to tickle the ear & stir up the feelings of the multitude, and it was received with much applause. . . .

1. George Phillips, clerk in the solicitor's office, Treasury Department.

2. Albert G. Brown (1813–1880), Democrat of Mississippi, was congressman, 1839–1841 and 1847–1853, and senator, 1854–1861.

3. Richard Mentor Johnson (1780–1850) of Kentucky was famed for his heroism in the Battle of the Thames in the War of 1812. George W. Hopkins (1804–1861) was Democratic congressman from Virginia, 1835–1847. John W. Davis (1799–1859) was Democratic congressman from Indiana, 1835–1837, 1839–1841, and 1843–1847.

4. Harvey M. Watterson (1811–1891) was Democratic congressman from Tennessee, 1839–1843.

Chester, Sunday, August 9. Folks all gone to meeting except Mr. & Mrs. Vose[,] Lem Barker, Frank & myself. I have *carried* him (Frank) to sleep & taken my seat at the desk to memorandumize a little. Since we arrived in N.H. I have visited Concord with Mr. Brown & spent one night there. We went up on Friday, July 31st, & returned the next day—saw Gov. Hill & his lady, took tea at Col. Stevens's on Friday, saw Hon. F. Pierce, Gen. Sweetser[1] & Mrs. S. & many other acquaintances, talked politics some & spent my time rather pleasantly. . . .

Everybody talks about politics nowadays—how rejoiced I shall be when the Presidential election is over. . . .

1. Henry S. Sweetser had been quartermaster general of the New Hampshire militia.

Washington, Sunday, September 27. . . . For the week past I have been at the Capitol daily, have purchased my winter's fuel, had a back building put up, been shooting twice, etc. Day before yesterday I received from Mr. Garland the appointment of Chief Clerk in the office of the House of Representatives, in place of Col. S. Burch removed. . . .

Friday, October 9. . . . Mr. Garland came up on Monday & came directly to my house, by invitation. He left for New Jersey on Tuesday & will return here tomorrow.

"The elections! the elections!" such is the cry everywhere and everybody seems to be excited. For my own part, though I am disgusted with the hard cider and log cabin *whoorah*,[1] & though the triumph of the Harrison party will affect me as much as anyone, still I feel none of the excitement that I have felt at former elections. I cannot account for it on any other ground [than] that I have passed through such exciting scenes during the past session that my nerves are hardened. . . .

1. Cider and the log cabin were the Whig symbols in the campaign, suggesting that Harrison drank the former and had lived in the latter.

Wednesday, October 14. Mr. Garland returned here Saturday morning—came directly to my house & has remained our visitor till eleven o'clock A.M. this day, when he left for Virginia.

Well, Georgia has gone for the whigs & such a rejoicing as they have had over their triumph I have seldom seen or heard. Yesterday evening the Log cabin was like a beehive and I presume the Whigs all got drunk on hard cider—they fired cannon a portion of the evening. But old Pennsylvania has said her say today & the boot is on the other leg—the glorious news from Philadelphia & its vicinity has depressed the Log cabinites amazingly. If we get Ohio we will elect Van Buren yet—tho but yesterday I confess I thought our chance *almost* desperate. . . .

Sunday, October 25. . . . On Tuesday last I heard of the death of my beloved Father. He died on Thursday the 15th inst. at 5 o'clock P.M. aged 71 years & 8 months, wanting 7 days. The news of his death was expected, and yet it had a deeper effect upon my feelings than I had anticipated. He had been sick a long time—and dangerously so for the last 6 months. On Monday morning, Sept. 14th, just before we left Chester, I went into his room with little Frank. Father was in bed, he clasped my hand for the last time and bade me good-by, and said[,] "God bless you Benjamin." He then said, "Lift Frank up to me that I may give him the last kiss he will ever receive from his Grandfather in this world." I did as he requested, & he kissed the little fellow while the tears were trickling down his cheeks, & he was so affected he could with much difficulty speak. Frank returned the kiss & bade his Grandfather good-by, & I led him out of the room. This was my last interview with my father—a man who has buffeted the storms of life and cast them aside, who has labored a long life, has brought up a large family of children, supported them all respectably till they were able to support themselves—had ample means to carry him comfortably to the end of life, and all this by his own untiring industry without the aid of anyone. Economy was always consulted in all his operations—he learned the lesson young, having no resources but his own brain & hands to apply to upon starting into life, & he never forgot it. I acknowledge I have often thought that he was too parsimonious, but *now* when I reflect upon the *prospect* before him I cannot remember a single instance wherein I think his economy went beyond the bounds of strict prudence. There were times during my youth when I thought he treated me harshly, but I do not doubt I deserved it, and for many years past he has evinced an interest in my welfare, and a sincere & abiding regard for my happiness which has erased from my memory every trace of harshness or unkindness which I once may have imagined. . . .

Tuesday, November 10. Well, the People of this Union have seen fit to elect General William Henry Harrison of Ohio President of these United States for four years from the fourth day of March next. This result, though not unexpected by me[,] was unhoped for—not that I have, *personally,* one particle of affection for Martin Van Buren, or a single dislike to Gen. Harrison. On the contrary I never liked the character of Van Buren. I believe him to be a coldhearted[,] *calculating* man, who cares more for his own personal aggrandizement than for anything else, while I believe General Harrison to be a warmhearted, generous and kind man, but not a man of very superior talents, and of great egotism. I have never, thank God, joined in the cry against his personal character. I believed him a brave man during the late war & that opinion I have never changed. If there is one thing I despise more than another, it is the miserable, shortsighted party policy of abusing a man—of endeavoring to detract from his well earned, personal reputation, merely because you happen to be opposed to him politically. Never have my lips breathed aught against Daniel Webster, nor has my pen *ever* written a line of slander upon his high & honorable character. On the contrary, I have taken occasion to speak of him in public in such a manner as I believed him to be worthy of being spoken of. I never will be guilty of the meanness of endeavoring to sully the lustre of the jewels of my country even if I cannot approve every act of the political lives of her great men.

I have opposed the election of Harrison. I have not been an active politician because I have not been in what I deemed a proper situation to take an active part, but, in my heart & in my language I have been his bitter & uncompromising opponent. I have been governed by principle in this opposition, I have been disgusted by the mummeries of his party, & the want of any avowed principle of action, and I never will justify any party in pursuing the course pursued by the party that has placed Harrison at the head of this nation. *Now* the principles that are to govern him & his party *must* be avowed. If he is for a Bank of the U.S., a protective Tariff, a patronage of internal improvements by the General Government, the abolition of slavery in the Dist. of Columbia, and the assumption of the State debts, then will I oppose his Administration with all the power with which I am able to do it, for on all these points I am fixed—unalterably fixed—in my opinions. If, on the contrary, he can devise any safe plan to receive & disburse the public money independent of a bank or banks, if he confines himself to a tariff of revenues alone, if he assumes the doctrine that the States themselves are the proper patronizers of internal improvements within their own borders & the Union has nothing to do with it as a Government, if he disapproves of any & all action in relation to Slavery in this District or the Slave states & Territories, except at the request of the people within the District or within those States & Territories, if he disapproves of involving the Government in debt to relieve those States which have by their own folly & extravagance involved themselves, then will his Administration be Democratic & every Democrat must approve it. Time will show.

Wednesday, November 11. . . . The weather, today, has been delightful— like a summer day. Col. Burch came to the office & manifested & expressed his great joy that *his party* had triumphed—until he was removed from office he pretended that he was no partizan, & took no interest in politics! The Democratic clerks are wheeling into the Harrison ranks by platoons, I understand. Dr. Barker, who used to be a Federalist & who has recently been a strong Van Buren man & was appointed within two years by Amos Kendall a Clerk in the Gen. P.O. Dept., has avowed to Mr. Childs[1] this day that he is and always has been a whig! What are such principles worth? . . .

1. Timothy Childs (1785–1847), National Republican and Whig congressman from New York, 1829–1831, 1835–1839, and 1841–1843.

Monday, November 16. . . . Have been down in the city this morning. All is politically still. There are nine white flags flying on the Log cabin flagstaff—indicating that they have the information that nine states have gone for Harrison. Well thank God, N. Hampshire & old Virginia[,] the Mother of States, have stood firm—they are the Gibraltar of Democracy. The army of Office seekers, Bankites, Tariffites, Abolitionists & all other *ites* which entered into a Holy Alliance to carry everything by fraud & humbug, have not been able to overcome the sturdy & sterling Democracy of these States. I wish they may stand alone, in the proud position where they now stand. The time will come, when every state which gives her electoral vote to Martin Van Buren in this contest will be looked upon as the citadel of liberty, which the Goths could not capture. I am proud that my native state stands firm where she always was & always will be, & I am proud that she has such a State as Virginia to back her.

Chapman's[1] picture, *The Baptism of Pocahontas*, was brought to the Capitol last Thursday, & on Friday morning I got a look at it[,] under great disadvantages, however, as it was not raised into the panel, & there was a large trestle before it, and it is not yet varnished. But very few have seen it even now as it is not open to the public. I do not profess to be a connoisseur of paintings, still I saw what appeared to me several great defects & some admirable points in the picture. The figure & position of Pocahontas is admirable, so are many other figures in the piece, but the hand of the priest which rests upon the edge of the fount is about the size of a child's at 7 years of age, and the foot agrees very well with the hand, though the figure of the priest is that of a man of ordinary size at 30 years, & his beard indicates fully that age. Near the priest is the figure of a man in armor whose hand is of the proper size, & the contrast is such that the most casual observer cannot fail to notice the defect. The face of the beautiful page who bears the helmet of the man in armor is that of a girl, whether intended as a female or not I do not know. The face of an aged spectator, seated in the background & covered with a flowing beard, is about the size of a child's at 10 years of age. I predict that the picture will be harshly criticized & do the painter little credit. Chapman has a good reputation, but this production will not add to it, though there are some points eminently beautiful. I saw it but a few moments, & had not time to note any excepting what struck me as glaring defects or surpassing beauties.

The new chandelier was put up in the Hall of the House about 2 weeks since. It is a magnificent affair, but it *leaks* & if that defect cannot be remedied it will be worse than nothing.

1. John Gadsby Chapman (1808–1889) was a well-known painter whose *Baptism of Pocahontas* is in the Rotunda of the Capitol.

Friday, November 20. . . . Yesterday was a cold[,] blustering day—staid at the Capitol till one P.M.[,] then went home & dined—returned to the Capitol—went down in the city—made sundry purchases & counted the little bits of white shirting which are fluttering like so many night caps hung out to dry, with their owners' names upon them, from the Log cabin flagstaff. There were 12, indicating that 12 states have gone for "Tippecanoe & Tyler too."[1] Cock-a-doodle-doodle-do! They may as well add six or seven more, & surmount them by a flannel petticoat bearing this inscription[,] "William Henry Harrison has received the votes of the states, the names of which are upon the flags below, by a system of frauds, humbugry & cheatery unparalleled in the History of this or any other country, & he is fraudulently elected the fraudulent president of these United States for 4 years from the Fourth day of March next, if the people who have been cheated, will permit him to assume the seat which has been but once before contaminated by a President placed in it by fraud." . . .

1. Whig slogan referring to Harrison's victory over the Indians in 1811 and to John Tyler (1790–1862) of Virginia, candidate for Vice President.

Tuesday, December 1.... Yesterday I called on Mrs. S. J. Hale of Boston, who is now in this city. Age is apparent on her brow. I knew her 15 years since at Newport & have kept up an acquaintance with her ever since. She is a remarkable woman & has exhibited a perseverance in stemming the torrent of adversity, which, with the death of her husband, seemed to overwhelm her, that is worthy of all praise and is an example to women that they well may follow. Left with nothing but a mind well stored and an imagination surpassed by few, she commenced Authorship & has succeed[ed] in rearing and educating three sons & two daughters, by her own exertions, & is now, I suspect, in the enjoyment of a competence. Her name now ranks high among the female authors of this Union.

Friday, December 18. Since my last writing herein Congress has convened and the second session of the 26th Congress is now almost two weeks old. The parties seem to have commenced a regular political onset. . . . It is evident enough that the Federal party are determined to have an extra session of Congress—to repeal the Sub Treasury law, distribute the public lands, create a national Bank and a new tariff of duties. Let them do it & if they can live long as a party after it is done[,] I do not know the American people so well as I thought I did. Since the commencement of the session I have been as entirely engaged as possible. I have hardly found time to eat my accustomed meals. In consequence of the removal of Col. Burch and my appointment in his place some expected the Whigs would not treat me with their usual kindness, but I am happy to be able to say that they have, and that nothing has been said to cause a feeling of pain or displeasure on my part, in relation to the subject. I shall, as I have[,] devote *all* my time and talents to my duty & if I fail to do it acceptably I am ready to relinquish it at any moment.

This day at 10 o'clock A.M. the splendid chandelier, which was suspended in the Hall of the House of Representatives in October last and which was composed principally of cut glass, fell and was broken in a million of fragments. It was a most magnificent affair—made by Mr. Hooper & Co.[1] Boston at an expense of something over 4,000 dollars. It weighed about 7,000 pounds, & had 78 lamps in two tiers. It was very ornamental to the Hall, & would have added much to the comfort of doing business in the evening—but it is now a mass of rubbish. One of the chains by which it was suspended broke at the link where it was fastened to the top of the supporting rod, which left it supported by only one chain, & half the friction being lost, & the counterpoise being much heavier than the chandelier, the latter ran up of its own motion, and when it struck at the top the jar was so great as to break the other chain and it came down with a tremendous crash. The large iron rod that sustained it fell across the Hall in such a manner that, had the House been in session, many members must have been hurt and some killed by it. Several desks, immediately under the chandelier were broken to atoms—but, happily, no one was injured. This is the second chandelier that has fallen, & I prophecy it will be the last. . . .

1. Henry N. Hooper & Co., 50 Commercial St.

Saturday, February 13. . . . Harrison arrived in the City on Tuesday last at ½ past eleven A.M. I never saw the snow fall faster than at the time of his arrival—the falling flakes were so large & fell so thick that it was almost impossible to see from the Capitol to the avenue. Notwithstanding all this, I am told that the streets were perfectly filled with people ready to "fall down & kneel" before their idol. I have not yet seen the General, but understand his dear friends have almost worn his right hand out shaking it. It is a fact that he has been under the necessity of leaving off the ceremony of hand shaking—*except perhaps when he takes his liquor.* He exhibits some spunk, for when asked in Baltimore where he should stop in Washington he replied he should not be guided by the recommendation of anyone—he knew where to go, & he should go "*where* he *damn pleased.*" We are to have an extra session, it is said. . . .

THREE

The Whig Interlude

William Henry Harrison's presidency lasted only a month. In March, French had looked down upon the inaugural ceremony from the upper windows of the Capitol; when Harrison died in April, he remarked that the President was "but as a clod of the valley."[1] Although he had misgivings about his own survival as a Democratic officeholder during the controversial days that marked John Tyler's rise to power, French managed somehow to hang on. In the midst of vetoes, cabinet changes, heated debates over banking, and a fistfight on the House floor, quelled only by the great bulk of Dixon H. Lewis, French pursued his rounds.

The actions of John Quincy Adams in the House could always be counted on to draw a response from French, ranging from contempt to profound respect. On January 24, 1842, Adams brought forth the famous petition of forty-six abolitionists of Haverhill, Massachusetts, to dissolve the Union, and in the weeks that followed the question of censuring Adams was the principal business of the House. French, viewing this at firsthand, now saw in Adams "the garrulity & ill temper of disappointed old age."[2] A year later, when Adams made a fierce speech against refunding a fine that had been levied against Andrew Jackson in New Orleans in 1815, French called Adams "a demon just from Hell."[3]

A welcome diversion was building a house at 37 East Capitol Street, close by the Capitol. When it was completed in 1842, Benjamin and Bess, with four-year-old Francis Ormond, rejoiced at leaving behind the vermin and other discomforts of rented quarters for the house that was to delight Benjamin for the remaining twenty-eight years of his life. In time vegetable and flower gardens were planted, walks laid out, additions made, adjoining lots acquired, and a stable built. A summerhouse facing a splashing fountain provided a special source of pleasure on hot summer evenings.

As he settled in comfortably as a substantial citizen of Washington,

French began to assume some of the responsibilities of that role, taking part in local politics and serving on the council, eventually as its president. He also joined the Society for the Promotion of Science and the U.S. Agricultural Society and moved easily into the world of business. He took careful note of the electromagnetic telegraph when his close friend F. O. J. Smith brought it to his attention in 1843, a year before the invention was formally demonstrated. Already astonished by the rapid transmission of information by printing press and rail, he now understood that electromagnetism would convert miles "into inches, & hours into seconds."[4] Investment followed interest, and active participation in the Magnetic Telegraph Company followed investment.

Because of the pace and demands of these years, only a single visit was made to New Hampshire. Once there, however, there was time for picnics, chowders, visiting the family mansion, roaming the old churchyard, rolling back the years, and indulging in the sentiments that all those pursuits implied. In Washington amusements and entertainments were both more and less sophisticated. The predictions of the Millerites that the world would be destroyed on April 23, 1843, was only a momentary distraction compared to the hilarity that followed the installation of Horatio Greenough's statue of Washington in the Rotunda. French was present, of course, and supplied the equivalent of an oral history of the proceedings. A lecture on phrenology brought French out in November 1841, and following the lecture he stepped forward with a dollar for a personal evaluation. Of the results, which were flattering, French wrote, "It becometh me not to say much."[5] Charles Dickens arrived in Washington in March 1842 and during the course of his visit captivated French entirely.

French, already displeased with the policies of the Tyler years, experienced a more personal disappointment in 1843. He had felt that he stood a chance to be elected Clerk of the House in December. However, because of divisions within his own Democratic party and because he knew that if elected he would be required to make wholesale removals, he withdrew from the contest. Caleb J. McNulty, the victor, eased French's pain by reappointing him as a clerk in the office.

A few months later, a real tragedy occurred when, on February 28, 1844, one of the huge guns aboard the visiting U.S.S. *Princeton* blew up during a demonstration, killing six, including two cabinet members. French, who had been invited to be aboard but was unable to attend, described the accident at length. When he tried to sleep that same night, his "dreams were of the dead."[6]

The final entry for this chapter announces the election of James K.

Polk. French rejoiced because his party was back in power and he could look optimistically to the future.

1. April 4, 1841.
2. Feb. 6, 1842.
3. Jan. 6, 1843.

4. June 19, 1843.
5. Nov. 18, 1841.
6. Mar. 3, 1844.

Journal

Saturday, March 6. At 12 o'clock midnight, on the 3d inst.[,] the 26th Congress finished its existence, or rather, its existence was finished. I have never seen a more harmonious ending of a session. Everybody seemed to be good-natured, & good humor prevailed. The Speaker's address, when he adjourned the House, was admirable & did him a great deal of credit. He is one of the most upright and amiable men I ever knew. I have had much official intercourse with him this winter & have been highly pleased with him.[1]

On Thursday, Mr. & Mrs. Brown[,] Bess[,] Frank & I attended the inauguration. We were at upper windows of the East front of the capitol where we could see all the crowd. The military escort was handsome & many of the banners were very elegant. The old General rode a white horse & was surrounded by his friends on horseback. He alighted and went into the Senate chamber, & from thence he came escorted by the Senate and accompanied by the Judges of the Supreme Court & the great functionaries of Government, to a platform erected for the occasion upon the blockings at the Eastern portico of the Capitol, where he delivered, or rather read from the columns of a newspaper, his inaugural. He was cheered many times by the crowd during the reading of it, which occupied something over an hour. I have heard 50 & 100 thousand people estimated as being present. I estimated the crowd by counting a line of soldiers who stood shoulder to shoulder within it, & there were between 20 & 22 thousand people in it. There might have been a thousand more upon the portico, and perhaps one or two thousand about on the terraces & in the grounds, but the entire number at and about the capitol did not exceed 25,000. I was much disappointed, as I expected to see two or three hundred thousand at least. The inauguration being over we went to the window of my office, which looks into Pa. Avenue from the West front of the Capitol, & saw the procession return, & then we all came home to dinner. Since then I have been constantly engaged at the office. . . .

1. Robert M. T. Hunter (1809–1887), of Virginia, served as speaker of the House for one term, 1839–1841. He was later a U.S. senator from Virginia and Confederate Secretary of State.

Sunday, March 14. Again has the hand of death been within the little circle of those near and dear to me—again am I called to mourn over one who was very dear to my heart. My sister Harriette died on Tuesday morning last after a gradual decay of more than a year. At the age of 25—an age when, if the world is to be enjoyed at all it is most lovely— she has been called from amongst us to repose in the silent grave. The news of her death reached me yesterday, &, though not unexpected, it brought with it a chill to my heart & I felt how uncertain are *all* things here on earth. . . .

Sunday, March 28. . . . *News*—aye, what saith the trumpeter who informs the world what the World is doing? The murmur of the *great world* on this side the Atlantic is all about the political & pecuniary aspect of the times—nothing but money & office is spoken of or written about. Some insist that Harrison behaves odd enough to justify a commission of Lunacy upon him, while others swear he is the very pink of chivalry & perfection. The Whig disappointees leave Washington with a flea in their ears & "a grumble in their gizzards," & to their distempered senses Harrison is not "the man they took him to be," while those on whom the President has smiled more propitiously are delighted with the *Classical* old hero! Congress is coming again on the 31st day of May, & then "To be, or not to be" in office? will be no longer a question with me. Come what will, I am determined to take the result calmly & without a murmur or an exultation. . . .

On the other side, Victoria & Prince Albert[1] are doing all they can to preserve the sovereign line of the Guelfs, & their subjects are scolding because the people of New York are determined to make a British murderer of an American citizen amenable to their laws.[2] Money affairs seem to be in as bad a state there as they are here, but *official life* is much more secure. . . .

1. Queen Victoria of England had married Prince Albert of Saxe-Coburg-Gotha in February 1840. Their first child, the Princess Royal, was born in November 1840, and a

male heir, afterward Edward VII, was born in November 1841. In all, the couple had nine children, six of whom survived their mother.

2. Alexander McLeod, a Canadian, was arrested in New York in November 1840 and charged with the murder of an American during the *Caroline* affair of 1837. The *Caroline* was an American steamer in the employ of Canadian insurgents.

Thursday, April 1. . . . All other news is now absorbed in the anxiety of the public mind as to the result of the dangerous sickness of President Harrison. He was taken on Saturday last, after dinner, with bilious pleurisy, & is now deemed in very great danger. I saw him in market on Saturday morning & he then appeared to me like a broken-down old man. He has been almost worried out of his life by applicants for office ever since he arrived in this city, & from accounts I had of him I came to the conclusion two weeks ago that he was deranged. On Saturday morning last a friend of mine called upon him, by appointment, upon some business. He then complained of a headache—my friend remarked that he probably did not take sufficient exercise. "Exercise[,]" said the General, "from seven in the morning till midnight I am constantly on the go. I am *bothered almost* to death with visitors. I have not time to attend to my person, *not even to change my shirt,* much less to attend to the *public* business. I must leave this House Sir. I must go and lock myself up somewhere where I can have some peace & be exempted from these interruptions." Poor old man. He is more to be pitied than the veriest slave that walks the streets of Washington, & if this sickness terminates fatally, I shall look upon William Henry Harrison as a martyr to the spirit of Humbuggery, which has for the past 18 months done more to overthrow this Nation than all its foreign foes have since 1776. Most sincerely do I hope for his recovery, for I believe him to possess a good heart & the kindest feelings, but he is led on by demagogues who make him the rampart to defend themselves from the shafts which would otherwise pierce them. I want him to live & I want the people of this country to learn a lesson, which I fear they will not learn if he dies now. I want him to live for his own sake, that he may see & be disgusted himself with the course which his leaders wish him to pursue. I want him to live, because, weak and imbecile as I deem him now, whatever he may once have been, & I doubt not his talents or his bravery in times past, he is, nevertheless, President of the United States, & I do not like even the *omen* of the death of a President while in office, & especially so soon after he has entered upon its duties. . . .

Sunday, April 4. At twelve o'clock & 30 minutes this morning died William Henry Harrison, President of the United States. I arose at 6 this morning to ride on horseback & on my way to the Capitol Stable met a neighbor who gave me the first intelligence of the President's decease. Mr. Brown & I then rode directly to the Presidential mansion & ascertained that the information was, alas, too true.

One little month has passed away & he for whom millions rent the air with shouts & whom thousands listened to with eager upturned faces, is but as a clod of the valley. What the political effect of this National bereavement is to be upon the country time, alone, will show. I can only predict, and I do predict that it will be the cause of a tremendous political excitement, & that it will render certain the triumph of Democracy in the next election. The ways of Providence are inscrutable, but they are always right, & this is for the best.

Tuesday, April 6. Yesterday at 12 o'clock I went to the Presidential mansion & looked for the last time on earth at the remains of him who was but the preceding day President of the United States. There was a great crowd in attendance at this *last levee,* & grief & solemnity was upon every countenance. It so happened that the gallant Col. Croghan,[1] the hero of Fort Stevenson, stood at the side of the coffin with me, gazing upon the calm[,] attenuated & pallid features of his old commander—what must his feelings have been at that moment? I could not know but I could well imagine. The corpse was in the coffin & was lying in the hall, which was hung with mourning. I stopped but for a moment, & then came away.

1. George Croghan (1791–1849), of Kentucky, had served under Harrison in the battle of Tippecanoe. In August 1813 he successfully defended Fort Stephenson in northern Ohio against a large force of British and Indians.

Wednesday, April 7. Have attended the funeral of Gen. Harrison today. I went to the Presidential mansion at 10 A.M. with a number of the officers of the House. The coffin containing the remains of the deceased was placed in the centre of the East room, where all who desired could view the face of the corpse. I went in & took *another* last look at that thin[,] attenuated, but calm & expressionless face. When I saw it on Monday I could not recognize any of its living features, but today I could, whether the time that had elapsed had changed them or whether I did not take sufficient note on the other occasion I know not, but certain it was that, to me, a change had taken place.

The Episcopal service was performed in the East room by Rev. Dr. Hawley[1] of St. John's Church. At 12 o'clock the procession moved, & I should think it was from a mile to a mile and a half in length. Everything was most admirably conducted. Having a bad headache I did not accompany the procession any farther than the Capitol, when I left the hack I was in & came home. . . .

1. William Hawley, pastor, St. John's Church.

Sunday, May 16. . . . The public mind is now considerably agitated on account of the steamship *President,* which sailed from New York on the 11th day of March, and has not since been heard of. The papers are full of conjectures as to her fate, & the Unitarian clergyman, Mr. Bulfinch,[1] alluded to her in his sermon of this day. There is, perhaps, more anxiety manifested for her fate in this immediate community than there otherwise would be in consequence of the departure of the Rev. Geo. G. Cookman,[2] late chaplain of the U.S. Senate, on board of her. Mr. Cookman is a worthy & eminent divine of surpassing eloquence, & for the past two years has been listened to by thousands on each alternate Sabbath, during the Sessions of Congress, while performing his official duties in the Hall of the House of Representatives. On the last Sabbath of the Session, the 28th day of February, Mr. Cookman preached to the largest audience I ever saw assembled in the Representatives' Hall—the Hall & its galleries were completely *crammed,* & hundreds, & perhaps thousands, went away, finding it impossible to gain admittance. I heard only a portion of the sermon, it being impossible to get a seat in the Hall when I found leisure *from my official duties in the office* to go in. I stood in one of the aisles a short time, & then gave up the attempt. Mr. C. was remarkably eloquent while I heard him, & Mrs. French[,] who was in the gallery through the services, thought his sermon exceedingly eloquent, & well adapted to the occasion.

The extra session approaches, or rather the time approaches when it is to be, & every politician is speculating upon what is then to take place. We have all sorts of prophecies as to what is to be done by Congress, & curiosity is on tiptoe to know what the President will recommend. From all that I can learn he will not recommend the charter of a U.S. Bank, & my belief is that if Congress passes a charter he will not approve it. I form this opinion from what I have heard in a very direct manner from the President. I judge from what I have heard, that the Whigs will be very much disappointed by the course which the President will feel himself constitutionally bound to pursue. . . .

1. Stephen Greenleaf Bulfinch (1809–1870) was a graduate of Columbian College, Washington, D.C. (now George Washington University) and taught and preached in the city for several years.
2. George G. Cookman (1800–1841), Methodist clergyman. The steamship *President,* which had sailed for England, was never heard from again.

Sunday, May 30. . . . The members of Congress are pouring into the city to attend the extra session which commences tomorrow, and a cloud of office seekers, equalled only by the locusts in Egypt accompany them. The only stranger to the city, now here, & not in search of an office[,] is Samuel L. Chase, Esq., of Vt. (my brother-in-law) who arrived yesterday—he assures me he does not want an office!! The great topics of conversation in the City is who will be Speaker & who will be Clerk of the House. The Whigs caucussed last evening & nominated Hon. John White[1] for Speaker & Hon. F. O. J. Smith for Clerk, & I hope & trust they will both be elected tomorrow. In the event of the latter election I have a deep interest, for on its result depends my office. . . . Nothing will save me, probably, but Mr. Smith's election, though I can, if I choose, be the candidate of the Democratic party, but I will not be the candidate just to be beaten. Mr. Clarke[2] & his friends & Col. Burch are, if rumor speaks the truth[,] pursuing a very dishonorable course, for, notwithstanding the caucus nomination which the minority was bound to respect, they are now doing all they possibly can to disunite the Whig party & obtain the votes of the Democrats. Col. Burch, in his usual fawning, lickspittle spirit, called on Mr. Smith yesterday & told him he had taken no part in the election of Clerk, & felt no peculiar preference for the one or the other candidate (Mr. Smith & Mr. Clarke), that I was willing he, Burch, should come back into his old place, etc., but such gammon did not take with Mr. S. & so the Col. has entered the political bear garden & is doing his utmost to defeat Smith. . . .

1. John White (1802–1845), a Kentucky Whig, was elected speaker on May 31. He served in the House from 1835 to 1845.
2. Matthew St. Clair Clarke, of Pennsylvania, served as Clerk of the House 1822–1833 and 1841–1843. He was also the compiler, with D. H. Hall, of *Legislative and Documentary History of the Bank of the United States* (Washington, 1832), and was associated with Peter Force in issuing some of the volumes in the *American Archives* Series.

Tuesday, June 1. Well, Congress has commenced its session. John White is elected Speaker, & Matthew St. Clair Clarke[,] Clerk of the House of Representatives. Mr. Smith being my personal friend, I was anxious he should be elected, though, had I been a member, stern political principle, if such a thing exists, would have forbidden my voting for him; but the manner in which he was defeated has convinced me that honesty in politics is only *a name,* that it exists alone in the imagination of political philanthropists. . . .My friends *bargained* for me & I am to be retained in the office—indeed the good feeling of my political friends toward me elected Mr. Clarke—but what a glorious political maneuvre they have overlooked, how short-sighted they have been, for, had they gone on steadily voting for their own candidates the Whigs could not have elected a clerk perhaps for days, & it would have led to a total disorganization of their party in the House. I would have taken this course. I cannot but be personally grateful to my friends for their interest in me, which *I know* induced some of them to vote for Clarke, but I had rather have been sacrificed, much rather[,] than to have had them vote either for Smith or Clarke. For their devotion to their avowed principles would have done more to divide the Whigs than any other course they could have pursued.

As it is, I am bound to make the best of the whole matter & shall do it.

Sunday, June 6. Well, one week of the extra session is gone, and the people are as wise as they were before it commenced, & no wiser! The week has been frittered away & nothing has been done by either House. The whigs are divided in the Ho. of Reps. The disunion in regard to the election of Clerk is not healed, & there is but little prospect that it will be, and I believe a portion of the whig party must split off from the remainder, & in my opinion there soon will be a Tyler party, which will consist of the Democrats & disaffected whigs, & a Clay party[,] which will be composed of a majority of the Whig party & the Conservatives. If such be the issue of the present disaffection, I predict that no Bank charter can become a law of the land this session, for Tyler must necessarily veto one if it passes both Houses. This he can do with perfect propriety & consistency with his former actions & expressed opinions. I do sincerely hope such will be the *end* of this beginning, for, if a Bank is chartered, I shall esteem the act as a blow at the liberties of the people from which they will not readily, if ever, recover. We have had enough of Banks, & God preserve the Country from being saddled with another.

The whigs, who voted for Mr. Smith as Clerk of the Ho. Reps.[,] are loud in their denunciations of the *bargain* that elected Clarke & express a determination to have the causes that led to Clarke's election investigated. Thank Heaven I knew nothing of the bargain until the election was over, & then I did not by any means approve of it. Let them investigate if they think proper. It can injure no *honest* politician, & if there has been dishonesty & corruption it ought to be exposed, the country ought to know it. . . .

Sunday, July 4. . . . Thursday evening Senator Pierce, Messrs. Atherton, Burke, Eastman & Shaw of the Ho.[,] & Col. Sylvester were here & we disposed of a couple of bottles of champagne very comfortably.[1] Mr.

Brown was also here. The House have adjd. at 3 o'clock P.M. every day
during the past week. They are to meet tomorrow, but it being the *quasi*
fourth, I doubt whether they will continue their session long. . . .

1. Edmund Burke (1809–1882), Ira Allen Eastman (1809–1881), and Tristram Shaw
(1786–1843), all from New Hampshire, were serving as Democratic congressmen at this
time. Burke later was commissioner of patents, 1846–1850. Henry H. Sylvester, chief clerk
of the patent office.

Sunday, July 18. Occurrences since I last wrote in this journal—July 5th.
People celebrated the 4th, Military turned out. Sunday schools marched
in procession to Capitol grounds & scholars partook of a collation, sundry speeches made. Temperance people met in a grove in Georgetown
& celebrated the progress of the Temperance reform, which has been
truly wonderful for the past year, and while all this celebration was in
progress the House of Representatives, to show their great economy to
time, sat and listened to speeches! till between two & 3 o'clock, and there
was I in the midst of them. . . .

16th. After House adjd. went with Pierce to Mr. Shaw's room & sat &
talked an hour & then Pierce came home with me & took tea & spent
the evening. Wife & I enjoy his company more this session than we have
for years. He is one of the best of companions, always pleasant and
amusing & interesting.

17th., yesterday. After House adjourned went out with Duvall & his
little son, W. W. Stewart & Mr. Berry, in the office carryall, to see Otto
Motly ride round the racecourse standing on two horses, upon the full
run.[1] Was much interested in his performances—riding[,] tossing balls,
playing with sticks & throwing up cannon balls & catching them on the
back of his neck! as they came down. They were bombshells of the size
of 44 & 62-pound cannon balls. Another performer did the rope dancing
feats that I have often seen before, such as hanging himself by the neck,
arms[,] legs, etc., while in full swing on the rope. He also threw a 56-
pound weight over his head, with his teeth, & balanced 4 wagon wheels,
lashed together, so as to be, say 10 feet high, on his chin. Did not get
home till about dark. . . .

1. Eli Duvall and Brook M. Berry were clerks, and W. W. Stewart was a messenger in
the office of the House of Representatives. Otto Motly, of Germany, a rider and equilibrist
called "Hercules on Horseback," had been the star of the circus show at New York's Bowery
Amphitheatre in 1840.

Sunday, July 25. . . . On Thursday Mrs. French, Frank & I walked down
into the City & saw a lot of French paintings, which were exhibiting,

preparatory to a sale of them at auction. Some of them were very beautiful. There was one winter scene that it almost made one cool to contemplate; it is most beautifully executed & I really longed to be its owner. Bess said she wanted all of them! I suppose 10 or 15,000 dollars would have purchased them! but that is rather more than I can afford to invest in pictures at this time. After examining the pictures & admiring them for an hour or two, we walked up the Avenue, & then to the Patent Office. The people were engaged in moving the curiosities belonging to the Historical Society of this city from the basement into the great Hall of the Patent Office building. My friend Col. [Peter] Force was there & very politely took us through the rooms, though they were closed to the public. The society has amassed an immense quantity of matter that is curious & interesting. There are numerous boxes & barrels which have not yet been opened, containing articles from the Exploring expedition.[1] The museum of the Society will probably, at no very distant day, be the best in the Union. . . .

1. The United States Exploring Expedition of 1838 to 1842, under the command of Charles Wilkes (1798–1877), journeyed to the Antarctic, the islands of the Pacific, and the American Northwest.

Sunday, August 8. Two weeks have passed since I journalized. The *private world* has gone along very much as usual. Last Sabbath I wrote a letter to Helen.[1] Col. Sylvester dined with us, & after dinner he, Frank & myself went down to the Navy Yard & saw the ship *Sea* which arrived the day previous with Greenough's statue of Washington[2] on board. Col. Pierce came in & took tea with us, & in the evening came in Messrs. Shaw[,] Burke & Atherton & Mr. Randall[3] of Maine.

The House of Representatives passed a bill to incorporate the Fiscal Bank of the United States[4] on Friday last. It had previously passed the Senate, & now everybody is anxious to know whether or not President Tyler will approve or veto it. I have never witnessed more excitement upon any event which depended upon the action of a single individual, and so uncertain is the public mind upon the subject that bets are making as to the result. I have long thought that the two Houses could not agree upon a bill the President would approve, & I have very little doubt as to his course. If he vetoes it *unqualifiedly*, the Democratic party will be bound to support him, & the World must regard it as a democratic triumph; if he sends in a qualified veto, stating what kind of a bill he will approve, etc., he will lose the support of both parties and sink into insignificance. I most sincerely hope he will pursue the dignified, manly course that becomes the president of these United States, and which accords with his formerly expressed opinions on the subject of a U.S. Bank—he will then stand high before the people of this country; on the other hand, if he pursues the course the Whigs desire, in defiance of his preconceived opinions, he will be hereafter regarded as a mere political hack, at the service of any party which chooses to flatter him. But I hope & believe better things of John Tyler, the man who has in former times expressed opinions that do him immortal honor, & stood by them up to this day, and why should he desert them. He will not!

1. Helen French (1824–1902), the tenth and youngest of Benjamin Brown French's half-brothers and half-sisters, was also the last to die.
2. Horatio Greenough (1805–1852), sculptor, was commissioned by the U.S. government in 1833 to complete a statue of George Washington to be placed in the Capitol.
3. Benjamin Randall (1789–1859), Whig congressman from Maine, 1839–1843.
4. The Fiscal Bank of the United States, sponsored by the Whigs, was, in effect, an attempt to revive the Second Bank of the United States. Such a bank, with headquarters in Washington, could establish branches only with the consent of the individual states.

Thursday, August 12. The President still *keeps dark* as to his intention in regard to the U.S. Bank bill, but no one seems to doubt now that it will be vetoed. We have a good deal of fun & joke going on about it. Yesterday about 2 o'clock there was a whirlwind passed along a portion of the city near Pa. Avenue, carrying with it various things, such as lumber, roofs of buildings, etc., and among other things it unroofed a portion of the Centre Market house, & while this commotion was going on "down in the city" & was very visible from the Capitol, at that place not a breath of air was to be felt, & so everybody said *it was the veto message* coming, & then everybody laughed. One member of the House said, yesterday, that he amused himself by rising early to see the negroes stand at the doors & windows on the Avenue watching for the Veto! They imagine it to be some great beast, like that spoken of [in] Revelation I suppose, which will come raving and tearing along the Avenue, *making all gee again.*[1] . . .

1. That is, making all right again, as in giving a command to a horse to turn to the right.

Sunday, August 15. Yesterday, according to a prophecy of Jo: Smith,[1] the Mormon prophet, this City was to have been sunk by an earthquake; but, alas for the *prophetical* reputation of Mr. Joseph Smith, the City still stands a permanent monument of the foolishness of man in attempting to assume the powers of Infinite knowledge. And yet there were those who were simple enough to fear the prophecied result, and I was told, seriously, that some of the citizens went to Bladensburg to avoid the expected destiny! It was a hot, damp, uncomfortable day. The House adjourned over from Friday evening to tomorrow, & many of the members went to Annapolis to visit the *Delaware 74*,[2] lying at anchor off that port. The President of the U.S. was to have gone, but did not. Why I have not heard, but some wag has got up the story that it was the intention of the Whigs to get him on board, & then, under pretence of shewing off the sailing powers of the noble ship, to get her under way & run out to sea, & there stay until the 10 days from the time the Bank bill was delivered to the President had expired, so that that bill would become a law by the provision of the Constitution! It would have been the best practical joke ever carried into operation, & the very idea is worthy of being recorded among the National Archives! The Senate sat, as usual, yesterday. No veto message yet, but rumor says it will come on Tuesday, that the entire cabinet will resign, that Congress will break up in a row, & that the excitement throughout the country will be tremendous. In this I hardly doubt that rumor is a prophet. The Whig party must break up. . . . It was conceived in the filthyness of the brothel, hard cider & profaneness were its midwives, the compost that nourished it was formed of the odds & ends of disappointed factions—Abolition, Antimasonry, old Federalism & humbug, mingled with drunkenness & dissipation—& in this hotbed it grew with the outward show of health & vigor, while disease and corruption was at its heart, like the bloated invalid, who wears the hue of health upon his cheek, while the fingers of death are grasping his very heartstrings. The light of Truth has dawned upon it & it *must* wither and die. God grant it a deep grave & an immovable monument of infamy! . . .

1. Joseph Smith (1805–1844), Mormon prophet and founder of the Church of Jesus Christ of Latter-Day Saints.

2. The ship-of-the-line *Delaware,* with 74 33-pounder cannonade, was launched at the Norfolk Navy Yard in 1820. In 1841 she was first used for local operations out of Norfolk, and later in the year sailed for a tour of duty on the Brazil Station. She was burned at Norfolk in 1861 to keep her out of Confederate hands.

Monday, August 23. The past week may be denominated *veto week.* A week ago this day President Tyler returned to the Senate the Bill to incorporate the subscribers to the Fiscal Bank of the United States, with his reasons for not approving it—of course nothing else has been talked about since. And now another Bank bill is under consideration in the House, & if it passes *it will be vetoed.* Such is my prophecy. . . .

Sunday, August 29. . . . On Monday last, Mr. Thos. F. Marshall[1] of Kentucky, having moved the adjt. on Saturday, was entitled to the floor as soon as the *Fiscal corporation* bill should come up in Committee of the whole on the State of the Union. Mr. M.'s fame as a debater had preceded him, & much was expected from him when he was elected to Congress. At an early hour the galleries of the House were crowded, & soon after the House met Mr. M. took the floor. He was, for a rarity, sober, & he spoke for an hour most eloquently, so that everybody was enraptured. The *gag rule* cut him off at the end of the hour in the middle of a sentence, and he was followed by Mr. Proffit[2] in, to my notions, a very capital speech. Many other speeches were made & at four o'clock the bill, by a previous resolution, was taken out of Committee & passed.

On Wednesday, an entirely different subject being under consideration, Mr. Marshall again got the floor, & being as much as "three sheets in the wind" he insisted upon finishing his speech of Monday, and so on he went, in spite of calls to order, on the same subject that he spoke upon on Monday, but how different his manner. Instead of the chaste style & manly eloquence of his *sober* speech, he ranted & raved, & played the mountebank. At one time he actually put one of his knees on his desk & stood for some time with the whole lower part of his leg lying across the desk; at another he leaned back against the side of his desk so far as almost to bring his back in a horizontal position, & so spoke for some minutes. To me it was a most disgusting exhibition, & lowered him exceedingly in my estimation. His speech was almost entirely in reply to one made by Mr. Wise several days before, & Mr. W. answered him in his usual manly, eloquent, & forcible manner. Marshall possesses first-rate talents & abilities, but he never can have the least influence for his habits of dissipation ruin him. . . .

1. Thomas F. Marshall (1801–1864), of Kentucky, was serving his only term in Congress.
2. George H. Proffit (1807–1847), Whig congressman from Indiana, 1839–1843, was appointed minister to Brazil in 1843 but was not confirmed by the Senate.

Friday, September 3. . . . After tea Madame & I walked round the Capitol grounds by moonlight. The moon was full, not a cloud to be seen, no air stirring, &, barring heat, the evening was as perfectly heavenly as an earthly evening could be; and as we passed along the magnificent eastern front of *our* Capitol, its white columns & balustrades appearing whiter, & its tremendous black dome if possible blacker, beneath the moonlight, I could not but ask myself if it could be possible that the immense pile before me, in all its beautiful proportions, was indeed the work of man, of pigmy man like me who, at that moment[,] stood almost as unnoticable [sic], & I am sure quite as unnoticed, as the veriest insect that was humming his adorations to the goddess of the silver bow from its lofty dome or beneath its magnificent portico? And then came the humbling reflection, that although man had erected it, that Time's corroding hand would level it with the dust about it, so that, in some distant age, no one could say *here* was the American Capitol—and perhaps long ere that time shall come the history of the *fall* of *this* republic will have been written. . . .

Saturday, September 4. . . . The House met, as usual, at 10, Mr. J. G. Floyd's[1] resolution of the 23d June, calling on the President for information in relation to the case of Alexander McLeod, was taken up & Mr. Floyd made his closing speech upon it in a manner that did him great credit. Mr. Everett[2] then took the floor and spoke until the morning hour elapsed, & then the House adjourned. . . .

Well, anyone who should read my journal of April 27th, 1838, *et seq.*, would hardly expect me to write complimentary charades on the name of Henry A. Wise, but what I then wrote was, as one may easily see, if other eye than my own ever sees it, written under a feeling that I had been insulted. From the uniform kindness always exhibited toward me by Mr. Wise from that day to this, & from what he once said to my friend F. O. J. Smith on the subject[,] I am convinced he did not intend to insult me or injure my feelings, & I therefore take back all I then said against him, & again record, what I have said both in public & private, that I believe him a man of high feelings of honor, generous & talented, & one who has been most deeply wronged & ungenerously dealt with by a party which he labored more zealously than any other person to bring into power. . . .

1. John G. Floyd (1806–1881), Democratic congressman from New York, 1839–1843 and 1851–1853.
2. Horace Everett (1779–1851), of Vermont, was a Whig congressman, 1829–1843.

Thursday, September 9. . . . Yesterday the House sat 5 or 6 hours & had the amendments of the Senate to the new Tariff bill under consideration. Mr. Wise moved an amendment to exempt salt from duty. Mr. Stanly[1] moved to add iron, cotton, sugar, and tobacco. Mr. Wise called for a division upon each & then Duvall & I had the pleasure of taking the yeas & nays on each. Salt[,] cotton & sugar were carried, iron & tobacco rejected. Then Mr. Birdseye[2] moved to reconsider the vote on salt—Mr. Morgan[3] the vote on iron—Mr. Wise the votes on cotton & sugar. Mr. L. W. Andrews[4] moved to lay the bill and amendments on the table, & in this beautiful state of *child's play,* Mr. Fillmore[5] moved an adjournment, and the yeas & nays being called for & ordered, the House after a vote by yeas & nays adjourned. Take it all in all it was the most ridiculous exhibition of child's play & disorder I ever witnessed, & it will probably take all day today to undo what was done yesterday.

1. Edward Stanly (1810–1872), Whig congressman from North Carolina, 1837–1843 and 1849–1853. He moved to California in 1854 and returned east briefly to serve as military governor of North Carolina, 1862–1863.

2. Victory Birdseye (1782–1853), of New York, had served in the Fourteenth Congress, 1815–1817, and was elected as a Whig to the Twenty-seventh Congress, 1841–1843.

3. Christopher Morgan (1808–1877), Whig congressman from New York, 1839–1843, and later secretary of state of New York, superintendent of the state's public schools, and mayor of Auburn.

4. Landaff Watson Andrews (1803–1887), a Whig congressman from Kentucky, 1839–1843.

5. Millard Fillmore (1800–1874), Whig congressman from Buffalo, New York, 1833–1835 and 1837–1843. Elected Vice President in 1848, he succeeded to the presidency upon the death of Zachary Taylor on July 9, 1850. He lost the nomination of the Whig party in 1852 to Gen. Winfield Scott, and in 1856, as the candidate of the Know-Nothing party, was defeated by James Buchanan.

Monday, September 13. . . . "King Caucus" now governs all the actions of Congress. It is all right and proper in my opinion that such should be the case for my party has acted upon that principle for years, but that the Federal party, the party which has denounced it for years & years, should now adopt & carry it to the extreme, is really amusing. It only goes to show that "there is no (political) honesty extant." During Thursday another of those scenes, so disgraceful to the House of Representatives, occurred in that body. Mr. Wise had made some remarks to which Mr. Stanly alluded in a manner that W. thought malevolent & unkind. He went to Mr. Stanly's seat to remonstrate with him when angry words passed between them, and Wise, as he says in his statement to the Committee, called Stanly "a mean, contemptible puppy and miserable wretch," to which Stanly replied[,] "You are a liar," when Wise struck him, and fight instantly ensued. Nearly all the members rushed to the spot where they were engaged. The House was in Committee[,] Mr. Samson Mason[1] of Ohio in the Chair; he left the Chair & the Speaker took it, & endeavoured for two or three minutes, in vain, to restore order. I was at the Clerk's table where I could see & hear all that transpired. The Speaker crying at the extent of his voice[,] "Order—order—order," exclamations from the crowd of "Damn him[,] down with him"—"Where are your Bowie knives"—"Order gentlemen, for God's sake come to order"—"Go it Arnold"[2]—"Knock him down," etc. Mr. Clarke, the Clerk of the House, seized the mace & went into the midst of the *melee* & exclaimed[,] "Gentlemen, respect the symbol of authority, respect yourselves." Mr. Arnold & Mr. W. O. Butler[3] of Ky. were seen in violent personal contest, & Mr.

Houston[4] of Ala. held an uplifted cane over Mr. Arnold's head, which some member arrested in its descent, & thus, probably saved Mr. A. a bloody coxcomb. In two or three minutes order was restored, mainly, I believe, by the exertions of Dixon H. Lewis, whose seat was at the head of the aisle where the tumult occurred, & who, as soon as he could[,] moved his tremendous form into the middle of the fight & instantly separated the first belligerents, & there he stood like an elephant among a parcel [of] dogs, keeping them all at bay, & separating any who seemed inclined to fight, until the House came to order. Mr. Wise arose from his own seat, apparently the calmest & coolest individual in the House, before order was fairly restored, and apologized in a most humble manner for the part he had taken in disturbing the order of the House, and after some debate, a Committee was appointed upon the matter, & the House resumed its ordinary business. . . .

1. Samson Mason (1793–1869), Whig congressman from Ohio, 1835–1843.
2. Thomas D. Arnold (1798–1870), a drummer boy in the War of 1812, served as a Whig congressman from Tennessee, 1831–1833, during which time an attempt was made to assassinate him on the west steps of the Capitol. He served again in the Twenty-seventh Congress, 1841–1843.
3. William Orlando Butler (1791–1880) served with Jackson at New Orleans and also as a major general of volunteers in the Mexican War. He was a Democratic congressman from Kentucky, 1839–1843, and an unsuccessful Democratic candidate for Vice President in 1848.
4. George S. Houston (1811–1879), Democratic congressman, 1841–1849, and senator, 1879, from Alabama. He was the Reform Democratic governor of Alabama, 1874–1878.

Tuesday, September 14. At 8 o'clock last evening the House of Representatives concluded their portion of the extraordinary session of Congress, & I venture to predict that it is the last extra session I shall ever witness, except some unforeseen *national event* like war or rebellion or insurrection demands it. Although it came together with a very powerful Federal majority, it has closed with the great end of its convention unaccomplished, & with a feeling of discord in the dominant party that cannot easily be reconciled. The Senate sat much later than the House, not having completed its Executive business. . . .

Wednesday, September 15. Yesterday all manner of reports were in circulation in this city. Early in the morning I heard that the President sent a special express to overtake the cars—then that the Canadians had seized Gen. Scott[1] & intended to hold him a prisoner, as a hostage for Alexander McLeod—then that the President, as a reprisal, had taken the British minister, Mr. Fox,[2] out of his bed the previous night & secured him in gaol as a hostage for Scott!!—then there were "rumors of wars," etc. But, in the course of the day, all these rumors died away. The members of congress that remained after the session closed left & the good citizens of Washing[ton] can now pursue the even tenor of their way without the excitement of the presence of Congress. Yesterday was a warm[,] pleasant day. I went to the Capitol in the morning, read the newspapers, went down in the city, called on Col. Force upon some business relative to the Corporation Affairs, & then looked over his valuable & immense collection of ancient books, among which to my great surprise, I found an original *manuscript* index to a portion of the Journals of the British House of Lords. How in the world it got into this Country nobody can tell.[3] . . .

1. Winfield Scott (1786–1866), a hero of the War of 1812, was appointed general-in-chief of the army in 1841. He later took part in the war with Mexico, capturing Mexico City, and was the unsuccessful Whig candidate for the presidency in 1852. Because of advanced age, he gave up command of the army in the fall of 1861.

2. Henry S. Fox (1791–1846), British minister to the United States, 1836–1844. After being replaced by Richard Pakenham he remained in Washington, where he died.

3. A large folio manuscript volume, "An Alphabetical Calendar of the Journalls of the House of Lords From the Restoration of King Charles Ye Second Anno 1660 Untill the Year 1723," is in the Peter Force Papers, Series VIII D, in the Manuscript Division, Library of Congress.

Sunday, September 26. . . . Yesterday was a beautiful day. Went to the Gen. P.O. at 8 A.M. with Henry's resignation of the Postmastership at Chester, & made arrangements for the appointment of my friend Thos. J. Melvin[1] as his successor. . . . After tea Mr. Johnston came in—stayed till 8 when we walked home with Ann & Mary,[2] & I accompanied him home. The evening was magnificent—heavens clear as crystal, weather cool, moon nearly at full. Aurora Borealis gleaming above the Northern horizon in a beautiful arch—it was an evening to be *walked* and enjoyed. It was a glorious evening for lovers. . . . I am now beset daily about a bill before the City Council for turning out the streets that are enclosed by individuals. It is referred to the Committee of which I have the honor to be Chairman, & of course everybody that has 10 feet of street enclosed is after me to report some modification to prevent them from losing the benefits of their enclosure. I never was at more loss to come to a conclusion as to the *right and wrong* of a matter as I am as to this. If I can ascertain what *right* is, I shall do it regardless of consequences. . . .

1. Thomas J. Melvin (1817–1881) was postmaster of Chester at several different times. The proprietor of a large general store, he served in both houses of the New Hampshire legislature.

2. Mary Brown, the daughter of Ann and Simon Brown.

Sunday, October 24. . . . During the week past the statue of Washington by Greenough has been brought from the Navy yard, under the direction of Capt. William Easby,[1] & was yesterday hoisted into the eastern portico of the Capitol, where it now is. It will be placed in the Rotundo this week.

This morning, before I was out of bed, the bells rang an alarm of fire. I looked out of the window & saw an immense smoke rising above the capitol, & supposing the fire to be but a short distance west of it, I, contrary to my usual custom, went out to see what was burning. It proved to be a stable, belonging to Brown's hotel,[2] on the corner of 6th & Missouri Streets. It was in the very midst of a nest of wooden buildings, but, in consequence of the contiguity of the Canal,[3] the fire was confined to the building wherein it originated, though others were several times on fire. I stayed till it was extinguished, & with a better opinion of the efficiency of the Washington Fire Department than I ever before entertained.

1. William Easby, a ship constructor, lived near Easby's shipyard.
2. Brown's Indian Queen Hotel, on the north side of Pennsylvania Avenue at 6th and C streets.
3. The Washington Canal, which incorporated part of Tiber Creek, connected the Potomac River with the Eastern Branch. It ran directly east to the base of Capitol Hill and then turned south and east to the Eastern Branch. It was covered over in the 1870s.

Saturday, November 6. . . . Recd. a letter from him [Henry Flagg French] day before yesterday stating that Mr. Fox[1] of Nashua was getting up a book to contain contributions from the pens of natives of New Hampshire, and requesting something from me. I this day sent Henry copies of several of my effusions which have never been published, telling him that he & Mr. Fox might make from them such selection as they see fit. I have no ambition to be an author, but as I have written some poetry that will not suffer, I hope, in comparison with much that I have seen *in print,* I have thought it well enough if natives of N.H. are to figure in a volume exclusively devoted to them, that my name should take its place therein for better or for worse. There has been poetry written by natives of that State that will not suffer in comparison with that of anyone, and some of the prose of her native sons exceeds, in vigor, elegance, & chasteness that of any prose within my knowledge. And who can doubt this when he considers that among her jewels are her Webster, her Cass, her Woodbury, her Richardson, her Pierce, her Atherton, her Hales, & a galaxy of others who have reflected honor upon her name, by their literary & political labors. I feel proud of my birthplace, and would not exchange the exalted title of "a native of New Hampshire" for any one the world could bestow upon me.

Arose about daybreak this morning, dressed warm & comfortable, it being a wintry morning and went round to Duvall's house, &, with him, went to Market—bought 80 pounds of beef at 6 cts. per lb.[,] 11 pounds of leaf lard for 1.00, turnips[,] crackers, etc. Then went to Parker's[2] & bought 109 lbs. butter at 23 cts. per lb.[,] ½ bbl. buckwheat at 3.75 & some other small matters. . . .

1. Charles James Fox (1811–1846), compiler, with Samuel Osgood, of *The New Hampshire Book. Being Specimens of the Literature of the Granite State* (Nashua, D. Marshall; Boston, James Munroe and Company, 1842). This work includes three poems by French.

2. G. & T. Parker, grocers, were located at the Centre Market, between 7th and 8th streets.

Thursday, November 18. . . . Day before yesterday I recd. a letter from Henry dated at Portsmouth, where he has located for the present. How odd it seems to me to think that Henry is not at Chester. For 27 years he has been a Citizen of that place & ever since I left it I have been in the habit of an almost constant correspondence with him *there*; from him I have expected, and recd.[,] *the doings* of my native town, & when I have gone there to visit he has ever been the first to welcome me & the last to bid me farewell. We have labored, studied, played together *there,* and now he is no longer a resident of Chester! I can hardly realize it. Washington without the Capitol would hardly seem to me stranger than Chester without Henry. There are those still left there whom I love & whose society I can most happily enjoy, but all, ay *all,* my desire to *reside* there is gone, and I almost dread to visit the old mansion, & *the tombs* of so many who were living when I was last there. . . .

Last evening I attended a Phrenological lecture by Dr. L. Hernis, a foreigner. His manner was good & his peculiarity of pronunciation rendered some sentences hard to understand, & it required the utmost attention to keep the thread of his discourse from escaping. I, however, managed to understand *all* that he said & I was amused & instructed. I am no believer in the science carried to the extent that its devotees carry it, though I do believe there is *something* in it. I never attended a lecture before, though I have read much *pro* & *con* on the subject & have very often heard it conversed about. After the lecture was over Dr. H. proceeded to examine the heads of any gentlemen who chose to submit to an examination & pay a dollar for it, & I, among others[,] underwent his manipulations & opinions consequent thereupon. Whether he spoke truly of my disposition, habits[,] etc., is not for me to say, because he was flatteringly inclined as I thought. He said some things of me, however[,] that *I know to be true, and the world does not.* He said that I was easily excited to anger, but could prevent its outbreak if I chose; that I was sensitive; that I was social in my disposition & habits; a good companion; liked a good dinner & a glass of wine & enjoyed company. That I was rather disposed to be indolent, though at times, I would devote myself with great energy and perseverance to labor, & when it was finished give myself up to indolence for a time. That I appeared at different times, like a different individual. That my mental faculties were very fully developed, & that my ideas were original—that I was no plagiarist. That I never argued without knowing what I was talking about, & that I went to the bottom of my subject & argued it closely & convincingly. That I was inclined to literature & a great lover of poetry. That I had much mechanical ingenuity, but that I had no individuality & did not remember persons well! That, upon the whole, my head was a well formed one, that I was a good neighbor, a good friend, & rather of a domestic turn.

Of all this it becometh me not to say much, but I will say that whether individuality is or is not much developed, I never forget a face that I have once seen, if my attention is particularly called to notice it, & that no one learns the 240 members of the House of Reps. quicker than I do, & retains their several physiognomies longer in mind.

I like to have forgotten that he said I was ambitious & fond of fame. I admit that *once* this might have been the case, but now—

> My feverish longings for Fame
> And dreams of distinction are gone. . . .

Wednesday, December 1. It is Winter & verily it looks like winter. The morning is cold & the earth is white with snow, but the clearness of the atmosphere & the stillness of the morning promise a pleasant day. Yesterday I was in the Rotundo of the Capitol nearly all day seeing them prepare to place the statue of Washington on the pedestal. Today it is to be raised.

Wednesday afternoon. The statue was placed upon the pedestal today. Nearly all the preparations were made yesterday, and at 10 o'clock this morning the President of the United [States] & the Secretary of the Navy (John Tyler & A. P. Upshur[1]) entered the Rotundo, & soon after they arrived the word was given to the men at the capstan bars to move. The statue rose beautifully to the required height in about 20 minutes, but, in consequence of some misarrangement of the derrick and guyropes[,] when they attempted to swing it over the pedestal one corner came in contact with one leg of the derrick, & in the effort to release it the upper part of the derrick became so twisted as to throw nearly the entire weight of the statue on to one side, & the consequence was that the whole concern was very near coming down. By great care, & the addition of other tackles & guyropes, & the shifting of those already upon it, it was brought back to its proper position and the statue was swung over the pedestal, & at one o'clock, precisely, was fitted to its place. Upon the announcement of the fact by Capt. Easby—the gentleman who contracted to put it up—three hearty cheers were given three times—or, to speak more nautically, "three times three" were given, which made the Rotundo ring again.

I have felt a deep interest in the placing of the statue, & have been in the Rotundo nearly all the time since they commenced work yesterday morning, and have been greatly amused at the different remarks I have heard about it. Some have condemned its position and its nudity, in no measured terms, others, they are few however, are perfectly satisfied with it & think it a masterpiece of art, worthy the subject & worthy the Nation. (I am one of the few.)

One gentleman remarked that if they would put a pair of runners under it, and place a whip in the right hand, it would add very much to the appropriateness of its position!

This man must have been, in his day, a Yankee stagedriver.

Another, probably a fiddler, said[,] "Well[,] the old fellow looks as if he was about to give us a tune. He has his fiddle in his hand, all ready."

Doctor ———— [sic] thought he looked as if he had just come out of a bath & was preparing to be bled.

Someone thought he must have jumped out of bed in a hurry & taken the sheet with him; "But[,]" said another, "I don't believe the old General ever slept without his shirt on, in all his life!"

An old gentleman said he remembered Washington very well & used to see him down at Mount Vernon walking about on his farm, but he never in all his life *saw him in such a dress!*

Another found great fault with the sandals. "Sandals!" said he[,] "General Washington with sandals on! Why the idea is ridiculous!"

One wondered what those *dogs heads*![2] on the front of the chair were placed there for.

Another wondered whether that thing in his left hand was a guitar. It looked to him as much like one as anything else, and he thought he must be preparing to play on it as he seemed to be *airing* his right forefinger for a nice touch of the strings! (I will here remark that the handle of the sword was not attached to the scabbard at the time.)

Many were very curious to know what point of time in Washington's life Greenough intended to represent, & a hope was expressed that he would publish something stating his own meaning as to the position, etc., of the figure.[3]

An opinion seemed to be general among the spectators that the statue with its pedestal was too large for the room, and that it would have had a much finer effect it it had not been placed in the centre. I am fully convinced the centre is not the place for it. The small figures are not yet placed upon the pedestal[,] but I presume they will be food for ridicule & praise. As I have undertaken to keep a record of the whole matter I shall add anything I may hear, as also the criticisms of those whom I think competent to judge of the beauty & propriety of the whole affair.

1. Abel Parker Upshur (1791–1844) of Virginia. He served as Tyler's Secretary of the Navy, 1841–1843, and succeeded Daniel Webster as Secretary of State. He was killed in an explosion aboard the U.S.S. *Princeton* in 1844.
2. Marginalia: The front of the chair is ornamented with *lions heads*.
3. Greenough memorialized Congress early in 1843 concerning the removal of the statue of Washington from the Rotunda to the grounds on the western front of the Capitol. In this memorial he discussed the positioning of the figure within the Capitol and took up some of the objections that had been raised to the manner in which Washington had been represented. A facsimile of the memorial is published in *The Miscellaneous Writings of Horatio Greenough*, edited by Nathalia Wright (New York, 1975), pp. 25–29.

Friday, December 3. Clerk's Office H.R. U.S. To continue the subject of my last journalization I will add my observations of yesterday on the statue. In the forenoon the back of the chair & the figures of Columbus & the Indian were placed in their positions, and when I entered the rotundo at one o'clock P.M. Hon. John Quincy Adams was, for the first time, viewing the statue. Gen. Scott was also there, in full uniform, having just returned from the funeral of Col. Hook[1] of the Army. I walked up to Mr. Adams & shook hands with him, it being the first time I had seen him since his return to the city, and accompanied him round the statue. He said nothing until he had viewed it on every side, but his countenance, which I watched somewhat particularly, manifested pleasure. At length I asked him what he thought of it. He replied, "My first impression with regard to it is very favorable. I think it a most finished production, but it will be subject to many objections on account of the nakedness of the figure, but that is a matter of taste altogether."[2] After some further remarks I left him & proceeded to another part of the rotundo to listen to what further I could hear.

One man asked[,] "If the man on the left of the chair" (the figure representing Columbus contemplating a globe, which he holds in his hand) "was *goin'* to take a game of trapball!!"[3] Another said the whole concern was so inappropriate & ridiculous that he would take it down and destroy it if he could have his way! What an exterminating man he must be; I should like to accompany him to a Phrenologist & ascertain whether the bump of destructiveness is not unusually developed upon his cranium!

Someone else said the position of the figure of Washington reminded him of a criminal at the bar when called on to plead to an indictment for a criminal offence—the right hand raised, the left extended, as if for mercy from the Court! This must have been a lawyer whose ideas never passed beyond the dock or the witness box, & whose mind was bounded like a yard of soil. . . .

A poor crazy fellow, who imagines himself the Major General of the Army of the U.S.[,] said he would have it taken down for it was too large. Someone replied that the statue was no larger than Washington really was, but that it weighed more, that Washington only weighed *two tons,* while the Statue weighed twenty!

My friend Johnston, who agrees with me in thinking the statue, & all its accompaniments, an almost, if not quite, perfect specimen of the sublime art which brought it into *existence*—if I may so speak—told me that he heard a trio of worthies ridiculing the costume, & expressing an opinion *seriously,* that it ought to have been formed of marble of different colors, & been dressed in the old Continental uniform—a three-cornered black hat, blue coat with buff facings, buff breeches & military boots & spurs!! Such a figure would be a curiosity at least, & might suit the taste of a Dutchman or New Zealander, but God forbid that the American taste should ever descend to an admiration of such monstrosities!

After hearing several persons criticise the countenance, in comparison with the best portraits, & after hearing an aged gentleman who was personally acquainted with the original & in whose opinion upon most subjects I have great confidence, remark that, "had he seen the head in the Louvre, he never should have mistrusted it was intended for a likeness of Washington." I was much pleased when Col. William Brent[4] told me that he was *well* acquainted with Washington, that he dined with him at Mount Vernon[,] but a few months previous to his death, & that the countenance of the statue was, to his view, a perfect likeness of the original.

Upon the whole I think the statue is growing into favor—there was not so much ridicule yesterday as [the] day before, & today I have heard none, but much praise. . . .

1. James Harvey Hook, of Maryland, had served in the War of 1812.
2. Marginalia: I remarked[,] "It surpasses anything of the kind I ever saw, but I suppose you have seen finer ones in the old world." He replied[,] "I have seen statues in the old world."
3. An old game played with a trap (a device for holding a ball), ball, and bat.
4. William Brent was clerk of the United States Circuit Court, Washington, D.C., 1824–1848, and agent for claims, 1824–1828, under the Treaty of Ghent, for property in the Chesapeake Bay regions carried away or destroyed by the British during the War of 1812.

Sunday, December 12. On the 6th instant commenced the 2d session of the 27th Congress, the advent of which was accompanied by nothing especially worthy of remark, and since its commencement there has been about the usual waste of breath in the House & about the usual quantity of rumor & running about out-of-doors. . . .

Last Sunday I read *Two Years Before the Mast*[1] and was exceedingly interested in it. I rose from the perusal almost impressed with the idea that I had just returned from a voyage to the coast of California, after experiencing all the roughness of the Cape Horn passage.

The statue of Washington continues to draw crowds of visitors into the rotundo, but I have not been in many times during the week past, for now it makes me angry to hear the ill-natured remarks that are made about it. I was much relieved the other day by hearing a lady, who *I know* possesses a correct taste & forms a correct opinion of almost everything she sees, remark that the beautiful proportions & admirable attitude of the statue, added to the faultless execution of the work[,] rendered the whole so perfect that she never should have thought of the nakedness of the figure had she not been told of it! She looked at it with an eye of veneration for the great original, & of pride that the country of which he was the Father had produced an artist capable of embodying his sacred form in marble in a manner worthy of the original!

She said to me[,] "I am astonished at the lack of classical taste among this free and enlightened people. It seems to me that the only thing in the Rotundo worthy to remain there is that statue. I could not but think that at the bronze statue of Jefferson, the uncouth sculpture about the walls, and the hardly less uncouth pictures in the 5 panels that are now filled, Foreigners were justified in laughing." She then expressed a hope that the 3 vacant panels would be filled with pictures worthy the place & the nation.

This was really an oasis in the desert of public opinion, which, I regret to say, is as barren as the sands of Sahara on this subject. The coat & breeches on the bronze Jefferson have risen 50 per cent in the opinions of many since *the* Washington, *in God's own costume,* was placed upon its pedestal. I think some of those classical genii who wanted Greenough's chanting cherubs *enrobed* in certain garments *incident to infancy,* when they were exhibited in Boston some years since, had better see to the covering up of the manly bosom and muscular arm of this glorious representation of the Pater Patria. It would then be *American*—and no mistake!

1. *Two Years Before the Mast,* Richard Henry Dana's classic of life at sea, was published in 1840.

Wednesday, December 15. . . . Monday, arose in good season, read till breakfast time, eat breakfast, went to the Capitol, was with the Speaker from ½ past 9 to 12 aiding him about the appointment of his committees, & getting them ready to be announced to the House. By the way, what a job it is for any Speaker to appoint those same Committees. How many sectional interests are to be considered when fixing upon 9 men to [deal with][1] a certain class of subjects bearing upon 17,000,000 of people scattered from Maine to Florida & from the Atlantic Ocean to the Rocky mountains! as, for instance, the Tariff, the Financial operations, Commerce, Agriculture, etc. How difficult to fix the suitable talent to the subject, & to apportion the political weight justly & impartially. The Speaker is like a man in a vortex where a hundred currents are eddying around him & he is at a loss which one to throw himself into that he may be borne into smooth water. No man ever labored with more assiduity than Mr. Speaker White did in forming the Committees of this Session, & with all his care I do not doubt there are heart burnings and disappointments in abundance. But to return to myself. At 10 m. past 12 the Speaker was ready to have his committees announced, & I went with him to the Clerk's table. There I remained till the Ho. adjd. about 2 o'clock. Came home & dined, went to the Mayor's office at 3 to attend a meeting of a Committee of the Corporation; staid there till 4 then went to the Council Chamber, & attended a meeting of the Council, which lasted till ¼ before 7; from the City Hall went to the Patent office where there was a meeting of the National Institution for the promotion of Science, of which I am a member. The meeting was held in the great room of the Patent office, & was fully attended, & exceedingly interesting. I think that Society—or rather Institution—is destined to be one of the most important Institutions in the U.S. The meeting of Monday adjourned at 9 o'clock, when I came home. Tuesday morning awoke with a most violent nervous headache, notwithstanding which I went to the Capitol at 9 A.M. & remained there till the Ho. adjd. at about 3 o'clock. The States were called for the presentation of petitions, & Mr. John Quincy Adams, as usual, got up a row about abolition petitions, & we had the yeas & nays & a call of the House, which operations did not minister to the ease of my head in the least. I came home almost sick— went into my chamber and there remained until evening. At about 8 felt much relieved—went to bed at 10 & arose this morning well. Today the House did little else than receive petitions, & adjd. about 3. I came home & dined, & returned & worked a while, then attended a meeting in the Hall of the House, for the formation of a National Agricultural Society, of which I became a member. . . .

1. French wrote "which" instead of "deal with." The sentence is unintelligible without the change.

Wednesday, December 29. . . . How pigmy-like it seems to be making a record of the observations and doings of a single individual! and yet the great mass of millions is made up of integers & were each to keep a record & publish it what a history of the world we should have!

But, of myself, the same dog-trot life that I have been pursuing for the past 8 winters has again commenced, & it will last, I suppose, if I live & am well, till next July, & then a little leisure may fall to my lot again. . . .

Monday, January 10. . . . Here I am, 10 days into a new year without a note thereof.

January 1st 1842. Was a delightful day. Went down in the City & bought some playthings for Frank & a cane for Mrs. French to present to Col. Pierce. At 12 noon Mr. & Mrs. Russell, Mrs. French, Frank & I went to the President's in a hack, and such a crowd as was there assembled I have never seen at the White House before. After being jammed in the crowd for an hour or two we succeeded, through much tribulation, in getting out, finding our hack & coming home. Frank could not imagine what it all meant, and asked me with great seriousness, if the people were going to *"head Captain Tyler."* Since January 1st but little of note has happened to me or mine. I have read considerably—*Barnaby Rudge—The Glory & Shame of England*—some of *Macaulay's Miscellanies*, etc.[1] The annual meeting of the Union Literary Debating Society was held last Thursday evening[,] and, after electing officers[,] 16 of us repaired to McGrath's Coffee House & had a supper. Wine & wit flowed till one o'clock—we had songs & speeches & fun & frolic & broke up well pleased with ourselves & with each other, and I did *not* have any headache *next day!* . . .

1. Charles Dickens's *Barnaby Rudge* was published in London in 1841 and *The Glory and Shame of England,* by Charles Edwards Lester (1815–1890), was published in New York in 1841. In 1842 Cary & Hart of Philadelphia published the first of five volumes titled *Political and Miscellaneous Essays,* by Thomas Babington Macaulay (1800–1859). *Macaulay's Miscellanies* is an interior, secondary title.

Saturday, January 22. On Thursday afternoon and evening it rained, notwithstanding which Mr. Russell and I went to the Debating Society at the Apollo Hall.[1] The debate was about the right of suffrage & whether it ought be subject to a property qualification. Of course *we* democrats were all on the negative side of the question. The debate was dull, though there was a large & respectable audience. . . .

1. Apollo Hall, E Street near 13th Street.

Sunday, February 6. . . . Congress are doing almost nothing for the benefit of the country, & the House of Representatives are doing more now towards dissolving this glorious Union than has been done, up to the 7th day of Jany. 1842, since the adoption of our Constitution. On the 7th day of Jany. the rules were suspended for the purpose of calling the States for the presentation of petitions, & the object of that suspension is not yet complied with! After much tribulation the State of Massachusetts was arrived at, the call having been commenced at Iowa, and as soon as Mr. John Quincy Adams opened his abolition budget, of course a storm commenced, & it continued with various changes until he presented a petition of 46 citizens of Haverhill, Massachusetts, for a peaceable dissolution of this Union! Immediately upon the presentation of that petition, Mr. Hopkins asked if it would be in order to move that it be burned in presence of the House. The Speaker said it would not. After some confusion & one or two motions Mr. Gilmer[1] moved a resolution of censure upon Mr. Adams; the next morning, Mr. Thos. F. Marshall moved an amendment setting forth the facts & deductions in a preamble, & proposing the *severest censure*. This has been the constant business of the House since the [7th][2] ult[im]o when the petition was presented. Mr. Adams commenced his defence on Thursday morning & will not probably conclude it for a week. He spares no one, & seems to be determined to give a full history of his own life & actions, & of everything else connected with this Government. He has exhibited more temper, more obstinacy, & more desire to attack everybody, friend & foe indiscriminately[,] than I ever saw either him or any other mortal exhibit before. And it seems to me, that notwithstanding his great memory, & his vigor of intellect, that I can perceive, what I never did before in him, the garrulity & ill temper of disappointed old age. He certainly has attacked his friends in a manner entirely unjustifiable, & with a grossness of speech & invective to which I did not suppose he was capable of descending. . . .

1. Thomas W. Gilmer (1802–1844), Whig and Democratic congressman from Virginia, 1841–1844. Resigning his seat in February 1844, he was appointed Secretary of the Navy by President Tyler, and was killed less than two weeks later in an explosion aboard the U.S.S. *Princeton*.
2. French had left this blank.

Friday, February 25. Nineteen days & no journalizing! In that time much has passed beneath my ken that I ought to have noted, but I did not & probably no other pen has or will do it, & so the world has lost so much, *if ever the world shall honor my record with its perusal*, which I very greatly doubt. But to go on from the time I left off above. . . . Mr. Adams after speaking two or three days, gave way to a motion to lay the whole matter, relative to his censure, on the table & the House thus disposed of it, and Mr. Adams triumphed! Since that time until yesterday they have gone on with the regular business before them. Economy is the order of the hour, & we poor Clerks have to take the whole weight of some of those *mighty minds* whose immense exertions seem to have invested them with the perfection of that elevated employment, *"the art of skinning flints."* The office of the Clerk of the House seems to have fallen particularly under their ban, & there appears to be a systematic effort to embarrass the Clerk & his office, but I trust there is too much good sense in the majority to fall into the foolish *small* economy proposed by the Committee!

Last week the statue of Washington was again moved from the centre of the Rotundo to a position just in front of the western entrance; it is placed several feet lower & looks much better than it did in the centre. It was moved on the same sort of "ways" used to launch vessels, & as it passed on the inclined plane from one position to the other the face was so elevated that the light from the dome fell directly upon it, & it made a most astonishing difference in the appearance of the features. When the figure is erect the shadow of the forehead & brows upon the lower part of the face destroys the effect of the artist's intention, & this was so exceedingly manifest when I saw it in its inclined position that I regretted to see it changed. . . .

Mr. Francis O. J. Smith came to this city a week ago last Saturday, & came to stay with us day before yesterday. He is now an inmate of my house. Yesterday I had a little dinner party consisting of Mr. & Mrs. Monroe,[1] Hon. Franklin Pierce, Senator, & Hon. Elisha H. Allen[2] of the House of Reps. We had a very pleasant time. Col. Pierce is about to resign his seat in the Senate, which, for my own sake & the sake of N.H.[,] I most deeply regret.

1. Probably Mr. and Mrs. Charles Monroe. Charles was F. O. J. Smith's brother-in-law and an early investor in the stock of the Magnetic Telegraph Company. The Washington directories for 1843 and 1846 also list a Charles Monroe as a clerk in the Post Office Department.

2. Elisha H. Allen (1804–1883), of Maine, served one term as a Whig congressman, 1841–1843. His subsequent career was spent largely in the service of Hawaii.

Sunday, February 27. After writing the foregoing on Friday evening, I went over to the Hall of the House, where the Congressional total abstinence Society held a meeting. The Hall was crowded almost to suffocation. Mr. Briggs[1] of Massachusetts was in the chair as President, & he opened the meeting with an address. He was followed by several speakers, and a number of resolutions were adopted. Dr. Sewall[2] addressed the meeting, & illustrated his remarks by 8 drawings of the human stomach, shewing the progress of drunkenness from health to death. Mr. Thomas F. Marshall made a most admirable speech upon a resolution offered by him discountenancing the fashionable habit of drinking healths at table. His great powers of ridicule, sarcasm and pathos were all brought into play, & he at one time convulsed the audience with laughter, & then dissolved them in tears—it was a glorious effort in a glorious cause. . . .

1. George Nixon Briggs (1796–1861), Whig congressman from Massachusetts, 1831–1843. He later served as governor of Massachusetts and as president of the American Temperance Union.

2. Thomas Sewall (1786–1845) graduated in medicine from Harvard in 1812 and became professor of anatomy in the medical college of The Columbian University, Washington, D.C. He wrote and lectured widely on the pathology of drunkenness.

Thursday, March 10. This day at two o'clock, Charles Dickens, the author, came into the House of Representatives with the Hon. N. P. Talmadge[1] of the Senate. I was introduced to him by Mr. Sutton,[2] the writer for the *New York Herald.* He stayed but a few moments. Soon after he left[,] a subscription paper for a dinner to be given him next Monday was handed me, and I signed it. I suppose Mr. D. will be the lion of a week.

1. Nathaniel P. Tallmadge (1795–1864), Whig senator from New York, 1833–1844, and governor of Wisconsin Territory, 1844–1845.

2. Robert Sutton was placed in charge of James Gordon Bennett's news bureau, the first to be established in Washington.

Sunday, March 13. . . . Mr. Dickens does not raise such a hubbub here as he did in Boston & New York, which is much to the credit of the Washington people. We are so used to *lions* here that we neither make gods nor beasts of them, but treat them with all the respect & all deference they merit. Dickens was in the House nearly through its session, day before yesterday. He was invited to a seat within the bar by some member, & occupied the selfsame chair in which Lord Morpeth[1] sat nearly every day while he was in the city. He is a very amiable looking man & has not a single mark of the Englishman about him; I should sooner have taken him to be a yankee. He seems to bear all the adulations heaped upon him with a modesty which does him infinite credit, & it makes me feel glad to see true literary merit & genius duly appreciated. . . .

1. George William Frederick Howard, 7th Earl of Carlisle (1802–1864). Lord Morpeth

was a courtesy title. Following the defeat of Melbourne in July 1841, Morpeth resigned a cabinet position and traveled in the United States and Canada.

Friday, March 18. I shall not soon forget the *doings* of the past week in which I have taken some little part. On Monday evening I attended a social dinner given by the Allegany club to Charles Dickens, Esq., at Boulanger's.[1] Hon. John Quincy Adams & Gen. Van Ness[2] were invited guests. Hon. Geo. M. Keim[3] was President, & Hon. M. St. Clair Clarke & Hon. Aaron Ward[4] were Vice Presidents. . . .

The party sat down at ½ past 7 o'clock P.M. and after partaking of a splendid entertainment Gen. Keim addressed them in a very happy speech of a few minutes length, complimentary to Mr. Dickens. Mr. D. replied in a most happy manner. Wit, sentiment, songsinging, storytelling & speechmaking occupied the time till eleven, when Mr. Dickens rose & in the most feelingly beautiful manner possible bid us good night. Mr. Adams & Gen. Van Ness soon followed; I left a little past 12, & I understand the party broke up at about 2. It was among the happiest evenings of my existence. Dickens, by his modesty, his social powers, & his eloquence[,] added to the high esteem in which I was previously induced to hold him. I believe every person present was delighted. . . .

. . . This morning the *diggers* have commenced digging for the foundation of my house. . . .

1. Joseph Boulanger, a Belgian, operated a popular French restaurant in Washington for years. He was also the White House chef and steward from the presidency of Jackson through that of Tyler.

2. John Peter Van Ness (1770–1846) had been a congressman from New York, 1801–1803, but forfeited his seat when he accepted a commission in the militia in the District of Columbia. Remaining in Washington, he became a banker, a society leader, and for the years 1830–1834, mayor of Washington. He had been made a major general in 1813.

3. George M. Keim (1805–1861), Democratic congressman from Pennsylvania, 1838–1843.

4. Aaron Ward (1790–1867), Democratic congressman from New York, 1825–1829, 1831–1837, and 1841–1843.

Sunday, May 1. . . . There has been considerable excitement in the House for a day or two past in consequence of the introduction, in a novel manner, to say the least of it, of the report of Hon. Geo. Poindexter[1] relative to the affairs of the N.Y. Custom House. Mr. Stanly reported it as the accompanying document to a report from the Committee on Public Expenditures. Mr. Wise opposed the printing of it, & expressed his strong disapprobation of the manner in which it was brought before the House. It was, however, ordered to be printed, & the President, in answer to a call of the House made day before yesterday, yesterday sent in a message accompanied by the reports of Messrs. Kelly[2] & Stuart,[3] the other Commissioners, & all the papers in the case, making a small basketful—they were brought by his Private Secretary *in a basket*, & delivered to the House, amid quite a laugh. . . .

A week ago last Thursday evening Bess and I went to Carusi's saloon[4] to see Daguerre's[5] magical pictures. There were 4 views—1st, the interior of the "Church of the Invalids" at Paris with Napoleon's remains, 2d, the Valley of Goldeau[,] 3d, "The Church of St. Etienne du Mont[,]" & 4th, a view of Venice. The pictures themselves merely as paintings are wonderful, but the marvelousness of the exhibition is the magic changes that are exhibited merely by the effect of light. In each picture, the gradations of light from sunrise to sunrise were all shown, & in the changes from daylight to candlelight the *pictures themselves were changed*, in character, though the canvas was the same! The church was silent & lone during the daylight scene. At midnight the altar was lighted for mass, & the church was full of people! & when daylight returned again, the Church was again empty, & all appeared as at first. It was the same with Venice, only to my eye Venice appeared the most perfect. Bess & I were perfectly delighted with the exhibition.

1. George Poindexter (1779–1853), delegate to Congress from the Mississippi Territory, 1807–1813; Democratic congressman from Mississippi, 1817–1819; and senator, 1829–1835. His report appears in *Reports of Committees, 27th Congress, 2nd Session, 1841–42, Serial 409, Report 669*.
2. Alfred Kelley (1789–1859), of Ohio, was Cleveland's first lawyer and a leading figure in the field of transportation.
3. William M. Steuart, of Montgomery County, Md.
4. The Assembly Rooms of Gaetani Carusi on 11th and C streets.
5. Louis J. M. Daguerre (1789–1851), French painter and inventor of the daguerreotype.

Sunday, July 24. On Thursday the 11th instant we moved into this house, and thus far it has answered all our expectations. It is cool & airy, & we have the great comfort of knowing that we are not surrounded with vermin, as we were in the Lindenburger house—roaches and *forty legs* abounded there, there were *some* bedbugs, & rats & mice were quite plenty. . . .

Since I made my last record here, my life has taken that *grindstone* round that has neither *cameo* or *intaglio* accompanying it—the surface has been as even as that of a lake in midwinter. It has been—up early—work—breakfast—work—to the Capitol—dinner—back to the Capitol—home—work—tea—*worn out*—to bed. The building of my house and the doings of the House of Representatives have engrossed all my attention. . . .

Thursday, July 28. This has been the hottest day of this hot season. At eleven o'clock I went with the Mayor[1] & President of the Board of Aldermen in my ex officio capacity, as Prest. of the Board of Com. Council, to visit the School for indigent female children kept in the basement of Mr. Smith's[2] church in 9th Street. There were between 40 & 50 scholars present and I was very much interested in the appearance of the school. The misses, although the children of poor people, were all neatly clad, & they appeared as intelligent as any like number of children that I ever saw together. The school usually consists of about 80 scholars, and is conducted by two instructresses, & is under the supervision & management of a number of benevolent ladies of this city. The Corporation give something to support it, hence the duty of the Mayor & Prests. of the two Boards to visit it. . . .

1. William W. Seaton.
2. John C. Smith, pastor of the 4th Presbyterian Church, New York Avenue.

Friday, August 12. . . . Since I wrote here, two weeks ago, things have moved along very steady with me. The House sits daily from 10 till 5 or 6, and of course I have little time to devote to any other than my official duties. Since the last veto the Whigs are cross & crabbed, & there seems to me to be a disposition among many of them to let the Government get along as it best can without any further action from them, but my opinion is, there will be enough honest men found in their party to unite with the Democrats & pass such a Tariff as will provide sufficient revenue for the support of the Government. The Whig party, as a party, is now perfectly reckless, and seem to care not a straw what may be the consequences of their action, provided they can embarrass President Tyler. Since the first veto their legislation has been aimed exclusively, almost, at the President, & their object seems to have been to get as many vetoes as possible. But in getting the last they have put themselves so clearly in the wrong that instead of "heading the Captain," they are, themselves, *headed*! Mr. J. Q. Adams has pursued a course, recently, disgraceful to his standing and his years. He has assumed to lead off the Whig party of the House, & has exhibited a virulence, an obstinacy, and littleness that it has pained me to notice. I think his judgment is failing, while his energies of body & mind seem to remain unimpaired. . . .

Sunday, August 21. . . . Congress has been considerably excited by the veto of the Tariff, & the House has been engaged most of the time in fruitless attempts to get up another Tariff bill. I think a week from tomorrow will wind up this session—this long & eventful session. Since the return of the Tariff bill by the President, John Quincy Adams has shown more temper, obstinacy, & bad feeling than any other man in the House, & it seems to me as if, in his ungovernable passion, he would rather see his Country sunk into a mobocracy than that *any* Tariff should pass. He appears utterly reckless, & I can compare him to nothing but a desperate gambler who stakes everything, in his madness, regardless of consequences. Mr. Adams, with all his knowledge, wisdom and learning, is a most dangerous man; his patriotism is a selfish one, and he cares not what becomes of his country any further than as his own political aspirations run parallel with her prosperity. His personal vanity is beyond that of any man of his age that I ever saw—indeed it amounts to a sort of coxcombry that is at times disgusting, & coarseness, vulgarity & clownism are often pressed into his service, of late, in his political tirades in order to get up a laugh among his degraded worshippers. I used to think better of the man, though I never placed the least confidence in his political integrity, knowing, as I did, his inordinate ambition, & his "feverish longing for fame."

His retentive memory and the intimate connexion of his entire life with the political history of this Country renders it easy for him to refer to the political events of the past 60 or 70 years, & his flatterers stand with open mouths & swallow all he says, with the assertion "Was there ever such a man!" as if, taking his life and connexions into consideration, there was anything very strange in his accumulated knowledge—would it not, rather, be strange, if it were otherwise. But with an egotism that would be disreputable to a Sophomore, he delights to talk by the hour together, of what *he* has been & what *he* has seen and what *he* knows! From his recent course I have not a doubt that if five hundred people were to cast off their allegiance from our republican government, & "offer him a kingly crown," he would not refuse it even a *first* time! All this I say after the most due consideration, & after having watched his course most closely for the past 8 years. He is the most dangerous man to the liberties of this country that is in it, and if he lives ten years longer, & retains his faculties, the whole country will agree with me in this opinion.

Yesterday Mr. Colt[1] blew up a vessel down in front of the arsenal, by the way of experiment. He applied the igniting power to his battery, from a distance of 5 miles. Mrs. French & Frank went down to see the explosion from Greenleaf 's point & were very much gratified. For my part I contented myself by looking at it through my glass from the top of the house, & its appearance was magnificent. A column of smoke, water and fragments rose several hundred feet in the air without any apparent noise & for a few seconds it seemed like a fixed mass of matter; it then dissolved & disappeared. The President & half the city were present at the exhibition, & the experiment appeared to be perfectly successful.

1. Samuel Colt (1814–1862), in addition to inventing his famous multi-shot pistol, was involved in the development of submarine batteries for blowing up enemy vessels as they entered or left a harbor. The spectacular demonstration of August 20 was Colt's second.

Sunday, September 4. My 42d "birthday" or, to speak more properly, the 42d anniversary of the day on which I entered this breathing world.

Last Wednesday [August 31], at ½ past two o'clock P.M. the second session of the 27th Congress adjourned, after a session of nearly nine months, and glad enough was I. On Thursday I commenced building a trellis in *our* garden, early in the morning, and finished it before night. On Friday after dinner Mr. Phillips & I commenced upon my summerhouse, & worked till nearly dark. Yesterday morning I arose before it was fairly day & went to work. Mr. Phillips came about 7, & between us we finished the summerhouse before sunset, and I never remember to have felt more fatigued in my life than I do today. . . .

Tuesday, September 13. Yesterday was the hottest day of this season, and it being the 5th Anniversary of Frank's birth, Bess & I concluded we would make him as happy as possible, so after breakfast I walked down in the city & purchased for him $1.50¢ worth of playthings, consisting of 12 horse soldiers & 12 footmen, a trumpet, a fish, a pair of swans & some candy. Got back about 12 almost roasted, dined at ½ past 1, recd. a notice from the Mayor convening the City Councils at 2, specially to attend the funeral ceremonies of Mrs. Tyler,[1] wife of the President of the U.S. Attended the Council, & from thence went to the Presidential mansion & attended the funeral ceremonies, got home about sunset. . . .

Mr. F. O. J. Smith came here the 5th inst. & staid till the Friday following—he made our house his home a portion of the time. Governor Isaac Hill was in the city at the same time & called upon me twice; the last time he met Mr. Smith here and they both took tea with us. They had quite a chat about farming, etc. There is something quite curious about the courses of those men. In December 1833, when I first came to Washington, Mr. Hill was a Senator & Mr. Smith a Representative in Congress; they both boarded at Mrs. S. A. Hill's where I also boarded, and were both of the same political school, & hand and glove with each other. Thus they continued until Mr. Van Buren started the Sub Treasury scheme, when a little party, styling themselves "Conservatives[,]" fell off from the Van Buren party, and among the recusants was Mr. Smith. The democratic journals fell to abusing this 3d party, & Mr. Smith, being a leader, was particularly selected as the target at which every *true-blue* democratic editor hurled his shafts. He was denounced as a renegade, a traitor, & all the slang of party was brought into requisition to overthrow him. I, among others, disapproved his course, but I did it in what I intended should be an open[,] honorable manner, & to himself, by letter, more than to any other person I gave my views & opinions freely, and without reserve. The political wheel of fortune rolled on, Harrison was elected Pr. of the U.S. & through the unwearied exertions of Mr. Smith, Maine gave her vote for him. He was inaugurated & in one short month he died! Mr. Tyler succeeded to the Presidential chair[,] and Mr. Smith & his friends were spurned as if they were worn-out tools that had done their duty & were only fit to be cast aside as worthless—and where was Mr. Hill?! He pursued such a course that the democracy of N.H. pub-lickly, but, in my opinion, unadvisedly, & with too great precipitation, read him out of their political church, and he, who had been the great champion of democracy in that State, who had but to issue his *fiat* against a partizan and "he was put right over," was himself shorn of his political honors & left to shape his political course as best suited his own judgment & taste. And so he became a sort of *conservative* of these days, & a sup-porter of the Administration of John Tyler! Both he & Mr. Smith are editors of Agricultural papers, & here they met, *probably* both of them for the purpose of, in some way, lending their aid to the present Exec-utive, and to make some arrangement as to who should take the field for the next Presidential campaign!

To me the political lesson was worth much, & I have given it deep consideration, and it has gone very far to sustain my previously formed opinions that the vane upon the steeple is as much to be relied on for steadiness to a single point, as is a politician! . . .

1. Letitia Christian Tyler (1790–1842), the President's first wife. Suffering since 1839 from the effects of a paralytic stroke, she had been unable to assume the role of first lady. She died of a second stroke on September 10.

Sunday, October 2. Last Sunday Mr. Horatio Hale,[1] the Philologist of the Exploring Expedition, dined with me. He returned to the U.S. last June, I think, having left the Expedition at Columbia River. He made a tour through many of the Indian tribes west of the Rocky Mountains, and then went to Mexico, & from that place came overland to the U.S. He called on us on the evening of the 20th Septr. & took tea. He was an apprentice boy in the *Spectator* Office at Newport, N.H. & lived in my house for more than a year. A more faithful & industrious boy never lived. Having read Barrow's[2] travels he took a fancy to compile a Chinese dictionary, and actually cut many of the letters in old type & *set up* a number of pages in some old *nonpareil* type we had in the office. He left Newport in October 1830 for Boston, to visit his mother (Mrs. Sarah Josepha Hale) and did not return. He then fitted for College, graduated at Cambridge, & went out in the expedition, was on board the *Peacock*[3] when she was wrecked, was robbed on his way to the U.S. near La Puebla in Mexico, but, through all the perils incident to the expedition, arrived home safe & sound. I have seldom been more interested than I was by Mr. Hale while with him. He gave me a sort of running history of the expedition—he told me of "hairbreadth scapes," & "of the many dangers he had seen," but, withal, in such a modest unostentatious manner, that I was highly pleased with him. . . .

1. Horatio E. Hale (1817–1896) was the ethnologist and philologist on the United States Exploring Expedition of 1838–1842.
2. Sir John Barrow (1764–1848), a founder of Britain's Royal Geographical Society, visited China, Africa, and the Arctic and wrote accounts of his travels. Young Horatio Hale undoubtedly read his *Travels in China* (1804).
3. The sloop of war *Peacock*, one of the vessels in the Exploring Expedition, struck a shoal in the Columbia River, July 18, 1841, and was battered to pieces.

Friday, January 6. . . . Monday was celebrated as the New Year's day. I went to the office as usual and staid till ¼ before eleven, then came home & while at home Miss Hale[1] came to accompany us to the President's. . . . We arrived at the Presidential Mansion at a little past 12, & found quite a crowd in attendance. We took our turn in pressing through the crowd & soon found ourselves *in the presence*. The President shook us all by the hand, & we passed on & were presented to Robert Tyler & his beautiful lady,[2] where we were again very cordially greeted. We then passed into the East room & mingled with the immense crowd. We staid more than an hour, saw a great many of our friends, then left, called at John Quincy Adams's & paid to him the compliments of the season. . . .

Tuesday went to the Capitol, & from thence down in the city, did errands & *paid bills*—returned to the Capitol. House sat till about 3. Hon. Isaac Hill came home with me & staid during dinner, but being out of health eat nothing. He left just before dark, & I attended the Capitol Hill Institute & listened with great pleasure to an interesting lecture on Electricity by Dr. Thos. P. Jones,[3] illustrated by experiments. Wednesday passed off as usual; in the evening went to the President's with Mr. Hill—there were about a dozen gentlemen present. The President talked about various matters & things, but most eloquently about his exchequer scheme. He went into quite an explanation of it & predicted its effect if once put into operation. He said that he presumed the Whig party thought that their bitter attacks upon him would give him great disquiet, but that they were entirely mistaken; he had witnessed them with the most perfect composure, that they had not disturbed his equanimity in the least, that they reminded him of a little spotted adder common in Virginia, who when enraged turned upon itself & inflicted a deadly wound. The Whigs, he said, had, in venting their spleen upon him[,] turned upon & destroyed themselves. . . .

Mr. John Quincy Adams made one of the most *ferocious* speeches in the House today, against refunding Gen. Jackson's fine,[4] that I ever heard; it actually made my blood boil, to hear one ex-president of the U.S. speak of another as Mr. Adams did of Gen. Jackson. Among other *flings* he said that Jackson was again to be used for party purposes— yes—he was to be made the President of the Democratic Convention which was to nominate a democratic candidate for the next Presidency. His manner was of that sneering, bitter, *devlish* kind that he so often assumes, that always makes him appear to me like a demon just from Hell, with all his passions under the influence of the red heat of the infernal regions. At such times, though I reverence & venerate his years, I cannot but feel sad that a man that might be all that is great, & worthy & good, should make himself what he does—a political harlequin, the laughingstock of his own party, & the despised of his opponents. I could not but think today how much, how infinitely superior the honest old veteran, Andrew Jackson, would appear, presiding over a National Convention in his stern & dignified manner, to John Quincy Adams, degrading himself into the partizan demagogue, & even burlesquing that character before the American House of Representatives. I wish, for the honor of the Country, for the honor of human nature, for the honor of *himself,* that the constituents of Mr. Adams would keep him at home— suffer him to write poetry or prose if he pleases, among the shades of Quincy, but prevent him from degrading himself here.

1. Sarah Josepha Hale (b. 1820), sister of Horatio Hale. Both Sarah and Horatio were children of the writer Sarah Josepha Buell Hale.
2. Robert Tyler (1816–1877), the oldest of President John Tyler's sons, married the actress Elizabeth Priscilla Cooper in 1839. Robert was his father's private secretary, and his wife acted as official hostess of the White House, due to the illness and death of Letitia Tyler.
3. Thomas P. Jones (1774–1848), editor of the *Journal of the Franklin Institute* and superintendent of the U.S. patent office, 1828–1837.
4. Jackson had been fined in New Orleans in 1815 for ignoring a writ of habeas corpus.

Tuesday, January 10. Yesterday there was a grand debate in the House on a report of the Committee of Ways & Means against Mr. Tyler's plan of Exchequer. Mr. T. F. Marshall closed the debate for the day in one of his eloquent speeches to which no reporter can do anything like justice, the *manner* producing at least one-half the effect. His speech is reported in the papers of today but some of the very best points are omitted. Today Mr. Botts[1] brought forward his resolution & specifications of impeachment vs. the President of the U.S.[,] & after considerable debate of one sort and another, & some maneuvering, the direct vote was taken & the resolution rejected by quite a large majority. Mr. Botts must feel mortified at this result, though he seemed to bear it with great equanimity. . . .

1. John M. Botts (1802–1869), Whig congressman from Virginia, 1839–1843 and 1847–1849. A Unionist upon the outbreak of the Civil War, he was imprisoned for a time by the Confederates.

Sunday, April 2. . . . Mr. F. O. J. Smith came here week before last & left last Thursday morning. He is now full of the idea of the electro magnetic telegraph in which he has some pecuniary interest, & which is to be laid down, under the direction of the inventor, Professor Morse,[1] between this city and Baltimore the ensuing summer, Congress having appropriated $30,000 for the purpose of testing its qualities & applicabilities for the purpose of transmitting information. It is one of the greatest inventions of the age, and will eventually be laid down all over the Union, if it operates as the philosophic world predict. . . .

1. Samuel F. B. Morse (1791–1872), artist and inventor of the telegraph. In 1843 Congress appropriated the funds for running an experimental telegraph line from Washington to Baltimore. The first formal message was sent over this line on May 24, 1844. French was soon to become associated with Morse, Amos Kendall, and F. O. J. Smith in conducting the business of the Magnetic Telegraph Company.

Sunday, April 23. This is the day set apart by the Millerites[1] for the end of this Sublunary Sphere. If they are correct my labor in making this record is perfectly superfluous, for I suppose my Journal will share the fate of everything else—but the prospects are anything but a burning up, for the rain has descended within the past ½ hour in torrents that portend another flood, rather than the prophecied fire! . . .

This is the first day I have sat down here in my little "Library," as it has been too cold to be without a fire, & there is no fireplace here. I have been sitting here nearly all day, reading and writing. Tomorrow wife & I expect to go out to Pierce's garden & get oceans of flowers to beautify our front yard with, and I hope the ground will be dry enough in the course of this week to enable me to sow my garden. My peas are just out of the ground.

1. The Millerites, or Adventists, followers of William Miller (1782–1849), preached that the Second Coming of Christ was imminent and that the world would be destroyed by fire.

Thursday, June 1. . . . Death in his most sudden & appalling shape has again visited our family circle. We yesterday recd. the intelligence of the death of Mrs. F.'s only brother, Samuel M. Richardson,[1] of Waynesville, Illinois, from wounds occasioned by the running away of a horse, Mr. R.'s arm having been caught by a running noose in the end of a rope halter. He died on the 12th May at 6 o'clock P.M.[,] the accident having happened at 10 that morning. Thus, one after another we pass away from earth. . . .

1. Samuel M. Richardson (1817–1843), the youngest of the seven Richardson children. Another brother, William (b. 1803), had died in 1819.

Sunday, June 11. . . . On Monday last [June 5] came on our Municipal election, & there was [sic] more *coalitions* & political chicanery than I have ever seen in this Ward. There were all sorts of bargains and combinations. All sorts of stories in relation to the candidates were put in circulation, & it all resulted in the reelection of Mr. Adams[,] Alderman for 2 years without opposition, Mr. Beck[,] Alderman, in place of Mr. Carberry resigned, over Mr. Watterston by a vote of two to one, a most astonishing result, & myself by 79 votes, Mr. Bassett by 58[,] & J. A. Lynch by 51, members of the Common Council.[1] There were 101 votes cast—80 is about the usual number given in this ward. Tomorrow the two Boards meet to organize. I shall again be a candidate for the Presidency of the Council, but there is not a member who cares less whether I am the successful candidate, than myself. My present intention is never again to be a candidate for Corporation honors. I may change my mind— men do sometimes! On Thursday at 10 A.M. I went to the Presidential mansion to pay what I considered due respect & courtesy to the Chief Magistrate of the nation on his departure for Boston, to attend the Bunker Hill celebration. There was something of a concourse of people, tho' not so many as I expected to see. At 12 a procession was formed, which escorted the President to the R. Road depot, & saw him off. Three, not very hearty, cheers were given as the cars started, & I, having witnessed one Presidential visit to N. England (General Jackson's in 1833 I believe—it *was* in 1833) pitied Mr. Tyler instead of envying him. Poor man, he will find it the most fatiguing piece of labor he ever undertook, especially under a June sun, & amid clouds of June dust. Though I deem him a weak, vacillating President, he is a gentlemanly &, as I believe[,] honesthearted man. May he enjoy his New England visit and be happy.

I have just dined—green peas & lettuce from *our own* garden, Lamb & potatoes constituted the dinner & strawberries, sugar & cream the dessert. I have eaten more magnificent dinners, but never better. I feel satisfied with all the world now.

1. James Adams, cashier of the Bank of Washington. Joseph Beck, messenger for the House of Representatives. James Carberry, inspector of timber at the Navy Yard. George Watterston (1783–1854), poet, novelist, third Librarian of Congress, 1815–1829, and Whig newspaper editor. Simeon Bassett, messenger at the Capitol. John A. Lynch of North Capitol Street. All were residents, with French, of the 4th Ward.

Monday, June 19. As evidence of the astonishing rapidity with which information is now spread over this land, I record here that I, this morning, at 9 o'clock read at the Capitol a large portion of Mr. Webster's speech delivered at the Bunker Hill celebration in Boston on Saturday last, probably about noon! It was in this city between 4 & 5 o'clock this morning. Thus, in less than 40 hours, from the time of delivery, we have a speech written out, printed & distributed more than 4 hundred miles from the place of delivery & all by the ordinary mail intercourse! Could the speech have left Boston instantly on its delivery and travelled at the rate of 10 miles an hour, it could not have reached here at the time it did. Then, when we deduct the time required to write it out from the rough notes of the Stenographer, the delay in printing it in New York (for it was the N.Y. *Herald* edition that I read)[,] the time required to fold, pack, & direct the papers, we may form some idea of the speed at which it travelled! What's the use of speculating about balloons, when information can pass from one end of the Union to the other at the rate of 20 miles an hour! But, astonishing as this is, only a few years will elapse when, by the aid of electromagnetism, miles will be converted into inches, & hours into seconds; the thought that occurs in the *heart* here in Washington, will be instantly known to all the extremities of this widespread Union! As the poor Irish woman said, upon some new invention being explained to her, "What a beautiful world this will be *when it is finished.*" . . .

Yesterday I attended the funeral of the Hon. Barker Burnell,[1] a member of Congress from Massachusetts. He died of Consumption, at his boardinghouse in this City, and the *Intelligencer* of last Saturday morning contains an obituary of him, written with more truth & in better taste than any obituary notice I ever read. I presume it was written by Mr. Gales. It is honorable to the head & heart of the writer be he who he may; and I will here say that although I disagree *in toto* with the politics of the *Intelligencer,* I esteem it one of the best, if not the very best, newspapers published in this Union. It is conducted with a truthfulness, a dignity of manner, & withal a simplicity which renders it always acceptable to my taste, & I feel lost when I do not read it before eating my breakfast. It possesses none of the stilted dignity of the *Globe,* which sometimes renders that paper ridiculous, & none of the puerile silliness of the *Madisonian.* Were I to compare it among newspapers, to any man among men, I should say it was the Chief Justice Marshall[2] of newspapers—simplicity, dignity, truth & knowledge characterized him, as they characterize *it.* Would that its politics were *right* as they once were, then it would be perfect! Both its gentlemanly editors[3] who I am proud to rank among my friends, are ornaments to society & to human nature. . . .

1. Barker Burnell (1798–1843), a Whig, served from 1841 to 1843.
2. John Marshall (1755–1835) became Chief Justice of the United States in 1801 and served until his death.
3. Joseph Gales and William W. Seaton.

Sunday, June 25. . . . On Friday at 11 o'clock A.M. the President of the U.S. returned to this city. He left Boston as soon as possible after the funeral of Mr. Legaré,[1] and came on as fast as steam could bring him without any parade whatever. I did not see him, but am told he appeared worn down with fatigue & care. It takes an iron constitution to endure such a triumphal progress as his was to Bunker Hill. The strong nerves of Gen. Jackson could not endure it without prostration, & such a progress from Ohio here killed Gen. Harrison, and if Mr. Tyler regains his health & spirits at once he may deem himself a truly lucky man. . . .

Yesterday, Mr. Clarke assigned the recording to the gentlemen of the Clerk's office. My share is considerable (338 pages) & will keep me employed pretty constantly for two or three months. Why could not he have assigned it sooner! But better late than never. It is the most useless labor ever performed by man.

1. Hugh S. Legaré (1797–1843), Union Democratic congressman from South Carolina, 1837–1839, was Attorney General, 1841–1843, as well as ad interim Secretary of State for about a month before his death.

Wednesday, July 5. How I spent the 4th, viz.—Arose tolerably early, breakfasted, went to the Capitol, rode down in the City, & as far as Mr. Clarke's, where I stayed an hour, & he showed me his arrangement of his papers (which is most admirable)[,] his curiosities, his parlors, his garden, etc. Left his house & did some errands, then went to 10th Street

Church where I attended the celebration by the Union L. D. Society, & listened with great pleasure & satisfaction to an eloquent oration by Jesse E. Dow, Esq.,[1] creditable alike to his genius, his patriotism & his research. Walked home with some of my friends[,] who I invited to come & drink lemonade at 4 o'clock. After dinner made a soup tureen full of lemonade, & at 4 came, Mr. Jas. Adams, Mr. S. Brown, Mr. Rogers, Mr. Payne, Major Barker, Dr. Towle, & Mr. Horatio King, & we drank lemonade, with such liquors as the drinkers saw fit to mix with it till about 6—passed the hours very socially.[2] Maj. Barker & I played on the flute together, & then I walked home with him & we played there. Came home, went down to Mr. Monroe's, came home by way of Mr. Brown's, & Frank & I went on top of the house & saw the rockets, & then went to bed, & so passed my Independence! . . .

1. Jesse E. Dow (b. 1809), a professor of mathematics and clerk in the patent office. He was also correspondent of several periodicals.
2. B. F. Rogers, clerk in the office of the first comptroller of the Treasury. Probably Orris S. Paine. James N. Barker, an assistant to the Secretary of the Treasury. N. C. Towle, clerk in the Post Office Department and later register of deeds. Horatio King (1811–1897) had been a newspaper editor in Maine. He came to Washington in 1839 as a clerk in the Post Office Department and eventually became Postmaster General for a brief period in 1861 under James Buchanan.

Wednesday, July 12. In consequence of Mrs. Brown's sickness[,] Mrs. French & Frank delayed their departure [for New Hampshire] until this morning, when, in company with Mrs. Monroe, they left in the cars for Baltimore. . . .

Sunday, July 16. . . . Hon. Caleb Cushing came here last evening to board with me till he sails for China.[1] He told me yesterday morning he was roasted out at the tavern, & I offered him *the sharing of my house,* while he remained, which he accepted. . . .

1. Caleb Cushing (1800–1879) had been a Whig congressman from Massachusetts, 1835–1843, but following Harrison's death he became increasingly identified with the Democrats. In 1843 Tyler appointed him commissioner to China where, in 1844, he negotiated the treaty of Wang Hiya. Cushing was later a general in the Mexican War, Attorney General in Pierce's cabinet, and minister to Spain, 1874–1877.

Wednesday, July 19. . . . I really enjoy the company of Mr. Cushing. Instead of being an odd, morose, unapproachable person, as he has been described to me, I find him social, interesting & like other men. He possesses a mind brimming with knowledge, and is always ready to impart it, at least such is his appearance to me. We eat, talk & smoke together, & during all those operations, he is ever giving me some information that is not only new but may be profitable to me. His habit of living is remarkably plain, & he makes as little trouble as it is possible for a man to make. . . .

Sunday, July 30. . . . Mr. Cushing intends sailing in the U.S. Steamer *Missouri* at 9 o'clock A.M. tomorrow. I shall miss his company nearly as much as I do Mrs. French's.

Since Mr. Cushing came here *we* have had plenty of *gentleman* company. Of course it was all his, but as it consisted of gentlemen with most of whom I have been well acquainted for years I enjoyed their visits as well as if they had come to see me. Mr. Joseph Gales & Cost Johnson[1] came today & paid *me* quite a visit, though their call was upon Mr. Cushing.

Went bathing day before yesterday with Mr. Cushing & yesterday with Dr. Towle, & found it a very refreshing operation after the extreme hot days. . . .

1. William Cost Johnson (1806–1860), Whig congressman from Maryland, 1833–1835 and 1837–1843.

Monday, July 31. . . . Mr. Cushing left my house at 8 o'clock this morning to go on board the *Missouri.* I bade him farewell with a sad feeling which I could not repress. Soon after he left, the thunder of the *Missouri's* guns told us that he was safe on board[,] & at eleven she weighed anchor & was off. I watched her movements through my glass till the thick weather almost hid her from my view. My best wishes went with Mr. Cushing for his health, his happiness & the prosperity of his mission. God bless him.

Since he left I have been to the Capitol & have done some work[,] & now it is about time for me to go to the Council. Were it not for that same Council I should now have been on board the *Missouri,* on my way to Norfolk.

Exeter, N.H., Thursday, August 10. I went to the Council, and, for all that was done, might as well have gone to Norfolk. Tuesday and Wednesday I did little else than oversee the building of my bathhouse. On Thursday I recd. a letter from Anne French (my brother's wife) expressing so much solicitude that I should visit them here, that on Friday at 4 o'clock P.M. I took the cars at Washington, arrived at Philadelphia the next morning about daylight, breakfasted, crossed the river & went on board the cars at Camden & arrived at Jersey City at 2 P.M. We crossed the river to N.Y. & I put my baggage on board the *Worcester,* bound to Norwich,

& walked up in the city, where I found Mr. Russell & Dr. Wells. Went with them to a *restaurant* in Maiden Lane & eat oysters, pie, etc. Returned to the boat—the Dr. endeavoured to persuade me to go on board the *Massachusetts* with him, but I did not. At 5 o'clock precisely, both boats cast off their moorings & we steamed down the river; our boat was soon a goodly distance ahead, & we saw nothing of the *Massachusetts* after dark. There was a heavy wind from the East & it rained in torrents. Still we held on our way & arrived at Norwich between 2 & 3 A.M. where we got on board the cars & arrived at Boston at ½ past 7. [The *Massachusetts*, as I have since learned, was obliged to anchor, in consequence of the weather, where she lay three hours; the cars were detained by a caving-in of a bank, or some such circumstance, so that her passengers did not arrive at Boston until 3 o'clock P.M.][1] On my arrival at Boston I went to Dr. Barker's at South Boston where I was most hospitably entertained till 6 o'clock Monday morning, when the Dr. procured a carriage & brought me to Boston where I took the cars at 10 minutes past 7, for this place. Arrived here about 9 on Monday, & on Tuesday evening my wife & Frank came up from Portland in the cars—so here we are, again, all happy.[2] . . .

I attended the annual examination of the students at the Exeter Academy on Tuesday, & dined at the Swamscot house[3] with the Faculty of the Academy. Dr. Bell[4] called here yesterday, & we have agreed to meet on the shores of the Massabesic to "roll back" as he says, "twenty years" on Monday next. I anticipate a pleasant time.

1. The brackets are French's.
2. Ariana French (1821–1865), French's half-sister, was with them at this time. She later married Charles Soule.
3. The Squamscott House was a hotel in Exeter.
4. Luther V. Bell (1806–1862), brother of Samuel Dana Bell, was a physician and superintendent of the McLean Asylum for the Insane.

Chester, Sunday, August 13. It is ten o'clock. I am again in the old paternal mansion—how changed since I was last here! This day I have visited the graves of my dear departed ones, & there in the old churchyard, beneath their monumental marble lie the mortal remains of two who were dwellers beneath this roof when I was last here—my father & my sister. I have been roaming over the fields where I have been often with them, & though I have worn a smile upon my cheek, there has been at times, sadness at my heart & a teardrop in my eye. Poor dear Harriette's bible lies upon the table below. In it are some stanzas in manuscript upon which are noted that they were sung to her only a few days

before her death, & I am told they were favorites of hers. I read *them*—
had I been alone—but why write thus here? . . .

Exeter, Friday, August 18. . . . Yesterday, Dr. Barker, Ned & I went to
Hampton Beach, where we spent the day. We rolled ninepins in the
forenoon, & in the afternoon went out fishing in a sloop. For the first
time in my life, I was a little seasick. We caught a few fish & returned
about 6 o'clock, and came up here in the evening. There were a great
number of people there. I should think there were a hundred at the
dinner table at the house on the hill, where we stopped. I met few whom
I knew. . . .

Chester, Sunday, August 20. . . . After we arrived here yesterday, Ned
& I went up to West Chester to fish & eat chowder. At about 2 o'clock,
Mr. Currier, Flagg Underhill, J. S. Brown, Thos. Montgomery, Mr.
Geo. P. Clarke, Ned & I embarked in two boats & went to "Pick nick"
island, in the Massabesic, where we landed our chowder *material,* & then
went out fishing.[1] We caught an abundance of fish for the chowder, & at
5 o'clock partook of it cooked in the most approved manner by Montgomery, who was the *Maitre de cuisine* in the affair. After *chowdering,* we
went ashore, and, as they say at the end of all *great dinners,* "the occasion
was marred by no unpleasant occurrence," but *per contra,* was *enlivened*
by a small shower of rain, & "the company separated at an early hour
highly delighted with their 'feast of reason & flow of soul'." Small beer
was the only *intoxicating* liquor upon *the board* (we actually had a *board*
there)[,] but cigars, not being prohibited in *the pledge,* were freely indulged in by some of the company. At 7 Ned & I started for home, where
we arrived at 8. . . .

1. Flagg T. Underhill was a successful manufacturer of edge tools in Chester. Thomas
Montgomery, of Chester, was a veteran of the War of 1812. George P. Clarke (1813–1890),
a lifelong resident of Chester, was postmaster in West Chester.

Washington, Wednesday, September 13. We arrived home last Saturday,
the 9th inst.[,] at eleven o'clock A.M.[,] and now, from memorandums
and recollection I intend to write up my regular journal from the time
I left off at Chester, as above to this date. . . .

[Thursday,] August 24. Spent the forenoon in Court [at Exeter]. Col.
F. Pierce was there, & after dinner he, Frank & I went to Hampton Beach
in a chaise. We "rolled ninepins" awhile, then went into the surf & had
a good wash, then took tea[,] & Frank & I returned to Exeter, leaving

Pierce at Leavitt's.[1] We did not get to Exeter till eight o'clock in the evening. Frank entertained me all the way home with his talk & singing. He sung two or three little songs to me, & his tongue was going steadily from the time we left the beach till we arrived in Exeter.[2] . . .

1. Leavitt's Hampton Beach Hotel.
2. Thereafter, French accounts for visits with relatives and friends in Exeter, Lowell, and Boston. While staying with the Lemuel Barkers in Boston, French saw an exhibition of painting for the Rotunda of Faneuil Hall, went to Bunker Hill, where he climbed the monument, visited the Insane Hospital at Charlestown, and walked to Dorchester Heights. On September 4 the family traveled by train to Providence, R.I., and Stonington, Conn., and took the steamer *Rhode Island* for New York. After staying in New York with the Charles Russells for three days, the Frenches left by train for Baltimore and Washington. They arrived home on September 9.

Sunday, October 1. . . . In the great world about me nothing has transpired within my observation worthy of a place on paper. The political horizon is amazingly beclouded just now, and no one can predict with any certainty what is to be. President Tyler is unpopular as a President, & he seems to be as changeable as the figures of a Kaleidescope—one moment he pursues one course of policy, turn him but a hair's breadth &, *presto*, the entire figure changes. The man who he appoints to office today he turns out tomorrow, and the *anomalic* expression "it's dangerous being safe" applies perfectly to the official incumbents of the present day. I do hope, be our next Administration what it may, Republican or Federal, Coon or Locofoco, Democratic or *Modern* Whig, that it will at least be consistent, & possess stamina sufficient to command the confidence of *someone*. . . .

Saturday, November 18. . . . When I was last in Chester I, as usual, visited the grave of my mother. The old slate stone having been broken, I directed a year or two ago that a handsome marble one should be erected to supply its place, which was done.[1] There were some lines upon the old stone, written purposely for it, by a Mr. Richards I believe. It was broken through those lines, so that a portion remained on one piece & a portion on the other, and, as I know of no copy of them except on that broken slab, I will endeavour to transcribe them here from memory. I committed them when a mere child.

> Peace to her gentle shade her soul is free,
> Eased from the pains of sad mortality,
> Enrobed with innocence, by virtue blest,
> For earth too good, she flies to Heaven for rest.
> Cease then fond husband, check the pensive sigh

The child of innocence shall never die—
She waits, a Seraph, at the Pearly gate,
To bid thee welcome on the wings of Fate. . . .

I have been shooting twice—spent an entire day each time—have read considerable, & among other things that horribly unnatural book the *Mysteries of Paris*.[2] It is deeply, breathlessly interesting, but it does not contain one natural character, & its tendency is decidedly immoral. I have written an essay on the writings of Bulwer, defending them, & read it before the Capitol Hill Institute. I have seen Marshal Bertrand,[3] the friend, the tried & faithful friend[,] of Napoleon. I called upon him at Col. Seaton's last Monday, & when I shook the hand of the old Marshal, & considered that he who stood before me was one who had stood by the great Napoleon in glory & in gloom, one who had earned upon the field of battle, from the Emperor, the glorious title of "Marshal of France," one who had followed the destinies of one of the mightiest men of earth till he received his last sigh at St. Helena, I *felt* that I stood in the presence of no common man. The Marshal has nothing in his personal appearance that would lead one to notice him particularly among a multitude. He is about 5 feet 8 inches in height, bald upon the top of his head, & what hair remains is white. He is rather robust in his appearance for a man of his age, and will compare nearest in size & appearance to John Quincy Adams, of any man I can think of. Goodness of heart is as apparent in his countenance as if it were written there in words, & were I to judge him from his looks, not knowing him, I should say he possessed a mildly peaceable disposition, was honest, upright & true, but that he was one of Napoleon's Braves I never should have guessed. . . .

   1. See September 27, 1835.
   2. Eugène Sue (1804–1857), originally Marie Joseph Sue, first published *Les Mystères de Paris* in installments in the French newspapers. In translation, *The Mysteries of Paris* was published in 1843. It was the most popular of Sue's many writings.
   3. Comte Henri Gratien Bertrand (1773–1844), a French general, was with Napoleon at Elba and St. Helena.

Sunday, November 26. After dinner. The Common Council, of which I have the honor to be President, supped with me on Friday evening last. . . . We sat down to supper at ½ past 8 & had a very merry time. The company left at about 11. During the past week I have been very busy in various ways, preparing for my supper, for the session, & in ascertaining the new members, and in electioneering for Clerk, for which I stand about a middling chance of an election. I have plenty of competitors, but, for me, the more the better. If I am elected I shall be thankful to the House for its confidence; if not, I shall make myself just as happy at the result as if I were. Next week will probably determine the matter.

This day I was introduced to William Cullen Bryant,[1] by Mr. Reding,[2] and he attended church with me. He is a man whom I have long desired to know. He is modest & unassuming in his personal appearance, but his countenance bears the impress of goodness of heart, & kindness toward all the world. I am happy to know the man whose poetry I so much admire.

1. William Cullen Bryant (1794–1878), poet and editor. By 1843 journalism had become his primary interest and, as editor of the New York *Evening Post,* he was strongly supporting the Democratic party.
2. John R. Reding (1805–1892), a Democratic representative from New Hampshire, 1841–1845, was also an editor.

Monday, December 18. I have just read my last preceding journalization. Since that was written 3 weeks have sped away & in that 3 weeks much has transpired affecting my own doings in the mortal world. I was *not* elected Clerk. I withdrew from the contest for several reasons, at a time when my prospects of success were perhaps as good as at any time during my aspirations for the office. Some of my reasons I will record here.

1st. I ascertained that the party with which it has been my pride and my pleasure to act were determined that the person whom they should elect should remove from office all the Whigs. Having for 10 years been associated with the then incumbents, I *could* not be made the instrument of such indiscriminate political slaughter. At first I thought I could march up to the required work were I elected, but reflection upon it day after day made me nervous—I could not sleep nights—& I thought[,] "If the anticipation troubles me so much what will the performance of the odious duty cost me in wear & tear of heart & feeling?" And proceeding upon this rule, I came to the result that it was my duty to withdraw from the contest.

2d. I found my party very much divided, & one member of the delegation of my own State (Mr. Reding) did not seem inclined to support me.

3d. I was assured that I should be restored to the Chief Clerkship of the Office, &, taking all things into consideration, I came to the conclusion that perhaps that place was better for me than the Clerkship of the House. . . .

. . . On Wednesday, Caleb J. McNulty[1] was elected Clerk of the House, &, immediately upon his election, removed Col. Burch from the Chief Clerkship and appointed me in his place. Since that time he has removed

Mr. Duvall, Mr. Patterson, Mr. Johnston, Mr. Berry, Clerks, & Mr. Stewart, Messenger. . . .

1. Caleb J. McNulty, of Ohio, served as Clerk of the House until dismissed on January 18, 1845. His place was taken by French.

Tuesday, January 9. . . . Last evening the Democratic members of Congress, with such citizens & strangers as chose to join them, celebrated the anniversary of the Battle of New Orleans. There were between one & two hundred present. The dinner was furnished by Maher[1] of the Globe Hotel, at the Apollo Hall. Toasts, songs, & speeches abounded. The party broke up at about 2 o'clock this morning. I came away at ½ past 12.

This is the 3d celebration of the 8th of Jany. within the past 12 years. Jany. 8th, 1832, at Chester, N.H., where I officiated as orator. In this city, Jany. 8th, 1835, for which I wrote a song, and that of last evening, for which I also wrote a song. It is a day that should ever be held sacred by every true democrat, for it was the day in which our arms triumphed over a haughty and vindictive foe, led on by some of the bravest generals that England could boast. It was the day when a man, only second in our annals to the Father of His Country, while he wove an imperishable wreath of glory for his own brow, performed a deed which has made the battle of New Orleans & American bravery synonymous and never to be forgotten terms on the page of history. Great in the field of Battle, Great in the Cabinet, & Greater still as a private citizen, he still lives the venerated[,] the admired, the beloved Chieftain, whom any true democrat delights to honor. God grant him many happy years to come.

Yesterday the bill to refund the fine to General Andrew Jackson passed the House of Representatives, only 28 members voting against it, and, to his infamy let it be recorded not only here but in every democratic paper in the country, at the head of its opponents stands the name of John Quincy Adams![2] I am more and more convinced, daily, of the *wickedness* of that bitterhearted old man.

1. James Maher, proprietor of the Globe Hotel on the corner of E and 13th streets.
2. Jackson had been fined $1,000 by Judge Dominick Hall in New Orleans in March 1815 for refusing to recognize a writ of habeas corpus. A bill to remit this fine was introduced in March 1842 and, after prolonged controversy, became law on February 16, 1844.

Sunday, March 3. The latter part of last week was a gloomy time for the people of this city, and far and wide will it spread to the uttermost bounds of the Republic, and even the sympathies of Nations far away will not be wanting upon this National calamity.

Wednesday last [February 27] closed on one of the most terrible accidents this community has ever known—two of the highest officers of this government, with three other gentlemen of high respectability and great moral worth, were hurried in a single moment from time into eternity.

On Wednesday morning the President, all the Heads of Department except Mr. Spencer, the Mayor of the City, many members of Congress, and a host of ladies & gentlemen—the elite of the city—went on board the U.S. war steamer *Princeton* at the invitation of her gentlemanly Commander, Capt. Stockton, to spend the day, & witness the effect of the discharge of the big guns on board her.[1] I was very specially invited to go, but my business prevented. The day was passed in the very height of hilarity and joy—everybody was happy; the ship made a trip down the river beneath, almost, a summer sky; the great gun (*the peacemaker*) was discharged several times and its effects witnessed by hundreds who surrounded it. The tables were spread & the feast was proceeding in the cabin, when (it is said at the request of Mr. Secretary Gilmer) one more discharge of the great gun was concluded upon. It was charged as usual, & Secretaries Upshur, Gilmer, & Wilkins, Commodore Kennon, Mr. Maxcy & Col. David Gardner of New York took their station in a group to witness the striking and bounding of the shot upon the water.[2] The gun was discharged. It burst near the breech; and one large fragment was thrown directly upon the group of gentlemen above named, & they were all, instantaneously, killed. A colored servant of the President stood near them & he was also killed. Many who were in the immediate vicinity of those killed were prostrated on the deck & stunned by the shock, among them Col. Benton of the Senate, & Capt. Stockton. Several sailors were badly wounded. Such is the accident that has clothed our city in mourning and in gloom. The scene has been described to me by several who were present as one of the most dreadful that can be imagined. The wife of Mr. Gilmer,[3] the daughters of Mr. Upshur & Col. Gardner were on board, and the feelings of all, who one moment before had been in the very height of enjoyment, were sunk to the very depths of woe. Grief, consternation, despair were all present, for, amid the confusion of the moment, no one knew the precise extent of the accident, no one knew who were the real mourners, who the sympathizers.

Secretary Wilkins, it is said, left the group who were killed but a moment before the explosion, remarking, "Though I am Secretary of War, I am afraid of these big guns."

Col. Seaton, the Mayor of this city, was at the table in the cabin with Messrs. Upshur[,] Gilmer, & the others, when they were invited on deck to witness the discharge, and rose to accompany them, but the berth into which he had thrown his hat and cloak was surrounded by ladies, and, as he himself told me, he did not like to crowd in among them & disturb them, so instead of getting his hat he entered into conversation with them, and while he was conversing the fatal gun was discharged. No one below mistrusted that an accident had occurred, & the word was instantly passed, "Three cheers for that gun," and they were given with a hearty good will, and were immediately followed with the information of the terrible catastrophe that accompanied the discharge!

The President was below. How it happened that he was, I have not heard, but can only suppose it to be another item in the *"good luck"* of the proverbially lucky John Tyler.

With Mr. Upshur I had no personal acquaintance. I knew him well by sight & by reputation.

With Mr. Gilmer I was well, and I do not know but I may say intimately[,] acquainted. He was a member of the 27th Congress, and resigned his seat in the 28th within the past month. He was an honest, upright, honorable, and strictly conscientious man, a ready debater, & though entering much into the debates upon the excitable subject of abolition petitions within the last two years, he never lost his equanimity of temper, & his remarks were always made, however severe the point or the application, with a gentlemanly courtesy which rendered him popular with everybody. He was emphatically *a good man,* and in his death the Nation has lost one of her brightest jewells.

I had a passing acquaintance with Mr. Maxcy, having been introduced to him when he was Solicitor of the Treasury.

Col. Gardner and Commodore Kennon I never saw that I know of.

The funeral obsequies were attended yesterday, from the Presidential mansion, by a vast concourse of people. The Corporate Authorities of this City, & of Georgetown & Alexandria attended. The four coffins (Mr. Maxcy's remains having been taken away) were placed in the centre of the East room, Mr. Upshur's & Col. Gardner's shrouded in black palls, Mr. Gilmer's & Com. Kennon's in the "star spangled banner" of their country. The room was crowded. The services were performed by the reading of the scriptures & burial service by Dr. Hawley, a prayer by Dr. Laurie,[4] & a sermon, or rather funeral address, by Mr. Butler[5] of Georgetown. The whole was performed with great solemnity and propriety, and the whole scene was one calculated to make a deep & lasting impression on everyone present.

After the services the procession formed in front of the Mansion, & under a large military escort proceeded to the Congressional burying ground, where the remains were entombed. The procession was about ¾ of an hour passing one particular point, and must have been considerably more than a mile in length. Minute-guns[6] were fired during the marching of the procession from the Capitol—from the centre of the city, and from the Marine Barracks—and half-hour guns were fired from the several military posts & from the ships during the entire day.

There was a fitness as it seemed to me, in the day itself, for the melancholy occasion. It was dark & lowering as if the very heavens were hung in mourning, and a few drops, like Angels' tears, fell at times from the murky canopy above.

When the news of the dreadful disaster first reached me, I was writing up the journal of the proceedings of the House of Representatives for that day, and never in my life do I remember to have experience[d] such a feeling as I then did—a suffocating sinking sensation, as if my heart was about to burst. I arose and walked the office a few moments, and vainly hoped the information was not correct. I finished my duties as soon as I could & then went down in the City and learned, alas, that it was all too true. My wife was invited to a little party that evening & had gone. I went but the calamity was all that was talked of, & at an early hour I came home, & during the whole night, when I slept at all, my dreams were of the dead.[7] . . .

1. John C. Spencer (1788–1855), of New York, was Secretary of War, 1841–1843, and Secretary of State, 1843–1844. William W. Seaton was serving as mayor of Washington at this time. Robert F. Stockton (1795–1866), naval officer, who, prior to his command of the *Princeton,* had taken part in the War of 1812 and in the war with Algiers.

2. Capt. Beverly Kennon, chief of the Navy's bureau of construction, equipment, and repairs. Virgil Maxcy (1785–1844), Maryland lawyer and diplomat, and a solicitor of the U.S. Treasury. David Gardiner (1784–1844), the father of Julia Gardiner, who, four months after her father's death, became the second wife of President Tyler.

3. Mrs. Thomas W. Gilmer, the former Anne Baker of Shepherdstown, Va.

4. James Laurie, Presbyterian minister from Scotland. Arriving in Washington in 1803 as a young man, he built the Presbyterian church on F Street, between 14th and 15th streets.

5. Probably Clement M. Butler (1810–1890), later chaplain of the Senate, 1849–1853.

6. Guns fired at intervals of a minute on the interment of an officer or other distinguished person.

7. The *Princeton* was the navy's first screw steam warship. She arrived at Washington on February 13 and made several trips on the Potomac, during which the "Peacemaker," one of her two big guns, which weighed over thirteen tons, was fired a number of times. On February 28, with President Tyler, the cabinet, and many other guests aboard, the "Peacemaker" was fired again and burst, killing six and wounding about twenty others.

Friday, July 26. Time has moved on just as if I had kept a regular diary for the 3 months & 5 days past.[1] I did keep the journal of the House up to the 17th day of June, on which it adjourned, and then I made the index, and performed such other duties as my office required. . . .

1. In a brief entry of April 21, French had remarked on the weather and the monotony of his existence.

Saturday, August 24. I awoke two or three hours ago and have not been asleep since. I laid & turned & shifted my pillow, arose & looked out of the window, went to bed again, counted, did everything I could think of to court the drowsy god, but come he would not, & so, with the first dawn of day I arose, dressed & came up here, to which place I yesterday moved all my books, writing apparatus, guns, pistols and ammunition. Wife thinks I have moved prematurely as garrets in Washington are rather hot places about this time of year. Perhaps I have, but when I get ready to do a thing I like to do it, and so here I am 10 feet nearer heaven than usual when I write, & of course so much more *attic*.[1] . . .

Cowbells—I wish every man who has put a bell on his cow in this city had to pay a fine of forty shillings. "Ding-dong-ding-dong-ding-dong"— there it goes & so it has gone all summer long. It is on one particular cow, & she never lies down or stops feeding. Night after night have I been waked & kept awake by that infernal bell, & though, like Othello I have commanded[,] "Silence that dreadful bell[,]" it would not be silenced, & so I have cursed it and borne it. . . . D—n that cow[,] how she does gingle it at this moment, as if she knew that I was writing about her. If I only knew who owned her I would buy her & cut the bell strap at once. What a glorious revenge it would be for all the waking hours that "ding-dong" has cost me! I believe I will go to market. . . .

    1. As in the classic style of Attic Greece.

Friday, September 6. My "birth day" has passed without a record, but I did not forget it. I am getting too much into the vale of years to forget birthdays now. 44 is a right venerable age for a young man, and I feel young yet. . . .

Sunday, October 20. . . . On the 12th [of September] was a mass meeting at Baltimore, where a goodly portion of the democracy of Maryland, and not a few from the District of Columbia, assembled to hold council on the political signs of the times, and to tender to each other the greetings of political friendship, and of the mass there assembled I was one. I went in the 6 o'clock train, arrived in Baltimore at 8, went to the Exchange hotel, which is one of the best hotels I ever put up at. After breakfast, J. C. Rives,[1] J. E. Dow & myself walked down to the wharf where the steamer *Oceola* [sic], on board which most of the Washington party had taken passage, was expected to arrive. She was not in, so we travelled onward to the height where the Baltimore signal station is, & where we could look miles down the Bay. We went to the top of a house & watched for more than an hour with a glass, the wind blowing almost a gale. At last we made out a steamboat, & ere long we knew her to be the *Oceola*; we then returned to the wharf, & at about 11 she arrived. The procession was formed & we marched to the grove where the meeting was held, about 3 miles out of the city. It is enough for my purpose to say that an immense crowd of people were assembled, & the pageant was gorgeous with banners, pavilions, etc. I staid two or three hours, when becoming excessively fatigued[,] I returned to the City, dined, & soon after went to the depot & got on board the cars & returned to Washington at ¼ past 7 P.M. So ended Sept. 12th, 1844. The anniversary of the battle of North point,[2] and of the birth of Master Francis O. French! . . . Saturday morning the 28th [of September] I arose as usual. The rain was pouring in torrents. I commenced coughing & at the 1st inhalation, or attempt at it rather, I became perfectly strangled, & continued so for about a minute, when I recovered just far enough to breathe, & then became strangled again. I thought death was near at hand, but by great effort I got over it. A doctor was sent for who prescribed, & after keeping my house two days[,] I again went abroad, but with a continual disposition to cough, which I suppressed with great trouble. On the succeeding Friday night, the 4th inst., I awoke in another suffocating fit, which lasted some time and was dreadful. It was followed by a copious discharge of blood from my throat & stomach. My neighbor Mr. King was sent for; he came in & went for Doctor May[,][3] who came and prescribed pills which stopped the bleeding, and I was again confined to my house for two days. . . .

1. John C. Rives (1795–1864), journalist and longtime partner of Francis P. Blair in the running of the Washington *Globe*.

2. The Battle of North Point took place over the period September 12–14, 1814, when the British landed a large force at the mouth of the Patapsco River but were turned back in their attempt to take Baltimore.

3. J. F. May lived nearby on New Jersey Avenue, near C Street.

Thursday, December 5. . . . Time has really gone like a racehorse since my last writing. How much of the doings of mankind that are to take a prominent place in future history have marked that little month! A Presidential election has taken place, and James K. Polk has been elected President of the U.S. for the next 4 years. No man has labored harder than myself to bring about this result, and no one has more sincerely rejoiced.

Since the result was known we have had rejoicings in abundance, and one Democratic jubilee in the City. It was held a week ago this day, & it was glorious. I enjoyed it more than almost any other festivity of my life. I illuminated my house as did nearly every democrat of the city.

I have, within the past month, had the 1st Canto of a poem (*Fitz Clarence*) which I commenced years ago, printed, & have distributed it among my friends who seem to be pleased with it. I have given some copies to members of Congress, & many have applied to me for copies. The few I had printed are nearly gone.[1]

Last Monday commenced the 2d session of the 28th Cong. It was with fear & trembling that I entered upon my duties, in consequence of an affection of my throat, which has followed the severe attacks of suffocation that have been visited upon me within the past 10 weeks. I am far from well even now, but am happy to find that thus far I have found no difficulty in performing my duties. . . .

1. *Fitz Clarence: A Poem* was printed in Washington in 1844 by Blair and Rives. The 1st Canto fills some twenty-five pages. Byronic in tone, the poem focuses on a fire at sea. French dedicated his work "To my sister Kate."

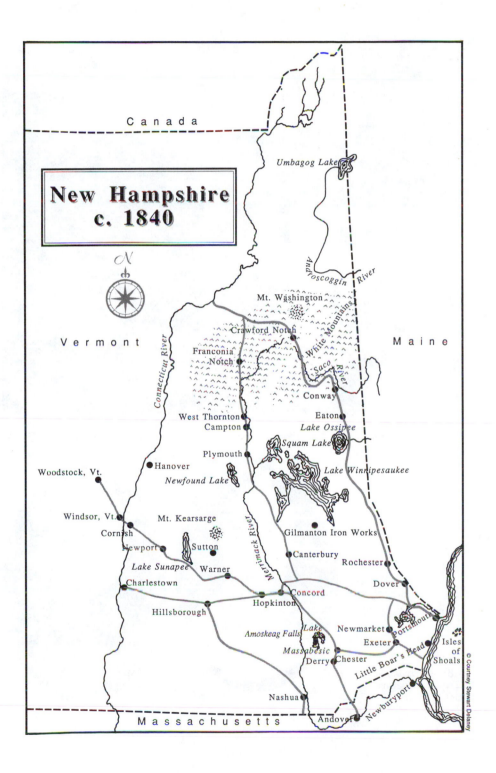

New Hampshire
c. 1840

Canada

Umbagog Lake

Vermont

Connecticut River

Androscoggin River

Mt. Washington

Crawford Notch

Franconia Notch

White Mountains

Saco River

Conway

Maine

West Thornton
Campton

Eaton

Lake Ossipee

Squam Lake

Plymouth

Hanover

Woodstock, Vt.

Newfound Lake

Lake Winnipesaukee

Windsor, Vt.

Mt. Kearsarge

Merrimack River

Cornish

Newport

Sutton

Gilmanton Iron Works

Lake Sunapee

Warner

Canterbury

Rochester

Charlestown

Dover

Hillsborough

Concord

Hopkinton

Amoskeag Falls

Lake
Massabesic

Newmarket

Portsmouth

Exeter

Isles
of
Shoals

Derry

Chester

Little Boar's Head

Nashua

Newburyport

Andover

Massachusetts

© Courtney Stewart Delaney

2. Daniel French house, Chester, N.H. Built 1800, burned 1902. (Courtesy Peter S. French)

3. Elizabeth Richardson French at thirty-three, from a miniature. (Courtesy Peter S. French)

4. Benjamin Brown French at thirty-eight, from a miniature. (Courtesy Peter S. French)

5. Benjamin Brown French house, 37 East Capitol St., Washington, D.C. Built 1842, torn down c. 1895 to make way for the Library of Congress. (Courtesy Peter S. French)

6. Benjamin Brown French's study, 37 East Capitol St., shortly after his death. (Courtesy Peter S. French)

7. Franklin Pierce during the 1852 campaign. (Courtesy Library of Congress)

8. The White House in 1861. (Courtesy Library of Congress)

9 The Capitol in 1862. (Courtesy Library of Congress)

10. Mary Lincoln in 1861.
(Courtesy Library of Congress)

11. Abraham Lincoln in 1864.
(Photograph by Mathew Brady;
courtesy Library of Congress)

12. Benjamin Brown French at Gettysburg the day after Lincoln's address. (Courtesy National Archives and Records Adminstration)

13. Benjamin Brown French and
his second wife, Mary Ellen, in
their garden.
(Courtesy Peter S. French)

14. Francis O. French at twenty.
(Courtesy Peter S. French)

15. Benjamin Brown French in Masonic regalia in 1864. (Courtesy Peter S. French)

16. Henry Flagg French. (Photograph in Daniel Chester French Papers; courtesy Library of Congress)

17. Andrew Johnson. (Courtesy Library of Congress)

18. Daniel Chester French at twenty-four. (Photograph in Daniel Chester French Papers; courtesy Library of Congress)

FOUR

Congress, Telegraphy, and Freemasonry

1845–1853

I n this chapter French reaches the prime of life. He is vigorous, optimistic, often ebullient, and intent on making his way in the world, so intent in fact that he neglects his journal more than at any other period in his life. Some important victories are earned, but there are also defeats. His resilience and good nature, however, see him through.

On January 18, 1845, French achieved his long-awaited election as Clerk of the House of Representatives, and at the start of the next session in December 1845 he was unanimously reelected. But what was given could also be taken away, and in December 1847, during an "accidental Whig majority,"[1] French was relieved of duty. Two years later his hopes for a return to office were high, but after prolonged balloting, marked by bitter Democratic factionalism, he failed once more.

His career in the Magnetic Telegraph Company also had its ups and downs. Already a director of the company, which operated the line between Washington and New York, he was elected its president in 1847. In the business world of the time this did not prevent French from going out on the line in the middle of a February snowstorm and working for three days, stretching a new wire across the Susquehanna River and securing it from the breakup of the ice. Earlier he had been on an expedition up the Hudson River, examining both shores for a suitable route for the telegraph. When, despite such efforts, the stockholders refused to reelect him in 1850, he spoke of his hurt in his journal. "I never had anything," he wrote, "which cut me to the very quick as that refusal . . . did!"[2]

Freemasonry came to the fore in French's life in 1846 when he was elected grand master of the Masons in the District of Columbia. On the occasion he reflected on his earlier Masonic membership in New Hampshire, where, because of the Anti-Masonic excitement of the 1830s, it became expedient to close the lodges. Dormant for a time, the craft was

165

now active again. As grand master he was often called to officiate at special events, such as the laying of the cornerstone of the Washington Monument on July 4, 1848.

In the larger world, where Manifest Destiny was at work, the war with Mexico came and went. Several months before it began in 1846, French could be found among the jingoes, thinking that nothing better could happen to the country than to have a war. A "new race of heroes" was needed because the old one had "nearly run out."[3] Once war came, French hoped for a swift conclusion but not before Mexico was taught that the American people "were not to be trifled with."[4] Subsequently, as the news of victories reached Washington, his joy was tempered by reports of the dead, many of whom he knew.

The events of a long wagon trip through New Hampshire's White Mountains in the summer of 1845 reveal French at his most exuberant. Once, while looking upon the majestic scenery, he could not contain himself and burst out with "Old Hundred." Glorious trout fishing, rambles through the valleys, and dining, drinking, singing, and dancing at inns and taverns—even a runaway horse—added up to one of the most enjoyable times of his life. On the return leg of the trip he stayed with the Shakers at Canterbury, persuading some of the Shaker women to fire his air rifle!

French's aptitude for being on hand at dramatic moments did not desert him. On his way home from the railroad station he passed through the Capitol just in time to see John Quincy Adams in the speaker's room, prostrated by the stroke from which he would soon die. Coming down the Hudson River, he steamed past Albany the day after it had been swept by fire. On the day he bade farewell to the outgoing James K. Polk, he also cordially shook the incoming Zachary Taylor by the hand. And on December 24, 1851, he rushed from his house to fight a fire in the Capitol that destroyed much of the Library of Congress.

As this period closed early in 1853, French resumed writing in his journal, which he had abandoned for a year. In that time Franklin Pierce, his friend of twenty years, had gained the Democratic nomination for the presidency and gone on to win the election. French's "whole soul"[5] had been in the matter; his expectations were correspondingly high. Yet even at this time of triumph there were portents that all would not be well, for the slavery question was now assuming new disruptive and dangerous dimensions.

1. Dec. 16, 1847.   4. May 25, 1846.
2. Dec. 21, 1850.   5. Jan. 2, 1853.
3. Aug. 24, 1845.

Journal

Sunday, April 19. Four months & 15 days ago I last wrote in this journal! How much has transpired in the great world since then—thousands have died, thousands have been born, the Earth has turned upon its axis 138 times, & everybody has said that many times, "It is sunrise" and "It is sunset." The morning and the evening gun has been fired around the world, and the *reveille* & the *retreat* has been daily beaten upon a million pieces of sheepskin, & millions of men have cursed the one, while rubbing open their sleepy eyes, & blessed the other, as they retired to their tents or barracks. But what has my record to do with *the world*! Nothing! Let the World keep its own Journal—it is enough for me to journalize the doings of one individual & what of the World is connected with his movements along the great highway of existence.

When I wrote last in this book Congress had been in session 3 days—now it has been gone 6 weeks. To me it was a most eventful session, inasmuch as one transaction of the House may make a very great difference in the aspect of my future existence in this life. On the 18th of January last Col. C. J. McNulty was unanimously dismissed from the office of Clerk of the House of Representatives, and I was unanimously elected to fill the vacancy. . . .

On the 4th day of February my second child was born, & my wife named him Benjamin Brown,[1] & now the prospect is fair that old Ben French & young Ben French will be often heard in future days, if we both live. He is a healthy, & a good child, & *we* think him handsome. . . .

1. Benjamin Brown French, Jr.

Sunday, May 18. . . . I am now getting into all sorts of extravagances. Since I last wrote in this book I have purchased a lot in addition to my house lot, a horse, carriage, saddle & bridle, and now I must build a stable & hire a boy! So one expense begets another, & men go on in extravagance until, almost imperceptibly, they find themselves a little too deep for their income. I hope I shall touch bottom before I get in "over head & ears." I have also entered into a stock company by the name of the "Magnetic Telegraph Company,"[1] which will call a thousand dollars from my purse, and I hope, in the end, will place it back with another to keep it company. . . .

1. The Magnetic Telegraph Company was the first successful stock company formed to construct telegraph lines. Its guiding spirits were F. O. J. Smith and Amos Kendall.

Exeter, Monday, June 16. At ½ past 5 o'clock P.M. on Wednesday last, I left my dear ones at Washington, and took the cars for Baltimore, on my way hitherward. Thermometer at 90. At ½ past 7 arrived in Baltimore, went on board the Steamboat *Geo. Washington,* & at 8 we were off for Frenchtown.[1] When I went into the cabin to take tea the atmosphere was very like what I should suppose the inside of a steamboat boiler would be just as the water was coming to a boil. I think I never suffered as much when taking any other meal in my life. Got on deck again as soon as possible [and] before we arrived at Frenchtown the wind came into the North East, & the weather became as uncomfortably cold as it was uncomfortably hot three hours before! At 12 or [a] little after we took the cars at Frenchtown, crossed over to New Castle & there went on board the *Robert Morris,* one of the swiftest boats in the U.S. I was lucky enough to get a good berth & had catnaps till ½ past 3 when we were aroused to "select out our baggage." At 4 we were at the Wharf in Philadelphia and there was no getting in anywhere, so I perambulated the streets, and saw the fire companies as they returned from the burning of the Atheneum, or gallery of Fine Arts.[2] At ½ past 5 the gate to the wharf where the N.Y. boat lay was opened & I got my trunk on board, then visited a barber's shop & was shaved, & then went to the U.S. hotel & took breakfast, & then went on board the steamer *New Philadelphia* for Bristol, at which place we took the cars and arrived in New York at one o'clock P.M.

I went to Brooklyn & visited Dr. Wells & his family. Went over to N. York in the afternoon & found Mr. [Amos] Kendall & Mr. [F. O. J.] Smith at the Mansion House, "Bunkers."[3] Mr. S. agreed to leave with me the next afternoon for Boston & I returned to Brooklyn. Friday morning visited N.Y. again, & Mr. S. & I took our berths on board the *Cleopatra.* . . . At 5 we were off, & at 1 o'clock at night reached Allen's point[,][4] where we took the cars & arrived in Boston about 9 A.M., having been detained between two and three hours by some accident to the boiler. Went to the Bromfield House with Mr. Smith, breakfasted on broiled fresh salmon—it was excellent. After breakfast called on Dr. Barker at the Custom house & was introduced by him to numerous persons. Wrote a letter to my wife, and returned to the Bromfield House where, at one o'clock, I dined & then took the cars with Mr. Smith and came here where I arrived about 5 o'clock P.M. . . .

So here is my history of a journey from Washington to this city, etc.— Actual time of travel—

W. to Balt.	2	hours	*Fare*	2.50
B. to Phila.	8	"	"	3.00
P. to N.Y.	6	"	"	2.00
N.Y. to Boston	16	"	"	2.00
B. to this place	2	"	"	1.50
	34			$11.00

deduct 2½ hours delayed
by an accident 2½ hours
31½

Pretty quick travelling, considering that, 40 years ago it was 3 or 4 weeks hard labor to go the same distance! . . .

1. A town on the Elk River in Maryland. Situated near the head of Chesapeake Bay, it was the western terminus of the New Castle and Frenchtown Railroad, connecting the Chesapeake Bay and Delaware Bay.
2. It was the Pennsylvania Academy of the Fine Arts that burned on June 11, not the Philadelphia Athenaeum. Some discussion of the fire is given in *Report of the Board of President and Directors to the Stockholders, June 2, 1851* (Pennsylvania Academy of the Fine Arts, Philadelphia, 1851).
3. Bunker's Hotel, or Bunker's Mansion House, at 39–41 Broadway, had been the Gen. Alexander Macomb mansion. It was called the Mansion House when George Washington used it as his residence while President of the United States.
4. Allyn Point, several miles north of New London, Conn., on the Thames River, was the steamboat terminus where through connections were made by rail for Boston.

Friday, June 20. Tuesday after breakfast Henry & I walked down to his office, & soon after we got there the cars came in & Col. Pierce, Judge Harvey[1] & others came to attend the session of the District Court. I was delighted to see Pierce; he appeared as in times of old. Talked with him some time at the Squamscott, & then went to the Court House, staid there a short time, & then Henry & I packed up & rode up to Chester, where we dined. After dinner Henry, Ned & I, walked into the South woods & visited many an old familiar place, particularly a beech tree on which several years ago I cut my name. After rambling about till nearly sunset we returned, took tea & spent the evening & night in the old mansion. Wednesday Henry & I went to Manchester with his horse & wagon, and there we took the cars at 10 o'clock & went to Concord. We went to the State House & were introduced on to the floor of the House & took our seats by the side of Mr. Speaker Hibbard.[2] After leaving the House I was introduced into the Council Chamber, & by the Governor to all the members of the Council, some of whom I have known for years. I then went into the gallery and met my old & much esteemed friend Saml. D. Bell, a man who was to me, during my early manhood, a mentor that I shall never forget. Dined at Gasse's[3] at the table with Gov. Steel[,][4] ex Gov. Hubbard, Speaker Hibbard & other distinguished men of my native State. At 3 we took the cars for Manchester and returned to Chester that evening. Yesterday we all went up to the Massabesic & fished. Had a glorious chowder on one of the islands, & enjoyed ourselves as well as a temperate party of 13 reasonably could. Just as we had finished our day's pleasures a party consisting of the Candia Band of music came over; they took our boat & went out on the pond & played, & the music sounded beautifully. We gave them 3 cheers & wended our way homeward, where we arrived about sunset. . . .

1. Matthew Harvey (1781–1866), born in Sutton, N.H., was Democratic congressman, 1821–1825, and governor, 1830, before being appointed judge of the U.S. District Court for New Hampshire in 1831.
2. Harry Hibbard (1816–1872), speaker of the New Hampshire House, 1844–1845, became a Democratic congressman, 1849–1855.
3. Gass's Eagle Hotel was considered the finest in Concord.
4. John H. Steele (1789–1865), a Peterborough mill owner, was twice elected governor of New Hampshire, serving from 1844 to 1846.

Washington, Sunday, July 13.[1] . . . Thursday, June 26. Henry & I concluded to start at 3 o'clock P.M. for the White Mountains, so I spent all the forenoon writing letters & getting ready for the journey. At 3 o'clock, all being ready, we got into the wagon, with grey "Oregon" harnessed thereto & all things packed, & off we went, Henry & I, for the Mountains. We passed through New Market, Durham, Madbury, & Squamnigonic [Squamanagonnick] Village, and arrived at Rochester, 24 miles from Exeter, at 7 o'clock P.M. where we "put up" for the night at Dodge's tavern. . . .

Friday, June 27. Breakfasted, and at ¼ past 6 started. The morning was beautiful, but the wind soon rose and blew as if it intended to blow everything over. We pushed on, found one large tree blown down across the road, but went round it; arrived at Ossipee corner about noon. Dined, & Henry & I went trout fishing. I took the brook the wrong way & caught nothing—came back to the tavern & wrote a letter to my wife. Just as I had finished Henry returned with a few trout, & at ½ past 5 left Ossipee for Eaton, where we arrived at ¼ past 8. Put up at Atkinson's tavern. Very democratic—house full of pedlers, etc., & we were all accommodated alike. Henry & I slept together surrounded by *chambers* filled with all sorts of people, the doors all destitute of any fastening whatever. Mr. Atkinson appeared to be a very clever man. He is a "Latterday Saint" & I suppose lives only *for the present,* as he expects the World to come to an end speedily. I will, however, give him & his good wife & family credit for *feeding* us well; they gave us enough & more, & did all they could to make us comfortable, & our bill for 2 suppers, lodgings, breakfasts & horse keeping was 134 cents!!

Saturday, June 28. Left Eaton at ¼ past 6 A.M. At Conway, 6 miles from Eaton, we were told that it was 21 miles to Old Crawford's by the stage road, and 18 by the *other road.* We took the *other road,* by what is called *the cliffs,* which are tremendous masses of rock standing perpendicular hundreds of feet high, & really worth seeing. We went on the *cliff road,* & found most of it remarkably pleasant & beautiful, though a portion of it was somewhat hilly & rough. Nearly all this day we seemed to be travelling among mountains, & Mount Washington reared his lofty head directly before us, showing large fields of snow upon his sides. The scene was exceedingly romantic. We arrived at "old Crawford's" (Abel Crawford's)[2] at dinner. Here we had our horse *put up* for the day, and after dinner Henry & I rigged up for trouting. I did not intend to wade, but he did, & we dressed accordingly. We had not fished long before, in jumping from one rock to another, in I went up to my knees, & being in, I thought I might as well stay, so we waded on. We fished till nearly sunset, & caught 130 trout, ranging in weight from ¾ of a pound down to 2 or 3 ounces. It was *glorious sport,* but I got tired at last, though I believe Henry would have fished all night if I would have staid. It was hard work to get him away; he is a devotee of old Isaac Walton. . . .

Sunday, June 29. At ½ past 9 A.M. we left Abel Crawford's—or rather Mr. Davis's[3]—for the house is now kept by a Mr. Davis, the old gentleman's son-in-law, after having experienced the utmost attention & hospitality. The morning was delightful though somewhat cold. We soon seemed to be involved among mountains, & the scene about us became awfully grand & majestic. It was a temple not made with hands in which all the aspirations of a man's soul must necessarily rise to the God who formed it. I felt that the day & the place were sacred. Though no great singer, I could not resist bursting out with "Old Hundred" & Henry joined me, and I declare that I never felt more solemn or more in the immediate presence of the God who made me, than when, among those everlasting & eternal hills[,] I sang—

> Be thou, oh God, exalted high,
> And, as thy glory fills the sky,
> So let it be on Earth displayed
> Till thou art here, as there, obeyed.

We soon came to the "Willey House," which is now painted white and converted into a tavern. Although I could not pass the scene of so deplorable a catastrophe as happened there in 1826 without feeling almost that I trod on holy ground, still, the life & stir about the once lone spot took away much of the inclination to reflect on, or rather the realization of, the deep tragedy which hurled a whole family into another world. We passed slowly over the fatal avalanche, underneath which, even now, the remains of some of the Willey family lie buried, but we did not stop.[4]

Sooner [sic] after leaving that fatal spot we commenced rising, & up-up-up was our course, till all at once there opened upon our view a scene which cannot be described. Off to the right towered the mountain hundreds of feet above us, & from its top leapt a little cascade which came winding & tumbling in its foamy course till it passed the road directly beneath our feet, through a rocky aperture many fathoms deep and only a few feet in width, from whence it went tumbling down into the Saco, which passes along the deep ravine on the left.[5] The eternal fastnesses of nature were all around us, and as we gazed back over the distance Eastward the tops of the highest forest trees were far beneath our feet. It was a scene which will live in my memory forever. After gazing about for a time, we passed on & entered the notch.[6] In this I was disappointed; it did not make the impression on me that I had antici-pated. It is a wild[,] romantic place, & some of the crags that overhang the roadway appear as if a single touch would hurl them headlong into the path below. I could hardly resist a feeling of pleasure when we had passed the one most threatening in appearance in safety! The notch is a singularly formed place. In the narrowest place the perpendicular rocks on either side are not 30 feet asunder, & through the narrow aperture passes the river Saco & the road. The rocks at this point are not very high, but they become higher & more majestic as you pass onward. . . .

At 12 o'clock noon we arrived at Fabyan's,[7] from which place Mount Washington is plainly to be seen. With my glass I could see the winding pathway up which the ascent is made. The weather was clear & cold. At Fabyan's we found Lieut. Parrot[8] of the Navy, & his mother. All the other visitors had gone on to Mount Washington. We dined, & rambled about until nearly night, when Mr. James P. Bartlett & his sister[,] Miss Sarah K. Bartlett, and Albert R. Hatch, Esq., and his sister[,] Miss Caroline H. Hatch, arrived at Fabyan's. Mr. Bartlett & his sister were elegant sing-ers[,] and our little party assembled in one of the parlors before a good fire & spent the evening very pleasantly. We made all our arrangements to ascend the Mountain on the next morning, and retired to rest.

Monday, June 30. Clouds and darkness were upon the mountain tops without a prospect of their dissipation. The wind was from the East, & every appearance indicated a storm, so about 9 o'clock we held *a council of war,* & determined to give up the jaunt to the top of Mount Washington & to proceed onward to Franconia Notch. Soon after 9 we were on our way. . . . We went on till we reached Franconia Ironworks,[9] where we dined. We all visited the furnaces, shops, etc., but the great furnace was not in blast[,] and we saw nothing new or strange. After dinner we proceeded onward and arrived at the *guide board* which is made thus[,][10] & following with our eyes the direction of the index we beheld the "Old man of the mountain." The resemblance to the human profile is most perfect. It seems to be the end of the mountain looking out upon the valley below. Its appearance is somewhat thus.[11] It is an astonishing curiosity. About ¼ of a mile before we arrived at the profile we passed Knapp's tavern, situated in the notch. Henry & Bartlett, who had visited the place before, were impressed with the idea that there was another tavern a short distance further on. So, at the guide board I mounted Hatch's horse & rode a mile onward, but found no house, so I returned, & our party retraced its steps to Knapp's where we *put up* for the night. The weather was cold, raw & cloudy, & there was no fireplace in the parlor, so we all adjourned to the barroom where we had a good fire built. After tea we all walked out, & Knapp's son took a gun with him & awoke the echoes. He fired several very heavy guns & the report reverberated among the mountains as if a park of artillery had been fired. After our return, we sang and danced & enjoyed ourselves mightily. Henry made a pitcher of Eggnog, the place of *ardent* being supplied with some wine which Hatch & Bartlett brought with them, which was duly disposed of and did not detract from the previous hilarity of our party. I have seldom enjoyed an evening more than that one, amid the mountains of Franconia, & I shall not soon forget it.

Tuesday, July 1. Henry & Hatch rose at about 4 o'clock & with Mr. Knapp's son, went trout fishing, promising to be back at ½ past 8. The ladies, Bartlett & myself rose at about 6. It was a cold, cloudy, drissly morning. Bartlett & I walked down to visit the "old man," but a thick fog cloud had embraced his venerable countenance. . . .

Returning to Knapp's we had a fire built in the dining room & there we waited for the truant trout fishers till between 9 & ten, when they returned with *four small trout!* At about 10 we sat down to breakfast, and at 11 bid adieu to Mr. Knapp's hospitable mansion, & pushed on toward West Thornton. Five miles from Knapp's we arrived at Knight's, where we were to turn off into a bypath to go to the "Flume." We left our horses at Knight's and with a boy 8 years of age for a guide, we went to visit the Flume. The path is over hills & through valleys, & is rough enough. They called it a mile—it seemed to me to be nearer two.[12] We all arrived safely, with the exception of a few rents in dresses, & a few scratches of the hands. The flume was, to me, the greatest natural curiosity I saw in my journey, & well worth a journey there to see. For about a quarter of [a] mile, the Merrimack—or rather the Pemigawasset branch thereof— runs through an aperture in the solid rock less than 20 feet in average width and, I should judge[,] more than a hundred feet deep. The side walls are nearly, & in most places quite, perpendicular. In the deepest part there rests, suspended about midway from the water to the summit, a large rock, say 10 or 12 feet long, & from 6 to 8 feet in diameter, which appears to have fallen, in some one of Nature's convulsions, and caught by the upper edge on one end & by the lower edge on the other, some- what thus.[13] We concluded that when the giants of old separated the rock, for the river to pass through, they *chucked* in this stone to keep the aperture from closing. It is quite a curious feature in the view, & looks as if it would come tumbling down at the least jar. I thought of Mahomet's coffin suspended between earth & heaven, & this rock may contain, for aught I know, some prophet of ancient days. Who knows but the Ma- homet of the Pemigawassets reposes within it, & perhaps, could the rock be liberated, it might ascend instead of following the usual laws of grav- itation! Directly over the rock, across the top of the flume, lies a large tree over which, the guide told us, people frequently walked. After ex- ploring the bed of the flume, the water being very low, we returned to the lower end & entered a path which led to its summit. It was laborious of ascent, but we arrived, at length, & all sat upon a large log & sung "Dundee" in full chorus. There were places where we could approach the margin sufficiently near to gaze down, & the view was romantic & to heads inclined to dizziness, somewhat appalling. . . .

Upon getting back to the river, we came to a place, about 10 rods in length, where the water spreads very thin and passes over a smooth rock, & at the bottom falls into a little pool. Mr. Bartlett took a fancy to see a large stone slide down the inclination, so, having procured one nearly as large as he could lift, he stood at the top of the inclination & threw it forward. The effort caused his feet to slide & away he went, following the stone on its downward course; for a short distance he slid, then he commenced running, then down he came, & away he went into the pool below. We all stood in silence till he got out on the opposite side, drenched from head to foot, then we gave a shout that made the old forest ring again. Miss Bartlett was very much frightened, & when I discovered it I felt really sorry I had indulged in such a laugh, but it was a scene too rich to pass *seriously* over, & Bartlett, with a few scratches on his hands, & some very serious rents in his clothes, joined as heartily & merrily in the laugh as any of us. . . .

. . . We returned to Knight's about 3 o'clock. Drank some egg nogg &

pushed on to West Thornton, where we arrived about 6 o'clock, cold and comfortless. We sat down by a good fire & got warm, took tea, sung & talked and laughed until 9 or 10 o'clock[,] & then all retired & slept—I can answer for one—soundly.

Wednesday, July 2. We all arose in good season & breakfasted, & at ½ past 8 A.M. Henry & I shook our good friends the Hatches & Bartletts by the hand, gave them our blessing & departed—they having determined to remain at Thornton that day to rest their horses.

Before we had proceeded a mile on our way toward Plymouth it commenced raining in earnest. In Campton we got out of the wagon to walk up a hill, & Henry threw the reins over the horse's back & was walking at his side, when away he went upon the run. We *poked* along after him, Henry consoling himself with the idea that the wagon & harness were strong & not *very* valuable. We walked on about a mile when we met a boy returning with our runaway & wagon, all in good order. We got in & rode on through Plymouth & to New Hampton where we stopped to dine. While dinner was preparing I wrote doggrel in a memorandum book in the shape of a sort of farewell to Miss Bartlett (which I afterwards copied into a letter & sent to her). After dinner we again *put out* in the rain & rode on to the Shaker Village in Canterbury, where we arrived about 6 P.M.[,] wet & tired. I went into the "Trustees Office" where I found a young man & asked him if we might pass the night with them. He very politely informed me that they did not often entertain travellers—that there was a tavern two miles below, etc. To which I said, "You see I am wet & tired, & I dislike to go further. I am the Clerk of the U.S. House of Representatives at Washington, & am on a visit here to my native state, & I cannot think *you* will refuse me a night's lodging."

"Are you French?" said my *Friend*, "Well, I think we *can* keep *you*. We always take care of respectable people who make themselves known to us, but we have been so often imposed upon by strangers whom we did not know that we have to be very careful."

Arrangements were immediately made to make Henry & me as comfortable as possible. Our horse was taken care of, a fire was kindled, & we were made truly welcome. . . . We retired about 10, into as neat a chamber as ever man need enter, & all the accompanyments were such as to make a man feel that he was not in a common tavern. I slept well till nearly 7 A.M. the next day.

Thursday, July 3. After breakfast I showed the Shakers my air gun, which I carried with me, and with which we shot various things. They were very much interested & amused with it. They fired it at a mark, & exhibited a skill which I hardly supposed they possessed. After we had done shooting[,] Gardner[14] asked permission to show it to the women[,] which of course we were happy to grant. He carried it to them, fired it in their presence, & persuaded some of them to shoot it.

We were then shown all about the farm & workshops, & were instructed & amused at their neatness & ingenuity. It rained in showers all the morning. At ¼ before 11 we started for Chester. It rained almost constantly till we arrived at Pembroke. . . . We remained at Pembroke till 3 or 4 o'clock & then left for Chester. Went down over the old Chester turnpike, and arrived at ½ past 6. It rained nearly all the way, & we were wet & tired enough.

Found Mother, Elizabeth & little Willy[15] (Henry's son) well. Took tea, and at an early hour retired to rest in the old mansion of my Father, where the days of my babyhood, boyhood & youth were passed.

[Friday,] July 4. A heavy gun awoke me at ½ past 4 A.M. Arose, dressed & went down into the kitchen and built a fire in the stove. Morning clear and cold for the season. Wrote a letter to Miss Bartlett, folks got up, talked till breakfast was ready, eat breakfast, & then, with little William in Henry's arms, we started for Exeter where we arrived at ½ past 10, not having passed over one rod of the road in returning from the Mountains, that we passed in going! . . .

Thus ended one of the pleasantest and most satisfactory journeys of my life. I had but one disappointment, & that was not being able to ascend Mount Washington. . . .

Saturday, July 5. Bid the dear ones at Exeter farewell at ¼ before 6 A.M. . . .

1. French had been summoned to appear in Washington on July 8 as a witness in the case of *U.S. v. C. J. McNulty*. Then, under date of July 13, he presented a journal within a journal, largely accounting for his actions during a trip through New Hampshire's White Mountains, June 26–July 4. Prior to that, from June 21 to June 25, French had made a brief excursion to Portland and Westbrook, Me.

2. Abel Crawford, the "patriarch of the mountains," was a pioneer settler and guide in the White Mountains. He was about eighty years old when French met him and had lived at this site for fifty years.

3. Nathaniel T. P. Davis.

4. On August 28, 1826, the hotel proprietor, Willey, and his family were killed while fleeing an avalanche that miraculously spared the hotel.

5. The Saco River rises near Crawford Notch and then flows south and east into Maine, emptying into the Atlantic below Saco and Biddeford.

6. Crawford Notch, a five-mile-long pass named for Abel Crawford.

7. Horace Fabyan (1807–1881), the premier hotelier of the White Mountains, operated the Mount Washington House from 1837 until it burned in 1853. The Fabyan House, built in 1872–1873, was named for him.

8. Enoch G. Parrott (d. 1879) retired from the U.S. Navy in 1873 as a rear admiral.

9. The Franconia Ironworks operated continuously from 1805 until the end of the Civil War. In its best years it produced 250 tons of pig iron and 250 tons of bar iron, used principally in the manufacture of implements and utensils.

10. Here French sketched a signboard with the word "Profile," and a hand pointing the way.

11. Here French made a small, rough sketch of the "Old Man of the Mountain."

12. Marginalia: I saw Mr. Richard Lea since I wrote this, and he is well acquainted with the localities. He says it *is two miles.*

13. Here French made a small sketch, showing a rock wedged between the perpendicular walls of the rocky aperture. According to a note appended to this account, Amos Tuck French searched for this rock on August 10, 1906, but was unable to find it. He learned later that it was carried away by an avalanche and freshet in June 1883.

14. Gardner Whitman of Boston, although only about twenty-two years of age, was considered by French to be one of the head men among his Shaker brethren.

15. William Merchant Richardson French (1843–1914), second child of Henry Flagg and Anne Richardson French and brother of Daniel Chester French. After service in the Civil War he settled in Chicago where he became director of the Art Institute of Chicago.

Sunday, July 27. . . . Thursday [July 24] went to the Capitol in the morning—at 11 o'clock went to Georgetown & attended the Commencement at the College. I was very much pleased with the services. The President of the U.S. & Heads of Department were present. I remained to dinner. A large number sat down at 4 o'clock to a very excellent & plentiful dinner. We had speeches from Mr. George Brent, Mr. Meek, Lieut. Maury & Mr. Hoban.[1] At 6 I came home. Mr. Brown & his family spent the evening with us, & we had music *& dancing* & considerable fun. Friday went to the Capitol early in the morning, at ten rode down in the City, did errands, went to the Dept. of State on business, from thence to the White House, saw the President & attended to some business with him. Met Mr. [Edmund] Burke there, & took him to the Patent Office in the office carriage, then finished my errand-doing & came home. Dined—Ned & Frank & I walked down East Capitol Street to give Frank an opportunity to shoot his little gun. He shot a sparrow which pleased him very much, it being the first bird he ever killed. . . .

1. George Brent (d. 1881) graduated from Georgetown University in 1833. He had a long career as judge of the Maryland Court of Appeals. Alexander B. Meek (1814–1865), of South Carolina and Alabama, was serving as a law clerk in the office of the solicitor of the Treasury in 1845. He then became U.S. district attorney for Southern Alabama, 1846–1850, and was later made a judge. Matthew Fontaine Maury (1806–1873) had already published a treatise on navigation and was at this time superintendent of the depot of charts and instruments. His masterwork, *The Physical Geography of the Sea*, was published in 1855. During the Civil War he served in the Confederate Navy. Mr. Hoban was either James or Henry Hoban, sons of James Hoban, the designer and builder of the White House. Both sons attended Georgetown College. James (d. 1846) was a lawyer and district attorney. Henry was a physician, but he gave up medicine and became a Jesuit in 1846. None of these men were on the program of exercises.

Sunday, August 24. What has been doing for the past month? Really I am much at a loss to tell. We have had hot weather—steady, unmercifully hot weather—we have had not wars, but plenty of "rumors of wars," and everybody supposed, a week ago, that Mexico was about declaring war against the U.S. The matter is not yet settled, but I doubt very much whether we shall have any war. The President is now concentrating the force of the U.S. upon our Southern Boundary & in the gulf of Mexico, & if the Mexican Government should have the hardihood to declare war they will find some hot work to attend to at the outset, though it is ridiculous to call our handful of men, and flotilla of ships, an Army & Navy! The policy of our government in relation to an Army & Navy has been "penny wise & pound foolish," and we must have a tough war with some nation that is worth going to war with & get most damnably licked at the outset before our legislators will learn wisdom enough to put the Country in such a posture of defence as she should be.

My own opinion is that nothing better could happen to the Country than a war with Mexico. It would wake us up—it would furnish a pretence, at least, to increase the Army and Navy and make our position for defence such as would be respectable for the Nation. It would settle, forever, the rights of this Country to annex territory in compliance with the wishes of the people residing thereon, it would furnish thousands of idlers & loafers something to do, and if we could have a few severe battles, it would furnish a new race of heroes, the old one having nearly *run out*! I really hope, for the benefit of the country, that Mexico will give us a chance to brush up a little. . . .

My own particular existence has been as monotonous as one could desire. I have gunned some, have attended to all my official duties, have had my cistern lined with lead, at an expense of some 40 dollars and a good deal of trouble, have had another enlargement of my stable, have read the 2d & 3d vol. of the Exploring expedition of Capt. Wilkes & have been greatly interested. Have almost roasted but enjoyed excellent health.

This community has been in much excitement during the past week in consequence of a rencontre last Monday evening between Mr. Wm. R. Elliot and Messrs. William Z. Kendall and Josiah F. Bayly, in which Mr. Kendall was shot dead and Mr. Bayly severely wounded by Elliot.[1] With Messrs. Kendall and Elliot I was well acquainted, & have esteemed them as gentlemanly, promising young men of excellent character & good disposition. Amos Kendall, the father of young K.[,] was absent at the time of the sad affair, in the City of New York. He returned on Thursday morning, and the funeral took place on that day. I was present, &, with a large concourse of people, followed the remains of the young man to their last resting place. It was a scene to melt the hardest heart. Mr. Kendall, considering all the circumstances, bore up under the severe affliction astonishingly well.

The entire week has been occupied in an examination of the case before the proper authorities & has resulted in the full committal of Elliot to answer at the next criminal court, for the offence. So far as I have examined the testimony and heard the case, the crime consists in Elliot's arming himself, as he did, after having a slight quarrel with one of the parties (Bayly) & then putting himself in their way with the evident intention of renewing the fight, and shooting one or both of them. The custom of carrying concealed deadly weapons is a bad one & should be frowned down by every community. In that consists Elliot's guilt. . . .

1. The *Daily Union* of Washington for the period August 18–26, 1845, is full of news of the "Distressing Occurrence," or "The Late Affray," involving William Rufus Elliott, William Zebedee Kendall (Amos Kendall's oldest son), and Josiah Bailey. Elliott was discharged by the criminal court on December 13, based on the presentment of the grand jury that he acted in self-defense. Elliott was the brother-in-law of John C. Rives.

Wednesday, September 10.

> The tenth of September, let us ever remember,
> When a fleet struck to Commodore Perry![1]

This morning's *Intelligencer* gave me the first notice I received that I was Chairman of the Committee of Arrangements to receive the "Old Defenders of Baltimore," who are to honor this city with a visit on the 12th instant—it being the 30th anniversary of the battle of North Point, which took place Sep. 12, 1814. The committee were requested to meet at the Mayor's office at 10 o'clock A.M. I attended, found a part of the Committee present, but having no information as to the number of guests expected, etc., we adjourned to meet again at 4 P.M.

In the meantime I was notified to meet at the President's office at ½ past 2 P.M. to take into consideration the most proper manner of proceeding to cause a statue to be erected to the memory of the illustrious Andrew Jackson. So, after dinner, I walked up and found the President (Mr. Polk)[,] Mr. Buchanan, Secy. of State, Mr. Walker, Secy. of the Treasury, Gov. Marcy, Secretary of War, Mr. Cave Johnson, P. M. General, Mr. Mason, Atty. General, Mr. Kendall, Mr. Ritchie, Mr. Dickins, Secretary of the Senate, and Mr. J. L. O'Sullivan.[2] The propriety of forming a central committee, to consist of the President, Heads of Department, Secretary of the Senate & Clerk of the Ho. Reps. and two citizens of Washington (Mr. Kendall & Mr. Blair) was discussed at considerable length. Mr. Bancroft[3] had been present before my arrival, & was opposed to the President & Cabinet being officially on the Committee. Mr. Mason suggested many things that might be said & objections made to the propriety of appointing such a committee. Mr. Buchanan was in favor of it, & thought it the proper manner to commence. Mr. Johnson & myself agreed with Mr. Buchanan. Mr. O'Sullivan urged very strongly the perfect propriety as well as the policy of forming the committee in the way proposed. The President avowed himself ready & willing to do all he could with propriety in the furtherance of so worthy & proper an object, & said when the formation of the Committee, as proposed, was first mentioned, without giving much thought to the bearing it might have[,] he acquiesced in the propriety of it, but upon consultation with Mr. Bancroft, & upon due reflection, he had come to the conclusion that his name had better not stand at the head of the Committee, but that he would most cheerfully do all in his power, and he would head the subscription list. Mr. O'Sullivan then read a paper he had drawn up, and took down a list of names (Mr. Cave Johnson's name standing at the head) as a Committee. My own name & Mr. Dickins's were upon the list, but Mr. D. peremptorily refused to be one of the committee, and his name was stricken off. The meeting then broke up and I hastened to the City Hall where I found the Committee to receive the Defenders in session. We agreed upon providing an entertainment[,] & Mr. Fischer[4] & I went to the Assembly rooms & then to Brown's hotel with a view of contracting for the dinner. Brown[5] was not at home, but Doctor Howe, his brother-in-law, agreed that he (Brown) should call on Mr. Fischer on his arrival home, & make the contract.

I then came home.

Day pretty faithfully spent for the public!

1. Oliver Hazard Perry (1785–1819), American naval commander in the victory over the British on Lake Erie, September 10, 1813.

2. James Buchanan (1791–1868), Democrat of Pennsylvania, was congressman, 1821–1831; senator, 1834–1845; Secretary of State, 1845–1849; and President, 1857–1861. Robert J. Walker (1801–1869) was born in Pennsylvania and moved to Mississippi in 1826. A Democrat, he served as senator, 1835–1845, and Secretary of the Treasury, 1845–1849. William L. Marcy (1786–1857), Democrat of New York, senator, 1831–1833, and governor, 1833–1838. He served President Polk as Secretary of War, 1845–1849, and Franklin Pierce as Secretary of State, 1853–1857. Cave Johnson (1793–1866), Democratic congressman from Tennessee, 1829–1837 and 1839–1845, was Postmaster General, 1845–1849, in Polk's cabinet. John Y. Mason (1799–1859) was Secretary of the Navy, 1844–1845; Attorney General, 1845–1846; and Secretary of the Navy again, 1846–1849. A supporter of Pierce, he was named minister to France in 1853. Thomas Ritchie (1778–1854), a founder of the Democratic party, was known as "Father Ritchie." He edited the *Richmond Enquirer*, 1801–1845, and the Washington *Union*, 1845–1851. Asbury Dickins of North Carolina was secretary of the senate from 1836 to 1861. John L. O'Sullivan (1813–1895) was founder of the Democratic journal *United States Magazine and Democratic Review* and its editor, 1837–1846.

3. George Bancroft (1800–1891), prominent Massachusetts Democrat and Secretary of the Navy, 1845–1846. He later served as minister to England and Germany. His *History of the United States*, covering the years down to 1789, was published between 1834 and 1885.

4. William Fischer, an importer and dealer in stationery on Pennsylvania Avenue.

5. Marshall Brown, owner of Brown's Hotel.

Sunday, September 14. Friday opened upon us, bright, clear & beautiful—not a cloud to be seen, & a cool bracing air from the northwest.

At 9 o'clock I was at the City Hall where everything was arranged for the celebration of the day, and I cannot give a better account of it, than is given by the Baltimore *Sun*, from which I cut the following.[1] In consequence of the indisposition of Gen. Hunter,[2] I had to act as Chief Marshal, as well as Chairman of the Committee of Arrangements. I announced the toasts.

There were a number of volunteer toasts which, I presume[,] will be in tomorrow's *Sun*, & so I will leave the space above to paste them in.[3]

After being exposed nearly all day to the sun, after attending, at the President's, at Mrs. Madison's,[4] at the Patent Office, at the dinner table, without eating or drinking until all were satisfied, & then hardly tasting anything, I attended the Defenders to the cars, expressed to the Chairman of their Committee the pleasure we had enjoyed in receiving their visit & entertaining them, apologised for any omissions or mistakes that might have unavoidably occurred & gave them my best wishes, then took leave of them. . . .

Frank went to the circus Friday P.M. with Edmund & was much pleased.

1. The cutting describes the reception in Washington for the Surviving Defenders of September 1814. A delegation from Baltimore came by train and joined the Washington Defenders. They were welcomed by the mayor and French before marching to "the President's mansion," where each defender was introduced by name to President Polk and his cabinet. Thereafter, the participants marched past Dolley Madison's residence, where they were greeted by her, and then went on to the patent office, the mayor's house, and finally to Brown's Hotel, where dinner was served.

2. Alexander Hunter, marshal of the District of Columbia, had taken the office under Andrew Jackson in 1834 and remained in it until 1848.

3. The space is blank, no volunteer toasts having been pasted in.

4. Dolley Madison (1768–1849), the widow of James Madison. She had been the leading figure in Washington society from 1801 to 1817. After her husband's death at Montpelier in 1836 she returned to Washington and resumed her place in society.

Saturday, October 4. On Sunday afternoon, Sep. 14, I started, with Mary Barker,[1] for New York, and we arrived there the next day at 11 A.M. after a very pleasant trip. I went immediately to Dr. Wells's in Brooklyn, where I found all well. Left Mary & returned to N. York in search of my friend F. O. J. Smith, who I found at about 1, and ascertained that I was to appear before a referee at 2. Appeared accordingly & after giving all the testimony I could relative to the case,[2] went . . . and dined at one of the splendid N. York eating-houses. Returned to Brooklyn at about 6 & spent the night at Dr. Wells's.

I remained in New York until Saturday morning the 20th, having visited the waterworks (Croton)[,] Castle Garden, the French opera at Niblo's, the great Hydrarchos skeleton, attended an oratorio, etc.[3] I came on home as fast as possible, arriving here at 3 A.M. Sunday, pretty much *fatigued out.* . . .

1. Mary Barker (b. 1830), daughter of Lemuel and Sarah Barker, married William O. Taylor in 1856.
2. French does not provide any particulars on this case.
3. The Croton Aqueduct, completed in 1842, provided New York City with an adequate water supply for the first time. Considered one of the great engineering feats of the mid-19th century, the distributing reservoir was on the site of the present New York Public Library. Castle Garden, a small island off the Battery, was the scene of many public and social events. Niblo's Garden was opened in 1829 by William Niblo (1789–1878) on the corner of Broadway and Prince Street. For years it was the most popular amusement center in the city and included a theater as well as gardens. *Hydrarchos (Basilosaurus) harlani*, an extinct, slender, toothed whale that attained a length of seventy feet. A specimen 114 feet in length had been inaccurately assembled by Dr. Albert C. Koch from several skeletons found in Alabama. Koch exhibited his construction as a sea serpent, "The Greatest Wonder of the Antediluvian World," at the Apollo Saloon, 40 Broadway.

Wednesday, December 17. How much of good, how much of evil, how much of interest & how much of commonplace in this mortal world, has come to pass since my last writing herein!

Congress has assembled, war has been talked of, the President has written a glorious message,[1] & I have worn out one month's worth of lungs in reading it to the House of Representatives, who on the 2d day of December honored me by unanimously reelecting me their Clerk.

On Friday last [December 12] Mrs. French and I dined at the President's. The party consisted of about 40 persons—we sat down to dinner at ½ past 5 & arose about ½ past 8. The evening was cold & the dining room was not well warmed, & all the excitement of quite a merry dinner party failed to keep me warm. Excepting the cold room, everything was as it should be, & everybody appeared to be happy. . . .

The monotony of *home* has been very much encroached upon within the past 48 hours. On Monday evening at about 10 minutes past 9, as Mrs. French & I were sitting in the parlor, we were alarmed by quite a disturbance overhead, which, upon rushing into the passage[,] we found was occasioned by Frank's having discovered that the stable was on fire. I ran out & attempted to get at the horse but it was too late, the flames had made so much progress that I found it impossible to get much within the door, & even at the short distance I did get in I was nearly suffocated, so I ran round and tore down the door of the cowhouse & let out the cow, & attempted to enter my woodhouse but could not on account of the smoke. My poor horse was burned up, with everything else my stable & woodhouse contained except my cow. By this I lost about $700—and most willingly would I have lost much more to have saved my horse. But it is all gone, & mourning and fretting is useless. Poor "Pet" (that was the name she bore when I bought her & by that name she lived & died in my service) was a kind & gentle beast, & many a pleasant ride have we all taken with her. Her troubles & trials are over, & what the fire left of her I have had deposited beneath the sod upon the spot where she died. And, though a poor dumb beast, many a tear was shed at her calamitous end.

The fire originated from my servant boy Charles having placed ashes in a wooden box in the stable! I was ignorant that it was done and I have been more particular, through life, to caution my family against such disposition of ashes than any other one thing, & with all my talk & caution here have I been put to all the calamity & expense by it!! But from this time hence I will try to forget it all, & start new.

McNulty's trial is now going on & I am under the necessity of attending daily at the Courtroom as a witness. I hope and trust it will not last long. . . .

1. President Polk's First Annual Message was sent to Congress on December 2, 1845.

Friday, January 2. Fairly started into another year. Yesterday we—Mrs. F.[,] Frank and I—visited the President's mansion where we got into the most dense & endless crowd I ever saw there. We could not & did not get near enough to the President to shake him by the hand, but it was a mercy to him for he had to shake, shake, shake, till I should think he had almost shaken his arm off. From the President's we went to Mr. Larned's,[1] from thence to Mr. Dickins's & from thence to Mr. J. Q. Adams's, at all which places we partook of refreshment. . . .

I suppose, now, Congress will go to work in earnest, & we shall have no more holidays. The great subject now is Oregon & whether we are to have war? Mr. Hannegan,[2] Senator from Indiana, introduced a string of very ill-advised resolutions into the Senate last week & the war question was considerably debated upon them. I have not a doubt the President will stand, firm as a rock, for the whole of Oregon, & if England does not yield, & chooses to have a war about it she can be gratified. But I do not believe there will be any war—wars are not fashionable nowadays, and it would be the very height of nonsense for England to rush into a war with us for a few degrees of land to which our title is most clear & undoubted, and which could be of very little service to her if she had it. . . .

1. James Larned, chief clerk, office of first comptroller, Treasury Department.

2. Edward A. Hannegan (1807–1859), Democratic congressman, 1833–1837, and senator, 1843–1849, from Indiana.

Sunday, February 15. . . . Friday evening we entertained about ½ a hundred of our neighbors, until past midnight. We had dancing, etc., & all "went merry."

I have not attended a ball this winter, although I have been appointed Manager to two. At the ball of the 8th January, there was a very full attendance. The President was there & the following anecdote is told of the manner in which General Felix Grundy McConnell[1] approached him.

The President was at the head of the supper table. General McConnell with a Miss Pulvermacher[2] on one arm & a Miss somebody else on the other, made his way up to the President, when he said[,] "Mr. President, shall I have the honor to introduce you to Mademoselle [sic]? *Par le vous Francaise?* This, Mademoselle, is the President of the United States, will you do me the favor to introduce your companion, whose name I have most unfortunately forgotten. Mr. Polk, will you permit me to drink your health in a bumper of champagne." The general here filled his own & the President's glass. "Jimmy Polk—may you be as great and as good a man as Andrew Jackson, whose victory at New Orleans we now celebrate—may you live to as good an age as that brave man, who is now dead, who died a patriot and a Christian & went straight to Heaven, where he is now sitting on Abraham's knee, who hails him as his only begotten son—by G—d!"

"No heel taps[3] Jimmy," exclaimed the general, draining the last drop in his own glass!

This was told me by a gentleman who was present and vouched its truth without exaggeration, and knowing McConnell perfectly, I do not doubt it took place nearly as it is told—if anything it is not sufficiently embellished. "The President," said my informant, "stood as straight as an arrow, with his glass in his hand, through the whole unique performance, but he looked as if he was *very much struck* with the manner and language of the General."

McConnell is a queer man. He unites, with a generous disposition, a perfect recklessness of consequences. When not excited by liquor he is gentle, unassuming, and kindhearted; but when intoxicated, he is rough[,] unmanageable & disagreeable. He is possessed, by nature, with much wit, & considerable mind & genius, but until he reforms it must be all lost to the world, except where it bursts out in vulgarisms among his pot companions. If the witty sayings I have heard him use could be divested of their vulgarity without losing their point, they would be worthy of being preserved, but they cannot. Hundreds of anecdotes are told of him, but they are all too vile to be repeated. . . .

1. Felix Grundy McConnell (1809–1846), Democratic congressman from Alabama, 1843–1846.
2. The Pulvermachers operated a "lace and fancy store" on the north side of Pennsylvania Avenue, between 4½ and 6th streets.
3. I.e., leaving any liquor in the glass.

Sunday, April 26. . . . If I had the time & the energy to jot down something of the past 2 months relative to the movements of the public, I could write this book through, but I won't do it. Congress has discussed the Oregon question *ad nauseam,* & have, at last passed *a notice*! War has been predicted & talked of till all the women began to dream of murder, rapine, guns[,] pistols & bayonets, but I have not yet believed that there was the least danger of war with England, & now I think peace is certain. . . .

Monday, May 25. . . . On Wednesday last Mr. F. O. J. Smith came to this city as a witness before the Investigating Committee—Ingersoll vs. Webster.[1] He has been engaged every day since he arrived in preparing & giving his testimony, & completed it yesterday. I have read it, & recommend it as a study to all politicians. There is in the 8th Vol., I think, of the *Democratic Review,* a story entitled, "Who governs then?" It is, of course, but *a story,* & it illustrates with great power, & in a very interesting manner, how great events germinate from very small causes, and the public impute to the movements of mankind any cause other than the one which actually creates the movement. This romance is *actualized* by Mr. Smith's testimony.

In June 1841, at the request of Mr. Smith, I called, with him, upon Daniel Webster, then Secretary of State. He was boarding at the House of R. H. Clements, in Green's row, 1 street East. It was intended as a mere friendly call. Many of the general topics of the day were commented upon & discussed, &, among other things, the Northeastern boundary question. Mr. Smith & Mr. Webster gradually withdrew from the other company present, & left Mrs. Webster[2] to entertain them, while they (Messrs. W. & S.) sat apart on a sofa very diligently engaged in a low conversation. From that conversation, thus held, resulted all the movements that finally led to the "Ashburton Treaty!!" From that time out Mr. Smith was the prime mover of the secret springs which led to the result which has been so *widely praised* & *cursed* as the only *effective act* of Daniel Webster's *public* life. And now, for the first time, six years having passed away, is it first known publickly, that Mr. Smith had anything to do with the matter! "Who governs then?"!! The praise or the censure belonging to that transaction, of right[,] all belongs to him.

On Friday last [May 22] at 1 o'clock I went to Baltimore to attend a meeting of the stockholders of the Magnetic Telegraph Association, remained there that night and returned Saturday morning. Our Telegraph is working its way slowly, and ere long the world will be astonished that it did not sooner see the vast revolution that it is to make.

Last week the great Fair[3] commenced in this City, & it is, indeed, *a great one.* I have been through the immense pavilion once & intend to go through it several times more ere the Fair breaks up, & then, if I am not too lazy, I will make some special record of it in this journal.

War with Mexico is now the main subject of conversation. It has commenced in earnest. God knows when it will end. I hope soon, but not until the perfidious Mexicans are taught that we are a people not to be trifled with.

This day ends the 43d Council of the City of Washington. I have represented this Ward 4 years in the Board of C. C. & this is, I hope & trust, my last appearance in the capacity of one of the Fathers of the City. I have prementorily [sic] declined being a candidate for either Board. . . .

1. Congressman Charles J. Ingersoll of Pennsylvania in February and April 1846 made accusations of corruption against Daniel Webster for his conduct while serving as Secretary of State under President John Tyler. A special committee of investigation reported in June and voted 4 to 1 in finding Webster blameless. The poor relations between Ingersoll and Webster that existed over the years are examined by Kenneth R. Stevens in "The Webster-Ingersoll Feud: Politics and Personality in the New Nation," *Historical New Hampshire,* 37 (Summer/Fall 1982), 174–192.

2. Caroline LeRoy Webster (1797–1882), second wife of Daniel Webster, was the daughter of Herman LeRoy of New York, once the head of one of the leading commercial houses in the United States.

3. The National Manufacturers Fair ran from May 21 to June 3, 1846. It was held to encourage the growth of manufacturing in the city.

Thursday, May 28. Tuesday—eat breakfast, mowed the grass in the garden & got into "a muck sweat[,]" changed my clothes & went to the Capitol, rode to the State Dept. & saw Dr. Brodhead,[1] who with me signed the bond of Wm. H. McLean[2] last July, he having been appointed a Constable, & we have just ascertained that he is a defaulter. Dr. & I rode to the Court House & commenced process to have him removed from office, & to secure ourselves if possible. *Mem.*[3]—sign no more Constable's bonds.

Returned to the Capitol just as the House met. Heard sundry speeches, & among the rest an admirable one by Hon. Martin Grover[4] of N.Y., a

strongminded, honest, straight-ahead democrat, who, without much education, has the natural power of intellect, which despises artificial cul-
ture, & which enables him not only to make himself understood, but *felt*.
I have no doubt many pronounced his speech of Tuesday demagogical.
I believe he was sincere & honest, & spoke exactly what he thought. He
has all the appearances & *marks* of an honest man.

House adjourned about 3, I came home, & soon after Mr. Simon
Brown came in. I sent for Mr. Norris,[5] & we three, with Mrs. French,
sat in the summerhouse & enjoyed ourselves. Norris & I drank champagne & smoked. Brown drank the wine but did not smoke, & Mrs.
French was only a spectator. . . .

Yesterday went to the Capitol as soon as breakfast was over, worked in
my office till the House met, then went to the President's & delivered
him a resolution passed as soon as the House met, calling on him for
Gen. Taylor's[6] official account of his battles. As I passed out of the Capitol
through the Rotundo, I beheld one of the most interesting sights I have
seen for many a day—all the pupils of the schools of this City assembled
therein. It was an oasis in the political desert. Those young & happy
faces, those bright & laughing eyes gazing about upon the to them new
things which surrounded them, called up in my bosom the most plea-
surable emotions. The hum & buzz of happy voices contrasted so with
the usual political din of the Capitol, that it seemed as if, with a single
step, I had gone from the turmoil of political life back to the days of my
own unclouded childhood. I passed out with a "God bless them all" sort
of feeling which lasted until a rascally *extortionate* hack driver wanted me
to give him *a dollar* for carrying me to the President's house & back to
the Capitol. I told him very plainly, I would not do it, & so I walked up.
I believe most of the hackmen of this city are the greatest rascals extant.
Returned from the President's just in time to be at my post when they
commenced voting on the general appropriation bill, in C. W. Union, (at
1 o'clock) & I do not think I ever saw three hours more demagogically
spent by the House than the three from 1 to 4. The main feature was,
to make a show of a desire to reduce the pay of members of Congress without
doing it! And most effectually was *the show made*. Without concluding,
however, the Committee rose *for want of a quorum*, & the House adjourned
between 4 & 5. I came home, dined & then wife & I went to the Fair. . . .

1. Dr. John M. Brodhead lived on New Jersey Avenue between B and C streets. He was
a clerk in the Treasury Department in the 1830s but by 1853 had become the Department's
second comptroller. He was also an early subscriber of Magnetic Telegraph Co. stock.

2. Constable William H. McLean lived on 14th Street between B and C streets.

3. *Memento*, remember.

4. Martin Grover (1811–1875), Democratic congressman from New York, 1845–1847.
He was later a justice of the supreme court of New York.

5. Moses Norris, Jr. (1799–1855), Democrat of New Hampshire, congressman, 1843–1847, and senator, 1849–1855.
6. Zachary Taylor (1784–1850) by this time had fought and won the battles of Palo Alto and Resaca de la Palma. These and later military successes gained him the presidential election in 1848.

Friday, August 21. . . . Since the last day of June, when Mrs. French left home, it has hardly seemed like living. Tomorrow she is to return. At 8 o'clock this morning I recd. a telegraphic despatch informing me that she left Boston at 5 o'clock yesterday afternoon!

Last Monday [August 17], Mr. [Simon] Brown, Mary Brown & Mary Barker (Major Barker's Mary) went, in company with me, to Piney Point, where we spent two nights and a portion of two days. The weather was hot, and the place was perfectly overrun with visitors, there being between two & three hundred where there was only accommodations for less than two hundred. Consequently those who came last, & I was among them[,] fared anything but sumptuously. We had enough to eat & drink, but sleeping was out of the question. The balls—one each evening—were very agreeable & quite brilliant, and, upon the whole, I enjoyed it pretty well. The young ladies wanted to stay longer, but Mr. Brown & I concluded we had seen enough of Piney Point, so on Wednesday morning we took the boat & arrived at the wharf here at 4 o'clock P.M. We went down on board the *Mount Vernon,* a most splendid new boat, commanded by Capt. Gunnell,[1] & returned to Aquia creek in her. There we took the *Powhatan,* Capt. Rogers,[2] & came up. The latter is a fine boat but not equal in beauty to the *Mount Vernon.* . . .

1. Captain Gunnell's *Mount Vernon* was built in Philadelphia in 1846. She was taken over by the navy during the Civil War and her name was changed to *Mt. Washington.*
2. Captain Rogers's *Powhatan* was built in Baltimore in 1845. She was renamed the *King Philip* when taken over by the navy in the Civil War.

Sunday, August 23. At ½ past 7 last evening Mrs. French, Frank, Ben and Maria returned, & I rejoiced to see them all in good health. I shall not soon suffer them all to leave again—it makes home so lonely—indeed, "home" is no home where a man's family is not. . . .

Friday, October 2. . . . I this day attended the funeral of Col. Samuel Burch, formerly, for many years[,] principal assistant Clerk of the Clerk of the House. I first became acquainted with him 13 years ago next December. For business talents & industrious habits he exceeded any person I ever knew. I have been constantly associated with him in some way ever since I came to Washington. We were Clerks together; he was a reporter & I was Clerk; we were again Clerks together; we were members of the City Council together; & again he was reporter while I was Clerk. His only failing was a vast eagerness for riches. He sacrificed health & office for money. Aside from this, almost mania, a better or more useful man never lived. As a man thoroughly acquainted with all matters appertaining to the Corporation of Washington, & to legislation in all its forms, he will be greatly missed. His funeral was attended by the old & respectable inhabitants of Washington, & they all felt that one of the "fathers of the city" had departed. . . .

Friday, November 6. Since I wrote last, nothing very special has occurred up to the commencement of the Week now about to terminate, to ruffle the smooth waters of my life's progress. The Russells came three weeks ago tomorrow. Mr. Russell is a Messenger in my office now; he deserves a better place, & I hope it will be in my power to give him one.

. . . On the 30th, a week ago this day, I was elected an Alderman from this Ward, in place of Alderman Beck, resigned. My term of office extends to June 1, 1848. I never gave my consent to be a candidate for office, with more reluctance, than I did to run for Alderman. A political and personal friend was my opponent (Peter Brady, Esq.)[1] and I beat him only 3 votes. Had I not been deceived by some of my democratic *pretended friends*—but who turned out to be traitors to me—& who assured me that, inasmuch as that Mr. Brady was a member of the other Board[,] he could not be supported for Alderman, I should not have consented to run at all, and, when I found that, but for my running he could have been elected[,] I felt sincerely sorry that I had consented to have my name used. The truth is I have, without any cause known to myself, incurred the bitterest enmity of some of the lowest & meanest men of this ward. These men *lied me* into the canvass, as it seems to me[,] for the sake of defeating me, & having done this, they used the basest & most despicable lies to defeat me. Under these circumstances my election was indeed a triumph, not over Mr. Brady, but over a set of scoundrels destitute of honor, honesty, or truth.

On Tuesday last I attended a meeting of the Grand Lodge of the District of Columbia, as one of the Delegates from National Lodge No. 12, of which I am a member, and was elected to the high & honorable station of Grand Master of Masons in the District. I shall endeavour to do my duty in this office so as to sustain the craft in that high and honorable position in which destiny has willed that they should stand. On Wednesday evening I had conferred upon me the degree of "Mark master"—a Mr. Delafield[2] of Tennessee presiding. It is a most beautiful degree, and it was conferred in a manner worthy of its beauty. I shall not soon forget the degree or the perfect gentleman, mason & scholar who conferred it.

Last evening, the same gentleman presiding, I received the beautiful & exceedingly interesting degrees of Excellent Master and Royal Arch Mason. I am more & more struck with the sublimity of this Ancient & Honorable order. In 1825, or 6, I was entered as an apprentice—passed & raised to a Master Mason in King Solomon's lodge in New London[,] New Hampshire. In 1827 I removed to Newport in that State & became a member of Corinthian Lodge, & soon after Master thereof, &, ex officio, a member of the Grand Lodge of the State. I was appointed a District Deputy Grand Master by Hon. James Wilson, Jr.[,] when he was Grand Master. The Anti-Masonic excitement soon after arose & it was deemed expedient not to work, so our lodges in New Hampshire were generally closed. I came to this city in 1833, and have attended but little to Masonry since.

Within a few years the Craft has left its dormant state & has become again active. It can never die. It may be depressed for a season, but the hand of Omnipotence reared it & will sustain it through all time.

1. Peter Brady (d. 1856), the father of Margaret Brady (1826–1906), who was to marry Edmund French, and of Mary Ellen Brady (1831–1905), who was to become Benjamin Brown French's second wife.
2. John Delafield was the first to be elected to the office of deputy grand master in Tennessee.

Friday, December 11. . . . Congress met last Monday—the President's message was recd. on Tuesday & read, & then the Whigs commenced their war upon it, upon the President, & upon the War with Mexico. The entire sessions of yesterday and day before were spent, in the House of Representatives[,] in denunciation by the Federalists & defence by the Democrats, of the President & his course of Policy. If the people of this Country will sustain the Federalists in their mad & unpatriotic course I do not wish any longer to be called an American citizen—for such poltroonism as they pretend they would have advocated had they been in power would disgrace the most arrant coward that ever existed. It would out Falstaff Falstaff, & cause a blush of shame on the cheek of him who avowed that "discretion is the better part of valor!" Let them go on with their base & cowardly attack, & we shall see how the brave & true-hearted people of our Country will view their actions!

For a week previous to the commencement of the session I was in constant attendance on the Regents of the Smithsonian Institution as their Assist. Secretary. It is really refreshing to be associated with such men. There is as much ability, learning, and general knowledge associated in that Board as I have ever seen among a like number of individuals, & in the keeping of such men the Institution must prosper. . . .

Sunday, January 3. . . . Prof. C. C. Jewett,[1] with whom I became acquainted at Providence some 3 or 4 years ago, came here a week or two since. He will doubtless be Librarian of the Smithsonian Institution. He spent considerable time with me & I enjoyed his visit very much. I anticipate great pleasure in his company when his residence shall be permanently fixed in this city.

On the 26th inst. [ultimo] I was installed as grand master of Masons in this District. We had a very pleasant meeting of the Grand Lodge. Last evening I attended Lodge No. 4 at the Navy Yard & installed the officers elect. Masonry is again taking the high stand that it ought to hold, if its principles are lived up to by the members of the craft.

New Year's day we had a dinner party, & our company staid until ½ past 10 at night. It was one of the most joyous occasions I have experienced for a long time. . . . In the morning Mrs. French & I went out calling—at the President's[,] Vice President's,[2] Mr. Larned's, Mayor Seaton's & Mr. Benton's. . . .

1. Charles Coffin Jewett (1816–1868), librarian at Brown, had been visiting the libraries of Europe. He became librarian of the Smithsonian Institution in 1848 and of Boston's public library in 1858. He was a pioneer in the field of planning and compiling a union catalog.
2. George M. Dallas (1792–1864) of Pennsylvania.

Sunday, January 10. *Friday.* . . . Head ached all day—weather very cold. After dinner slept an hour or two in my chair, dressed for the ball. Mr. & Mrs. Russell came in, & Mrs. R. aided Mrs. F. to dress. At ¼ past 9 we went down to Jackson Hall & the people began to come thick & fast. The dancing commenced, the President & his Cabinet arrived and were duly marched in to the tune of "Hail Columbia." Everything seemed to be progressing beautifully when, all at once, smoke & fire came rushing out of one of the apertures by which the hall was heated by a furnace in the cellar. The people began to move slowly to the dressing room, some of the ladies manifested alarm, but no rushing was seen. Mrs. F. found her cloak, etc. I took them & we went back into the hall & staid until the *knowing ones* exclaimed that there was actual danger. Then we, with a pretty considerable of a crowd, got down the stairs & out of doors. My cap & cloak was left in the carriage & had gone home, to return at 12 o'clock! The weather was freezing cold, but we trotted down the street.

The smoke was pouring out of the lower story of the building in dense volumes & I had no doubt then that it would be burnt, so we walked as far as my friend Purdy's[1] & rang him & his good wife up. I left Mrs. French at his house, borrowed a hat of him, & tripped it home, got my carriage & returned to Mr. P.'s. He had been up to the Hall & gave me the pleasing information that the fire was out & that the folks were about renewing the ball. We concluded it would be best to come home, & so home we came. The dancers returned & kept up the frolic until nearly or quite morning. The fire was caused by the closing of the register when the furnace was in full blast, which caused so great a heat that the wood-work took fire, & the storeroom beneath the hall was pretty thoroughly on fire when it was first discovered.

Yesterday from 10 A.M. to 2 P.M. I was engaged, in company with the Vice President, Secretary of the Senate[2] & Speaker of the House[3] in opening and examining proposals for furnishing the printing of Congress. At 2 the debate ceased on the bill for raising 10 regiments of troops, & from that time till dark the Committee & House were engaged in voting & did not pass the bill after all. I suppose it will pass tomorrow.

The House has got into a strange political situation, & it is difficult to tell who are supporters of the Administration. Parties seem to be breaking up & no mortal can foresee what is [to] be the result. But, as Mr. J. Q. Adams once said, "We shall see what we *shall* see." . . .

1. John Purdy operated a wood and coal yard on 7th Street, near the Washington Canal.
2. Asbury Dickins.
3. John W. Davis.

Sunday, February 14. Yesterday Mr. John Quincy Adams made his appearance in the Hall of the House of Representatives for the first time this session, having been detained in Boston by severe indisposition. It was really refreshing to see the din & tumult of politics give way for a time, & to note that the feelings that do honor to the human heart triumphed. The members present rose spontaneously as Mr. Adams entered the Bar. Hon. Andrew Johnson,[1] who has occupied Mr. A.'s seat all the session[,] gave it up at once[,] making some remarks as he did it, to which Mr. Adams replied briefly. After he took his seat nearly every member present walked up & shook hands with him. As I shook the venerable gentleman by the hand I felt that a tear was gathering in my eye, & I have no doubt that many a one felt the same.

Mr. Adams looks & appears feeble, & cannot last long. He has many failings, but he is a great & a good man notwithstanding them all. . . .

Yesterday the Senate of the U.S. by a vote of 27 to 21, I believe, expelled the Editors of the *Union* from their privileges on the floor of the Senate. Thomas Ritchie, the father of Democracy, almost, has been thus, by a vote of all the Whigs & John C. Calhoun, David L. Yulee, Mr. Westcott & Mr. Butler—4 Senators *pretending* to be democrats—expelled from the floor of the Senate of the United States for publishing in the *Union*, Newspaper, an article reflecting upon the Senate![2] Will the democracy—*will the people*—of this country submit quietly to this high-handed & outrageous proceeding of the Senate? Not they. Those who have done this unclean & dastardly act will rue the day that they did it. The brand of infamy will be so indelibly stamped upon them that like the old & infamous "Alien & Sedition" it will not "out." It will burn on, deeper & deeper, like the Greek fire, unquenchable, as long as their lives shall last, and the name of *Thomas Ritchie* with that of *William Duane*[3] shall stand enrolled on the banners of pure democracy, long after he shall sleep in his tomb, as an editor & a man, who, when the Palladium of the Liberty of the People, a free press[,] has been attacked, stood boldly forth in its defence, nailing his colors to the mast and defying the Aristocracy of the U.S. Senate to do their utmost against him!

1. Andrew Johnson (1808–1875), Democratic congressman from Tennessee, 1843–1853, and senator, 1857–1862. As Lincoln's second Vice President, he succeeded to the presidency in 1865.
2. John C. Calhoun (1782–1850), of South Carolina, held national office almost continuously for forty years, as a congressman, Secretary of War, Vice President, senator, Secretary of State, and, at this time, once again as senator. David Levy Yulee (1810–1886), until 1846 David Levy, territorial delegate from Florida, 1841–1845, and senator, 1845–1851 and 1855–1861. James D. Westcott (1802–1880), Democratic senator from Florida, 1845–1849. Andrew Pickens Butler (1796–1857), Democratic senator from South Carolina, 1846–1857.
3. William Duane (1760–1835), editor of the Jeffersonian *Aurora* in Philadelphia, had vigorously opposed the Federalist Alien and Sedition Acts, which had restricted freedom of speech.

Sunday, April 11. How many things have happened, since Sunday, Feby. 14, the time I last wrote herein! The blank page of the *then* future, all fair & stainless, now contains a record which in future times will be referred to as one of the most brilliant pages in the history of this Nation, if not of the world. Buena Vista, & the Hero of Palo Alto, Resaca de la Palma, & Monterey, will hereafter be spoken of as we are accustomed to speak of the victories of those great Military leaders with whom we associate the Military glories of the past, Leonidas, Hannibal, Napoleon, & no battle even of these warriors stands so gloriously *enlaureled* as that of Buena Vista, where, under the gallant Taylor, 5,000 Americans overthrew & routed 20,000 Mexicans! I was not mistaken when I wrote the two following lines in a song sung at the New England celebration in this city, last December—

> Old Zack to carry on a war's
> The Rough & Ready man sir!

But, with all this glory to our arms, the voice of grief over the gallant dead is heard. Yell, Hardin, Clay, Lincoln, & a host of others, whose hearts beat high with patriotism, have gone, covered with laurels, & mourned by a Nation's grief, to their long & last homes.[1] They fell, as it is glorious for patriots & soldiers to fall, in the front of battle, bravely fighting for their Country's honor.

Two of these brave men were well known to me, & with one I could claim all the intimate connexions of an associate & a friend—the generous, the noble-minded, & lion-hearted Yell. Twice since I have been connected with the House of Representatives has he been a member, & his course while here was a guarantee that the honor of his country was safe in his hands. The gallant & fearless Hardin was known also to me as a member of the House, during the 28th Congress. . . .

Yesterday came the news of the surrender of Vera Cruz & the Castle of St. Juan d'Ulloa to our army & Navy.[2] Glory heaped on Glory! I hope these victories may not make us so vainglorious as to deem ourselves invincible! though I believe we can beat any troops on earth in a fair field of equal numbers, & as to the Mexicans three to one in their favor is we deem as no odds at all against us. I trust now, that peace will soon follow the brilliant results of the past 60 days. If Mexico is not more than demented such must be the case; otherwise Old Zack & his gallant men will soon be "revelling in the Halls of the Montezumas." . . .

1. Archibald Yell (1797–1847), Democratic congressman from Arkansas, 1836–1839 and 1845–1846. He was also governor of Arkansas, 1840–1844. He was killed in the Battle of Buena Vista. John J. Hardin (1810–1847), Whig congressman from Illinois, 1843–1845, had served in the Black Hawk War. Henry Clay, Jr. (1811–1847), oldest son of Henry Clay, was an aide to Gen. Zachary Taylor and was killed while leading a charge at Buena Vista. George Lincoln of Massachusetts had been brevetted captain for gallantry in the battles of Palo Alto and Resaca de la Palma.

2. Vera Cruz and the island fortress of San Juan de Ulloa surrendered to Gen. Winfield Scott on March 28, 1847, opening the way for the advance upon Mexico City. Commodore David Conner (1792–1856) was in command of the naval forces up to March 20, at which time he was succeeded by Matthew C. Perry (1794–1858).

Thursday, June 24. . . . April passed away. May 1 came & with it the ceremonies of laying the cornerstone of the Smithsonian Institution which, as Grand Master of Masons of this District[,] I performed in presence of some thousands of Spectators. The President & Vice President of the United States were present, the one being ex-officio President of the Institution, the other Chancellor of the Board of Regents. It was, take it all in all, a most imposing spectacle. . . .

Exeter, Sunday, August 8. Up to the 5th day of July I remained in Washington. Prepared a 4th of July oration & delivered it on the 5th before the Democratic Association, & it was published in the *Union* of the 6th. . . .

After delivering the oration of the 5th at ½ past 10 A.M. I went to the R. R. depot where Mrs. French, my two boys & Mary Jane (the nurse) met me, and at 12 we started for Philadelphia where we arrived at 11 o'clock P.M. Miss R. Russell accompanied us.

We remained in Phila. at Jones's hotel, until the 8th. On the 6th I was elected President of the Mag. Telegraph Co. between Washington & N.Y. which rendered it necessary that I should devote much of my time to the interests of that Company. . . .

. . . On Monday 11th, left N.Y. for Washington, leaving my family at Dr. Wells's. Stopped at Princeton from 12 noon until 6 P.M. on Telegraph business. Called on Prof. Henry[1] at his house & spent an hour or two with him. I never was better entertained during the same time in my life. He is one of the most scientific men of the age. Remained in Philadelphia that night & arrived in Washington the next evening. Remained in Washington Wednesday & Thursday, & attended to various things connected with my several offices. On Friday, July 16, at 12 noon started again for New England. . . .

Stayed in Brooklyn Sunday & spent most of the day with Prof. G. B. Glendining.[2] Monday morning Mrs. Wells, Glendining & I walked over to the City & went making purchases & seeing sights until noon, when they left me. Dined at Delmonico's with Mr. Haley[3] & went on board the Chinese junk—a great awkward curiosity. At 5 went on board the Steamer *Vanderbilt* & at 6 were underway for Boston, which place I reached at 8 A.M. on Tuesday. Wife & Ben absent at Lancaster. Spent 20, 21, & 22d in Boston. Wife returned on Wednesday, & on Thursday 22d we came from Boston to this place, where we all remained until Monday 26th when we went to Chester. . . . Ned & I spent Tuesday [July 27] in gunning. We killed birds enough for a breakfast for the family. On Wednesday we made up a "gander party" to Auburn, & went out on the Massabesic fishing. At 2 P.M. we partook of an admirable chowder on picnic Island—there were 14 of us—& we all enjoyed it. . . . Thursday 29th Mrs. French & I went to Pelham in Henry's chaise to visit Gen. Richardson. We dined with the General & his Lady, & were received &

treated with a most cordial welcome. Stayed until 3 P.M. & then returned to Chester.

On Friday 30th we all[,] except Frank[,] came down to this place in the Stage. Frank came with Ned on Monday, and for the past week we have been luxuriating in various ways—spent two days at Hampton Beach—one in Boston—boated—fished—shot, etc. . . .

1. Joseph Henry (1797–1878), a leading physicist in the field of electricity, was professor at Princeton from 1832 to 1846, when he became the first secretary and director of the Smithsonian Institution.

2. George B. Glendinning is listed as a teacher in the Brooklyn directory of 1846–1847, and as residing at Warren Street near Henry.

3. J. J. Haley, a relative of F. O. J. Smith and an early subscriber of telegraph stock.

Washington, Tuesday, September 7. . . . After writing the foregoing on the 8th of August . . . I remained in Exeter until Wednesday, Aug. 11th, on which day we all left for Washington. . . .

Sunday, September 19. . . . Saw an account of the death of my old friend Richard Henry Wilde[1] in the newspaper today. He died of yellow fever in New Orleans. A *man* & a *gentleman* has departed. With an accomplished mind, he united one of the kindest hearts that ever beat in mortal bosom. He was a man of high literary attainments and a poet of considerable distinction. His morceau, "My life is like a summer rose," etc., is well known to every person of any reading. I formed my first acquaintance with Mr. Wilde in 1834 & have met him often since he left Congress. Peace to his ashes! . . .

1. Richard Henry Wilde (1789–1847), poet and Democratic congressman from Georgia, 1815–1817, 1825, and 1827–1835. He was later professor of law at the University of Louisiana.

Thursday, December 16. After having been in the daily habit of repairing to the Capitol between 8 & 9 A.M. & seating myself at my desk for the past 14 years, it seems somewhat odd to be all at once relieved from that duty.

On the 7th day of this month it pleased that august body, the House of Representatives of the United States, having an accidental Whig majority, to elect Thomas Jefferson Campbell[1] of Tennessee[,] Clerk of the House of Representatives.

The vote stood

For Thos. J. Campbell	113	Whigs
For Benj. B. French	109	Demos.

For Geo. Kent[2]	1	Abo. [Abolitionist]
For Nathan Sargent[3]	1	do.
For Saml. L. Gouverneur[4]	1	nondescript

It is proper to add that among the votes for me, were those of John Quincy Adams, & Lewis C. Levin.[5] Isaac E. Holmes,[6] from some foolish personal pique, connected with his love for a whig for whom he wanted an office, voted for Gouverneur. Holmes is a Whig in all his feelings and actions, & I trust the people of Charleston will have sense enough to permit him to repose on his laurels, after his present term of service expires. The evening previous to the election Henry Nes,[7] of Pennsylvania, held up his hand & swore before the God that made him, in presence of Mr. Levin, that he would vote for me, and then perjured himself by voting for Campbell! Let the unprincipled, perjured wretch answer to his conscience and his God for this crime! I despise him. Mr. Pillsbury[8] of Texas did not arrive until the evening of the day on which I was defeated. Had he been here to vote, I should probably have been elected.

To me personally, it is matter of little moment, as I stand in that blessed position, having "neither poverty or riches." I can live without the office full as well as the office can live without me! But to my friends in the office, some of whom are really poor, it is likely to be a source of distress. The political guillotine has already been set in motion, and five or six of my good fellows, & excellent clerks, have been decapitated. Two years hence[,] if I live, I will make an effort to get back & if I succeed Mr. Campbell's appointees will hardly have time to wink before their political heads will be off!!

I am now a happy man, with just enough on my hands to keep me busy, and without the terrible responsibility of the Clerkship of the House—the most laborious & most responsible office, during a session of Congress, under this Government.

Since Sep. 19, the day on which I wrote last in this journal, nothing very especial occurred, until the 7th day of December, to jostle the smooth running of the wheels of my existence. I was absent several times on the business of the Magnetic Telegraph Company, of which I still have the honor to be President.

Congress imposed upon the Secretary of the Senate and myself the duty & responsibility of contracting for lighting the Capitol & Capitol grounds with gas, which duty we attended to, and the result is now manifest.

This is a tremendously windy & stormy evening, and up here in my attic it makes everything tremble. My room is getting cold, so I will close my journalizing.

1. Thomas Jefferson Campbell (1786–1850), Whig congressman from Tennessee, 1841–1843, was Clerk of the House from 1847 to 1850.

2. George Kent (d. 1859), of Concord, N.H., was a friend of William Lloyd Garrison and an early adherent of the antislavery movement.

3. Nathan Sargent (1794–1875), Whig journalist who used the pen name "Oliver Old-school," was Washington correspondent for many northern newspapers.

4. Samuel L. Gouverneur was the nephew of Mrs. James Monroe. He married his cousin, Marie Hester Monroe, the daughter of President and Mrs. Monroe, in 1820. He was the postmaster of New York City until dismissed by Jackson.

5. Lewis C. Levin (1808–1860), one of the founders of the American party in 1842, was American party congressman from Pennsylvania, 1845–1851.

6. Isaac E. Holmes (1796–1867), South Carolina lawyer and nullifier, served as Democratic congressman, 1839–1851, before moving to California.

7. Henry Nes (1799–1850), Pennsylvania physician, served as an independent congressman, 1843–1845 and 1847–1850.

8. Timothy Pilsbury (1789–1858) served first in the legislature of the Republic of Texas and then as a Democratic congressman from the state of Texas, 1846–1849.

Sunday, February 6. And now, after this year has proceeded on its march thirty-seven days, here I am making a note of my existence. . . .

Since the 16th day of December I have been a daily laborer upon matters connected with that wonderful application of natural effects, produced by natural causes, known as the Magnetic Telegraph. As the President of the Company which established the line between Washington & N. York, and as Trustee of the Washington & N. Orleans Company, I find my hands full, and am not likely to rust out for lack of business. When I add to these *vocations*, the other business that necessarily devolves upon an Alderman, an Ex-Clerk of the Ho. Reps. & a man who has the weight of the Masonic Fraternity of the District on his shoulders, as their Grand Master, to say nothing of some dozen little offices "too numerous to mention[,]" it may be justly concluded that I have but little time to myself—hence the many *hiatii* in this journal. . . .

. . . I went to the Telegraph office this A.M. & we tried to connect the line through to Jersey City, but it was no go. . . .

Friday, February 11. Since my last writing, herein, I have read an address delivered by the Hon. Geo. P. Marsh[1] before some Historical Society in Vt. I think. If it were not such a journey from this attic down to my basement where the book is, I would get it, but as I cannot afford so many steps now I will leave a place for a note to describe it exactly. The subject matter of the address is the manner of writing History, and I have been forcibly struck with the views taken by Mr. Marsh. He assumes the position that History, when written as it should be, goes into the minutia [sic] of existence—that the good historian, instead of contenting himself with the great, prominent public actions of a nation, seeks individual history as it affects national history &[,] mingling them, gives a daguerreotype of the times he writes about. He instances Prescott[2] as one who writes *upon this* model. Mr. Marsh is a most sensible man and one of the best writers of this day, and his address has pleased me much. He is, no doubt, right, & upon meeting him yesterday I told him he was the very man to write a history of this country on the plan prescribed in his address.

If every man competent to such a thing would keep a journal of the events passing about him, what a splendid history might be made of a collection of such journals from all parts of a country.

Company has come & I must go down.

1. George P. Marsh (1801–1882), Whig congressman from Vermont, 1842–1849, and minister to Turkey, 1849–1854. A scholar and author, he was later the first U.S. minister to the kingdom of Italy, serving from 1860 to his death in 1882.
2. William H. Prescott (1796–1859), the American historian of the Spanish conquests in America.

Tuesday, February 22. On Thursday last at 5 P.M. I left this City for Philadelphia on Telegraph business, and arrived there at 2 A.M. on Friday. Went to Jones's hotel. After breakfast went to the Telegraph office and spent nearly all of that day and the next there. At 4 P.M. on Saturday left Phila. for Havre de Grace,[1] where I spent the Sabbath. That evening went to Perrymansville[2] in the cars & spent the night there. Mr. Park,[3] Ch. operator at Phila.[,] was with me. At 7 A.M. yesterday morning rose and breakfasted, and then Park and I started on foot for Bush river bridge, about 3 miles from Perrymansville. We tested the wires at that place and remained until nearly 12 o'clock, then walked on with Mr. Cleveland, who came from Baltimore in the morning train, to the Magnolia House, 5 miles, near the Gunpowder river. There took the cars for Baltimore, where I spent last night, & came home this morning.

Yesterday John Quincy Adams was prostrated by a stroke of palsy, while in his seat in the House. I came through the Capitol as I came from the cars, & went to the Speaker's room & saw him. I shall probably never look upon him again in life. He was perfectly unconscious, and appeared as if in a sound sleep. And, although I stood over his venerable and venerated form but a moment, many a thought crowded through my mind in that brief space. The tears came up unbidden to my eyes, and I turned and left the sad & melancholy scene.

I heard of his sudden attack yesterday at Baltimore, & it had such an effect upon my feelings that I hardly slept, but thought of him continually.

1. Havre de Grace is located at the mouth of the Susquehanna River, 35 miles northeast of Baltimore.
2. Perrymansville, the present-day Perryman, Md., is several miles southwest of Havre de Grace.
3. John D. Park had earlier been associated with the telegraph office at Fort Lee, N.J., opposite Manhattan.

Thursday, February 24. Mr. Adams lingered until 17 minutes after 7 o'clock last evening and then his spirit departed to the God that gave it. His mortal remains lie in the Capitol—the last scene of his earthly existence. I stood beside them this morning. No one was in the room save myself & the form—the cold senseless form of him who for so many years has been the observed of all observers—who but a short time since was well entitled the greatest & the most learned Statesman of his country. I could hardly realize that what I saw before me but yesterday contained the brilliant intellect, the almost unbounded information, the almost Godlike mind of John Quincy Adams—and that now it was but a clod of the valley[,] as unconscious & inanimate as the bier upon which it was extended!! A great man has gone down to the tomb, but his works & his deeds of usefulness shall continue as long as his Country shall be known among the nations of the earth.

Sunday, February 27. On Friday the City Councils were convened at 4 o'clock P.M. & a message was laid before them from the Mayor, notifying them officially of the decease of Mr. Adams. A committee was appointed to report suitable resolutions of which I had the honor to be one. They were reported, and I addressed the Board of Aldermen as follows.[1] . . .

Yesterday the funeral ceremonies took place, and seldom has such an immense concourse of people assembled to pay the tribute of their respect to the memory of an individual. It is estimated that there were 15,000 people in attendance. I was at the capitol in the morning & looked for the last time upon the face so familiar to me, as he lay in his coffin. But my head ached so badly before the ceremonies commenced that I was forced to come home & go to bed, where I laid nearly all day. . . .

1. At this point French pasted into his journal a newspaper clipping of two columns eulogizing J. Q. Adams. In this, French quoted a poem on the sundial, written by Adams, and given to him, in which Adams said:

> Snatch the retrieveless sunbeam as it flies,
> Nor lose one sand of life's revolving glass.

Sunday, April 9. . . . Spring with all its greenness and beauty is opening upon this portion of the world, and I hail it with more than ordinary pleasure. Having added to my land, I am now endeavouring to convert the barren lot which I have purchased, and from which I have removed two old dwelling houses, into a garden.

My business hours are devoted to the Telegraph. Everything like literature, either in reading or writing, seems to have departed from my thoughts. Business, straightforward, unpoetical business, engrosses nearly all my time and attention, and I can say with all sincerity, that if I have failed in any duty which I owe to the Telegraph Company, it has not been for lack of exertion to do everything deemed by me necessary for the honor and prosperity of the Company.

Had radishes from my own hotbed for breakfast this morning. Had lettuce a week ago.

Tuesday, May 23. Arose at ¼ past 5 o'clock this morning, and walked out on the Railroad, where I met Mr. McDuell[1] by appointment, and we went to examine a route by which to bring the Telegraph wires into the office in a better & more direct manner. Traced out a route to the office. Then walked down to the Centre Market House, & then home. . . . Have read Edward Everett's[2] eulogy on John Quincy Adams. It is eloquent and truthful.

I will now return & fill up some of the blank time between the 9th of April & this day. . . .[3] In addition to my usual business I aided some in preparing my grounds for a garden—read a little & wrote a little in the way of friendly correspondence—attended masonic and other meetings—in fine[,] pursued the even tenor of my way until the 5th inst. when, at 6 o'clock A.M.[,] I started in the cars for Philadelphia. Left Baltimore at 9, & soon found that I was surrounded by a most respectable company of M.D.'s who were just wending their way homeward from a Medical Convention which had been held in Baltimore. Among them was Doctor Oliver Wendell Holmes[4] of Boston. Having read his poetry for the past 20 years, & laughed over and admired it, I took the liberty to introduce myself to him, and we chatted together much of the way to Phila. He made a very favorable impression upon me, and I separated from him at Philadelphia expressing a hope to him that we should meet again, & with an invitation to him to visit me should he come to Washington—all which was of course reciprocated by him.

At the usual hour (3 P.M.) I arrived in Philadelphia & stopped at the Washington House, where I was well taken care of both as to bed & board. Stayed in Philadelphia until Sunday morning [May 7] at 9 o'clock, at which time started with Mr. Park, Ch. operator, for Princeton. Arrived there at 11, dined & walked out 3 miles on the R. Road to examine telegraph—weather very hot—at 6 P.M. took the N. York train & arrived in N. York a little after 9. Stopped at Bunker's. Monday did telegraph business, went over to Brooklyn & visited my relatives, etc. . . . Remained in N. York until Sunday morning, when I left, and came on home as fast as possible & arrived here at 8 o'clock Monday morning.

On my return, I found forty or fifty letters nearly all requiring answers, or causing some business, which, with the current business of the Telegraph occupied nearly all my time for a week. . . .

The reading of Mr. Everett's eulogy on Mr. Adams calls back his venerable form to my mind, and reminds me of the last interviews I had with him.

He had written to me, in answer to a letter to him, that he should vote for me as Clerk of the House at the commencement of the present Congress. Soon after his arrival in the City, I met him in the Hall of the House, in company with Mr. Marsh of Vermont, & we held a conversation of some half an hour, in which Mr. Adams was very pleasant & seemed to be disposed to mirth. He asked Mr. Marsh, among other things, if he could inform him why dog days commenced on the 24th day of July & continued to the 24th of August. He said he knew the usual reason assigned but there was nothing in that, & he doubted whether any good reason could be given. He had searched much, but in vain, for one. He continued this subject of conversation half serious & half in jest, apparently, for some time.

A few days afterwards he called at my office at the Capitol & desired to see me. I happened to be out. The next morning I called at his house & had considerable conversation with him. He alluded to his promise to me that he would vote for me, and said, in his peculiar tone and manner, "Mr. French, you are to be opposed. I am sorry for it. I hoped that they would suffer you to be elected without opposition—the newspapers say that no whig will vote for Mr. French—I care not what the newspapers say. I profess to be a whig, and I *shall* vote for Mr. French."

The main object of Mr. Adams's desire to see me was, that I would aid him in getting a poor orphan boy appointed a page in the House. I set myself about the matter at once, & was successful.

When the day of election came, as is well known, Mr. Adams voted for me. I was defeated by a small majority. A day or two afterwards, happening to be in the Hall on business, I went to Mr. Adams to thank him for his uniform kindness to me, but, before I had time to address him he said, "Well Mr. French, they beat you. I am sorry for it—your friends did all they could for you." I then thanked him and bade him good-by, little supposing I should never hear his voice again in this world. It was the last time I ever heard him speak, though I saw him on his deathbed.

1. George McDuell ran a business in coal, wood, sand, and gravel at the corner of 14th and C streets, near the canal.
2. Edward Everett (1794–1865), of Massachusetts, scholar, statesman, and orator, was congressman, 1825–1835; president of Harvard, 1846–1849; Secretary of State, 1852–1853; and senator, 1853–1854. An unsuccessful candidate for the vice presidency, he delivered the major address at Gettysburg in 1863.
3. This is French's ellipsis.
4. Oliver Wendell Holmes (1809–1894), writer, and professor of medicine at Harvard, 1847–1882. He published "Old Ironsides" in 1830 and his first volume of poems in 1836.

Sunday, June 4. "Watchman, what of the night?" "Vel and vot of it?" Not much. Since I wrote herein last the Democratic National Convention has assembled in the City of Baltimore & nominated Lewis Cass as their Candidate for the Presidency and Wm. O. Butler for the Vice Presidency. Two good men & true, who will, doubtless, if they live, be elected. I shall go into the field with all the talents I have for them, & hope I can do *something*. I believe the selection to be admirable, and have not a doubt the Democracy of the Country will respond heartily. This week the Whigs hold their Convention in Philadelphia. Although the Democratic prospects of union were, at the outset, somewhat dismal, I think the whig prospects are darker than were ours. If Taylor should be nominated, neither Massachusetts, Vermont, Connecticut or R.I. can be counted on as sure for the Whigs—at least for Taylor. Cass, it is said[,] is sure of Ohio anyway, but if Taylor is nominated it will render Ohio certain for Cass. Clay has set his heart on being the nominee, & if defeated he & his friends will be lukewarm. So eager is Clay for the nomination that I have heard one who knows all about it say that if he does not get it he will not live six months! Should he be nominated Taylor will run as an independent Candidate. Scott is spoken of, and I believe him to be the strongest man the Whigs can select. Let who will be selected, he will only be set up to be beaten!

The news is that the Treaty of Peace with Mexico has been ratified by the Congress of that Nation. I hope it may turn out to be true. . . .

Sunday, June 25. The Whig Convention met and nominated Zachary Taylor for President and Millard Fillmore for Vice President, and never have I seen so much discord reign in any party as now distracts the Whig ranks. The N.E. Whigs swear[,] "so help them God," they will not support Taylor, and I am confirmed in my prediction that he will not receive the vote of a single New England State.

The N. York "Barnburners,"[1] a division of the democratic party, have held a convention at Utica and nominated Martin Van Buren! as their candidate for the Presidency, & Henry Dodge[2] of Wisconsin for the V. Presidency. It is said the former will accept the nomination, & I presume he will. He is just that coldhearted, selfish man to do it. After having been the cause of the shipwreck of his own party, who adhered to him after it was perfectly evident that defeat was certain beneath the Van Buren banner, it is like him to show *his gratitude* by endeavouring to distract the Democratic party by suffering a disaffected few to use his name against that of the regular nominee! But that true democrat, Henry Dodge, will suffer no such use to be made of his name! If he does, I have mistaken the man.

Let the Barnburners do their worst. Lewis Cass, if he lives, is bound to be the next President of the United States! . . .

1. The Barnburners were antislavery Democrats who were considered to be so radical that they would burn down the barn to get rid of the rats.
2. Henry Dodge (1782–1867), territorial delegate of Wisconsin, 1841–1845, and senator, 1848–1857.

Sunday, July 30. Just as I predicted on the preceding page[,] Van Buren accepted & Dodge declined. It is like the *men*[;] one is a cunning, conceited coxcomb, though a man of great talent, the other an honest, upright old soldier, with a heart as open as the day, above deceit of any kind & far above anything like ingratitude to the party that he has always acted with, & that has always nobly sustained him. The political cauldron is now filled with all sorts of ingredients, & God only knows what the result is to be. The prospect, however, is that the election will be made by the House of Representatives—*if there happens to be one.* W. O. Butler will without doubt be the Vice President, & if so, & there is no election by the House, he will be President—with that result I shall be satisfied.

Since the 25th of June, when I last wrote here, my life has been a busy one. Up to the 4th day of July I was engaged all the time either in attending to the Telegraph, or in preparing for the imposing ceremonies of the 4th. On the latter day the city was crammed with people & the cornerstone of the National Washington Monument was laid. I officiated as Grand Master of Masons & performed the Masonic ceremonies, as the newspapers of the day will show. Everything went off gloriously.

On the 10th the Directors of the Magnetic Telegraph Company met at Barnum's hotel, in Baltimore, & on the succeeding day the Stockholders met & I was reelected President of the Company. Returned on the 12th. Remained at home until the 25th then went to Havre de Grace on Telegraph business. Examined the line around by Port Deposit on the 25th & 26th & returned on the evening of the 26.

Events of the month to remember.

3d   Edmund F. French married to Miss Margaret Brady, in Washington.

4th   Sister Elizabeth[1] died in Chester, N.H.

"   Cornerstone of Washington Monument laid.

11th   I was reelected Prest. Tel. Co.—was at Baltimore 10th[,] 11th & 12th.

25th   Went to Port Deposit.

26th   Returned.

It is my present intention to leave this city on Tuesday morning for New York, & to go up the North River[2] to examine a route for a Telegraph up on one side & down on the other to the City of N.Y.

Mrs. French is to leave the latter part of the week & meet me in N.Y.[,] & we intend to visit Saratoga. . . .

1. Elizabeth French (1817–1848) had been unmarried.
2. That part of the Hudson River that flows past New York City.

Sunday, August 27. On the 1st day of this month I left this City for New York, for the purpose of going up the North River to examine a route for our Telegraph. Staid at the Washington House[,] Philadelphia[,] that night. Arrived in New York about noon on Wednesday the 2d. Thursday morning the 3d[,] Messrs. Norton,[1] Hart[2] & I went on board the Steamer *Hendrick Hudson* & went to West Point, where we remained that night. It was my first run up the North River, & my first visit to West Point. I was interested & instructed with what I saw & heard. Nature has worked on a large scale on the Hudson River and all appears grand & majestic.

Public House at W. Point filled with visitors, & Messrs. N.[,] H. & I had the *pleasure* of being all deposited together in an attic, where we found three narrow[,] hard beds & where, with some joking[,] some sleeping, & much wakefulness we managed to pass a pretty hot night.

We saw the Cadets drill on the afternoon of the day we arrived, visited the public buildings & the burying ground and interested ourselves as well as we could where no amusements are permitted.

Friday the 4th, after breakfast[,] we took passage on board the Steamer *Alida* for Rorah Hook,[3] where we examined "the lay of the land" & questioned the good people with a view of ascertaining how we could get along, on that side of the river, with a line of Telegraph. We there procured a small boat & crossed over to Caldwell's Landing, where we examined further, dined, pitched quoits for amusement, & at about 3 P.M. took the *Hudson* on her downward trip & arrived at New York before dark.

Remained in New York until Thursday morning. Wife & family with Mrs. Adams[4] arrived there on Tuesday & we all stopped at the City Hotel. On Tuesday afternoon a meeting of the Directors of the Telegraph Co. was held & it continued until Wednesday afternoon.

On Thursday morning[,] Aug. 10th, Mrs. French, Mrs. Adams, Frank, Ben & I went on board the *Hudson* & "put out" for Albany. We all started with a determination to see the beauties of the Hudson & be pleased (except perhaps little Ben, whose main wish seemed to be to "push along[,] keep moving"). We viewed the pallisades, the highlands. We all took a special look at West Point in passing, saw "Monterey," "Vera Cruz[,]" "Buena Vista" cut upon the rough Ledges upon one side of the eminence, & the word "MEXICO" in letters 8 or 10 feet in diameter I should judge on the face of a ledge on an opposite angle—with the date of its capture "Sep. 13 & 14, 1847," I think.[5] We also saw Kosciusco's[6] monument & all the other *visibilities* from the Boat, worth looking at. All these things I had visited on the previous Thursday, at the expense of a goodly flow of perspiration.

Onward moved the magnificent *Hendrick Hudson,* & onward we moved with her. We saw "Cro'nest" & "Breakneck," "The Catskills" & the towns & villages along shore, & in the neighborhood of 5 o'clock P.M. we brought up at the pier in Albany, which then lay a city of fair proportions and inviting aspect, before us. We did not go on shore, but took passage in a little steamer alongside for Troy, where we were safely landed in less than an hour, & took lodgings at "The American." We were excellently fed & taken care of until 8 the next morning, at which time we started in the cars for Saratoga, where we arrived about 10. Three thousand visitors, at least[,] had taken precedence of us, & we could hardly find a place big enough to crawl into. After much search & trouble we succeeded in getting housed, after a fashion, over the "Bath Houses" attached to Congress Hall, & there we spent the residue of as hot a day as I ever desire to encounter. In the evening of that day came off the grand Fancy Ball at the U.S. Hotel, which all our party except Benny attended. It was magnificent & we enjoyed it until 1 o'clock A.M. on the 12th when we "gave in," went home—home!!—& retired. All arose in good season & went & drank of the water of health at the Congress Spring.

After breakfast took a carriage and rode out to Saratoga lake, where we rolled ten pins—Mrs. Adams, Frank & I—Mrs. F. would not roll. Returned by the way of the Pavilion High Rock & Flat rock springs, &

drank at the two former. We visited the racecourse as we went out, & saw some beautiful trotting.

We spent one week at Saratoga. On the morning of our second day we were provided with good rooms at Congress Hall & were well attended to and cared for.

We passed our time in amusements of various kinds, & were merry and happy. On Friday afternoon, the 18th inst., we left at 4 o'clock in the cars for Troy, where we arrived at 6. Mrs. Adams there left us, to take the cars the next morning for Boston, & we went on board *The Empire*, steamer, which immediately got underway for New York. Passed Albany at dusk—what a change since we passed it a week & a day before! Fire had swept a fair portion of it into nonexistence, & nothing but burning embers and blackened walls remained where on the preceding morning stood a goodly city!

At 9 we took our stateroom & there remained until 6 A.M. on Saturday the 19th when we hauled in at the pier in New York. Again took lodgings at the City Hotel, & remained there until Monday at 1 o'clock P.M. when we left for home. Stayed in Phila. at Jones's Hotel that night, & came to Washington the next day, where we arrived at ¼ past 7 P.M. finding everything right & in good order. . . .

1. J. W. Norton, after opposing a submarine telegraph line from New Jersey to Manhattan, financed a line crossing the Hudson River at Anthony's Nose, several miles above Peekskill, N.Y.

2. George H. Hart had been made a director of the Magnetic Telegraph Company in May 1846 and was elected treasurer in July of that year.

3. Roa Hook is located on the eastern shore of the Hudson River, just above Peekskill.

4. Mrs. James Adams, wife of the alderman from Ward 4, and French's neighbor.

5. Mexican War battles.

6. Thaddeus Kosciusko (1746–1817), the Polish patriot and soldier who served in the American Revolution.

Sunday, January 21. . . . I read the speech of Hon. J. R. Giddings, in the Ho. Reps. made the day previous, on the claim of Antonio Pacheco for payment for a slave hired by Major Dade as a guide to his command, and who escaped to, or was captured by, the enemy at the time Dade & his troops were defeated & killed by the Indians, during the Florida war.[1] When "Jumper,"[2] the Indian chief, came in & surrendered he brought in this slave with him, & Gen. Jesup,[3] deeming him a dangerous person, sent him west with the Indians. This act of Gen. Jesup was deemed to constitute a claim in favor of Pacheco against government for the value of this slave *as the property* of Pacheco. The point made by Mr. Giddings was that slaves were not property, and when the time shall come, as come it surely will, when slavery in this Union shall be spoken of as a thing *that was,* that argument of Joshua R. Giddings will be universally admitted to be an able and an unanswerable one in favor of the position assumed by him. However the "Chivalry of the South" may ridicule it *now,* they will, hereafter, *be glad* to refer to it and use it *in their own defence.* It is a great argument of a mind well informed on the subject upon which it treats. It is the argument of a high-minded[,] fearless *man,* who is ready, I know, to become a martyr in a righteous cause. No one has disagreed with Mr. Giddings farther, in some of his positions, than I have. But, I confess, while many of those with whom I have heretofore acted, have spoken & written of him as if he were a degraded human being, unfit to associate with their "high mightinesses," I have always viewed him as an honest man, devoted to what he believed to be right, who would not vary one iota from the path he had marked out for himself upon any terms which this world could offer. While, I presume, by most of my political friends he has been viewed with dislike, & by many with absolute hatred, I have seen him in an entirely different light. I have ever respected him as a man, & appreciated his talents, as far more than merely respectable. Now I view him as one of the great men of this Nation, and the time will come when others, who now differ with me, or *pretend to do so,* will be proud to come out & openly defend the opinions & sentiments of him whom they now so affect to despise.

So far as I am concerned I have nearly sacrificed myself in defending the South. I am now ready to let them sacrifice themselves, if they choose to do so, to their own folly. Mr. Giddings is right!

After reading his speech, I walked round to his boardinghouse, and had an hour's conversation with him, not only upon the subject of the speech, but upon slavery in general, and in this District in particular. I am ready to do all I can to aid in its abolition here. . . .

1. Joshua R. Giddings (1795–1864), Ohio abolitionist, was in turn a Whig, Free-Soil, and Republican congressman, 1838–1859. Maj. Francis L. Dade, with two companies of soldiers, was massacred by the Seminoles in an ambush while marching to reinforce Fort King in December 1835. The slave, Lewis, survived and remained among the Indians.

2. Jumper was a Seminole chief active in the Seminole Wars. He came into one of the military posts in Florida in the spring of 1837, accompanied by Lewis. Pacheco claimed his slave, but the military commander refused to deliver Lewis and ordered him sent west with the Indians. In 1848–1849 Pacheco was claiming compensation from Congress.

3. Thomas Sidney Jesup (1788–1860) was quartermaster general of the army, 1818–1860, but had a field command during the Second Seminole War.

Sunday, March 11. . . . On Thursday, Feby. 22d, I left Washington at 5 P.M. amid a snowstorm & went to Baltimore. Attended a Masonic Festival that evening at the Grand Lodge Room given by one of the Lodges. . . .

At 9 A.M. Friday, took the cars for Havre de Grace, where I arrived at 11. Mr. Morrow and I immediately commenced the labor of so arranging the Telegraph wires as to place them out of danger from the breaking up of the ice. We labored all that day. Mr. Griffin[1] arrived in the evening train from N. York with two miles of steel wire, & on Saturday we stretched it across the river,[2] working steadily all day. Sunday Mr. Morrow and I made all the necessary connexions, and I returned on Sunday evening to Baltimore. . . . I returned to Washington Monday evening [February 26]. During the week the City began to fill up, and on Monday last it was *full*. On some day of Week before last, Thursday I believe, the Mayor and Corporate Authorities visited President Polk & took leave of him. The Mayor addressed him in his usual happy manner, and Col. Polk replied with much feeling and eloquence. We then all shook hands with him and bade him an affectionate farewell. I really felt sad when I reflected that it was probably the last time I should ever see him. I bade Mrs. Polk good-by at the closing of the levee the evening previous. They both have my most sincere wishes that they may enjoy happiness unalloyed during the remainder of their lives.

On our return from the President's mansion we called on General Taylor at Willard's Hotel,[3] were all introduced, and shook the old General cordially by the hand. I saw him for the first time, & made up my mind at once that he was an honest-hearted, happy old man, who would, if he could, have his own way, do his duty faithfully and impartially. He will not, I fear, be permitted to have his own way, although I believe there is a streak of honest obstinacy about him that his advisers will find it hard to get around, or over.

. . . Monday last [March 5] was the great day here. Anyone who passed through our streets would have supposed that "all Creation" had made Washington their headquarters. The procession was formed, the Senate convened, the Inaugural was spoken, the snow fell in flakes at intervals during the day, and the clouds wept in abundance during the evening and night. Notwithstanding all this the three Balls went on, and were numerously attended, and in the course of Tuesday morning Washington went to bed, & quietness was within her borders. As for me, abhorring a crowd, I subscribed to the "No party ball" at Jackson Hall, & attended it. It was a brilliant, beautiful, & genteel Assembly, and I enjoyed it until 1 o'clock, when I came home and went to bed. . . .

1. Daniel Griffin of Georgia was the first president of the Washington and New Orleans Telegraph Co., 1848.
2. The Susquehanna.

3. Willard's Hotel, replacing the old City Hotel, was opened at the corner of Pennsylvania Avenue and 14th Street in 1847 by Edwin and Henry A. Willard.

Tuesday, September 11. Considerable of a *skip* since my last—six months exactly, equal to six years of olden time. . . .

In April I know I must have been in Philadelphia, for the Directors of the Magnetic Telegraph Co. met there on the 2d Thursday. On the 26th day of June I delivered a Masonic Address in Portland[,] Maine. On the 12th day of July I was reelected President of the Mag. Tel. Company. I have spent nearly half the time since April, out of this City. On the 31st day of July I started for the East, on a visit to my N. England friends. The next day Mrs. French, Frank & Ben followed & overtook me in Philadelphia. At 9 the next morning we left Phila. for N. York, Prof. Jewett, Lady & child accompanying us. At Princeton we overtook the 6 o'clock train which had met with a terrible accident. Two persons lay dead, one in the cars, the other at the roadside. Several of the cars were smashed, & many of the passengers were wounded, some very severely. The passengers in the train in which we came on walked by the broken train, & took the train from N.Y. which returned. We staid in N. York until Saturday & then proceeded to Boston. . . .

Tuesday, November 27. The members of the two Houses are fast coming in, and the city is filling up not only with members of Congress, but with the usual accompaniment of office seekers which attends the advent of a new Congress. How many must necessarily be disappointed! I am a candidate for the place from which two years ago I was ejected, because *I was a democrat,* and, much to my surprise, I find several of my democratic friends in the field against me. John W. Forney[1] of the *Pennsylvanian,* James C. Berritt,[2] late Chief Clerk in the Pension Office (which place he resigned)[,] are the most prominent of my opponents; indeed, in my belief, Forney is the only one who stands the least chance of being nominated over me, &, if nominated he cannot be elected! It is a free country, they say, & any man has a right to aspire to whatsoever office he may desire to obtain, but my notions of honor do not exactly square with the idea of placing myself *in the way* of any democrat who has been immolated on the political altar, when he is seeking a restoration of his rights! And the *Honorable* James Buchanan & the *Honorable* William R. King,[3] have taken the field against me, or rather, in favor of Forney. The time *may* come when I shall have a chance to give them a Roland for this Oliver,[4] & if it does, I will do it.

My chances for the nomination are deemed best, & I think I can lick Forney, if I try, even if he be nominated. . . .

1. John W. Forney (1817–1881) was the editor and proprietor of the Philadelphia *Pennsylvanian*. In 1854 he became a partner in the publication of the Washington *Daily Union*. He twice served as Clerk of the House, 1851–1856 and 1860–1861, and as secretary of the Senate, 1861–1868.

2. Probably James G. Berret, Democrat, elected mayor of Washington in 1858 and again in 1860. He was arrested and removed from office in 1861.

3. William R. D. King (1786–1853), Republican congressman from North Carolina, 1811–1816; Democratic senator from Alabama, 1819–1844 and 1848–1852; and Vice President for six weeks, 1853.

4. "A Roland for this Oliver," meaning blow for blow, comes from the legend of Roland, the leading peer of Charlemagne, who fought for five days with another peer, Oliver.

Tuesday, December 25. It is nearly one month since I wrote the foregoing, & no Clerk of the House of Representatives is yet elected. On Saturday evening, upon the sixty-third vote, and after 18 days labor, the House succeeded in electing a Speaker by a plurality vote—Mr. Cobb[1] of Georgia receiving two more votes than any other person. The manifestly unconstitutional proceeding of electing *by a plurality* was cured by passing a resolution, declaring Mr. Cobb elected, by a large majority.[2] Thus the House became organized, and immediately adjourned over until yesterday, when the President's message was recd. & read. The members drew for seats, & adjourned over until Thursday. It is not probable the Clerk and other officers will be elected before next week.

Mr. Forney was nominated by the Democratic Caucus over me for Clerk. Very well—let him get elected—if he can. I shall not be in his way, but, if he cannot be elected, I can. But, whether elected or not, I have learned what the sincerity of the Democratic party is! and, hereafter, shall govern myself accordingly. I am not to be *driven* from the Democratic ranks, but, if ever it happens to be in my power to pay up some of the old scores that are due to my *professed* Democratic *friends*, they shall be paid *with interest*! . . .

1. Howell Cobb (1815–1868), Democratic congressman from Georgia, 1843–1851 and 1855–1857; speaker, 1849–1851; and Secretary of the Treasury, 1857–1860.

2. A plurality resolution was adopted on December 22, the day of Cobb's election.

Sunday, December 30. The Russells & Ned & his wife dined with us on Christmas day, & considering how cold it was we managed to keep very comfortable and had a pleasant time. The Children enjoyed it very much. . . . At 4 o'clock P.M. [December 26] . . . the G. Lodge of Freemasons met at Masonic Hall, and at 5 proceeded to the Unitarian Church, where a very eloquent and appropriate address was delivered by Hon. Joseph R. Chandler,[1] P. G. Master of Pennsylvania. I was then installed as G. Master of the District by Hon. W. C. Dawson,[2] G. Master of the State of Georgia, & then proceeded to install the Grand officers of this Grand Lodge. The Choir performed its part of the duty most admirably, & the whole thing went off most satisfactorily to all. . . .

Yesterday afternoon Mrs. French, Frank, Ben & I went to see Bayne's panorama.[3] It is a superb affair. The illusion is so perfect that one cannot get rid of the idea that he is moving past the scenes upon the canvas & that they are real, instead of their moving past him, & being upon canvas. The paintings are exceedingly well done, and the exhibition is one of the most interesting I have ever witnessed. I almost believe that I really passed out of Boston Harbor in a steamboat, encountered a storm at sea, entered the river Mersey, passed the packet ship *Washington Irving,* went to Liverpool—then visited London, passed *under* many of the bridges across the Thames, saw the Lord Mayor's show, etc., on the river, then from a height, witnessed the whole scene at a single view—visited the Rhine & passed up & down, viewing its banks, covered with castles, towns, villages, & broken into mountains and valleys. . . .

Nothing further done as to election of the officers of the House of Representatives. I think they will not commence upon them until Thursday next, by which time the absent members will have returned. If all prophecy does not fail, I shall be elected Clerk, notwithstanding Mr. John W. Forney's attempt to push himself into it. Had he possessed one particle of honor, he never would, under the circumstances, have attempted to undermine my prospects of being restored to a position from which I was ejected because I was a democrat. Elected or not, I will pay him for this interference before I die, if my life is spared for any length of time.

1. Joseph R. Chandler (1792–1880), Whig congressman from Pennsylvania, 1849–1855, was later minister to the Kingdom of the Two Sicilies, 1858–1860.
2. William C. Dawson (1798–1856), Whig congressman from Georgia, 1836–1841, and senator, 1849–1855.
3. Walter M. Bayne (1795–1859) was an English landscape and panorama painter who exhibited his panorama of a voyage to Europe in a number of American cities between 1847 and 1856.

Monday, December 31. Farewell old year! I owe you far more of happiness than of misery, and not without a feeling of regret do I bid farewell *forever* to 1849. . . . The great public events are written down in ten thousand places, & the record can never be erased—but the private events! the events of the hearthstone, and beneath the rooftree—the song of marriage, and the dirge of death—the welcome of the newborn infant, and the last farewell to departed loved ones—the thousands and tens of thousands of little events of which the public know nothing, but which seem to those whom they immediately effect [sic] of more importance than the falling of all the thrones of earth—who can count them—who can appreciate their effect! . . .

Tuesday, January 1. Mrs. French & I have just returned from the President's, where we went at 12 o'clock with all the world of Washington to take Old Zachary by the hand. . . . Mr. Clay was there, and his movements carried with them a mass of the visitors—indeed it seemed to me as if he was "the observed of all observers" instead of the President. As his tall form passed along the East room, surrounded by a crowd who seemed eager to obtain some notice from him, I could not but think that, after all, he was the idol of the occasion. "Henry Clay" is a political war cry that will at any time and in any part of this Union create more sensation among men of all parties than any other name that can be uttered. Although he has never been able to obtain a majority of the electoral votes of this Union for the Presidency, I have no doubt that, perhaps with the exception of Andrew Jackson, he has been and is now the most popular man in this broad nation. He now stands, at the age of three score years & ten, the *beau ideal* of a patriot, a statesman, a great man! Opposed as I have ever been to him politically, I always liked the man. Bold and uncompromising in all his actions, fearless of consequences, he has always assumed to be a leader & always sustained himself well. I had rather be Henry Clay as he is, than to have been President of the United States! . . .

Sunday, January 6. . . . The House of Representatives tried twice to elect a Clerk and did not succeed. Mr. Forney came within two votes of an election, but I trust this is the nearest the House will ever come to committing Forneycation. Tomorrow they are to try again. Until Thursday evening I kept out of the field—determined, although I have been, as I conceive, very badly treated by my party, not to do a single act in opposition to the regularly nominated candidate. On that evening it came to my knowledge from a reliable source that there were *democrats* who were determined that I should never be Clerk of that House—that they were pledged to go against me to the "bitter end"—& rather to vote for whigs than for me! My Yankee blood was up at once, & I placed myself in the field, ready to take any chances that might come.

Sunday, March 3. On Friday, Jany. 11, the House of Representatives elected Mr. Campbell Clerk by one majority. It was effected by the desertion of Southern democrats from their own party. I was content, for, of all the miserable, mean, despicable and dishonorable efforts ever made to defeat a man no one ever exceeded those made by Col. John W. Forney & his coadjutors to defeat me. Lying was among the most worthy of their movements. If my life is spared I'll pay them up to the last political farthing. . . .

. . . On the 21st day of February I went to Richmond, as G. M. of Masons, to assist in laying the cornerstone of the Washington Monument in that City, on the 22d. I went down in Company with Gen. Taylor, President of the U.S.[,] & my position enabled me to see more of him than I ever had before. He is an honest, plain, unpretending old man, who, if left to his own course, would be as honest as it is possible for a man to be, but about as fit for President of these United States as any New England Farmer that one might select out of a thousand, with his eyes shut. I heard his speech at Aquia Creek; it was very commonplace. He made almost the same in the Ho. of Reps. at Richmond, and again at the laying of the cornerstone, and again at Fredericksburg on his return. I heard him only at the Creek & at the cornerstone, but judge of the others from the reports in the newspapers. At the cornerstone he made one addition which struck me as very happy, and, as I have not seen it in print I will record it as near as I can recollect it. He said[,] "Although a native of Virginia—of the Old Dominion—the Mother of States, I left her soil so young, & have been so much absent, that I cannot claim to be one of her citizens. I, however, return to her with pleasure— I come back, fellow citizens, as an affectionate son, after a long absence, returns to throw himself into the arms of his beloved mother." This was received with immense cheering. . . .

Sunday, December 21 [22]. Nine months and some odd days have elapsed since I wrote in this book, but my life has passed *right along*, just as fast as if I had written herein daily.[1] Up to July 11th I went on taking care of the interests of the Magnetic Telegraph Company as its President, slaving myself in its interests and doing all I could to make it profitable and respectable, as a reward for all which the Stockholders refused to reelect me at the annual meeting in July. I never had anything which cut me to the very quick as that refusal of those who placed me in that office did! I was deserted by those I deemed my friends, men whom I would have gone any length to serve. They did it, however, under a sort of duress, & I think it very likely they will repent what they did, if they have not already. I have *freed* my mind about the manner in which I was treated, to Messrs. Morse, Geo. Vail,[2] Kendall & others, & will *free it* no farther here. . . .

After my dismissal from the Presidency of the Telegraph Company I made up my mind to be independent until October, and so moved all the matters & things appertaining to my office at the Telegraph Office, to my house, and enjoyed the *otium cum dignitate* of life until August when I left for New England. . . .

Soon after my return I opened an office down in the City, as an agent, etc., and since (on the 19th of November) Col. H. H. Sylvester has joined me. *Ecce signum*.[3] So now I am fairly launched into business on my own account. Would to heaven it might give me enough to do, so that I may never again be dependent on office. We have plenty of business, but it is of that sort which only pays *if we are successful*. We have not taken a hundred dollars in cash since we commenced. But we mean to test it thoroughly.

Jenny Lind[4] came here last Sunday evening, and left on Thursday morning. She gave concerts on Monday & Wednesday evenings, the latter of which Mrs. French and I attended. We were delighted of course. . . .

1. During this interval, on July 9, President Zachary Taylor died suddenly and was replaced by Millard Fillmore.

2. George Vail was a silent partner (through his younger brother Alfred) in the implementation of Samuel F. B. Morse's invention of the telegraph.

3. French inserted in his journal at this point two announcements carried in Washington newspapers. One of these indicated that French and Sylvester would attend to the "purchase and sale of stocks and real estate, claims before Congress; claims for pensions, patents, and bounty lands, and all other transactions where an agent or attorney is necessary in the city of Washington. . . ."

4. Jenny Lind (1820–1887), Swedish soprano (the "Swedish Nightingale"), was brought to America by P. T. Barnum, 1850–1852, after great successes in Europe.

Saturday, January 4. . . . At 12 noon Mrs. French, Frank and I went to the President's, where, after squeezing through as dense a crowd—no, not *squeezing through*—but going along with, as dense a crowd as it has been my fortune to get into for many a day, we at length had the pleasure of reaching *the presence,* and shaking by the hand our excellent Chief Magistrate, Mr. Fillmore, & paying our respects to the Presidentess & her daughter.[1] We passed on to the East Room, which I have never seen so sparsely *inhabited* on a new year's day. After staying half an hour, I left Mrs. F. & Frank, and took to my feet, for a grand round of visits. I went first to Mr. Secretary Corwin's,[2] thence to Mr. Wm. R. King's, thence to Col. Seaton's, thence to Mr. Webster's, who greeted me with the familiar, & flattering salutation[,] "How are you countryman?"—alluding to our being natives of the same State. . . .

1. Abigail Powers Fillmore and her daughter, Mary Abigail.

2. Thomas Corwin (1794–1865), Ohio Whig who served as a congressman, 1831–1840 and 1859–1861; senator, 1845–1850; and Secretary of the Treasury, 1850–1853.

Wednesday, January 16 [15]. On Tuesday the 7th inst. at 5 o'clock P.M. I left this city (Washington) for N. York. . . .

. . . [On the 10th] invited Mr. Norton to dine with me at the Astor. After dinner went to his "Telegraphic Rooms" & there met Miss Julia Turnbull[1] (the danseuse) & her niece, who were there to invite N. to spend the evening with them. He introduced Miss T. to me and I was very much pleased with the modesty & unassuming deportment that she exhibited. She is, as a dancer, what Jenny Lind is as a singer, of irreproachable character, and an ornament to her sex. Her niece is a mere girl, & was on a visit to her aunt from a nunnery in the vicinity, at which she was at school.

In the evening Norton and I attended the Astor Place Opera & heard Parodi,[2] the far-famed & accomplished singer. The opera was "Giovanna di Napoli."

I do not pretend to be a judge of opera, but was tolerably well pleased with the performance. Parodi was admirable as an actress, & if I had not heard Jenny Lind I suppose I should have been satisfied with her singing, but according to my judgment she does not come within "a long shot" of my favorite Jenny. Beneventano[3] was very good, but he amused me very much, in the midst of a beautiful solo, by turning his head one side & spitting upon the stage! "Well[,]," exclaimed Norton[,] "that's cool," which, with the action, set me off in a laughing fit that I like not to have got over during the evening. . . . Came home Sunday morning.

I never was more completely disgusted in my life than at the mean, miserable picayune action of our Board of Directors. I think God never made two meaner men than Merrit Canby[4] & R. M. Hoe;[5] I hold them both in the most utter contempt—the 1st because he is mean & cowardly, inasmuch as he fears to record his avowed opinions on the record—the other because he is simply mean-spirited, & has treated me in a manner that must ever render him, in my estimation, a man unworthy of my confidence or respect, & one whom, if ever Providence places it in my power, I shall not fail to pay back with interest the injuries he has heaped upon me.

No dividend yet!! Our new President is *a manager* so far as spending goes, for the income of the Company was never larger than during the 3 past months. But he is *repairing* the line! Well, he can do what best pleases him. Had I done it I should have been crucified at once. But, after all, I like Swain,[6] for he is a free-hearted[,] open & aboveboard man, & I like Abell too—*very much,* for, if I do not much mistake him, "in his heart there is no guile."[7] Sailer[8] & Clark[9] are mere cyphers. Mr. Kendall is the great gun of the Board, & can do pretty much what he pleases. I think he did not treat me as he ought, in voting against me, but I never shall lay that up against him. He has had trouble enough with his Telegraph connexions to vex a Saint, & I can hardly blame him for being out of sorts at times. I wish him well with all my heart. . . .

1. Julia Turnbull (1822–1857), Canadian-born American ballerina, had only recently taken on acting roles.
2. Teresa Parodi (b. 1827), Italian dramatic soprano, was brought to the United States by the impresario Max Maretzek (1821–1897) as a rival to Jenny Lind. She made her debut in 1850 at the Astor Place Opera House.
3. F. Beneventano, also active in New York operatic circles, was said to have been "rough in method" but to have had a voice of "magnificent natural quality."
4. Merrit Canby (1783–1866), a businessman and financier of Wilmington, Del., had invested $200 in the Magnetic Telegraph Co. in 1846. He had been in the sugar refining business in Philadelphia from 1815 to 1836.
5. Richard M. Hoe (1812–1886), inventor and manufacturer of printing presses, was an early stockholder in the Magnetic Telegraph Company and became one of its directors.
6. William M. Swain, proprietor of the Philadelphia *Public Ledger,* early saw the advantages of the telegraph for news. He became the president of the Magnetic Telegraph Company in 1850, replacing French.
7. Arunah S. Abell (1806–1888), publisher of the *Baltimore Sun,* was a pioneer in speedy news service, using Morse's telegraph. The quotation is adapted from John 1:47.
8. Joseph Sailer (1809–1883) was for many years the financial editor of the Philadelphia *Public Ledger* and one of the country's leading financial authorities. He was for several years secretary of the Magnetic Telegraph Company.
9. Thomas M. Clark, like Sailer, was an early secretary of the Magnetic Telegraph Company. He also functioned as a superintendent of the line between Philadelphia and New York City.

Sunday, March 9. I labored like an ox from the time I wrote herein last until the 3d of March, in attending to business before Congress as an agent & attorney.[1] . . .

My old friend, Hon. Isaac Hill[,] is now very sick, at Mrs. Durham's in Green's row (Carroll Place), & it is doubtful whether he will recover.

1. Among other things, French's business affairs involved two steamship lines, French spoliations, a Mexican indemnity case, revision of patent laws, Canadian reciprocity, and a number of private claims before Congress. He earned about $400 for the firm, January 16 to March 3.

Sunday, April 6. Gov. Hill died at Mrs. Durham's on Saturday, March 22d, at 4¼ o'clock P.M. I wrote an obituary of him for the *Union* of the succeeding Tuesday. Hon. Samuel Green,[1] formerly a Judge of the Superior Court of New Hampshire, died in this City on the same day that Gov. Hill died. Judge G. had been a Clerk here for 12 years, having left the Bench in N. Hamp. at the age of 70. He was between 82 & 83 when he died. . . .

Attended church this morning—Rev. E. E. Hale[2] preached—sermon very good, but nothing extra. . . .

1. Samuel Green (1770–1851) had been a lawyer in Concord, N.H., and a judge of the state's Superior Court, 1819–1840. He came to Washington in 1841.

2. Edward Everett Hale (1822–1909), at this time minister of the Unitarian Church in Worcester, Mass. He later wrote "The Man Without a Country" and was chaplain of the Senate, 1903–1909.

Sunday, June 1. . . . Last Thursday, by invitation of Mr. John Pettibone,[1] a small party, of which I was one, made an excursion up to Little Falls in the little canal steamer *Roselia*—she being a new invention, and it being her first trip up this canal, by way of experiment. Her propelling power is a *scull,* & her motion is precisely that of a boat sculled by hand. She went along beautifully, & with very little wash to the canal banks, perhaps no more than that of a boat propelled at the same rate by horses towing it from the bank. She made at least 5 miles per hour. . . .

1. John Pettibone, a lumber merchant, lived on 14th Street between B and C streets.

Sunday, June 22. . . . On Thursday Capt. Easby, Commr. of Public Buildings, informed me that the cornerstone of the Capitol would be laid on the 4th proximo with masonic honors, and saying to me that I might as well be preparing. Knowing that the Capt. was a true Mason & desired what he said was to be, I asked him if he had the President's directions. He replied in the negative, but said he should get them—that he had no doubt on the subject, etc. I told him I was not quite so sure, having heard that Fillmore was rather inclined to anti-masonry, and knowing him to be from the hotbed of that miserable disease. Yesterday the Capt. came & told me that the cornerstone could not be laid with Masonic honors, that the President would not consent—that he said if he invited the Masons he must invite the Odd Fellows!!, etc. In fact[,] trumping up excuses to screen his anti-masonry behind. I was not disappointed, because I believed whiggery in the shape of Millard Fillmore was *little* enough to sneak behind anything for an excuse. But when the Freemasons of the United States take into consideration that the Cornerstone of the present Capitol was laid by George Washington, *as a Freemason,* and as President of the U.S.[,] they will not be likely to overlook the insult of being *deprived* of even assisting in the ceremonies, and when the Odd Fellows ascertain *the reason given,* they will not be likely to consider it very flattering to their order, I think! But let him work it out. I shall not be there, if I cannot be there in my appropriate place of G. Master, unless I am compelled to attend as President of the Board of Aldermen. . . .

Sunday, July 20. In my summer House, in the Garden.

I must first *explain*. As mentioned in my last journalization, all thought of laying the cornerstone of the extension of the Capitol with Masonic honors was given up until Monday, July 1st[,] when Mr. Wallach,[1] the Marshal of the District, sent for me and informed me that the President had directed that the Masonic Fraternity should be invited to assist in the ceremonies.

After considerable conversation and explanation I agreed to make the necessary arrangements and proceeded, accordingly, to invite the Gr. Lodges of Va.[,] Md. & Pa. & our brethren of Alexandria. The best arrangements possible, in the time given, were made, & on the 4th nearly 200 Freemasons were in the procession and everything passed off satisfactorily to all. I delivered an address which was well recd. considering that it preceded Mr. Webster. All the proceedings of that day are published, and I intend to paste a copy into my scrapbook for future reference. They may be published in pamphlet form by the Govt. as they should be. It is a little curious to observe that the President had once decided that there should be no masonic ceremonies, & then reversed that decision. I am inclined to think the "power behind the throne, greater than the throne itself," was, in this instance, the reflection that there were quite a large number of Freemasons in these United States, & among them some of the first and most influential men of this Union! I may be wrong, & I have the kindest feelings & the highest regards for President Fillmore. I believe him to be an honest, upright, well-meaning man.

On the 24th of June according to previous arrangements, some 300 persons—Freemasons & their families—went on board the Boat *Thos. Colyer* to Mount Vernon, where I delivered an address standing at the Tomb of Washington. . . .

On the 10th day of this month, "The Magnetic Telegraph Company" held its annual meeting in Baltimore. I left Washington at 6 o'clock A.M. The Directors met at 10 at Barnum's hotel, and after the adjournment of the Board the stockholders held their meeting. Our meetings are not very pleasant. There has been a feeling of jealousy existing ever since the first organization of the Company, between the managers at Phila. & those of N. York & Washington, which always shows itself at our meetings. At the last meeting, by a Union of the Washington stock, we elected

Wm. Selden[2] of this City[,] Treasurer, thus removing the Treasury of the Company from Phila. to Washington. This act created quite a tempest, and an effort was made, by one of the Directors of last year, Mr. Sailer, to defeat me as a Director. He did not, however[,] succeed, and I had the honor of defeating him! Considering the position he has always assumed towards me, and the bitter feeling he has often exhibited, I confess I gloried in his defeat. . . .

1. Richard Wallach had been appointed marshal of the District of Columbia by Zachary Taylor in 1849. He served until 1853 and was later elected mayor, serving from 1861 to 1868.

2. William W. Selden, prior to this time, had been the Treasurer of the United States for eleven years. At this time he was head of the banking firm of Selden, Withers and Co. He was later marshal of the District of Columbia, 1858–1861.

Friday, July 25. Wife, Ben & I went to Nottingham, Maryland, yesterday & returned today.

Isaac[1] says the horse is sick, so I will go & see what I think of him & write about our journey at some other time.

1. A servant in the French household.

Sunday, July 27. The horse was only tired & heated. On the 24th I drove him to Mr. Carroll's near Nottingham,[1] 25 miles, resting several times, and the next day back, in 4 hours, thermometer about 90. We were in a buggy & in reasonable weather it would have been nothing, as it was we were all pretty well tired out. . . .

. . . At Mr. Carroll's we were received with a hospitality that could not be surpassed & enjoyed every luxury that his mansion could afford. He and his good lady are as kindhearted and hospitable people as I have ever met, and I want to repay them for their kind attention to us, if possible, at my own house. Mr. C. has a magnificent farm of 430 acres. His house stands on an eminence, & is surrounded by forest trees & handsome lawns. It is a lovely location. He raised 1,600 bushels of wheat this year—his usual crop of tobacco is between two & three hundred hogsheads—his lands are well cultivated, & *abundance* of almost everything is there to be found. I almost envied him his situation. He has 50 slaves, all appear happy & contented, & while all were *well* clad, those about the house were dressed better than N.H. Farmers' wives & daughters are ordinarily dressed. Mr. Carroll informed Mrs. French how one of his slaves died last Spring, in consequence of an injury from the kick of a horse, and he could hardly tell it without shedding tears. What Northern fanatic shall have the impudence to say that those 50 negroes are not, by far, better off than if they were free! Freedom to them would be ruin, & I presume no one could give them more distress than to go and announce to them that they were free.[2] . . .

Indeed the old Testament abounds with evidence of the *ownership of men by men*, and Jeremiah says, by way of simile[,] "Is Israel a servant? *Is he a home born slave?*" Jer. 2.14. Showing most certainly that there were in the days of Jeremiah "home born slaves." The Decalogue, itself written with the finger of God on Mount Sinai, contains the words "man servant" & "maid servant," and there cannot be a doubt that, from the day when Cain went out from Adam, down to this, *servitude* has existed, & has been sanctioned by the Almighty! But our new light fanatics, for the want of something better to do, have set themselves out *to repeal the laws of God*, & make what they in their vainglorious selfishness believe to be better ones! Alas poor human nature, how frail, how shortsighted thou art, especially when wrapped in the cloak of the fanatic!

1. Michael B. Carroll (1801–1851) owned several large tracts of land in southeastern Prince George's County, Md. The plantation visited by French probably was Brookefield, known today as Brookefield at Naylor. Nottingham was a small port on the Patuxent River.
2. At this point in his account of the visit to Michael Carroll's farm, French pasted a newspaper clipping in his journal. It contained antislavery resolutions adopted by the Hillsborough, N.H., Conference of Congregational Churches. French declared the resolutions to be "impudent & uncalled for" and felt that they denounced "in spirit, the Holy Word of God."

Thursday, September 4. . . . My last record of July 27th gives an account of our visit to Mr. Carroll's down in Maryland. Little did I think when I made that record that, before I should write in this book again, I should be called upon to perform the Masonic burial service at his grave! But so it is. Michael B. Carroll now sleeps in the dust, and the places that knew him shall know him no more forever. He died suddenly, of apoplexy, on Saturday afternoon last, at 5 o'clock. We were notified of his death on Sunday, & at 3 o'clock Monday Morning ten of us (Masons) started for his residence, where we arrived at 8. All the arrangements were made, and at 3 P.M. we laid his mortal remains in their final resting place on earth, with all the honors men can bestow & with hearts bowed down with grief.[1] . . .

1. French wrote an obituary notice of Carroll's death for the *Intelligencer*. Pasted in his journal, it dwells on the esteem in which Carroll was held by his slaves and touches on the "false and foolish sympathy of Northern fanaticism" where slavery is concerned.

Sunday, September 28. . . . *Friday* [September 26].[1] At my office & about the City all the morning. Recd. a letter from John Gedge, Esq.,[2] G. M.

of La.[,] asking me to exert my influence to get the son of a Bro. Mason pardoned. He is between 16 & 17, & ran away to join the Cuban invaders & is now a prisoner at Havana, or on his way to Spain as a convict. Wrote a letter to President Fillmore asking advice. Dined at 3 P.M. & immediately afterwards started in my buggy with Mr. White for Marlborough to shoot ortolan.[3] Arrived at M. at 6. Carried White down two miles & left him to make arrangements for the morning. Returned to Marlborough and at 8 o'clock went to bed. Arose at 5 o'clock, breakfasted & rode down to the river[4] (3 miles)[,] found White & the boat ready & we got on to the marsh just as the sun was rising. We had elegant shooting for about 4 hours—got 75 birds, & killed at least 20 that we did not get. We had 4 down at a time often, & in consequence of the thick grass could not find more than one or two of them, the living ones being so thick we would not stop to hunt for the dead ones. I did all the shooting & missed only five or six times, in killing the 95. Killed each one single— of course.

My gun got so dirty after killing 60 that I had to stop and wash it. Otherwise I should have shot 20 more at least, as it took from 20 to 30 minutes of the best shooting time to wash & dry the gun. We went to the house of White's brother-in-law[,] a Mr. Smith, about noon, got some dinner, and then crossed slowly over in a boat & walked up to Marlborough. At 3 P.M. we started for home & arrived at 6 P.M. pretty well tired out. . . .

1. Retrospective.
2. John Gedge had been elected grand master of the reorganized Grand Lodge of Louisiana in 1851, thereby uniting two rival groups.
3. I.e., bobolink.
4. The Patuxent River.

Sunday, November 23. . . . I am now a candidate for Secretary of the U.S. Senate and of course I have many friends laboring for my success, and they are more sanguine than I am that I am to succeed. I begin to believe *something* in destiny—at all events, I believe that an overruling Providence "shapes our ends, rough hew them how we will," & if it is His will that I shall be Secy. of the Senate, I shall be—if not, *not!* Time will show. . . .

Thursday, December 25. Something over one month has passed since my last record. Of my own individual life I can recall nothing of moment. I have been out of the City but once, & then to attend a meeting of the Stockholders & Directors of The Magnetic Telegraph Company, especially called at Baltimore, on Wednesday last. We had a pleasant meeting and arranged all our difficulties with the Bain Line, or rather North American Company, by buying them out.[1] Now, I suppose, we may calculate upon our Telegraph Stock, between this City and New York, being as good as any stock in this Union. . . .

. . . During the night the Franklin Hotel, corner of 8th & B streets, was burned, and, just as I had finished my breakfast in the morning [December 24], Frank came in [and] told me he believed the Capitol was on fire. I hurried over & ran up the Eastern steps, and found the Congressional Library in flames. It was about 5 minutes past 8 when I got there. There were perhaps 20 persons in the rotundo & the passage. Gen. Cass came up to me and said that he thought the whole Capitol would be burned, & advised me to telegraph to Baltimore & Alexandria. I sent a man down in haste to do so, & seeing the great want of water ran down and assisted in getting the sucking nose of two suctions into the fountain, but neither would suck, one being frozen up and the hose of the other not being tight. After trying for some time, I ran back to the Capitol & down the steps of the western front where, with the aid of others, I succeeded in forming a line from the fountain up the steps & aided for some time in passing up water. I then returned to the Rotundo & assisted in getting the Columbia Engine (I think it was) into the Rotundo, & by that time the *Perseverance* was working at the eastern fountain, & forcing a stream into the engine in the rotundo. Soon after the Anacostia got to work, then the Union came (for which I sent a special messenger). A hose was passed up through the passages onto the roof of the South wing, & I went up & assisted there a while, then down and up on the North wing where it was said there was danger, and finding it so, I ran down & aided in getting a line of men to pass up buckets of water. Then I went down and assisted in getting a hose up on that side, & so I worked on, sometimes in one place, sometimes in another, till the fire was completely subdued.

I came home pretty much exhausted, about 11 o'clock, & changed my wet clothing for dry, and then went down in the city and did some business, & then bought the Christmas toys for the children, & came home. About sunset I walked over to Mr. Meehan's[2] to have a talk with him about the supposed origin of the fire, etc. He was still at the Capitol, but Wharton[3] was at home, & we talked the matter all over. He assured me that there had not been a spark of fire in the Library, as anyone knew of, for several years. A candle or lighted segar was never allowed there. The Library was closed, as usual, at about ½ past 4 on Tuesday, the doors locked, and when the fire was discovered from without, the doors were burst open by the Capitol Police. The Police were never allowed to have the keys, & had no means of getting in except by breaking in. When they first entered the fire appeared to be in the North East part of the room, & as one of the chimnies from the committee rooms passed up on that side of the Library, we concluded the fire must have caught from a defect in that chimney.

This morning I went over with the determination to satisfy myself. The chimney alluded to passed up directly back of the place where the fire was seen first. It is now perforated by several holes for the ends of joists, and into one of those holes a person, in my presence, introduced a piece of iron, as he said, quite *into the flue of the chimney!* He went up on a ladder to reach it. As there seems to be no other possible manner of accounting for the fire, I conclude that it must have caught from that flue. I *know* that enormous wood fires are kept in the Committee rooms, particularly in such intensely cold weather as we have recently had. I know also that there are not many chimnies in the Capitol that have not, at some time been burnt out, & I also know from my own experience while there, that those chimnies are more or less burst whenever they take fire. One of the chimnies in the office of the House of Representatives was so injured while I was there, that a portion of it had to be taken down and rebuilt with brick. They are generally, if not all, of stone. My theory is, that a flue of the chimney passing up on the side of the Library, had been on fire, or partially so, on Tuesday or some previous day, that the flame in seeking vent, had pressed out sufficiently to ignite the end of a joist, which may have been seasoning & charring for years— that the fire worked slowly back upon the joist until it burnt outside of the wall & into the library. The moment that was done there was, of course, a draft from the library into the flue, which enlivened the fire sufficiently to ignite any combustible matter near it, & thus the fire took. Until some more plausible manner of accounting for its origin comes to my knowledge I shall account for it in that way.

Mr. Meehan told me that about 25,000 volumes were destroyed. The library consisted of 52,000 volumes, including the Law Library, which was in a different part of the Capitol. One large room, attached to the main Library, containing all the books on Politics & Religion, was untouched by the fire. The books were moved out, but were not injured. There are also a large number distributed in the Committee Rooms for lack of room in the library, so that there is now quite a respectable library left. . . .

1. The Bain Line was a telegraph line from Washington to New York built by the North American Telegraph Company in 1848 using the patents of Alexander Bain. After Samuel F. B. Morse won an infringement suit against Bain, the line was incorporated into the Magnetic Telegraph Company.

2. John Silva Meehan (1790–1863), fourth Librarian of Congress, 1829–1861, served under ten presidents.

3. C. H. Wharton Meehan (d. 1872) was employed under his father in the Library of Congress. He eventually became custodian of the Law Library. Authorship of *The Law and Practice of the Game of Euchre* (Philadelphia, 1862) has been attributed to him.

Thursday, January 1. My theory of the cause of the fire at the Capitol turned out, upon thorough examination, to be true. The fire did not commence at the exact point I supposed, but in the same flue at a point lower down which, when I was present, was covered with cinders. The end of one of the timbers was actually found by the sweep inside of the chimney in a burned state! No public building should be erected in these enlightened days which is not made fireproof.

The only important event that has transpired since I last wrote, in this city, was the arrival of Louis Kossuth,[1] late Governor of Hungary, at eleven o'clock A.M. on Tuesday last[,] the 30th inst. [ultimo]. No previous arrangement had been made to give him a public reception. Still, the street was crowded with people as he came from the Depot to Brown's hotel, where lodgings were prepared for him. As one of the Committee of the Jackson Democratic Association, I was at Brown's when he arrived, and as soon as we conveniently could, after his arrival, the committee waited on him and delivered the address of the Association. He replied very handsomely and appropriately. He certainly is a most remarkable man. . . .

I went to my office at ½ past 9 this morning, wrote some letters, went into Brown's & The National, Hotels, & looked about to see who was to be seen. Returned to the office. At 12 noon, Thomas came down with the carriage, & I took Maj. Weightman, Del. from New Mexico, & Phil. Barton Key in with me, and we rode out to Judge Douglas's.[2] Paid our New Year's respects to Judge & Mrs. D.[3] . . .

1. Louis Kossuth (1802–1894), leader of the Hungarian insurrection of 1848–1849, fled into exile and visited the United States, 1851–1852.

2. Richard H. Weightman (1816–1861), first delegate to Congress from the Territory of New Mexico. He was killed fighting for the Confederacy in the Battle of Wilson Creek, Mo., in 1861. Philip Barton Key (1818–1859), a Washington lawyer and the son of Francis Scott Key. He was district attorney of the District of Columbia, 1853–1859. Stephen A. Douglas (1813–1861), Democrat of Illinois, served as congressman, 1843–1847, and senator, 1847–1861.

3. Martha Martin Douglas (d. 1853) married Stephen A. Douglas in 1847.

Saturday, January 10. Last Monday I was in the Senate of the U.S. when Kossuth was introduced. The Senate Chamber, galleries & lobbies were crowded with people. The galleries were exclusively devoted to the Ladies & presented as brilliant a galaxy of beauty as the eyes of man would ever desire to look upon. The area back of the Senators presented the same aspect, & among those was Madame Kossuth, who stood in a position where I had a full and fair view of her features. I never saw her at any other time. She is by no means handsome. Kossuth came in, attended by the Committee at 1 o'clock, & was introduced by Gen. Shields.[1] The Prest. p. t.[,] Mr. King, welcomed him & invited him to a seat, which he took, & the Senate adjourned. . . .

Wednesday [January 7]. At one o'clock Kossuth was introduced into the House of Representatives very much as he was into the Senate, excepting that he made a short speech. There was an immense crowd present, as at the Senate. I was present & liked the way it was done much better than at the Senate.

Thursday 8th. Board of Directors of Mag. Tel. Co. met at my office at 10 A.M. Did up all our business by ½ past 3. I dined with Mr. Swain at the National, & soon after went to Jackson Hall to attend the Dinner. It was crammed with Ladies & Gentlemen, & at ½ past 7 between 5 and 6 hundred sat down to as magnificent a Banquet as ever need be provided. Kossuth was there, & on being toasted rose & responded eloquently in a speech about ¾ of an hour in length. It was a most happy & beautiful speech. The Company was addressed by Messrs. Cass, Douglas, Lane, Dodge, Maj. Stevens of the Army & others & at 12 o'clock we broke up after a celebration that would have made the shade of Old Hickory rejoice, if shades ever do so.[2] I almost split my lungs reading the toasts. . . .

Came home & dined. After dinner a Miss Minor[3] & a Miss Inman, from Providence, R.I., called & informed me they had come here to teach negro schools for girls. Miss Minor had commenced & was getting along well, & Miss Inman had gone into a white school until scholars enough should attend to require the services of both. They called on me by advice of the Mayor, because I am President of the Board of Aldermen. The why and wherefore did not seem to be very apparent, as no one has yet made any opposition to their teaching, & I hope and trust will not. They are engaged in a good cause, & I say God speed them. They appeared to be sensible, ladylike, well informed girls, & I was much pleased with my interview with them, though I must say I do not admire their taste in the selection of an occupation! They think, doubtless, as Kossuth does, that it is their calling, their destiny (if there is such a thing as destiny)[,] & I surely would not attempt to dissuade them from it. . . .

1. James Shields (1810–1879), Democratic senator from Illinois, 1849–1855; later senator from Minnesota, 1858–1859, and from Missouri, 1879. He had been brevetted major general for gallantry in action in the Mexican War.

2. Joseph Lane (1801–1881), Democrat of Oregon, was territorial delegate to Congress, 1851–1859; senator, 1859–1861; and vice presidential candidate with John C. Breckinridge in 1860. Isaac I. Stevens (1818–1862) had been on Gen. Winfield Scott's staff in Mexico. He later commanded an exploration party seeking a railway route to the Pacific and was delegate to Congress from the Territory of Washington, 1857–1861. He was killed in battle at Chantilly, Va., in 1862.

3. Myrtilla Miner (1815–1864) founded a school for training free black girls in Washington, 1851.

Sunday, January 2. . . . From early last Spring up to the 1st Monday in November last, the public pulse was feverish in relation to the election of President and Vice President of the U.S. All sorts of speculation was afloat as to who should be the nominees of the two parties. I corresponded with my Friend Gen. Pierce on the subject of his nomination & in consequence of his letters, recd. in April, I used all the efforts I could, honorably, to cause his name to be taken in the event of a failure to nominate one of the prominent candidates. I was first for Lewis Cass, after him, for Frank Pierce. My whole soul was in the matter, and I labored with all my energies both here & at Baltimore, and my efforts were crowned with success. What I did to secure the nomination of Pierce I have written at length in a letter to Hon. F. O. J. Smith, which I asked him to preserve.

As soon as Pierce was nominated I came home and devoted the entire time up to the day of election to his election, & perhaps no one man in all this Union rejoiced more sincerely over his triumphant election than I did.

During the past year I have scarcely been out of this City, except to attend to the business of the Telegraph Company. In April I attended our meeting in Baltimore, in July in Phila. and in October in New York. I was also in New York in August, on business of the W. & New Orleans Telegraph Company, & I was in Baltimore a week in June attending the National Convention. . . .

Gas was brought into our House Dec. 2d, 1852, & lighted for the first time.

Friday, January 7. . . . Arose at a little before 8 this morning, and on opening the *Intelligencer* read the account of the accident that had befallen my friend Gen. Pierce, President-elect, by which his only son (Benny)[1] was killed. It went to my very heart, & I have thought of nothing else all day. How utterly insignificant to that noble, warmhearted, affectionate man, must, at this moment, appear the Presidency, to which he has been elected! a mere bauble, ten thousand of which he would give to restore the breath of life to his dead boy. Oh God, be merciful to the bereaved mother, whose heart must be well nigh broken by the sad bereavement. They have all the sympathies of my nature, but human sympathy will avail them nothing. If it would, that of a whole Nation is theirs. "He who tempereth the wind to the shorn lamb," can alone heal up their torn hearts.

I have written a brief note to Gen. Pierce today expressive of my feelings—it seemed a duty that I could not resist. I have felt all day as if some great calamity had befallen me. . . .

1. Benjamin Pierce (1841–1853), the only remaining child of Franklin and Jane Pierce, was killed in their presence in a train accident on January 6, 1853. As a result, the Pierces entered the White House in a state of nervous and mental exhaustion.

Sunday, January 16. . . . The 8th was a splendid day, the weather as warm as summer, the sky unclouded, and the air hushed & still. At 10 A.M. the troops and the citizens began to assemble in front of the City Hall preparatory to the interesting services attending the inauguration of the Equestrian Statue of Andrew Jackson. By eleven the space in front of the Hall and the streets leading therefrom were filled. At about 12 the procession moved, and arrived at Lafayette Square before 1. The ceremonies there were according to the programme which I preserve here.[1]

There were at least 20,000 people present at the ceremonies at the Square, and I should think as many more on the pavements, at the windows and on the housetops along the Avenue. It was a most beautiful sight, and everything went off admirably. . . .

. . . The statue is magnificent and meets the approbation of everybody I believe. It will immortalize Clark Mills.[2]

After the Oration by Judge Douglas, I led Mr. Mills forward and introduced him to the immense audience and he was received with that enthusiastic and soul-stirring applause which he so richly merited, by three times three heartfelt cheers. He then waved his hand & the statue was unveiled, when the cheering and clapping of hands gave evidence of the pleasure of all who gazed upon it.

In the evening there was a banquet at Jackson Hall, got up by The Democratic Association, which was very thinly attended. The tables were spread for 500 & scarcely a hundred and fifty were present. Considering *the manner* in which it was started, and *the purpose* for which it was got up, I did not greatly regret that it turned out to be a failure. I was present, and saw all the flummery of a cane presentation to Mr. Jonah D. Hoover,[3] of whom some interested individuals are endeavouring to make a very great man. They cannot do it for the reason that "you cannot make a silk purse of a sow's ear"—the raw material is not right! . . .

Wednesday [January 12], passed the day at my office and the Capitol, and in the evening attended a meeting of the Encampment of Knights Templars, and conferred the orders on Albert Pike, Esq.,[4] of Arkansas. He is a scholar and a poet. Was an officer in the Mexican War and a man whom I am disposed to hold in high estimation. . . .

1. The program, affixed to two pages of French's journal, lists B. B. French, John C. Rives, and John W. Maury as the Committee of Arrangements. Stephen A. Douglas was the principal orator.
2. Clark Mills (1810–1883) introduced bronze casting to the United States with this statue. He later made the bronze casting for Thomas Crawford's "Freedom" surmounting the Capitol dome.
3. Jonah D. Hoover, a wealthy Washington shoe merchant. He was marshal of the District of Columbia, 1853–1858.
4. Albert Pike (1809–1891), prominent lawyer and a leading Freemason. He took part in the Mexican War and commanded Indian troops for the Confederacy.

Sunday, February 6. . . . Thursday evening, Washington Encampment met and we conferred the orders of Knighthood on Gen. Sam Houston.[1] We had a full encampment, and everything went off admirably. After we had closed, about 20 of us went to the Columbian and partook of an oyster supper which had been prepared for us, and we separated at about 10 o'clock well pleased with *ourselves* and all the world. . . .

Friday the 4th was Benny's birthday—8 years old. At his own particular request I bought him a fiddle for a birthday present. . . .

1. Samuel Houston (1793–1863), Democratic congressman from Tennessee, 1823–1827; governor of Tennessee, 1827–1829; president of the Republic of Texas, 1836–1838 and 1841–1844; senator from Texas, 1846–1859; and governor, 1859–1861.

FIVE

Changing Parties

1853–1857

s the American political party system fell apart in the 1850s, French made the transition from Democrat to Republican. He had started to edge away in the early 1840s, when his conservative views enabled him to hold his job in the Clerk's office even after the Whigs took over the White House. When the Democrats returned to power in 1845, French was elected Clerk of the House, but Whigs and Southern Democrats forced him out in 1847. Even so, he remained a Democrat, worked hard to elect Franklin Pierce President in 1852, and looked forward to sharing the spoils when Pierce took office.

Hoping to be named to the lucrative position of marshal of the District of Columbia, French was disappointed when Pierce appointed him commissioner of public buildings instead. During his first year as commissioner he began to dabble in the nativist Know-Nothing movement, submitting articles to a Know-Nothing newspaper in Massachusetts to help his brother-in-law, Simon Brown, get elected lieutenant governor. When Pierce learned of this in 1855, he dismissed his friend from office.

By this time French had already lost interest in nativism and was turning to the antislavery movement, which came to his immediate attention when his minister was accused of being an abolitionist. In 1854 Pierce's support of the Kansas-Nebraska bill, which repealed the Missouri Compromise and established popular sovereignty in the new territories, disturbed French and his brother Henry. According to French, Henry, who was in Washington that winter, "made no secret of his opposition" to the Kansas-Nebraska bill.[1]

When Pierce asked Benjamin to send a letter to New Hampshire in favor of the bill, he demurred. His long, convoluted reply revealed how torn he was by the slavery issue. Though insisting that he supported the principle of popular sovereignty, which stood behind the bill, he admitted that at first he had opposed repeal of the Missouri Compromise. He would defend repeal in Washington but not in New Hampshire, where antislavery feeling was growing.[2] His position was similar to Martin Van Buren's at the time.

Despite his rift with Pierce, French declared in 1855 that he was still a Democrat, though not an "*Administration* Democrat."[3] As far as slavery was concerned, he was "so much a Freesoiler as to be opposed to the addition of any more slave territory to this Union—but utterly opposed to the agitation of the question of slavery if it can be avoided."[4] From that point on French's journal is full of sharp criticism of Pierce. In June he attended the Republican convention, and at the end of the chapter he noted that he had taken his seat as president of the Republican Association of Washington.

As French vacillated over parties and slavery, he was making similar adjustments to the changing economy. Deep-rooted in the rural tradition of New Hampshire, he found great pleasure in serving as treasurer of the U.S. Agricultural Society. In the fall of 1853 he traveled to Lexington, Kentucky, for meetings of both the Agricultural Society and the Freemasons, one of several trips undertaken during Pierce's presidency. Others included one to New England to visit his family and several to New York for the Magnetic Telegraph Company. With his dual interest in agriculture and telegraphy French was typical of many Americans who yearned for the old agrarian order but were beginning to make their living from the new technology.

French also typified most nineteenth-century Americans who continually faced untimely death in the family. He was so distressed by the nearly simultaneous deaths of two of his nephews, one sixteen months old and the other only one day old, that he composed a poem on the sad occasion. When Henry's wife, Anne, died before she was forty-five, Benjamin could only comment that she was "now a saint in Heaven."[5] In previous years he had already noted the deaths of two stepmothers, one father, one brother, two sisters, and a number of in-laws, many younger than he.

At the same time French fully enjoyed happier family moments. His older son, Frank, graduated from Phillips Exeter Academy in 1854 and from Harvard in 1857. When French visited Henry Flagg French in Exeter in 1855, he was entertained by Amos Tuck, who had recently organized the Republican party in New Hampshire and would soon be a force behind Abraham Lincoln. French also met Tuck's daughter Ellen, who later married Frank. By 1857, at the end of this chapter, French was fifty-six, his political direction had been set, the story of his family had begun to take shape, and the forces leading to the Civil War were gathering momentum.

1. July 1, 1855.   3. Ibid.   5. Sept. 4, 1856.
2. Ibid.   4. Ibid.

Journal

Sunday, March 27. I am about half sick today. Have written a letter to Hon. Stephen Adams,[1] Senator[,] telling him I should decline the office of Reading Secy. in the Senate if it should be offered to me, as the newspapers say it is to be, if a certain resolution should pass. I have also written to Frank, and now, after my journal has had a seven weeks rest, I will try to bring it up to this time. Up to the 4th of March, I was principally engaged in attending to any business before Congress—since then most of my time has been *filched from me* by office beggars. If anything can vex a man it is the having men intrude upon him without the least shadow of right. There are many who I am pleased to serve, but I can see no propriety in persons whom I have before never heard of or seen, coming to me to aid them to obtain office—no matter where I am or what I am doing they *must* be attended to as a matter of right. At first I tried to bear it with patience, but it got to be such a bore that I had to speak out plainly, offend or not, & now I believe they are getting to understand my position, & I am somewhat relieved from the enormous burden that was upon me.

On Monday, Feby. 21, Gen. Franklin Pierce, the President-elect, now President, arrived in this City at about ½ past 8 P.M. He came on very privately, and tried to evade even the Telegraph, but did not succeed. I knew all his movements from the hour he left Concord till he arrived here. I heard, by Tel. from Baltimore, of his leaving that city in less than an hour after he left, and, as a matter of curiosity, have filed away 4 despatches showing how accurately I was informed of his movements. No man can dodge lightning! I did not go to the cars to see him, although I was at the City Hall & could have done so, but would not annoy him, believing he desired to see no one.

On Tuesday morning, I called & paid my respects to him at Willard's. He received me kindly, almost affectionately. Two or three days afterwards he came to my house & spent half an hour. I was one of the aids to the Marshal of the District at his inauguration on the 4th of March, and was near Gen. Pierce through the day. He performed his part of the ceremony like a man, & there was unbounded admiration expressed of his bearing & the manner in which he did every part of his inaugural duties. The Marshals attended him to the *White House* and saw him introduced to thousands of his fellow citizens. The day was not very favorable, as it snowed slightly all the morning. About noon the sun struggled through the clouds & could be dimly seen for a couple of hours, but, when I returned from the President's, I faced quite a severe northeast snow storm, and was covered with snow when I dismounted at my own door. The crowd was immense & everything went off well & happily.

And so my old friend & companion, Frank Pierce, with whom I have passed many & many a happy and jovial hour, was duly inaugurated into the highest & most honorable office on earth. Has he forgotten, *in his elevation,* his old friends? We shall see! Up to this time[,] I confess, I am disappointed about some things, but I do not give up that good & true heart yet.

Since the Inauguration, I have not seen General Pierce except officially or in a crowd. I have had perhaps one minute's private conversation with him, when he promised to see me before he made any changes in the offices of this District. I presume he will not forget that promise.

Doctor and Mrs. Barker came here on the Tuesday preceding the Inauguration & intend to leave tomorrow. We have enjoyed their visit much. I have tried to do all in my power to make them comfortable & happy. We have rode, and walked, and visited, & been merry.

Thursday evening we all went to the President's levee. It was a throng, and the President did the duties of receiving the immense crowd in the most urbane and gentlemanly manner possible—the ladies all fell in love with him! Mrs. Pierce (poor afflicted woman) was not present, and Mrs. Means (formerly Abby Kent)[2] did all the feminine honors with that grace & dignity which always marked her, even in her girlhood. We were boy & girl together in Chester, N.H., where we were both born, & now we are here amid the hurly-burly of Washington. Mrs. Pierce & Mrs. Means came on a few days after the Inauguration. I called on Mrs. M. a day or two after she arrived, & had a very pleasant chat of half an hour with her. I hope we may see something of her while this great City is our home.

Since I wrote here last, our First Fair of the Metropolitan Mechanic's Institute has been held. As one of the officers of the Institute, I had considerable to do with it. It was most successful, and we all feel proud that it went off so well.

Spring is coming upon us fast—our garden is beginning to show itself some. I am now preparing to build an addition to my house, which will greatly improve it, I think.

I suppose no poor devil of a politician has been so annoyed and embarrassed about office as I have been since the 4th of March.

I am a candidate for the office of Marshal of the Dist. of Columbia. The office is very valuable. There are many other candidates, and their main object is to get me otherwise provided for. So, without any effort of mine, I was first placed in the position of candidate for Secretary of the Senate. Dickins was re-elected. Then there was an effort to make me Chief Clerk—that failed. Now there is a resolution pending before the Senate to have a reading Secretary appointed, with a view of giving me that place. I have declined it. All these things are terribly annoying to me, and are all tending to injure my prospects of being Marshal as by some they are intended to do!

Now I go straight ahead for the Marshalship, & shall take no other office.

I have written enough for once.

1. Stephen Adams (1807–1857), Democratic senator from Mississippi, 1852–1857.
2. Abby Kent Means, second wife of Jane Pierce's late uncle, Robert Means, acted as Jane's companion while Pierce was President and often presided over official receptions.

Sunday, April 3. The last has been rather a busy week to me. On Monday P.M. the President of the U.S. with his private Secy. Mr. Webster[1] came to my door and invited me to walk with them. We walked about ½ a mile down East Capitol Street, & our talk was of office. Gen. Pierce commenced by saying[,] "Major, I want to say something to you about this office of Marshal. You cannot expect me to appoint you merely because we have been so many years personal friends." I replied, "Certainly not, I have not, and do not ask it on that ground. I ask it on the score of competency on my part, and the wishes of the people of the District, of whom I believe ¾ at least are in my favor." He replied, "Do you mean democrats or citizens without reference to party?" F. "I mean citizens generally, but have little doubt a majority of the democratic party of the District are in my favor." P. "Why do you not get them then?" F. "Because I have said to my opponents, if the Senate make me their Secy. I will accept it, & have not therefore exerted myself to procure names— neither did I suppose an array of names would be necessary."

We went on conversing on this subject for some time, the General alluding to the long time I had held office, etc., & closing his remarks by admitting my faithful & useful services to the Democratic party, my long and unwavering personal friendship for him, and his for me, & assuring me that he had not made up his mind as to who he should appoint Marshal. We talked of other offices, etc. On arriving at my door on our return, I said[,] "Well General, am I to understand that if you do not appoint me Marshal I am to be provided for in any other way?"

He replied, "I desire to provide for you, and it is now necessary that I should have another private Secy. to sign land patents, as Mr. Webster is so constantly engaged that he cannot possibly do it. It will be but temporary, and if you will accept it you shall be appointed."

The reading Secy. of the Senate was then alluded to, & he advised me, with much emphasis[,] to accept it, if the resolution should pass & it should be offered to me, assuring me that, in his opinion, it would be the stepping stone to the Secretaryship. He was so earnest about it that I at length promised to abide the result of the resolution, and, should it be defeated, to accept the temporary office proffered by him. I then said, "Will it have any effect on you[r] decision as to the Marshalship, if I procure a majority of the Democrats of the District to petition for me?" He replied, "Certainly it will," and we separated.

On Tuesday the resolution about the reading Secy. was modified in such a manner that I would not have accepted office under it, and was then postponed to the next session.

I went to the President's and told him I would accept the temporary place offered by him. He said he would give the order at once for my appointment.

On my return home that evening it occurred to me that there might possibly be an impression in his mind that if I accepted that place I should withdraw as a candidate for Marshal. Determined to place myself right on that score, I addressed a note to the President informing him that in accepting the temporary place offered I must not be understood as withdrawing my application for Marshal, as I intended to show him by an expression of public sentiment how I stood in the *hearts of the citizens of the District*.

I went to work at once to start my friends up to make an effort in my behalf which, considering the short time they have had to operate, I consider crowned with complete success, as I have now got petitions signed by more than 800 democrats of the District for my appointment and shall send them in tomorrow. I have not heard from the President on the subject of the temporary appointment since my note was written.

On Wednesday morning last Mrs. Fillmore died at Willard's Hotel. The Mayor called the Councils together to take proper action on the occasion. . . . In accordance with the second resolution I went to Willard's at 5 o'clock Thursday morning and accompanied the remains, with Mr.

Fillmore & his family & a few others, to the Depot, where I bade the Ex-President & his son & daughter good-by.[2] They bore their deep affliction in a manner that rendered their grief dignified, while it created a sympathy for them all, that boisterous & unmanly bowing down could not have done. The current was evidently deep, but it rolled placidly & solemnly along.

At 5 o'clock precisely, I was at the Mayor's door with my carriage to take him with me to Willard's, but he had gone. Within the next two hours I heard of the very sudden decease of Mrs. Rives,[3] the wife of my friend John C. Rives, who resides next door to the Mayor, at 5 o'clock. Mrs. Rives took tea with her family the previous evening in her usual health & died in child bed at 5 o'clock the next morning! I attended her funeral at 4 o'clock Friday afternoon. Poor Rives—he adored her—& no heart but his own can know the bitterness of the cup from which he was so suddenly called to drink. He, too, bore his affliction like a man. How thick the shafts of death seem to be flying about us! High place, & riches, and even health seem to be no shield or panoply from the attacks of the Great Destroyer. "Prepare to meet thy God"—are words too lightly said and too lightly thought of. Would that I could be more deeply impressed with their solemnity and importance.

Let them be my subject for reflection this day!

1. Sidney Webster (1828–1910) was a young lawyer in Pierce's Concord law firm, who accompanied him to Washington in 1853 to be his private secretary.
2. Abigail Powers Fillmore (1798–1853) married Millard Fillmore in 1826. Ill during much of his presidency (1850–1853), she died from pneumonia less than a month after he left office. Their only son was Millard Powers Fillmore.
3. Mary Rives had been one of the workers in Rives's bindery.

Sunday, April 10. . . . On Tuesday I called with a friend to introduce him to the President. After the introduction, the President said, "I cannot appoint you Marshal." I said, "Have there been any representations made to you derogatory to my character, or which have induced this result?" He replied most emphatically in the negative, and added, that he could give me reasons which would be satisfactory to me for not appointing me. I asked for a time to hear those reasons, & he appointed 9 o'clock that evening. I went up & had an interview of ½ an hour. His reasons were, that I was in a position to get a better office from the Senate next December, and that, being an intimate friend of his and a New Hampshire man by birth, it would be construed as an act of favoritism which he wished to avoid. I asked him who he intended to appoint. He replied that he did not know, but *the person most fit for the office, whom the citizens seemed most to desire.* I told him I had presented the petitions signed by a large majority of the democrats of the District and did not doubt a very large majority of the citizens were for me. He spoke of the uncertain character of petitions, etc. I asked how he intended to ascertain who was the choice of the citizens. He replied by saying that he should consult with prominent citizens, and named the Mayor,[1] J. C. Rives, Gen. Armstrong[2] &, I think, one or two others. I told him I was content. And after considerable other conversation as to the different candidates & many offices, he told me I had better accept the place he had proffered me, of Assistant Private Secy. I told him I would, on condition that it should not be in my way for a more lucrative and better office. He promised me it should not, & so we separated.

He appeared worn down by fatigue, & I told him I would not undergo what he was undergoing to be President of the U.S. He said it was hard, & he wished all the offices were elective.

On Thursday I applied to the Department of the Interior for my appointment as a Clerk in the Genl. Land office, to which it was necessary I should be appointed before I could receive any pay as Assist. Private Secy. On Friday I recd. it & was appointed by the President Assist. Private Secy. & entered on my duties at the Presidential Mansion.

I cannot help feeling that I am degraded. But may reasonably hope to hear the promised words, "Friend go up higher." . . .

1. The election of John W. Maury, Democrat, mayor in 1852 ended eighteen years of Whig mayors.
2. Robert Armstrong (1792–1854), brigadier general in the Seminole War in 1836, was later proprietor of the *Washington Union*.

Sunday, April 17. Monday, Tuesday & Wednesday I was at the President's House signing Land Patents. Thursday morning went to Baltimore to attend a meeting of the directors of the Magnetic Telegraph Company, which was held at 4 o'clock that afternoon at Barnum's Hotel.[1] We got through about dark, & then had a game of billiards in Barnum's private billiard room. . . . After breakfast rode back to the city in an omnibus, & went up into Cathedral street, and tried to find my old friend Charles Gilman,[2] Esq., but did not succeed. Returned to Barnum's—then to the Sun building where our Tel. office is kept. After returning to Barnum's, I read the newspapers & "loafed round" till ½ past 2, then dined & at three went to the cars, left at ½ past 3 & arrived home at about 7 P.M.! The cars ran off the track the evening before & injured the locomotive, so that we had to come on with an old worn-out one, that *could not* make over 15 miles a hour! Slow travelling for this month of April in the year of grace eighteen hundred and fifty-three.

On my return, found that the bricklayers had commenced work on my home during my absence. They commenced laying brick on Thursday at 1 o'clock P.M. . . .

1. Zenus Barnum (1810–1865), proprietor of Barnum's Hotel, had been a competitor of Samuel F. B. Morse in the telegraph business.
2. Charles Gilman, 6 Cathedral St.

Sunday, April 24. I now go daily to the President's & sign Land Patents. I *can* sign 150 an hour, but probably do not sign over 100. There are now 10,000 ahead to be signed, & the Commissioner informs me they intend to issue about 500 daily. Well, if I keep this office, I have a job before me and it is *so intellectual*!

FRANKLIN PIERCE
by B. B. French Asst. Secy.

That's it—day in and day out—I expect my brain will become a sheet of parchment all scribbled over with those words, that my heart will become a sort of vague idea of *something* that once beat with "feverish longings for fame," but went out under the quenching operation of neglect and ingratitude from those who have been dearer to me than my own life!

I need not have taken the office, but having done so I will do all my duty, be my feelings what they may.

The President is getting rid of some of the pressure upon him, and often appears to me like that same Frank Pierce with whom, twenty years ago, I frolicked, and was merry & happy—in those days when Thornton and Webber were with us, and we felt, if we did not sing,

Begone dull care I prithee begone from me, etc.

He appears happy & seems to bear the infliction of greatness as if he was created for the place he fills. I cannot but marvel when I recall the first time I ever saw Frank Pierce and compare his position then with what it now is!

I went to Sutton, N.H., to practice law in 1825 & remained there two years. Either in the summer of '25 or '26, I cannot now remember which, as I was casually passing the old meeting house in the North Village, near which I resided, I saw a genteel young man, apparently about 20 or 21, full of fun and frolic, standing with some others, & so prominent over all in his conversation and action, that I inquired who he was. I was told it was Frank Pierce, son of Gen. Pierce[1] of Hillsboro. I do not now remember whether I was introduced to him or not, but I took such a look at him as never to forget him.

I next knew him in 1830, when residing in Newport, the first year he

was a member of the House of Reps. of N. Hamp. In 1831 I was a
member from Newport, & on my way to attend the session, I met Pierce
at Hopkinton. I was in a chaise, he on horseback, and the little mare he
rode is just as prominent in my memory now, as she was visible before
me then. We went on to Concord in company—we took rooms at Gass's
Eagle Hotel, nearly opposite each other, & then commenced a friendship
between us that has been, on my part, almost an affection. From that
day to this I have not wronged Frank Pierce in thought[,] word or deed,
nor have I suffered him to be wronged in my presence, without at once
placing him right.

And now, in his 49th year, he is President of the U.S.

While my life has gone along evenly and smooth, his has been bap-
tised in events of stirring importance, of brightness and of gloom. His
pathway, from the fiat of the people, to the Presidential chair, was bathed
in the blood of his only child, and the tears of a Nation fell, as it were,
upon the bier of that mild and gentle boy. How sorely *he* was afflicted
we cannot know, for only the heart that suffers, "knoweth its own bitterness," but feel it as he might, he bore it *like a man,* who looked higher
for consolation than this earth or the vain human bubbles that float upon
its surface!

Twice, since I have been at the President's house, I have looked upon
the portrait of poor little Benny, & for half an hour afterwards I could
not speak to anyone—if I had attempted it I should have burst into tears,
in spite all my manhood. It affects me strangely. Why should it? I cannot
tell, but the thought that that mild, innocent countenance, that beautiful
forehead covered with fair hair smoothed down by the hand of a doting
mother, should in a single instant pass from life to death, and in such a
manner!—even now I can scarcely endure the thought. . . .

I met Messrs. N. Hawthorne, Ticknor of Boston & J. B. North yesterday at the Patent Office, & they agreed to come up this afternoon, and
walk down to the Congress burial ground with me, but I think the rain
will prevent.[2]

Mr. & Mrs. Monroe spent last evening with us, & we played whist.
Monroe was removed from office yesterday. Why no one can tell. It is
wrong!

1. Benjamin Pierce (1757–1839) served at Bunker Hill before becoming a tavernkeeper
and general in the militia in Hillsboro. He was elected governor of New Hampshire in
1827 and 1829 as a Democrat.

2. Nathaniel Hawthorne (1804–1864) had written a campaign biography of Franklin
Pierce in 1852 and was about to sail for England as consul. George Ticknor (1791–1871)
was the author of *History of Spanish Literature* (1849). John B. North worked in the office
of the first comptroller.

Sunday, May 29. . . . I returned to Washington on Tuesday.[1] Hon. John Y. Mason came up with me, and we talked politics most of the way after we took the boat at the Creek. We discussed the President & his policy & his appointments. I soon saw that all had not gone exactly to Judge Mason's mind. Still he seemed willing to sustain the President all in his power. As soon as I could see the President the next morning, I took pains to let him know Judge Mason's feelings and views &, I believe, put in train an opportunity for an explanation which should make all right. . . .

    1. From a speaking engagement in Richmond, Va.

Sunday, July 31. I am writing in this journal for the first time in my new library, although we have occupied it about six weeks. I have had no time to journalize since I wrote herein on the 29th of May.

About that time the President appointed me Commissioner of Public Buildings, my duties to commence on the 1st July. As soon as it was publickly known that I was appointed the rush upon me for office commenced, and such a time as I had for the month of June was enough to disgust any man with public office. My doorbell was ringing almost continually from 6 A.M. to 10 P.M. when I was at home, & my office at the President's was continually filled with applicants for office—until I was forced to bring my work home, & evade the hordes of office seekers by denying myself to them. I went on with my duties of Assist. Secy. until the 1st of this month, & then entered on the duties of Commissioner of Public Buildings. But there were about 10,000 land patents left for me to sign, which at my leisure I have been at work upon, & hope to finish the present week, and this has prevented my writing in this journal.

At the annual meeting of the W. & N. O. Telegraph Company on the 6th inst. I was elected Treasurer, which adds considerable to my other duties, but as I have an excellent clerk, Chs. E. Thomas, all goes along smoothly & comfortably & I hope to do my various duties acceptably to my employers. I find the duties of Commissioner very arduous, as my attention is required all over the city. It is a hard office with very inadequate pay—$2,000 per annum. . . .

Last evening I rode horseback with the President. We passed over the long bridge,[1] & on to the heights beyond, where there is a magnificent view of the city, which I saw for the first time from that point. Our talk was of all sorts of things, but principally of *our own past*. I enjoyed it much. I got home ¼ before 9, & feel today wonderfully stiff on account of my jolting. . . .

My addition to my house cost $1,400 & is all paid for!

    1. Now the Fourteenth Street bridge.

Sunday, August 21. The past 20 days—A few days after I rode with the President as recorded on the preceding page, I went again with him & Sidney Webster. My horse fell down & I went over his head, but was not injured any to speak of. I immediately mounted again & rode on. Came home about 9, & have not been on horseback since. Barring my fall, our ride was exceedingly pleasant. Mr. Webster (Sidney) was with us, & we talked & laughed & told stories & were merry. . . .

A fortnight ago tomorrow, the President put in my charge the moving up from the Navy yard of the statuary made by Horatio Greenough for the Eastern portico of the Capitol, and the placing it on its pedestal.[1] I employed Clark Mills to superintend the work, & yesterday we got up the first box on to the blocking. The weight ten tons. All the others will be got up this week. . . .

Tomorrow Frank is to leave for Exeter again. He has been at home five weeks and we have enjoyed his visit much. Edmund Flagg is now in the City and is coming to take tea with us this evening.

1. Greenough, already famous for his statue of Washington (1843), completed this colossal group in 1851. Entitled *The Rescue*, it showed a pioneer family saved from Indians.

Wednesday, January 4. On Monday I went to the President's at ½ past 10. Found the arrangements all made to receive the visitors of the day. At 11 the President & his Cabinet took their stations in the circular room, & the doors were thrown open to the Diplomatic corps, who came in and paid their respects. Mrs. Pierce was not well enough to undergo the fatigue of receiving, and did not make her appearance. General Pierce received those who called with his usual graceful and polished manner. Those whom I knew of the foreign corps were Chevalier Haldemann, Mr. Crampton, Gen. Almonte, Baron Gerolt, Mr. Marcoleta.[1] I knew many of the others by sight but could not affix their names. Mr. Palmer,[2] Consul general of Ecuador[,] came in with General Vilanül,[3] the Minister from that place, and introduced him to me as a brother Mason & Grand Master of Masons for Ecuador. He is a venerable looking man, with hair & long beard as white as snow. He was altogether the best looking man in the room. Many of our own Army & Navy officers were present in uniform, and among the uniformed gentry was the nephew of Mr. Bodisco,[4] in the uniform of a Russian curaissier [sic]—which was white kerseymere jacket & pantaloons fitting as tight, & if possible, tighter than his skin, long military boots coming far above the knees, a horseman's sabre at his side, a splendid gilt helmet surmounted with an eagle in his left hand, supported against his breast, & all set off with epaulettes and a profusion of gold lace. Take him all in all he was "a sight to behold." He is, however, a fine looking, well built young man of perhaps 25 years.

The diplomatic reception ended at 12 noon, and then commenced the reception of the *sovereign people,* who for two mortal hours passed on in a continual stream of humanity, & the President shook hands with all. I counted for several minutes at different times, and the shaking of hands averaged full thirty per minute, making, in the two hours, 3,600. It would be within bounds to fix the number who shook hands with the President during the entire levee at 4,000. The thing went off well. As soon as it was over, Henry, Anne and I set off in our carriage on a calling expedition, but we found it too late to do much in that line. We called at J. C. McGuire's,[5] Col. Benton's, and Mayor Maury's, and then came home. In the evening Henry and I walked over to Mr. Adams's & spent an hour or two, and drank a glass of eggnog, and so ended our New Year. . . .

From the 21st of August, the time of my last journalization, to the 7th of September nothing occurred worth writing about, in my beat.[6] On the morning of Wednesday, Sep. 7th, Mrs. F.[,] Benny and I took the cars for Baltimore. At that place we met Mr. & Mrs. Gilman and Ellen Gilman, & then all started, at 8 o'clock for Lexington, Ky., via Pittsburgh. Arrived that night at Hollidaysburg[7] where we remained until the next morning at 11 o'clock, when we started for Pittsburgh. It being our first passage over the inclined planes,[8] we were very much interested. The scenery about us was magnificently grand—mountain seemed piled on mountain, and we enjoyed the passing over the mountains very much. We arrived at Pittsburgh in the evening, put up at the Monongahela House—or, as all the servants called it[,] "the Mongola House." At 6 the next morning we left Pittsburgh expecting to reach Cincinnati that evening, but the train of the evening before coming in to Pittsburgh ran over some cows and was thrown off the track & the engine and cars were considerably smashed up. The wreck was not cleared away when we arrived and [we] were detained about two hours. We then went on and arrived at Crestline, Ohio, so much behind our time that we did not connect with the train from Cleveland, so we had to remain at Crestline till 12 o'clock at night when the train from Cleveland came along & we took it & arrived at Columbus the next morning early. Left Columbus at ½ past one[,] I think, & arrived at Cincinnati in time to go on board the Steamer *Lady Franklin* for Louisville. We arrived at Louisville on Sunday morning [September 11], and spent the day at the Galt House— the dirtiest & meanest house I ever remember to have stopped at. On Monday morning we left Louisville & arrived in Lexington about noon. As the great Agricultural fair was about to be held there, it seemed as if all the world had there assembled. . . .

At 12 o'clock noon on Tuesday, Sep. 13, the G. G. Chapter & G. G. Encampment met & went on sitting alternately, until the Tuesday following when they both adjourned, and Wednesday afternoon we started for home, intending to return by the way of Niagara. We arrived in Louisville on Wednesday evening the 21st, where we remained until the next morning, & then took the *Ben. Franklin* for Cincinnati, expecting to arrive there before daylight the next morning, but in consequence of fog on the river we were detained & did not arrive until too late for the Cleveland cars. This kept us from our intended visit to Niagara, so we went to the Burnett House—as splendid a Hotel as I ever stopped at—where we remained until afternoon and then went on to Columbus. The next day we arrived in Pittsburgh . . . and on Monday, Sep. 28, at 11 o'clock A.M. arrived at our home.

The journey was a delightful one. We saw much of Lexington, and pronounced it the most beautiful city we had ever visited. . . . We also visited Henry Clay's house and farm—Ashland—about a mile from the City. I was there on the day on which it was sold.[9]

After our return home I went on doing the various duties required of me, nothing happening of much moment. In October I went to New York & attended a meeting of the Directors of the Magnetic Telegraph Company. Stayed at Doctor Wells's. . . .

My brother Ned lost two children in October. Edmund F. aged 16 months, & Arthur L. an infant of a single day. . . .

1. French meant Chevalier Hulsemann (not Haldemann); Hulsemann was chargé d'affaires from Austria-Hungary, 1841–1855. John F. T. Crampton (1805–1886), British minister to the United States, 1852–1856. Juan Nepomuceno Almonte (1804–1869), minister from Mexico to the United States, 1841–1846 and 1853. Baron Fr. Von Gerolt, minister from Prussia, 1844–1868. Baron Don José de Marcoleta of Nicaragua was at the time trying to have a canal cut through his country.

2. Though no such official is listed in the *Register of the Department of State*, this may be Robert M. Palmer, U.S. minister to the Argentine Confederation, 1861–1862.

3. José Villamil, chargé d'affaires, 1853–1854.

4. Baron Alexander de Bodisco, Russian minister to the United States, when fifty-six had married the sixteen-year-old daughter of a government clerk in Washington.

5. James C. McGuire, a merchant.

6. What follows is a retrospective passage describing French's trip to Lexington, Ky., in September 1853.

7. A town in central Pennsylvania where a portage railway carried canal boats over the Alleghenies to Johnstown.

8. An inclined track on which trains or boats were raised from one level to another.

9. Clay, who died in 1852, had left Ashland to his wife Lucretia with permission for her to sell it in her lifetime.

Sunday, January 8. . . . *Evening*. Mrs. French, Henry, Benny & I went to church. . . .

After the services we had a meeting of the society, during which, a malignant article, abusing Mr. Channing,[1] & accusing him of being a bitter abolitionist, and tinged with all sorts of "isms[,]" published in the Georgetown *Independent* of yesterday morning, was alluded to and by request read. It will not hurt Mr. Channing. Such ribaldry disgraces the writer far more than the one against whom it is aimed. . . .

1. William Henry Channing (1810–1884), Unitarian minister, nephew of the famous Unitarian William E. Channing.

Sunday, January 15. . . . After dinner. Attended Church, and heard a good sermon by a Mr. Brooks[1] of Boston. After church we had a society meeting, & Mr. Channing having been mentioned as a candidate for settlement over our church, & being a known abolitionist, the question of abolition was incidentally raised & discussed. The election of a pastor was postponed for the present. . . .

Wednesday evening, Henry & I dined with Judge Douglas.

1. Charles Brooks (1795–1872), Unitarian clergyman and author.

Sunday, January 29. . . . Congress is moving along at its usual rate; they have done a little more business this session, thus far, than usual. The great question now is the Nebraska bill.

A few weeks ago Judge Douglas reported a bill from the committee on Territories to the Senate to establish that Territory, accompanied by a long report, in which is proposed the repeal of the Missouri compromise. This, of course, has raised a political storm. The South are unanimously in favor of the measure. The North & West, one would suppose, would be as unanimously against it, but the President has taken ground in favor of it, & the N.H. Senators and Representatives are *in a stew*. The President has had them all up before him & they have "argufied the topic." [Moses] Norris, as I was told, demolished the President's argument in favor of the act in about a minute, but still, they all dislike to differ with their own President.

The opinion seems, now, to be that it will pass. Perhaps it is as well that it should, & let the question be forever settled. The Union will be in danger if it passes, but I trust that the Power which has so long sustained it will save it. For the past 8 or 10 years we have been nearly all the time in a state of turmoil and excitement on the subject of slavery. That accursed institution was engrafted on our system of political polity by our ancestors, and like the "old man of the sea," sticks to us, & will[,] I fear[,] through all time to come! On the principle that "what can't be cured must be endured," we had better let those who have slaves take care of them, and manage the matter in their own way; and, I suppose, if the Missouri compromise could be repealed without endangering the Union, and the North would settle down peacibly on the *old constitution,* as our fathers left it, it would be the best thing that could happen! But, will they do it? "Aye there's the rub." I think they will not. I prophecy— I hope I am a false prophet—but I do prophecy that if this matter is pressed through, that not a single northern man, from President Pierce down to the most insignificant politician who goes for it, will be sustained by the people of the free states! . . .

Friday, February 10. . . . Since Anne & Henry came we have had a very pleasant and agreeable time both at home and in visiting. Wednesday of last week Henry & I dined with Doct. Kittredge[1] at the National, and after dinner walked up to Willard's & spent an hour with Gen. Cass. We had a very interesting interview with him. He & Henry talked about the old inhabitants of Exeter, N.H., where the General was born, & he seemed much to enjoy his reminiscences. The General spoke of the Nebraska bill, expressed his regret that it had been brought forward at this time, but avowed his intention of voting for it, said he was committed to its principles as everybody knew by his Nicholson letter,[2] and could not do otherwise than vote for it. He spoke with great animation of the manner in which everything was done in these days of progress, said that everything, even the most minute, must be accompanied with a flourish to give it weight. "Why[,]" said he[,] "a mason can hardly lay a brick in a building without saying, as if to enforce the act with some emphasis, *there— G—d d—n you, lay there!*" He ridiculed severely this tendency to make a great uproar about little things. . . .

1. Since there is no Dr. Kittredge in the Washington directories, this is probably Dr. Rufus Kittredge (b. 1794), of Cincinnati, brother of George Kittredge of Chester.
2. Letter from Lewis Cass to Alfred O. P. Nicholson in 1847, in which Cass introduced the doctrine of popular sovereignty.

Sunday, February 26. . . . On Thursday evening last I delivered a lecture on "Lecturers & Language" at the Columbia Engine House, before the Fire Company. My audience was not large but was respectable—many ladies were present, & my lecture was well received. . . .

Friday morning I met a Committee of the Pomological Congress, at the National. They have voted to erect a monument in Washington to the memory of A. J. Downing,[1] and desired to consult me officially in relation to the place where it should be placed. I agreed to consult with the President in relation to it. From the National I went to the Smith-sonian Institution & attended the meeting of the Agricultural Society. Mr. Fox[2] of Michigan delivered a lecture, and it was, in my estimation, an admirable one. While he was speaking the President of the U.S. came in, and was received by the Society standing & with cheers. The President remained until the lecture was concluded & for sometime after. He then rose, and with a grace of manner which few men possess in a more eminent degree than Frank Pierce, he addressed the President (Mr. Wilder),[3] thanking him for the invitation to be present, regretting that official engagements, probably not near so important as the business they were engaged in & certainly to him not so agreeable, demanded his presence elsewhere, & expressing a hope that their deliberations might result in great benefit to the Country, he retired amid the enthusiastic cheers of the audience & the verbal expression all around the Hall of admiration at his manner & his remarks. It *was* Frank Pierce as I have seen him a hundred times—& although it was, no less[,] the President of the U.S.[,] I forgot the President in the *man*—& a higher compliment I could not pay him!

I remained and heard several good speeches, among them one by Prof. Mapes,[4] the tone of which I admired. It was strong, eloquent, & to the point on which he spoke—viz. the establishment of *a Department* of Agriculture, not a Bureau. He "had no idea of seeing all the Agricultural interests of the Country sifted down into a well hole of the Patent Office."

All I have to say to him or to any other farmer is this—"You have it all in your own hands, Farmers, you form the constituencies of nine-tenths of the Representatives in Congress, & all you have to say to your candidates for Congress is, Sir[,] you can go if you will make it a *sina que non,*[5] that a Department of Agriculture shall be established. Unless you will do this you cannot go!" This would do it. If they say[,] "We can find nothing in the Constitution to warrant this[,]" the reply will be[,] "Then give *us* a chance to amend the Constitution, for we are determined that the immense Agricultural interests of the Country shall not be disre-garded as they have been heretofore!" Let the Farmers talk in this way to the candidates, instead of instructing them on some political dogma of no sort of interest to any but professed politicians, and they shall obtain their wishes. They shall obtain too what will be of more impor-tance *to this* country than all the other Departments combined!

At 12 I went to the President's, but he had not returned. I then went to my office and worked till about 3 o'clock, and then came home to dinner. At 4 went to the Encampment & conferred the orders of Knight-hood on Major Howe[6] of the U.S. Army, & returned home between 7 & 8, almost worried out. Went to bed early.

At 9 o'clock yesterday morning, I called by appointment for Major Howe at Brown's Hotel & went with him to the President's. Saw the President & introduced the Major. Spoke on some other matters—the monument to Downing among them. The President advised me to consult with some members of Congress as to the course best to be pursued. Major Howe & I left the President's together. He commenced a conversation relative to Spiritual manifestations. I expressed my entire disbelief in anything *spiritual*, at the same time acknowledging my curiosity relative to the matter, & my desire to investigate. He mentioned the family of Mr. Cranston Laurie[7] as being remarkably under the spiritual influence. Being acquainted with Mr. Laurie, and being strongly urged by Major Howe to go with him and to witness what he regarded as the wonderful demonstrations of spiritualism by them, I confessed to a desire to see them & converse with them. I accordingly accepted an invitation of the Major to go directly there. We went. . . .

Mrs. Laurie . . . spread a large sheet of paper before her (it is wafered in to the last page of this book) and taking a pencil, apparently with the utmost firmness in her fingers, placed the point on to the paper, and holding it as it appeared with great exertion for a few seconds, started off with a rapidity of writing such as I have never seen in the most accomplished stenographer. She would write perhaps a line & a half & then stop as short as if her hand had actually struck some hard substance. The pencil would then work to and fro in her fingers—the fingers would be apparently cramped & drawn into different contortions—then, away the hand would go again over the paper with a rapidity that I should have supposed, had I not seen it, impossible. Thus she went on until she had made the signature—"Andrew Jackson," when she dropped the pencil, & asked me to feel her hand. I did so—it was as cold as ice itself. . . .

The entire message as finally completed is as follows.

"To Major French: Major you are welcome. I hope you will not think *to* [sic] lightly of the matter before you but judge for yourself. I feel that I am remembered and that a word from me will be regarded by you I so highly regard [sic] while in the form" "Andrew Jackson."[8] . . .

I then wrote[,]

"Do you remember Franklin Pierce?"

The answer, written just as the former was written, was[,]

"You ask the question in doubt but I will convince you the question can be answered in more ways than one. I can answer yes."

I then asked—keeping it to myself—"Will he carry out your own principles as President of the U.S.?"

Answer.

"If you will attend to the matter it will meet your wishes—No[,] all you desire cannot be given at once."

The pencil was laid down, & I was asked by Major Howe, "Are your questions answered?" I replied, "They *are* answered to a certain extent, but I will read them & you can judge." I then read the two questions.

Mrs. Laurie then took up the pencil & away went her hand like a racehorse, & the following was the result.

"I do. You know me well and can appreciate all my counsel. And he *needs* a guide more than *any* ever in the white house of the same way of thinking with yourself and me."

"Andrew Jackson"

The pencil was dropped—Mrs. L. sat a few moments & then rolling up her eyes, & placing her thumb & finger on either side of her forehead brought to my mind the idea of the Pythoness. They said[,] "She is in a trance, & will speak in a moment."

She commenced speaking slowly and solemnly as the spirit of Jackson addressing me. The old General was so very complimentary that I should blush to write down what he said. Had he been half as complimentary when President I should have been at least one of the Cabinet! According to Mrs. L. the fate of this Nation is mostly in my hands. I have held office, I have been in responsible situations. I should hold higher office & be in more responsible situations. I was a man, I possessed talent, & what was more, I had a heart. I had influence, standing. I must exert them for my country. Those high in office now must soon go out—the people would demand it. The President would have a rough path to pursue, difficulties would surround him, he would need all his friends, I was one of them and must not desert him, etc. She spoke three or four minutes in the foregoing strain. I may not have given her language exact, but very nearly so in what I have given above. . . .

I then wrote on the paper I had, keeping it from all others—

"Do you remember what you once said in my presence, relative to the prospect of a duel between Forsyth & Poindexter?"

Answer. "You know your duty. Follow it[,] your own mind will direct you from imposition."

I said, "That is no answer to my question." Mrs. Laurie at once wrote[,]

"No, I am not permitted to answer it." And here ended my interview with the General!

1. Andrew Jackson Downing (1815–1852) was the first great American landscape gardener.

2. Charles Fox (1815–1854), of Ann Arbor, Mich., was senior editor of the *Farmer's Companion and Gazette*. His address: "The Necessity of Agricultural Instruction."

3. Marshall P. Wilder (1798–1886), of Boston, was president of the Massachusetts Hor-

ticultural Society, 1840–1848, helped establish the Massachusetts board of agriculture, 1852, and directed the U.S. Agricultural Society.

4. James J. Mapes (1806–1866), of New York, was editor of *The Working Farmer* and a pioneer in developing fertilizers.

5. French meant "sine qua non."

6. Albion P. Howe (1818–1897) was an artillery officer in the Mexican War.

7. Cranston Laurie was a clerk in the Post Office Department.

8. French attached this paragraph (written by Mrs. Laurie supposedly under the influence of Andrew Jackson) at the end of this volume of the journal (Vol. 6). The writing, especially the signature, looks surprisingly like that of Jackson, and the spelling of "to" and "regard" is also typical of Jackson.

Sunday, March 5. Since writing the foregoing about spiritual manifestations, I have neither witnessed nor sought to witness any. I have been told enough respecting the Laurie family to render anything I might hear from them of no effect, & I now entirely disbelieve any spiritual agency whatever, in what I saw and heard there as described in the foregoing pages. Still, as "men of mark" do believe in it, I intend to investigate further. . . .

Our Administration which has now stood one year, has undertaken to do curious things. What the doing thereof will result in, time alone will determine.

The Nebraska bill passed the Senate, at 5 o'clock yesterday morning, repealing the Missouri compromise. It has been so modified, however, on its way through as to be shorn of many of its objectionable features. It will not go down at the North, and I now prophecy that every Northern man who votes for it will find that he has sacrificed himself politically. The power of the President over Congress is such that he can control the vote of the Senate and perhaps the House (the latter remains to be seen and is in my view doubtful)[,] but he cannot control the *people* of the Free states, and *that* he will ere long discover. Had he asked me, I could have told him this beforehand. There never was so great a political blunder committed, as the bringing forward of this repeal measure at this time, in my opinion. It may be right in itself, & according to Gen. Cass's Nicholson letter, is, but the expediency of doing right under certain circumstances is questionable. Wrong should never be done, but Mr. Calhoun's "masterly inactivity" is sometimes nearer right, than *right* itself is. As Father Ritchie used to say[,] "*Nous verrons.*"

On Wednesday last I bought a little black mare, saddle & bridle for $75, to ride horseback, in the performance of my duty as Commissioner.

It seems to me as if there was a studied effort on the part of the *officials* above me to give me as much *official* trouble as possible. Yesterday I received a parcel of ridiculous questions from the Secretary of the Interior—ridiculous, inasmuch as that *he knew* it was not in my power to answer some of them. I spent the entire *official* part of the day, writing him an answer. And so my time is frittered away, & I am kept from my real duties to take care of the moonshine that comes dimly down from the Department of the Interior.

Robert McClelland[1] is an honest man, but he is afraid of his own shadow, & *anyone* can go to him & complain of some imaginary wrong, & he sets to work to investigate it—spending valuable time, & causing those under him to do the same—to find out whether A. B. is employed inside or outside of a certain fence, when it matters not a bauble which! I have written pages upon pages of reports to him since I have been in office on matters of the very smallest importance, & which eventuated in just nothing. . . .

1. Robert McClelland (1807–1880) was Democratic congressman from Michigan, 1843–1849; governor of Michigan, 1851–1853; and Secretary of the Interior, 1853–1857.

Sunday, May 7. The Columbia Fire Company are doing themselves great honor in the course they are now pursuing. They have fitted up their saloon elegantly & are collecting a valuable Library. How much better than to be rowdying & spending their money in dissipation, as fire companies have, heretofore, been prone to do. . . .

J. W. F[orney] is now wholly in the confidence of the Executive. He is emphatically a Buchanan man, & *he means* that Buchanan shall be the next President of the U.S. Mr. Oakford,[1] Chief Clerk in the G. P. O. Dept.[,] is an intimate friend of Forney's, & was brought in there by Mr. P. M. G. Campbell,[2] on account of his political shrewdness, smartness, & deep devotion to Buchanan. He has his understrappers about him, & they, not being altogether prudent, have said, "We support Pierce as long as it is for our interest *to use him,* but as soon as the proper time comes, we shall break ground openly for Buchanan. Forney will manage the thing. He is hand & glove with the President, & he will know the proper time to move." Such, in substance, has been the conversation held in the Gen. P. O. Dept. Such are the lessons inculcated by those Judases whom General Pierce has taken to his bosom, while he has kept his old, tried & true friends at more than arm's length from him!

As my former friend, as one whose honor was as dear to me as my own, as one for whom I would have made any reasonable sacrifice, I feel sad at these prospects, but I cannot help it, & I can truly say to Pierce, when the event comes

Thou canst not say I did it.

1. John O. Oakford, of Pennsylvania.
2. Postmaster General James Campbell (1812–1893), of Pennsylvania.

Tuesday, July 4. Since midnight there has been no such thing as rest. The bells have been ringing—guns firing—crackers snapping—and young America has been wide awake and rejoicing. Besides the weather is like a fiery furnace. I arose about an hour ago, & have been looking on the morning joy of our Washington Republic. Although somewhat annoying to a staid & sober individual who likes his rest, my heart, *particularly at this time,* rejoiceth in this demonstration of regard for the Union & Constitution. So, go it young America—with your cannons, guns, pistols, crackers, bells & whoorahs! . . .

Sunday, July 9. Well, after writing the foregoing on the 4th I eat breakfast, and went to the Capitol where Doct. Towle and I made up my report as Treasurer. Then I came home & *sweltered* through the day—the hottest I ever felt in Washington—thermometer 94° in my house. On the 5th the Tel. Co. met. Mr. Kendall introduced resolutions reorganizing the Company—making a stationary President—with two privy counselors to be selected from the Directors. We all believed the resolutions proper, and they were adopted. I was urged by some of the best and most influential stockholders present to be a candidate for President, but declined, and myself nominated Mr. Kendall. He was elected.

I was nominated for re-election as Treasurer, & a Mr. Musgrove from the south, who holds Daniel Griffin's stock, nominated John E. Kendall[1]—Amos's nephew—and Amos, with a coolness which did him credit, voted all his stock for his nephew, and he was elected. I never witnessed a meaner transaction in my life. Had they let me know that they wanted the office for Johnny, I would have withdrawn from it, but I did not even mistrust such a thing, & so they *kicked me out.* This is Amos Kendall's second exhibition of friendship for me! I forgave his removing me from the Presidency of the Magnetic Tel. Co.; but if I ever forgive this cold-blooded, & unfeeling movement, may God forget me!

More than 20 years ago Amos Kendall was denounced as an ungrateful, dishonest, & dishonorable man. I defended him in the newspaper with which I was connected. I came to Washington & met him. He professed to hold my wife's father, with whom he studied law, & who acted towards him like a father, in the highest veneration, & I respected him for that, if for nothing else. Time moved on and we became in some manner connected as members of the Mag. Tel. Co. He was President, and resigned, & with his aid I was elected—being, at the time, Clerk of the Ho. Reps. U.S. I did not want the office, but accepted it. I held it for three years and labored like a dog in it, and then that same Mr. Kendall ousted me. He had good reasons for it—reasons satisfactory even to me—and I forgave him. Last July[,] he being Treasurer, & a feud having sprung up between him & Mr. Alexander,[2] President of the Co.[,] a compromise was entered into and Mr. Mowry was elected President, and I Treasurer, I hardly having been consulted about it. I accepted the Office of Treasurer and performed the duties, & this year, as above stated, was very unceremoniously ejected. . . .

1. John E. Kendall had played a large role in completing the New Orleans and Ohio Telegraph in 1851.
2. Elam Alexander had also been president of the Washington & New Orleans line.

Tuesday, August 8. . . . I think, so far as appropriations for this City were concerned, this has shown itself the meanest House of Representatives I ever knew—they even refused *fuel* & *a furnace keeper* to the President's House! The U.S. has built a furnace that burns an immense quantity of fuel, warming the entire mansion with heat from steam, & requiring the constant attention of one man, & have thus saddled upon the President an expense of some 12 or 1,500 dollars per year, & the House of Representatives, with a contemptible economy, amounting to meanness, has refused to grant an appropriation of $1,365, to meet this expense! I wonder they do not impose upon the President the warming of the Capitol! His House is equally as public. . . .

Sunday, September 3. My well diggers came to water in abundance at 48 feet, & my well was finished & everything working first rate a week ago yesterday, since which we have pumped up thousands of gallons with no apparent diminution of the water in the well. The spring is "rapid" & yields abundantly—my cistern is now full, & the fountain playing into a full pool. These waterworks are invaluable. Frank left here for Exeter a week ago last Thursday evening, & telegraphed his safe arrival on Saturday. He went to Cambridge on Monday, & evening before last we recd. a despatch that he was admitted as a Sophomore. So now he is fairly entered [in] college. He has started well—may he end as he has begun. . . .

Sunday, September 10. . . . Got the new fountain at the President's playing last evening—looks handsome. I have written a long, reminiscent letter to sister Kate today. Nothing especially new. Last Tuesday afternoon, Sep. 5th, they laid the cornerstone of a Methodist church at the corner of 3d & A Streets on Capitol Hill. Bishop Waugh[1] conducted the services. I was present by invitation & was pleased. It was said to be the cornerstone of the first Protestant church, ever laid on Capitol Hill. This, I think an error, as the Church South of the Capitol, now occupied by the negroes, is, I believe[,] a Protestant church. But, I hope the one laid last Tuesday will not be the last. It is time Capitol Hill should begin to grow, as well in grace, as in population. God bless Capitol Hill!

1. Beverly Waugh (1789–1858) became American Methodist Episcopal bishop in 1836 and senior bishop in 1852.

Tuesday, January 2. My first work of yesterday morning, after eating my breakfast, was to write some poetry addressed to Mrs. Pierce.

At 10 I walked to the President's & performed my official duty of seeing that all was prepared for the reception. At 11 the Diplomatic Corps were received by the President and Mrs. Pierce, and the scene in the Reception room was very brilliant—all the foreign corps being in gaudy uniforms—or rather, court dresses. The contrast between *our* President and his cabinet, and the glitter of gold & epaulettes on the Foreign representatives was great, and in my judgment very much in favor of *us*. No man dresses more appropriately on all occasions than Gen. Pierce. Yesterday he wore a suit of plain but rich black, & wore, as he ever has since the death of his boy, black gloves. Mrs. Pierce wore black except her headdress which was white. She looked better than usual. The General looks to me, as if the cares & troubles of his office wore upon him; still he appears cheerful, and is affable.

At a few minutes before 12, the Diplomatic corps withdrew and the doors were opened to the multitude—and *such a multitude* as thronged the White House for two or three hours, I have seldom—I am not sure as ever—witnessed. Many thousands shook the hand of their Chief.

After remaining as long as was necessary, at the President's, I left. I called at Gov. Marcy's and George Riggs's[1] first. Then Mrs. French came up in our carriage, & we went calling together. We called at Judge Blair's, & saw Mrs. Blair & Mrs. Woodbury & Ellen, all splendid women.[2] Mrs. Woodbury holds her age better than any woman I ever saw. I thought as I saw the mother (Mrs. W.) & daughter (Mrs. Blair) across the room that the mother appeared certainly as young as the daughter. . . .

1. George W. Riggs (1813–1881) was a prominent Washington banker.
2. Montgomery Blair (1813–1883), son of Francis P. Blair, had served as judge of common pleas in Missouri and was now practicing law in Maryland. His second wife, Mary Elizabeth, was the daughter of Supreme Court justice Levi Woodbury, who had died in 1851, and Elizabeth Clapp Woodbury. Ellen C. deQ. Woodbury was the sister of Mary Elizabeth Blair.

Sunday, January 28. . . . Yesterday I was at the President's and he showed me all the pretty things that the Emperor of Japan sent to him. Those

that are proper to be kept at the President's House as ornaments &
furniture are to remain—the rest are to be sent to the Patent Office.
Some of the things are magnificent. . . .

Sunday, February 18. . . . Powell's picture arrived about a week ago, and
on Thursday Powell himself came.[1] I had made all the necessary arrangements before his arrival, to expedite the putting up of the picture,
and at 4 o'clock Thursday P.M. we all "set in," & had it in the frame and
all right at ½ past 9 that evening. Yesterday and day before the Rotunda
was visited by thousands to look at it. I think the general impression
concerning it is good. It is, however, in some points, justly subjected to
severe criticism. I had a new clock 3 feet in diameter, with a gilt frame,
put up in the rotundo, yesterday. It is handsome. . . .

1. William Henry Powell (1823–1879) was commissioned in 1847 to paint a panel com-
memorating the explorer Hernando de Soto for the Rotunda of the U.S. Capitol.

Tuesday, March 13. The N. Hampshire election came off today. I take
it for granted that the Administration party is whipped—and who can
wonder. Franklin Pierce of N.H. was elected President a little more than
two years ago by an overwhelming majority. He took his seat as President
on the 4th of March 1853, and no man ever retired to his rest a more
popular man than did General Pierce, on the night of that 4th of March!
But he had already whistled his best friends down the wind, & taken to
his embrace a set of scoundrels who were sure to mislead him and then
betray him. Time servers—men of no principle, worshipping only at the
shrine of Mammon, and ready to betray anybody for *forty pieces of silver*!
With as ill assorted a cabinet as well could be assembled. Marcy[,] really
a great & good man. Guthrie,[1] whom nobody out of Louisville, Ky., ever
heard of before, rich, honest, & parsimonious, & about as fit for Secretary of the Treasury as any clodhopper that could be picked up in an
Irish bog, a proslavery Kentuckian. McClelland, a really clever fellow,
but with little mind & no nerve, a man of doubtful views on many of
the leading questions of the day, a cross between an abolitionist and a
proslaveryist, & probably about as weak a piece of timber as ever was yet
worked into an American Cabinet! Davis,[2] a gentleman and a scholar,
smart as a steel trap, with a strong tendency to disunion, and a decided
inclination to the maintaining of slavery and slave power; & ready to go
all lengths in order to enable the Military power to walk roughshod over
the civil. Dobbin,[3] as amiable & clever a little man as the Lord ever made,

true to his friends & to his Country, & whose name stands out honorable and fair & without reproach, worthy to stand by the side of Marcy, although not so great, still great enough for his position, and good enough for *any* position. Campbell, a seven-by-nine pane of dirty glass set among half a dozen large ones of the best plate, a fifth-rate Attorney at Law, whom the office of P.M. Gen.[,] so much beyond all his hopes or expectations, has puffed up into such an inflated piece of humanity that it may be asked as of the Roman—

> Upon what meat does this our Caesar feed,
> That he has grown so great!?

Cushing, brilliant and cold as an icicle. A man of splendid intellect & of the best possible education, but of unbounded ambition. A man whose motto always seems to have been "the end justifies the means." A man who has been "everything by turns and nothing long!" A federalist, a Tyler man, a conservative, a democrat—*anything* for office or place. As a member of the House of Representatives he was despised for his duplicity, as a General in the Mexican war the only laurel he won was tumbling down and breaking his leg while walking with a lady in the street of some Mexican city—perhaps Jalapa. As a Judge on the Massachusetts bench he stands in the annals of jurisprudence—a blank—& as Attorney General of the U.S. he is enough to damn the prospects of the purest President that ever lived! He has not one particle of principle! With such a Cabinet, and with Mr. Private Secretary Webster[,] who never learnt the manners of a gentleman, to receive his visitors, and with John W. Forney, a drunkard and a most unprincipled & dishonest man[,] as his bosom & confidential adviser, & who stands ready to give him the betrayal kiss when the Buchanan men are ready to pounce upon him, who can wonder that Franklin Pierce has done, in two years, what all the enemies of democracy have striven in vain for 50 years to do—*broken down the Democratic Party!* He has done it! & New Hampshire will, this day, bear witness to the fact!

No man prayed more heartily than I did that General Pierce might be a successful President, and leave the chair of State with the blessings of the American people upon his head. . . . I sacrificed my time and my business to make him President & gloried in his election, and he has treated me as if he deemed me of about as much importance as his bootblack or his coachman. He has hardly extended to me the common courtesies of life, and has placed me in the poorest office within his gift. . . .

1. James Guthrie (1792–1869) was a Kentucky railroad promoter, who was Secretary of the Treasury, 1853–1857.

2. Jefferson Davis (1808–1889) had already served in the House of Representatives, 1845–1846, and the Senate, 1847–1851, before being appointed Secretary of War, 1853–1857.

3. James C. Dobbin (1814–1857), of North Carolina, reorganized the U.S. Navy during his term as Secretary of the Navy, 1853–1857.

Sunday, March 25. . . . My last writing herein was on the 13th, inst., the day of the N.H. election. I wrote some truths on that day, & my prophecy has been fulfilled, & my old friend Ralph Metcalf is elected Governor of N.H. I do not regret it, although some of my means were *squeezed out of me,* to aid the Democracy of that State. I *knew* it was money thrown away, & so told *them* when I gave it. . . .

Sunday, June 3. On the 24th of May came off the Election in Virginia. No state election was ever anticipated with more interest all through the Union, and this City was for a week or two prior to the day & for several days afterward filled with excitement. Betting was entered into without stint & it is said that many thousands of dollars changed hands. Mr. Wise was triumphantly elected Governor & every member of Congress elected is a democrat. I consider that election the death knell of Know Nothingism. Had that party triumphed I should have regarded it as indicative of the election of a Know Nothing President of the U.S. at the next election. Although, at one time, I was, under a misrepresentation, induced to join that order, as soon as I ascertained its real principles and ends, I left it. No honest democratic republican can belong to it. Its outside principles are good—its inside ones damnable![1] . . .

1. This final sentence in the paragraph was added later by French.

Sunday, June 10. I do not believe that ever a humble individual who was striving to do right, ever was persecuted with such devlish bitterness as I have been for the past week! Talk about hunting Indians with bloodhounds—it is mere child's play compared with the howling pack of human dogs that have for the week past been on my track. "Tray, Blanch, & Sweetheart, little dogs & all."[1] Know Nothings and Democrats, Catholics & Protestants, great men & little men, & many *very small* would-be-great men have all united in the cry, and never poor hunted hare was pursued with greater lust for its blood by Huntsmen & Hounds, than I have been pursued by these Harpies and Hyenas, who lust for my ruin because I have dared be honest, & have regarded the Truth as more sacred than any forced obligation to lie! I now wish I had kept a diary of the past week, entitling it "The diary of a hunted politician!" I did not, & cannot probably recall, from the uproar that has attended me, one half of the sayings & doings of the week. I will, however, try to recall what I can, beginning with—

Tuesday, May 29. On which day I was at the Treasury on official business, where I met the President. He said that he wanted to see me at his house. I went up & in a conversation he informed me that he was greatly annoyed by a constant complaint to him that I was a "Know Nothing." He said he assured those who said so that I was not—that I had assured him I was not, & he believed me. [In that he was mistaken, for that was the first time he had ever spoken to me on the subject.][2] He said that Gov. McClelland had told him that I had said to him that I was not, which I did. I wanted to tell him *all* the truth about it—that I had been initiated & withdrew—but he went off on to the Know Nothings, & the way he did abuse them was not slow. He avowed his intention to remove everyone who belonged to the party from office as soon as he ascertained the fact, etc. In the midst of his conversation the messenger came in & informed him that someone had come who desired to see him, and he bid me good-by, & left the room. I returned immediately to my office, & had scarcely got seated before Capt. Dunnington[3] came in and said that he had ascertained from whence came the story that I was a K.N.— that a person in full communion with them had publickly avowed at the Navy yard that he was present and saw me initiated. I told him that he probably told the truth for once, as it was a fact that I was initiated more than a year prior to that time. I then went on & told the Capt. all about my initiation & immediate attempt to withdraw by sending my verbal resignation, etc. I came to my house, dined, & then wrote a letter to the President, informing him of all the facts. . . .

Wednesday, May 30. I went early to my office, & after doing up my morning business went up into the Senate Chamber & there had a long conversation with my friend Peyton Page[4] on the subject of my position. From thence went back to my office & was informed that the President had called to see me, & was probably then about the Capitol. I started to find him, and did so, after a while, in the Office of the Clerk of the House of Representatives. I went in, & he fastened the door, & we sat down & had a long talk. He avowed to me his satisfaction at my full disclosure of my position, advised what course to pursue in future, reasserted his own intentions as to those in office who continued their allegiance to the K.N. party, etc. Our conversation was the longest, I believe, that I have ever had since he became President, and was of the "old times" character, such as to bring up the intimacies of our former years fresh into my mind. I separated from him feeling that I had been talking with "Frank Pierce" as he was in the days when he seemed more like my brother than any man ever did who was not related to me!

I returned to my office & pursued the duties of the day, feeling cheerful & happy. The City was rife with rumors of my removal, & with all sorts of lies to my prejudice.

Thursday, May 31. Was early at my office, having agreed to meet a Mr. Nason[5] of N.Y.[,] a hot water furnace builder, at the Patent Office, at ½ past 10, to make arrangements with him for the erection of a furnace in the West wing of that building. Between 9 & 10 I started for the Patent Office; at the gate of the Capitol grounds I met Henry, the President's coachman, with a note from the President asking me to call up & see him. I walked directly up—found him in his office & he handed me a note signed "Wallach" & addressed "Mr. President," in which it was stated that "I belonged to a Know Nothing Lodge" & he could prove it—that it was stated that a certain Mr. Sheets, who was employed with many men by a Mr. Stewart[6] (my superintendent)[,] had given notice to his men that if they went away to vote on Monday, he would discharge them, they being foreigners. I told the President I did not believe one word of it, and as to my belonging to a K.N. Lodge, he had all the truth about that. He advised me to see Mr. Wallach. I left and went as fast as possible to the Patent Office, where my business detained me till 12 o'clock, & it was there arranged that I should go to my office and write my acceptance of Mr. Nason's proposition, who was to call at 2. I went to my office, & sent for Mr. Stewart, and, while waiting for him, wrote to Mr. Nason. He came, & our bargain was concluded. By that time it was so late that I found it would be impossible to see Wallach personally, so I wrote him a letter [a portion of which was published in the *Star* of June 2d.][7] Mr. Stewart came in & upon enquiry I found, as I expected to, that the story about the men was utterly false, & I wrote a note to the President and sent Stewart up with it, and then came home. . . .

Monday, June 4th. Municipal election day. As soon as I was up in the morning Mr. Nokes called & told me that Doct. Busey had told him that, in consequence of my letter in the *Star*, the *Organ* was coming out on me that afternoon.[8] That articles written for the *Organ* by me had been kept, and were in my own handwriting at the *Organ* office. I had forgotten that I had written those articles, & could not recall them, or the subject of them, to my memory. . . .

In the evening I went to the President's. I went immediately into his office where, as near as I can remember[,] the following dialogue took place.

The President, "Well, Major they have got you now!"

F. "Yes, they have so, but no editor who had a spark of honor or gentlemanly feeling would betray a person as I have been betrayed."

P. "What were those articles about?"

F. "Two short ones about the Massachusetts election, I think, and one long one about the Baron de Kalb,[9] but not one word against democracy or the Administration. I wrote them in another person, had forgotten the facts and cannot now recall them."

P. "When I recd. your resignation this morning, I thought I would not accept it, & so told Dunnington. What do you think I had better do?"

F. "Accept it by all means. It was sent to be accepted, & should it not be, it will be said there was some understanding between us."

P. "Well, Major, I think it will be better for both of us, under the circumstances[,] that you should be, for the present, out of office, and I will accept it." . . .

Tuesday, June 5. My resignation & Doct. Blake's[10] appointment announced by the *Union*. After my morning office business, went to the President's and had an interview. He told me that Doct. Blake was reluctant to accept the office, & could not at present, & that I must remain until he could enter upon its duties. I agreed to do so. All sorts of lies in circulation against me, & my office a perfect hell on earth.

Wednesday, June 6. Doct. Blake called & it was arranged that he should enter on duty July 1st.

1. Loosely quoted from *King Lear*, Act III, scene 6.
2. Brackets French's.
3. Charles W. C. Dunnington was captain of the Capitol police.
4. Yelverton Peyton Page, a clerk at the Capitol at the time, was later grand master of the Masons in the District of Columbia when he died in 1863.
5. Joseph Nason of Nason & Dodge, makers of iron plates and steam warming and ventilating apparatus in New York City.
6. Richard H. Stewart, a carpenter.
7. Brackets French's.
8. James Nokes, a Capitol policeman. S. C. Busey of Georgetown. The *Daily American Organ*, a Know-Nothing newspaper, was published in Washington, 1855–1857.
9. Baron Johann de Kalb (1721–1780), a German professional soldier, fought on the American side in the Revolution.
10. John B. Blake was commissioner of public buildings, 1855–1861.

Sunday, July 1. . . . My mind is now made up as to the *political* future— my platform is established, & there I stand openly and avowedly. No more time-serving, no more equivocation, no more "Know Nothingism." For my Country and her Constitution first of all!

A Democrat, so far as living up to the principles of those fathers of Democracy, Jefferson, Madison, Monroe, & Jackson, is being a Democrat: But no city of Washington, present *Administration* Democrat, that has established the principle of taking into the Democratic ranks every Whig who was not a Know Nothing, or, being one, left their ranks to *get into those* of the Democratic Party! Poor Pierce, I actually pity him, when driven to such shifts to sustain his weak & unprincipled Administration.

An American in heart and principle—so much a Freesoiler as to be opposed to the addition of any more slave territory to this Union—but utterly opposed to the agitation of the question of slavery if it can be avoided, &, although abhorring slavery in the abstract, defending it to the utmost of my power so far as it is tolerated or justified by the Constitution.

I am for letting every State in this Union enjoy its rights fully under the Constitution. I regarded the repeal of the Missouri Compromise by the last Congress, as the greatest political blunder that ever was committed, although I defended the principle, inasmuch as I always thought the original compromise wrong in principle, & should have voted against it if I had been in a position to vote at all.

To show, however[,] in what manner our present immaculate Administration makes its officers *toe the mark* I will state a few facts. My brother Henry F. French was here much of the winter of 1853–4 and was violently opposed to Douglas's repeal act, & made no secret of his opposition. I was taken into the President's office & told by his Excellency that my brother's opposition to that bill was injuring me, & many took occasion to say that his opinion & my own coincided. I said to the President that my brother had his opinions and I had mine, & in this matter we did not agree. That when I first knew of the movement I denounced it as impolitic, & was sorry it was started—that I thought it was a firebrand that would set the whole Union on fire. But that I had defended it as a *principle* and should continue to do so, but that I really was astonished when I first found that *he* was sustaining it. His words, as I now recollect them, were[,] "Good God, Major, what could I do? Dixon,[1] a Whig[,] had started it, and it would not do to let the Whigs carry it through, & I was forced to assume the responsibility of doing it. Many think Douglas was the originator of the movement on the Democratic side, but he was not." After a long conversation, the President suggested that I should write a letter to some friend in N.H. taking strong ground in favor of the repeal, and he suggested Col. Henry E. Baldwin[2] as the person to whom I should write it, and I then, without much reflection, consented to do so. I left, & having reflected more seriously on the subject, I wrote the President a letter which I now copy here. I really believed what I then wrote & think I can now defend it, but I wrote under a sort of duress which prevented me from saying what I thought then and think now that the repeal was an impardonable political blunder, and the sooner the *compromise* is restored, the better will it be for the Union!

The Letter.

Washington March 27, 1854.

General Pierce.

My Dear Sir,

Since I conversed with you on Friday last, I have reflected much on the proposition to which I then assented, that I should write to some friend in New Hampshire expressing my views of the principles of the Nebraska Bill. I am satisfied that such a letter from me, when all the circumstances which surround me are considered, would be rather an injury than a benefit to both of us in New Hampshire. I hold a public office here to which you appointed me, and it would be trumpeted through the State that I was not only interfering improperly with questions before Congress, but that every official was expected to defend the views of the President. Our former intimacy in N.H. and present friendly personal relations would also be paraded to render futile any argument I might use. . . .

Lest you should misunderstand my position, I say that I have deeply regretted the opposition to the Nebraska bill. There may be, and doubtless are, some who oppose it because they honestly believe the Missouri Compromise ought not to be disturbed, but I believe the bitterest opposition proceeds from those who are actuated by the most malignant feelings, induced by disappointed ambition.

The principles upon which the legislation contained in that bill is founded are as eternal as truth itself. . . .

If, through the intervention of wicked men[,] they shall be broken down, and trampled underfoot, the death knell of popular liberty will be tolled, and the footprints of freedom on earth will be overtrodden and "crushed out" by the iron heel of despotism.

All the arguments I have read and heard have not convinced me that the compromises of 1850 did not virtually repeal the compromise of 1820. It is true Congress did not in so many words say that the people should have their rights restored to them North of 36° 30' in the Louisiana Purchase, but they did say that the people should exercise their legitimate rights in the Territory ceded to the United States by Mexico along the same line of latitude, thus recognizing a principle which the Missouri compromise annulled. There can be no doubt that Senator Dixon took this view of the matter when he introduced his amendment on the 16th of January last proposing to repeal that compromise. His desire probably was to remove all doubt as to the position & right of *all* the people inhabiting the same line of territory, and Judge Douglas, adopting the same view, introduced the principle of restoring to the people in the Territories of Nebraska & Kansas the same rights which had been given to those in New Mexico and Utah.

When this measure was first brought forward, like many other of its warm friends, I was startled at it, and expressed myself against the policy of moving it at this time. I looked upon it as unnecessary but nevertheless defended strenuously the principle. I was not then aware (not having watched closely the proceedings of Congress) of Mr. Dixon's proposition and supposed that the proposed legislation was originated and brought forward by Senator Douglas, without any special reason for so doing, and that the Union would be thrown into a state of excitement (as it since has been) with no apparent necessity for the act which should produce it. But as soon as I became aware that there were others who were determined that the question should be moved and that it *must* be met, I was among those who were ready to meet it in the most legitimate manner possible.

I regret, even now, that the necessity was presented which compelled the movement, but it having been done, as one who has advocated the great principle of popular rights from my boyhood, I shall not be found a deserter at this late day, and throwing aside all personal considerations, I shall do all in my power to sustain the measure & to sustain those in whose care it now is.

> With sentiments of the highest
> regard, I am your Obt. Servt.
> B. B. French.

Thus I wrote—I stand as firmly by the principle of *popular sovereignty* now as I did then, and think that the people everywhere should rule the political division (whether State, Territory, Empire or Principality) that they occupy. But the Missouri Act was regarded by everyone as *a compromise* of principles between the North and the South; in any other view it could not have received, probably, a single vote from either section of the Union. It was acquiesced in by those who opposed it most strenuously, the *people* of Missouri agreed to it, and it became, in fact, a compact, and notwithstanding my letter, I think it never should have been annulled. Besides, circumstances have since occurred showing that, as regards Kansas, there is a *determination* among the slavocracy that the people of that Territory *shall not* make it free if they are ever so much disposed to do so, and as it is now perfectly evident that the repeal was for the purpose of establishing more slave territory in this Union, which

I am decidedly opposed to, I am as decidedly for a restoration of that compromise, & shall do all I can to bring it about.

1. Archibald Dixon (1802–1876), who served as Whig senator from Kentucky, 1852–1855, moved to repeal the Missouri Compromise on January 16, 1854.
2. Henry E. Baldwin (1815–1855), a journalist in Newport, N.H., in 1839 created the first illustrated political campaign publication.

Lancaster, Mass., Sunday, July 22. . . . Friday morning I called to see the President, being the first time I have seen him to speak to him since June 5th. We had a long talk & he gave evidence in his conversation that he at least remained my warm friend. We conversed on various matters, & I have no doubt from what he said that he has some expectation of being renominated for the next term. He cannot again be elected under any circumstances! . . .

Chester, Sunday, July 29. On Tuesday morning last, at 20 minutes after 7 Mrs. F.[,] my sons & I left Lancaster for this place. At Groton Junction Frank & Ben took the cars for Boston, & Mrs. F. & I for Lowell. From Lowell we went to Lawrence—from thence to Derry, & from thence in the stage here, where we arrived at ½ past 3 P.M. Our *home* is at John S. Brown's, where we are taken excellent care of. We spend most of the daytime at the old Mansion which my father built and where are this day—Mrs. French, senior, Henry & his wife & their children (Harriette, Willie, Sarah & Dan)[,] my sister Helen, Mrs. L. M. Barker, & Simon and Ann Brown—considerable of a household![1] Mrs. Barker is on a visit for her health. Lt. Gov. Brown & his wife came yesterday on a short visit. At this house we have, besides the family, William C. Brown, his wife & two children. He is here for his health. We are *all* related thus. Simon, William & John are brothers. Simon married my sister, which brings the families into connexion, & we were all *brought up* together here in old Chester, so that it seems to me just as if we were *all* brothers. . . .

After all, this Old Chester, my native town, is one of the most naturally beautiful places on earth! The street—or road—from the common to the top of the ascent is one mile in length, & the rise is some 100 or 150 feet in that distance, & very regular. Good-looking country dwellings and their appendages are scattered all along the distance, & much of the way the sides of the road are ornamented with trees. On the North side, for nearly ½ a mile, is a continuous row of as handsome trees—nearly all planted by my brother Henry (Judge French now) some 25 years ago—as I ever saw, which gives an elegant appearance to the street, & the location is so high that the prospect, especially from the upper end of the ascent, is magnificent—in all my travels I have seen few more so. Well here we all are, & when I have more time I will write more fully of all the old familiar things about me.

1. Mrs. French, Sr., was Benjamin's stepmother, Sarah Flagg French. Sarah French (b. 1846) and Daniel Chester French (1850–1931), the sculptor, were Henry's youngest children.

Exeter, Wednesday, August 1. Yesterday at 2 o'clock, Henry & I started from Chester in his wagon and came down here, where we arrived at 6 o'clock. . . .

Thursday, August 2. Henry and I went to Mr. Tuck's[1] and took tea last evening. We staid till nearly 11 o'clock & then came home & retired. We had a very pleasant time. Mr. Nelson & his wife & baby (she was Abby Tuck) were there, & Miss Ellen Tuck, Mr. T.'s daughter[,] who is pretty, & they tell me, a sensible girl.[2] I never saw her before, that I remember. Mr. Hoyt[3] came in, in the evening, & we enjoyed our visit first rate. . . .

1. Amos Tuck (1810–1879), Whig congressman from New Hampshire, 1847–1853, took part in forming the Republican party in Exeter in 1854.
2. William R. Nelson (1822–1864); his wife Abby (b. 1835) (daughter of Amos Tuck); their daughter, Laura Nelson (1853–1955); and Abby's sister, Ellen Tuck (1838–1915).
3. Joseph G. Hoyt, professor at Phillips Exeter Academy, took part in the state constitutional convention in 1850 and was later chancellor at Washington University in St. Louis.

Chester, Sunday, August 5. Henry & I left Exeter Thursday evening at precisely 6 o'clock. The sun was shining brightly right into our faces, & he carried a palm leaf fan to protect his eyes—as for me I faced it. At ¼ past 7 it descended & then the cool of a Northern summer evening came so that I was obliged to wrap my thick shawl about me. How different is the weather here from that of Washington! We arrived here (as the Judge said we should when we started) at exactly 9 o'clock; the town clock was striking as we turned around the "Meeting house."
. . . Friday was at the old mansion all day, mostly engaged in making & putting up a hammock, which I succeeded in doing quite well, & in which the family will, I trust, take much comfort, especially the children. Dan calls it "the hang-up." It is suspended between two large trees about 15 feet apart—it took about 150 feet of rope and an old canvas sacking bottom of a bedstead to make it. Hatty[1] & I sewed on a piece of cotton, doubled to strengthen it & made *islet* [sic] holes in it, & then secured it with ropes to the canvas, which was the work of several hours. . . . In the evening it cleared off, & we had a most magnificent sunset. Mr. W. C.

Brown, Mrs. Brown, & Emma[2] entertained us with music in the evening—they sing the old tunes that I love to hear, & sing them admirably. The Judge,[3] Helen, & Hatty were down here, & we got out a table and tried to entice the spirits to give us an exhibition of their doings, but they came not. I believe they are afraid of me! and I am getting more & more skeptical as to spirit rappings, etc. I am much inclined to believe that it is either deception or delusion, though I cannot doubt that there is some phenomenon about it, that leads the most honest person to believe in it. . . .

I have conversed considerably with "knowing ones" here about politics in the course of the past week. There is no doubt a crisis is approaching, and the removal of Gov. Reeder[4] of Kansas will hasten it. The Union is soon to receive such a shock as it never received before, and I deem it very problematical whether it can go safely through the danger which now threatens it! I hope & pray that it may, but I am ready[,] for one, to stand by the North in resisting the unjustifiable attempts now making by the South to add more slave states to this Union, to which movement I am sorry to see a Northern President of the U.S. lending his aid! How terribly Franklin Pierce has disappointed all his friends!

1. Henry Flagg French's daughter Harriette.
2. Daughter of William C. Brown.
3. Henry Flagg French.
4. Andrew H. Reeder (1807–1864), of Pennsylvania, was governor of the Kansas Territory, 1854–1855.

Concord, Mass., Sunday, August 26. We came up—myself, wife, Frank & Ben—from Boston last Tuesday evening. In the morning Gov. Brown took me to the State House and I was introduced to Gov. Gardner[1] and many members of his Council. I had a long conversation with the Gov. in his private room, and was very much pleased with him. He appears to be an offhand, sociable, free and easy man, with plenty of firmness and determination. . . .

1. Henry J. Gardner (1818–1892) was the Know-Nothing governor of Massachusetts, 1855–1858. Simon Brown was his lieutenant governor in 1855.

Boston, Friday, August 31. . . . Tuesday morning I came down to Cambridge with Col. John Keyes,[1] Sheriff of the Co., in his buggy drawn by two spirited horses. The morning was lovely—but rather chilly. The mercury [was] at 38 when I arose at 5 A.M. at Gov. Brown's house. We came over that never-to-be-forgotten, and most interesting road over which the British troops passed in going to, and returning from, Lexington &

Concord on the memorable April 19, 1775. Col. Keyes pointed out all the interesting localities connected with that expedition—the precursor of such mighty events. I do not think I ever enjoyed a ride more in my life. The Col. landed me safely between 8 & 9 at the door of Massachusetts Hall, where Frank rooms, in College, and where he was to meet me. He came in a few minutes after my arrival, & I assisted him two or three hours in arranging the things in his room. I came into Boston about noon and he about one o'clock. . . .

1. John S. Keyes (b. 1810) was sheriff of Middlesex County and father of Mary Brown's husband, George Keyes.

Sunday, September 2. Henry & his wife & Dan came yesterday to dinner, and today Henry, Frank & I went to hear Theodore Parker[1] preach. His sermon was excellent, and I was deeply interested, and was very much gratified. This is a hot day.

1. Theodore Parker (1810–1860) had recently been active in efforts to assist fugitive slaves in Boston.

Brooklyn, Tuesday, September 4. . . . At ½ past 8 o'clock yesterday morning, Bess, Ben & I left Boston in the cars, & after a very monotonous journey of 10 hours arrived here safe, & found the Doct. [Wells] & his family all well and glad to receive us. . . .

Washington, Tuesday, September 11. We left Brooklyn at 7 A.M. Friday, the 7th, & came home that day, arriving here at 7 P.M. Our visit to N. England was pleasant throughout, and we all enjoyed it exceedingly.

We found all well and *right* at home. Saturday I spent answering letters. Sunday attended church. Yesterday worked all day fixing mosquito bars[1] for the beds. This day if my head will permit (it aches badly now) I shall go to the Departments on business. We are having very hot weather.

1. I.e., mosquito nets.

Friday, September 28. Since Sept. 11 up to last Tuesday, nothing of any special moment occurred in my own walk of life, & therefore I made no record. I saw the President once & he was exulting over the recent election in Maine and claiming it as an Administration triumph. I did not, I do not, regard it in that light. I look upon it as a triumph of a fusion party of Democrats & Whigs, over the ultra-Maine-Liquor-Law party,[1] and Know Nothingism. I do not believe the Kansas question had any-thing to do with it, although the President assured me that all his infor-mation from Maine asserted that the Kansas question (slavery or not slavery in that Territory) was the one at issue, & the Slavery party triumphed, and that Connecticut, N.H.[,] N.J.[,] Ill.[,] Inda., Iowa, and[,] he thought[,] Michigan would follow. He named other States, but I will not attempt to specify them. I am sure he named those above enunciated. He said in 18 months Democracy would be again firmly in the ascendant and all over the Union, & the Constitution and Union would stand firmer than ever. I told him I doubted his premises, but sincerely hoped & prayed his conclusion might be verified. Time will prove the correctness of his prophecy. . . .

1. The election result in Maine was part of a state reaction against the strict prohibition law which was enacted in 1851.

Tuesday, January 1. . . . I have been daily at the Capitol and have wit-nessed the vain efforts made to elect a Speaker. Yesterday I was there nearly all the time of the session of the House, and witnessed the uproar that ensued the sending in by the President of his Annual Message, to an unorganized House of Representatives. It was a bold and strange proceeding on his part, and I was not at all surprised that a tempest followed. However, he has succeeded in getting his Message before the Country, and it is generally a good one. The latter portion is "a bid" for Southern support for the next term, & will probably be accepted by the South, & render the President still more unpopular at the North than he now is—and he is almost as unpopular as possible now! His argument in favor of the repeal of the Missouri Compromise is weak & puerile, and will be attacked without mercy. . . .

Wednesday, January 2. . . . Went to Bank of Washington on business, and then to Mr. Adams's & Capt. Dunnington's, & then home. Dined—read Mr. Giddings's speech of the 18th Dec.—a capital one—strong, eloquent, & to the point. I intend to make it my platform in my future political course.

At ½ past 3 went round to Mr. Adams's & he & I walked down to the Firemen's Insurance Office where there was a meeting of the Directors, at 4 P.M. We made a *semiannual* dividend of 10 per ct.! did some other business, and Adjd.

Came home, took tea, read Mr. Giddings's speech aloud to Mrs. French. . . .

Sunday, February 17. . . . Mr. & Mrs. Tuck[1] took tea & spent last evening with us, and we enjoyed their company very much. The bell rings for breakfast—no one except the servants up to eat it. Breakfast eaten by three of the family, self, Mrs. F. & Mary Eliza.[2] Frank and Ben still in bed—lazy boys—½ past 8 o'clock.

I must go to church today if it be cold. Our minister, Mr. Conway,[3] preached an Abolition sermon three or four Sundays ago, at which many of the Society took offence, and at a Society meeting last Sunday—at which I was not present—they passed resolutions of censure. I think Mr. C. was imprudent in preaching it, although it hit both North & South, but I am for a free pulpit, and approve of a minister's speaking from it just what he thinks. If a majority of his people do not approve his sentiments, their course is a very plain one; they can dismiss him. I would no more have my minister trammelled in his preaching than I would my wife in her management of her household affairs. I may see and hear things in both that I do not entirely approve, but never will attempt to dictate. Mr. Conway is a man of splendid abilities—rather transcendental, & sometimes a little extravagant in his ideas. Still, his heart is all right, and I like him, and if he dissolves his connection with our society it will be broken up, I fear. . . .

1. Catharine S. Tuck, second wife of Amos Tuck.
2. Mary Eliza Wells, daughter of French's half-sister, Catharine French Wells.
3. Moncure D. Conway (1832–1907), minister of the Unitarian church, was later discharged for his antislavery views.

Sunday, February 24. . . . *My* past week. Gone, & little to account for! Attended church Sunday. Mr. Conway preached from Gal. 5. 1st. "Stand fast therefore in the liberty wherewith Christ has made us free."

The sermon was an admirable one, and had it not *followed* the one of three or four Sabbaths ago, no one would ever have dreamed of finding fault with it. . . . In allusion to his former sermon, however, Mr. Conway made some comparison between Indians as our fathers treated them, & slaves as now treated. He said that one might discuss in the most severe manner possible the treatment of the Indians, and no fault was found. It would not be so if Indians could be used in cultivating cotton, rice & sugar! This was the idea, and it was sufficient to stir up some of the members of the society, & the threats at the door of never hearing another sermon from Mr. Conway were many & loud. I was sorry to hear them, but it cannot be helped. I shall attend Church today to see how those threats are carried out. . . .

Sunday, March 2. . . . New Hampshire election takes place a week from next Tuesday—Pierce and his understaffers here have sent thousands of dollars to that State to buy up the voters & carry the state for his cause. My belief is that they will not succeed—I hope not certainly. . . .

Saturday, March 29. . . . Yesterday the *Union* contained the withdrawal of John W. Forney from its editorial chair. He has gone out in order to act in Pennsylvania for his friend James Buchanan, who will be a prominent candidate for the Presidency. General Pierce has folded Col. Forney to his bosom for the past 3 years as if he were his dearest and best friend. He is not the first man who has warmed a viper into life to be bitten by it! Col. F. will now go to Philadelphia &, with "the Pennsylvanian" under his control, will do everything he can to defeat Pierce's nomination. . . .

Sunday, April 13. . . . On Thursday, at 6 A.M., I left for Baltimore to attend a meeting of the Directors of the Mag. Tel. Co. We met at 10 A.M.[,] did up the business by ½ past 12, & then Mr. Canby & I played four games of billiards. Then returned to Barnum's & prepared to attend a dinner party at Mr. Abell's. At 4 o'clock we were at Abell's, & a few minutes after we arrived[,] all the guests being assembled, we sat down to one of the most elegant dinners I have ever seen served—and I have eaten at the best of tables. . . .

Monday, May 25. . . . Politically we [are] getting upon troublous times— not only troublous, but fearful. I cannot but feel that the Union is now really in danger. The Kansas difficulty is ominous of widespread difficulty. The attack of Preston S. Brooks[1] of So. Carolina, a member of the House, upon Charles Sumner,[2] Senator from Massachusetts, while seated in his seat in the Senate Chamber on Thursday last, for words spoken in debate, although, *in itself,* a personal matter, must and will create a feeling throughout the Union that cannot easily be calmed. No one can tell what the end is to be, but it must necessarily be *bitter.*

The political *presidential* cauldron is boiling fiercely. The friends of Pierce and Buchanan are at open war, & between them, I rather think Hunter or Rusk[3] will get the nomination next week at Cincinnati. I do hope Pierce will not be in the field. Cruelly as he has treated me, the old personal feeling of friendship for him remains in my bosom & I cannot eradicate it. Whoever may be nominated will be opposed by me—although I can do but little.

---

1. Brooks (1819–1857) beat Sumner with a cane because of Sumner's verbal attacks on Brooks's uncle, Andrew P. Butler, senator from South Carolina.

2. Sumner (1811–1874) was so badly injured that he did not return to the Senate for three and a half years.

3. Thomas Jefferson Rusk (1803–1857), Democratic senator from Texas.

Friday, June 6. . . . I am reading, daily, the proceedings of the Cincinnati Convention. Fourteen ballots took place yesterday. Pierce recd. his highest vote on the first, shewing that there was no intention on the part of *anybody* to nominate him. He is getting his pay now for hugging his enemies to his bosom and discarding his friends! His heart, if he has one, is not in the right place! He has been false to himself, and all his friends, & will be laid on the political shelf, there to become moth-eaten for the rest of his life. No man ever had a better chance and a better prospect for a renomination and election than Frank Pierce when he commenced his Presidential career. The game was in his own hands, he held excellent cards, but he played them like a fool, and has lost the game.

I hope Buchanan will not be the nominee—anyone else, I care not whom—but not old Buck. He and his understrappers have been laboring the whole of Pierce's term to compass his defeat & Buchanan's elevation. I have seen it all, and deprecated and denounced it, and I hope most sincerely that the mean, contemptible, underhanded game they have played to betray Pierce, while they pretended to be his friends, will not result in their triumph. . . .

Saturday, June 7. At 20 minutes before 11 A.M. yesterday, I was in Todd's building[1] when Mr. Barnard,[2] who keeps his office there[,] recd. a Telegraphic despatch announcing the nomination at 10 o'clock of James Buchanan as Democratic candidate for the Presidency of the U.S.

Well, I hoped for a different result, but now we know whom we have to beat, & it behooves us *to unite* and beat him, as we can. Pierce made no show for a nomination, and the entire desertion of his friends was evidence that he had, long since, been betrayed. Why was this? He had gone *the entire* for slavery, and the South were satisfied. He had done all in his power to put down Freedom in Kansas, but alas that could not save him. There must have been a reason—yes there was a reason which they dared not avow openly, and dared not print. It was that he was the supporter, if not the instigator[,] of the repeal of the Missouri Compromise. . . . The Democrats of the Cincinnati Convention knew very well that the man who had done this could not be re-elected, if he were renominated, & so they made choice of one whose escutcheon was not covered with "great gouts of blood," and one who, being out of the

Country during all the excitement of the past two years, cannot be identified with the war on Freedom, & who, mark my prediction, will try to escape the odium that has attached to the Pierce Administration on account its unholy & unjustifiable course on the subject of slavery!

There has been no popular outburst here yet, but we shall have it, with those whom Pierce has cherished, to lead off with it!

J. C. Breckinridge[3] of Ky. is nominated for Vice President. A good and a true man. I know him well & respect him highly. He is a democrat to the backbone, and of course proslavery, and must be beaten, if possible.

Yesterday Mr. Postmaster General Campbell removed from office, my brother-in-law, Rev. Charles P. Russell, and avowed as his reason that Mr. Russell voted for Silas H. Hill[4] for Mayor! . . .

1. William B. Todd, a furrier, owned Todd's Marble Building on Pennsylvania Avenue.
2. Theodore Barnard, agent for the New York Associated Press.
3. John C. Breckinridge (1821–1875), Democratic congressman from Kentucky, 1851–1855.
4. Hill, the Know-Nothing candidate, was narrowly defeated on June 2.

Sunday, June 15. . . . I wrote a note to the President on Monday stating my views as to the removal of Russell, & asking him to right that wrong. He has neither done it or noticed my letter. Just as I supposed. Mr. Russell went up to see him. He expressed regret at his removal, but could not interfere. Held Judge Richardson's family in high estimation! etc. Hypocrite—base, heartless Hypocrite! I did feel a lingering respect & even affection for the man till this thing was done. Now I despise him, and never desire to see his face again, and I do really think he had better, for his own honor, have been four years in the Penitentiary here, than 4 years in the Presidential chair, & he would return to New Hampshire less a disgrace to the State & to himself. He is a cold-blooded, heartless man! . . .

Sunday, June 22. I went to Philadelphia as I expected, and attended the Republican Convention. . . .

Our Convention was very harmonious, and I hope our candidate will be elected, but *now* I doubt.[1] I have not yet seen enthusiasm enough to make up my mind.

I am writing in the Arbor in the garden. The weather is hot and I am too sleepy to write more, so I will defer.

1. John C. Frémont (1813–1890), Republican candidate for president, famous for his

western expeditions and his role in the seizure of California, had been senator from California, 1850–1851, and was married to Thomas Hart Benton's daughter Jessie.

Monday, July 21. On Tuesday last at ½ past 4 P.M. I started for New York, and, riding all night, arrived there at 5 A.M. Wednesday. Went over to Doct. Wells's Brooklyn and found Kate and her new baby[1] as well as could be expected. Attended the Telegraph Directors' meeting at 4 o'clock P.M. which kept us together till dark, then played a game or two of billiards, & then returned to Brooklyn, tired out completely, & to bed & asleep. After dressing in the morning (Wednesday) at Doct. Wells's I went over to the city of N.Y. and *walked* up to Col. Frémont's[,] 56 9th street—I should think 3 miles from the Astor House. Saw the Col. and Mrs. Frémont, and had a very pleasant interview. The Col. is a modest and gentlemanly man, & appears as I expected he would, well. The honor of *being nominated* by a great party is by no means a small one, and he wears it gracefully, and should he be elected he will, I have not a doubt, be the man he ought to be. I talked, say ½ an hour[,] with him & Mrs. F. & came away well pleased. . . .

    1. Anna Wells.

Thursday, September 4. . . . Mrs. French, Frank and Benny left 3 weeks ago this day for New England. They remained in Boston until the following Wednesday and then went to Exeter where, I suppose[,] Mrs. French now is. She went to be with her Sister, Mrs. Anne R. French, who was in the last stage of a consumption, and is now a saint in Heaven. She died at ¼ past 4 o'clock A.M. on Friday, Aug. 29th. . . .

Thursday, November 20. . . . James Buchanan is to be President on the 4th of March next, I suppose. A majority of the Electors elected on the 4th inst. are Buchanan and Breckinridge men, & unless some "slip between the cup & the lip" occurs, they will be elected Prest. and Vice Prest. of course. My own opinion from all I could learn was that there would be no election by the people. I had no hope of Frémont's election from the day he was nominated. I was for John McLean,[1] and counselled as strongly as I could his nomination, but was overruled by the majority, and now they see the fruits of their *headstrong preference* for Frémont. Had McLean been nominated, he would this day have been President-elect of the United States! The Republican Party seem to me to have no political wisdom or foresight. They throw away all the influence they have, and I now begin to despair of their success, ever. . . .

On my way to Baltimore I heard of the death of Hon. John M. Clayton.[2] He died at his home, Dover, Delaware, on Sunday evening Nov. 9th. He was my personal friend, and many a most pleasant evening have I spent with him, & been entertained & deeply interested in listening to his conversation, in which he excelled almost any man I ever associated with. He seemed to have read everything, & never to have forgotten anything. He was a great man, and had he possessed the industry of James K. Polk, might have been a man of more mark than he actually was, although he was among the acknowledged great men of his time. He will be very much missed.

The last time I ever remember to have seen him at his own room, was one day last summer, not a great while before the Republican Convention at Phila., perhaps the day before I left. He was then quite unwell, but sat and talked for an hour or more about the political prospects. He knew I was a delegate to the Convention, and urged me to do all I could for the nomination of Judge McLean. "For[,]" said he[,] "let that Convention nominate McLean, and he will be elected—there is no doubt of it, but let them nominate any other man, and it elects Buchanan. Now, French, you go there and use all your influence in favor of McLean, if you wish your party to succeed."

He gave me his reasons, at much length, for this conclusion[,] and agreeing with him in sentiment, I, of course, followed his advice.

When I took my leave, he walked to the door with me. It was a beautiful summer afternoon, and he stood upon the doorstep and remarked, in a manner so feeling, & so full of expression that it made me very sad, upon the beauty and mildness of the weather. "Oh how beautiful[,]" said he, "how lovely, and I sick, yes, French, too sick to enjoy it. Oh the blessing of health—we know not till we lose it, how to appreciate it—it is one of God's best blessings. Oh if I could only get well again." He went on in this way for five or six minutes, & the tears were in his eyes & in mine too, when I bade him good-by.

I saw him many times afterwards, in his seat in the Senate, but never had any conversation with him except on business.

How our great men are going, one by one, away, and how few seem to be coming on to take their places! The age of statesmen seems to have gone by, and that of upstarts, striving to be great without the first germ of intellectual greatness within them, has taken its place. We have now left of the old stock, only Cass, Benton, Marcy, and Buchanan. They are truly worthy of the name of statesmen. Seward is at the head of the next younger generation and possibly Hunter, Pearce, Foot, & Rusk of the Senate may yet take positions to be known as leading statesmen.[3] So may Banks, Howell Cobb, Humphrey Marshall, & Israel Washburn, & perhaps others, now of the House of Representatives.[4] Giddings is far beyond any of them, but he has taken such a bold, uncompromising stand on Free Soil ground that he never can stand purely as a statesman *by general consent,* though he is one in reality, & one of the most honest and best we have! Would to God he could be President of the United States! *He could be depended on!* God bless him!

One man I have seen within the past three months who could, if the opportunity were given him, and he would profit by it, take a stand amongst the great men of the United States, inferior to no one—and that man is Henry Champion Deming[5] of Hartford, Conn. He possesses *all* the elements of a truly great man, & may Heaven so shape his destiny as that those elements may be brought into requisition & be exerted for the good of our Country, which needs every talent of every individual citizen. I had a good opportunity to form an opinion of Mr. Deming[,] for I was ten days an inmate of his family, and our Masonic connections were such that I was with him nearly all the time, and I speak of him with no mere snap conclusion, but because I know, & can appreciate the man! Our political views are wide asunder, so that I surely formed my opinion without any political predilection in his favor. If in my power to call public attention to his merits, it will assuredly be done. . . .

1. John McLean (1785–1861) was a justice of the U.S. Supreme Court, 1829–1861. He received 196 votes at the Republican Convention of 1856.

2. John M. Clayton (1796–1856), a Delaware Whig, served in the U.S. Senate, 1829–1836 and 1845–1849; as Secretary of State, 1849–1850; and in the Senate again, 1853–1856.

3. William H. Seward (1801–1872) was Whig governor of New York, 1839–1843, and Whig (later Republican) senator, 1849–1861. James A. Pearce (1804–1862), of Maryland, was Whig (later Democratic) congressman, 1835–1839 and 1841–1843, and senator, 1843–1862. Solomon Foot (1802–1866), of Vermont, was Whig (later Republican) senator, 1851–1866.

4. Nathaniel P. Banks (1816–1894) was first Democratic and later Republican congressman from Massachusetts. He had been elected speaker of the House in February 1856. Humphrey Marshall (1812–1872), Whig (later American party) congressman from Kentucky, 1849–1852 and 1855–1859. Israel Washburn (1813–1883), Whig (later Republican) congressman from Maine, 1851–1861, was one of four brothers to serve in the House.

5. Henry C. Deming (1815–1872), Whig (later Republican) mayor of Hartford, 1854–1858 and 1860–1862, also served in the U.S. House, 1863–1867.

Friday, January 2. . . . After writing one or two letters, went down, dressed *in my holiday clothes,* & at 12 started out to New Year my friends. Day very dismal, & before I got home (at ½ past 3) it commenced raining.

My first call was on Messrs. Tappan & Cragin, at Mr. Alden's.[1] Both out. Left cards, & went to Doct. Bayly's,[2] Ed. *Era.* Saw the Doct. & his family—drank a cup of coffee, & ate some chicken salad, & then called on Col. Benton. He seemed to be very happy to see me, & we talked about his recent visit to New England, & his lecture, & the manner in which it was received. He was evidently much elated at his success. He told me he should start at 6 this morning for Cambridge, Mass., & he should then give the "she-doctors" a benefit. . . .

Hon. James Bell,[3] senator from N.H.[,] is now boarding with me. He came Dec. 10th. We were boys together, although I am 4 years & 2 months his senior, and we studied law within a few rods of each other at the same time—his brother's[4] office, where he studied, being within a stone's throw of my father's[,] where I studied. It is very—*very*—pleasant to have him with me, as he is ever ready to join in our amusements, and to talk of the olden time.

1. Mason W. Tappan (1817–1886), Republican congressman from New Hampshire, 1855–1861. Aaron H. Cragin (1821–1898), American party and Republican congressman from New Hampshire, 1855–1859. Alden was a boardinghouse keeper.

2. Gamaliel Bailey (1807–1859), briefly a doctor in Canton, China, and in Cincinnati, was editor of the antislavery *National Era* in Washington, 1847–1859.

3. James Bell (1804–1857) had been the unsuccessful Whig candidate for governor of New Hampshire, 1854 and 1855, before being elected to the Senate in 1855.

4. Samuel Dana Bell.

Tuesday, January 19. On the evening of the day I last wrote herein my brother Henry & my brother-in-law Soule came. Soule remained a week, & Henry until last Friday morning. It was a great gratification to me to have them here. On the morning that Henry left Frank came home to spend his winter vacation.

I was engaged nearly all of last week in attending to my duties as Treasurer of the U.S. Agricultural Society. It held its annual session Wednesday, Thursday & Friday—perhaps the most interesting one it has ever held. It was well attended and the debates were exceedingly interesting. On Thursday we all went by invitation to the President's, & were introduced individually by Col. Wilder, Prest. of the Society[,] to Gen. Pierce—speeches were made by both Presidents, & they were both peculiarly happy in what they said. I had not before been in the President's house for 16 months! I used to go there daily. May Frank Pierce, whom I have cherished in my heart's core for many a long year, & by whom I have not been treated [as] I hoped to be, be a happy man during all of life that is left to him, is the solemn & sincere wish of my heart! Me, his course has politically ruined—I would not, in retaliation, injure a hair of his head.

Saturday at ½ past 2 P.M. I went into the House of Representatives. Mr. Giddings was speaking in opposition to a bill for the relief of Asbury Dickins. I walked round to *his* seat—he was standing in another member's near—& stood leaning on his chair listening to him, when in the middle of a sentence, as suddenly as if he had been shot through the heart, he sunk senseless into his seat. There was an immediate rush towards him, & those nearest took him up as soon as they could, & carried him into the area back of the Speaker's chair, and laid him on a sofa. It was some 5 to 10 minutes before he showed any signs of life. Then he commenced breathing, accompanying each breath with a groan, &, there being a great crowd about him, I left & came home. As soon as I had dined I returned—they had then removed him to the Speaker's room where he lay, slowly reviving. He was carried to his lodgings in the course of the evening, and is now comparatively well. This is the second time Mr. Giddings has been attacked in the same way while speaking. I talked with him about it ½ an hour yesterday. He deems it a disease of the heart, & says he is perfectly aware of his situation, but, like a true man, as he is, avows himself ready & willing to go at a moment's warning, hoping, as he says, for a happier life hereafter, where there will be no heart diseases to trouble him. . . .

Sunday, February 1. . . . I spent the evening of Saturday before last (the 24th) with Judge McLean, at his room. I never was introduced to him before, but found him one of the most pleasant & agreeable men I ever met. Oh if he had only been nominated at Phila. last summer as the Republican candidate for President, but he was not! Well, all is perhaps for the best.

Last Tuesday evening I called at Messrs. Tappan, Cragin, & Colfax's[1] boardinghouse at 7. . . . On my way home heard of the death of Preston S. Brooks, Member of the House from S.C. He had just died at Brown's hotel, very suddenly and unexpectedly. From peculiar circumstances attached to him, connected with his unfortunate attack on Senator Sumner, & his associations since, his death caused a profound sensation, & was the talk of the City. It was officially announced on Thursday in both Houses, and he was entombed in the Congressional Burial ground on that day.

The first time I ever saw Preston S. Brooks to know him, was at a dinner at Mr. Levin's room, at the National Hotel. . . . He made a most favorable impression on me then, & from that time onward till his attack on Mr. Sumner, I regarded him as a most amiable & worthy gentleman. Only a short time prior to that attack, I saw him in the House, urging his fellow members, in private conversation, to vote for a pension to a poor old soldier friend of his—I introduced him to Gen. Granger[2] of New York, whose favor he was seeking in behalf of his old friend. He made sufficient interest to get the bill passed, & I honored him highly for it, & congratulated him on its passage. That congratulation was the last word I ever spoke to him. The last time I ever saw him was perhaps 10 days before his death, when I met him on Pa. Avenue while I was walking with my friend Albert Pike. He shook hands with Pike, & they conversed for several minutes with each other, while I held Pike's arm, but a mutual nonintercourse seemed to be established between Brooks & myself, & we, neither of us, recognized the other. Poor fellow—he was then in the very prime of health and manhood, nearly 20 years my junior—now "he sleeps that sleep that knows no waking." . . .

I was at the P.O. Dept. on business last Thursday, & had quite a political talk with my friend, First Asst. P.M. Gen. Horatio King, to whom I attempted to define my political position and views. We seemed to agree in most points & yet consider ourselves at political antipodes to each other!

Last Monday evening I took my seat as President of the Republican Association of the City of Washington for the first time and made a few remarks expressive of the same ideas and principles exactly that I avowed to Mr. King, & they were received with applause & apparent gratification. . . .

1. Schuyler Colfax (1823–1885), Republican congressman from Indiana, 1855–1869, was speaker, 1863–1869, and Vice President, 1869–1873.

2. Amos P. Granger (1789–1866), Whig (Republican) congressman from New York, 1855–1859.

SIX

The Gathering Crisis

1857–1861

uring these years the politics of the nation, the debate over slavery, and French's personal life each moved rapidly toward an ominous climax. As the tension rose, so too did the pace of French's life. Between the election of Buchanan and the election of Lincoln he took at least a dozen business and family trips that carried him to many parts of the nation.

Even though French had shifted to the Republican party, he was still the same old moderate who had friends of various persuasions. In December 1858, for example, he remarked that he favored a Whig, John M. Botts of Virginia, for President. A few months later he had shifted to a Democrat, Stephen A. Douglas. He had, however, no uncertainty about President Buchanan, whom he accused of being "in league" with treason as secession loomed.[1] In 1860 he was not an original supporter of Abraham Lincoln, but once Lincoln was nominated, French backed him enthusiastically.

French's antislavery views were just as moderate and as wavering. He first insisted that Kansas must be free but then conceded that he would accept Douglas's popular sovereignty there. After John Brown's raid he attacked the "dangerous sympathy of the unholy & bloodthirsty abolitionists of the North for the old murderer and traitor." When Brown was executed, French wrote that the abolitionist had "met his just deserts."[2] French was above all "an ultra Union man,"[3] and when South Carolina seceded, he called their leaders "arch traitors."[4] As he made his way down this middle path on the slavery question, he typified millions of Northerners who had no desire to end slavery in the South but who would fight to save the Union.

In private life French had become an aging patriarch who rejoiced in his family triumphs but reacted fearfully when youthful rebellion, illness, or death threatened his family. In the years before the Civil War, Frank brought nothing but happiness and pride as he graduated from law school and became a lawyer in New York City. The chapter ends with the Frenches preparing for Frank's marriage to Amos Tuck's daughter Ellen. Ben, on the other hand, the proverbial prodigal son, was "given to fine dressing and rowdyism" and "hate[d] to study or to do anything useful."[5] Hints of what lay ahead for Elizabeth appeared in June 1860 when she went to New York to seek medical advice. She returned no better and in November underwent a mastectomy for breast cancer. A striking picture of French's domestic life can be found in his letters to Elizabeth while she was away, which he included in his journal. Trying to entertain her, he described in detail the beauty of their garden, his experiences shopping and running the house, and his own foolishness in hurting his leg playing baseball.

The chapter also contains valuable descriptions of French's many trips. In 1857 alone he took no less than six—three to New York on legal and telegraph business, one to Cambridge, Massachusetts, for Frank's graduation, and trips to Syracuse and Louisville for the Agricultural Society. A year later he found time for two short sailing trips along the New England coast. The remarkable acceleration in the speed of travel can be judged by comparing one of French's early trips with one taken a quarter century later. He had spent fifty hours in 1835 covering the 500 miles from Chester to Washington, ten miles an hour; in 1859 the 700-mile trip from Washington to Chicago took thirty-two hours, or twenty-two miles an hour.

As the winter of 1861 neared its end, French's story and the history of the nation were both approaching a grim climax. While Elizabeth lingered on after her operation, South Carolina and other southern states were seceding from the Union. On March 3, 1861, the Frenches were awaiting Lincoln's inaugural on the fourth and Frank's wedding on the fifth. The outbreak of the Civil War and Elizabeth's death were not far off.

1. Dec. 30, 1860.
2. Dec. 4, 1859.
3. Nov. 27, 1860.

4. Dec. 25, 1860.
5. June 17, 1860.

Journal

Monday, March 8. . . . I was in pretty constant attendance on the sessions of the Senate and house during the last month of the session. Some of my business came to a favorable conclusion, & I shall get enough out of it, "to keep the wolf from the door," till Congress comes again, I hope. The last morning of the session—the Clerks being pretty much worn out—I aided at the Clerk's table of the House from the close of the recess till 12 o'clock, & then went, with the members, to the Senate & saw the President and President elect—Pierce & Buchanan—enter the chamber & seat themselves, & then rise & go out to the front portico where the ceremonies of the inauguration took place. I went out with the crowd, but the air being chilly, I did not remain long. I could not hear the inaugural, so I came home & made myself comfortable. There was an immense crowd of people in the city, & it is rather a mystery to me where they all found accommodation. . . .

Thursday, March 19. . . . I was at Willard's hotel day before yesterday, & such a crowd! as I saw there assembled I have seldom laid eyes upon at a hotel. Men in office seeking[,] I presume, to be retained. Men out of office seeking to get in. And men who have come here to buttonhole their friends in, or their enemies out. There I saw at least 50 whom I knew, and some hundreds whom I did not know, from the North, South, East & West! This is one of the curses of our republican system of rotation in office. . . .

Saturday, April 25. . . . The political *world* is now pretty much out of my beat. I see precious little of the "Powers that Be," & have no aspirations to know anything of them more than that they keep the Country peaceable & prosperous. I want to see Kansas a Free state, & I bless God that the prospects now are that Slavery will, some day, end in North America; I hope & trust peaceably & with the concurrence of all good men both North & South! I have said a thousand times, and say now, that I would not aid in depriving the South of a single hair's breadth of her rights under the Constitution, *in all particulars,* and there exists not a man in all the South who would go farther than I would to sustain and defend those rights. I am by no means an Abolitionist, nor would I, if I had the power, abolish slavery "at one fell swoop." I would abolish it gradually and peaceably, & in no way to the prejudice of the South—but for its ultimate benefit and happiness! I do not want slavery to extend one inch into territory now free, and if anything I can do will prevent it, it shall not! . . .

Tuesday, June 9. . . . On the first day of this month came our Municipal election, when we had "high times" at some of the polls. This Ward was as quiet as a Sabbath day, and I cast my vote about 3 o'clock P.M. without let or hindrance.

The chief difficulty was at the 4th ward polls up 7th street, at the Northern Liberties Market.[1] It seems that an organized body of scoundrels, calling themselves "Plug Uglies"[2] (a rascally name), came on from Baltimore to *regulate* our elections. Their first demonstration was made at the polls above mentioned between 10 & 11 o'clock. The first I knew of it was at 11, when I was on my way to the P.O.

A crowd was assembled at J. F. Callan's[3] drugstore[,] corner of E & 7th streets, and upon enquiry as to what it meant, Mr. Callan, who was standing on the sidewalk in front, informed me that two hundred rowdies from Baltimore had attacked the polls, driven away the Commissioners of Election & broken up the polls. That a man was then in the store, who had a pistol bullet shot through his arm, and had his chin injured, and that they were then dressing his wounds—that Capt. Goddard[4] had been severely hurt, etc. I told [him] that every scoundrel of those who had come from Baltimore ought to be killed, & I would make one to go and help kill them. I . . . walked home . . . & I heard no more until about ½ past 3 when the news came that the Marines had been called out and had fired on the mob & killed seven persons. I went out to ascertain the facts, but there were so many contradictory stories that I could not tell what to believe[,] the Union Party justifying & the American Party bitterly condemning the actions of the Marines in firing.

The story of one party was then, and is now, that there were as many as 200 "Plug Uglies" brought here by the Americans to overawe our polls. On the other hand the Am. party say that there were not over 35 here.

The public accounts that I have seen represent the polls as having been broken up and a cannon procured and loaded and a determination manifested to prevent the elections from proceeding—the firing of pistols at the Marines, and the throwing of stones and other missiles. It is also represented that the crowd was addressed, both by the Mayor[5] and Capt. Tyler[6] of the Marine Corps, & they were earnestly solicited to disperse. That the Mayor ordered the polls open, but that the crowd swore they should not be again opened, etc.

Upon this state of things the firing was, in my view, perfectly justifiable. But, on the other hand, I was yesterday told by Mr. James Nokes, a good citizen and credible man, who was present and at whose side a man was shot down, that the "Plug Uglies" had all left before the Marines came. That the cannon was dragged up from the Navy yard by a parcel of boys, and there was, probably, no intention of firing it. That he begged the Mayor, "for God's sake" to have the Marines leave, and Capt. Goddard to use his influence with the Mayor to have them leave, but that no regard was paid to his request. He said only two pistols were fired when the Marines took the cannon. That when they fired it was deliberately done, first in one direction, then another, & then in another. That they even fired at persons who were running away, & that he regarded it as deliberate murder.

I asked him how it happened that the cannon was loaded with ball cartridges, stones, etc. He replied, that boys would act foolishly, or something to that effect.

I have been inclined entirely to justify the President, the Mayor, and all concerned, but if Mr. Nokes's story is true they certainly are not justifiable. His sympathies are strong with the Americans, & he may not have seen the affair in an unprejudiced light, though he is a cool, truthful, and reliable man.

So I have written down both sides and will leave Monsieur Time to decide which is right.

1. Located on the south side of Mt. Vernon Square.
2. The "Plug Uglies" were Know-Nothing (American party) supporters.
3. James N. Callan.
4. John H. Goddard served as the first captain of the District of Columbia night police force, 1842–1854 and 1858–1861.
5. Dr. William B. Magruder, representing Democrats and Republicans, had barely beaten the Know-Nothing candidate in 1856. He was reelected in the election of 1857.
6. Henry B. Tyler of Virginia was stationed at the Marine barracks.

Sunday, June 28. A clear cool morning—not a breath of air stirring; appearances indicate a hot day.

I left this city at 6 o'clock A.M. of the 11th inst. for Boston. . . . & then went to Concord, Mass., arrived at Lt. Gov. Brown's at ½ past 1 [June 13]. Frank met me at the gate. The Gov. trimming his apple trees, Mrs. Keyes confined to her chamber with her new baby,[1] then about a week old, Mrs. Brown pleased at being a *Grandmarm*—and all well as possible under the circumstances.

Frank read his class poem to Mrs. B. & me in the afternoon. A little after 7 Mr. Keyes came home from Boston with a monstrous lobster, which we fed on for about 3 days! It was excellent too. . . . Monday morning [June 15] at 7 I went down as far as "Porter's" in the cars, and then walked down to the Colleges at Cambridge. . . .

Thursday [June 18] I was all about the City, doing errands & calling on my friends. Friday was Class day at Cambridge, & at ½ past 8 Mrs. Barker, Hattie French, Nell Tuck, & Fanny Gilbert[2] (the three latter came down from Exeter the day previous) went out to Cambridge. We made Frank's room our headquarters, & witnessed with great pleasure and satisfaction the ceremonies of the day. Everything passed off admirably, notwithstanding that the day was rainy, by spells, throughout. Frank acquitted himself well, and received much praise from those whose praise was worth having.

. . . Arrived home at 7 P.M. Monday [June 22]. Found all well, but my garden pretty much ruined by the hailstorm of last Sunday. It was the most tremendous one ever known here, & did immense damage. There were tens of thousands of panes of glass broken in this city, & the shrubbery was cut all to pieces. . . .

Tuesday [June 23] I was engaged all day in writing on an address to be delivered at Mount Vernon Wednesday, and in mending my skylight, which, though of very thick glass, was completely smashed. The west window of my attick, entirely exposed, but of triple thick glass, was not injured at all. One half the blind of the west window in my sleeping room was open, and one pane was broken. The glass in the roof of the Capitol was much broken, and I have a piece now before me which is of this thickness—| |—as was all the glass in that roof. Men walked about on it! . . .

1. Elizabeth Keyes.
2. Fannie W. Gilbert (d. 1897) of Exeter later came to live with the Frenches in Washington.

Sunday, July 26. Now for the record of the past month. . . . I left here on Monday evening, June 29th, for New York, to attend a meeting of Telegraph Committees. . . .

I remained in New York till Friday morning, July 3d, when I came home. On Thursday I did some errands—called on my friend Robert Macey (Deputy G. Master of the G.L. of N.Y.)[,] upon Wheeler and Wilson, sewing machine makers,[1] & they agreed to send my wife a new sewing machine & take her old one, in consideration of my efforts to aid them at the start, & did other errands. . . .

I remained at home until Wednesday evening, July 8th, when I left for Philadelphia to attend the annual meeting of "The Magnetic Telegraph Company," and two meetings of Directors—the old Board & the New. We commenced at 10 o'clock A.M. Thursday, & closed up at 8 P.M.

I stopped at the La Pierre House—a first-rate House—the best I have ever staid at in Philadelphia. At 7 o'clock Friday morning I took the cars for New York City, on my way to Syracuse to attend the Exhibition of Mowers and Reapers, etc., held at Syracuse, N.Y., by the U.S. Agricultural Society. Arrived at the wharf in N.Y. at ½ past 11—went to the Depot of the North River R.R. and started from thence for Albany at 12 noon. Arrived in Albany between 5 & 6, & started on the N.Y. Central R.R. for Syracuse at ½ past 6. Arrived at the Voorhees house[,] Syracuse[,] about 1 A.M. Saturday [July 11] & went to bed. Arose at 7 o'clock, met Col. Wilder & Maj. Poore[2] & after breakfast commenced my duties as Treasurer & continued in the performance of them until Wednesday at 2 o'clock, when I left for Lockport to visit my sister Sarah (Mrs. S. L. Chase)[,] intending to return the next Monday.

Arrived at Lockport at 7 P.M. Found all my relatives well. I had not seen Sarah since August 1838, when my brother Edmund & I visited her at Woodstock, Vt. Since then what changes! Her only living child then was Daniel F. Chase,[3] now a fine young man in business as a dentist with his father. She has also three other sons, George 18, now in College at Geneva, N.Y., Saml. Logan 16 & Arthur Livermore 14. George came home on Saturday, & Frank arrived the same day, so we had quite a houseful, and all enjoying ourselves.

On Thursday, the 16th, I visited, for the first time, Niagara Falls. I left Lockport at 9 A.M.[,] arrived at Niagara at ¼ before 11, & went to the "International." From thence I walked to Goat Island and around it, went on to "Prospect Tower," then took a carriage & rode round by the suspension bridge to the Canada shore. Went under the fall on that side, and then rode to Lundy's Lane battleground,[4] & from the top of a sort of tower there saw Brock's[5] monument by the aid of a telescope, returned to the "Clifton House" where I staid a few minutes—then back over the suspension bridge (I walked over on the Railroad part) to the International, where I dined, and then returned to Lockport. . . .

Tuesday morning [July 21] at 6 o'clock & 20 m. I took the cars for Syracuse, leaving Frank at Lockport, and arrived at Syracuse at ¼ before 11, expecting to find the Exhibition going on, & all my friends there. I was greatly disappointed, & not a little mortified[,] to find that all was over and closed up, and all my friends had departed. I dined at the Voorhees House, & at ½ past 2 started for Albany—arrived there at 8, & went on board the steamer *New World* in which I arrived at New York at 7 A.M. Wednesday, and at 8 A.M. started for home, and arrived here at ¼ before 7 Wednesday evening. Never in my life was I more rejoiced to get home, for I was thoroughly tired out. . . .

1. Wheeler & Wilson Manufacturing Co., 343 Broadway.
2. Benjamin Perley Poore (1820–1887) was the Washington correspondent of the Boston *Journal* and secretary of the U.S. Agricultural Society.
3. Daniel F. Chase was 20.
4. Lundy's Lane, a road in Canada leading westward from the Niagara River, was in 1814 the scene of an inconclusive battle between the British and the Americans in the War of 1812.
5. Sir Isaac Brock (1769–1812) was a British major general killed in the Battle of Queenston Heights in 1812.

Wednesday, August 6. Frank returned home last Saturday morning, and is to commence the study of the law at once. Where & how is not yet exactly settled. I have been pretty busy since I wrote last herein, attending to my household matters, as I expected to have left this day for New York to attend a Telegraph meeting. . . . Mr. Kendall was appointed chairman of the Committee of Delegates from the Mag. Tel. Co., & Mr. Barnum and myself made up the Committee. Mr. Kendall ascertained a few days since that some of the Companies who entered with us into the Articles of Agreement did so with the intention of deceiving us & some other companies, and that they had played us *as false as possible*. So he notified me, day before yesterday, that so far as the Mag. Tel. Co. was concerned no meeting would be held; I am thus relieved from going, much to my satisfaction. . . .

Wednesday, September 16. . . . On Thursday, Aug. 27, at 20 m. past 4 P.M. I started in the cars for Louisville, Ky., to attend the Annual Exhibition of the U.S. Agricultural Society. Arrived at the "Relay House" 9 miles this side of Baltimore, at a little before 6, & there waited for the western train for Wheeling. It came some 20 minutes behind time, having on board about 300 U.S. soldiers bound for Ft. Leavenworth, Kansas. I got on board, & on we went. At Harpers Ferry we took supper. . . . We went on very well till daylight, when [we] were going over the mountains, when we ascertained that a freight train ahead of us had been thrown from the track by a slide. This detained us two hours, when we again got under way expecting to breakfast at Grafton.[1] When about 6 miles from that place, it being[,] I think[,] about 10 o'clock, news came that two freight trains had come in collision, that both were completely smashed, one of the engineers killed, & it was very uncertain how long we should be detained, but, at least 6 hours!

Our soldiers were almost in a state of mutiny, & the officers had hard work to control them. It was a very unpleasant state of affairs, so Gov. W[illard][,][2] Mr. Ricketts,[3] . . . a gentleman from Chicago whose name I have forgotten, two others who I did not know, & I hired a man, who happened there, with his two-horse farm wagon to carry us by the common road to Grafton. We laid boards across for seats, & off we started. Had a pleasant ride, although rather *a hard one*. All were disposed to be merry[,] and joke & pun abounded. In something over an hour we arrived at Grafton, & there sat down to a good dinner, which we all enjoyed, not having eaten since the previous evening. . . . At about 5 P.M. our train came along, & we got under way again for Wheeling where we were due at 9 o'clock A.M. *the previous morning*. Being so much out of time, we had to wait for every down train to pass us, & when we came to the "Broad Tree" tunnel, which had caved in a few weeks prior, we were "zigzagged" over, which took some hours.

Finally we arrived at Benwood, some 4 miles below Wheeling, at about 12 o'clock, midnight, & there it took at least an hour to get the soldiers, their baggage, & the passengers on board the boat to cross to Bellaire, Ohio, where the cars started for Columbus. We got across at last, & all went to the Norton Hotel, where we arrived between 1 & 2 A.M. of the 29th—16 hours behind time! We routed up the hotel people, & after some little expostulation with the landlord, who seemed at first inclined to send us supperless to bed, we got a good supper, & Gov. Willard, Mr. Ricketts, Col. Drew & I were shown into a room with one double bed & one single one, as the best that could be done for us! I had gone up first, supposing that only two were to follow, & had appropriated the single bed. When the other 3 came, I offered my bed to Gov. Willard, but he declined, and wrapping himself in his shawl camped down on the floor. An army of musquitoes were soon upon us, & none of us slept much[,] I believe. . . . I had a very pleasant run to Columbus, where we arrived at 2 P.M.[, and] eat a miserable dinner in the depot. At ½ past 2 left for Cincinnati, where we arrived between 5 & 6, went straight to the other depot & took the train for St. Louis. I left it at Seymour [Indiana], & took another train for Jeffersonsville [Indiana], where we arrived between 4 & 5, & about 5 I got across the river & to the Gault House at Louisville. The journey was the hardest one I ever made, and I was thoroughly tired out. I found that no provision had been made for my accommodation. I routed Major Poore, & he referred me over to Col. Wilder, in whose room he told there was *an extra bed*—the rascal knew it was occupied but kept that to himself! So I routed Col. Wilder, who, with his eyes about a quarter open, told me to go and find a cot, as the other bed in his room was occupied. . . ! So I left him & went roaming along the passage, & seeing the door of "No. 50" open[,] I enquired of the porter if that room was occupied. He said he did not believe it was, as the door had been open all night. So in I went, fastened the door & went to bed, where I slept gloriously till between 8 & 9, when I arose, washed & dressed & took breakfast. Major Poore kindly permitted me to have a single bed placed in his room, and during my tarry at L. I occupied his room with him, with great pleasure, happiness, & comfort.

Monday Morning, Aug. 31, the Exhibition commenced. I went out to the grounds daily & rather enjoyed myself, although I had but little to do—the local committees *relieving us regulars* of all the labor of receiving & paying out *money*. My friend Major Poore did *all* his duty & worked, as he always does, like a steam engine in trowsers.

Thursday evening Col. Preston,[4] formerly a member of Congress, gave a magnificent party, which Col. Wilder, Maj. Poore & I attended, & where we met many whom we knew. The V.P. of the U.S.[,] Maj. Breckinridge, was there[;] so was Secy. Guthrie. . . . I left the fair grounds about 11, went into town in the cars, packed up, wrote a letter to Poore, & at noon of Friday, *Sep. 4th, my birthday,* I left in the Steamer *Moses McClellan* for Cincinnati. . . .

. . . Arrived home at 6 o'clock [A.M.] Saturday, Sep. 12. . . .

My brother Henry left Liverpool, on board the steamer *Europa,* on the 29th Sep.—the day I was at Bellaire—& I saw his arrival at Halifax in the *N.Y. Herald* while at Elmira. Today recd. a letter from him written at home, & enclosing one written on board the *Europa.*

1. A railroad junction in what is now West Virginia.
2. Ashbel P. Willard (1820–1860), governor of Indiana, 1857–1860.
3. President of the railroad from Seymour to Jeffersonville, Ind.
4. William Preston (1816–1887), Whig congressman from Kentucky, 1852–1855.

Thursday, September 17. . . . I have had some men building a hencoop, & while overseeing the work I thought I should have roasted alive. . . .

Monday, October 5. . . . *"The Times"*—good gracious what Times we are having—Banks suspending, Firms failing, Brokers breaking, the money world all topsy-turvy, & no specie to be got unless at ruinous discount. A great beer barrel of public credit is now pretty well stirred up, & the froth is working off like fun. It will soon work itself clear & emit a pure & healthy stream from the spigot—they have been pouring from the bunghole too long!

Wednesday, October 14. . . . On Wednesday of last week I went to New York to attend a meeting of our Board of Telegraph Directors. I staid at the Astor House, where we held our meeting on Thursday afternoon and evening. . . .

In New York the talk was of nothing but the panic—breakages, suspensions, banks, etc., and everybody's face was as long and melancholy as possible. . . .

Sunday, December 6. . . . Although on paper the Democrats have a majority, they will find themselves in a minority the moment the Kansas question, coupled as it must be with slavery or no slavery, comes up. I deem it impossible that a man born and bred north of Mason & Dixon's line can advocate the establishment of slavery in Kansas. That will be the great question of the session, and I am not certain that even the question of Union or no Union, as it now exists, may turn upon the decision! I hope and pray not, however, although, if I had a vote to give upon it, I would not hesitate a moment to cast it for Free Kansas, be the consequence what it might.

I have not seen half a dozen members of Congress yet, but shall probably see hundreds tomorrow.

The new Hall of the House of Representatives is nearly finished. Capt. Meigs[1] has *rushed* the work upon it so as to show it to Congress. It will not probably be occupied by the House till May or June. It is a gorgeous affair—too much so, to my taste, for a business room. The ceiling is magnificent, & perhaps not too elaborately ornamented, but the gilding about the Speaker's chair, the doorways and panels looks, to my eye, tawdry & out of place, worthy only of a theatre, lager beer saloon, or steamboat cabin! It is in very bad taste. . . .

1. Montgomery C. Meigs (1816–1892) of the army engineer corps supervised the building of the Washington Aqueduct, 1852–1860, and the wings and dome of the Capitol, 1853–1859. He was quartermaster general of the Union army during the Civil War.

Sunday, December 20. . . . Last Wednesday morning—the 16th—the House of Representatives occupied, for the first time, their new Hall. I wanted to see them meet there merely as a matter of curiosity, but my health would not permit. I went over Thursday & saw them assemble there. It is the most dismal looking place I have ever seen for a Public Body to meet in. There is no question that it is a better room for hearing in than the old Hall, but in every other respect it is vastly inferior, nor do I believe the Representatives will be satisfied with it. . . .

Sunday, December 27. . . . Our poor Unitarian Society became very much shattered by the imprudent preaching of Mr. Conway—although I believe he was sincere & meant to do no more than he conceived to be his duty—still it was unfortunate, & came near breaking up the society. Doct. Dewey[1] came and healed the troubles in a great measure, by his influence, and now Mr. Haley[2] follows, & is, I believe, to be the instrument, under God, to keep us united. May it be so, is my sincere hope & prayer. . . .

. . . I hoped much of Buchanan, although not one of his supporters—still I considered him an accomplished statesman and a man of talents. I am disappointed—his course in regard to Kansas has been vacillating and weak, & unbecoming a President of the U.S. Even some of his warmest friends and supporters have deserted him—even Douglas, the Champion of Kansas, etc., has taken a *chute* wide from him, & will eventually land in the Republican party, unless I am very much mistaken.

Douglas is a man of splendid talents, & is a man of too much good sense and of too high political aspirations to throw himself away, & his only hope for future political preferment is to go for free Kansas, & let the South take care of herself. She has got to succumb to Northern views—I mean *liberal* Northern views—or go to the wall! Pierce ruined himself in his attempt to conciliate the South. Buchanan seems to be pursuing the same track, & now is Douglas's time to make himself just what he desires to be!

1. Orville Dewey (1794–1882), Unitarian minister and lecturer, filled the pulpit of the Washington Unitarian Society in the winter of 1857.
2. William D'Arcy Haley was a prominent Mason as well as a minister.

Sunday, January 10. . . . Wednesday morning Ned came up and informed us of the sickness of his infant son (Charles Soule). We went down & Dr. Wells at once pronounced it a hopeless case. The child died at 4 o'clock P.M. & was buried Friday. Ned's 7th child, & now only three left! Poor Margaret, how I pitied her. She appeared so filled with grief. Ned bore it like a man & a Christian. . . .

Sunday, January 17. . . . Monday afternoon Doct. Wells left. At nine o'clock Wednesday morning, the U.S. Agricultural Society met at the Smithsonian building, and it continued in session Thursday & Friday. As its Treasurer I had to be present during its sessions. The meeting was a very interesting one. Col. Wilder declined re-election as President, & Gen. Tench Tilghman[1] was elected. . . .

1. Tench Tilghman (1810–1874) of Maryland was general in the state militia and president of the Maryland and Delaware Railroad.

Sunday, January 31. . . . I *puttered* about Monday, cleaning up my desks, putting my papers in order, burning letters & other old & useless papers, & getting ready to move my office down in the City, which I did Tuesday morning, and now occupy as my City office a corner of the Agricultural office in Todd's Building, 365 Pa. Av. Major Ben: Perley Poore, Secy. of the U.S. Ag. Soc., has charge of the room, and I find him so sensitive & so ridiculously particular in the vindication of his official prerogatives that I doubt whether I shall be able to remain in the same room with him. He absolutely flew into a violent passion on Friday because I suggested the putting of some wedges under a bookcase to keep it from falling over. Although an excellent Secretary & a sensible man in most things, he is absolutely a fool in this matter of official prerogative, and I intend to treat him as one. I certainly shall not humor his nonsense, nor regard his passionate & silly outbursts.

I was requested by one of the Executive Committee to keep my office as Treasurer & do my private business there, and on my suggesting as much to him (Maj. Poore) he replied that it was done at his request, & he was delighted to have me there, etc., but that room was wholly in his charge and *no one* should interfere with his arrangement of it. He got into such a passion Friday that he would not let the office boy use my dust brush, when offered by me, to dust out some pigeonholes, but made him do it with old newspapers! He must be a most unhappy mortal in his intercourse with his fellowmen! . . .

Monday, February 15. Pretty cold weather at last. It snowed all day Saturday, & four or five inches fell—enough to make *some* sleighing. The weather has been freezing for two or three nights.

On the 10th inst. I moved my office again to my house. Major Poore and I could not get along comfortably. . . .

Sunday, March 7. . . . I was out nearly all day. At 9 to the P.O.—then to Gen. Quitman's room, where I met Messrs. Henry O'Reilly, Tal. P. Shaffner & J. J. Speed—our object to converse with Gen. Quitman, as Chairman of the Com. of the House of Representatives, on the subject of the erection of a Telegraph from the border of Missouri to Salt Lake City.[1] After quite a conversation with him we went to the War Department & had a long and very satisfactory interview with the Secretary of War, Gov. Floyd,[2] who avowed himself most favorable to the project. He recommended it in his annual report. . . .

1. John A. Quitman (1798–1858) was Democratic congressman from Mississippi, 1855–1858. Henry O'Reilly (1806–1886) was an Irish immigrant newspaperman who in 1845 made a contract with Samuel F. B. Morse and Amos Kendall to raise capital to build telegraph lines from Pennsylvania to St. Louis. Taliaferro P. Shaffner had constructed the telegraph line from Nashville to St. Louis, 1848–1850. John J. Speed, a merchant in Ithaca, N.Y., was F. O. J. Smith's telegraph agent in the Old Northwest.
2. John B. Floyd (1806–1863) was Democratic governor of Virginia, 1849–1852, and Secretary of War, 1857–1860.

Sunday, April 11. Five weeks have trotted away since my pen has performed any journalizing duty. And what has been going on during those weeks? So far as I am personally concerned hardly anything worth spending ink about. I have been "dawdling" about attending to the business of my clients and a very little of my own. I have seen Mr. Gardiner apply his electrical apparatus to the chandelier of the Senate, and light it elegantly. I have written his memorial to Congress asking the purchase of his Patent and had it presented in each House of Congress. I have "been about" with O'Reilly and Shaffner & Speed[,] doing all I can to induce Congress to contract with them to lay a telegraphic wire from Missouri to Utah. I wrote the Report made by Gen. Wilson,[1] from the Com. on Military Affairs to the Senate. I have watched the Kansas question and rejoiced at the defeat, *thus far*, of the "Lecompton swindle."[2] . . .

The public all over this Union have been in a fever of political excitement about Kansas. Crowded galleries and lobbies have borne witness to the intense feeling which has existed here, & from this political centre has radiated the fever heat to all quarters of the Union. Both Houses have acted, but the question on the adoption or non adoption of the Lecompton Constitution is by no means settled. I hope & trust, ere another week passes, it will be, and that Congress will proceed with its regular business.

Yesterday morning Thomas Hart Benton died at his own dwelling house in this City. He died a death worthy of his indomitable life—no Roman ever gave up his life more nobly. He *worked on* to the day before his death, & had an interview with the President, Mr. Buchanan, the evening before he died.

Thomas Hart Benton was a great man, and a century hence his *greatness* will be more fully appreciated than it now is. I have known him well for over 20 years, and I pronounce him the most untiring man I ever saw. While in greatness he ranked among the first of our American Statesmen, in vanity he was unsurpassed by any man I ever knew. As one small instance that came within my own knowledge I will record the following.

I was called on as a magistrate, some 7 or 8 years ago, to take the acknowledgment of a paper to be used in England, when Col. Benton was present and signed it, with me as a witness. He wrote his name, and straightening up in his chair & placing his finger upon it, he said in a tone & with a manner that Doct. Johnson could not have surpassed, "There, Sir, is a name that is known as well in Europe, Sir, as it is in America. Yes, Sir, the name of Thomas H. Benton is sufficient to verify a paper anywhere." And this was said with a seriousness that gave perfect evidence of the sincerity of belief in the assertion.

It was one of Col. Benton's peculiarities, & very many instances of the same sort of vanity could be found well authenticated.

But he had a right to be vain. And he was peculiar in using language regarding himself as if he were talking of another—as "Benton said this[,]," "Benton did so & so," "Benton was thus & thus."

Col. Benton had his failings[,] but he was a true, noble hearted, courageous man, & his Country will be proud of him. . . .

1. Henry Wilson (1812–1875), of Massachusetts, was elected to the U.S. Senate by a coalition of the Free-Soil, American, and Democratic parties in 1855 and served until 1873, when he resigned to become Vice President. He was a brigadier general in the Massachusetts militia.

2. The House had just blocked a Senate bill to admit Kansas under a constitution guaranteeing the right to slave property. This constitution had been drawn up by a pro-slavery convention at Lecompton, Kan., and was ratified only when Free-Soil settlers refused to vote.

Sunday, April 25. . . . On Thursday morning last I started for Philadelphia to attend a meeting of the Board of Directors of the Mag. Tel. Company. . . . At 4 we met, & immediately adjourned to Mr. Swain's house where he was confined by lameness. Our meeting lasted till Friday evening at 9 o'clock. We held it in 3 sessions[,] & I worked steadily all the time when I was not asleep, being on an important Committee to form a contract with Mr. Douglas[1] of Louisville, Ky., an agent of the "New Orleans & Ohio Telegraph Lessees." I found him a very gentlemanly man & we formed the contract. . . .

This evening Mr. Clark[2] has been reading Bryant's poetry to me— "Thanatopsis," "Hymn to the North Star," "June," & several other poems. Bryant is his favorite poet, as he is mine. . . .

1. George L. Douglass, vice president of the New Orleans and Ohio Telegraph Lessees, a rival of the Magnetic Telegraph Co. in the South. At this meeting they agreed to divide up the territory.

2. Daniel Clark (1809–1891), Republican senator from New Hampshire, 1857–1866.

Sunday, May 2. . . . In the evening [April 27] attended a meeting of the Republican Association. Officers elected. I was elected President. We adopted the form of an address & voted to submit it to the Congressional Committee, and then adjourned to Tuesday evening next. . . .

The past week has been politically remarkable on account of the agitation and final settlement in Congress of the Kansas question. On Friday both Houses agreed to the report of the Conference Committee, & the so called "English compromise" was passed.[1] The Democracy rejoiced as if they had achieved a *real victory*—cannon were fired—processions marched—and great things were done! My own belief is that no victory has been won. Kansas, if her people are the men I take them to be, will spurn the bill, *bribe* and all, and come to Congress by & by with a free constitution & demand a place in the Union. This action of the Democracy will react "& plague the inventors." . . .

1. The English bill, sponsored by Democratic congressman William H. English of Indiana, was a compromise measure that insisted on a popular vote on the Lecompton Constitution. The constitution was rejected by the voters of Kansas on August 2.

Sunday, June 13. . . . Last Monday came off our Municipal election, and, as considerable political excitement preceded it, fears were entertained that rowdyism might be in the ascendant on that day. Therefore a strong special police was appointed, a portion of which was mounted & under the command of the Marshal of the District. I was one of the mounted men & was on horseback nearly all the time from 8 A.M. till 7 P.M. We were of some service I think in preventing more bloodshed than actually took place at the City Hall, as we were called there to suppress a row, and did it effectually. Four men were wounded by pistol shots before we arrived. Upon the whole, the election passed off quietly. James G. Berret[1] was elected Mayor. I voted for Richard Wallach, and but for illegal voting I think he would have been elected. Barret is a good fellow, & I think will make a good Mayor. Magruder has proved himself totally unfit for the office, & it is well for the City that we are rid of him. He has done me personally grievous wrong & I shall not soon forget it. . . .

1. Berret, a Democrat, served as mayor, 1858–1861.

Rainsford Island, Boston Harbor, Monday, July 12. . . . Here we have, at this present writing, Dr. & Mrs. Barker, William B. & his wife and baby, Lemuel B., William Taylor & his wife, Mrs. French, self, Frank & Ben, Docts. Green & Nichols (the Doctor's Assistants here) and Miss Taylor (Wm.'s sister) making a pretty sizeable & very pleasant family.[1] *We,* with the Assist. Superintendent & his family, none of whom have I seen, and some two hundred Hospital patients, and a few vagrants sentenced here by the Police Court, one horse, one cow, several dogs, and numberless cats compose the habitants of Rainsford Island. This Medical Principality of eleven acres over which rules "Monarch of all he surveys" My Honorable Bro. in Law, Doct. Lemuel Maxcy Barker. Long life to him, and especially to his Monarchical sway here, for it is a right pleasant little kingdom.

1. William and Lemuel Barker were the sons of Dr. Lemuel M. Barker. William's baby's name was Mary. William O. Taylor was married to Dr. Barker's daughter, Mary. Probably Dr. S. A. Green, 19 Kneeland St., Boston.

Exeter, Thursday, July 29. . . . Doct. Barker had fixed Tuesday the 13th for the beginning of an excursion in his yacht *W. S. Thacher,* & as a matter of course we were on the *qui vive* all Tuesday morning preparing. The yacht went up to Boston after the party who were to accompany *us* of the Island on Monday, & we expected her back about noon on Tuesday. A gale from the South was blowing. At about 2 she rounded the headland of Long Island [Boston Harbor], coming like a racehorse, the water all foam about her—it was almost fearful to look at her running at the rate of at least 12 knots an hour! She passed the wharf at Rainsford, and the Capt. brought her up into the wind & about in true seamanlike style, and she was soon safely moored to the leeward side of the wharf, and the party welcomed on shore. . . .

Copy of the
Log of the yacht *W. S. Thacher*
during an excursion
of Pleasure. . . .

Tuesday, July 13th, 1858, 4 o'clock & 54 minutes past meridian, cast off from the wharf at Rainsford Island, Boston Harbor, bound on an excursion of pleasure. Capt. Macomber[1] and three sailors in charge of yacht and 12 excursionists ripe for fun. Wind over the taffrail—a stiff 12 knot breeze and chopping sea—Schooner, under single reefed main-sail and jib, behaved beautifully. Passed Boston outer Lighthouse . . . at 5 o'clock & 5 minutes. Shipped three or four seas over the lee beam, and the water came swashing aft, to the terror and mighty speedy moving of the gentlemen who were seated on the larboard cushions of the stern sheets! Faces beginning to turn pale—whether from fear or seasickness this deponent saith not. . . .

½ past 8, cast anchor in Gloucester Harbor, and those of the excursionists who desired it were landed in the small boat, and went to the Pavilion House. Sat down to an excellent supper about 10 o'clock. . . .

. . . At 2 P.M. [Thursday, July 15] we hove up anchor, hoisted all sail, fired five pistol shots, gave Gloucester three cheers, and put the *Thacher* before the wind—what there was of it—it would not have filled a modern lady's bonnet—much less her nightcap! But the *Thacher* is "a live crit-ter"—and, as Major Jack Downing[2] said about Martin Van Buren's going up Gen. Jackson's ladder, "Nobody saw how he did it, but, somehow, the first they knew, there he was, up at the very top"—so of the lively *Thacher,* nobody could see how she did it, but the first we knew, we were in the midst of the "bounding billows." Off "halfway rock" every man that could raise "a red" threw it on the rock for luck, it being an old custom, still sacredly followed, for every captain who sails near enough to halfway rock to throw a cent on it, to do so, otherwise his voyage will be attended with bad luck! We did not think it was a custom "better followed in the breach than in the observance," & so there was a flight of at least a dozen coppers *toward* that rock as we passed by—how many *reached it* is an open question!

On—on—singing and storytelling, now and then a splice, all hands sober, & all hands merry. Swift eloquent *in imitation,* eloquent in originality, eloquent in kind feeling—indeed there was a regular spread of kind feeling and fun all over the stern sheets, till even the Captain mounted the rudder cap, and with the helm between his feet burst out into one of the most elegant hifalutations of western eloquence—rich with the spread eagle, the Fourth of July and the Rocky mountains. It must not be supposed that the Captain's speech was original. If it had been I have no doubt it would have been much better, in point of good language and good sense. It was one of those western extravaganzas, purporting to be a speech of some candidate for office, of the half horse & half alligator stripe, which we often see in the newspapers. It was, however, admirably spoken, and received with all the honors. The Captain really came out and proved himself "up to snuff" and "a trump card." We were delighted that we had a Captain who could administer to our pleasure, as well as to our safety.

At 6 o'clock P.M. we cast anchor in Marblehead harbor and came ashore.

Under command of Major General Sutton,[3] our forces were marshaled, and we proceeded to attack the office of Hon. Wm. Fabens,[4] Counsellor at Law, and Philanthropist; who received our attack in the warmest manner possible, and soon silenced us with a display of gin bottles that it was found hard to resist—so we surrendered at discretion. . . .

Mr. Fabens told me among other most interesting things, that Skipper Floyd Ireson—

> Old Flud Oirson, with his horrd horrt,
> Torrd & fortherred & corry'd in a corrt
> By the women of Morblead—[5]

died within the last six months. He also told me that "Old Flud" went out fishing a few years ago and was blown off to sea and supposed to be lost, but was picked up, carried into Boston and sent home. After which the boys used to follow him through the streets, crying

> I Floyd Ireson, for leaving a *wrack,*
> Was blown to sea in a dory & couldn't get back. . . .

Salem, Saturday morning, July 17, 1858. After writing up the log yesterday morning at Marblehead, most of our party, under the lead of our

Friend Fabens walked through the town and saw some of the lions, but *nary* [an] elephant.

Queer old place that ancient town of Marblehead; venerable in its aspect, unique in its arrangement. There live some 7,000 human beings, in good houses, no two of which are alike, and it seemed to me no two of which were on a line with each other. Built originally on rambling cow paths to suit the convenience of the builders, there they stand, monuments of the independence of those ancient builders whose bones now rest 'neath the clods of the old churchyard, in the very centre of the town. Young America[6] has, however, got a foothold even in old Marblehead; its ancient and peculiar dialect is dying out, very few now use "corrt" for cart, "corry'd" for carried, etc. I did not hear those barbarisms at all, although I was assured that they were used now by some, & only a few years ago by nearly all. At the hotel I asked a woman to bring me up a pitcher of water, & she replied very nearly thus—"I'll bring ye some *worrter,* ef ye'll hond me *the pucher."* I do not recollect any other specimen of Marblehead dialect, although I conversed considerable with various persons, and they all used good & properly pronounced English.

It will not be long before the young scamp (young America) will be marking out his broad streets and straight lines, and probably in 50 years Marblehead as it was and is will be almost as much a myth as Utopia or Robinson Crusoe. Even now the town is ornamented by some very elegant dwellings erected in modern style, which would not be out of place in the most aristocratic parts of the largest cities of the Union, and there is now one building erected nearly a hundred years ago by a Col. Lee, and now used for a Bank, which in palatial proportions & lordly finish will compare with any building within my knowledge—not even excepting the Presidential mansion at Washington.[7] It is a grand old monument of the liberal notions of the olden time.

Among other of young America's innovations on lapstones, waxed ends, pegging awls, and shoe hammers,[8] there are sundry shoe manufactories which turn out machine made shoes in any quantity. We visited the largest in the place, where the whirr of some scores of sewing machines gave evidence that there were a few live folks left yet. All these machines were operated by girls, and really it was a goodly sight to see them so busily and profitably employed. Some of them were exceedingly pretty, even my rather venerable eyes could appreciate that. . . .

. . . We reached this port of Salem at about 5 o'clock P.M. [Friday, July 16] and made the Essex House our headquarters (where this present writing is in progress). . . .

Rainsford Island, 4 o'clock P.M., Saturday, July 17, 1858. . . .

At ½ past 9 we were all on board, and at precisely ¼ before 10 were under way, with a fine breeze, and all sail set for Rainsford. The breeze was from the South, and the *Thacher* did her duty on a wind bravely. We passed Marblehead rock, on which is enclosed in a monument, by the Marbleheaders, the first pulpit of the Old South Church in Boston. Many years ago that old building was repaired, and a new pulpit placed in it. The old pulpit, being considered of small value, was asked for by the Marbleheaders, to be placed on that rock, and was given to them. It was placed there, and after standing exposed for some time[,] was seen to be decaying, when they went to work and built over it a stone monument of masonwork; and there it stands a lasting monument to their piety, generosity, and public spirit; and there, probably[,] it will stand till "That day of wrath that dreadful day, when Heaven & Earth shall pass away." . . .

At 10 o'clock & 24 m. we passed the lighthouse with a stiff breeze, but we lost it all before we arrived at the wharf at Rainsford, which we did at 2 o'clock P.M. and were received with warm demonstrations of welcome by those whom we left nearly a week ago. . . .

1. Probably Calvin D. Macomber, boatbuilder, Boston.
2. Jack Downing was the imaginary Yankee in Seba Smith's humorous letters poking fun at the Jackson administration.
3. William Sutton was major general in the Marblehead Light Infantry.
4. William Fabens (1810–1883), for many years a trial justice in Marblehead.
5. Ireson was immortalized in John Greenleaf Whittier's "Skipper Ireson's Ride" as the sea captain who refused to rescue the crew and passengers of a sinking ship and was tarred and feathered by the women of Marblehead.
6. "Young America" was the name given to a movement identified with nationalism, manifest destiny, and sympathy with the European revolutions of 1848.
7. The Lee Mansion on Washington Street was built in 1768 by Col. Jeremiah Lee, a prosperous merchant. Presidents Washington, Monroe, and Jackson all held receiving lines in this building.
8. Tools used by the old shoemakers.

Rainsford Island, Friday, August 6. . . . As we neared the wharf at Rainsford, Dr. Nichols sang out[,] "Major, the Atlantic Telegraph cable is laid," and on getting on shore I found Theodore & David Taylor, Wm. Taylor's brothers, who confirmed what Doct. N. said.[1]

Judge French has been, ever since I arrived, pretending to read to me, in every paper, the laying of the Atlantic cable. He dined with Wm. Taylor in Boston yesterday, & the brothers dined with him. It is *barely possible* that he has put these young gentlemen up to humbug me a little. I do not, at any rate, put the most implicit confidence in the information, because I have always believed it could not be laid. It may be so, as the days of miracles may return. *Nous verrons!* . . .

1. Theodore was actually William's cousin. The cable was completed August 5.

Exeter, Tuesday, August 17. . . . Queen Victoria's Message to the President of the U.S. & his reply came in the papers today, & we have listened one hour—from 12 noon to 1 P.M.—to the ringing of all the bells in this town, and some particularly patriotic individual has wasted at least two ounces of powder, next door, in firing a pocket pistol for the last 2 hours![1]

Well, the Atlantic Cable is laid and *they say* it works. I suppose it does, and it is not only a great, but a marvellous triumph of science and art. I, who was among the first to aid in bringing forward the Telegraph in the U.S. & who have superintended the putting up of thousands of miles of wire & seen all its workings, did not believe the Atlantic cable could ever be successfully laid & worked. I was mistaken, and now I will believe that *anything* can be done that man really undertakes to do! . . .

1. The messages were to celebrate the laying of the cable.

Isles of Shoals, Appledore House, Thursday, August 19. I left Exeter in the cars at ½ past 9 yesterday morning, for Portsmouth, & arrived there at ¼ past 10. . . .

The boat was a small schooner of 40 tons, & a good sailer. We cast off from the wharf at 5 minutes before 11, and arrived here at ¼ past 1. Had to beat all the way. . . .

As soon as the boat left[,] Mr. Clark[1] & I walked over this Island. It is a rocky & somewhat romantic place, composed of two eminences, with a valley between. The Appledore House is a large building, capable of accommodating say 150 guests. It is kept by Mr. Laighton,[2] and, I should think considering the situation, well kept. There is one other house on the Island, owned by Mr. L.—who owns the entire Island—which is used as an outbuilding for boarders. That with the bowling saloons, bath-houses, etc., composes all the buildings here. There are now, I should judge, between 50 & 100 visitors, people apparently moving in the first circles of life. Fishing, bowling, & walking seem to be the principal amusements. Mr. Laighton has not been away from the Island for 13 years! He was formerly an active politician, and a member of both Houses of the N.H. Legislature, but becoming disgusted, as Mr. Clark told me, with the world, he purchased this Island, came here & built this house, and here he intends to die. He is now a man of goodly size, weighing perhaps 250, & so lame as to be under the necessity of using a crutch and a cane.

The group of Islands forming the Isles of Shoals consists of seven, a part of them in Maine & a part in N.H.[3] This one [Appledore] is in Maine. Star Island, on which is the town of Gosport, is in N.H. It has something over 100 inhabitants, and sends a Representative to the "General Court" of N.H. This Island once contained quite a Colony, & the foundations of the old houses are now to be seen.

There is, upon the eastern eminence of this Island[,] a "cairn" made of stones, some 10 or 15 feet high & perhaps 20 or 30 feet in circumference, which Mr. Laighton says was erected by John Smith[4] of Virginia & Pocahontas memory. I do not know whence comes the tradition—it may be so, but I doubt it. It looks old enough to have been erected by Noah, but I do not believe it was![5] . . .

1. Senator Daniel Clark's wife and son Frank had accompanied them to the Isles but returned immediately on the boat.
2. Thomas Laighton (1805–1866), of Portsmouth, N.H., purchased four of the islands in 1839. His daughter, Celia Thaxter, published her first poem in 1861.
3. There are actually nine islands.
4. John Smith (1579–1631), who is better known for his contributions to the Virginia Colony, made a trip to New England in 1614 and brought back information about the value of fisheries in that area.
5. During this visit to the Isles of Shoals French took part in a celebration for the laying of the Atlantic Cable. His account of the affair, published in the *New England Farmer,* is included in the journal entry for August 29.

Exeter, Monday, August 23. I staid at Appledore till Friday at 2 o'clock, then came up to Portsmouth in the *Golden Eagle.* . . .

Tuesday, August 24. The Judge and I went to Rye Beach yesterday. The ladies thought of accompanying us, but the cold[,] windy weather prevented. We left there at ½ past 10 & arrived at the Ocean House about 12. . . . Had rather a pleasant ride & time at Rye. Dinner served with all the ceremony of the Revere, Astor, Girard, or National Hotels. Servants summoned up by a bell with military precision—and courses all served regularly so that the dining is a good long hour's work. How much better I like the free & easy style at Laighton's, Isle of Shoals, Appledore House, where everybody help themselves as fast as they choose, & sit 10 minutes or two hours at the table just as they fancy. . . .

Chester, Wednesday, August 25. . . . Mr. Tuck told me that J. G. Whittier[1] was in town, and had been at his house. I expressed a desire to form his acquaintance, and Mr. Tuck promised to go with me to his Hotel in the morning, so at 8 yesterday morning I walked over to Mr. T.'s & he went with me to the Squamscott House, where Mr. W. stopped. He had just left for Mrs. Chadwick's[2] to accompany his sister,[3] who was staying there, about the town. We went there & saw him & his Sister. I had a talk of perhaps 20 minutes with him, and found him just what I expected, a plain gentlemanly man with a heart full of the milk of human kindness. We talked of politics—of poetry—of Mr. Giddings, of Doct. Bailey, of the *Atlantic Magazine,* of trees, etc. And we went out and measured the stump of an elm that some vandal had cut down last year, in Mrs. Chadwick's yard, for fear it would fall on the house! About as much danger of it as that Mount Washington will blow over some windy morning! The stump was seven feet, good measure, in diameter—21 at least in circumference. An "Autocrat" tree.

I enjoyed my call on Mr. W. exceedingly. . . .

1. John Greenleaf Whittier (1807–1892), the poet and abolitionist, lived in Amesbury, Mass. French had this talk with him in Exeter, before leaving for Chester.
2. The widow of Peter Chadwick (d. 1847), who had been clerk of courts.
3. Elizabeth Whittier (d. 1864) kept house for the poet until her death.

Concord, Mass., Saturday, August 28. Henry, Hattie & Sally left Chester at 4 P.M. on Thursday, for Exeter. After they left[,] Helen and I walked down & made a call on Mrs. Aiken.[1] She, as usual[,] asked a quantity of questions, and answered most of them herself. She has with her a little granddaughter—Mary Richardson[2]—Isabel's daughter, who married Mrs. French's cousin Daniel. She is a beautiful girl, but apparently of weak intellect, so much so as to distress me while with her. . . .

This morning arose at 5 & read. Breakfasted with Mr. Keyes[3]—he having to leave between 6 & 7 for Boston.

Now it is about 9 o'clock, and all the folks are talking around me in the sitting room, so, with a memorandum that I walked down to the old Chester burying ground after breakfast yesterday morning & stood at the graves of all my relatives & plucked from my Mother's some little bits of foliage, I will defer writing any more at this time.

1. Nancy Marston Aiken, mother-in-law of Elizabeth French's cousin, Daniel S. Richardson.
2. Mary A. Richardson (b. 1845), daughter of Daniel S. Richardson and his wife, Isabella.
3. George Keyes, husband of French's niece, Mary Brown.

Sunday, August 29. After writing the foregoing yesterday I walked down—*or over*—into the town with Mary Ellen.[1] . . .

[At this point French inserted his description of the celebration on the Isles of Shoals that appeared in the *New England Farmer* on September 4. The following are excerpts.]

It was a bright thought of two of the most respected guests of this house, from Boston only three or four days ago, that this Island, in the midst of that Ocean that now rolls its billows above the cable, should duly celebrate the momentous event of its successful working; and to their untiring energy do we owe one of the most beautiful festive results that the writer of this has ever witnessed. . . .

At precisely half-past 7 the signal rocket from Little Island was sent up, and the word was given by the gentleman from Boston who, by common consent, commanded the fleet, and was duly dubbed Commodore, for all to repair on board the boats; which order was promptly obeyed, and the boats, well stowed with Roman candles, left the shore. A large, eight-oared barge, on board of which was a very fine choir, led, followed by several large sailboats, and quite a fleet of rowboats from this and Star Island.

The fleet passed round Little Island, the choir singing, with beautiful effect, "God save the Queen" and "Hail Columbia," and rounded too in line in front of the Hotel.

At a signal from the Commodore's barge, the rockets ascended from Little Island, and a general discharge of Roman candles from all the boats took place. While this was in progress the sweet voices of the choir came across the water in beautiful cadences, and the whole scene was as beautiful as can well be imagined.

This part of the display over, the boats returned from the shore in the same order in which they left, the officers and crews disembarked, and proceeded in procession to the piazza of the house, which was densely crowded with individuals. The Commodore returned his thanks to his officers and crews for the prompt and efficient manner in which they had performed their duties, and invited all to repair to the North Parlor (a room capable of containing more than a hundred people) where the *inside* festivities were to take place. . . .

In due time Father Neptune, in full *sea costume*, bearing his trident, accompanied by Mrs. Nepture and three little Neptunes, all appropriately clad, entered and proceeded through the room, and at its head were welcomed in a most amusing and capital manner, by Hon. Daniel Clark, who happened to be present as a guest, and whose remarks were received with great applause. Neptune responded briefly, and then the dancing commenced, and was kept up to a late hour.

The dresses of Father Neptune and his interesting family, which were the *chef d'oeuvres* of the female department, deserve more than a mere passing notice. Neptune was clad in a frock trimmed entirely with the vegetable products of the deep, with a sash of kelp and sea-grass over his shoulder, the tops of his boots turned over with the same, his crown ornamented in front with a star-fish, and behind with the shell of a lobster, his beard of some sort of moss or sea-grass, exactly resembling a long grey beard, and which, in these days of long beards, would do no dishonor to the first drawing-room in the land.

Mrs. Neptune wore a white robe duly and tastefully festooned, and flounced with sea-weed, kelp, etc., and the little Neptunes were almost walking *kelpies* personified. Nothing short of genuine lady-genius could have got up a rig so beautiful and so appropriate. . . .

1. Mary Ellen Brady.

Sunday, September 5. . . . *Thursday* [September 2]. Commenced making a well sweep before breakfast, worked on it steadily, alone, until 11, when I had it finished & put up at the well where the drains come in, and where the water for drinking is now procured for the household. Gov. Brown & Mary Eliza Wells went to Westboro Wednesday and returned at noon Thursday. Spent the afternoon reading & *dawdling* about. Evening sick with a violent pain in my stomach, lasted nearly all night—but arose well.

Friday . . . visited Lowell. . . . We went to the Washington House, where our friend Doct. Whitmore[1] boards, and became his guests for the day. He took us to the Carpet Factory[,] which we went all over, and I was very much interested, it being my first visit to one.

After dinner we called at Daniel Richardson's & spent an hour with him & his wife very pleasantly, then on Mrs. William Richardson—her husband being away at Boston—then on Mr. Joseph Keyes at the Jail— he was at his office, so we saw only Mrs. Keyes.[2] The attendant showed me over the Jail, which is one of the best—perhaps the very best—in the Union. Cost $300,000! I was almost sick enough to be in bed all the time, but worried through my visit, & enjoyed it all I could under the circumstances.

Started for this place at 17 minutes before 5 & arrived home at 7. . . .

1. Brother of Mary Whitmore Richardson, the widow of Elizabeth French's brother Samuel.
2. Anna M., wife of Elizabeth French's cousin, William A. Richardson (1821–1896), who was judge of probate and insolvency for Middlesex County, Mass., and later served as Secretary of the Treasury. Joseph Keyes was brother of John S. Keyes and later assistant U.S. marshal for Massachusetts.

Lancaster, Friday, September 10. . . . After breakfast, Kate Vose, Mrs. French, Ellen and I walked over to the State Industrial School.[1] Ellen and I started first—the other ladies expecting to ride. We went and measured a large elm between here & the school, about 40 rods off the main road to the left as we went out, near a lane. It measured, 5 feet above the ground, 21 feet 7 inches in circumference. At the ground it would measure, I should think, at least 26 feet. We arrived at the School grounds and went to Mr. Peirce's[2] house by whom we were received with the utmost kindness and urbanity. After sitting with him 15 or 20 minutes, Mrs. French & Miss Kate came on foot—they could not get a horse and carriage—and Mr. Peirce then took us thro' the several buildings. Everything was in perfect order, & the inmates all appeared clean & nice— were all employed & seemed happy. There are 97 inmates. Mr. P. had about 20 assembled on the green under the lofty & elegant shade trees, and all seated and while busy at their work—knitting—they sang to us perhaps half a dozen pieces, beautifully. They are not instructed in music, but choose their own songs, and take their parts as they think proper. They sang in excellent time and tune. The leader was a bright young girl of apparently 15 years, who[,] Mr. Peirce told us, came there a year or two since, a dirty[,] swearing slut. All the language she knew was oaths, & she was covered with filth. Now she is a handsome, black-haired, neat-looking damsel, uses good language, & can cut and fit a dress as well as any dressmaker. Mr. Peirce remarked *emphatically*, "That girl is saved." . . .

1. Kate and Ellen were daughters of Bess's sister, Mary Vose.
2. Rev. Bradford K. Peirce.

Washington, Sunday, October 3. . . . The G. L. [Grand Lodge] closed about 6, & while we were consulting—Ingle,[1] Rhees[2] & I—in the hall, we heard two pistol shots & the explosion of one cap, down at the door that opens upon D Street, & were immediately told that someone was shot. On going down we found that a stranger had fired two shots into the open door[,] one of the bullets taking effect in the great toe of Bro. Heiburger.[3] The man was arrested & proved to be a monomaniac by the name of Minant Streng, who imagined that the Freemasons were trying to oppress him, and were, *as a Body,* in league against him, & he desired to kill one so that they would kill him, and thus put an end to his troubles. Poor fellow, he is to be pitied, rather than condemned.

Heiburger's toe was amputated the next day, & yesterday he was doing well. Streng is in jail, & will probably be sent to the Insane Hospital. . . .

1. Christopher Ingle, a lawyer, was secretary of St. John's Lodge, No. 11.
2. William J. Rhees was chief clerk of the Smithsonian.
3. Francis J. Heiberger, a tailor on Pennsylvania Avenue.

Monday, October 11. . . . The city seems to be infested with burglars and petty thieves. On the night of the 20th August, while I was away &

Mr. Russell & family in the house, some thief or thieves broke in and stole nearly a hundred dollars worth of silver-plated ware, & some silver, from the basement. Articles stolen—

Two silver-plated teapots, coffee pot, creamer[,] sugar bowl & slop bowl, cost			$40.00
One silver-plated caster		cost	18.00
1 cake basket, silver-plated,		"	12.00
2 " "		"	25.00
1 table silver spoon		"	2.50
4 silver teaspoons and two salt spoons		cost	5.00
1 " fork		"	2.50
1 plated ladle		"	2.50
			$107.50

The thief or thieves got in at a window of the basement—broke open the sideboard, where the plated ware was, wrapped it up, as we suppose, in napkins, which they stole also, put it into a market basket—also stolen, & cleared out without disturbing any of the household, or the Police!

Soon afterwards somebody broke open the hencoop and stole 4 hens. Last Friday morning at 5 o'clock the hencoop was again visited by one man, & we heard him. I got up and frightened him by shoving up the window and firing a pistol. He got off with two chickens. We have killed off nearly all our hens since we returned and intend to kill the 3 remaining, for there is no protection for us, as I see, though we pay taxes enough to be entitled to some!

Sunday, December 12. . . . Since I wrote last herein, . . . time has passed almost without note by me. Benny has been here and enjoyed every moment of his time. He leaves at 6 A.M. tomorrow for Exeter to resume his studies. It is hard to be separated from one's children so, but, if we would have them men of the right sort, there is no help for it. I think Benny is doing well at the Academy, & hope much for him. . . .

I have gone in pretty strong to make Hon. John M. Botts the next President of the United States, and if the Republican party act wisely, they will unite on him and he can easily be elected. Mr. Clark boards with us again this session. He is now alone, but is going after Mrs. Clark and Frank next week. Mr. Fessenden[1] & Mr. Foot of Vermont came over last evening and we had a game of whist. Last Wednesday evening Mr. Clark and I were at their rooms at Mrs. Carter's,[2] & played there. It is very pleasant to have these social interviews, and these Senators are all pleasant men, and it is to me a source of much gratification to have a chance to associate with them. . . .

1. William Pitt Fessenden (1806–1869) was a Whig and Republican senator from Maine, 1854–1869.
   2. M. A. Carter, 4 A St. North.

Tuesday, January 4. . . . Today the Senate of the United States took possession, for the first time, of their new Chamber in the new North wing of the Capitol. I was present in the gallery and saw the "potent, grave and reverend seignors" enter in solemn procession, preceded by their Sergeant at Arms, Col. McNair,[1] and Vice President Breckinridge. The speechmaking had been previously done by Mr. Crittenden[2] and the Vice President agreeably to programme, in the old Chamber, around which is festooned a thousand memories of the Past which can never be forgotten—of Great Men & Great Things, and I much doubt if ever associations as sacred and as soul-stirring can ever be connected with the new Chamber.

The old Senate Chamber is a beautiful room, convenient for business, well lighted, and gracefully formed. The new Chamber is simply an oblong, or parallelogram, in form, lighted wholly from the ceiling, and *aired* solely from an artificial apparatus, carried by a steam engine, similar to the *blower* of a furnace. It is very beautifully finished with iron, and is far more creditable to whomsoever had charge of the style of decoration than the gaudy Hall of the House. As a business room it is not to be compared to the old chamber. As a *pleasant room*, it is[,] in comparison to the old Chamber, about as a cellar to a beautiful & well-lighted drawing room. In the old Chamber the want of a gallery room was a very great defect, which is entirely remedied in the new, which affords gallery room for 1,000 persons. The galleries were filled today, but they will not be often. Clay, & Webster, & Calhoun, and Wright,[3] and a host of others whose voices could attract a sufficient number of auditors to fill the Capitol are gone, and there are none—no not one—to fill their places! Will there ever be? I doubt if there ever will. I do not know of a single Statesman now living, who promises to fill the place of either of those men of the past. God save the Republic, is all I have to say in regard to this want of living talent! . . .

1. Dunning R. McNair of Kentucky.
   2. John J. Crittenden (1787–1863), of Kentucky, was a Whig senator, 1817–1819, 1835–1841, 1842–1848, and 1855–1861. He was also U.S. Attorney General, 1841 and 1850–1853; and Unionist congressman, 1861–1863.
   3. Silas Wright (1795–1847), Democratic senator from New York, 1833–1844.

Thursday, January 27. Twenty-two days and not one word! What have I to say of them? I do not think much. I have been moving about considerable and accomplished very little.

The U.S. Agricultural Society met on the 13th inst. and being Treasurer I attended. While that was in session there were four Telegraph Meetings, all of which I attended. I almost lived away from home that week, there was so much going on.

Then the Burns festival was preparing for and I had promised to make a speech at that, and so I wrote a poem, and collected some facts & flourishes in my mind for a speech. The festival came off evening before last, at the National, & it was one of the best conducted festivals I ever attended. The speeches and songs were first-rate. I made my speech and read my rhymes, and they were well received. I think the best speech of the evening was made by John Mitchell,[1] the Irish Patriot. He is a very eloquent speaker. Senator Pearce of Maryland and Speaker Orr[2] were the Presiding officers, and they did themselves great credit. We finished up with "Auld Lang Syne" in full chorus at 2 o'clock, and I walked home in company with my friend Hon. J. A. Bingham[3] of the Ho. Reps.[,] who, by the way, made one of the best speeches of the evening. . . .

I saw Mr. Buchanan, the President of the U.S.[,] at the funeral today.[4] I have not seen him to shake hands with him before, since he became President, although I have known him personally & well for twenty years or more. He looks hale & hearty, and as if he might last several years to come.

1. John Mitchell (1815–1875), of the Young Ireland movement, advocated repeal of the Act of Union and armed resistance to England. He escaped to America, where he did newspaper work and lectured, 1853–1875.
2. James L. Orr (1822–1873), Democratic congressman from South Carolina, 1849–1859, and speaker, 1857–1859.
3. John A. Bingham (1815–1900), Republican congressman from Ohio, 1855–1863 and 1865–1873.
4. The funeral was Mrs. Robert Beale's.

Thursday, February 3. . . . Harriette Flagg[1] died very suddenly, although her death was expected soon, on Tuesday morning, and today we followed her remains to Glenwood Cemetery & saw them there deposited in the Tomb. . . .

How my mind was carried back to my birthplace—Chester, N.H. Standing at the door of the tomb[,] where they were depositing the precious burden we had accompanied thither, were six persons who, at one time, all made the old town *their home,* with her whose remains lay cold in death before us. Mrs. Flagg[2] and Edmund, Mrs. Louisa Russell, my brother Edmund, & Mrs. French & myself. Years long since gone came back upon me & I felt sad & solemn. . . .

I do not feel like writing any more tonight. Mr. & Mrs. Clark are gone to dine at Gov. Seward's. Mrs. French is sick in bed with headache. Frank is preparing to go out to a party at Senator Douglas's, & little Frank Clark is my only companion here in the library. Still as a little mouse he sits at the opposite side of the table reading. He is the best boy of his age I ever knew.

The wind is blowing, & I believe it is becoming colder. *Exeunt omnes.*

1. Harriette Flagg was the niece of Benjamin French's stepmothers, Betsey Flagg French and Sarah Flagg French.
2. Harriette Payson Flagg, mother of the deceased, lived on until 1868.

Sunday, February 13. . . . Yesterday I went down in the city in the morning & called on Mrs. Thos. P. Smith, a lady from Medford, who keeps the "Mystic Hall Seminary." She brought to me a letter of introduction from Doct. Lewis[1] of Boston. I found her a dashing widow of some 40 years—agreeable, accomplished & smart. She is here for the purpose of making her school known among the Southern people, and she will do it! I spent ½ an hour with her very pleasantly, & promised to call at ½ past 8 P.M. & accompany her to Doct. Bailey's. . . . Miss Abigail Dodge[2]— who writes under the *nom de plume* of Gail Hamilton—is an inmate of Doct. B.'s family, and was there of course. She is a wonderful girl, for she is only a girl I should think. She looks as if she were not much, if any, over twenty. She is an oddity too. Hair worn like a boy's. No combs or curls, but smooth & parted on the top of her head. Features decidedly homely—cross-eyed—but the handsomest set of natural teeth I ever saw in the jaws of any mortal. Her dress striped silk, & by no means fashionable in its make or set. But, under this unpromising exterior there is a mind—a soul—of as much brightness and beauty as was ever placed in the body of a mortal. It is a diamond of the first water, in a very ordinary setting, but when you see its flashing beauties, you forget the baser metal with which it is surrounded. I never remember to have seen a person from whose lips flowed, as if without an effort, such a continuous stream of bright thoughts, clothed in beautiful language. She was, evidently, the cynosure of the constellation of literary gems that graced Doct. Bailey's parlors last evening. I enjoyed my visit very much, and left at 10, by permission of my elegant widow, who promised to find her way back to the National without me, she having a carriage in waiting & insisting on my taking it home. I, however, chose to walk. . . .

1. Winslow Lewis (1799–1875), a prominent Boston surgeon, was at one time a grand master in the Masons.

2. Mary Abigail Dodge (1833–1896) wrote witty essays for the *National Era*, 1858–1860. She was a well-known editor and author for the rest of her career.

Saturday, February 26. About as dismal, uncomfortable morning as we have had for a long time. Ground covered with snow—trees covered with sleet, and raining fast. Thermometer 32° & wind northeast.

Great times in Congress—Senate fighting over the acquisition of Cuba, and the House over the appropriation Bills. As for President Buchanan[,] he seems to be nowhere! His Administration is "a dead cock in the pit," and he will wind up two years hence, if he lives so long, a despised President.

I have just read the proceedings in Congress yesterday, as published in the *Intelligencer,* and they do no credit to the Honorable members of either house. In the Senate they were at work fighting between the Cuba & Homestead bills at ½ past 12 when the report closes. Mr. Senator Clark came home sometime between 10 o'clock & daylight, but he is not up yet & so I have not yet learned the grand *finale* of the wise doings of the night. There was some very sharp shooting between Toombs[1] on one side & Wade,[2] Fessenden, & Seward on the other—severer things were said than are usually said in the Senate. Things look rather squally as regards the doing of the necessary business. My experience is, however[,] that it gets through *somehow,* and I think it will this time. There is, however, a good deal of unkind feeling between the different parties, & they now are many.

1. Robert A. Toombs (1810–1885), of Georgia, was a Whig congressman, 1845–1853, and a Democratic senator, 1853–1861.
2. Benjamin F. Wade (1800–1878) was a Whig and Republican senator from Ohio, 1851–1869.

Monday, February 28. . . . Last evening about 7 o'clock Abbott Moore[1] came in and told us that Hon. Daniel E. Sickles, Member of the Ho. Reps. had killed Philip Barton Key, by shooting him with a pistol near Lafayette Square.[2] It was quite a shock to me, Key having been my personal friend for several years, and always esteemed by me as an upright, honest gentleman. I was too unwell to go out and ascertain the facts and circumstances, but Senator Clark went down to the National Hotel where he ascertained all that could be known.

It seems Mr. Key has been criminally intimate with Mr. Sickles's wife. The fact was brought to Sickles's notice by an anonymous letter a few days since. He at once took measures to ascertain the truth, and Saturday evening Mrs. Sickles confessed all to her husband. She also told him that

Key was to meet her at 2 o'clock yesterday P. M. and that signals were to pass between them by the waving of handkerchiefs.

Mr. Sickles armed himself and watched. He saw Key coming down Pa. Av. opposite Lafayette Square making the signal. He met him, and after a few words between them drew a pistol and shot him through the heart. He shot three times. Key threw an opera glass at him, which was the only resistance he made.

The *Intelligencer* gives an account of the affair this morning, but meagre and unsatisfactory.

Poor Key—I can hardly realize that he is dead. He was the son of Francis S. Key[,][3] author of the "Star-Spangled Banner." His brother was shot dead in a duel, several years ago, by a Mr. Sherburne[4] of N. Hamp.[,] an officer in the Navy.

1. Abbott Moore of New York was a clerk in the patent office.
2. Daniel E. Sickles (1825–1914), Democratic congressman from New York, 1857–1861, was acquitted in the trial that followed, the first person ever to be acquitted on a plea of temporary insanity.
3. Francis Scott Key (1779–1843) spent most of his life in Georgetown and Washington.
4. Midshipman John H. Sherburne killed Midshipman Daniel Key in a duel in 1836.

Friday, March 11. . . . Mr. P. M. General Aaron V. Brown[1] was taken sick two weeks ago next Monday, and died at 9 o'clock and 20' A.M. on Tuesday at the age of 63. He was a good man. I knew him well, and while a Member of Congress from Tennessee was very intimate with him. . . .

So they go—my old and valued friends. Grundy, Jackson, Polk, Hugh L. White & Brown, all distinguished men, and all well known to me, all from Tennessee[,] have departed long since I became a resident of Washington. And how many others from other states—alas, alas[,] they count by hundreds. My generation is fast passing away—*passing away!* . . .

I have been at the Patent Office today with Doct. L. Bradley, to see his new Telegraph invention with our Chief Operator[,] Mr. Caldwell.[2] I saw it a few days ago. It seems to me to be an important invention for us Morse folks. I have written Swain, Barnum, Hoe & Smith about it. If they view it as I do, they will be awake about it. . . .

1. Aaron V. Brown (1795–1859), of Tennesse, served as Democratic congressman, 1839–1845, and governor, 1845–1847, before being named Postmaster General in 1857.
2. A. Harper Caldwell was later chief cipher operator for the Army of the Potomac.

Sunday, April 3. Three weeks since I have made a record. Nearly two of them passed in severe sickness. I think that my digestive organs became very much deranged last Autumn. I did not take proper care of myself & kept growing worse all winter. On Wednesday evening, March 23d[,] I went to bed at about 8 o'clock P.M. in much pain at the pit of my stomach. It increased rapidly, & my wife put cloths wrung out of hot water upon me. I was in agony, and commenced vomiting—took morphia, but got but little relief. As soon as morning dawned sent for Doct. Johnston.[1] He came and prescribed—I now forget what. About 2 P.M. the pain left me, but so sore & weak that it seemed to me as if I never could get over it! The Doct. came again about 2 or 3 o'clock and gave me calomel. I got through Thursday night tolerably well. Friday morning took castor oil, and in the afternoon the medicine commenced doing its duty. Saturday better, but oh the feeling of *deadness* at my stomach that night—it was absolutely horrible—no pain, but a feeling as if my stomach *was gone!* I drank some raw brandy, which helped me. Sunday[,] much better, and thence onward I have been nearly free from pain—indeed I have had none since last Monday—and now I call myself *well.* I am not strong, but gaining daily, & I think, with care, I shall have no return of the disease.

We have had a remarkable early spring. There has been no frost for nearly a month, and vegetation is in all its glory. The hyacinths, crown imperial, wall flowers, magnolias, etc., in our garden make quite a display of flowers, & our peach, plum, pear, and cherry trees are white with bloom. . . .

1. William P. Johnston.

Monday, April 11. On Tuesday last, about 1 o'clock, I recd. a despatch asking me to start for Philadelphia that evening to attend a meeting of the Board of Directors of the Magnetic Telegraph Company. So, at 3 o'clock & 40 minutes I started, and arrived at the Girard House in Phila. at about 11 o'clock. Took tea & went to bed. Saw Mr. F. O. J. Smith before he was up in the morning, and ascertained that our Board was to meet at 10 A.M. Went to the Telegraph office, and thence to Mr. Swain's house. Found him & Col. Hoe at breakfast. At 10 we went to the office & held our meeting, but could do nothing until we had an interview with our Counsel—St. Geo. Tucker Campbell, Esq.[1]

He appointed 12 o'clock, at his office, to meet us, & at that hour we repaired there. Mr. Russell,[2] a lawyer from N. York, was the agent & attorney of the Telegraph Companies with which we were trying to negotiate, & met us at Mr. Campbell's. We proceeded to consider a long &

intricate contract that had been drawn up to which there were to be seven parties, as follows.

The American Telegraph Co.	1st part.
Magnetic Telegraph Co.	2d "
N. Y. & Washington Printing Tel. Co.	3d part.
Trustees of the House Tel. Co.	4th "
Morris[3] & Russell	5th "
Morse, A. Kendall & Vail	6th "
Trustees of all the foregoing (new Co.)	7th "

Besides these parties, Hon. F. O. J. Smith's Telegraph stocks & interests were to be purchased at $300,000.

This contract was proceeded with item by item, & discussed. At ½ past 2 we adjourned till ½ past 4. Then met again, & proceeded with our examination and discussion, with at times no little exhibition of temper between Mr. Russell & the members of our Board who were present, viz. Messrs. Barnum, Kendall, Swain, Hoe, & myself. We held our meeting till nearly 9 & then adjourned to meet again at 11 Thursday morning.

I was entirely exhausted, & could hardly drag myself along to my hotel. Took a cup of tea & something to eat & went to bed. Arose Thursday morning much refreshed & at the hour appointed we all met again at Mr. Campbell's, where we had another session, with an intermission for dinner, till between 9 & 10 at night, and then adjourned till ½ past 10 Friday morning—our directors to meet Mr. Campbell at 9 to have a private interview.

At 9 Friday morning we met Mr. Campbell, & took his advice as to certain unsettled points in the agreement, the main one of which was that we could proceed no further until we had the consent of each individual stockholder of our Company.

At a little before 11, Mr. Russell & Mr. Smith came.

Our seven propositions were read to Mr. Russell by Mr. Campbell, & he at once said he must consult his principals before he could agree to them. Mr. Smith announced that he should not wait another day, & that, if we were to postpone action until our individual stockholders were to be consulted, there was an end of the matter so far as he was concerned.

We then had a general talk for an hour, which ended in no certain conclusion, & we separated. Our Board repaired to the office and held a regular meeting and adopted a resolution appointing a Committee to draw up a paper for our Stockholders to sign, & to take measures to procure their signatures, and then we adjourned.

At 8 o'clock Saturday morning I took the cars & arrived home at ½ past 5 in the afternoon. . . .

Our meetings with Mr. Campbell at Philadelphia afforded me much amusement & much study. There we were, shut up with him in his office not less than 18 hours, discussing an intricate, *illegal* contract, hard to understand, & about which there occurred dispute after dispute between Mr. Russell (a keen[,] shrewd Lawyer & an Englishman, who thoroughly understood every point) and Mr. Campbell & our Board of Directors— Mr. Smith occasionally volunteering his views. . . .

1. St. George Tucker Campbell had successfully represented the Magnetic Telegraph Co. in dealing with the New York and Washington Printing Telegraph Co. in 1852.
2. Robert W. Russell represented the New York and Washington Printing Telegraph Co., which was absorbed by the American Telegraph Co. at this meeting.
3. Francis Morris of New York.

Friday, April 22. . . . While in Baltimore[1] I went with Mr. Gilman to see a card manufactory—cards to card cotton & wool with. The machinery is the most ingenious I ever saw, & seems the most like *iron life* of any I ever saw. I thought the machinery for making percussion caps very ingenious and very perfect, but this excels that.

This evening is election evening in our Commandery of Kts. Templar and I *must* go, rain or shine.

I have not been to the Court House since the trial of Sickles commenced, and have no desire to go. I have read all that has been published in the *Intelligencer,* & some from other papers. It only shows how depraved men & women can be, who lose respect for themselves, and for all about them. They have been trying to prove that Sickles was temporarily insane when he killed Key. I think *they have proved* that Key and Mrs. Sickles were *permanently insane,* for a year and more, or they would not have acted as they did!

The whole thing places frail humanity in rather a disgusting attitude.

1. French was in Baltimore on April 14 for a telegraph meeting.

Sunday, April 24. . . . I fear Mr. Haley is attempting to do too much *out-of-door* work, and thus paying too little attention to his *inside* duties as a Pastor. His sermons recently have not been at all studied, and consequently were loose and slipshod. I was sorry, more for his sake than my own, that they were so.

As soon after Mr. Sickles was committed to jail as he possibly could get there[,] Mr. Haley was there, and he has been a constant visitor there since, and has attended the trial as constantly as if he were one of the counsel, as I have been told.

In one point of view this is all to be commended—in another it is not.

I do not doubt that Mr. Haley's good heart and kind nature has prompted all his action in this matter, and that he is governed by the best & purest motives. But when I consider that he is *my* Pastor, & ought to be my spiritual adviser, and that he has not entered the doors of my dwelling for nearly or quite a year! even though I was severely—perhaps dangerously—sick, & he knew it, I cannot overlook the fact of his constant devotion to Mr. Sickles, where he has even exceeded his Christian duty, and his total neglect of me! It is not right.

As a man I like Mr. Haley very much; as a Minister—as *my* minister— I have much reason, as I think, to be dissatisfied with him, and unless he *changes*, in some measure, his course, I shall be compelled to change my place of worship. If I have a right to any religious sympathy, I ought to have it, most certainly, from the Clergyman I pay to minister to me! . . .

Sunday, May 15. Three weeks have past without a record! Perhaps it [is] as well that there is not one, as I have witnessed, personally, little worth recording. Sickles, who murdered Key in cold blood, has been acquitted by a Washington jury, and perhaps, in view of *all* the circumstances, rightfully acquitted, but the blood is on his hands, & the "damned spot" will never "out" as long as he breathes mortal breath.

I was at Philadelphia last week. Left home at 20 m. before 5 Monday morning & returned Wednesday evening at ¼ before 6. Our Board of Telegraphic Directors met, & there were representatives from the various Telegraph interests in the U.S. present. Peter Cooper, F. O. J. Smith[,] Cyrus W. Field, Mr. Sibley, Prof. Morse, Amos Kendall, etc., were there, and we *all* tried to consolidate the Telegraphic interests of the Union into one great company.[1] Whether we did, or did not succeed is yet to be seen, as we left the matter in the hands of Committees. . . .

1. Peter Cooper (1791–1883), a pioneer in the iron industry, was president of the company laying the Atlantic cable. Cyrus W. Field (1819–1892) was associated with Peter Cooper in laying the Atlantic cable. Hiram Sibley (1807–1888), who believed in consolidation, formed the Western Union Telegraph Co. in 1856.

Thursday, August 11. . . . Judge French's court was legislated out of existence last June by the N.H. "General Court" and his term of office expired on the 1st inst. New Hampshire ermine is mean stuff, & I am not sorry it is off the Judge's shoulders. Now he contemplates going to Boston, where, I think he will make money. He has selected a lady to do the wifely honors of his house, in place of our dear departed Anne, Miss Pamela Prentiss[1] of Keene, daughter of my old friend John Prentiss[,] former Editor of the *Keene Sentinel*. From all accounts he has probably selected well, and I hope they will both be happy. Although the idea of seeing anyone in the place of Anne is not a pleasant one to contemplate, still I rejoice that he has concluded to marry again. He will be happier, and if his new wife appreciates the memory of the Angel whose place she supplies, she will make his future in this world far more happy than it would be were he to move on his lonely way in widowerhood. God grant them years of happiness.

The weather since I last wrote herein has been generally comfortable. Some hot days, & now the season is rather dry. I am very busy preparing for my various duties at Chicago, where the Masonic G. G. Boche's,[2] & the U.S. Ag. Society meet the 2d week in Sept.

Frank has taken all the Masonic Degrees and orders since he returned, up to the Knight Templar which he is to take this evening. I expect him to be with me at Chicago, to aid me in my various & ardent duties.

1. Pamela Prentiss (1828–1895) was fifteen years younger than Henry Flagg French.
2. Name of the General Grand (G.G.) U.S. Masonic chapter.

Sunday, August 14. Soon after I finished the above I went down to the Asylum and conferred the Order of Knight Templar on Frank. . . .

Frank is very much engaged in making a table of cases for Prof. Parsons[1] of Cambridge, which takes all his time—8 or 9 hours a day— hard work and poor wages I fear, but I like to see him engaged, even if he does not put much money in his pocket. . . .

Mr. R. W. Latham has been here since I wrote the foregoing. He is just from N.Y. and ardent for the nomination of Mr. John Minor Botts for the Presidency. I am warmly a friend of Mr. Botts and sincerely believe that a union of all the opposition on him will insure his election. And I just as sincerely believe that the nomination of W. H. Seward by the Republicans will insure the defeat of that party, for Seward cannot get the support of the old Americans, & I doubt if he can of the old line Whigs, & no opposition man can be elected without their cooperation. I will be true to my Republican principles, but can support Botts with all my heart if my party will agree to go for him. I have done all in my power in a prudent manner to bring his name before my Republican friends. John M. Botts for President and Solomon Foot for V. President would be a Ticket that could be carried without a doubt! I go for its nomination!

1. Theophilus Parsons (1797–1882), professor at the Harvard Law School, 1848–1869, was a productive scholar whose *Law of Contracts* went through nine editions.

Sunday, August 21. What of the past week? Tuesday morning, the 16th inst.[,] the bell of the Columbia Engine House commenced ringing at ¼ before 4. I arose & looked out and saw the workshops at the North of the Capitol on fire. Benny & I dressed and went over & saw them burn down. They were of light, combustible material and made a brilliant fire. From the time the bell commenced ringing till they were all flat down, I did not hear a cry of fire, or even a shout! Several engine & hose, & hook & ladder Companies were there, & they worked some, but were as still as if a Quaker meeting instead of a fire was in progress. The remarkable stillness seemed to strike everybody. There were hundreds of people—perhaps thousands—on the ground, all with their eyes open, mouths shut, & arms folded! . . .

After dinner Mr. Stevens[1] came in, and we walked over to Judge Douglas's, & he talked in the most interesting manner, on the construction of the Constitution, for at least one hour, presenting views that had never struck me before, & citing historical data of which I had never heard! His argument was

1st. To prove that the Constitution has nothing to do with establishing slavery, but that it is established by the local law of the place where it exists.

2d. That Congress can neither legislate Slavery in or out of the Territories of the U.S.[,] but that the people of the Territories have the sole power over it, as much as the people in the States have.

3d. That wherever the word States is used generally, in the Constitution, the word applies to Territories. For example—where a fugitive from justice flees from one *State* to another—Territories are the same as States, otherwise a fugitive to a *Territory* could not be arrested there.

His arguments were specious[2] and convincing, & I now prophecy that he will convince the people of the whole Union—North & South—that he is right, & the eternal slavery squabble will be healed through him, and if he live[s] he will [be] President in 1864 by almost the unanimous vote of the people!

I always thought Stephen A. Douglas very much of a man, but today he seemed to me, indeed, the political giant! I can hardly find the words to express my admiration of his views as expressed to me, in that short hour.

I saw Mrs. Douglas[3] for the first time, to know her. She is a magnificent woman, and considerably advanced in a certain state.

It is 9 o'clock P.M. & all the folks have gone to Mr. Russell's.

The drums are beating tattoo, & I will lay aside my pen.

1. Ezra L. Stevens, a clerk in the Interior Department.
2. Obsolete meaning of "specious" was "pleasing."

3. Adèle Cutts Douglas (1835–1899), Douglas's second wife, was pregnant at the time. Her child, Ellen Douglas, was born September 30 but died ten weeks later.

Sunday, September 4. 59 years of my life gone today!

How much left? Aye that's the question! Seems as if I had lived a *master while* now. I have lived it very satisfactorily to myself, and hope the remainder, long or short[,] will be ditto.

Heard Mr. Haley preach—couldn't preach much—cold & bronchial affection. What he did preach was good & according to my notions. He alluded to Horace Mann[1] & spoke of him as he deserves to be spoken of, as a first-rate man, & one who did great good in the world. I knew Horace Mann well, & I know what he did for the cause of education, and he did much—very much—and he did it *first best.* He deserves a monument in every schoolhouse in America!

I sat in the Choir today, and tried to help my friend Stevens sing bass— my bass was probably *base* enough! But the place was cool, & I *saved a quarter,* as the contribution box does not come into the choir!!

A hot, muggy, dog day.

I won't write another word!

1. Horace Mann (1796–1859), of Massachusetts, did much to reform American public education and served as congressman, 1848–1853.

Sunday, October 9. Two days after I wrote the foregoing—viz. on the 6th day of Sept. [Tuesday] at 3 o'clock & 20′ P.M. I left this City of Washington for Chicago, Ill., to attend the Exhibition of the U.S. Ag. Soc. & the meetings of the Grand Encampment and G. G. Chapter of the U.S. . . .

At Baltimore, we all took the 6 o'clock train for Pittsburgh. We arrived at Harrisburg at ¼ to 9 & staid till 3 A.M. the next morning. Stopped at a Hotel (the U.S. I believe). At 3 A.M. Wednesday we were off for Pittsburgh. We all slept I believe till daylight. We passed over the Alleghenies in the forenoon—a most romantic scene it is, as we climb the mountains with two locomotives attached, puffing their way up as if they must get out of breath! turning sharp angles away up the mountain, where from the car windows we could look down—down—down into almost a fathomless abyss. Nobody was sleepy then! At the top of the mountain we passed thro' a tunnel, a mile long, and then commenced our descent. What an improvement on the old stationary power & iron ropes, as it was when I crossed six years ago!

At 20 m. before 1 we arrived at Pittsburgh. . . . At ½ past 1 we left

Pittsburgh and arrived at Crestline [Ohio] at 8 o'clock & 40 m. P.M. There we took the sleeping car—it being my first experience in that way.

As soon as the sleeping arrangements could be made, we all "turned in," and, being pretty well tired out, it was not long before I was asleep, and I think I slept as well as ever I did in my bed at home. About sunrise we were called, & arose & washed & prepared, as well as we could, to arrive at Chicago. At 9:40′ A.M. Thursday, we arrived at Chicago. . . .

Friday & Saturday I attended to my duties as Treasurer. Sunday morning Frank arrived, & we spent the day in our room pretty much. . . .

Tuesday morning the Grand Masonic Bodies met, & from that time till I left for home on Friday evening, Sep. 24th [23d], I was in a constant whirl of business & excitement, so much so that I can hardly remember when any particular event occurred, although I have a general remembrance of everything. I know that on Thursday, the 15th, I was elected Grand Master of Knights Templar, and was installed & took my seat as G. M. on Saturday. I, of course, declined a reelection as G. G. Secy. of the G. G. Chapter. The Masonic bodies closed, to meet again at Memphis, Tenn., in 1862, on Monday evening the 19th, & from that moment until Friday evening, Frank & I were constantly engaged paying bills & premiums. . . .

. . . On Thursday of the 2d week I dined there [Richmond House] again with our President & Executive Com. & Maj. Poore and Frank, by invitation of Mr. Cyrus McCormick,[1] the Reaper-man. I also breakfasted there once with my Masonic brethren, & Gen. Tilghman, Gov. Crittenden & I had a private dinner together one day at the Tremont. . . .

At 8 o'clock Friday evening the 24th [23rd] Gen. Tilghman, Mr. & Mrs. McGowan & I started for home. We took the sleeping car & arrived at Crestline the next morning, at Pittsburgh in the afternoon, where we again took a sleeping car, and at Harrisburg at 2 A.M. on Sunday morning. We remained there until 8 A.M.[,] then came down to Baltimore where we dined & spent Sunday night. (Mr. & Mrs. McG. left us for Phil. at Harrisburg.) I left Gen. T. at Balt. Monday morning, and came home, where I arrived at 10 o'clock, after the hardest 3 weeks' labor I ever had in my life. . . .

1. Cyrus H. McCormick (1809–1884) invented the reaper in 1831 and opened his own factory in Chicago in 1847.

Sunday, December 4. . . . Within the time covered by this journalization John Brown's raid[1] into Western Va., his fight, seizure, trial & execution has taken place. But the Newspapers are filled with all the details of this most insane, unfortunate, & melancholy affair, so I will do no more than

to record my entire, utter, & sincere condemnation of the movement of
John Brown. I am at a loss to determine whether he was crazy or not. If
sane, he assuredly merits the sympathy of no one, & has met his just
deserts, and most emphatically do I denounce and regret the uncalled
for and dangerous sympathy of the unholy & bloodthirsty abolitionists
of the North for the old murderer and traitor. That he was brave &
fearless no one can deny, and so much the more dangerous man was he.
I can feel no admiration for the high qualities of any man who uses those
qualities to overturn the Constitution and Laws of my Country! When
Republicanism becomes in the least treasonable, I am no longer a Republican. My Republicanism teaches me to stand by my Country & her
Constitution, & when I show the first symptom of any other course let
my fellow citizens denounce me—but not till then! . . .

1. John Brown (1800–1859) seized the U.S. armory at Harpers Ferry, Va., on Oct. 16,
1859, and after being captured by Robert E. Lee, was hanged for treason on Dec. 2, 1859.
Lee (1807–1870) was at the time lieutenant colonel in the cavalry.

Tuesday, December 13. . . . The two Houses of Congress convened last
Monday week. The House has been laboring to elect a Speaker ever since
but has not yet done it. The time is mostly wasted in speeches of bitter
crimination and recrimination. The Southern Democrats affect to believe
all Republicans Abolitionists, and the Southern Democrats & Americans
are fighting among themselves. It is all wrong—wrong—wrong! But,
while political aggrandizement takes the place of true patriotism & a
determination to preserve the Union & Constitution, they (the Ho. of
Reps.) must remain as they are. *Ten* true patriots from each party, who
would cast aside all personal consequences and pledge themselves to do
what they honestly believed to be right, could exert an influence that
would lead to happy and harmonious results. . . .

Sunday, January 22. . . . In the 22 days since what?—*Let me see.* Rode
once in a sleigh—down to the office of the Firemen's Ins. Co. Tuesday
P.M. Jany. 3d—not first-rate sleighing. Went skaiting once with Benny,
and found I could skait tolerably well—that is I could *do* the straight
forward work and *gradual curving,* about the same as 40 years ago! but
when it came to "grinding bark," skaiting backwards, "squaring the
yards[,]" & such like, it was no go. I could "scull" just as well as ever—
indeed I found *that* came back to me better than striking out in the
graceful movement of common skaiting. I skaited about ½ an hour when
my ankles became "plenty tired" & I took off my skaits & came home. . . .
    The House still persists in remaining without a Speaker. Seven weeks

now have they been a disorganized mob—for they are nothing else—bringing disgrace upon the Country & upon themselves. The *people* must take measures to reform this kind of thing or the Nation will soon be—no nation, but a disorganized & broken up people. Let us hope for the best. . . .

Sunday, January 29. . . . The House came very near choosing Hon. Mr. Smith[1] of N.C. Speaker Friday. Indeed at one stage of the vote he was actually elected, but a change by members from him to some other person prevented an election. Mr. S. is an old Whig, with American proclivities, & the Democrats, except 3, and Americans united upon him. It gave the Republicans a terrible *scare!* and tomorrow they will unite on Pennington[2] of N.J. and probably elect him, although the Americans are very sanguine in the belief that Smith is to be the man. I think I have heard enough today to warrant me in the belief that Pennington is to be the man. The absence of C. B. Cochrane[3] is a misfortune to the Republicans, & it is said that unless they can *pair him,* they will *stave off* the election till he can get here. . . .

1. William N. H. Smith (1812–1889) had just been elected to the House.
2. William Pennington (1796–1862) had also just been elected.
3. Clark B. Cochrane (1815–1867), of New York, was elected as a Democrat to the House in 1857.

Sunday, February 5. . . . The weather during the week past has been very cold. On Wednesday the House elected Mr. Pennington[,] Speaker, & adjourned over to Friday, when they elected Col. J. W. Forney[,] Clerk[,] & Mr. Hoffman[1] of Md.[,] Sergt. at Arms, & then adjourned over until tomorrow. . . .

I have felt as if the Republicans of Washington were not being very well treated, but I was with Senator Clark last evening, who assured me that the party were doing the best for their future interests, & that we of Washington should not be forgotten, if the Republican party eventually triumphed.

I read Forney's speech of Friday evening, in yesterday's *Herald.* It is a smasher, & I agree with him in his political views as therein expressed, in toto, although I disagree to the "meat-axe" style in which he attacked his old friend James Buchanan, especially when I know that he (Forney) as Clerk of the House is bound, as a duty, to carry, *in person,* all messages (Resolutions, etc.) from the House to the President. Their personal meetings must be particularly cordial!!

1. Henry William Hoffman (1825–1895) represented the American party in Congress,

1855–1857, but failed twice at reelection. He served as sergeant at arms February 3, 1860, to July 5, 1861.

Thursday, February 16. Frank left us for New York, at 6:20′ on Tuesday morning, to enter into the "rough and tumble" of life's business in that City. I have great faith in his success, for he is industrious, with a good education, & good habits, and an analytical mind. . . .

Sunday, March 4. Fifteen days recordless.

On the 22d of Feby. *We* inaugurated the Equestrian statue of Washington, made by Clark Mills; & with the morning flood of rain, the afternoon depth of mud, the delay of the 7th Regiment of New York troops to arrive, etc., we had "*a Time of it.*" . . .

Politically, the Congressional Republican Committee, & the Republican Association of Washington, are endeavouring to arrange their operations so as to carry on the ensuing campaign harmoniously. We—The Ex. Com. of the Assn.—met the Cong. Com. at Mr. Clephane's[1] one evening last week & proposed, pro & con, but came to no definite conclusion. The Cong. Com. do not seem inclined to do us justice—they are desirous to overshadow us, but we do not intend to be overshadowed! I hope & trust all will be harmoniously arranged. I have never seen such an entire disregard to justice in making subordinate appointments, as manifested by the newly elected officers of the House of Representatives. They were elected by Republican votes, & have kept in and appointed rank democrats to office! I hope and trust a day of retribution will come!

On the 29th Feby. (last Wednesday) I listened for nearly an hour and a half to the speech of William H. Seward. The vast galleries of the Senate were crowded, and hundreds who came to listen had to go away. It was a great speech.[2] Let the *N.Y. Herald* and other papers of that *genus* say what they please against it—I say it was a great speech, and will *tell*.

On Friday evening last I attended a reception at Senator Seward's. It was large and elegant, and I enjoyed it exceedingly. I was introduced for the first time to Hon. *Charles Francis Adams*[3] and had a very interesting conversation with him. He introduced me to Mrs. Adams.[4] Mr. A. resembles his father, my old and beloved friend John Quincy Adams, very much, and his manners are exceedingly like his father's. I was very much pleased with my interview. I was also introduced to Gen. J. W. Nye[5] of N. York, and listened with admiration to the scintillations of wit and humor which were continually sparkling from his conversation—no matter with whom. Mr. Seward seemed particularly to enjoy his company. I left about 10, bringing Hon. Senator Preston King[6] to his lodgings on A St. North with me in my carriage. . . .

1. Lewis Clephane, an early Republican and business manager of the *National Era,* was appointed postmaster for the District, 1861.

2. Unlike Seward's speech on October 25, 1858, in which he said that the slavery struggle was an "irrepressible conflict," this one was conciliatory and therefore met the approval of moderates such as French.

3. Charles Francis Adams (1807–1886) served as a Republican in the House of Representatives, 1859–1861.

4. Abigail Brooks (1808–1889) married Charles Francis Adams, 1829.

5. James W. Nye (1814–1876) was at the time president of the board of police, New York City.

6. Preston King (1806–1865) of New York served in the U.S. House of Representatives as a Democrat, 1843–1847, and as a Free-Soiler, 1849–1853, and in the Senate as a Republican, 1857–1863.

Sunday, April 22. . . . I am never idle—Much of my time in the month, has been devoted to Freemasonry, & something of what I have done will be found in Morris's *Voice of Masonry*[1] to be published May 1st. I sent him a long account of certain doings here which he says will appear in that publication. . . .

1. Robert Morris (1818–1888) began publication of this periodical in 1859.

Saturday, April 28. Missed my Journalizing yesterday! I arose at 6 A.M. and as soon as I had breakfasted I went out in the garden and worked till afternoon, then rode down in the City & did some errands & returned & again went to work mending the western summerhouse. Found it in such a rotten condition that I had to take out two of the old joists and put in new ones. It took me all the afternoon, & I came in at ½ past 6 tired enough. Read to Mrs. French all the evening. She had a severe headache all day. Went to bed at 9 o'clock. . . .

Friday, May 4. . . . This week has been rife with accounts from Charleston as to the doings of the Democratic Convention—what a farce it has turned out to be! First it was broken asunder, and then the Northern half could not agree on a candidate, & finally adjourned to meet at Baltimore on the 18th of June. The Republicans are in high glee at the result. We had a glorious meeting of the Republican Association last evening—speeches from Case[1] of Indiana, Farnsworth[2] of Illinois and Montgomery Blair of Maryland. Our meeting lasted from 8 till 11. Case read, among other things[,] the preamble of the act passed in 1783, I think, abolishing slavery in Pennsylvania. It is strong, and shows how determined our fathers were that the Declaration of Independence should not be a farce of mere words!

Dinner!

1. Charles Case (1817–1883), congressman, 1857–1861.
2. John F. Farnsworth (1820–1897), congressman, 1857–1861 and 1863–1873.

Monday, May 13. This has been a great day in Washington. The Japanese Embassy, consisting of ever so many dignitaries, an army of servants & 80 tons of baggage, and a treaty in a box covered with red morocco and strapped with iron, arrived at the Navy yard at precisely 12 o'clock meridian.[1] All Washington seemed to be out to receive them— and plenty of American Dignitaries to boot. They were received with a salute of cannon, & in carriages and omnibuses were borne to Willard's Hotel, escorted by the Military of the District, the Marine Corps, & the Ordnance Corps from the Arsenal, and a street full of people. That red box rode *on the top of an omnibus,* escorted—or guarded—by three police officers! *I* think it should have been carried in "a coach and six" & guarded by a Regiment of Cavalry! To think of a hundred men coming all the way from Japan, to bring a treaty, & then to see it ignominiously riding on the top of an omnibus, from the Navy yard to Willard's—"Ye Gods & little fishes," it is too—too bad. It is, however[,] safe I presume!

I had no idea of seeing any of the great show. At 11 o'clock I went to the Capitol & meeting Senator Clark we walked to my house & went to the top of it with a glass & saw, very plainly, the steamer having on board the Embassy, accompanied, apparently, by two others, approaching the Eastern Branch from Alexandria. The stripes and stars were flying from the stern flagstaff, the Japanese flag from the centre of the Boat, & a white flag with something on it, from the forward staff (probably the steamer's with her name "Philadelphia" upon it). We could distinctly see the people on board, & distinguished the red coats of the Marine Band in the bows very plainly, & could read the steamer's name on her paddle box, as she rounded into the mouth of the Anacostia. . . .

1. Townshend Harris had negotiated a treaty with Japan in 1858, calling for diplomatic representatives at the capitals of each nation.

Sunday, May 20. It is ½ past 9 o'clock of as beautiful a morning as need be. I awoke this morning with a violent headache, but it has now nearly gone. Since last Monday P.M. when I last wrote herein, the City has been in a state of excitement consequent upon the presence of the Japanese Embassadors and the doings of the Republican Convention at Chicago.

Friday afternoon came the information of the nomination of Abraham Lincoln[1] as the Republican candidate for the Presidency, and in the evening that of Hannibal Hamlin[2] for Vice President. Of course the City was all agog with the news. Many were, of course, disappointed, but all agreed that the nominations were judicious & must be unanimously and heartily supported.

The Republican Association was called together last evening, and I took the chair at a little past 8—made a brief speech, & then called on Hon. Mr. Pettit[3] of Indiana, who was present, and spoke well and eloquently for about ½ an hour. Mr. Frank[4] of N.Y. then spoke. A procession was formed for the purpose of proceeding to the residence of Senator Hamlin at the "Washington House" to serenade him. The Marine Band was in attendance, & the procession, numbering perhaps 200, marched to the Washington House, which was handsomely illuminated. The Band played the "Star-Spangled Banner." I made a few remarks, from the balcony, introducing Senator Hamlin, when he was received with vociferous applause. He addressed the assembled multitude, by this time numbering thousands of all sorts of politics. No interruption, however, took place. Mr. Campbell[5] of Pennsylvania followed Mr. Hamlin. As soon as he concluded[,] three hearty cheers were given for the nominees, the band struck up, and the procession moved to Senator Trumbull's[6] on 8th street, opposite the P.O. Dept. The Senator was serenaded, & came out & made a good speech. While he was speaking it was evident that there were "uneasy spirits" in the crowd who were determining on a fuss. He was many times interrupted with taunting remarks, but went on and concluded. Hon. E. B. Washburne[7] followed & spoke eloquently. He had spoken from 5 to 10 minutes, when an organized rush was made from F St. down 8th by a gang of drunken rowdies probably (for I cannot believe sober citizens would be guilty of such an act)[,] it is said, with ropes stretched across the street, at all events with sticks held across. It was so sudden & unexpected as to sweep all before it, & the street was emptied in a moment. The Association, however[,] rallied almost as quick as it was *rushed* away, & Mr. W. concluded his remarks, expressing manly indignation for the cowardly effort that had been made to suppress public speaking on the part of the Republicans. There was no further interruption. As soon as Mr. W. concluded, I stepped forward, called for 3 cheers for the nominees, which were given *with a will*, and then adjourned the meeting and came home, where I arrived at ½ past 11. Take it all in all, & considering the state of political affairs in this Administration-ridden city, it was a glorious triumph of Republicanism. We shall have a ratification meeting next week—and perhaps a row, but I hope and trust not.

Last evening at ½ past 5 Mrs. French, Mrs. Russell & myself went to the President's where the Marine Band were to play & the Japanese to be present. Such a crowd I think I have never witnessed. The grounds seemed to be densely packed with human beings. The "Embassy" was upon the South Portico, the observed of all observers. We saw them well & saw the President come out & shake hands with them, amid much bowing & genuflexion. We staid about an hour and then came home.

We received a letter from Frank yesterday announcing his admission to the practice of law in New York on one day of last week.

What a world this is!

1. French met Lincoln during the latter's term as congressman, 1847–1849.
2. Hannibal Hamlin (1809–1891), of Maine, was a Democratic congressman, 1843–1847; senator, 1848–1857; and Republican senator, 1857–1861.
3. John U. Pettit (1820–1881) was a Republican congressman, 1855–1861.
4. Augustus Frank (1826–1895) was a Republican congressman, 1859–1865.
5. James H. Campbell (1820–1895) was Whig congressman, 1855–1857, and Republican congressman, 1859–1863.
6. Lyman Trumbull (1813–1896) was Republican senator from Illinois, 1855–1873.
7. Elihu B. Washburne (1816–1887) was Whig and Republican congressman from Illinois, 1853–1869.

Monday, May 28. The attack upon the Republican Association last Saturday evening week, has made more sensation, and operated more to the detriment of the City than I supposed it would. All respectable people heartily condemn it, and its effect has been to reduce the appropriations for the benefit of the City materially in the House of Representatives. I have ascertained since I wrote the preceding account that stones were thrown into the crowd & some of the Republicans were hit pretty hard. The thing will operate as its own cure, and there will be no more disturbance, I think. We are to have a ratification meeting this evening, which the Mayor says *shall not* be disturbed.

I was very busily engaged all last week in attending to my business before Congress & political matters attendant upon the preparation for our meeting tonight. We had a very full & interesting meeting of the Association on Thursday evening, & I believe all our arrangements for this evening are completed.

Last Monday I happened at the Patent office when the Japanese Embassy visited it. I had an excellent opportunity to see them, as, with the crowd, I passed around the rooms near them. The Chief Embassador[1] seemed to appreciate fully everything that was shown to him. The cases were unlocked, & the Commissioner of Patents, Hon. Philip F. Thomas,[2] who accompanied him, took great pains to show him, & to hand to him, when he could, such specimens of Yankee inventive skill as seemed particularly to attract his attention. He, the Chief Embassador, has an expressive and intellectual countenance, & withal, a mild & pleased expression—at least he then had, as if he were perfectly satisfied with his peculiar position. He has a Roman nose, & is the only one I saw with a nose of that character. He was dressed in a light grey silk coat, or blouse, of some stiff texture like brocade, and very full trowsers about the same color. He wore two swords, the handles of them highly ornamented. His attendants, of rank, were dressed very much, *in the form* of their habiliments, as he was, but no other wore grey. Those who seemed to be of far less rank wore what seemed to be knee breeches & dark stockings with shoes. Their legs had very much the appearance of old Judge Bibb's,[3] who, to the day of his death, wore the old gentlemanly dress of '76, & his legs were very slender, giving him the appearance of being mounted on a couple of stout walking sticks!

Yesterday I was down in the City, & met quite a number of the Japanese both in going down & returning. They were, as usual, attended by a crowd of people. I saw them, for the first time, with their heads covered. They had on curious hats—if hats they may be called—of different patterns & kinds. Some of them looked like black house roofs in miniature. One had on a sort of broadbrimmed hat appearing like metal. They moved along with much dignity, scarcely noticing the crowd about them. It was a warm afternoon and they carried ordinary fans, & were constantly fanning themselves. . . .

1. Simme Boozen-no-kami.
2. Philip F. Thomas (1810–1890) had been Democratic governor of Maryland, 1847–1850.
3. George M. Bibb (1776–1859), senator from Kentucky, 1811–1814 and 1829–1835; and Secretary of the Treasury, 1844–1845.

Sunday, June 17. . . . Mrs. French left home on Tuesday morning the 5th inst. She went to New York[,] where she now is, in the hope of improving her health. Ben is at home with me, but I see precious little of him, and am much troubled about him. He has a parcel of boys about him and is given to fine dressing and rowdyism. He hates to study or to do anything useful—likes to run off with the fire companies, sit up late nights and lie in bed till nearly noon mornings. I do not know what to do with him, but am convinced something *must* be done or he will be ruined. He is now out somewhere with his playmates.

Since Mrs. French left[,] most of my days have been spent at the Capitol endeavouring to get my business before Congress acted upon. Thus far my success has been small, and I am about discouraged. I am very thankful[,] however, that, in consequence of my election as Clerk of the Com.

of Claims, to take effect on the 1st of July, I can have no more engagements in relation to claims before Congress, and once out of that business
I am done with it forever. It is disgusting business at the best. . . .

The outside world has been rumbling on as usual, nothing very strange
or exciting having happened since I wrote herein on the 28th of May.
Our ratification meeting on the evening of that day was a very large one
and went off well. The Police kept the most perfect order, and the speaking was good. Our election on the 1st Monday in June resulted in Mayor
Berret's being *declared* elected, though there is not a doubt on my mind
that Richard Wallach was rightfully and legally elected. He has commenced contesting the matter &, if our Court has any impartiality, he
will in due time be declared Mayor.

My garden looks finely now. Michael has got it well cleaned up, &
everything is flourishing. It is now ¼ to 6. The shower is over, & it is
about time for somebody to come home.

Sunday, July 8. I have been lame with a sprained tendon in the calf of
my left leg since Tuesday, June 26th, & it has kept me pretty much
confined to the house. I did it in running while playing a game of baseball. I wrote Mrs. French on the 27th, & on the 28th she started for
home at 6 P.M. & arrived the next morning at 6. I met her at the cars,
though pretty lame, but have been very much lamer since.

[At this point French incorporated into his journal a series of letters to
Elizabeth, written between June 5 and June 27. Salutations and complimentary closings have been omitted.]

As the best journal of the time she was absent[,] I will put my letters
to her in here.

Journal for Mrs. French's amusement

June 5. Bid Mrs. F. good-by at 10 m. past 6 A.M. in the cars. Came
home feeling more like sitting down and having a good cry than anything
else. Gulped down my grief—read the *Intelligencer* & eat breakfast *alone*.
Ben not up. Mr. Russell came in and we talked over the election. . . .
Everybody talking about the election. "Disgraceful frauds"—"Much
fighting in the evening in the 4th Ward"—"Wallach's house stoned"—
"Nokes's house stoned in the 6th ward"—"A member wounded with
pistols in the 4th ward." Wallach, I am told, is determined to test the
election legally.[1] There is no doubt he is legally elected. Remained about
the Capitol till 1 P.M. Then came home, and wrote this. . . .

Wednesday morning June 6th. ½ past 7. Have just eaten breakfast alone—4 eggs, one cracker & a cup of coffee. Ben not up. . . . Michael just came in & announced that he could not find our cow. Told him to eat his breakfast and start again. Hope she is not stolen.

¼ to 6 Evening. Mike found the cow. I awoke with a severe headache this morning. Cause uncertain. Must have been either the excitement of your departure—or laughing at Mr. Fessenden's jokes & stories—it could *not* have been the trifle of St. Croix rum I tasted at Judge Chipman's![2] *Tea bell.* After tea. I had to take tea alone, Benny gone to recite. He has taken *one* meal with me since you left. He got up at ½ past 11 this morning. Bridget & I did our best. Willey Russell[3] came in a little after 11 and succeeded in rousing him. He did not recite yesterday, notwithstanding my request to him to do so. I think we had better make a tinker of him. He does not seem to care about anything but his clothes. I have just read the *Star.* It shows a state of rowdyism in this city that is really appalling. Congress *must* do something for us to make an efficient police or we shall all be murdered or burned up. . . .

Friday, June 8th. . . . Arose at a little past 5. At 5 m. before 6 Michael brought round the horse & buggy. I went down & got Gov. Grimes[4] & we went over to the Asylum. The morning was beautiful. Doct. Nichols[5] treated us as if we had been princes. We went over the building considerably till breakfast. Eat breakfast—coffee, fried chicken, beefsteak, fish balls, cakes, bread, & strawberries. Mrs. N. & Doct. Stevens[6] with us. After breakfast the Doctor showed us all around the premises. There was old Tilda Wathon, among the women—tidily dressed, singing & keeping time with her foot, happy as a clam. She arose when we went in and followed us around, walking as straight and as dignified as if she were a queen. There, too, was my old crazy friend Robinson, with whom I had considerable talk. He gave me a white transparent stone in payment of $50 that I once lent him, insisting that it was a diamond, & that if I would take it to Gault's & have it cut it would make a very elegant jewel!

Tell Frank he must consider Mr. Sumner's speech *a personal matter,* and not *a party one.* It is terribly, vindictively, savagely severe—a mortal tongue stab at the South, for every blow Brooks gave. *The party* do not endorse its severity, though they admit of its truth. Heaven avenged him first and now he has avenged himself. . . .

Sunday, June 10. . . . Yesterday . . . I met Mr. Clephane and some other gentlemen who seemed quite excited about something, and one of them, a visitor here from Kansas, wanted to borrow a revolver. I asked what for. He said[,] "To protect a friend, & Clephane can tell you all about it." So Clephane & I stepped aside, and he told me that there was an evident determination on the part of some Southern Hotspurs to assassinate Charles Sumner.[7] That men had been at his room & had tried to see him alone. That the evening previous (Friday) a man forced his way upstairs with some other gentlemen, & when they entered Mr. Sumner's room, he stood in the doorway & announced himself as "Mr. Draper," who desired to see Mr. Sumner alone a moment. Mr. Clephane was present. Mr. Sumner said[,] "I am Mr. Sumner[,] Sir; if you have anything to say to me you can say it in the presence of these gentlemen. I shall not see you alone." The man then said that he should say nothing unless he could see Mr. Sumner alone, & began to back toward the stairs. He went down, & was followed, but as soon as he got out of the door moved off so quick as to be lost sight of, & Mr. Sumner's friends have been unable to trace him. Clephane staid with Sumner till 2 o'clock in the morning, when he (S) went to bed. He told Clephane he had no dread of being killed outright, but that he had a perfect horror of being maimed. He will not consent to go armed, or to resist. He is a noncombatant on principle. His friends are determined that he shall not be left alone, and that they will attend him, armed. And the gentleman who wanted a revolver was one who had agreed to attend him. I lent him my revolver, & hope, if anyone attacks Sumner he will have a chance to use it effectually. I got so excited about the matter that I did not get over it all day. I went down in the City & bought one of those little pistols that I can carry in my watch pocket, & I mean to carry it for the present, despite of the law—for, if we are to be bullied for our republican principles, I think we ought to be prepared to defend ourselves. I also bought two pairs of knit drawers—a dollar a pair—& have one pair of them on now. They are very comfortable. . . .

June 14. . . . Michael is at work daily in the garden. He has cleaned out the walks & dug up the dock, and will commence weeding this morning. We had a mess of the peas two or three days ago—they were the largest & sweetest I ever saw or ate. I picked the last of them this morning. I have picked the raspberries every morning. . . .

Mr. Russell & I talked over Benny this morning, and concluded it was useless to attempt to make him study until Charley[8] & Willey [Russell] left. You remember I told you about his going to the fire & I not knowing when he came in. I found out yesterday that, having forgotten his night key[,] he climbed up on the hinges of the front door blind, and got into his chamber window!

Tell Frank that Gov. Grimes was in college with Mr. Tuck, and knew all about *the romance* of his courtship, and gave me a history of it when we went to the Asylum. It was quite funny. How *we* do always find out the youthful indiscretions—or rather the *discretions*—of the aged of the present day! Senator G. said Tuck's children ought to be handsome[,] for their mother[9] was. Ben recd. the *London Illustrated*, sent by Frank, yesterday. . . .

June 15. . . . Weather hot. Ben got up about daylight & went to a fire without my knowing it, came home before I was up, eat all the raspberries I had picked for breakfast & went to bed again! . . .

June 20. It is 8 o'clock Tuesday [Wednesday] evening. I have been all day at the Capitol. . . .

At home, here, things are going on first-rate, except that I cannot make Ben get up mornings, or make him study. He pretends he has commenced again today, and is to recite, at Mr. Russell's request, tomorrow. . . .

Mr. Russell just came in with my letters and papers and told me Douglas's chance of a nomination was desperate. I hope it is, for I consider him the worst man *for us* that the Democrats can nominate. I will leave my letter for tonight. . . .

June 24. . . . I am in the summer house in the garden—it is my second summer house epistle & the first on this iron table. The other was written to Helen about the 1st of May I think. Everything around me looks beautiful. This arbor is covered with roses (such as they are). I shall pluck the leaves of *one* and put it in this letter. The fountain is playing—it is now surrounded with coreopsis[10] nearly as high as my head, and *flauntingly* in bloom. The bed west of me is perfectly yellow with esfoltzia,[11] mingled with poppies, verbenas,[12] lots of little fine white flowers, blue flowers, that little red flower that used to grow in such abundance round the fountain—strange as it may seem I have forgotten its name—pinks, coreopsis, etc. In the round bed there is a row of flaming red poppies as double as possible, a few roses, many verbenas[,] some blue flowers—no, purple—are they snapdragon? South is the green grass just mowed—East[,] the side of Mr. Russell's house so covered with vines that you can hardly see the boarding. I think every summer the garden is as handsome as possible, but it seems to me now handsomer than I ever saw it. Michael has been faithfully over it. The weeds are all out, & the walks as clean as possible. The fountain is full & the water perfectly clear, & what is strange to me[,] it has been clear all summer. Not green & slimy as it was last summer. . . .

. . . Congress will adjourn tomorrow, & I shall rejoice to see its coattail buttons receding! "That d—d old wry-necked[,] squint-eyed, white-livered scoundrel"—as I heard a *democrat* elegantly term him the other day—"who disgraces the white house with his presence" has pocketed one of my clients' resolutions, & thus cheated *me* out a hundred or two. . . .

June 27. Instead of being on my way to New York now, as I supposed I should be at 5 o'clock last evening, here I am, a fixture to the house. It is with the utmost difficulty & with great pain that I can hobble from one side of the room to the other, & yet, when I sit still I hardly know that anything ails me.

I got all ready to leave, after dinner yesterday—took down the parlor curtains & put them away, & then went down with Benny to the ball club, & went to playing. As I was running I felt a sensation like a tremendous blow on the calf of my left leg & thought someone had hit me with a stone, and had to stop & get down on one knee. They all said I had merely strained a muscle of my leg & that it would soon be well. I staid an hour, sitting on the grass, & hoping, but, instead of getting well[,] it got worse, & I started to try to walk home, but finding I could not, & seeing a carriage in the street[,] I hailed it & rode home in it. Mr. [Ezra L.] Stevens was here & he sent for some arnica flowers and having soaked them in [   ],[13] bathed my leg thoroughly. Between 8 & 9 I went to bed. Mr. Russell came in & soaked a rag well in the liquid & bound it on. The leg was swollen half as big again as my other. Soon after I went to bed the pain, which had been very severe, ceased, & I thought I should certainly be able to go this morning. I slept pretty well till ½ past 4 & then waked & tried to get up, but it was no go. I could not touch my foot to the floor without agonizing pain; so I hobbled to the bell & rang it & told Bridget, who was grinding the coffee, I could not go & went to bed again. I lay till after 7 & then got up & tried to dress, but had to get Benny to help me on with my stockings. . . .

. . . My pay as Clerk will begin to run next week, & I think on $1,800 & what I shall receive *outside,* we can live till "Old Abe" gets in & then look out! . . .

1. In an election marked by fraud, James G. Berret was barely reelected mayor.

2. Possibly Norton P. Chipman, patent attorney, later one of the prosecutors in the trial of Henry Wirz, commandant of Andersonville Prison.

3. Young Ben's cousin, who lived next door.

4. James W. Grimes (1816–1872) was born in New Hampshire and moved to Iowa, where he became governor, 1854, and served as congressman, 1859–1869.

5. Charles H. Nichols, first superintendent of the hospital for the insane, which opened in 1855.

6. B. N. Stevens, assistant physician at the hospital, was born in New Hampshire.

7. The Southerners were responding to Sumner's four-hour speech, "The Barbarism of Slavery," delivered on June 4, 1860.

8. Another of Ben's cousins.

9. Sarah Nudd Tuck (1810–1847) had ten children, of whom five died early.

10. A plant with daisylike flowers.

11. Eschscholtzia, a yellow-flowered plant called the California poppy.

12. A plant with showy clusters of variously colored flowers.

13. Word illegible.

Wednesday, July 25. . . . The wonderful meteor, which seems to have
made a sensation all over the area of the U.S. from Boston to Norfolk,
and from Buffalo to 200 miles out at sea, which shot from West to East
on Friday evening last, the 20th inst.[,] was seen from my house by the
servant girl, Bridget Conolly. She had just gone out, & it was about ½
past 9 o'clock. She said nothing about it that evening, but early the next
morning told Mrs. F. about it, describing it almost exactly as it has since
been described in the newspapers. She said it scared her so that she
thought the day of Judgment had come and could not go to sleep until
nearly morning, and she seemed very anxious to be informed what *it
would do*—anticipating some great calamity, it would seem.

Last Saturday Joseph Gales, Senior Editor of *The National Intelligencer*[,]
died, and yesterday he was buried. He has been very feeble for several
years, & has gone, very gradually, down to the tomb. He was one of
Washington's most respected citizens, & one of the most liberal men that
ever lived—ruining himself, and embarrassing many of his friends, by
his extravagant generosity. He might have left hundreds of thousands of
dollars behind him, but it is doubtful whether he has left a dollar; indeed
it is most likely he has left an estate encumbered much beyond its value.
He was a man of a comprehensive mind, & of great ability to commu-
nicate to others. For more than a half century he has been the mainstay
of the *National Intelligencer*, & has exerted an influence all over these
United States that, perhaps, no other man in his position has ever exerted. The time was when "Gales & Seaton" shaped the political ends of
this Government, & emphatically led public sentiment.

As an editor "Jo: Gales" (as he always subscribed himself) was dignified, truthful, conscientious and eminently forbearing. I doubt if he ever
wrote a line that his best surviving friends would wish to blot. For more
than twenty-five years I have been personally acquainted with Mr. Gales,
& I write here that in all that time, & in the hundreds of interviews I
have had with him, I have never seen aught that was not characteristic
of the liberal gentleman & the well-informed scholar. I have *heard* from
others accounts of bursts of passion that certainly did him no credit, but
which charity has led me to impute to sickness & pecuniary embarrass-
ment, both of which, I *know*, have weighed heavy upon him for several
of the past years. I know he was as sensitive as a child, & would, when
speaking of his troubles, burst into tears. Is it then to be wondered at
that he should, at times, be thrown off his equilibrium, & manifest anger. . . .

Friday, August 3. The next morning after I wrote the last foregoing, I
started with about 40 Knights Templar for New York. We had a pleasant

trip on, were received with all kindness and courtesy by our N.Y. and Brooklyn Brethren, & escorted in good style to the "Smithsonian House" two miles up Broadway. Friday, the 27th, we visited the *Great Eastern*[1] in a body, and went over her as much as the immense crowd on board would permit, and were reasonably surprised at her immense size, & the beauty of her main saloon. When in the latter I could not realize that I was in a ship, & floating. . . .

1. With a displacement of 22,500 tons, the *Great Eastern* was several times larger than its closest rival in the Atlantic steamship trade.

Brooklyn, Sunday, August 12. Well here I am with Mrs. French, at Doct. Wells's. We left Washington at 3:20' on Friday, & stayed at Phila. that night. At 9 A.M. yesterday we left Phila. and arrived here a little before 2.

We have started on a regular *bust* of 6 weeks. Left the house closed up, & no cares behind. Frank & Ben are both here. Ben came on last Wednesday and is to go to Exeter to School. Frank met us at Jersey City & came over to N. York with us. He came over and passed the evening. We had a very hot ride from Washington to Phila. In the night it rained, and yesterday was more comfortable. Mrs. French[,] who is rather an invalid, bore the journey better than usual—escaping a sick headache. Doct. Wells's family are all at home[,] which makes a houseful.

Chester, Sunday, August 26. On Tuesday last, the 21st, inst.[,] Mrs. French, Ben & I arrived here at about 4 o'clock P.M. . . .

On Wednesday last (the 22d) I went [to] Concord and organized the Grand Commandery of Knights Templar of New Hampshire. . . . Thursday morning arose feeling well; eat my breakfast, & was immediately taken with my old spasmodic pain in the stomach which lasted five hours, & was so severe that I thought it would kill me. At about 12 it left me with a spasm that seemed almost to tear me to pieces, & I was at once easy: In the afternoon I had a regular chill.[1]

So here I am at Chester where I came *to enjoy myself*. Visions of shooting & fishing and rambling about my old haunts preceded my arrival, & here have I been cooped up in Mr. Batchelder's[2] house, sick about all the time! I am afraid this visit will cure me of all desire ever to visit my native town again. . . .

1. French was suffering from an attack of gallstones.
2. David L. Batchelder (1823–1882).

Rainsford Island, Tuesday, August 28. At 10 o'clock A.M. yesterday, Doct. & Mrs. Wells, Mrs. French, Willie French & myself left Chester in the stage—or, rather, Mr. Batchelder[,] its owner & driver[,] took Mrs. F.[,] Mrs. W. & I, in a carryall, & the Doct. & Willie rode in the coach[,] which was full, & reached Derry so as to take the ½ past 11 train for Boston, where we arrived about one. Went on board the *Morrison* (steamboat) & came down here, where we arrived at 4 P.M. Found Doct. Barker & family all well, and Mrs. Vose & Johnny[1] here. We all went down and bowled for an hour after dinner, then returned & took tea & spent the evening in conversation. . . .

1. Son of Mary and John Samuel S. Vose, born 1845.

Cincinnati, Ohio, Sunday, September 23. . . . Mrs. French & I visited Exeter—spent two or three days with Hon. Amos Tuck most pleasantly. I went to Boston and out to Cambridge, on the day my brother moved into his new residence there. . . . Left for this City by way of Albany, Buffalo, etc. Arrived at Cleveland Sunday morning Sep. 9th. Remained there that day & Monday, on which latter day I joined in the glorious celebration of the Inauguration of the statue of Commodore Perry. It was one of the largest gatherings of people I ever saw, and all went off gloriously. I left Cleveland that evening, and arrived here about daylight the following morning, and entered immediately on my duties as Treasurer of the U.S. Agricultural Society. From that hour to this I have been constantly engaged in as arduous a labor as I ever performed. So far as money is concerned, the Exhibition has been a failure, & this very evening a thousand dollars of our funds on hand before this exhibition commenced, have been devoted to the payment of premiums and expenses. . . .

Rainsford Island, Tuesday, October 2. . . . I left Cincinnati at ½ past 7 A.M. last Tuesday (a week ago this morning) and had we connected regularly at Buffalo, should have arrived in Boston the next afternoon at 4 o'clock, but between Cleveland and Buffalo the Engine gave out in some way, & we were delayed so long that we did not arrive in Buffalo till two hours & more behind time. I remained there till 5 A.M. Wednesday morning and then left & arrived at Boston at 12 midnight. The next morning at 9 o'clock found the *Thacher* at the wharf with my son Benjamin & all his "traps" on board, he having left Exeter, on his own responsibility. The Lieut. Gov.[1] & nearly all the Council came on Board with Gen. Sutton at 10 o'clock[,] and all came down here to make an official visit to this Institution. We had a pleasant sail down, found all well here, except Mrs. French, who had not been well for a long time, was considerably out of health then, & so continues now. . . .

1. Eliphalet Trask.

Washington, Sunday, October 21. I left Rainsford Island on board the *Thacher* at 25 minutes before 12 on the 10th inst. We arrived at Long wharf in Boston at 1, and I went immediately to the Judge's office where I remained with him till 3. . . . At 7 packed up my Templar's costume, and with Sir Knights L. M. Barker & W. O. Taylor went to visit Boston Encampment, where I was received with all the honor to which the Grand Master is entitled. I delivered an address to a large crowd of Templars, saw the Order conferred on Judge Wells,[1] & then was escorted to a Banquet, where "all went merry as a marriage bell" till toward midnight, when we all dispersed. I returned to the U.S. [Hotel] & spent the night and at 9 o'clock on Thursday morning, Oct. 11, bade Mrs. Taylor & Doct. Barker farewell & was off for New York.

Arrived in that City about 5 and found the streets thronged with people, all out to see the Prince of Wales,[2] who had arrived from Philadelphia that afternoon. I made my way as best I could toward Brooklyn, crossed at Wall St. Ferry about dusk, & when I got into Clinton street who should I overtake on the sidewalk [but] my wife, . . . over to see the Prince, and she had a good look at him too from a window in Broadway. We walked to Doct. Wells's together, & in a short time all the family were assembled, they coming home one by one, after having seen the Prince. . . . At 6 Saturday morning Mrs. French, & Mrs. Margaret French (my Bro. Ned's wife)[,] baby[3] & nurse, & myself left Doct. Wells's &, crossing Fulton Ferry, went to Jersey City Ferry, where at 7 o'clock we took the cars for home. . . .

Mrs. French has been tolerably well through the week, but is sick in bed again today with headache. Her sickness is very discouraging, & I hardly know what I ought to do about it. She is trying homeopathy, but I think some more powerful medicine ought to be given her. . . .

1. George D. Wells was killed in the Civil War in 1864.
2. Edward, Prince of Wales (1841–1910), the eldest son of Queen Victoria, was extremely popular because of his social charm and tact. He did not succeed his mother as Edward VII until 1901, when he was nearly sixty.
3. Mary French (1859–1939) married her cousin Daniel Chester French in 1888.

Sunday, November 4. . . . I have been attending to my duty as Clerk of the Committee of Claims at the Capitol daily for the past two weeks. All the losses of individuals[,] citizens of Kansas[,] consequent upon the Kansas troubles, have been, by order of the Kansas Legislature, audited by a Board of Commissioners in that Territory and have been sent to Congress with a request that they may be paid by the United States. There are nearly 500 of them[,] and the House of Representatives referred them to the Committee on Claims, and the no small job of examining them one by one has been assigned to me and is my daily labor. I have gone through about 160 of them & intend to finish the lot before Congress comes, so I must work hard.

Political affairs are in a dreadful state just now. The hotheads of the North and South are threatening to burst up the Union, but cool, Union-loving men of *all parties* are laboring to preserve it, and I think it will be preserved. Lincoln will be elected President of the U.S. next Tuesday, & then the crisis will come. There will be many threats and probably *some action*, but my belief is wise counsels will prevail in the end, and the Union be saved &, I hope, perpetuated for years & years. . . .

Sunday, November 11. Lincoln is President-elect of these United States. My political hopes so far are realized, but my fears that the threats of the South are really to bring trouble upon the whole Union, by being carried into stern action[,] almost render me joyless at the grand result. But if Disunion is to come merely because the South cannot have *all* the old sow's teats to suck, then I say in John Quincy Adams's words[,] "Let it come!" The sun will rise & set, the world will revolve, men & women will be born & marry and die, & posterity will say[,] "What a set of shortsighted fools our fathers were, who broke up the fairest nation, & the best government that was, under God's blessing, ever formed." I have determined to be calm about it & let what will come, take it coolly & philosophically.

What a week has the past been to me! On Monday Doct. Johnston announced to me that a tumour that has been forming in my dear wife's breast for more than a year *is a cancer,* and the discouraging manner in which he spoke of it so affected me that I felt as if I had rather die than live. For two or three days & nights I was most wretched. On Thursday we had a consultation with Doct. May[,] and upon his representation Mrs. French has determined to undergo an operation. The *hope* that it may be in all things successful has raised me from utter despondency to some feeling of interest in the world, *but not much.* On the evening of Jany. 11, 1825, we were married, and for the almost 36 years that have passed since then, we have gone on living & loving together, our hearts, hopes, aspirations & interests as perfectly united as if we were one being. The severing of *such a union* is like tearing the heartstrings of the survivor from the bosom—thus it seems to me, & I have almost hoped, and should quite, were it not a cowardly hope, that I might not be the survivor! I pray God, oh how sincerely, that the dear wife of my bosom may yet be spared to me, if I am to live for any length of time, & if it must be different, that I may be enabled to say sincerely, "He doeth all things well."

Friday, November 16. Yesterday between ½ past 1 and ½ past 2 P.M. Doct. J. F. May, assisted by Doct. W. P. Johnston, cut from my dear wife's bosom the cancer mentioned in the foregoing journalization. The entire right breast was taken away. She was placed under the influence of ether, & suffered no pain. During the time of the operation I was as nervous and excited as possible, & have hardly got it over yet.[1] Mrs. French rested tolerably well through the night, they say, & seems as well as I could expect her to be this morning. Thanks be to God for this much of his mercies & his kindness, and oh may she be restored & may years of happiness[,] health & comfort be hers.

Frank came home Tuesday morning & it is a comfort to have him with me.

1. French meant "over it."

Tuesday, November 27. Mrs. French has been steadily, though slowly, recovering since the 15th. Doct. May (the surgeon) visited her for the last time Saturday. Doct. Johnston continues his daily visits. The wound did not heal by the first intention & is still open, though, as Doct. J. says, healthy in appearance, & promising to do well. Mrs. French has been up and about the chambers daily for nearly a week, & could, I think, come downstairs if she chose to do so, but is very careful of herself and does not intend to run any risks. Mary Ellen Brady has been with us all the time since the operation, & if I feel true gratitude to any mortal above all others, it is to her for her kindness. Can I ever repay it[?] All our friends & neighbors have been as kind as possible. . . .

. . . South Carolina seems *determined* to secede, & if she could do so alone, I think it would be the best thing possible, for there have been certain men there who have desired to form a separate government for years, and there are men there now who only want *an excuse,* no matter how frail, for secession, and I, for one, am willing they should try it for a time. It would be the ruin of the State, and right glad would they be in a few years to return. We must all wait coming events, and make the best of what may "turn up."

I am an ultra Union man—I am for concession & conciliation. I think the Northern states have done outrageously wrong in passing their "personal liberty bills" & am ashamed of them for it, for it is nothing less than nullification. So far as I can I press upon my friends their repeal, & the carrying out in good faith the fugitive slave law. I am utterly opposed to any intermeddling with Southern rights and will go as far as anyone to defend them. I pray for Union everywhere! . . .

Sunday, December 9. . . . My dear wife is improving, but slowly. She keeps about house, and the wound on her breast is nearly healed up, but she does not get strong as fast as we could wish.

"Secession"—"Disunion"—"Southern Confederacy"—"Monarchy" are now the leading words in the Southern states, especially in So. Carolina. No one knows what a day may bring forth, & the great result—whether happy or dread—is known only to that Providence who rules, for ultimate good always, the destinies of man! Hon. Amos Kendall, God bless him for it, is now writing a series of articles in favor of Union, which are published in *The Evening Star.* That of last evening is so excellent, & gives such a proper view of the effect of an *attempt* at secession, that I will cut it out and preserve it here. There are many truehearted Union men, of great talent & influence, whose hearts & souls are now in this effort to save from destruction our Citadel of Freedom—the last rallying point of Liberty on Earth. The *National Intelligencer* is working nobly in the Holy cause, and may it be richly rewarded. Col. Seaton is my personal friend, & I glory in calling him so, & in having such a friend. . . .

Tuesday, December 25. Christmas. A dull, dark, snowy morning. Frank & Ellen Tuck arrived by this morning's train. We knew they were coming, and I slept by "catnaps" all night, getting up every now & then to ascertain what time it was and finally rising at 5 to prepare for receiving them. . . .

South Carolina resolved herself out of the Union on Thursday last the 20th inst. The earth did not quake, the sun shone on, & Nature did not mark the event with any uncommon convulsion. Still, in reading the "hifalutin" and bombastical debates of those arch traitors to their Country, who without reason have been guilty of so damning an act as that of endeavouring to break up our Federal Union, one would suppose that this act of secession of an insignificant, nigger-ridden state was really one of the greatest & most sublime events that the World ever witnessed! when in fact it has about the effect in regard to our great Union that the sailing of a jack o' lanthorn[1] across a swamp has upon the solar system. . . .

1. Archaic for "lantern."

Sunday, December 30. . . . All sorts of speculation are rife, & South Carolina & her hotheaded traitors are doomed to remitless perdition a thousand times a day, if the words of honest, patriotic men can so doom them.

James Buchanan, President of the United States, is generally believed to be in league with the treason that is working its way through the South, and which now threatens to overwhelm in disaster the fairest fabrick of political empire that God ever permitted to exist. If he be so in league, & it is certainly ascertained, I think he had better never return to Pennsylvania. True old Keystone that she is, she will repudiate her traitor son, though he has heretofore been so highly honored. . . .

Tuesday, January 1. . . . I finish the record in this journal with a sort of melancholy feeling. "The Times are out of joint"—I am fast approaching old age—my own health & my wife's are not so good as they were years ago, & I shall this day commence my new Journal with a feeling of sadness with which I have never before commenced one. But I shall commence it with an abiding Hope that its pages will show much of prosperity, much of happiness, and a settlement of all the National troubles that now surround my Country. Dangers are now staring us all in the face. Secession of a State without any other cause than a desire to break up as glorious a Union as ever man waked upon, for the sake of the individual aggrandizement of a few hotheaded traitors who are determined to rule or ruin—whose motto seems to be, "It is better to rule in Hell than serve in Heaven."

May they be put down by the strong arm of Righteousness & Right!

I will now commence Journal No. 8.

Tuesday, January 1. I commence this Journal at what still continues to be the seat of Government of "The United States of America," although the sovereign state of South Carolina has Resolved herself out of the Union, & will be followed in her suicidal *attempt* to secede by other states equally foolish.

There is at the head of this Government now a weak old man, who fears to exercise the proper functions of President of the United States, & whose course is looked upon as next akin to Treasonable. Would to Heaven we had another Andrew Jackson there instead of James Buchanan. The name of the latter *must* go down to posterity associated with shame, infamy, & I fear with *Treason*! But enough of this on this first day of the year. . . .

At 3 P.M. Frank expects to leave for his place of business—New York. On the very day that I commenced the Journal preceding this (March 1, 1858) he left to commence his studies at the Law School at Cambridge. Since then he has become an Attorney, & located himself in the City of New York.

Everybody seems to be getting excited, & some even frightened, in anticipation of what *may* happen in the attempt of some misguided scoundrels who, it is said, intend to prevent, by force, the inauguration of Abraham Lincoln as President of the U.S. Even Senators & Members of the House enter into excitement, & are *earnest* in their advice that we all be on the alert to counteract any attempt at forcible prevention. The Republican Party are by no means asleep on their posts. Measures have been taken to keep our sentinels on the watchtowers, & we shall not be caught unprepared for any exigency, at any time. It is said that secret organizations already exist to consummate the unholy intentions of these traitor villains. It may be so, but I am one of those who do not believe it. I have tried to ascertain whether any such organization exists, but can learn of none, and I do believe, with all my knowledge of my fellow citizens of all parties, that if there were any organization of the sort I should know it. Still, I shall not fold my arms in fancied security, but shall hold myself ready at a minute's warning to aid in putting down any unlawful attempt to interfere with the proper preliminary or final proceedings in consummating the election of Lincoln. . . .

Wednesday, January 9. Frank, instead of leaving as he intended, on Tuesday, was so unwell with a cold that he did not leave until Friday morning.

Since my last writing political matters have not improved, and the excitement in relation to the danger of a general breakup of the Union is intense, though by no means noisy.

The President has changed his ground, if not his views, within the week past. He was insulted by the *Lords Commissioners from Mighty South Carolina,* and returned their insulting missive unreplied to, when they made hurried tracks for home with several fleas in their ears. They came & went so suddenly that it is very doubtful whether "their mother knew they were out." I suspect Northern pressure on the President, from his own political friends, drove him to review his course. Secy. Thompson[1] of the Interior Department resigned yesterday, and Philip Francis Thomas[,] Secy. of the Treasury[,] is the only one now left of the secessionists to counsel the President.

For the 8 days past, I have been doing precious little beyond going daily to the Capitol and attending to my duties as Clerk of the Committee of Claims.

For the past two days I have been attending, as one of a Committee of Appraisers, to appraise the real estate in the squares North & South of the Eastern grounds of the Capitol, with a view to the purchase of the same by Congress for extending the Capitol grounds. Also a triangular piece on Pa. & Md. Avenues at the foot of Capitol Hill. We finished our appraisal yesterday afternoon. . . .

1. Jacob Thompson (1810–1885) was a Democratic congressman from Mississippi, 1839–1851, before becoming Secretary of the Interior, 1857–1861. He later served in the Confederate Army.

Thursday, January 24. . . . Last evening Mr. and Mrs. Gallaudet[1] & Miss Mary Gordon[2] came to see us & spent the evening, & we had a very merry time. Mr. G. is a son of the Mr. Gallaudet[3] so long & favorably connected with the Deaf & Dumb Institution at Hartford, & whom I knew. He is now engaged in the Institution at Kendall Green.[4] He is a very interesting man, & the evening seemed like one of the times of old. We had puzzles & conundrums, & some excellent imitations of various animals, etc., by Mr. G.[,] who is quite an adept in the art of imitation. He is the only person I ever saw who could articulate distinctly in *two voices* at the same time!

1. Edward M. Gallaudet (1837–1917) was brought to Washington in 1857 to found the Columbia Institution for the Deaf and Dumb. The advanced department later became Gallaudet College.
2. Mary Gordon of Exeter, N.H., was a young instructor at the Columbia Institution.
3. Thomas H. Gallaudet (1787–1851).
4. Kendall Green was a real estate development of Amos Kendall near the corner of 7th and M streets Northeast. Kendall gave one of his houses there to the institution.

Sunday, February 3. . . . Mrs. French still in her chamber, but convalescing slowly. She has been down here (in the Library) twice. The Doctor told her yesterday that it would be two months before she would be entirely well.

"These awful times!" "What is to become of the Nation?" This exclamation and question are on everybody's lips. The latter nobody can answer. We Union men all hope on, & the last few days have given us reason to hope. Tomorrow the "Peace Convention,"[1] as it is called, is to meet & something may grow out of that. Men of all parties seem to be more conciliatory than they were some weeks ago, but there are still maniacs from the North and South both who seem to gloat over the anticipated destruction of our glorious Union. The general feeling now seems to be to let the cotton states go, & save the rest of the Union. South Carolina has always been a brawling termagant and is better as she now is than in the Union. She has made her bed, let her lie in it for all time to come! If she does not find it one of thorns[,] I am greatly mistaken.

It is a curious state of things just now. Six States have *seceded* within the past month, and one has *acceded*. Kansas was admitted on Thursday, & yesterday thirty-four guns were fired by the U.S. Lt. Artillery in honor of her admission. I believe the game of secession is about played out and that of *accession* has commenced.

My head aches quite badly & I will shut my book.

1. The Peace Convention, with John Tyler in the chair and delegates from all parts of the Union, met in Washington for several weeks, starting February 4. It failed to find a compromise.

Sunday, February 10. Treason is progressive! Six States gone out of the Union! Immense amounts of property stolen by the Secessionists! They denominate it "seized"—yes it has been *seized* just as I might thrust my hand into my neighbor's pocket and *seize* his money! What the end is to be no one knows—but as God orders all things right, I have no doubt this seeming "partial evil" will result in "universal good!" We must wait patiently & prayerfully, do *our* duty & *Trust*! The end must come!

My past week has been rather a pleasant one notwithstanding the excitement and turmoil of the times. Last Monday morning my excellent friend Hon. Amos Tuck arrived & has made my house his home since. Hon. William B. Hubbard,[1] my beloved and esteemed Masonic Brother[,] came Tuesday evening & was most welcome. . . .

1. William B. Hubbard, grand master of the Knights Templar, lived in Columbus, Ohio.

Tuesday, February 12. . . . Mr. Tuck & I had a long and interesting talk yesterday about our family affairs, & seemed to have an excellent mutual understanding regarding all we talked about. Last evening we played euchre—Mrs. Wells & Mr. Tuck vs. Ellen & I—Mrs. French *advising* Mrs. Wells.

Frank expects to be home tomorrow morning.

Sunday, February 24. Much, for weal or for woe, has transpired since I wrote 12 days ago in this book. So far as household and family affairs are concerned, although the usual calm has not been broken[,] great changes have been planned. Frank came home on the morning of the

13th as we expected, and it was very soon arranged that he and Ellen should be married, and that they should go to Exeter and occupy Mr. Tuck's house, & should Mr. T. leave Exeter, as he expects to do, that Frank should take his business—if he do not leave, they will become partners. We are all delighted with this arrangement, and the wedding is fixed for the 5th of March. In the meantime all is doing by way of preparation that might be expected in view of so important an event.

Mrs. French continues miserable in health, and at times I am almost discouraged about her. Then she seems better, and I think she will get right up and be well again.

This morning (I write by gaslight) when I got up she was complaining of headache. These constant headaches are what keeps her weak & sick. Pray God she may soon be restored. . . .

Matters & things in general. For the past 12 days political events have seemed to tend more towards a healing up of our national troubles. Virginia, Kentucky, Missouri & Arkansas, have spoken *through their people,* and have spoken trumpet-tongued for Union. The Peace Convention has been moving slowly along in the good work it assembled here to do, & the prospect was yesterday that it would come to a happy conclusion of its labors tomorrow, and that the result would be harmony among the states still remaining in the Union.

Abraham Lincoln, President-elect, has been making a pilgrimage from Springfield, Illinois, to this city. It seems to have been one glorious ovation to New York, & thence to Phila. & Harrisburg, and would have been, doubtless[,] to this City, but that, for some reason not now known, he was telegraphed at Harrisburg day before yesterday to come on here with all despatch. In consequence of which he took the evening train day before yesterday and arrived here at six yesterday morning, to the great surprise of everybody, except a few who knew of the movement. By the programme he was to arrive at ½ past 4P.M. He is now safe at Willard's & we must keep him safe and inaugurate him on the 4th, & then he must take care of himself!

The 22d was greatly honored here. The House of Representatives adjourned over in honor of the day, and an immense military parade took place.

I am to act as Chief Marshal on the 4th & have had labor and fuss enough to prepare my programme and appoint my Assistants & Aids. I finished it yesterday & sent it to the printer. . . .

Tuesday, February 26. Sunday was spent by me in reading and writing, and was a very quiet day. Mrs. French deathly sick all day with headache.

Yesterday I went early to the Capitol, & then down in the City and did some errands. Returned to the Capitol, and was almost annoyed all day with visitors, some on one sort of business & some on another. Marshal Selden[1] informed me, early in the morning, that Mr. Lincoln was to call on the Supreme Court at 3, at their consultation room. I walked over & saw Mr. L. as he entered the room and came out. He then visited the Senate, and then the House. I happened to be in the rotundo when he passed through on his way to the House, and followed him in. The members congregated around him at once & such a shaking of hands commenced as one seldom sees—cordial—even enthusiastic. After being surrounded for say 10 minutes by his political friends, he passed over to the democratic side where he was quite cordially greeted by his political opponents. He remained some 15 or 20 minutes, and then left for his lodgings.

I came home at 4 o'clock, dined, was called on by at least a dozen people before 7 o'clock, and then played cribbage with Mrs. Wells till I became so sleepy I could not play. Talked a short time with Mr. & Mrs. Russell, & then lay down and slept.

1. William W. Selden.

Friday, March 1. It is morning, and March opens beautifully. This is like a summer morning, clear & beautiful.

Tuesday [February 26], at the capitol all day, and harrassed beyond measure by continual calls on all sorts [of] matters relating to the Inauguration ceremonies and applications for assistance to get men into office. Came home about 4. Went down in the City to meet my Aids at the Washington House and do errands.

Wednesday. Rode down in the city immediately after breakfast, did errands & saw Mr. Clephane, who agreed to meet me at the Capitol at 12. Returned to the Capitol. Mr. C. came as agreed, and we went to see Gen. Scott at his office opposite the War Dept. where he detailed to us all the information, anonymous and otherwise, that he had recd. threatening the assassination of the President-elect, himself & others, and then went on to give us his theory of what the assassins expected to gain by such action. Which was, briefly, that all who could act as President of the U.S. should be got out of the way, thus leaving the U.S. Govt. without any head, when the Southern Confederation was to step in and assume the Government of the whole Country. I told him I thought if any such effort should be made I thought that the Southern President would not be very likely to reach Washington alive. While conversing with Gen. Scott, Gen. Wool[1] came in & gave us the first information of the result of the action of the "Peace Congress." Gen. Scott was exceedingly pleased, & we all had a jubilation over it.

On leaving Gen. Scott[,] Mr. C. & I went to the White House to call on President Buchanan. While there the Mayor & City Councils called to take official leave, the ceremonies of which we witnessed.

We then called on Mr. Lincoln[,] the President-elect, & while conversing with him, the Mayor & Councils arrived to pay him their respects and welcome him to the Federal Metropolis.

I had considerable conversation with Mr. Lincoln, & was very much pleased at his offhand, unassuming manner, and I believe he will make a first-rate President.

1. John E. Wool (1784–1869) was in command of the army's Department of the East.

Saturday, March 2. Yesterday & today I have done little else than attend to the duties devolved upon me by the Chief Marshalship of the Monday procession. My room at the Capitol has been thronged with people, and when at home I have but little peace.

We are making preparation for Frank & Ellen Tuck's wedding, which is to take place at 8 o'clock Tuesday evening. The folks are beginning to arrive. Mr. & Mrs. William R. Nelson arrived this evening[;] so did Mr. Starr[1] of Phila. We expect Doct. Wells in the morning. At tea this evening we had besides our own family—Mr. Tuck, Mr. & Mrs. Nelson, Edward Tuck,[2] Mr. Starr, Miss Mary Gordon, counting Mrs. Wells & Ellen as our own family.

The servants we now have are Darby McCarty (came yesterday morning)[,] Ellen O'Brien, Margaret & Bridget Grant.

The weather is very hot—it has been like summer for the 3 or 4 past days.

1. James Starr, a student, 1414 Arch Street.
2. Edward Tuck (1842–1938) was the brother of Ellen Tuck. In 1900 he founded the Amos Tuck School of Administration and Finance at Dartmouth College.

Sunday, March 3. My dear wife had a very restless night—nervous & wakeful. She is very weak & the arrival of so many last evening doubtless excited her uncommonly, so that she could not sleep. Her sleeplessness disturbed me considerably, as I was up several times. I arose a few minutes after six this morning, and, as Doct. Wells had not arrived *here* at ½ past, Mrs. Wells and I walked down to Edmund's to find out whether he was there, but he was not. We returned & sat till ½ past 7, about, & then I went to the Depot and found the Doct. just arrived in a special train—the regular train having missed the connexion at Baltimore. The Doct. & I walked home together.

Eight o'clock & nobody but Mrs. Wells and myself down yet, although the others are moving. The breakfast bell rings.

SEVEN

Marriage and Death, Marriage and War

1861–1862

I n looking back over these eighteen months French remarked that he never wanted to write such an account again. The time was "streaked," he said, "with the record of great happinesses and great miseries. Marriage and *Death*, and Marriage, and War, and suffering mark its pages, and many a sigh and many a tear [had] accompanied the record."[1] In this chapter the beginning of the Civil War is seen through the eyes of a man whose personal losses and gains often overshadowed the history taking place around him.

Two themes run through these pages: French's struggle to cope with the illness and death of his wife, and the efforts of Lincoln and the North to rally from the breaking up of the Union. The two stories advance side by side—Bess's operation and secession, Frank's marriage and the inauguration of Lincoln, Bess's death and the outbreak of war. When Bess died in early May, Frank had difficulty getting to Washington from New England just as Northern troops did in relieving the beleaguered Capital. As French was taking tentative steps toward marrying Mary Ellen Brady, Lincoln was trying to fortify the Union by holding the border states. French's alternating hope and despair over his relationship with Mary Ellen was similar to emotions in the North during the uncertain first months of the war.

French interweaves personal anecdotes of family and friends with descriptions of Washington before and after the first Battle of Bull Run in July. In a series of graphic entries he portrays the naive optimism of the North before the battle and the horror that followed as soldiers and spectators poured back into the city. A group of friends from Concord, Massachusetts, came to witness a victory over the Rebels, only to get caught up in a disaster. On returning from the battlefield at midnight John S. Keyes was so frightened that he shouted up to his mother, who was staying with the Frenches, "Pack your trunk and be ready to leave in the ¼ past 4 o'clock [A.M.] train." When asked why the haste, he replied, "We are whipped all to pieces."[2]

Once past its unrealistic optimism and pessimism, the North settled down to a long war, and French set out to remarry and find a position in the Lincoln administration. By September he had made up his mind that he could not live without Mary Ellen, and he had also been made commissioner of public buildings. The rest of the chapter revolves around the efforts of the North to invade the South and French's efforts to win Mary Ellen and make good in his job.

Since he saw Abraham Lincoln on a regular basis, French was able to record a series of sharp vignettes of the President. He was on hand when Lincoln was forced to use all of his vaunted strength raising a giant flag to the top of a pole outside the White House. When French called on Lincoln to ask about being appointed commissioner, the President deftly turned the question aside by offering his spyglass to French so that he could look at the enemy on the other side of the Potomac. Finally commissioner, French was in a position to describe Lincoln in a rare moment of relaxation as he watched Monsieur Hermann demonstrate his skill at sleight of hand.

French's interest in his own concerns and those of Lincoln did not keep him from observing the early progress of the war. Like many in the North he was enthusiastic when General George B. McClellan replaced Winfield Scott as commander in chief, but grew restless when McClellan hesitated before starting south. He reflected Northern cheer as reports came in of successes in Tennessee and Northern gloom when McClellan failed to capture Richmond after coming within four miles of the city.

The journal is dotted with personal incidents that complement the larger story. On her way to church one day Mary Ellen had to pass by a company of marching soldiers who were barracked near French's house. Since there was barely eighteen inches between the fence and the troops, Mary Ellen's hoop skirts "brushed against the regimentals all the way, and no doubt gave those inside of them a thought of the dear ones at home."[3] Mary Ellen was also close at hand when McClellan reviewed the Union forces, "escorted by about *two miles* of cavalry."[4] It was typical of French's life at this point that when he made two trips north late in the chapter, one was official, the other personal. In July 1862 he visited a foundry in New York in order to secure ironwork for the dome being erected on top of the Capitol. Two months later he was back north again, this time to marry Mary Ellen in Concord, Massachusetts. As the North fought back the Southern invasion of Maryland in September, Benjamin and Mary Ellen were honeymooning at Niagara Falls.

1. Sept. 26, 1862.
2. July 22, 1861.
3. Feb. 2, 1862.
4. Nov. 20, 1861.

Journal

Wednesday, March 6. Monday was Inauguration day. At ¼ before 9 A.M.[,] as Marshal-in-chief, I mounted my horse & rode immediately to the City Hall where my Assistants & Aids to the number of 60 or 70 reported to me. At 10 the Military began to arrive, and at a few minutes after 11[,] the procession being formed in line, wheeled out into column of march, & moved towards Willard's. It was the most imposing procession I ever saw. In front of Willard's it was again formed in line & so remained until 10 m. past 12. Mr. Buchanan[,] being detained at the Capitol to approve Bills, did not arrive until that time. On his arrival at Willard's, he, President Lincoln, with Col. Baker[1] & Mr. Pearce of the Senate, were all seated in an open carriage & received into the column of march with a proper salute from the military & music & cheering of the populace. The column then moved toward the Capitol. No more imposing or more orderly pageant ever passed along Pennsylvania Avenue. At the North door of the Capitol The President & President-elect were received & passed in. In a few minutes they, with their attendants[,] appeared on the platform on the Eastern portico, and Mr. Lincoln delivered his inaugural and was sworn into office. I got a position where I could hear every word and was delighted.

I have since read it carefully, and am of [the] opinion that words could not have been selected & framed into sentences that could better express the ideas of those who have elected Abraham Lincoln to the Presidency. The Inaugural is conciliatory—peaceable—but firm in its tone, and is exactly what we, Union men, want. And let the Southern hotspurs say what they will, it will have more tendency to bring back the seceding States than anything else that could have been said. It is in the right tone and spirit, & is evidence as strong as proof from Holy writ that the United States of America is no longer to be triumphed over as if it were a coward and dared not protect itself! Some of us will now try to show the South that we have a Union to defend and that, by the aid of the God of Battles, we are determined to defend it—"peaceably if we can, forcibly if we must."

The inauguration ceremonies over, we escorted the new President to the white house where he received all comers with that cordial welcome that so strongly marks the sincerity of the man.

In the procession was a sort of triumphal car, splendidly trimmed, ornamented and arranged, in which rode thirty-four young girls. On our return, the girls all alighted, & I took them in and introduced them to the President. He asked to be allowed to kiss them all, & he did so. It was a very interesting scene, & elicited much applause.

After we had finished the reception, a large body of my Marshals escorted me to my house, and at 5 I was out of my saddle & pretty much used up. But it was a glorious occasion, and went off without an accident or a blunder. I tried to do *all* my duty, & all those under me did theirs nobly.

Yesterday morning [March 5] I arose early but pretty sore from my day's ride. Frank & Ellen Tuck were to be married in the evening, & the entire day was devoted to preparation for that momentous family event. . . . We had from 30 to 40 present, and everything went off well. Doct. Butler[2] performed the marriage service and did it admirably. At 3 o'clock today, Frank & his wife and Mrs. Nelson (Abby) left for the North. . . . Mrs. French has stood all this excitement well, & is now sitting on the sofa talking to Mr. Geo. Nelson,[3] & bright as a new dollar.

1. Edward D. Baker (1811–1861), senator from Oregon, 1860–1861, introduced Abraham Lincoln at the inauguration. Appointed major general in 1861, he was killed at the Battle of Balls Bluff, Va., October 21, 1861.
2. Clement M. Butler.
3. George Nelson, probably the brother of William Nelson, Abby Tuck Nelson's husband.

Tuesday, March 19. I am, as it were, all alone. . . . Mr. Tuck left last Thursday afternoon. Mrs. French has been confined to her chamber most of the time since, & Ben lies in bed till nearly noon, & is off most of the time when up, so that, except when I sit in Mrs. F.'s chamber, I see no one but the eternal callers after office, with whom I am disgusted. . . .

Friday, April 5. . . . Mrs. French has continued apparently about the same in health. She has had a few quite ill turns—headaches, faintings, sickness at stomach, etc., and then rallied & been quite comfortable. For more than a week her general health has been better than for a week or two previous, but her pleurisy, which has become chronic, has troubled her considerably. She is now suffering under the infliction of blisters, which seem to relieve her. She has not been downstairs for three weeks, but, if ever a pleasant day comes, when she is well enough to ride out, I shall take her to ride. Mary Ellen Brady is with us, and has been for three weeks. She is our good Angel. God bless her. . . .

My time is spent in reading, writing, going to the Capitol, down in the City, & sitting with Mrs. French. I am with her as much as possible from the time I have eaten my dinner until she retires for the night.

I have been incessantly annoyed for the past month with applications to sign petitions for office and write letters for candidates. Last evening, as I see by the *Republican,* the annual election of officers of the Republican Association took place, and J. J. Coombs, Esq.,[1] was elected President in my place, for which I am very thankful. Had I been aware that it was election night I should have attended and withdrawn, but it is perhaps as well as it is. I have tried to serve the Association faithfully for four or five years—have done all I could for it & seen it increase from about a dozen to more than a thousand—but am sorry to believe that at least one-half of its members have become so for the sake of office! There are some true men in its ranks. I fear that the Powers-that-Be intend to ignore it root and branch. That is Mr. Seward's policy I know, & Mr. Seward is now "The Administration." . . .

. . . This week I have had the water from the street brought into my premises and connected the street service pipe with the pipes in my garden. Have had my well covered, & converted into a sewer for the sink drainage in the basement. . . .

   1. Joseph J. Coombs, of Weston & Coombs, publishers.

Sunday, April 14. . . . My week has been a dreadful one to me. Mrs. French's sickness and the terribly unsettled state of the national affairs have combined to make me nervous & almost sick. . . .

I saw the President twice Friday. Once at about ½ past 9 A.M. when he said[,] "Mr. French, you call at 3 this afternoon *and I will try to let you in.*" At 3 I called. There were several present who had precedence, & I waited patiently till 4 when *all* having departed, I went in & had a cosey chat with the President of about half an hour. He avowed much kind feeling toward me, said I was often in his mind and that I had claims which should not be forgotten. He specified two offices with which he said he would connect my name, and give me one of them if possible. He did me the honor to ask my advice about several matters and seemed pleased when I gave it to him. He appears to me to be as honest, upright, & firm a President as we have ever had. God prosper his Administration, and bless him. . . .

Friday, April 19. Awful times! Civil war all around us; secession tramping on; Proud Old Virginia tailing on after crazy South Carolina & the other Cotton States. I *think* this whole thing has been most damnably managed by the President and his advisers. When it was seen that secession was determined upon by the seven States where it halted, it would have been better to let them go, than by fighting to hold them, driving out six or seven more! I do not believe in secession—I do believe in revolution—but have no idea that the South had any reasonable ground to justify them in it—they were maddened by misrepresentation, & thought they had. The North will gain nothing by attempting to hold them, and can get along better—far better—without than with them; so let them go in God's name, & peace go with them if they can maintain it!

Besides[,] *one Nation,* ½ of which tolerates, and the other ½ opposes, slavery can never last long, any more than one man can serve two masters. In my judgment the South are to be greatly the losers by severing their connexion with the North, but that is their lookout & not mine.

This City is now filling up with troops, & many are expecting that it will be attacked. I am not one of them. I do not believe it will, and I do believe that "the sober second thought" of all concerned will lead to a speedy settlement of all the existing difficulties. . . .

Sunday, April 21. Never did I sit down to write in my journal with gloomier feelings or gloomier forebodings. Mrs. French *is* no better, my hope of her recovery is gone. She is becoming weaker daily. She cannot sleep nights, is short breathed, & sick with headache & its consequence[,] with her a sick stomach and vomiting. Oh my God—my God sustain me in this affliction.

My poor country too! Here we are in Washington, cooped up by the cutting off by the crazed secessionists of Maryland of all communication with [the] North either by mail, railroad, or telegraph. Day before yesterday some Massachusetts troops in coming through Baltimore were attacked by a mob and some of their number killed. They were forced to fire & killed some of those who attacked them. At once mob violence commenced—the R.R. track was torn up—bridges burnt—the telegraph wires cut, & all the troops on their way here forced to return. We have all sorts of rumors here today. It is said that a large body of troops left Philadelphia in vessels yesterday for Annapolis, & that they will be here today—also that the steamer *Baltic* left New York crammed with soldiers, & that she will come up the Potomac tonight. Further, it is said, that a sufficient number of troops will be raised at the North and sent forward

to *insure* their passage through Baltimore *at all hazzards,* and to open &
keep open communication with the North & East! . . .

Tuesday, April 23. . . . Yesterday rumors upon rumors were abroad. At
one time we had news of the arrival of the expected troops and then it
was ascertained that there was no truth in the story. Rumors came of
fights here and fights there, but the day wore off & no troops came &
there was no fight anywhere, as we could learn. About ½ past 8 my old
friend Doct. George Gross[1] came to see me; he had just arrived from
Virginia and was full of the war news of that State. He told me how
reckless the inhabitants had become & how perfectly determined they
were to capture Washington, that they talked of raising troops by the
hundred thousand, and of all other extravagant and impossible feats.
He said the rumor was that Jeff Davis was on his way to Richmond with
50,000 men, etc. He staid till about ½ past 9 & gave me a sort of history
of all the doings in Virginia, partly what he had witnessed, & partly what
he heard. I became, I confess, considerably excited[,] & it added none
to my night's rest! At 5 A.M. today I arose & after reading the papers
and writing some letters & eating my breakfast, I went to the President's
& had a long talk with him about the times. I found that he knew but
little more than other people, all communication being cut off from the
outside world. I then saw Gen. Scott. He seemed wide awake to the crisis,
but bold and determined, & his talk was that of an old soldier and true
patriot. I religiously believe in him, and came away in much better spirits
than I went.

I have purposely refrained from giving either the particular conversation of the President or of Gen. Scott. The latter is full in the faith
that he can successfully defend this city, and that he shall soon reestablish
railroad & Telegraph communication with the North. . . .

1. A Dr. George Gross, who claimed to be a resident of Fairfax County, Va., was arrested
in Virginia in the summer of 1861. He had been taken prisoner by the Confederates at
the Battle of Bull Run and was charged with having led the Union army to that place.
However, Gross took the oath of fidelity to the Commonwealth of Virginia and to the
Confederate Government and was released.

Thursday, April 25. . . . We have just heard that the 7th Regt. has arrived
all safe & sound, and in good order! *After dinner.* They have arrived about
1,000 strong. Ben was at the R.R. & saw them. He says they shot 6 men
who were tearing up the R.R. track. That part of the story I doubt. I
am rejoiced that they have arrived. The report I understand—8,000

troops at Annapolis, ready to come on. We shall soon have enough to render the City secure. . . .

Sunday, April 28. Since my last writing my poor dear wife has changed so much for the worse that she must soon go. God give me strength to bear this terrible affliction. Yesterday I had a dreadful day until toward evening when I became more calm. Last night I slept tolerably, waking up many times. This morning I feel as if I should be deranged in mind. I can stay nowhere for 10 minutes at a time. I have been on my bed, on the sofa, walking out, reading, or rather trying to read, at my wife's bedside holding her hand and conversing with her, and all this in less than 2 hours! I arose at 5 & now it is seven.

Telegraphed Frank last evening to come on if he could. Oh how I hope he will come.

I can write no more now.

Tuesday, April 30. My dear wife became easier toward noon on Sunday, and was quite comfortable through the day. She gave me specific directions at her bedside, how to dispose her jewelry and who especially to remember. She was as calm as possible, & I took down all her directions in writing, to be carried out, if God permits me, to the letter. Rev. Mr. Russell was with her twice in the course of the day to administer the consolations of our holy religion. . . . She is entirely reconciled to die & says[,] "How glorious it will be to meet my friends who have gone before me, in another world." Her energies are wonderful considering her situation. Yesterday morning she insisted that I should take down the parlor curtains, which I did, & then she ordered the servants to wash the windows, which was done. In the afternoon she had some clothing brought down from the garret & laid on her bed, and she selected out such as she desired appropriated to certain purposes. . . .

A telegram came Sunday night from Frank that he would start Monday, and one yesterday forenoon from him at Boston that he should leave Boston yesterday morning, and desiring me to Telegraph him at the Astor House, which I did. I also Telegraphed Gen. Butler[1] at Annapolis of all the circumstances, and requested of him, if possible[,] to facilitate Frank's passage here. He replied that all that he could do should be done.

The City is very quiet considering the hosts of troops that are in it. I think now we are secure from any attack. I go daily to the Capitol & look about & have found several old friends whom I knew in Massachusetts. . . .

1. Benjamin F. Butler (1818–1893) had reached Annapolis at the head of the 8th Massachusetts Infantry on the night of April 20–21. The arrival of the New York 7th and the Massachusetts 8th in Washington a week or so later eased the fears concerning the safety of the city.

Friday, May 3. Frank arrived at 10 o'clock Wednesday. He came by the way of Annapolis and had no trouble in getting through. It was a great joy to his mother, and she seemed to be happier all day. . . . Yesterday she suffered much of the day with shortness of breath. She passed a pretty good night, Mrs. Vose taking care of her. All this morning she has been very much oppressed, & about an hour ago seemed to me to be in much agony. She got over it, & when I left her a few minutes ago appeared quite easy.

Frank & I walked up to Willard's after breakfast. We called on Col. Lamon[,][1] the Marshal, & had a very pleasant interview. . . .

1. Ward Hill Lamon (1828–1893) became Abraham Lincoln's law partner in the Eighth Judicial Circuit of Illinois in 1853. A heavyset, rough-and-tumble fighter, Lamon served as Lincoln's bodyguard on his journey to Washington in 1861 and was appointed marshal of the District of Columbia. He was later the official author of two books on Lincoln, actually written by others.

Monday, May 6. My poor dear wife is now a saint in Heaven. At quarter after four o'clock this morning her pure spirit winged its way to the realms of bliss, and the mortal remains now lie quiet and beautiful as if she only slept. I cannot realize, when I look upon her, that she is dead. Saturday night she passed with tolerable comfort. Mary Ellen & Miss Goldsmith[1] staid with her. At one time she awoke from a sweet sleep & said to Mary Ellen[,] "Is this a dream? Oh I have been in such a beautiful place, where I was so happy, & all was so pleasant. I thought I was invited out to dine there, and was very happy." Yesterday morning she appeared so comfortable that Frank & I went to ride by her advice. We returned about ten—found her in much agony—the Doctor with her. He did all he could for her, but we all saw that her disenthrallment was fast approaching.

About one her distress amounted to agony, & I was so overcome that I could not remain with her without exhibiting so much outward feeling as to distress her. After that paroxysm was over, she lay comparatively quiet. I was suffering very severely with nervous headache but was at her side occasionally all the afternoon. At ½ past 8 I felt entirely worn out, not having slept much the previous night, and went in [and] gave her my last kiss, which she returned, & I went to bed. I slept until 1 o'clock, then lay awake a long time. Got up & walked my room, looked at my watch—it was ½ past 2—went to bed and was very restless, but heard nothing. In my imagination I looked into a place that seemed filled with people innumerable, and there, in the midst, in white, was my dear[,] dear wife. Then I slept till daylight, and about 6 on opening my door Mary Ellen came & told [me] Mrs. French was *at rest*. I *felt* that it was so before, but I hardly dared to ask. She breathed her life quietly away, and died without a struggle. Oh God I thank thee that it was so.

And now what is the short remainder of my life to be? Alas—alas I know not. . . .

Same day—4 o'clock P.M.

Oh how the day drags on. It has rained steadily as if the heavens were weeping at my calamity! I have tried to read Theodore Parker's sermon on Immortality, but my mind would wander. My friends have been to see me, and I have talked with them, but while talking of ordinary subjects my mind would revert to the one great trouble of the day. I have been in many times where her dear form lies[,] & it is a melancholy pleasure to behold her. Frank & I have been looking over many things preparatory to his leaving for Exeter, for he is to take with him some of her clothing for Ellen, and much of my silver. . . .

Here I sit now, in my back parlor all alone. The women have gone to lie down[,] & Frank & Ben have gone out somewhere. Oh how lonely—lonely—lonely.

1. Perhaps the daughter of Martha Goldsmith, who ran a boardinghouse in the neighborhood.

Thursday, May 9. Yesterday! Oh what a day. In the morning after breakfast my desolation came over me so that I felt that it was *impossible* for me to stay *anywhere*. . . .

Three o'clock and the people began to assemble. At about ½ past[,] Washington Commandery of Knights Templar, in undress uniform[,] came up & marched in procession as an escort. God bless them one & all for this kind mark of respect to me. It touched me to the very soul. It was kindly and beautifully done.

At about ½ past 3 Rev. Mr. Cutler[1] performed the funeral services in the parlor where my Angel's remains lay. He made a short address portraying her character, oh how truly, then read the funeral service and made a prayer, and then that form that I have worshipped so long & loved so dearly left my house & my home *forever*! He placed her in the receiving tomb, and I came back trying to resign myself to God's holy will, but oh how desolate were my feelings. . . .

1. Probably Clement M. Butler.

Friday, May 10. . . . Frank & Ben left for Exeter at ¼ before 11 yesterday morning. I went to the Depot with them. . . .

Tuesday, May 14. . . . The shortsighted Virginians burned the chain bridge, above Georgetown, last evening.[1] I do believe there never was since the world was created such a blind raid upon the dearest interests *of themselves* as the South is now making, and particularly Virginia. As if the natural consequences of secession were not swift enough in ruining all their prospects, they have added the incendiary torch, to burn up all that can add to their comfort. Surely the chain bridge was of ten times more use to Virginians than to anybody else. They will all come to their senses by & by and wonder that they could have been so deluded! . . .

    1. Marginalia: An error—it was not burned. But such was the report here.

Sunday, May 19. . . . Tomorrow morning I intend to leave this city for New England, where there are hundreds of warm hearts to welcome me, and with them I shall, I know, enjoy as much happiness as, under the circumstances of my life[,] it is possible that I should.

I have been endeavouring for the past week to see the President but have not succeeded. When I have been there he has been so engaged that I could not ask to be admitted. Yesterday he was out riding. I desired to see him that I might, if possible, ascertain whether he intended to do anything for me. I have been true to him, and I thought I did all my duty in the canvass that preceded his election. Everybody but me seems to receive a reward, while I am *entirely* overlooked. . . .

Last Thursday afternoon [May 16] Mr. Thompson[1] & I rode out to the 7th Regt. camp with Mrs. Vose & Mrs. Russell in my buggy. We visited the tents and then saw the Regiment in line as it was inspected. There were a great many spectators, and the Regiment appeared well. On our return we saw the Regiment at Franklin Square (the 12th New York)[2] in line, and when we arrived at Willard's Col. Corcoran's Irish Regiment,[3] from N.Y.[,] passed us in column of march[,] making a very handsome and imposing appearance. At 4½ Street we passed quite a body of troops marching. I did not know from whence or whither bound. They looked rather rough, and I think had been out drilling. . . .

    1. J. Raymond Thompson, of Maine, was a clerk in the sixth auditor's office of the Treasury Department.
    2. French had corrected this, crossing out "the R.I. I believe."
    3. Michael Corcoran (1827–1863), commander of the 69th New York Infantry, had recently been court-martialed for refusing to march his regiment in honor of the Prince of Wales, who was visiting New York. The charges were dismissed so that Corcoran could

lead his troops to Washington. After fighting at Bull Run and around Norfolk, he died when he fell from his horse.

Brooklyn, Tuesday, May 21. At ¼ past 4 o'clock yesterday morning Mrs. Vose[,] Mr. J. Raymond Thompson, and myself, left Washington. The morning, & indeed the whole day, was rainy & dark & dismal. . . .

We came on without accident and arrived at Jersey City depot at 3 o'clock & 20'. Just before we got into the depot the car we were in ran off the track. We were moving slow & were *jounced* along several rods pretty considerably. The car, being out of the line, struck one of the large posts[,] knocking the foot out & carrying the lower part of the post up so that, when I got out[,] it rested on the top of the car at an angle, thus.[1] Nobody was either frightened or hurt, but things were considerably broken. . . .

1. French incorporated into his text at this point a minute sketch of the railway car and the broken post.

Lancaster, Wednesday, May 22. I went over to N.Y. with Mr. Soule, & instead of finding the Boat at pier No. 3 as we expected, we found it at pier No. 39, a mile or more up the city. We walked all the way. I took two staterooms, then walked to the largest dry goods store in the world, as they say—Claflin Mellen & Co.'s[1]—and all over it. It is enormous, being 375 feet long and 80 feet wide! Four or five stories in height. We went all over it, & I got pretty well tired out. . . . At ¼ to 4 we left Doct. W.'s for the Boat, & at 5 the Steamer *Connecticut* left her wharf. We had a beautiful run to Allyn's Point which we reached at 1 o'clock this morning, where we took the cars and arrived at Worcester at 4. We remained in the Depot there till 6:20, when we left for this place & arrived here at 7:20. . . .

1. Horace Brigham Claflin (1811–1885), a successful New England merchant, removed to New York City in 1843. In 1851, with William H. Mellen, he formed the wholesale dry-goods firm of Claflin, Mellen & Co., doing business throughout the United States. In January 1861 he had opened a new and capacious warehouse at the corner of Worth and Church streets.

Concord, Mass., Thursday, May 23. I left Lancaster at 7.20 A.M. today and arrived here at ½ past 8. . . .

Mr. [Simon] Brown had to go to Boston in the early train today, and is to return at 12 noon. Mrs. Brown & Mary received me with all the affection possible, and we have talked over the dreadful events of the past few weeks freely & tearfully. . . .

Rainsford Island, Sunday, May 26. Here I am, at this most pleasant of all pleasant places in New England that I have ever visited, and where I have passed so many happy hours during the three past years with her whom for so many years I adored, and whose memory is now so precious to me. I arrived here in the *Thacher* at noon yesterday. No one except the Captain (my friend Macomber) and his crew came with me. . . . I came up the wharf alone, and the Doct. met me near its shore end. Our meeting was almost a silent one, for no living mortal has a tenderer heart than Doct. Barker, & his feelings came out in a burst of grief which, of course[,] overcame me, and it was some time before either of us could speak. . . .

This is a perfectly lovely morning—no clouds—the ocean as calm as possible, and all Nature bursting into life. It is probably the last Sunday morning I shall ever pass here, for the Doct. is to surrender his office next Friday. It[,] with all the other associations, makes me feel sad enough.

The news published in the Boston papers of last evening was very exciting to me, but as it only pretended to be rumor, I do not place any confidence in that part that states that the 7th Regt. & other troops were being driven back towards Washington. I long to hear more. I feel as if I ought to be at Washington defending my home, but doubt if I should have an opportunity to do so if I were there, for I have been strangely overlooked considering my position as a politician. I do not believe that the rebel traitors can take Washington. If they can I shall, of course, be ruined, and I doubt if there ever will be any need of my return there.

Exeter, Tuesday, May 28. At 11 o'clock yesterday morning I bid adieu to beautiful Rainsford, perhaps forever. . . . On arriving at Boston I called at the Custom House to see Mr. Tuck, but he was not in. I then went to the Cornhill Coffee House, changed some of my clothes, saw Geo. Keyes at his dinner, & then went to my brother's [Henry Flagg French's] office. At 1 he & I dined at the Coffee House. At ½ past 2 I left his office for the cars & left the depot for this place at 3. Arrived here at five, the rain pouring about as fast as I ever saw it. Frank met me at the Depot, and we came down in a stage. Found Ellen, Hattie, & Fanny Gilbert ready to give me a cordial welcome. At 7 Mr. Tuck arrived, and Ben came up. . . .

Chester, Thursday, May 30. Frank, Ben & I left Exeter at 9½ o'clock this morning and arrived here at ¼ before 1. Found Mother and Helen the only occupants of the old mansion. . . .

Exeter, Sunday, June 2. At 8 o'clock A.M. yesterday Frank, Ben & I bade farewell to Mother & Helen and left the old mansion at Chester for this place. we arrived here at 11 after a very pleasant ride, the weather being superb. . . .

Monday, June 3. . . . I read "Denmark Vesey"[1] in the *Atlantic*, it being quite a minute account of the effort of the So. Carolina negroes to get up an insurrection in 1821 & *ante*. They nearly succeeded, & it seems to me good evidence that the South now stands on a domestic volcano that may burst out at any hour. If it should, with their foolish—aye mad—attempt at secession on their hands, they will be in an awful condition, and to be sincerely pitied by the world. In such a case I, for one, should not certainly rejoice over their calamity, for tens of thousands of innocent people would suffer such horrors as the world has seldom witnessed. . . .

1. Denmark Vesey (1767–1822), a free black of Charleston, S.C., was hanged on July 2, 1822, for conspiring to lead a slave insurrection. The article in the *Atlantic* to which French alludes appeared in June 1861 and was written by Thomas Wentworth Higginson (1823–1911).

Tuesday, June 4. . . . Frank & I had a long talk about Ben just before I went to bed, and I was greatly troubled, so much so that I dreamed of him all night when I slept. . . .

Concord, Mass., Sunday, June 9. I went to Boston Friday afternoon and went out to Cambridge with my brother Henry and passed the night. He and I walked all about the town after tea and viewed the magnificent residences. Cambridge is a lovely place, and with something to employ my time about I could spend the remainder of my life there, as it now seems to me, very pleasantly. It seems, however, as if Washington were my destiny. . . .

On Friday afternoon, when in Boston, the Judge and I visited the Aquarial gardens.[1] We took seats in the gallery and watched the whale and porpoise flou[r]ishing around the large tank. They were very lively, rushing round it continually. After we had been there about ½ an hour, we noticed that the porpoise seemed to be distressed. Soon he showed evident symptoms of something wrong by throwing himself ½ his length out of water & then sinking back tail downward nearly to the bottom. After a few spasmodic efforts the poor creature began to fail, &[,] in say 5 minutes, went to the bottom a dead porpoise! They got a pole & fished him up and took him out. He was a plump, fat, handsome fellow, but as dead as a doornail. What killed him no one could tell. Only a few moments before he began to fail, Henry remarked that Prof. Agassiz[2] had prophesied that the whale would not live long, & that perhaps if we staid a little longer he would oblige us by dying in our presence. He did not, but the porpoise did! . . .

1. The Grand Aquaria, located at 21 Bromfield Street, was said to have been "filled with rare marine animals."

2. Jean Louis R. Agassiz (1807–1873), Swiss-born Professor of Natural History at Harvard, 1848–1852 and 1854–1873, was noted for his lectures, exploration, and theory of epochs of creation, which was in opposition to the Darwinian theory of evolution.

Tuesday, June 11. We have had a picnic and chowder on Egg-rock[1] today. . . .

. . . At 2 o'clock all was ready—the table elegantly set, & all arranged for eating. A pot full of chowder, a goodly lot of fried potatoes, plenty of lobster salad, pies, doughnuts, oranges, pineapples, claret wine, etc., constituted the food & drink.

Two milk cans full of hot coffee, added to the drinkables by Mrs. Brown[,] were very acceptable indeed. We had "all sorts of a time." I think I never saw fun & frolick & enjoyment more fully carried out. Judge French & Geo. Keyes seemed to be perfectly possessed with the spirit of fun & deviltry—they knocked everybody about as if they were so many ninepins. *I*, portly as I am, & inclined rather to sobriety as I was, got rolled up in a carpet, had an india cracker exploded in my face, & a mug of coffee which I was drinking suddenly hit so as to spill it into my face & bosom. As for the women, they met with no mercy in being tormented & hustled about, & all sorts of fun was perpetrated on everybody. We voted it, unanimously, the best picnic & chowder that ever was. At about 5 we broke up & went our several ways. . . .

1. Egg Rock is a small promontory where the Sudbury and Assabet rivers join to form the Concord River.

Washington, Saturday, June 15. I am again at home. . . .

Mr. & Mrs. Russell came in to see me on my arrival, and Mary Ellen Brady, who is to take care of my house and of me for a time, now indefinite, but I hope for the rest of my life, came up soon after my arrival and was like a gleam of the brightest sunshine in my house. During all my Angel wife's sickness she was with us, and oh so good, so kind, so gentle that she took a hold upon both our hearts—the love of one has gone to heaven with an emancipated soul, the love of the other still remains here as true as it is possible for human love to be. The comforts of life are all around me, and I will now try to be happy. . . .

I find very little apparent excitement here. True[,] I have not been out, but here at my house it is as still as ever I knew it in my life. . . .

Wednesday, June 19. . . . On Monday I went to the Capitol. Found my room still occupied by "The Quartermaster's Department." Staid a short time & then went down in the city. . . . On my return I found Mr. Tuck here, and he is still with me. After dinner he and I rode out in the buggy. Saw the troops in various parts of the City and saw the 4th Pa. Regt. march out for Alexandria. . . .

. . . After dinner Mr. Tuck and I rode over to Arlington in my buggy and saw the fortifications, troops, etc., over the river, Mr. Tuck having procured the passes. We had a very pleasant ride. Saw the evening parade of the 8th New York Regiment, stationed at Arlington, which was very handsomely done. We arrived home about 7, took tea, and Mr. Tuck went to the President's and has just arrived home—10 o'clock.

Saturday, June 22. . . . I went to the Capitol, where I spent the morning. Saw the Commissioner of Public Buildings[1] and spoke to him in favor of several of my friends. . . .

At ½ past 1 we had dinner, and at a little past 2 Mr. Tuck left for N. Hamp.

I enjoyed his visit very much, and regretted to have him leave. If I should by any good luck get the office of Marshal of this District—Col. Lamon having resigned—I shall impute it entirely to Mr. Tuck's influence. He has labored well for me. . . .

1. William S. Wood, although appointed commissioner of public buildings by Lincoln, and serving as such for some months, was not confirmed by the Senate. Early in the favor of Mrs. Lincoln, he accompanied her on a controversial shopping trip to New York but soon fell out of grace and was displaced by French.

Wednesday, June 26. Oh what an indolent, inefficient life I am leading! My office, as Clerk of the Committee on Claims, furnishes me no work *now*, the Committee room still being occupied by a Captain in the Army as a Quartermaster's Office. . . . I am, daily, bored more or less by people after office, who seem to think I am bound to assist them *all*. So goes my time. I am ashamed of myself to fritter it away so. . . .

Sunday, June 30. . . . Yesterday afternoon at ½ past 3 I rode down to Mr. Adams's, where Mary Ellen was spending the day, and took her and

Alice Adams up to see the President raise a flag on a large tent, or marquee, in the grounds South of the Presidential mansion. There was a large assemblage of people, and quite a parade of military. The tent pole extended up some twenty or thirty feet above the tent cloth, and the latter seemed to be fastened *closely* around the pole, & the flag, being in the tent, was expected to be drawn up between the pole and the cloth *by main strength*. At ½ past 4 The President and a portion of his Cabinet and General Scott appeared on the south piazza of the house, and were greeted with cheers and a salute. In a few minutes The President and Mrs. Lincoln, accompanied by Mr. Seward[,] Secy. of State, Mr. Chase,[1] Secy. of the Treasy.[,] and some other gentlemen whom I did not recognize, and by Rev. Smith Pyne,[2] left the piazza (Gen. Scott remaining) and approached the pavilion, the band playing very beautifully "Hail to the Chief."

As soon as the distinguished party had ascended the platform, Mr. Pyne read an ecceedingly [sic] appropriate prayer, in a very distinct and impressive manner, and concluded by repeating with great fervency the Lord's Prayer.

The President then took hold of the halliards & commenced raising the flag. At the place where the cloth surrounded the pole it hung hard, but the President tugged away *with a will,* and up it went, but, alas, when it blew out in the breeze the two upper stripes and about three of the stars were separated by a rent, and just hung like a ribbon to the rest of the flag. Although a thousand hearty cheers went up, and the band played "the star spangled banner," and the guns of the Artillery, stationed on the Monument grounds, thundered a salute, I felt a sorrow that I cannot describe, at seeing *the torn flag.* It seemed to me an omen of ill luck. My only consolation was observing the determined energy with which the President pulled away at the halliards—as if he said, in his mind, "It has got to go up whether or no." And I thought, "Well, let what reverses may come, he will meet them *with the same energy,* and bring us out of the war, if with a tattered flag, still it will *all* be there!" . . .

1. Salmon P. Chase (1808–1873), senator from Ohio, as Free Soil-Democrat, 1849–1855, and as Republican, 1861. Served as Secretary of the Treasury, 1861–1864, and Chief Justice of the United States, 1864–1873.
2. Smith Pyne, pastor of St. John's Episcopal Church, opposite the White House.

Thursday, July 4. . . . Last Monday I carried Mary Ellen out in the buggy to visit the 2d N. Hampshire Regiment. It is encamped on a hill out 6th Street, beyond Boundary Street. We rode to Col. Marston's quarters, and saw him, Major Stevens, Doct. Hubbard, & Chaplain Parker, who was sometime at the White House when Gen. Pierce was President.[1] . . .

... Tuesday morning was as clear as possible, and cold. I went on top of the house and could see Alexandria through my glass, as plain as if it were within ¼ of a mile. I could see all the camps about the city, and the soldiers about them. Tuesday was a cold day. Tuesday evening I saw the comet for the first time. It was very brilliant, and we watched it some time. I arose in the night and saw it again. It was nearly down to the horizon, and the tail was immense.[2] Yesterday we were all day at work putting up the flagstaff and rigging the flag. . . .

The war seems to remain about as it was. Troops are pouring in, and I think soon Secession must fight or run. If it stands to fight it must get whipped[,] unless I am wonderfully mistaken in the vigor and valor of Northern men!

1. Gilman Marston (1811–1890), commanding officer of the 2d New Hampshire Infantry, was an Exeter lawyer. He was badly wounded at the first battle of Bull Run but recovered and was promoted to brigadier general in November 1862. He was also a Republican congressman, 1859–1863 and 1865–1867, and senator, 1889. Probably Josiah Stevens of Concord who was commissioned major in May 1861 and resigned in July 1862. George H. Hubbard (1823–1876), of Hopkinton, N.H., was practicing medicine in Manchester when he was appointed surgeon of the 2d New Hampshire Infantry in 1861. He served throughout the war in many localities. Henry E. Parker, who had been pastor of the South Congregational Church in Concord, N.H., was the first chaplain of the 2d New Hampshire Infantry.

2. The Great Comet of 1861, described as extremely bright, was first discovered on May 13 in Australia. Shortly after the earth passed through its tail on June 29–30, the comet's brilliance gradually began to diminish until its position was determined for the last time on May 1, 1862. A patriotic postal cover of the time depicted a hurtling Lincoln as the Comet of 1861.

Sunday, July 7. . . . Since the 4th nothing very special in my own particular existence has happened. The Nation is going on, and wars & rumors of wars are about us. Congress is setting in vigorously. The House did the proper thing in electing Galusha A. Grow[,][1] Speaker. He is entitled to the place, for his eminent services in the Republican cause and the cause of his country for years, & is eminently qualified for the place. Hon. Emerson Etheridge[2] succeeds Col. Forney as Clerk, at which *I* rejoice. Col. F. was elected at the commencement of the last Congress, with no claims whatever to the place, for he never was a Republican. A compromise elected him. I have no fault to find with the man, although he once treated me shamefully. He is now a candidate for Secy. of the Senate—so am I. I have no expectations that either of us will get the place, & I care very little whether I do or not. I should like it, but have so often been disappointed when endeavouring to get office, that I am prepared, *always*, for defeat. . . .

1. Galusha A. Grow (1823–1907), Free-Soiler and Republican congressman from Pennsylvania, 1851–1863; speaker, 1861–1863.

2. Emerson Etheridge (1819–1902), Whig congressman from Tennessee, 1853–1857 and 1859–1861; Clerk of the House of Representatives, 1861–1863.

Thursday, July 11. . . . I desire to write here, lest by some accident I should not find time to give the directions by will or otherwise, that it is not only my *will*, but my *solemn order* to whoever administers my estate, that there be given out of it to Miss Mary Ellen Brady, one thousand dollars. Her great care of my dear departed wife, and her kindness to me makes her seem like a dear, dear daughter, and Mrs. French said to me on her deathbed, "I leave Mary Ellen to you." I will never forget the injunction, and consider myself as much bound to carry it out, in some way, as if I had been placed under a solemn oath to do it. I impose the duty on my son Frank to see this wish sacredly complied with, unless it should be in my power, as it is not now, to carry out this legacy while I live, as I shall surely do if I can. That there may be no mistake about this, I sign it.

B. B. French

My conscience is somewhat relieved by making this provision. I know it is not legally binding, but it *will bind my heirs,* if I know them as I think I do.

Saturday, July 13. I was called to my door yesterday morning when nearly dressed, by a rap, & on going to it found Mary Ellen, Louisa Russell, and Nannie French.[1] Mary Ellen told me that Margaret was sick and had sent for her, and she left. At 8 o'clock Margaret gave birth to a son, her 10th child.

I went to the Capitol and down in the City after breakfast. Did errands & invited Senators Clark, Foot, and Hale to spend the evening with me. Returned from the Capitol about one, & dined at two. After dinner walked down to Edmund's & gave Mary Ellen a diamond ring that I purchased at Gault's. It was *partially* to carry out my dear wife's injunction. . . .

Senator Clark came about 8 o'clock, and Mr. Jo[seph] Keyes & Edwin Barrett[2] came soon after. Ned & Mary Ellen came up about 9. Senators Foot & Hale did not come. We played euchre and passed a very pleasant evening. All left before 11. . . .

1. Nannie French, probably Anne Rainsford French, one of the daughters of Edmund and Margaret French.
2. Edwin S. Barrett (1833–1898), of Concord, Mass., was in the hide and skin trade.

Wednesday, July 17. . . . The outside world has been moving on with more than ordinary vigor—battles have been fought, Congress has been exceedingly busy & exceedingly patriotic. There has been a vast movement of troops in this vicinity, & there are more than 50,000 now embodied over the river in Virginia & moving forward toward Manassas. A fight or a run of the secession army is deemed certain with 24 hours. I prophecy *a run*. . . .

I am, somehow, pretty much disgusted with the world and wish all my property here was converted into cash. I think, if it were, I should go to Europe. I want to be as far as possible from this scene of my desolation. At times it seems as if I could not endure it any longer.

Friday, July 19. . . . The Federal army, more than 50,000 strong, is pushing on as fast as possible toward Manassas Junction where it is expected that the Traitor rebels will make a stand. Thus far they have run on the approach of the Federal troops. This day *must,* I think[,] tell the story of a decisive battle, or an ignominious rout of the rebels. The Federal troops either reached Manassas last night, or must this morning. . . .

. . . I went to the Navy Department on business for a friend, but did not succeed in seeing the Secretary. Hon. Truman Smith[1] was with me. We waited two or three hours, but the place was besieged by Members of Congress, who have the preference in seeing the Secretaries. . . .

1. Truman Smith (1791–1884), of Connecticut. A Whig congressman, 1839–1843 and 1845–1849, and senator, 1849–1854, Smith was practicing law in Connecticut in 1861.

Saturday, July 20. Soon after eating breakfast yesterday I walked to the War Department—found it would not be possible to see the Secretary—heard all sorts of rumors about battles, etc., but could not ascertain the truth of any of them. One was that Gen. Tyler's[1] brigade had marched up to a masked battery at Bull Run, and that 500 were killed and an immense number wounded! which all turned out to be gammon. I staid about the War Department perhaps an hour, saw President Lincoln pass through the lower passage, which was crowded with people. He was dressed in a common linen coat, had on a straw hat, & pushed along through the crowd without looking to the right or left, and no one seemed to know who he was. He entered the East door, passed entirely through & out at the West door, & across the street to Gen. Scott's quarters. I was somewhat amused to see with what earnestness he pushed his way along & to observe his exceedingly ordinary appearance. . . .

1. Daniel Tyler (1799–1882), Union brigadier general from Connecticut, was criticized for not attacking vigorously enough at a key point in the battle.

Sunday, July 21. . . . At 3 Misses Emeline Barrett[1] & Lizzie Bartlett[2] came with their heads full of exciting news of a battle now in progress at Bull Run. Emeline, whose nephew is with the Mass. 5th Regt. *as a spectator,* was very much troubled. She came with tears in her eyes. I told her not to believe anything she heard until it was officially confirmed. We soothed her as well as we could, & she left at ¼ before 4 in much better spirits than she came. . . .

1. Emeline Barrett, the aunt of Edwin Barrett, ran a very popular boardinghouse in Concord, Mass., for more than forty years. Her nephew later wrote an account of the Battle of Bull Run for a Boston newspaper.
2. Lizzie Bartlett (b. 1830), of Concord, Mass., was the daughter of Dr. Josiah Bartlett II.

Monday, July 22. I am sick in body & in mind. The battle yesterday was disastrous to our troops. Forty-thousand men in the open field undertook to fight 70 thousand well entrenched, and of course were whipped. At 12 o'clock, midnight, Col. John S. Keyes, who had been at Bull Run, came to my door, called up his mother, & said[,] "Mother pack your trunk and be ready to leave in the ¼ past 4 o'clock [A.M.] train." I asked why such haste? He said, holding up both hands, "We are whipped all to pieces." He then went on to describe the battle and the retreat, & said when he left the whole army was in full flight. Mary Ellen was down at my brother's & I went immediately after her. She came up & aided Mrs. Keyes to pack, got her some breakfast, etc., and at ¼ past 4 accompanied her to the depot, & she, with Doct. Bartlett,[1] Miss Emeline, Mrs. Jo. Keyes, & Lizzy Bartlett, went. . . .

At ½ past 8 I walked down in the City and soon found, to my sorrow, that our "grand army" had made a grand run, and has been terribly cut up. As I passed along the North side of the Avenue I saw a baggage wagon marked "2d Reg. N.H.V." which stopped opposite the door of a house on the other side. I walked across, & behold Surgeon Hubbard of Manchester was the driver and he had inside Col. Gilman Marston, badly wounded, with a bullet through his shoulder. So great a crowd collected at once around the wagon that I could see nothing, so I walked on, and on my return called at the house and was told Col. M. seemed inclined to sleep, & it was thought best not to disturb him as there was no hemorrhage, so the wound had not been examined, & no one could tell how bad it was. I then came to the Capitol. Soldiers were straggling into the city in all sorts of *shapes*. Some without guns—some with two. Some barefooted, some bareheaded, & all with a doleful story of defeat.

Ambulances & wagons also came. At the Capitol everybody's face was gloomy. A gentleman sat in one of the member's seats in the Hall, who was present from the firing of the first gun at 10 A.M. till ½ past 9 P.M.[,] and seemed to have had all his wits about him. He gave a very full description of the fight & the retreat. On being asked if the retreat was in good order, he said, it was in the worst order that could be imagined, that it was actually led by the officers. That he saw two officers throw away their swords, cut a horse loose from a wagon & both get on and ride away. He said the ground was strewed with all sorts of provisions from Bull Run to Centreville, where a rally was made [and] the troops again formed.

It is now 3 o'clock P.M. and all sorts of rumors come along. Col. Keyes was here about the time I commenced writing, on his way to Alexandria to look after his brother-in-law, Capt. George Prescott,[2] of the Mass. 5th. He said the report was that the U.S. troops were retreating in good order, with some 3,000 cavalry in pursuit, and that they intended to make a stand somewhere, perhaps at Fairfax, & give battle again.

As for me, I am almost too sick to be up, but, eager as I am for news, I cannot go to bed. . . .

1. Dr. Josiah Bartlett II (1796–1878) practiced medicine in Concord, Mass., for fifty-seven years. He was the president of the Massachusetts Medical Society in 1862.

2. George L. Prescott, captain of the 32d Massachusetts Infantry. He was brevetted brigadier general of volunteers in front of Petersburg, Va., where he was mortally wounded.

Tuesday, July 23. Another day has passed and Washington is fast settling down into its usual calm. The rain fell steadily all of yesterday—the city was filled with excitement & *demoralized* soldiers most of whom, I suspect, ingloriously fled on Sunday. This morning opened bright and beautiful. I had occasion to ride down in the City immediately after breakfast, and found that the Companies were resuming their old quarters, & reorganizing fast. The soldiers seemed to be individually engaged in drying their wet clothing, cleaning their guns, cooking, etc. The smoke and dust of battle having cleared away, we all begin to see the field as it was actually left, and the loss on our side, currently reported yesterday at 5 or 6,000, has dwindled down to 5 or 600! It is believed that the rebel loss far exceeded ours, but nothing certain is known. They did not follow our retreating army—so much is certain—& no reason is given but that they were too much cut up to do so.

I met Gen. [Henry] Wilson—Senator—this morning, and speaking about *the battle*, he said, "Don't call it *a battle*, it was nothing but a tuppenny skirmish, with about 500 killed on each side—that was all it was, and all it ought to be called."

I have succeeded in keeping myself pretty busy all day. Arose early, read the papers till breakfast was ready. As soon as I had eaten breakfast went to market. Thence to the P.O. & to Jo. Keyes's boardinghouse. Found that Capt. Prescott & Edwin Barrett had both returned to the city unhurt. Called on Barrett, who showed me the trophies he had brought from the field of battle, consisting of a very nice pair of secession saddlebags, a handsome revolver, belonging to one of the Black-horse Cavalry, pretty much all of whom are said to have been killed by the Zouaves, an India-rubber blanket, & a woolen ditto, picked up on the road & both belonging to our troops, [and] a button cut from a secession coat. He also brought in a horse with his equipments, taken from the rebels.

After having a very minute and interesting account from Edwin of what he saw (& being with Gen. McDowell,[1] he had the opportunity to see a great deal)[,] I went to see Capt. Prescott. Found him with most of his company quartered at Jimmy Maher's old tavern house.[2] He was looking finely. . . .

Edwin told me that he saw a lively fight between the 2d N.H. Regt. and a Georgia Regiment in a small piece of woods, in which the Georgians were badly beaten. After the troops had left he said he went into the woods and saw the dead bodies of 42 rebels & 10 wounded on a space of ground not larger than the parlor in which we were sitting when he told me the story. . . .

1. Irvin McDowell (1818–1885) was in command of Union forces at the first battle at Bull Run.

2. James Maher, a grocer at this time, once had a hotel at the corner of E and 13th streets.

Friday, July 26. . . . [On Wednesday, July 24] I rode down to Col. Marston's room & saw him. He looked quite well and his physicians told me was doing well, & they had strong hopes of saving his arm. The bullet was a common musket bullet & struck his right arm just below the shoulder, passed through it, & lodged in his breast, from which it was extracted. At Marston's room I found Senator Clark, and we rode out to the encampment of the 2d N.H. Regt. in my buggy. We saw Col. Fisk[1] and Major Stevens, and many others. Ned was out there & introduced me to Dearborn Morse,[2] a son of Josiah Morse, whom I knew from my childhood till his death. He lived at my grandfather Brown's when I was a boy, and I was glad to see his son, who is the very image of his father.

Major Stevens gave us a very interesting history of the battle, explaining it by diagrams which he drew as he proceeded. He was in it from first to last. He said he saw one of the "Black horse cavalry" undertake to sabre a Zouave. He parried the sabre stroke with his musket, seized the trooper by the breast of his coat, dragged him from his horse and cut his throat, all within a single minute. . . .

1. Probably Francis Skinner Fiske, lieutenant colonel, 2d New Hampshire Infantry.
2. Josiah Dearborn Morse, of Chester, a private. He was discharged as disabled in August 1861 but subsequently served in another New Hampshire regiment.

Sunday, July 28. . . . Had the horse harnessed & rode down to Edmund's, took him and Harry into the buggy and rode out to the N.H. Camp— 2d Regt. Saw Col. Fisk, Chaplain Parker, & the soldiers. Maj. Stevens was in the city dining with some friend. Nothing has yet been heard of our friend Jo. Morse,[1] & it is uncertain whether he was killed or is a prisoner. Chaplain Parker was holding his afternoon Sunday school, & I remained through the exercises. He had under consideration the mission of our Savior, & his explanations were very touching and convincing. After the explanation was through the class all arose & sang coronation, beautifully. There were excellent voices among them, & they sang with great feeling. The exercises were closed with a fervent prayer by the Chaplain. Each soldier present had his pocket bible & hymn book. As I thought of the wide difference between their occupation on the last Sabbath & this, I felt a solemnity and a heart sympathy that I cannot describe in words. . . .

The Regiment is not yet over the disorganization of last Sunday's fight, but, as Col. Fisk told me, is fast getting back to its former discipline. . . .

1. Joseph R. Morse (1823–1877), of Chester, a private. He was captured at Bull Run and paroled in May 1862.

Tuesday, July 30. . . . At 7 A.M. Senator Hale called and *invited me* to have my horse harnessed and carry him to the encampment of the Minnesota Regt. about ½ a mile East of my house, where he desired to see an officer. I *accepted the invitation* and we rode out. Found Col. Gorman[1] and his staff at breakfast. Staid perhaps ½ an hour, & the Col. told us about the fight at Bull's Run. His Regt. was in the thickest of it. Mr. Hale did his errand, & we returned. . . .

1. Willis Arnold Gorman (1816–1876), colonel of the 1st Minnesota Infantry. He had been a Democratic congressman from Indiana, 1849–1853, and, as a supporter of Franklin Pierce, had been appointed territorial governor of Minnesota, 1853–1857. He became a brigadier general following the Battle of Bull Run.

Saturday, August 3. . . . This morning I rose about 5, read the newspapers, walked in the garden & picked a few peaches, the first of the season. Breakfasted at about ½ past 7 and then rode down to Market & to the P.O. Got back a little past 9. At 12 o'clock Mrs. Keyes and I went to the Capitol. Went first into the gallery of the Senate; while there Prince Napoleon[1] and his suite, accompanied by Secretary of State Seward, came into the Chamber. We knew the Prince instantly from his striking resemblance to the portraits of Napoleon 1st.

Mr. Seward introduced him to many of the Senators, and he remained for, perhaps[,] ½ an hour. Mrs. Keyes & I went over to the House & sat awhile in the gallery there & then came down to come home, when we met The Prince & Gov. Seward in the passage where we had a fine view of him & saw still more distinctly the great resemblance to his Great Uncle. . . .

. . . After tea Mary Ellen came up and spent the evening, and I have just returned from accompanying her to Edmund's. I hope she will soon make one of my household again. I miss her beyond measure. . . .

1. Napoleon Joseph Charles Paul Bonaparte (1822–1891), oldest son of Napoleon Bonaparte's brother Jerome, and called Prince Napoleon, returned from exile in 1847 and commanded French troops in the Crimean War. He was sent to America in 1861 to avoid a duel with the Duke d'Aumale.

Thursday, August 8. . . . It is now ½ past 1, and I have been since ½ past 11 trying to write here. But the report is out that the President has appointed me Commissioner of Public Buildings, and my house has been filled with people after office, or in relation to office, so I could not write. Now I will stop.

Saturday, August 10. It is 3 o'clock P.M. At the time of the above writing, as mentioned, the town rumor was that I was appointed Commissioner of Public Buildings. It was true, but I was not *commissioned,* and before the President signed the commission, some new light burst upon him in relation to the position of Commissioner Wood before the Senate[,] & he held up my commission for advisement, and still holds it. I have this day seen both The President & Mrs. Lincoln,[1] and am satisfied that I shall be Commissioner within a few weeks, if not on Monday. . . .

What the future is to bring forth God only knows. One thing is certain, I cannot and will not live as I have been living for the past month. There must be someone with me, who is dear to me & who will stay!

1. Mary Ann Todd Lincoln (1818–1882) married Abraham in 1842.

Saturday, August 17. . . . Mary Ellen returned, to stay at my house again, on Wednesday, and it adds, oh so much to my happiness. She makes my home cheerful and like *home*. Would to God I could have her with me the rest of my life, for I find my happiness depends upon her presence, and I would try—oh how earnestly—to make her as happy as a mortal woman could be.

Friday, August 23. Thirteen men have called today for my recommendation to office. Signed all their petitions. Easier to sign than to talk!

Mr. & Mrs. Keyes left at ½ past 7 this morning, and Mary Ellen & I miss them exceedingly. Mrs. Keyes was so lively & interesting that we have both become greatly attached to her. . . .

After breakfast this morning I rode down to the Plumb gallery[1] and was photographed in my K. Templar costume complete, for my friend [F. O. J.] Smith. They then took me for an album card. Two or three days ago I was taken in ordinary clothing at Brady's,[2] for an album card. . . .

1. Plumb's Daguerrean Gallery at the Concert Hall, Pennsylvania Avenue, between 4½ and 6th streets.
2. Mathew Brady (1823–1896), whose photographic studio was on Pennsylvania Avenue, had already started compiling his monumental photographic history of the Civil War.

Monday, August 26. . . . Early Saturday morning my friends Capt. Williams[1] & R. H. Stewart came up and informed me of the arrest, by the Govt.[,] of Mayor Berret. The City was full of *quiet excitement* about it all day—i.e., everybody talked about it but there was no outward demonstration. Several others were arrested, & among them Mrs. F. A. Hassler,[2] formerly Miss Betty Hanson, & now known among all my friends as "Betty Hassler." Her sister is the wife of William Barker,[3] formerly a Clerk in the Treasy. Dept. & now an officer in the Rebel Army. Last summer or spring, Mrs. R.[4] went to Manassas to visit her sister; when she arrived there she ascertained that her sister had gone to Culpeper C[ourt]-H[ouse]. She saw Beauregard[5] who offered to permit her to visit Culpeper but would not permit her to return, so she gave up proceeding onward and returned here full of praise of the rebel general, and when my brother's last child was born in July, she said to Mrs. French, "I wish that child was mine. I would name him Beauregard." She has been open in her praise of the secessionists, & of expressions of sympathy with their movements, and I have for quite a length of time suspected her of complicity with those who were carrying on correspondence with our enemies. I think she was arrested none too soon.

Yesterday was a most lovely day. I accompanied Mary Ellen to St. Aloysius's Church, *saw* the morning services, and listened to an admirable discourse on the efficacy of prayer. It is a long time since I have, before, attended the services at a Catholic Church. The last time I was ever in one was at the funeral of Mr. Peter Brady, Mary Ellen's father (1856), the services on which occasion were performed at St. Matthew's Church. Mary Ellen is a devoted Catholic and, although she could not, probably, make a proselyte of me, she could very easily induce me to become a worshipper in her church, for I am one of those who do not believe in particular creeds as necessary to salvation. I believe in universal worship, and if all sects and denominations who believe in the Saviour would surrender their creeds and become one great body of worshippers of God under the general name of *Christians,* & live as the sacred volume requires them to live, they would be in no danger of eternal punishment hereafter. . . .

I do not believe in praying on the housetops or in the presence of others, but alone, in the solemn stillness of one's own chamber. . . .

1. Probably Thomas J. Williams, a clerk in the office of the commissioner of public buildings.

2. Mrs. F. A. Hassler was arrested by order of the Assistant Secretary of War and committed to the 13th Street Prison on August 23, 1861. From there she was transferred to Rose O'Neal Greenhow's 16th Street residence, which was also being used as a prison. Betty (or Bettie) Hassler was charged with being a courier and holding contraband correspondence with the insurrectionary states. She was released by order of the Secretary of War on oath of allegiance and parole, October 30, 1861.

3. William N. Barker had been an officer in the National Volunteers, a military organization of Southern-rights men formed in Washington in September 1860. He was to become the chief of the signal bureau, C.S.A.

4. French undoubtedly intended "Mrs. H.," for Mrs. Hassler.

5. Pierre G. T. Beauregard (1818–1893) was one of the commanding officers for the Confederacy at the first Battle of Bull Run.

Thursday, August 29. . . . The war does not seem to lead to much fighting about here now, but there must be some soon; things cannot remain as they now are long. Two armies, *looking each other in the face,* must fight soon!

20 minutes to 2 P.M. A Regiment of soldiers has just passed on its way down East Capitol St. The street is almost ankle deep with mud, and the troops, for some unaccountable reason, were marched through it, when there is a good pavement 30 feet wide that they could just as well have occupied almost dry-shod. It seems to me as if the officers always endeavoured to make every movement as uncomfortable as possible to the soldiers! When the weather was burning hot they seemed to take special pains to move the troops beneath a meridian sun, clothed & burdened as heavily as possible! . . .

Saturday, August 31. . . . Things are moving on and, as it seems to me, toward some definite result. I was told that 6,000 troops came into the city yesterday. *I know* a great many came. A gentleman who ought to be well posted, and I believe he is, told me evening before last that our army across the river, and within call at a very short notice on this side, amounted to 150,000 men, *well* armed, equipped, and disciplined; and that that of the enemy amounted to 120,000. It cannot certainly be that two armies of such numbers, whose defences are almost within hail of each other, can long be kept from a general battle. There is now a war of pickets daily.

I know that our officers & soldiers are eager for a fight, and I believe, when it comes, that the Bull Run disaster, if disaster it was, will be redeemed. I think, also, that the movements in other quarters are tending to bring on some sort of a denou[e]ment that will go far to decide this question of Union or disunion. Troops were moving all last night across the Navy Yard Bridge, which seems to me to be an evidence, unmistakeable, that another great battle is soon to be fought. . . .

Wednesday, September 4. . . . My family this day consists of Miss Mary Ellen Brady, Ben, Dan. F. Wells,[1] & my three servants. Mary Ellen is a special blessing bestowed upon me by Providence, as I view it, for without her presence here I would not be here myself! A few evenings since she told me of some of the privations of her younger life. She endured more than I was aware of, in consequence of a family connexion, after the death of *her* mother. . . .

I saw the President of the United States yesterday. I called at the Mansion at a little past 2 P.M. & was told that he was out, but expected in every moment. In about 5 minutes a carriage drove up to the door with 4 gentlemen in it. The President was one, but no mortal man would ever have suspected that it was "The President." He was dressed in gray woolen clothing, and had upon his head a most ordinary broad-brimmed slouch. He was covered with dust and came in alone with the peculiar swinging gait that characterizes the old "Rail splitter." I was in the passage that is at the foot of the stairs leading up to his office. The moment he entered the door of the vestibule he saw me and[,] although twenty feet, at least, off, and an open door between us, he said in a most hearty, offhand manner[,] "Mr. French how do you do," & approaching me, we shook hands, & he invited me to walk up to his office with him, which I did, holding a conversation all the way about the Times & situation of affairs. He expressed himself very well satisfied with the position of matters and things now. We reached the office and were seated. The last time I saw the President he told me he should appoint me Commissioner of Public Buildings "the first of Sept." I opened the conversation yesterday by saying that, as the first of Sept. had come, I thought I would call & ascertain his intentions. He looked up with his peculiar smile and eye-twinkle, and said[,] "The fifth, Mr. French, the fifth; *you* understand." And then he laughed. I replied, "Yes Mr. President, I do understand, and no more need be said on that subject."

We then conversed a few moments on ordinary topics, looked at the opposite shores of the river through his glass, which he adjusted for me, and I took my leave. . . .

1. Son of Catharine and P. P. Wells.

Saturday, September 7. Yesterday I received from the President of the United States the appointment of Commissioner of Public Buildings. I spent all the day up to ½ past 1 P.M. in getting and executing my bonds. Mr. James Adams and Mr. John Purdy being my sureties. The Commissioner's Bond is for $20,000 penalty—the Bond as Agent for disbursing the Appropriation for the Patent Office Building[,] $40,000.

Before I left my house in the morning applicants for office began to annoy me. They met me on the streets, & as soon as I returned to my house at 2 o'clock, they began to come[,] & I had no peace until I left at 7 P.M. to spend the evening at my brother's. Today I am to call at 9 A.M. on the Secy. of the Interior and consult, and as soon after that as possible I shall go to the office & enter upon the duties. . . .

This new office will place me in a very unpleasant position in regard to many things, especially removals and appointments. The applicants are legion, & I do not know that I can remove many, if any. Mr. Wood, my predecessor, has "shelled out" nearly all that he found in, & left me the mere gleanings. I shall, however, try to do my duty faithfully.

Yesterday I sent to Mr. Fenton,[1] Chairman of the Com. of Claims of the Ho., my resignation of the Clerkship of that Committee.

1. Reuben Eaton Fenton (1819–1885), Republican congressman from New York, 1853–1855 and 1857–1864.

Sunday, September 8. Yesterday, from 8 A.M. to 9 P.M.[,] when I was where people could reach me, I was annoyed by applicants for office and I have not been free from them today, although they have sufficiently reverenced Sunday not to annoy me much. I had a long interview with the Secy. of the Interior, Hon. Caleb B. Smith,[1] yesterday, in which he gave me some excellent advice as to the conducting of the business of my office and avowed his determination of not interfering in the least with my appointments.

I was at the President's and saw Mrs. Lincoln & the President. Mrs. L. expressed her satisfaction at my appointment, and I hope and trust she & I shall get along quietly. I certainly shall do all in my power to oblige her and make her comfortable. She is evidently a smart, intelligent woman, & likes to have her own way pretty much. I was delighted with her independence & her ladylike reception of me. Afterwards I saw the President[,] & he received me very cordially. . . .

1. Caleb Blood Smith (1808–1864), former congressman from Indiana, was appointed Secretary of the Interior in 1861 and served until 1863, when he resigned to become U.S. judge for the District of Indiana.

Thursday, September 12. . . . Mary Ellen and Margaret went to Georgetown today to visit a sick friend, Mrs. Cissell,[1] who is very near her end with consumption. She has been sick three years. "Fading still fading"— what a disease it is, and how it has laid many of my dear ones in the tomb! My Mother, when I was only 18 months old; a beloved uncle (Prest. Brown of Dartmouth College)[;] two Aunts (his sisters)[;][2] a brother (Arthur)[;][3] a sister (Elizabeth)[;] my brother's wife (Anne, who was my wife's sister & very dear to me)[;] and my own dear, dear wife, all died of consumption! . . .

1. Mrs. Cissell's death was announced in the *Daily National Intelligencer,* September 16.
2. Nancy Brown Sweetser (d. 1799) and Lydia Brown Robie (d. 1811).
3. Arthur L. French (1806–1825) died while a student at Dartmouth.

Friday, September 13. . . . There never was so still a time in Washington, I do believe, as this is! Although soldiers by the 100,000 are about us, there is a stillness that is ominous. Just as I wrote the last word the President's carriage drove up to the door, he and Mrs. Lincoln being in it. He came in & we had a talk about the charges preferred vs. Watt, Stackpole, etc., at the White House.[1] I am to go up tomorrow at ½ past 8.

1. Charges of disloyalty had been made before the House Select Committee on Loyalty of Clerks, chaired by John F. Potter of Wisconsin. John Watt, head gardener at the White House under Presidents Pierce, Buchanan, and Lincoln, had also been suspected of petty corruption ever since he served under Commissioner of Public Buildings French in 1854, but he had held his position and was much in the favor of Mrs. Lincoln in 1861. He was finally removed from office in 1862 for his role in leaking part of Lincoln's first annual message to the press. Thomas Stackpole, doorkeeper of the President's office, survived despite similar accusations of disloyalty, but after becoming steward in 1863, he was removed in 1865 for other reasons.

Saturday, September 14. I went to the Capitol about 8 o'clock and then to the President's. Dan went with me and the President gave him an order for a pass to Alexandria. The President handed me the communication from Mr. Potter, of the special Committee of investigation, as to the loyalty of public officers, in which Maj. Watt, Mr. Stackpole & Edward McManus,[1] are all implicated. I read it over carefully, and Watt gave me testimony *per contra,* which, considering it goes to prove a negative, is very strong. I do not believe Watt guilty. As to the others[,] no rebutting testimony yet appears. I brought it all home with me & think I shall analyze it tomorrow as a matter of curiosity.

Returned to my office about 11, and from that time till 3 P.M. had not a moment to myself. Will this rush for office ever abate! At 3 came home to dinner and was annoyed from that time till ½ past 4 with applicants for office. At ½ past 4 Mrs. Russell, Mary Ellen & I rode down to the Congress Burying Ground to witness the removal of my poor dear wife's remains from the tomb to the grave. . . . Oh how sadly I felt, as I stood at that last home on earth of my dear one; and I thought[,] "Now indeed have I *an interest* in the soil of Washington"—that never can be taken from me, & it will not be long before kind friends will place me by her side. . . .

1. Edward McManus, who was also accused before the Potter committee, held his post as doorkeeper of the north entrance to the White House until French discharged him in 1865.

Tuesday, September 17. I rode over to the Insane Asylum on Sunday afternoon; Mary Ellen accompanied me. We were taken to the top of the main tower by Doct. Nichols, the gentlemanly Superintendent, and through a fine glass that he had could see Munson's Hill[1] so distinct as to see the horses move their tails in switching off the flies. While we were looking they[,] the rebels[,] raised their flag, which Doct. Nichols said had not been up for a week or more before. We looked about in all directions & saw what was going on about us, so far as erecting fortifications, etc., was concerned. . . .

1. Munson's Hill, near Bailey's Crossroads in northern Virginia, was skirted by the railroad line from Alexandria to Leesburg. The site was abandoned by the Confederates later in the month.

Sunday, September 22. . . . The troops are pouring into the city. I am told that 15 or 20,000 have arrived during the past week. Hundreds have passed my house this morning. I think the army within an hour's march of this city, & in it, can scarcely be less than 250,000 men. Something *must* occur in the way of battle soon.

Sunday, September 29. . . . The *Chronicle* of this morning announces the bloodless capture of "Munson's Hill" from the Rebels. The Supt. of the "Old Capitol Prison"[1] was just here and informs me that six prisoners are on their way to that place. He told me, what I did not before know, that the supervision of that Prison is under me as Commr.!

1. The Old Capitol Building was erected on 1st Street in 1815 for the use of Congress while the Capitol, which had been burned by the British, was being rebuilt. It was later used as a boardinghouse and then turned into a prison during the Civil War.

Saturday, October 5. . . . Yesterday we drove to the camp near Bladensburg accompanied by Mr. Tuck (who came Thursday evening) and three other gentlemen—they in a hack, M. E. & I in my buggy. I saw all the troops—the 2d N.H.[,] 12th Pa. and one or two other Regiments, all under the command of Gen. Hooker,[1] to whom I was introduced by my old friend Doct. L. V. Bell, Brigade surgeon. We staid and saw the afternoon drill and the sunset dress parade. I was very much pleased with Gen. Hooker and spent the afternoon very pleasantly. . . .

1. Joseph Hooker (1814–1879) had graduated from West Point, served in the Mexican War, and then retired before being appointed brigadier general of volunteers in the Army of the Potomac in 1861. He had full command of that army during the first half of 1863 but was defeated at Chancellorsville and replaced by George G. Meade before the Battle of Gettysburg.

Friday, October 18. . . . 9 o'clock A.M. I have been out, and at work. Last evening I dined at the President's. The party consisted of Gen. Anderson (of Fort Sumter fame)[,] Mr. Holt (formerly Secy. of War)[,] Mr. Clay (eldest son of Henry Clay)[,] Caleb B. Smith (Secy. of the Int.)[,] Mr. Shaw of Ky.[,] Gov. Sprague of R.I.[,] Mr. Speed of Ky. & myself.[1] The President & Mrs. Lincoln, of course. We sat down to the table about ½ past 5 & arose about ½ past 7. The President was in excellent spirits and we all seemed to enjoy ourselves. I sat between Mrs. Lincoln and Mr. Holt, & we carried on quite an interesting private conversation about many things. After dinner I sat at Gen. Anderson's side & was delighted to find how fully he recognized his Religious and Masonic obligations. He is a Royal Arch Mason, and intends to become a Knight Templar. He told me much about the bombardment of Fort Sumter. He regards the entire transaction there as Providential. He is a very modest man, and benevolence is as clearly marked on his countenance as if the word were written on his forehead. I enjoyed very much the entire visit. . . .

1. Robert Anderson (1805–1871) had been put in command of the forts in Charleston Harbor in November 1860. After the fall of Fort Sumter he took command of Union forces in his native Kentucky. Joseph Holt (1807–1894), Democrat from Kentucky, had been Secretary of War, 1860–1861. He supported the Union and was appointed judge advocate in 1862, and as judge advocate general he presided over the trial of Lincoln's assassins. Thomas H. Clay (second, not eldest, son of Henry Clay) was later named minister to Nicaragua and died in 1871. Mr. Shaw was probably Hiram Shaw of Lexington, Ky., for whom Thomas Clay was seeking an appointment as paymaster. William Sprague (1830–1915), wealthy Republican governor of Rhode Island, 1860–1863, accompanied a regiment from his state to Washington in 1861 and was elected senator in 1863. His marriage to Kate Chase (1840–1899), daughter of Secretary of the Treasury Salmon P. Chase and famous for her elaborate entertainments, was the social event of the winter of 1863–1864. James Speed (1812–1887), brother of Lincoln's close friend Joshua Speed, was a prominent lawyer who helped hold Kentucky in the Union. He was later Attorney General of the United States.

Sunday, October 27. . . . I was at the President's last evening, and took occasion to intercede as warmly as I could for Mrs. Hassler, who is now confined on account of her secession proclivities. She has doubtless been a very imprudent woman, but from a knowledge of her for 20 years, I do not believe it possible for her to be wicked or malicious. She is naturally volatile and merry and outspoken, but her heart has no guile, if I can read it aright. She is very smart and very witty, and *now* I think she has been sufficiently punished for any dereliction of patriotic duty of which she may have been guilty. The President promised me that he would speak to Mr. Seward about her, and ignored any knowledge of the cause of her arrest and confinement. I hope and trust she will soon be released. Her poor old mother called on me yesterday and made a most earnest appeal that I would do all I could in her daughter's behalf. I shall comply in earnest with her wishes.

Thursday, October 31. . . . Early yesterday morning I went to the President's—had an interview with him, and a very pleasant one—returned to my office, rode over the Eastern Branch to see what my workmen were doing, went to the Insane Asylum, & with Doct. Nichols & Mr. Forsyth,[1] the surveyor, who accompanied me over, walked out and examined a route for a change of the road, which change would be *a very great* improvement in the approach to the Asylum. . . .

1. William Forsyth, surveyor of the City of Washington.

Sunday, November 3. . . . Afternoon ½ past 2. Just after breakfast two or three thousand troops, with all their equipments on, passed here on their way towards the Navy Yard. I have since been told that 10,000 have gone down to Port Tobacco today in consequence of some demonstration of the rebels to cross the Potomac. . . .

The newspapers of yesterday contained the correspondence between Lt. Gen. Scott and the Secy. of War,[1] in which the "Old Hero" asks to be retired, and the order of the President granting his request. It all does honor to the three individuals. Ever since I can remember, the name of Winfield Scott has been in my mind the synonym of valor, honor, & military glory. For more than twenty years I have been personally acquainted with him, and I felt, on read[ing] his withdrawal from active duty, as if a calamity had befallen the Nation—and yet it seems to be a necessity, and it was so admirably done that I could but feel glad that, after so long a life of heroism, the good old man was to have a season of rest before he should leave a grateful people forever. The young hero, McClellan,[2] who fills his place, will doubtless fill it well, for he too is the soul of honor, gallantry and industry. He has already made his name a watchword, and his fame will increase with his years, unless his bravery overcomes his prudence and places him, as it did the generous & noble-hearted Lyon[3] and [Edward D.] Baker, a mark for rebel bullets. God grant he may long be preserved to his country. He is now our Hope and our Stay in this hour of peril! Oh this war—this war—wherein brother is pitted against brother, & friend against friend, and all for no earthly cause that can justify it. But it must be fought through to the bitter, bitter end, and God will defend the right!

1. Simon Cameron (1799–1889), of Pennsylvania, was still Secretary of War, but in January 1862 he was replaced by Edwin M. Stanton because of corruption in the awarding of war contracts.

2. George B. McClellan (1826–1885), who had taken command of the Army of the Potomac after the first Battle of Bull Run, replaced the aging Scott as general-in-chief of the Union armies on November 1, 1861. McClellan was removed from his command in November 1862 after his defeat in the Peninsular Campaign and his limited victory at Antietam.

3. Nathaniel Lyon (1818–1861) was killed in the battle of Wilson's Creek, Missouri, while leading Union forces fighting to keep Missouri in the Union.

Friday, November 8. Yesterday I was engaged much of the day on my official report. Went to the Interior Department at the Secretary's request and staid awhile on official business. Came home between two & three P.M.[,] dined, and then took M. E. & "Maimee" (little Mary) down to Mountjoy Hanson's[1] where Mrs. Margaret French was spending the day. Saw Mrs. Hassler, wife of F. A. Hassler, who has been imprisoned during the last ten weeks as a secessionist, and who was released a week ago last Tuesday. She was very glad to see me & profuse in her thanks for the trifling exertions I made for her release. She is a funny woman. Her husband had just returned from *his* home in N.Y. & he also thanked me. . . .

1. Possibly T. M. Hanson, who was active in Masonic affairs with French.

Sunday, November 10. . . . Mary Ellen went down from Church & came home about 10. After dinner she & I rode down—Willie French[1] with us—to the Congressional Cemetery & saw the new gravestone I have had erected at the head of my lost & loved one's grave. It is, I think, a beautiful stone. Marble on a granite base, and in elegant proportion. The inscription upon it is

> Mrs. Elizabeth S. French,
> Wife of B. B. French.
> Born in Groton, Mass. July 13, 1805.
> Died in Washington, May 6, 1861.
>
> And now thy smiles have passed away,
> For all the joys they gave,
> May sweetest dews and warmest ray,
> Lie on thy peaceful grave.

The stanza is from Doct. O. W. Holmes's poem entitled "A Metrical Essay," in which is embodied a description of Cambridge churchyard, among the finest, in my opinion, of the Author's poems, and they are all good. . . .

1. Son of Edmund French.

Wednesday, November 20. . . . Today there was a review of some sixty or seventy thousand troops by Major General McClellan, about ten miles from here. Mary Ellen & I went in the buggy. We left here about ½ past 9. On arriving at the Long Bridge we found it covered with carriages, & men on foot & horseback from one end to the other. We got into the line as soon as possible, & moved slowly about ½ way over, when Major Gen. McC. escorted by about *two miles* of cavalry passed us. All had to stop till they had passed across. Then came a parcel of baggage wagons from the other side, & we had to wait for them to pass, then a vessel came up and the draw was opened, & we had to wait for *that,* & so, after all sorts of delays, we got safely to the other side in one hour from the time of starting from this end. I say safely, but not damageless, for the back panel of my buggy was split by the pole of a hack. We joined the vast caravan of life which was moving onward in all sorts of ways toward the grand review. A portion of the road was good, but another portion was about as bad as any road I ever travelled over. At one place the clay was so deep that carriages went in halfway to the hubs of their wheels, and we passed one, stuck therein, as we went, and one as we returned. My stout old horse put us through "just as easy," & he did all his duty both ways. We arrived at the scene of review about ½ past 12. We could not get within a ¼ of a mile of the troops, the interval being filled with carriages [and] people on foot and on horseback who had arrived before us. We could see the paraded columns & some of the movements, & the smoke and sound of the saluting batteries of heavy cannon as McClellan passed around in reviewing were very *apparent* as well as *resonant,* for the smoke was visible & the sound almost deafening. As soon as the salutes were over we, thinking we had seen all that we cared to see, & dreading to be mixed with the returning crowd, set our faces homeward. We met thousands of people pressing toward the scene of review, and had very few to accompany us. We arrived home safe at 3 o'clock, pretty well tired out. . . .

Sunday, November 24. Mrs. Margaret, Mary Ellen & I went in the buggy, Darby driving, & Edmund & his son Harry, Henry Wells,[1] & Ben on foot, to the President's last evening to witness the performance of Mons. Hermann.[2] We arrived at 9 o'clock, & by ½ past 9 all the invited company had assembled—perhaps a hundred. Secretaries Seward, Cameron, Smith & Welles, were there, Generals Meigs & Porter, Com. Dahlgren, & many officers of lower rank whom I did not know, and some whom I did know.[3] There was quite a number of ladies, some handsome, some homely. The President looked natural & easy. He is Old Abe, & nothing else, place him where you will. Everybody that knows him loves him, I believe. Mrs. Lincoln looked remarkably well & would be taken for a young lady at a short distance. She is not very old, say 40 to 45. She seemed much at her ease, & strove to be very agreeable & was so.

The performance did not commence until toward eleven, when Hermann astonished his audience by some of the best slight [sic] of hand performances I ever saw, and I have seen a great many. . . .

1. Henry Wells, French's nephew, son of Catharine and P. P. Wells.

2. A "private exhibition" at the White House by Monsieur Hermann (or Herrmann), the "Great Prestidigitator," was mentioned in the *New York Times* of November 24, 1861. He had performed séances in magic at the opening of New York's Academy of Music in September 1861 and was considered the sensation of the hour.

3. Gideon Welles (1802–1878) of Connecticut, a former Jacksonian Democrat, was Secretary of the Navy, 1861–1869. Fitz-John Porter (1822–1901), brigadier general under

McClellan, took part in the Peninsular Campaign. He was cashiered in January 1863 following Second Bull Run. Commander John A. Dahlgren (1809–1870), inventor of the revolving turret guns used on the ironclad gunboat *Monitor*, took command of the Washington Navy Yard in 1861.

Sunday, December 8. Yesterday, from 1 o'clock till 3, I attended Mrs. Lincoln's first reception, officially. The President was present a portion of the time, and I had to introduce visitors to both. I got through the duties without any difficulty, although I very much dislike that part of my duty. I went in, however, to do all that may be required faithfully, and I intend to do it.

Yesterday was a busy day to me. I went to market with Mary Ellen, & then we went shopping. Got home about 11 o'clock. I went to the Capitol & about ½ past 11 Mrs. Lincoln's message came. I came home and dressed, & went to the President's. Got home about ½ past 4. Dined at 5 and felt about used up. . . .

Monday, December 16. . . . About 7 [Friday, December 13] Mrs. Lincoln sent down for me to go up and see her on urgent business. I could not go, of course, but sent word I would be up by 9 A.M. Saturday.[1] Although suffering with a severe headache I went & had an interview with her, and with the President, in relation to the overrunning of the appropriation for furnishing the house, which was done, by the law, "under the President." The money was actually expended by Mrs. Lincoln, & she was in much tribulation, the President declaring he would not approve the bills overrunning the $20,000 appropriated. Mrs. L. wanted me to see him & endeavour to persuade him to give his approval to the bills, but not to let him know that I had seen her! I accordingly saw him; but he was inexorable. He said it would stink in the land to have it said that an appropriation of $20,000 for furnishing the house had been overrun by the President when the poor freezing soldiers could not have blankets, & he *swore* he would never approve the bills for *flub dubs for that damned old house*! It was[,] he said[,] furnished well enough when they came— better than any house *they* had ever lived in—& rather than put his name to such a bill he would pay it out of his own pocket! So my mission did not succeed. It was not very pleasant to be sure, but a portion of it very amusing. Mrs. Lincoln was to have a reception in the afternoon, but on account of my headache insisted upon my not attending. . . .

1. French was entertaining company Friday evening.

Wednesday, December 18. I am a Grandfather! I recd. a Telegraphic despatch from Frank yesterday, informing me that his wife, Ellen, had given birth to a daughter. I wrote to him immediately, congratulating the young couple upon the happy event & requesting that the child might be named Elizabeth, & *called* Bess.[1] . . .

Last evening I attended, officially, the first public reception at the President's. It was a jam, & well might the President exclaim *jam satis*! My particular duty consisted in introducing the guests to Mrs. Lincoln, and I found it no sinecure. For two mortal hours a steady stream of humanity was passing on, & there *we* stood[,] I saying[,] "Mr. or Mrs. or General or Col. or Gov. or Judge, so & so, Mrs. Lincoln," & she curteseying [sic] and saying[,] "How do you do," & sometimes to a particular acquaintance, "I am glad to see you," & giving the tips of white-kidded fingers in token of that gladness. She bore herself well and bravely, & looked Queenly. At ½ past 10 the Band played "Yankee Doodle," & in 5 minutes the East room was deserted. I arrived home at 11. . . .

1. Elizabeth Richardson French (1861–1945). In 1892 she married an Englishman, Herbert F. Eaton (Lord Cheylesmore).

Sunday, December 22. . . . Saturday afternoon I attended Mrs. Lincoln's reception and introduced the callers. I like Mrs. L. better and better the more I see of her and think she is an admirable woman. She bears herself, in every particular, like a lady and, say what they may about her, I will defend her.

Notwithstanding all my efforts to do my duty as a public officer, to be honest in the discharge of every duty, to treat everybody with courtesy & kindness, an effort is making to defeat me in the Senate. Well let those who are traitors to me work, and if they can defeat me, let them do so. If they cannot[,] let them beware, for my eye is upon them, and they shall rue the day they undertook, without the least particle of cause, to assail me. . . .

Monday, December 23. . . . I had a long talk with Senators Clark and Grimes today, about the extravagance at the President's house. Gov. Grimes is peculiarly worked up about it.

Wednesday, December 25. . . . I have recd. as Christmas presents, from Mr. Forsyth a gallon of excellent brandy and a box of prime cigars. From Mary Ellen two silver labels for decanters, on which are engraved "Whiskey" & "Brandy." From Ben two silk pocket handkerchiefs, from Mrs. Russell a beautiful Prayer Book, & from Mrs. Adams, a Backgammon

Board. And so my Christmas of 1861 has passed away, and just at this moment it seems to me as if I little care whether I ever see another. . . .

My eyes are heavy. I am lonely & sad—sad—sad. "Is there no balm in Gilead and no physician there?" I think there is, & by & by the balm will come and the physician too, and I shall be healed. . . .

Wednesday, January 1. . . . I went to the President's at ½ past 10, & remained till 20 m. past 2. The reception was a very fine one. The Diplomatic Corps commenced coming before 11. Mr. & Mrs. Lincoln came down at about 10 m. past 11, & the reception of the Diplomats, The Supreme Court, & the Officers of the Army and Navy was elegant and imposing. Lord Lyons[1] was received with peculiar distinction, & seemed to be particularly pleased to be present. If this attendance today indicates anything, it indicates that our Government stands well with all Foreign Nations with which it is in amity. The crowd of people at the *public reception* was immense. . . .

1. Richard B. Pemell Lyons (1817–1887) was the British minister in Washington, 1858–1865.

Wednesday, January 8. . . . Last evening a reception at the President's. I was there officially to introduce "The American Queen" to her numerous and most brilliant visitors. I never have seen so elegant a reception, or one that went off better. Mrs. Lincoln in light silk, pearl headdress & ornaments, with a wrought lace scarf, or shawl, valued at $2,500! She was "got up" in excellent taste, and *looked* the Queen. Mr. Lincoln in plain black, and as kind & cordial as it is possible for a President to be. Everybody loves & respects him & deservedly, for he is one of the best men who ever lived, and the Union ought to prosper under his mild but firm & kindly rule. God bless him. . . .

Friday, January 10. . . . No fighting, or rumor of fighting[,] yet!

I was walking with Hon. Owen Lovejoy[1] day before yesterday, when we met a long train of cars going down Maryland Avenue loaded with timber, boards, scantling, etc., when he remarked very emphatically & sneeringly, "Winter Quarter—winter quarters." As much as to say, "There's to be no fighting, & we are cowards." . . .

1. Owen Lovejoy (1811–1864), Republican congressman from Illinois, 1857–1864.

Friday, January 17. Mr. Hubbard[1] left as he expected at 3 P.M. Sunday. Henry Wells left at 5 P.M. Tuesday[,] since which I have been without company in my house. Tuesday, Wednesday and yesterday I suffered much with stiff neck, soreness in my left shoulder, and headache. The two former days I did not go out of my house. Yesterday, although suffering the most excruciating pain in my head, most important business, relative to myself[,] demanded my presence before the Committee on Public Buildings and grounds of the Senate, before which is my nomination as Commissioner, & to whom the most damnably false charges have been made by two ingrates and liars whom I put in office 7 or 8 years ago, and removed since I entered on the duties of Commissioner under the present appointment—George W. Dant[2] & James H. Upperman.[3] For the past 3 months these scoundrels have done naught else than go about this City lying about me. They gave their entire budget of falsehoods to a Senator, Mr. Pomeroy[4] of Kansas, & he brought the charges before the Senate, which induced a recommitment of the nomination to the Committee, before which I was summoned to appear yesterday, and, notwithstanding one of the most severe headaches I ever had, I went over and heard the lies one after another as detailed by Mr. Pomeroy, with all patience, and then answered them in about ½ an hour's speech, as I think effectually. . . .

1. William B. Hubbard, of Columbus, Ohio, had been staying with French since January 1.
2. George W. Dant had been a messenger in the office of the commissioner of public buildings.
3. James H. Upperman was a gatekeeper at the Capitol during Pierce's administration. In 1863 he was a "tinner" on the Washington and Georgetown Railroad.
4. Samuel C. Pomeroy (1816–1891), one of the first two senators from Kansas, served 1861–1873.

Friday, January 24. . . . My daily life is somewhat monotonous. About 9 I go to my office & remain there, annoyed beyond measure by persons after office, or after *something*, constantly. I do not think I have been ten minutes alone in my office for ten days! At about ½ past 2 I come home, dine, and have some peace. Every Saturday from 1 to 3 P.M.[,] & every Tuesday from ½ past 8 to ½ past 10, I am required, as an official duty, to be at the President's to introduce visitors to Mrs. Lincoln. It is a terrible bore, but, as a duty[,] I *must* do it, and it leads to an acquaintance with very many celebrities of whom I should otherwise have no personal knowledge. . . .

Tuesday, January 28. . . . Mr. Hawkes,[1] Mr. Foot's Clerk, came over [on January 27] and informed me that I had been unanimously confirmed by the Senate. Now for the office borers!

1. Moses Hawkes, a Senate clerk for the committee on public buildings and grounds, was a neighbor of French's.

Sunday, February 2. It is ½ past 8 o'clock and a cool, pleasant morning. For the last half hour we have been watching two companies of 4th U.S. Infantry who were paraded directly in front of the house in full marching rig, where they were duly inspected. They appeared to be in perfect readiness for a move—knapsacks packed & cartridge boxes filled. After inspection they were marched back to their barracks just below here. Mary Ellen started for church and had to pass down the whole line between the soldiers and the fence—having about 18 inches space for hoops and all—the skirts of her garments brushed against the regimentals all the way, and no doubt gave those inside of them a thought of the dear ones at home. The sight of a pleasant female face has much inspiration to a soldier's heart, & the brushing of her robes against him must be a perfect luxury of inspiration!

> Daily, with souls that cringe & plot,
> We Sinais climb and know it not.

Perhaps Mary Ellen has climbed a Sinai with some of those poor soldiers this morning and knows it not!

The weather has been about as disagreeable for the past 3 or 4 weeks as need be. I do not remember ever to have experienced such mud anywhere as our streets have exhibited lately. An officer who came up from Sickles's Brigade day before yesterday told me that he absolutely *swam* his horse through the mud in the high road! There *could* be no military movements. Yesterday the weather cleared up, and there was frost last night, and this is a lovely, cool, bracing morning. One week of weather like this will enable our troops to move, and I have a strong premonition that as soon as a possible opportunity presents[,] something effective will be done. I hope we shall not suffer the 22d of February to be desecrated by the inauguration, at Richmond, of that Arch Traitor Jeff Davis, as President of the Traitor Confederacy! If I were Abraham Lincoln I would stop it or sacrifice the whole Army & Navy of the United States. I would test the great question of who is to rule these United States—the legitimate or bogus rulers!

Last Tuesday evening I attended the President's reception and introduced the sovereigns to Mrs. Lincoln. It was a great reception—such an one as I never saw before except on the 1st of January. It seemed to me as if there was to be no end to the crowd, and when I left at ¼ past 10 it was rushing on as fierce as ever. . . .

Yesterday I was at my office all the morning, and at Mrs. Lincoln's reception all the afternoon. The weather being rainy, & the walking awful, there was not a very large or very brilliant attendance. N. P. Willis, Mr. Sumner (Senator)[,] Mr. Stark of Oregon (appointed Senator in place of Baker but not yet admitted)[,] Miss Seward, *without any hoops on,* and other celebrities graced the occasion.[1] Mrs. Don Piatt (Belle Smith of the Newspapers)[2] came before Mrs. Lincoln made her appearance, to see her privately, & I had ½ an hour's very pleasant chat with the elegant, beautiful, and accomplished lady. . . .

1. Nathaniel P. Willis (1806–1867), editor and author, was associated with New York's *Home Journal* at this time. Benjamin Stark (1820–1898), Democrat, served only from October 1861 to September 1862. Frances Adeline (Fanny) Seward (1844–1866), daughter of Secretary of State William H. Seward.

2. Louise Kirby Piatt (1826–1864) married the journalist and editor Donn Piatt in 1847. The two contributed to various newspapers, and some of Mrs. Piatt's writings were gathered and published as *Bell Smith Abroad* in 1855.

Saturday, February 15. The drum is beating, the snow is falling, and it is 7 o'clock. . . .

I was at the War Dept. & saw the Secy. and his Assistants yesterday, and did some business with the Secy. (Mr. Stanton).[1] He is prompt, energetic, and decided—the very man for the place. While there Gov. Fish[2] and Mr. Ames,[3] the Envoys of Mercy to Secessia, returned. The Traitors & Rebels refused to permit them to perform their charitable mission, and they returned with the coin entrusted to their care that would have relieved many a worn and weary prisoner. May God deal with the Traitors in their hour of need, as they have dealt with the prisoners they have taken!

After finishing my business at the War Department I went to the Treasury, and then to the President's, & then back to my office, where I remained till nearly 3, & then I came home. . . .

1. Edwin M. Stanton (1814–1869), of Ohio, served as Attorney General under Buchanan, 1860–1861. He replaced Cameron as Secretary of War and served under Presidents Lincoln and Johnson until 1868.

2. Hamilton Fish (1808–1893), governor of New York, 1849–1850, moved from Whig to Republican during his term as U.S. senator, 1851–1857. In February 1862, Fish was serving as a commissioner for the relief of prisoners.

3. Edward R. Ames (1806–1897), Methodist bishop, was also a commissioner.

Sunday, February 23. The past week has been a very busy one to me, and perhaps I may say an eventful one for my entire future in this world may hinge upon a single hour of the latter part of it.

The Nation has been wonderfully excited, & Washington has, of course, been in a tumult. The news of victory after victory over the rebels has come and over them we have all rejoiced, and appearances indicate that the game of secession is nearly played out.[1] The Southern press is despondent, and every prestige of success is now with the Union-loving portion of the people.

Early in the week Congress ordered the Commissioner of Public Buildings to illuminate all the public buildings on the evening of the 22d. They had previously ordered a celebration of the day by the reading, in the Hall of the House of Representatives, of Washington's Farewell Address in the presence of the two Houses, the Supreme Court, the President and his cabinet, the officers of the Army & Navy and such citizens *as could get in to hear it.* My entire time, after the illumination order passed, was devoted to preparation for it. Thursday afternoon [February 20] Willie Lincoln,[2] the second son of the President, died, and the illumination was, on that account, postponed. The other order was carried out yesterday, & such a multitude as thronged the Capitol I have never, or seldom, seen. I hardly think I ever saw so many inside of it at one time. Among my duties was that of seeing that order was preserved, and a very hard & exciting duty I found it. It was, however[,] performed, and all went off well. Col. Forney read the Address and, although there were but very few in that immense audience who had not read it many times, it was listened to with a silence and a decorum worthy the solemn and grand and imposing occasion. I am inclined to think that almost every Senator & Representative, all the Heads of Department[,] & all the Judges of the Supreme Court[,] except Ch. Justice Taney,[3] were present—a very large number of the high officers of the Army and Navy in full uniform, a great many citizens who recd. invitations, the Diplomatic Corps, the officers & attendants of both Houses[,] & a pretty good sprinkling of ladies were on the floor of the House—and the galleries were crammed to suffocation, while thousands upon thousands were outside who could not get in anywhere. I think everybody was impressed with the idea that we had a Government still.

The President, in consequence of his family affliction, was not present. . . .

1. French and the North were unduly excited by the capture of Fort Henry and Fort Donelson in Tennessee and by Lincoln's war order setting February 22 for the start of a great Union offensive.
2. William Wallace Lincoln (1850–1862) died of typhoid fever.

3. Roger B. Taney (1777–1864), Democrat from Maryland, was Chief Justice of the United States, 1835–1864. He gave the majority opinion in the Dred Scott case.

Sunday, March 2. . . . One week ago this morning I wrote herein. What have I been doing since?

On Sunday [February 23] Senator Browning[1] of Illinois called and told me it was the desire of the President & Mrs. Lincoln that I should take the entire charge of the funeral arrangements at the White House on the succeeding day, which I promised to do. . . .

Monday [February 24], as soon as I had eaten breakfast, I went to the President's. I found everything properly arranged for the funeral. The body of little Willie lay in the green room, in the lower shell of a metallic coffin, clothed in the habiliments of life, and covered with beautiful flowers.

After looking about the house for a while I walked up into the President's office and read. He came up after I had been there about ½ an hour and appeared quite calm and composed. He talked about his family and about the war. The servant came in and told him "Tad" (Thomas[,] his youngest son)[2] desired to see him. He left immediately for his son's room. Gov. Seward came in, and soon after the President returned. I was sent for to go down and see someone about further preparation & did so. I did not see Mrs. Lincoln at all. About noon, The President, Mrs. Lincoln & Robert[3] came down and visited the lost & loved one for the last time, together. They desired that there should be no spectator of their last sad moments in that house with their dead child & brother. They remained nearly ½ an hour. While they were thus engaged there came one of the heaviest storms of rain & wind that has visited this city for years, and the terrible storm without seemed almost in unison with the storm of grief within, for Mrs. Lincoln, I was told, was terribly affected at her loss and almost refused to be comforted. At two o'clock all were assembled in the East Room. The President & Robert, all the Cabinet officers; Gen. McClellan; the entire Illinois delegation in Congress; Vice President and Mrs. Hamlin,[4] and a large attendance of persons in official positions, and citizens. Doctors P. D. Gurley[5] & John C. Smith, conducted the services with great solemnity and propriety and then, followed by a procession in carriages about ½ a mile long, the body was borne to Oak Hill cemetery in Georgetown and temporarily deposited in the tomb of the Chapel, finally to be removed to Illinois. I returned to the President's, and then home, where I arrived about 5 P.M. So passed Monday. . . .

1. Orville H. Browning (1806–1881), Republican from Illinois, was appointed to succeed Stephen A. Douglas in the U.S. Senate in 1861 and served until 1863. His published

diary covering the years 1850–1881 contains a record of important conversations with Lincoln.

2. Thomas ("Tad") Lincoln (1853–1871).

3. Robert T. Lincoln (1843–1926) attended Phillips Exeter Academy, graduated from Harvard in 1864, and served on the staff of General Grant. The only Lincoln child to survive both of his parents, he was later Secretary of War and president of the Pullman Car Company.

4. Ellen Emery Hamlin, second wife of Lincoln's vice president, Hannibal Hamlin.

5. Phineas D. Gurley, pastor of the New York Avenue Presbyterian Church.

Sunday, March 9. . . . I have been looking over my last year's record of "about these times." I perceive my ideas in relation to the treatment of the rebellion were different then from what they now are. Up to "Sumter" I was in favor of letting the Southerners, who desired it, go. I was for peace. I dreaded the terrible issue of war & bloodshed. The rebels had their own election—they elected war—they began it—and now, as the old song goes—

> If they still advance,
> Friendly caution slighting,
> They may get, by chance,
> A belly full of fighting!

"Let the dead Past bury its dead." My business now is with the *Present*. And what of the Present? In the week that has gone by since my last writing what? Of my private life all I can say is, I am one week nearer to the grave. I do not think of a single act of my own worthy of a record. Gen. Lander[1] died—his remains were brought to this city and, with all the pomp and circumstance of *glorious* war, they were conveyed from Secretary Chase's residence to the R.R. Depot and thence sent to his native town in Massachusetts where they are to rest. Another of the braves of our Country sacrificed to that damnable ambition of the Rebel leaders to rule or ruin! I only knew Lander casually, having been once introduced to him, and had a conversation of perhaps half an hour. He was a noble specimen of mankind. Tall, admirably formed, noble in all his aspirations, and fearless as if he had been made of bronze. He was a man to be depended on, and his loss is one that will be most sensibly felt.

Mary Ellen, Helen, & I viewed the vast procession from the Capitol during its march from the upper end of Pa. Avenue till the remains were carried into the Depot. It was solemn, grand, and imposing. I went to Secretary Chase's house but was too late to look upon the face of the dead, the coffin having been closed before my arrival.

We are now biding *a time*. The newspapers are not permitted to publish much war news, and all we can do is to guess what will come next. A gentleman told me yesterday that by Saturday next our troops would be in possession of Richmond. I hope it may be so, but it has been said so long and so many times that I hardly credit it, though there is evidently great preparation making for a general movement of our Army on the Potomac. The 4th U.S. Infantry is "hutted" within a stone's throw East of my house, and they have been all ready to move for several days, and will doubtless disappear from this encampment today or tomorrow. That a heavy blow is to be struck no one can doubt, and, *if successful,* it will break up rebellion in Virginia. If not successful, God only knows what the effect will be—but I do not mean to tolerate the idea of a *failure.* . . .

1. Frederick W. Lander (1821–1862), who had taken part in several important exploring expeditions in the West, died of illness while in command of Union troops in western Virginia. His wife, Jean Margaret Lander, was one of America's foremost actresses.

Monday, March 10. . . . I think the 4th Infantry, encamped just below here, are preparing to move this morning. They have just hurraed, and now there is a pounding going on as if something uncommon was taking place.

As I cannot write, *even here,* what is now most in my thoughts, and before which all else gives place, for it involves the happiness or the utter misery of my future life in this world, I will close my book.

Sunday, March 16. . . . The soldiers all left last Monday, and such a moving as this city presented the eye of man has seldom seen. They all went over the river to fight, but they could find no enemy! and so they are pushing on South in search of one! . . .

We have had all sorts of stories for the week past. McClellan has been vilified and glorified, and many doubt very much which "fied" of the two best applies. It does seem to me as if there had been *laches* somewhere. Caution is a good thing, especially in such sinners as the rebels are! But when it comes to being stopped entirely for months & months, by a little mud—or even a good deal of mud—it seems to go one step beyond caution, and gets into the neighborhood of *Fear.* When the mud is too deep for our troops to *march,* it is passing strange that the enemy should not find it too deep to *run!* There are various stories about our vast overestimate of their force—about "quaker" guns[1] mounted on their ramparts, etc.

I am slow to believe anything not official, and do not believe one-half of the stories that are told to prejudice McClellan. I never worshipped the man as some have, but I did believe in him and, until he has had his "great go" & failed, I won't give him up.

The stirring times in Hampton Roads last Saturday & Sunday rather stirred us up here for two or three days. When we look at it in the most favorable light possible[,] it was a sad affair. At least 200 of our brave men were sent to "Davy Jones's locker" at one fell swoop of what was once our eagle of the seas—now changed, alas, in consequence of our own folly, into a poor beast of a rebel ram—*but,* yes, *butt,* he can, as the *Cumberland* and *Congress* found to *their* cost, and considerably to the cost of this Government. Had it not been for the Providential arrival of the tough little *Monitor* God only knows what the result would have been. All praise to Capt. Erricson.[2] . . .

1. A dummy gun or cannon, so named because of the opposition of the Quakers to war.

2. John Ericsson (1803–1889), Swedish inventor of the screw propellor and builder of the ironclad *Monitor.* He came to the United States in 1839. There was great consternation in Washington when the ironclad *Merrimac* destroyed both the *Cumberland* and the *Congress* in Hampton Roads on March 8, 1862, but fears were eased the next day when the *Monitor* battled the *Merrimac* to a draw and forced it to withdraw.

Sunday, March 23. Another week and nothing special in my horoscope, *that I know of.* . . .

Yesterday the monotony was a little broken by a visit early in the morning to the President's, when I had quite a long, and quite a satisfactory interview with the President & Mrs. Lincoln, it being the first time I have seen either since poor Willie was buried. The President looks & appears careworn. Mrs. L. looks distressed & pale, but as if she would in time get over her sad bereavement. She feels it very much and wept bitterly yesterday while talking of her loss. . . .

Saturday, March 29. . . . At least 100,000 men have gone down the Potomac during the week or two past, no one *outside* knows whither, but we all suspect they will be heard from in the vicinity of Richmond ere long. Since the *Merrimack* came out "on the rampage" three weeks ago, and was sent back into Norfolk like a whipped hound with his tail between his hind legs, the rebels have not dared to send her out. When she again makes her appearance in Hampton Roads, I prophecy, from what I have heard, that she will be made as short work of as she made of the *Cumberland* and *Congress*. She will find more than one *ugly customer* to deal with. The next week must be full of events, it ought to settle the question of Union or Disunion, and I hope and trust that if it does settle it it will be Union forever!

Sunday, April 6. . . . That "forward movement," that "onward to Richmond" that we all expected last Sunday has not yet taken place that we know of. Everything relating to the war is now done so privately that I should not be much surprised if Richmond & New Orleans, and a few other large cities[,] should be *privately* captured & we common folks know nothing about it! *I* have, however, been let partially into some of the state secrets, far enough to induce me to think that not over two days more will elapse before we shall hear of something that will wake us all up. May it be Victory or Death—no backing out. One week may crush out the damnable rebellion! and when it is crushed out I do hope the Government will have nerve enough to hang all the "head devils" that they can catch.

Arthur L. Chase,[1] my sister Sarah's son, is now here. He has been a soldier for seven months in a New York Cavalry Regiment, which has been kept all that time *horseless* and idle, and is just disbanded. It has probably cost the Govt. somewhere in the neighborhood of $200,000, and done nothing! "And that's the way the money goes." What a Government this is to throw away money! Millions upon millions have been wasted since this rebellion broke out, and millions more will be wasted before it is closed. . . .

Yesterday I saw the President and had a long and very pleasant interview with him.

1. Arthur L. Chase, the youngest son of Sarah and Samuel Chase, died while in service in 1864.

Sunday, April 20. . . . The week past has not been one of great military doings & events, so far as we outsiders have learned. McClellan, with a large army, is near Yorktown, Va.[,] & Franklin,[1] with quite a force, has gone down to aid him, while McDowell and Banks are *doing something* on the opposite side of the Potomac. McDowell has made a demonstration down at Fredericksburg, & the Rebels have run across the bridge there and burnt it. I suppose our troops will follow as soon as they can repair the bridge. At Fort Monroe & thereabouts matters have been, seemingly, quiet. Something stirring must occur ere long.

My own week has been rather a pleasant, though a somewhat tame[,] one. Monday I was at the Departments, the President's, etc., I believe. Mr. Stevens introduced me to Mr. Brown, who amuses the world under the *"nom de plume"* of "Artemas Ward."[2] He lectured at Willard's Hall that evening, and I was invited to be present, but I got too much tired during the day, so Helen went with Mr. Stevens, and was very much amused. She gave us an account of the lecture on her return.

Tuesday I was at my office all day, and in the evening had Doct. Brod-head, Wharton Meehan, and Thos. M. Smith[3] here to play Euchre, and in order to inaugurate Meehan's book on Euchre, just published "at some little cost," at 9 o'clock we, with the ladies (Mary Ellen and Helen)[,] sat down to one of the best oyster suppers I ever ate part of, prepared by Mary Ellen. We did it ample justice both in eating and in language, as it deserved—"God bless *my* Queen!" . . . Friday at the President's all the morning arranging for the sale of some old furniture. . . .

1. William Buel Franklin (1823–1903) successfully commanded a corps of the Army of the Potomac in the Peninsular Campaign and the Battle of Antietam but was held partly responsible for the Union defeat at Fredericksburg.
2. Charles Farrar Browne (1834–1867), American humorist, wrote under the pseudonym Artemus Ward.
3. Thomas M. Smith, of New Hampshire and Indiana, chief clerk in the fifth auditor's office, Treasury Department.

Sunday, April 27. . . . Arose yesterday morning early and attended to some little matters about the house, then went to my office. From there walked up to the office of Gen. Wadsworth,[1] Military Governor of the Dist. of Col. On my way up my brother Edmund overtook me & we walked on together. We broached a subject of conversation never before alluded to between us, and had quite a talk. It was of domestic purport, deeply interesting to us both and to our families, in which some disagreement of opinion has existed. We talked plainly and strongly, but, thank God, good naturedly, and my belief is that a result will follow that conversation that will be, in the end, most satisfactory to all concerned. . . .[2]

I walked to Gen. Wadsworth's, transacted business with him and found him a perfect gentleman. . . .

. . . Edmund and I walked down to the Congressional burying ground [later in the afternoon], where I stood at the last earthly resting place of the loved one who was "all the world to me." . . .

Oh how much I have thought of *her* recently, and, although my living affections are given in all their intensity to a living woman, they are only given to her because I regard her as the very similitude of the one who has gone, and it seems to me as if in loving the living presence I was also loving the departed Angel!

After roaming about the burying ground for a time, we returned to Edmund's, where Edmund, M. E. & myself had a conversation interesting us alone. I mention the fact here that, if need be, I can hereafter recall the time. . . .

1. James Samuel Wadsworth (1807–1864) was later killed in the Battle of the Wilderness.

2. French's brother, who opposed the marriage of Benjamin and Mary Ellen, was apparently relenting.

Wednesday, April 30. . . . She [Mary Ellen] intends leaving me in a month to spend the summer in New England—what shall I do? If her absence from the house a single night deprives me of my rest, what may I expect from her absence a whole summer! My heart & soul are set upon her, & she is cruel to think more of the world's opinion than of my comfort & happiness! *Miserable me.*

Friday, May 2. . . . Day before yester The Secretary of the Interior (Mr. Smith)[,] Mr. Walter the Architect,[1] and I went all over the Capitol extension, making a thorough examination to see what is necessary to be done to *preserve* the building, as the law provides. We also went on the dome. Spent something over two hours in our *reconnoisance* [sic]. . . .

1. Thomas Ustick Walter (1804–1887) was in charge of the extension of the U.S. Capitol from 1851 to 1865, during which time the wings were added and the dome completed.

Sunday, May 4. . . . I went to the President's about noon, desiring to see him. Cabinet in session. I remained alone in the private Secretary's room perhaps an hour and was not a little amused at hearing vociferous laughter in the President's room as if the "grave and reverend Signors" were having a precious good time. I saw the President, did my errand, and came home. . . .

I invited [Mary Ellen] to accompany me to Mount Vernon yesterday, and she agreed to go. So, at about 8 yesterday morning I walked down, and she returned with me, and she, Helen, Doct. Barker, Mr. Cook & myself, went down in the *Thos. Colyer*, with about 150 others. The day was as perfect as possible[,] and we enjoyed the trip vastly. At Mount Vernon the party roamed over the grounds *ad libitum* for an hour and a half. Mary Ellen and I went with many others into the chamber where Washington died. It is a small[,] low room, with two doors leading from it into small rooms or closets besides the door of entrance. In one corner stood an old-fashioned[,] high-posted mahogany bedstead with common wooden slats across it, which looked to me as if they were new. The room contained nothing else and looked dismal and bare and comfortless enough. . . . We went through the house—or so much of it as was open— and "a Godforsaken" looking place it is. The only appearance of comfort we saw was in the old kitchen which M. E. & I visited and where we found a handsome, fat negro woman sitting at the side of an ancient table, preparing vegetables for cooking. The table was undoubtedly a relic of the days of Washington, as it looked a hundred years old. It is about 6 feet long, by about 3 wide. Is more like a rough high-post single bedstead than a table, the posts forming not only the legs, but projecting upward 3 or 4 feet, and the table, formed of thick plank, worn by use into deep creases, being at the height of an ordinary table, somewhat in this form and proportion.[1]

The woman told us she had been there but a short time, and came from Washington. The floor of the kitchen was of brick, and the cooking was done by the aid of a common cooking stove, very like, as M. E. remarked, the one in my kitchen, evidently made since Washington died! I could not but think how many a roaring time of merriment that kitchen had seen when the walls probably resounded to the thrumming of the banjo accompanyment to some nigger voice, while perhaps some "Ole Virginny neber tire" footsteps rattled over those very bricks in a regular plantation breakdown, while the "cha-cha-cha" of the ebony spectators applauded the performance, and, mayhap[,] even the stately form and composed eye of the Great General was there to enjoy the merriment, for there is not, and never has been in this world a human nature so restrained or a human form so stiff and so dignified, that the one could not be melted & the other bent by the unsophisticated merriment of a happy assembly of negroes, every aspiration of whose souls, and every fibre of whose bodies[,] indicate unmitigated joy. The thought passed, & we left to see other things. . . .

1. French drew a small sketch of the table at this place in his journal.

Wednesday, May 7. . . . One year ago yesterday my blessed wife became a saint in Heaven. I tried to devote yesterday to her memory. About noon Mary Ellen & I rode down to her grave & carried with us such flowers a[s] could be gathered from my garden, and placed them on the sod that covers her dear remains. . . .

Thursday, May 8. . . . Last evening I attended a ward meeting to nominate candidates for city offices for the June election. It was quite a full meeting, but I did not exactly fancy its manner and action & do not believe I will ever attend another. It is too much of a farce, for my experience is that no one seems to feel at all bound by the doings of such a meeting.

McClellan seems to be doing his whole duty now. He is making the rebels skip down on the Peninsula between York & James River, and I think, now, the rebellion is on its last legs. McClellan has been shamefully abused, but I have never lost faith in him. I have believed him, ever since Scott retired, the master spirit of the War, and he is now proving himself so, or, at any rate, the successes under his masterly plans are proving him so. Hurra for George B. McClellan! . . .

Saturday, May 10. . . . Yesterday I was at the President's—he is still at Fort Monroe [Old Point Comfort, Virginia]. I then went to the Department of the Interior, and then swapped buggies with the McDermotts,[1] am to give $100 to boot. Then returned to my office and remained till 3 P.M. Came home and dined, took a nap, and in the evening went with Mary Ellen & Helen to the opera at Grover's Theatre[2]—the old National. *The Barber of Seville* was the performance, and Gottschalk[3] gave us some exquisite pianoforte playing. I was never so well pleased with an operatic performance. . . .

Mancusi[4] as Figaro, was admirable. Madame D'Angri[5] did not come up to my idea of a Prima Donna especially after hearing Parodi. But I came away satisfied. . . .

1. The McDermott family had a coach factory (John McDermott & Bros.) at 455 Pennsylvania Ave.
2. Leonard Grover was the proprietor of this theater. At this time it was located at 14th and E streets.
3. Louis Moreau Gottschalk (1829–1869), American pianist and composer.
4. Mancusi had been performing in various theaters in New York City since the fall of 1861 and was often on musical programs with Gottschalk.
5. Elena D'Angri made her first musical appearance in New York City in 1856 with the pianist-composer Sigismund Thalberg. A contralto, she was called "a superb artist."

Sunday, May 18. . . . In the afternoon [of May 11] I took Senator Foot in my buggy and in Company with Mayor Wallach, Caleb B. Smith, Secy. of the Interior, Senators Grimes and Morrill,[1] (they in a carriage) went to the Insane Asylum. We had a pleasant ride and a pleasant visit. Doct. Nichols, the gentlemanly and admirable Superintendent, showed us all over the building and premises, and everything was in such perfect order and so neat that all were delighted with the visit. . . .

1. Lot M. Morrill (1813–1883), Republican of Maine, was one of three Morrills in Congress at the time. Another was his brother, Anson P. Morrill, of Maine, and the third was Justin S. Morrill, of Vermont. Lot Morrill was a senator, 1861–1869 and 1869–1876; and Secretary of the Treasury, 1876–1877.

Wednesday, May 21. . . . At about 2 A.M. [May 20] Mary Ellen awoke me out of as sound a sleep as possible by saying[,] "The shop is on fire!" I was out of bed in an instant and putting on only a pair of pantaloons and slippers, I was out in, say[,] two minutes. The building was so completely in flames that I saw it would be useless to do more than endeavour to save the contiguous buildings—my coalhouse, woodhouse, etc. So I got out the hose[,] coupled it on to the hydrant, and in 5 minutes had a stream of water on to the coalhouse—just in time to save it. My shop, tools, and quite a quantity of lumber were burned. It caught in the second story, but how[,] no one can tell. I cannot think it was set on fire by an incendiary, although it may have been. My opinion is that matches had carelessly been left in the chamber, & that the mice in some way set them on fire. The loss was about $150. . . .

At 3 Mary Ellen and I rode up in the Capitol Extension carryall to see a match game of baseball played by the National & Jefferson clubs. We staid till about 5, saw that the National were likely to beat, & then came home. In the evening I prepared an address for the presentation of a flag at 5 P.M. today, which I am to make in behalf of some ladies to the Second Regiment of Dist. Volunteers, calling themselves "The President's guard." . . .

On Saturday last [May 17] I recd. the appointment of Disbursing Agent of the Capitol Extension and New Dome and gave a bond in the penal sum of $40,000. . . .

Tuesday, May 27. What a stirring day I have had. I did not get up in my usual good season, it being ¼ to 7 when I got out of bed. On coming down I found a note from one of the drawkeepers on the Long Bridge informing me that a locomotive had broken down a portion of the bridge so that the draw could not be opened, and no passing could take place. As soon as I eat my breakfast I went to the Capitol, had the carriage brought to the door and went to the Bridge. Found it badly broken—a locomotive[,] having crushed through the upper planking, rested on the trestles—it being at a place where the bridge had been planked on some cross joist, to raise it to form an inclined plane. It had been done under Military supervision, and miserably done too. Saw Col. McCallum,[1] the Military Supt. of Railroads, and he promised to have it put in repair at once. Returned to the Capitol, where I staid awhile, then went to the Interior Department, saw the Secy. & did, perhaps, half an hour's business with him. Returned to my office, then went up to the Architect's office in the 3d story of the Capitol. He made his report as to the necessary work on the Extension, and I wrote to the Secy. of the Interior and enclosed it. Down to my office & wrote a letter to Mr. Train[,][2] Chn. Com. of P. B. & G. of the House, and a Resolution relative to painting dome. While writing them, news came of all sorts of disasters to the Union army. I believed not a word of it and went on with my business. Saw Mr. Train & gave him my letter and resolution. . . .

1. Daniel Craig McCallum (1815–1878), engineer and authority on the construction of railway bridges, had been appointed military director and superintendent of railroads by Secretary of War Stanton in February 1862. He was made a major general in March 1865.
2. Charles R. Train (1817–1885), Republican congressman from Massachusetts, 1859–1863, was later aide-de-camp to General McClellan.

Sunday, June 1. . . . Wednesday afternoon [May 28] I rode out to Clark Mills's place with the Secy. of the Interior, Mrs. Smith,[1] Mr. Walter, and Mr. Mills. It was rather a funny *cavalcade*. The Secy.[,] Mrs. S. and Mr. Walter in Mr. Smith's carriage—Mills in his own carriage with two horses and a servant in livery to drive. I in my own buggy, alone. Our object was to inspect and accept the bronze statue of Freedom that Mills had been casting for the dome of the Capitol. It is a magnificent figure and exceedingly well done. The Secy. accepted it, and it is to be brought in and placed in the Eastern park. Mills rode a part of the way back with me and called at my house[,] & we took a drink together. It might have been water, but it was not! . . .

1. Mrs. Caleb Blood Smith.

Sunday, June 8. This is the last day Mary Ellen is to be in my house for a time. She, with Margaret and her five children, expect to leave at 6 A.M. tomorrow to spend the Summer in New England. I shall miss Mary Ellen very much, but she deems it a necessity, and I will submit with [as] good a grace as possible. According to her notions, if I am ever to call her my own there must be a separation for a time, and the sooner one commences, the sooner can the other happen. . . .

On Friday I took M. E. in the buggy, and we visited the Convent at Georgetown, where Mary Ellen has a cousin—her Mother's sister's child[,] "Sister Blondine,"[1] to whom I was introduced, and with whom I shook hands through the lattice work. . . .

1. Sister Mary Blandina Brown, VHM (d. 1882). Sister Blandina was an "Out Sister," not as strictly cloistered as most in her convent. She taught music and was especially proficient on the harp.

Monday, June 16. . . . As soon as I got my breakfast I went to my office, then to the Dept. of the Interior, then to the President's where I saw the President and Mrs. Lincoln. She was just going out to her summer home[1] and gave me a very strong invitation to visit her out there, which I shall certainly do. She seemed to be in excellent spirits, and delighted at getting out of the city. . . .

1. The so-called "summer White House" was a stone cottage on the grounds of the U.S. Soldiers' Home, north of the city. The Lincolns spent much of the summer and autumn there, 1862–1864.

Monday, June 30. . . . Saturday at 8 A.M. with quite a party, I went up the river to the Great Falls. We left the city in omnibusses and carriages and rode as far as "Cabin John" Bridge, which is a famous structure to carry the aqueduct across the creek of the same name. I believe it is the longest span in the world. It is a great work and does Gen. M. C. Meigs, under whose supervision it was constructed, infinite credit.[1] From that place to the Great Falls, we went in a canal boat. The party consisted of between 20 & 30. . . .

We arrived at the Great Falls about 2, looked about, and sweltered, for the weather was very hot. There was plenty of liquor on board the boat when we started[,] much of which went on shore *inside the human skins,* and I have seldom seen a merrier party. After running about & frolicking for two or three hours, we started on our return and dined on board. We had an excellent cold collation, plenty of champagne and ice water. The boat *would not* keep in the middle of the canal but kept constantly running against the bank—either the helmsman or the Boat was evidently a little corned. . . .

Monday 5 P.M.

I went to the Capitol about 9. Was engaged all the morning examining testimony on charges made by Mr. Henshaw against Nathan Darling.[2] It was an exceedingly unpleasant business. I got through at one and then went to the Deaf and Dumb and Blind Asylum at Kendall Green, as one of the Committee of Examinations, to examine the pupils. I dined there and remained till 4 P.M. I only saw the Blind examined, but was much interested. . . .

1. Cabin John Bridge, designed by Meigs and completed in 1861, was the longest masonry single-arch bridge in the world and remained so for years to come.
2. Nathan Darling, captain of the Capitol police, in the office of the commissioner of public buildings, had arrested two persons during a commotion in the lobby of the gallery of the House of Representatives on February 22, 1862. He was charged with assault, pleaded guilty in the June term of the criminal court, and fined. Lincoln remitted the fine and pardoned Darling on February 18, 1863.

Friday, July 4. . . . I have been looking over my journal and am considerably amused to find how long we have all been expecting that Rich-

mond would be taken! And now the doings of the past week have driven
back our immense army from within 4 miles of Richmond to 20! The
loss of life has been immense. Our generals call it a strategic movement
of McClellan to obtain a better base of operations! Two or three such
strategic movements would annihilate our army. Our soldiers have,
doubtless, fought gloriously, but they have been overwhelmed and driven
back by numbers—of that I think there can be no doubt, and I now
almost despair of our ever taking Richmond. . . .

Brooklyn, Monday, July 7. In accordance with an order from the Secy.
of the Interior I left Washington day before yesterday evening at 5 o'clock
to visit, first, the iron foundry in N. York, where the iron work of the
new Dome of the Capitol is cast, and, second, the marble quarries at
Lee, Mass.[,] where the marble for the Capitol Extension is got out. We
desire to know how the work at both places is progressing. With my
friend Hon. Amos Tuck, who had been at my house a week, I took the
cars at Washington. We took sleeping berths. While crossing the river at
Havre de Grace the sleeping preparations were made and soon after we
left the river we went to bed. I never slept as well in the cars before.
Indeed, I had a very tolerable night's sleep. . . .

There were with us in the cars many wounded officers & soldiers from
McClellan's army. In the car with me were three officers, two of them
captains. One shot through the leg below the knee, and one through the
arm, and one in the neck. They all expressed the greatest confidence
and enthusiasm in McClellan. They think he managed his forces admirably, & were exceedingly indignant that he was not reinforced. One of
them told me his army was perfectly safe now, that no force that the
rebels could send could overcome it, and he added, "As soon as he is
decently reinforced he will take Richmond." At Baltimore three fine-
looking gentlemen came on board, one of whom seemed to be dreadfully
excited. I soon found that he was from New Jersey, and that his only
son had been killed in the recent battles. He[,] with his two friends, had
come on to get the remains, but, in consequence of a military order, they
could not be permitted to visit the battlefields. The man's name was
Danforth,[1] one of the great car builders of New Jersey, and a man of
ample fortune. He had, I think, taken some stimulant which, added to
his natural grief and excitement, made him almost frantic. He would sit
still awhile, and then burst out into the most terrible imprecations against
the rebels, and against slavery. He would quote scripture, smite his fists
together, roll up his sleeves, cry, & laugh a sort of laugh that made me
feel worse than his crying. Then he would rise up and vow most solemnly

that he would devote every dollar of his fortune, which he said was ½ a million of dollars, to the emancipation of slaves. He was a very large, tall, fine-looking man, and seemed to mean exactly what he said. I felt a great deal of sympathy for him, and could not but think that although

Old John Brown is mouldering in the grave

how many were left who were actuated by the same principles he was, and that, in due time those principles would take firm root in the free hearts of the American people, and would walk over slavedom and reb-eldom with a stride that no earthly power can resist. Slavery is doomed, and the rebels themselves have doomed it. . . .

1. Charles Danforth (1797–1876), self-made man, president of Danforth, Cooke & Co., which manufactured locomotives that were sold worldwide.

Concord, Mass., Thursday, July 10. At ½ past 5 o'clock last evening I arrived here (Gov. Brown's) well, but hot and tired. . . . I found Mary Ellen well and glad to see me, and now my great regret is that I must, so soon, leave her again to go into my lonely home at Washington.

As soon as I had taken breakfast on Monday, I left Brooklyn and went to the St. Nicholas Hotel in New York. . . . Mr. Walter came about ½ past 12. We dined at 2, and ½ past[,] Mr. Fowler[1] came with a hack, and we rode out 8 miles to the Foundry where we found the iron work for the Dome progressing rapidly and satisfactorily. On our way we passed through Central Park, and by direction of Mr. F. the Driver carried us to all the prominent points. After inspecting the work at the Foundry we visited the house of Mr. Janes,[2] one of the partners, who lives in elegant style, & who entertained us very handsomely. . . . At 8 A.M. Tuesday we left N.Y. for Lee, Mass. At Bridgeport we took the cars over the Housatonic road—a better road—more clean, comfortable and airy cars—and a better conductor—it has never been my lot to find in all my travels. The valley of the Housatonic, through which we passed[,] is a perfect romance, broken into hills, mountains, and valleys, and dotted with villages. It is a scene for a painter or a Novelist, & might be richly wrought up on paper.

At 3 P.M. we were at the airy and comfortable mansion of Mr. Charles Heebner,[3] one of the contractors for furnishing the marble, in Lee. Here, again, we were excellently well taken care of by Mrs. Heebner. We visited and inspected the quarry and found everything progressing to our sat-isfaction. The men were splitting out the bases for the columns—the parts now most wanted. We spent the night at Mr. Heebner's. At ½ past 6 Wednesday morning I bade the hospitable Heebners, and my friend

Walter, good-by, was taken in Mr. H.'s carriage to the R.R. Depot, and at 7 left for Pittsfield, 9 miles distant. At Pittsfield I took the cars for Boston where I arrived at ½ past 2, dined at Young's with my brother, and at 4 took the cars for this place, and arrived here as per commencement of this journalization. . . .

1. Charles Fowler, a partner in the company of Janes, Fowler, and Kirkland, which supplied the ironwork for the Dome.
2. Either George or Edward R. Janes, both partners in Janes, Fowler, and Kirkland.
3. Charles Heebner was a partner in Rice, Baird and Heebner of Philadelphia, which supplied marble for the Capitol Extension. Their quarry was in Lee, Mass.

Exeter, Sunday, July 13. . . . , Mary Ellen and I took the cars for this town of Exeter, where we arrived at 7 & came to this (my son Frank's) house. We found a right down good welcome, and I found a little beautiful granddaughter whom I had never before seen[,] Little Elizabeth Richardson French—she will always be "Bessie"—born last December. Right glad were we to get here. Frank is most comfortably and pleasantly situated in a little box of a house on Pine St. . . .

Tuesday, July 15. . . . At two o'clock yesterday afternoon Frank, Mrs. Ellen, Mary Ellen, Laura Nelson, the baby & myself, packed ourselves into a two-horse carriage and went excurtioning. We went first to Hampton Beach over a road which I never before travelled, by the way of Kensington, Hampton Falls, etc. We passed the house where old Meshech Ware,[1] 1st President of N.H., resided and died. . . .

My Mary was very much pleased with the view of the ocean & seemed rather inclined to "sail in." I think, had she been in proper tog I should have seen her among the breakers. . . .

1. Meshech Weare (1713–1786), of Hampton Falls, N.H., served between 1776 and 1784 as president of the Council, the executive branch of the new state government. He was elected president of the state in 1784 but resigned in 1785 because of bad health.

Monday, July 21. I sit here at Frank's Library table to make my last record, at this visit. At ½ past 11 I shall start for Washington where, if good luck attends me, I hope to arrive tomorrow evening. This visit to New England has been an uncommonly pleasant and happy one to me, notwithstanding the unhappy episode that made a portion of my visit to Chester unpleasant.[1] From my arrival at Gov. Brown's at Concord to this time, Mary Ellen has been constantly with me, and I have enjoyed her company beyond measure. She has been so kind, so good, so entirely unselfish, that had she not become wrought into my affections as the woof is wrought into the warp, before she left Washington, this communion with her of eleven happy days would have done all the weaving that had been done by her presence in my house for nearly a year. Now, life to me, without her, would not be worth a single sunrise! . . .

1. Two pages, apparently for July 19–20, have been cut out of French's journal. Two additional pages have blank sheets pasted over them, but it does not appear that there is any writing under these blank sheets.

Washington, Wednesday, July 23. Here, in *my lonely home,* I again open this volume to write down my experiences and thoughts—my blessings and my troubles—my hopes and my fears.

On Monday morning, at the happy home of my son Frank, I made the last record in this book. At ½ past 11 on that day, I bade my dear ones at Exeter farewell, and was soon on my way to Boston. At 2 I dined in Boston at Young's with my Brother Henry and Mr. Tuck. After dinner the Judge & I went *Photographing.* I ordered a dozen of Mary Ellen's at Whipple's and then went to Black's with Henry, who holds him in high esteem as a Photographer, and sat for my own. Then we walked to the Worcester Depot and, at ½ past 5, I started by the Worcester and Norwich line for N. York. We took the Steamer, *City of Boston,* at New London, about 10 P.M. I got an elegant stateroom, No. 74, and had a good night's sleep. At 6 A.M. I was landed at the Jersey City Depot and left for this city at ¼ past 7 and arrived here at 6 last evening. Thus ended a very pleasant "abroad" of two weeks & three days—the only drawback on the pleasure of which was the unfortunate affair at Chester.[1]

The more I see of Mary Ellen the more am I convinced that on my union with her depends the happiness of what remains to me of life— be it much or little—and the thing that pleases me best of all other things connected with this matter is the *almost* universal approbation—and warm too—of my relatives and friends. The Judge & his family, the Browns, Mother & Helen, & Frank & his wife have expressed themselves with the utmost kindness, much pleased at the anticipated union. I have, as yet, had no talk with Ben about it but do not doubt his pleasure, for he is very fond of Mary Ellen. I should have added the Wells's [sic] & the Soules & the Russells. I do not think that there is *now* any actual feeling of opposition to the match, although Ned did oppose it bitterly, through, as I think, a mistaken idea, which having been corrected, he has come round to a sort of tacit submission—not a hearty approval, like all the rest. . . .

1. There is no subsequent explanation of the unfortunate affair in the journal.

Sunday, August 3. . . . Since I wrote herein last the times have been tame enough considering that there are so many wild traitors about. There must be some stirring events soon. I saw the President day before yesterday morning. He was in good spirits and looked well. We talked of the number of efficient troops in the field, and he told us that, although the army consisted nominally of 600,000 men, from the best information that he could get there were not, at that moment, over 362,000 available fighting men in our army. Sickness, wounds, and absence on leave had thus thinned our ranks!

We must hurry up the volunteers!

We are to have a great war meeting here next Wednesday evening. I am one of the *arrangers* and hold the important position of Chairman of the committee on Finance and intend to make the folks fork over if possible. I commenced yesterday morning, but my headache interfered and I had to give it up. . . .

Sunday, August 10. . . . We had our great War meeting Wednesday afternoon and evening [August 6]. It commenced at 5 and ended between 10 & 11 and was a rouser. I have never seen more persons assembled in front of the Capitol except at an inauguration, which it very much resembled. The speaking was first-rate. *The feature* of the occasion was the presence of the President of the U.S.[,] who made quite a speech. I never witnessed more enthusiasm than was manifested at his appearance. It shows how he is beloved. He is one of the best men God ever created. . . .

Sunday, August 24. . . . I am chairman and treasurer of the Committee of the District to raise money for the support of the families of enlisted soldiers. We had quite an interesting meeting at my office last Wednesday. Nearly all the Committee were present, and we discussed matters quite freely. Distributed the subscription books to the Ward Committees & agreed to meet weekly. I made my first deposit at Riggs & Co.'s yester of about 1,700 dollars. I think we may raise $50,000—not over—although $200,000 was talked about at the great war meeting! We will do our best. I was also honored with the position of a corporator of the Guardian Society, and last Monday we met and organized. . . . If the object can be carried out as intended it will be one of the most humane, charitable and useful institutions ever established in Washington, and will be of unlimited benefit to everybody, as well as to those who partake of its bounties. . . .

One week from tomorrow the Grand Encampment of the U.S. is to meet in the City of New York. One week from today I shall be there, if alive and well, & nothing now unforeseen prevents. I trust we can finish up our business by Friday evening so that I can leave for Boston. I *must* be in Concord, Mass., before Tuesday, the 9th, for on that day Mary Ellen & I are to commit matrimony at Concord, and when I return here I shall bring her as my own dear wife. I hope then to have some happiness in the married state once more. . . .

New York, Thursday, September 4. Were this not the anniversary of my birth, I do not think this page would be written. On Friday last I left Washington at 5 P.M. and arrived here early the next morning, since which time I have been *immersed* in the business of the Grand Encampment of Knights Templar of the U.S. I trust we shall finish our business today, and I shall leave in the Fall River Boat for Boston & be with my Mary Ellen tomorrow morning. . . .

Concord, Mass., Sunday, September 7. I left New York in the Steamer *Metropolis* (Fall River line) at 5 o'clock P.M. on Thursday last, and arrived in Boston at ½ past 6 Friday morning. Went direct to the Judge's office and left my carpet bag—took breakfast at Young's, went to the Custom House, saw Frank, returned to Henry's office, found him in, then went again to the Custom House with him, and at 11 took the cars for this place, where I arrived at 12 noon. Found all well and glad to see me. . . .

. . . Day after tomorrow, Mary Ellen and I are to commence our journey of life together. Most happy am I in anticipation of this great happiness.

Montreal, Canada, Saturday, September 13. . . . Monday afternoon [September 8] we were all pretty busy preparing for the great event of Tuesday. Nathan[1] procured flowers to dress the rooms, and George came from Boston Monday evening with the wine & cake, etc. Mary Vose came Monday evening. . . .

Tuesday the 9th we were all up early and all joined in preparation for the wedding. The friends began to arrive before noon. . . . Our good Father McElroy,[2] who was to perform the marriage ceremony, did not come as expected in the noon train, but at 10 m. past 2 he came in a private carriage, having missed the train by 4 minutes, for the first time, as he said, in his life. At about ½ past 2, all having been prepared & the wedding guests assembled in Mr. Brown's north parlor, I went in & took my station with the Rev. Priest, and in a few minutes Mary Ellen entered, leaning on my son Frank's arm, as beautiful a bride as I ever desire to see. He handed her to my left side, and the wedding ceremony was performed by Father McElroy in a very impressive manner. We plighted our troth to each other in the most solemn form possible, and I do not doubt it will be kept "until death do us part."

After the ceremony an elegant entertainment, prepared by my good sister, was given, and all went merry—very merry indeed, for two hours or more[,] when the party began to separate. At 6 Mary Ellen & I (being one) left for Boston, Frank, Ellen, & Col. Keyes & Ben accompanying us. Mrs. French & I, with Frank & Ellen, took rooms at the Tremont House. Ben left for Washington. . . . At ½ past 8 o'clock Thursday morning we took the cars, booked for "Montreal" at 11 that evening. On arriving at Middlesex, Vt., we learned that a burden train had been smashed about a mile from that station, and it would take two or three hours to clear off the wreck. So Mary Ellen and I left the cars and *put up* at the Middlesex house (a very common tavern, but where they did all they could to make us comfortable) until 8 o'clock yesterday morning, when we left that place for this. We arrived at "Rouse's Point" about 1 & left there at 3, under the promise that we were to be here at 7. We arrived here a few minutes after 10! and I think it will be about my last trip in a car attached to a freight train. I never was more tired or more impatient in my life. We stopped, it seemed to me, every five miles, & our stops were very long, but we got here at last! & came to the "Donegana" Hotel, in a chamber of which I am now writing at one side of a table while my dear one is writing to her sister Margaret at the other.

Today we have rambled about the city, visited the "Cathedral," and went to the top of one of the towers, from whence this great & magnificent city is all to be seen. From that place we went to the "Hospital of the Gray Nuns," all over which we were most politely shown. It is filled with poor patients, from the infant in swaddling clothes to the old man over 100 years of age! It is not only sectarianly Catholic, but truly catholic in the broadest meaning of that comprehensive word. Oh the good that is done in this world by good Catholics! I have seen it & keep seeing it daily.

This house seems to me to be filled with secessionists. I am almost disgusted with the continual rejoicing, or rather, exulting, over the success of the Rebels. I hope & trust their exultations will be brief, and that soon my turn will come. . . .

1. Nathan Henry Barrett (b. 1830), brother of George Keyes's Concord friend, Edwin S. Barrett. Nathan Henry later came to Washington and took a job in the Post Office Department.

2. Perhaps John McElroy, S.J. (1782–1877), who had served at Georgetown College, at Frederick, Md., in the Mexican War, and in Boston, where he founded Boston College.

Lockport, N.Y., Thursday, September 18. . . . Monday morning the 15th. We left Montreal at 8 o'clock, and after a very fatiguing day's ride, arrived at Toronto, 333 miles, at 11 o'clock P.M. . . . We remained at Toronto, at the "Rossin House,"[1] one night and left for Niagara at about 8 o'clock.

Tuesday, 16th. We arrived at Hamilton at 12 noon and had to wait there for the Great Western train till 3:20. . . .

Wednesday, 17th. . . . Mary Ellen and I started out as soon as we got breakfast, and viewed the various wonders of Niagara, until 12. Then we returned to the Hotel. . . .

After dinner Mary Ellen & I took a hack and visited the Whirlpool on the Am. side. The afternoon was excessively hot. We returned to the Hotel and at 5:30 started for this place, where we arrived at 6:30. . . .

1. The Rossin House, A. C. Joslin, proprietor, was at the corner of York and King streets.

Washington, Thursday, September 25. At home again, thanks be to God, with a dear, dear wife to love me and take care of me, and whom I dearly love. If any mortal could make the place of my lost Bessie good, it is the one I have chosen—my dear Mary Ellen. We arrived home at 6 o'clock on Tuesday evening. We left Lockport, with Mrs. Wells[,] Tom, & Annie[1] at 8 o'clock A.M. Friday morning, and we arrived at Albany after rather a pleasant day's ride at 8 o'clock P.M. & went on board the steamer *Isaac Newton.* Found her crammed with passengers, partly composed of a Regiment of troops. Mrs. F. and I got a good stateroom and were very comfortable. At 9 the boat started from the wharf and grounded in a few moments in the middle of the river, and "there she lay 'till next day"—or till 1 o'clock the next morning—so we did not arrive in New York until ¼ past 12 P.M. on Saturday, and at Doct. Wells's in Brooklyn between 1 & 2. . . .

1. Tom and Anna Wells, children of P. P. and Catharine Wells.

Friday, September 26. Yes it *is* Home, now, and I am again happy in it. May this happiness continue as long as it pleases God to let me live. Yesterday I visited the War Department on business connected with obtaining an exchange of some prisoners now at Richmond who were taken at Manassas, when on an errand of mercy there to minister to wounded soldiers after the recent battle.[1] Among them were some of my employees at and about the Capitol. . . .

And now I have come to the *last page* of this eventful journal, commenced Jany. 1st, 1861. Oh God, oh God, may I never have occasion to write such an one again. It is streaked, as it were, with the record of great happinesses and great miseries. Marriage and *Death,* and Marriage, and War, and suffering mark its pages, and many a sigh and many a tear has accompanied the record. What is written is true! Farewell to it. Faithful companion of many a weary day[,] *Farewell.*

1. The Second Battle of Bull Run, or Manassas, was fought on August 30.

EIGHT

The Lincolns and the Civil War

1862–1865

appily married, and with his domestic life in order, French becomes less introspective in this chapter, and his journal focuses on the rich life of Washington in wartime. Abraham Lincoln was at the center of this life, and French, by reason of his position, appears to have been able to drop in on the President almost at will. He saw him when he was careworn and when he was "full of fun and story."[1] Often critical of others, French's words about Lincoln are invariably approving, respectful, and caring.

Two events stand out in French's association with Lincoln—the dedication of the National Cemetery at Gettysburg and the assassination. Both are covered at length in his journal. At Gettysburg, French assisted in making arrangements for the ceremonies and wrote the words for the consecration hymn. Seated on the speaker's platform on November 19, 1863, he listened admiringly to Edward Everett's long oration and then heard Lincoln dedicate the cemetery "in a few brief, but most appropriate words."[2] French learned of the awful event at Ford's Theater when he awoke at daylight on April 15, 1865, and saw a sentry pacing outside the house. After visiting the room in which Lincoln lay dying, and realizing that there was no possibility of survival, French busied himself for the next several hours looking after Mrs. Lincoln and making the necessary preparations at the White House and the Capitol for the funeral. Toward the day's end he turned to his journal and wrote: "We have supped full with horrors."[3]

As with Lincoln, a special relationship existed with Mrs. Lincoln. Whenever the receiving lines formed at the White House, French took his place at her side, introducing her to visitors. On these occasions he sometimes remarked in his journal on the appearance, manner, and dress of "The Queen." There were other meetings, however, that were clouded by her thoughts of Willie Lincoln's death. When French went to see Mrs. Lincoln for the last time, on May 22, 1865, as she left Washington with her sons Robert and Tad, he was concerned that the death of the President had unhinged her mind.

French attempted to follow the course of military operations, but news was often fragmentary and slow in reaching Washington. In June of 1863, however, he conveys something of the "blaze of excitement"[4] that was aroused as two great armies moved toward Pennsylvania and the fields of Gettysburg. A year later he was indignant when the Confederates raided north again, threatened Washington, and cut the rail lines to Baltimore. He remained confident in eventual Union victory but passed through periods of uncertainty and longed for Washington to become "*a civil* city" once more, and not a city of "Camps, corrals, and soldiers."[5]

The end did finally come, and when word of the fall of Richmond reached Washington at noon on April 3, 1865, everyone took to the streets as bands played and cannons were fired. Commissioner French had the Capitol illuminated on the following day, displaying on the western portico an enormous lettered transparency declaring "This is the Lord's doing; it is marvellous in our eyes."[6] A few days later he was in Richmond, viewing the ruined city, visiting the abandoned defense works, and riding through the camps holding Confederate prisoners. At Jefferson Davis's mansion, which was still intact, French had "Yankee Doodle" played on Varina Davis's piano.

The great review of the Union army in Washington offered one last memorable spectacle. French watched it from East Capitol Street and then from the dome of the Capitol. More than 50,000 troops were in sight, filling all of the principal avenues. To French it was "a grand and a brave sight."[7] The war was over and the world had changed. Lincoln was dead, the conspirators were captured, and Andrew Johnson had succeeded to the presidency. French stayed on as commissioner of public buildings, but he was in his sixty-fifth year, had suffered excruciatingly from gallstones, was growing restless under a new Secretary of the Interior, and was beginning to think that his working days could not last many more years. But on Christmas Eve of 1865 he could review his condition and that of his household and conclude with his old enthusiasm that "if we are not comfortable and happy we ought to be whipped!"[8]

1. Mar. 23, 1864.
2. Nov. 22, 1863.
3. April 15, 1865.
4. June 18, 1863.

5. Sept. 25, 1864.
6. April 6, 1865.
7. May 24, 1865.
8. Dec. 24, 1865.

Journal

Friday, October 10. . . . Last Sunday . . . Mrs. Mary Ellen French, my sweet wife, Mr. Alfred G. Taggart, & I, in the Capitol extension carriage, rode out to the Hospital at Columbia College to see some sick soldiers. . . . Mr. Taggart had some young friends there, to whom he introduced us, and also to Surgeon Taft[1] who very politely accompanied us and directed us to whom to give the grapes & figs which we took out with us for distribution. We went through the hospital tents and saw men wounded in all sorts of ways—some convalescent, some very badly wounded, but of whom there was hope, and some who were apparently doomed to death. It was a sorrowful and melancholy round, and the only consolation afforded us was to witness the gratefulness with which the poor fellows received the trifling offering we gave. I only wished it was a hundredfold greater. Mary Ellen was very much moved at the distress around her.

Monday I devoted the time entirely to the duties of Treasurer of the Volunteer Family Fund, up to dinner. After dinner Mary, Edm[und], Taggart & I rode down in the carriage to the Navy Yard to see the *Monitor.* We were readily admitted into the yard and drove down to the wharf where the World-renowned *iron clad* was lying. We got almost to her before we saw her, and such an insignificant looking craft for a war steamer I never saw or dreamed of. "A cheese box on a raft" expresses her appearance better than anything else, and those on board the *Merrimack* must have been utterly astonished to see such *a thing* come boldly up and give the monster battle, and still more so when they had to skedaddle off into Norfolk pretty essentially used up! We went on board, Gen. & Mrs. Banks[2] happening to be with us, and examined the wonderful craft—saw the very slight effect which the shot of the *Merrimack* had upon her iron sides, deck and turret. She has been so many times described, technically, that a description by me, here, would be a waste of time and paper. We spent perhaps half-an-hour on her deck, then went on board a vessel loaded with iron from Norfolk, among it one of the guns of the *Merrimack,* which was struck about midway by a shot from the *Monitor* and cut off as smooth as need be. It was one of the largest sized Dahlgren guns. After seeing these things my friend Geo. R. Wilson, Master Machinist, took us all through the Machine shops, and explained all the wonderful mechanical operation going on. We left about sunset, after having our curiosity very much gratified. . . .

. . . Day before yesterday (Wednesday)[,] after dinner, we rode down to the Congressional Cemetery and placed flowers on the graves of our dear departed ones. . . . From there we rode to the Insane Asylum, where I saw my friend Doct. Nichols, and General Hooker, who is there getting well of his wound. I saw there several gentlemen of my acquaintance, and among them Col. Solomon Meredith[3] of Indiana, who was with Gen. Hooker in his battles. . . .

1. Charles Taft, assistant surgeon, U.S. Army.
2. Mary Theodosia Palmer Banks (1817–1901) had been a Waltham factory worker. She married Nathaniel P. Banks in 1847 after an eight-year engagement.
3. Solomon Meredith (d. 1873), of the 19th Indiana Infantry, rose to the rank of major general.

Sunday, October 19. . . . [Friday] evening Mr. James Brown,[1] our Concord soldier, came. He had got a furlough and was going home. He staid with us Friday night and gave us a very interesting history of his campaign down on the Peninsula under McClellan. The reminiscences were not pleasant. He left for home at 6 yesterday morning. He has a severe cough, although otherwise looking well. I fear he is sicker than he supposes. . . .

I have seen the President but once since my return, and then on business of my office. He was very pleasant and agreeable and did what I asked of him without any hesitation, which was to give a preremptory [sic] order for the removal of the Army Bakery from the Capitol. The removal has been made since! . . .

1. Probably James A. Brown, who was later a watchman at the Capitol, in the office of the commissioner of public buildings.

Sunday, November 2. . . . Thursday five Regiments from Vermont, which had been in camp below here for a time, passed my house on their way to the war. They looked well, and will give a good account of themselves I do not doubt, if called on to fight. . . .

Friday, November 7. The snow has been falling all this day, and the weather is uncommonly cold. Notwithstanding the snow storm, Mrs. Russell & Mrs. French have been to two hospitals contributing food & clothing to the sick. The Emory Hospital is a mile below here and they give an account of it that makes one shudder, and ought to disgrace those who have the control of it. The buildings are mere rough board shanties, not a fire or the means of having a fire in them, and the poor sick soldiers lying on beds covered with snow! The women carried down clothing, contributed by the citizens of Concord, Mass., & sent to Mrs. Russell for distribution, which they distributed to such as they thought most in want. . . .

Sunday, November 9. . . . Today I attended St. Aloysius Church with Mrs. French. I do not fancy the Catholic form of worship, but I am sufficiently *catholic* to believe that Religion does not consist in forms, and that it is of little consequence how man worships if he be sincere. . . . Although not particularly interested in the ritual of the service, which I have so often witnessed, I *was* interested in Father McGuire's[1] sermon. It was eloquent, truthful, and well spoken. . . . I like Father McGuire, & wish I could listen to him every Sunday of my life! . . .

McClellan is, at last, relieved from the command of the Army of the Potomac! I hope his successor will turn out to be *a live general,* be he whom he may. We have had enough delay already!

1. B. J. Maguire, the pastor of St. Aloysius Church.

Sunday, November 23. . . . I wrote herein last, the day after McClellan was deposed from the command of the Army of the Potomac. Many prophecyed disaffection in the Army, and disaster everywhere, but as yet we have not seen any such result, and Burnside[1] has moved onward toward what seems to promise *good* results & perhaps *glorious.* I felt bad at Mac's removal, but sincerely believe it will result for the best. . . .

1. Ambrose E. Burnside (1824–1881), who had captured Roanoke Island earlier in the year and had taken part in the Battle of Antietam in September, was given command of the Army of the Potomac on November 5. He was badly defeated at Fredericksburg in December.

Monday, December 8. We have had since Saturday morning very cold weather, thermometer has not been above 30 since Friday, and as low as 19 above o (13 below freezing) after sunrise in the morning. Ben had a pointer pup which he kept in the stable, and the poor little fellow froze to death night before last. I think I never grieved as much over the death of any animal as I did over that poor little dog. . . .

Sunday, December 21. . . . Amelia [Barnard] staid with us till last Thursday, and we enjoyed her company very much. We had the Gallaudets here to tea on Friday evening the 12th inst. from the Deaf & Dumb & Blind Asylum at Kendall Green. Of mutes we had old Mrs. Gallaudet,

Mr. & Mrs. Dennison (he is not entirely deaf & can talk) & Mr. Phelps of Vt.[1] The mutes seemed to enjoy themselves as well as the gabblers. Young Mrs. Gallaudet & Mary Gordon came with the party from the Asylum. Mr. G., being sick, could not come. It is almost wonderful to observe the difference in the appearance of Amelia when her mute friends are with her & when they are not. She is always cheerful, but the moment a deaf mute who can converse rapidly visits her she becomes all animation, her countenance lights up & she seems almost a different person. . . .

The war! I have no heart to write about either it or the political aspect of affairs. Defeat at Fredericksburg—the Cabinet breaking up—our leading men fighting with each other! Unless something occurs very soon to brighten up affairs, I shall begin to look upon our whole Nation as on its way to destruction. . . .

1. Amelia Barnard was a deaf-mute. Mrs. Thomas H. Gallaudet, wife of the founder of the school for the deaf in Hartford, Conn., and mother of Edward M. Gallaudet. James Denison was an instructor of the deaf and dumb at the Columbia Institution and principal of the primary school. His sister Susan married Edward M. Gallaudet in 1868. Phelps was the son of former senator Samuel S. Phelps of Vermont.

Friday, December 26. Christmas has come and gone since last I wrote. Mrs. F.'s birth anniversary has also come and gone. Dec. 23d she was 31 years of age. I gave her a Prayer Book as a birthday present, and a sewing machine and diamond ring as Christmas presents. She gave me *Folk Songs*—a superb book—and the 2 first volumes of Pierre Irving's life of Washington Irving.[1] I value them beyond price. My friend Wm. Forsyth sent me a gallon of brandy, six bottles of Champagne, and a box of cigars. Harry French[2] gave me a gutta-percha ring, which he made on purpose for me, and being a little too small for my smallest finger I shall wear it on my watch chain, where it now is. I value it very much because he made it expressly for me. These are *all* the Christmas presents I have rec'd. . . .

We spent our Christmas very soberly. All the morning I was engaged about house *fixing up things*. After getting regularly shaved, *bathed*, & dressed for the day, I wheeled a barrel of apples round to Duff Green's row,[3] partly, and the remainder to the Casparis Hospital. I remained at the latter place and saw the sick soldiers eat their Christmas dinner. Came home at ½ past 1, and at 2 dined. We had an admirable Christmas dinner, and Lem. Barker and Taggart as guests. Ben, an unmannerly cub, did not come to the table at all, but ate at his workbench where he was working on his steam engine. . . .

Congress has adjourned over to the 1st Monday in Jany. I believe the

Country would be better off were they to adjourn finally for wrangling seems to be the order of the day.

1. Pierre M. Irving (1803–1876), nephew of Washington Irving (1783–1859), in addition to writing his uncle's biography had helped with his financial and literary affairs.
2. Harry (Henry) French, one of Edmund French's sons.
3. Duff Green's row was a large block of houses located one block east of French's residence. It was used to house contraband slaves for a time and later as an annex to the nearby Old Capitol Prison. It had been owned by Duff Green (1791–1875), journalist and one-time Jacksonian, who aided the Confederacy by operating ironworks.

Sunday, February 15. . . . From tea till after ten I read aloud to Mary Ellen from Pierre Irving's life of Washington Irving. I had read the 1st Vol. ¾'s through to myself, and I finished it aloud last evening. I have seldom read a more interesting book. How it brings back the times when I used to long for the arrival of *another* number of the *Sketch Book,*[1] and when it did come, the supreme pleasure that I enjoyed in reading it aloud to a bevy of young ladies (she who was afterwards and for so many years my own beloved Bessie, being one) who enjoyed the quaint humor and wept over the pathetic descriptions with me, and appreciated all that the beloved author so elegantly and forcibly portrayed. We laughed tumultuously over the "Legend of Sleepy Hollow," "Rip Van Winkle," & the like, and wept over the "Broken Heart[,]" "The Pride of the Village," etc. I believe we all fell in love with Irving, & my own affection for him has been constant. I once had the pleasure of seeing him while he was absorbed in some investigation in a room in the Department of State. He was poring over old books as if he were absolutely devouring their contents. I was in the room on business, and a Clerk present whispered in my ear[,] "That is Washington Irving." I took a good, long look at him and never shall forget his appearance. He was to me[,] "Geoffrey Crayon, Gent." and not "Deidrich Knickerbocker." I never had the pleasure of an Introduction to him. No writer, not even Walter Scott, ever made such an impression on my young mind as did Washington Irving. His writings charmed me, & when I was once launched on the river of beauty which seemed to flow in waves of silver, from his facile & elegant imagination, I never could cast anchor until I had reached that final haven[,] "The End"; & even then, like Oliver Twist, I longed for "more." . . .

1. *The Sketch Book of Geoffrey Crayon, Gent.* (1819–1820).

Wednesday, February 18. Monday morning as soon as I had eaten breakfast I went to the President's to see him on business. I was with him about

½ an hour. He certainly is growing feeble. He wrote a note while I was present, and his hand trembled as I never saw it before, and he looked worn & haggard. I remarked that I should think he would feel glad when he could get some rest. He replied that it was a pretty hard life for him. My main object in calling was to get him to appoint my friend N. C. Towle[1] Register of Deeds, which he has done. I walked back to the Capitol. . . .

1. N. C. Towle was at the time a clerk for the Senate committee on claims.

Sunday, February 22. . . . Attended The President's and Mrs. Lincoln's reception, as usual, yesterday. Mary Ellen, Ariana & Nathan accompanied me. It was a very crowded and brilliant one. The President and Mrs. L. affable and pleasant as they always are on such occasions. "The skeleton," if there be one, is always kept out of sight.[1] Robert was at home looking fresh and healthy. He is a fine looking young man. . . .

1. Probably a reference to the feelings that could be expected to arise so close to the first anniversary of the death of Willie Lincoln.

Tuesday, March 3. . . . Yesterday at the Capitol most of the time. . . . In the evening a reception at the President's. Mrs. Lincoln sent a carriage for me at 7. I dressed and was up there at 8. Mary Ellen, Ariana, Nathan & Ben from this house, and Abbie Thomas,[1] were there. They came up between 9 & 10. The reception was exceedingly crowded. I think I never saw such a crowd in the White House in my life, and it was a steady stream of humanity for 2½ hours of all sorts and kinds of people. Ladies in magnificent toilets and in the plainest imaginable garb. The Major General in his dress coat, & the common soldier in his patched great coat, and boots covered with mud halfway up the leg. Every grade of every arm of the service seemed to be there, from Gen. Halleck[,][2] Com. in Chief[,] down to the private. Epaulettes & shoulder straps, cheverons [sic], & scales were as thick as leaves in valambrosa.[3] Citizens in all sorts of dress, from the finished & perfumed dandy down to the shabbiest of the shabby[,] passed along & oh

> The white arms and raven hair,
> The braids and bracelets
> The swan-like bosoms and the necklace,
> An India in itself, but rapturing not
> The eye, like what it circled

that passed before my vision, as I stood at the side of "The Queen" of all this show—she, herself[,] habited as it became her in rich black satin and jewels of the richest kind. The President, too, "honest old Abraham," looked better than I ever saw him before at a reception. The whole thing passed off admirably, and by midnight I was at home and in bed.

The President told me, prior to the reception, of the capture of our Steam ram *Indianola*[4] by the rebels, which made me feel sad. It does seem as if we were meeting with too many reverses, considering our resources and strength. But when it is considered that not only the Rebels but the monied men of England are against us, I do not know as it is to be wondered at that there is now and then a triumph over our arms. . . .

1. Abbie M. Thomas of Chester, Pa., married Ben on May 9, 1866.
2. Henry W. Halleck (1815–1872), military adviser to President Lincoln, July 1862–March 1864, with the title general-in-chief; he never succeeded in devising a grand strategy for the war.
3. Vallombrosa, the name of a Benedictine abbey in the thickly wooded Vallombrosa Valley near Florence, Italy. The abbey became the Royal School of Forestry in 1866. Milton wrote of the "autumnal leaves that strow the brooks in Vallombrosa" in *Paradise Lost*.
4. The *Indianola*, an ironclad gunboat on the Mississippi River commanded by Acting Master Edward Shaw, ran past the Confederate batteries at Vicksburg on February 13–14, 1863, but was forced aground and captured by Confederate vessels on the Red River on February 24, 1863.

Thursday, March 19. Yesterday, early at my office. At 10 A.M. started for the President's to serve a friend. Went to the Navy and War Departments, to the Second Auditor's Office, and then to the President's. Saw the President, and after doing my business with him, I went to the Treasury Department, then back to my office where I remained till between 2 & 3 and then home. . . .

The drum in the camp just East of us is beating tattoo, and I will also beat it and close my journal till a more propitious season.

Still reading "Gurowsky's Diary."[1] He seemed to see things pretty clearly, but is unbearingly abusive of those in power.

1. Adam Gurowski (1805–1866), a Polish radical and exile who came to America in 1849. He was an adviser to William H. Seward in 1861 and in 1862 published his *Diary* containing criticism of Seward and Lincoln.

Sunday, March 22. . . . I finished "Gurowski's Diary." The book is a thoroughly disgusting one. Vanity of vanities runs through every page. Count Gurowski knows everything and no one else knows anything! General Scott is no soldier but an old weak granny, and almost a secessionist!! President Lincoln is a poor, weak, proslavery man, but rather honest & well meaning!! The Cabinet generally a set of nincompoops—for a while

Blair was somebody, but even he degenerated before the end of the book into a nobody. McClellan was the greatest imbecile who was ever born, and nobody seemed inclined to follow the advice of the *allwise Gurowski*!!! and so, after swallowing the dictionary of quotations, his Sapiency commences a book & throws up his overcharged stomach on every page. Poor Gurowski—it is evident that you knew a little something; but I believe most of your *prophecies* were made after the happening of the event pretended to be prophecied! I think the man who would write such a book and print it, ought to be put in a military prison, or an insane asylum. So much for Count Gurowski's book. . . .

Saturday, March 28. . . . Mrs. Lincoln has no reception today—cause unexplained—nevertheless I am glad, as I supposed the last one was to take place and that it would be a large one, & I should be well tired out. . . .

Yesterday we all went to the President's to see & hear the Indian powow. There were nine chiefs of different nations[,] I believe, and two squaws. As I do not wish to write out a description of the scene I will cut a slip from the *National Intelligencer* giving an account of it. The *Chronicle* contains a full account with the speeches, but it is too long to put in here.[1]

The *Intelligencer* has omitted the interesting fact that after the President took his leave, the Indians were all conducted to the Conservatory, where a photographist was in waiting and they were photographed in groups. If the first group comes out well[,] the face of the Com. of Public Buildings will appear looking over the shoulder of Miss Kate Chase. . . .

1. Two columns, titled "Our Indian Relations," are pasted in French's journal at this place.

Sunday, April 5. . . . Yesterday opened cold and blustering. Pa. Avenue was a cloud of dust during the day. I was invited by the President of the Washington & Alexandria R.R. Co. to accompany the Secy. & Assist. Secy. of the Interior—Judges Usher[1] & Otto[2]—to the Potomac Bridge to examine it & its vicinity in connection with the plans for building a R.R. bridge alongside of it. At ½ past 3 we got into a car on Maryland Avenue and, drawn by a first class locomotive, went to and across the bridge. We all got out on the bridge to see the draw opened, & the wind, which was blowing a gale from the N.W.[,] cut like a knife. We were all glad to get back into the warm car. After crossing the bridge, it was decided that we should run down to Alexandria, which we did[,] and had a very pleasant visit to our R.R. friends. I met there a Mr. Devereaux,[3] who has charge of the U.S. trains there, and who is a very fine man. He is a Kt. Templar from Mississippi, and I think he told me, was G. Commander there when the rebellion drove him away. At ¼ past 6 we left for Washington and went from the cars to 14th St. where a very elegant entertainment was prepared at the "Occidental[,]" opposite Willard's on 14th St. We sat down at ½ past 7, and I left after the 4th or 5th course at ¼ past 9. . . .

1. John P. Usher (1816–1889), of Indiana, had moved up from assistant secretary to the position of Secretary of the Interior in January 1863.
2. William Tod Otto (1816–1905), of Indiana, assistant secretary of the Interior Department, 1863–1871.
3. John H. Devereux (1832–1886), superintendent of military railroads, was later president of several railroads in the Great Lakes region.

Monday, April 20. . . . Scarcely a day passes in which some occurrence of years ago is not referred to in conversation. I turn to my journal of the time, and lo! a hiatus—no record of the event in question! I am, however, very often enabled, in consequence of my journal, to come at the truth relative to long past occurrences that would otherwise remain in doubt, for, when I have made *any* record it can always be entirely relied on.

For all of last week the 10th N.J. Regt.[,] stationed in the barracks on the next square East, were under marching orders and expected daily to be off. At 4 o'clock this morning the revellie [sic] was beaten, & when I arose at 6 there the good fellows were, knapsacks and tin dippers all on, paraded for a start. Between 6 & 7 they were drawn up in column of march in the centre of the street, the drums & fifes struck up, and "forward" was the word. They passed towards the Capitol 1,000 strong, bound, as we understand[,] for *Dixie*. They made a noble and gallant appearance, with their officers at their head and their splendid banners in their centre. Since they have been on duty here they have proved themselves by their conduct, soldiers & gentlemen, and it made me feel sad to see them depart. I formed the acquaintance of only one of the officers—Adjt. Kennard[1]—and we all liked him much. May good fortune go with them all. I suppose their deserted barracks will now be tenanted by some other corps. May it be as good as these men have been. All East Capitol Street turned out to see them off. . . .

1. Edward E. Kendrick was the adjutant of the 10th New Jersey Infantry, serving in that capacity from September 1861 to the end of the war.

Sunday, April 26. . . . Monday about noon a broken Brigade of Penna. Reserved Corps came from someplace across the Potomac & occupied the barracks evacuated by the 10th N.J. in the morning. They make the camp a perfect beehive. They have hardly had an opportunity yet to show what they are, for until yesterday morning the weather has been awful. . . .

Died on Friday last at 4 P.M. my friend John Silva Meehan, Esq., aged 73. I have known Mr. Meehan ever since I came to Washington—30 years next Dec. He was then, and until 1861 I think, Librarian of Congress. If ever a pure-hearted, honest, upright, honorable man lived, it was John S. Meehan. He lived a cheerful, happy life and died without apparent pain, of apoplexy. On Friday, at breakfast, he was apparently well, and in possession of all his faculties, and at 4 o'clock he was dead! Oh how much preferable is such a death to one after a lingering & painful illness. Today at 4 P.M. I am invited to aid in his burial.

Evening. At 4 P.M. Mrs. French & I walked over to Mr. Meehan's late residence and attended the funeral. I was one of the "pallbearers." . . . There was quite a concourse of our old citizens present. The services were conducted by Rev. Mr. Morsell,[1] and the address was very good. I have seldom heard a more appropriate one, or a truer one, at a funeral. . . .

1. J. Morsell, pastor of the Episcopal Church, Christ Church (Navy Yard).

Thursday, April 30. *National Fast day.* This is the day set apart by the President of the United States to be observed throughout the U.S. as "a day of humiliation, fasting and prayer."[1] I for one intend to endeavour to keep it. . . .

1. Lincoln, in a proclamation of March 30, in response to a Senate resolution, appointed April 30 to be National Fast Day.

Sunday, May 10. . . . I am sitting here, in my library all alone . . . and only the tramp of feet and the ripple of the fountain, as the water falls in the basin, disturb the perfect stillness of the atmosphere. A thousand troops are quartered within a moderate stone's throw of this house, & if they were all dead, they could not be stiller than they are this quiet & beautiful afternoon. . . .

Tuesday, June 9. . . . At a little past 11 left office for Provost Marshal Todd's headquarters, 19th Street. Did what I had to do there, then went to Navy Dept. to make enquiries about my friend Thos. W. Gilmore's[1] son, of Newport, N.H., who was on board the *Preble* when she was burned, and desires to be ordered North. Had an interview with the Chief Clerk,[2] but not *very* satisfactory. I suppose all these officers, like myself, are overwhelmed with all sorts of enquiries. Some of them very impertinent, and make as few words as possible in answering questions. From the Navy Dept. went to the President's; thence to the Treasury Department, all over the new part of which I was very politely shown by the Chief Clerk in the Architect's (Mr. Rogers) Office.[3] It is very much nearer completion than I had any idea of, and is one of the best jobs, take it all in all, that I have ever seen. It gives striking evidence of the immense labors and ramifications of the Treasury Department and of the absolute requirement that its head should be the best that this Nation can produce. Chase is equal to the task!

From the Treasury I went to the grounds South of the President's and gave directions relative to the fences; then back to my office where I remained till about 3. . . .

1. Thomas W. Gilmore was the president of the First National Bank of Newport. His son was uninjured when the sloop-of-war *Preble*, serving in the Gulf Blockading Squadron, accidentally caught fire on the night of April 27, 1863, and blew up.
2. William Faxon of Connecticut.
3. Samuel F. Carr was the chief clerk in the office of the supervising architect, bureau of construction, in the Treasury Department. Isaiah Rogers (1800–1869) was the supervising architect in 1863 and served until September 1865. He was one of the leading architects of his time, having designed Boston's Tremont House and New York's Astor House and Merchant's Exchange.

Wednesday, June 10. . . . Went to the Capitol between 8 & 9, then rode all along the new line of Telegraph, the Res[olution] of Cong. making it the duty of the Secy. of the Interior & Com. of Pub. Buildings to approve in writing the route over which the wires shall pass—then to the Dept. of the Interior, where the Secy. & I approved, in writing, the route. The day hot & dusty. Returned to the Capitol and was informed that I had been sent for to attend at the Court House as a witness. Went immediately to the Court House and there ascertained that my testimony was wanted as to the character of John A. Goss (our plumber, Jack) who hit a man over the head with a piece of gas pipe on Saturday, & he died on Monday. The hearing had been postponed until 2 P.M. I came home and eat something and returned at 2. The hearing was to see if the court would allow the prisoner to be admitted to bail. The testimony was clear that it could not be more than manslaughter, & bail was admitted, Angus,[1] [R. H.] Stewart, Goodall[2] & I being bail in the sum of $2,000. . . .

1. Job W. Angus, general superintendent in the office of the commissioner of public buildings.
2. Probably George W. Goodall, plumber and gasfitter.

Tuesday, June 16. . . . Yesterday came stirring news from the war *in these parts*. Lee with his entire army is moving toward the Shenandoah valley. Quite a large force has reached Martinsburg, Hagerstown, etc., and all seem to be preparing for a general invasion of Pennsylvania & the North. The President has ordered out a hundred thousand of the militia, and the North seems to be generally rising, and Hooker is moving up this side of the Rappahannock. It seems to me as if this was the golden moment for a general movement that shall annihilate Lee's army. I suppose they will fight to desperation, but, if I do not mistake the Northern spirit & feeling, we can meet them with five to one and Hooker can then flank them and they are gone! We shall see what can be done, but if an invasion of the North can be made with success, then I am ready to give up!

Thursday, June 18. . . . The country, now, is in a blaze of excitement. Some of the Rebel troops have crossed into the upper part of Pennsylvania, & the North is wide awake and are pouring out their troops to aid the old Keystone in her defence. If, as things look now, a hundred thousand troops gather at Harrisburg this week and find no enemy to encounter, and will press onward till they meet Lee's army and attack him, while Hooker takes him in flank, a victory may be gained that will cover the victors with immortal glory! I make no pretence to military strategy, but this seems to me to be so feasible that I hardly see how it can be overlooked! And furthermore, I do not see why Richmond is not left an easy conquest to our troops at Fort Monroe, N.C., etc. Time will develop, for good or for evil, what is to be done. I have more hope for a speedy overthrow of the Rebellion, at this moment, than I have ever had before. If it is not done *now,* & the Rebels are permitted to get off scot free, or to triumph over our troops, then our cause is, to say the least, doubtful. But that *cannot be,* with the uprising of the North, and the determination exhibited by the Army proper, it cannot be! We *must* triumph.

Yesterday was a terribly hot day. It is now over 5 weeks since rain enough has fallen here to lay the dust, even, and the heat & drouth are almost unbearable. I was out nearly all day yesterday. In the afternoon across the Eastern Branch, and in ascending "Good Hope" hill in a buggy[,] we met a pontoon train coming into the City from the Rappahannock, ½ a mile long, with its mules, waggons, etc., and I really thought I should be suffocated by the dust. I could not see the faces of men four feet from me! I returned home at about ½ past 6, as nearly worn out as ever man was. . . .

Saw the President yesterday morning and he was in excellent spirits. I wonder whether he ever has a moment of leisure when he is awake! I should think this constant toil and moil would kill him. The more I see of him the more I am convinced of his superlative goodness, truth, kindness & Patriotism.

Monday, June 22. . . . General excitement has marked the time; the Rebels have been raiding into Maryland and Pa.[,] and there is some prospect of an attempt on Washington. Well, ever since the war began Washington has been in danger as often as once per quarter, and I have not yet been frightened and I do not mean to be until the rebels come, and perhaps not then! They have chosen war & we must endure the consequences or be written down "cowards" by posterity. . . .

Friday, June 26. Well, we went to the Convent. . . . Sister Mary Blandina, Mrs. French's cousin, welcomed us with as much cordiality as if she were not a Nun! She took us through the Academic part of the Convent, and we admired the neatness and order that was manifest throughout. I do not think there was as much dirt through the immense collection of school rooms, class rooms, society rooms, music rooms and dormitories as the respectable gentleman who has just visited me with his feet a little muddy has left on the floor of this room wherein I write!

My first visit to the Convent was, I think, in 1834—twenty-nine years ago! I have been there many times since but do not remember to have gone through the building as I did last Monday, and I was very much struck with the *like appearance* of everything then and now. It seemed as if but a single hour had intervened!

After showing us all through the Academy, the good Sister took us to the music room, where half-a-dozen young ladies gave us some of the best music I have listened to for many a day. Three harps and two grand pianos formed the instrumental music, and several of the young ladies sang admirably. One of the young ladies played "The Carnival of Venice" with great skill & power of execution. We were all delighted with the music. . . .

Sunday, July 5. The 4th of July for 1863 is over and gone. It was a glorious day in Washington. Everybody seemed determined to make it known publickly that secession was at a low ebb in the Federal City. Early in the morning the noise of juvenile firecrackers, the exploding of muskets, pistols and, what seemed to me, some uncommonly noisy explosive firework, commenced & was kept up without cessation till nearly, or quite, midnight. . . .

I felt proud of the manner in which the day was celebrated in Washington. I[t] was really a glorious Independence, and its effect was very much heightened by the exhilarating news from our army which was received about 10 o'clock A.M. and was soon spread all over the city. Meade has, thus far, met with a great success, which, I trust, will be followed up by a greater. I have great hope that my prediction on page 106[1] of this journal may be fulfilled.

The Honorable Secy. of the Interior J. P. Usher—Jackass Puny Usher —has taken special pains to annoy me because I will not knuckle and kneel to him, which, "by the Eternal[,]" I will never do. So far as he has the legal "supervisory and appellate" power over my office I will gladly submit, but not a single hairsbreadth beyond. On the 30th inst. he addressed a letter to me "relieving" me from the Disbursing Agency of the Capitol Extension, New Dome, & Patent Office Building. He had an undoubted *right* to do so. But there is a gentlemanly way to do an act and a boorish way, and he chose, as his nature is, to take the latter. My only notice of his *brutem fulmen,* was to reply with as much dignity as I could to him, asking no questions, but notifying him that I should comply with his request, and writing a note to the President informing him of the coarse treatment I had received, but requesting no interference whatever from him.[2] I am impressed with the belief that I can checkmate the outrageous official doings of the Secy. when Congress comes. I think, if my life and health are spared, I will show him that *he* is the most unpopular Secretary of the Interior who ever held that office. I shall, at any rate, try what I can do. He is the meanest and most contemptible man I have ever had anything to do with. Let him rest for the present. Through my influence he was confirmed. He has broken every solemn pledge he made to obtain influence, and is *a Liar.*

June 30th & July 1st I was engaged in the examination of the deaf and dumb and blind pupils in the Columbia Institution at Kendall Green. Doct. Sampson[3] and Rev. Mr. Chapman[4] of Georgetown & myself compose the Committee of Examination. I do not remember ever to have been more interested in the performance of any duty. Mrs. French accompanied me out the second day, when the Exhibition took place.

For the week past I have been gradually removing my office of Commissioner from the front basement of the Capitol to the attic story. The rooms I now have are far more pleasant and convenient than the old ones, but not so accessible, which is rather in their favor, as persons who merely call to *loaf* will not annoy me, as they often did in my old office. . . .

1. See June 16, 1863.
2. French wrote to Lincoln on July 2, remarking that he had been relieved by Usher

"without notice or reason," and expressed the hope that he still retained Lincoln's "confidence and kind feeling." Lincoln Papers, Library of Congress.

3. George W. Samson (1819–1896) had been pastor of Washington's E Street Baptist Church and from 1859 to 1871 was president of Columbian College. Later in life he was the president of Rutgers Female College.

4. William H. Chapman, pastor of the Methodist Episcopal Church in Georgetown.

Wednesday, July 8. *"Vicksburg has fallen!"* Since 2 o'clock yesterday I suppose I have heard that said a thousand times. "It is a glorious victory," and I trust we shall soon have more of the same sort. Rumor already has it that Port Hudson is captured, and I believe if our army does all its duty Lee's army will scarcely ever see old Virginia soil again *as an army.* It is already awfully used up and is fast being pushed to annihilation. Richmond must soon go, and then poor Jeff will be driven to his wits end. My guess is that the Rebs. will soon find themselves a set of poor[,] miserable wretches, and they will cry to come back into our glorious Union! I see National glory in the future such as the past has never seen. Slavery forever abolished! The South populated and thriving under Free labor & Free rule! No more Cotton lords, but plenty of Cotton Commons, and all the land pouring out its productions & becoming immensely rich! Industry, Wealth, Happiness, Virtue, all marching hand in hand, and millions of voices raising their thanks to God for His goodness in doing good to all. Oh how manifest it is to my mind that *He* is now working out the future goodness and greatness of this, his chosen people[,] by the sore affliction and sacrifice of War! My Faith in the glorious result has not wavered a single instant since the Rebel cannon opened on Fort Sumter, and I think now I have a perfectly realizing sense of what our future is to be; and to the goodness and honesty of Abraham Lincoln, who has acted, in my beliefs, as the servant of the Most High God in all that he has done, do we owe all that we are to be.

The weather was very dry nearly all June. The Potomac was very low and easily fordable. Lee's army crossed as easily as the Israelites crossed the Red Sea, but no sooner were they well away from its Northern bank than the rain began to fall, and it has been raining almost continually till the river has risen so much as not to be fordable at any point, & Lee & his whole army are caught, & must be captured! Is not the finger of Providence as clear in this as it was to the Israelites of old when they escaped so miraculously from Pharaoh & his Hosts? I think it is. Then—

> Sound the loud timbrel o'er Egypt's dark sea,
> *JEHOVAH* hath triumphed! *His* people are *FREE*!

Friday, July 10. About 10 o'clock last evening the 34th Regt. Mass. Volunteers, Col. Wells,[1] left their barracks a few rods below here and marched for the depot, there to take the cars for Harpers Ferry. We had all formed strong attachments to many of the officers of that noble regiment, and it seems today as if half the City had departed. Col. Wells, Capt. Leach, Lt. Horton & Lt. Macomber visited us, and we became acquainted with several others; the whole Regiment knew me, and as they passed two companies gave 3 cheers for "Major French."[2] I felt as if my personal friends, who had been making me a visit, were departing! They are gone to fight the battle of Freedom; may God be with them and protect them.

No more special news of victory has come since I last wrote herein. . . .

1. George D. Wells, who was a judge in Boston, was killed at Cedar Creek, Va., on October 13, 1864, one day after he had been brevetted brigadier general.
2. William B. Leach, of New Hampshire, had been made a captain and assistant adjutant general of the 1st Minnesota Infantry in May 1862. Jere Horton, a teacher of Westfield, Mass., was commissioned as a second lieutenant in the 34th Massachusetts Infantry in August 1862. George Macomber was commissioned as a lieutenant in the 34th Massachusetts Infantry in July 1862.

Friday, July 17. . . . The war news has been exciting. Port Hudson is captured, and the Mississippi opened—a tremendous triumph to the Union cause! The news from the vicinity of Charleston looks well. Lee's army has escaped across the Potomac, but with vast losses, and the chances seem to be that it will yet be badly beaten. He is rushing, it is said, for Richmond as fast as possible. Meade is not idle & will endeavour to head him. Things look well all around for the triumph of the Union and Constitution over Rebellion & Treason. The recent awful riots in N. York will eventuate in good. They were initiated by desperate men for a purpose which has signally failed, and the result must be disgrace & shame to those who initiated them, and among them[,] I regret to say, is my old Friend Frank Pierce, late President of the U.S.[,] who by his miserable, weak speech at Concord on the 4th inst. disgraced himself and the name he bears.[1] I thought better of him, but now I give him over to Secesh & Rebeldom. "Ephraim has gone to his idols. Let him alone."

Wednesday I aided at Jay Cooke & Co.'s Banking house in forming "the 1st National Bank of the Dist. of Col.," under the new Banking law.[2] H. D. Cooke is President, William S. Huntington[,] Cashier, Fahnstock, Wills, and myself[,] Directors.[3] They intend to get it under way by the 20th inst. . . .

1. Ex-President Pierce at a Democratic gathering in Concord, N.H., on July 4, had attacked Lincoln and denounced the war as a "fearful, fruitless, fatal civil war." Widespread

rioting, in response to the implementation of the Conscription Act of March 3, 1863, broke out in New York City on July 13 and continued for four days.

2. The National Currency Act of February 25, 1863, had established a national banking system under a comptroller of the currency.

3. Henry D. Cooke (1825–1881), banker, journalist, and brother of banker Jay Cooke. Harris C. Fahnestock (1835–1914) later directed the New York branch of Jay Cooke and Co., 1866–1873. John A. Wills, attorney with Magraw and Wills, 261 G St. Huntington lived at 326 H St.

Wednesday, July 22. Monday the 20th at 6 A.M. a son was born to Frank and Ellen, at Roxbury, Mass. I recd. a Telegram at 10 o'clock & 20 minutes from Frank announcing the fact. (Child named *Amos Tuck*).[1] . . .

Monday the 153d New York Vol. came to occupy the barracks below us. They appear well. Had their first dress parade this evening.

The war seems now to be doing well for the Union & I hope is drawing to a close. A few weeks will decide whether a peace is *to be conquered,* or whether the war is to continue. . . .

1. Amos Tuck French (1863–1941) annotated this entry in 1902: "My grandfather does not seem enthusiastic over the arrival." Like his father, Amos Tuck French was a successful banker, serving as the director of the Manhattan Trust Co., 1893–1908. He edited the privately circulated *From the Diary and Correspondence of Benjamin Brown French* (New York, 1904).

Sunday, July 26. . . . Yesterday was a very hot day. I was at the President's at 10 A.M. by appointment with my friend J. Q. A. Fellows[1] of New Orleans, and a Mr. May,[2] a young planter from near that City. They came to see what could be done to reorganize the civil government of Louisiana on the basis of Free labor. The President received them in a most friendly and cordial manner, and we conversed at least an hour, and our interview ended very hopefully, with an appointment for another next Monday or Tuesday. From the President's we went to the Treasury and had a very pleasant interview with Secy. Chase on the same subject. I got back to my office at about 1 o'clock. . . . In the evening my friend Collins called and talked to me about various things. Among others he spake of the *organized* persecution I was to undergo for not removing Capt. Darling from the place of Captain of the Police. The attempt is to be made to prove him guilty of various improper things & then to connect me with them as being privy thereto.

Now the fact is that there has been a studied effort for the removal of Darling ever since I became Commissioner. Vague charges of improper conduct have been *scattered about,* but not a single thing proved, and no one charges him of neglect of duty! That he is strict in his discipline I have no doubt, & perhaps sometimes harsh when he finds his subordinates neglectful of their duty, but I never had a man under me who seemed so earnest to do all that was required of him as is Capt. Darling. This is, however, one of the secret plans of the outs to get in and sponge the Govt. Let them try. We will see who can beat! Perhaps they can. . . .

1. John Q. A. Fellows is identified in a letter of July 24, 1863, from French to Lincoln, as "one of the true Union, Administration men of N. Orleans." Lincoln Papers, Library of Congress. An eight-page plan by Fellows on the reestablishment of civil government in Louisiana is in Lincoln's papers under the date of June 26, 1863. Fellows was defeated as a candidate for the governorship of Louisiana in 1864.

2. Mr. May was characterized in the same letter from French to Lincoln as one who had "freed all his slaves & hired them as laborers."

Friday, August 14. . . . Last Sunday William Ellison[1] of Boston, and J. G. Stephenson[2] of this City, Librarian of Congress, dined with us. Mr. Ellison came, by invitation, about 11 A.M. & staid till dark. Doct. Stephenson came about 1 & staid till 4. He gave us a very full and interesting account of the battles up in Pennsylvania, in all which he took an active part. He was a Col. on Gen. Meredith's staff. According to his notions a great blunder was made in not attacking Lee at Williamsport. He thinks, had that been done, we should have had a complete and decisive victory! I was of the same opinion when I first heard of the position of things there, though, of course, I could know nothing certain, but so it looked to me, and I felt chagrined when I heard that Lee had crossed the Potomac unmolested. But, I suppose, it was so ordained, & all will turn out for the best in the end! . . .

1. Perhaps William P. Ellison (1835–1903), who was to become prominent in Boston's financial circles.

2. John G. Stephenson (1828–1883), fifth Librarian of Congress, 1861–1864.

Sunday, August 23. . . . At 6 A.M. Mrs. French and Ben left for Baltimore, she to visit her sister Sarita[1] at Mount de Sales, a convent about 6 miles out of the City, and Ben to do some errands of his own I believe. At ¼ past 11 I followed. . . . Found Mrs. French at the Convent, and just bidding good-by to start for the City. She introduced me to the Mother Superior[,] to several of the Sisters and to Sarita. Sarita is a lady-like little body, and very interesting in her appearance. She has seen much of the world, & appears much older in her conversation & manners than she really is. She is neither handsome nor homely. She appears full of vivacity and declares she "won't be a nun." I have not seen her before since she was, perhaps 5 years old. . . .

1. Sarita Brady (1848–1884) was Mary Ellen's half-sister, the daughter of Peter Brady and his second wife, Sarah Morrison Brady. When Peter Brady died, Sarah took Sarita

with her and went to live in Spain. Following Sarah's death, Sarita was sent to the convent outside Baltimore. When she was eighteen, she went to live in Washington with Margaret French, her half-sister.

Sunday, August 30. . . . On Thursday evening The two Commanderies of Knights Templar paid me an official visit. There were about 60 in all, and they made a very creditable appearance. We entertained them with cake, liquors, ice cream, peaches, sandwiches, jelly, lemonade, ham, etc. They seemed to enjoy themselves, & take it all in all, it was an exceedingly pleasant occasion. They came a little past 6 and left at ½ past 8. Mrs. French had a goodly number of her lady friends who mingled with the Knights. At one time the garden was pretty well filled, and the full moon shining down from a perfectly clear sky on the white plumes of the Knights & white dresses of the ladies gave the scene in the garden a most romantic effect. The fountain was in full play & sparkled in the bright moonbeams, the water in the pool shimmered & shone as if it were polished silver, the shrubbery, the green arbors, the marine band discoursing eloquent music, all combined, seemed to call up scenes of romance of which I have read, but never expected to see actually illustrated, especially on my own premises! . . .

Monday, September 7. I have been busily engaged all day, from 8 to 11 in getting William A. Taliaferro[1] free of service under the draft, on the ground that he has an old & infirm father & mother to take care of. Then at the office till nearly 3, all the time engaged. Then home & dined. At 4 to Doct. Sigismond's,[2] Dentist, & had a very bad tooth filled with artificial bone filling—charge $8—if it is good[,] little enough. Mary Ellen is off to see Gen. Benham's[3] pontoon bridge put together. . . .

    1. William A. Taliaferro, a messenger at the Capitol.
    2. S. B. Sigismond's dental office was at 260 Pennsylvania Ave.
    3. Henry W. Benham (1813–1884), military engineer, was in command of the pontoon depot in Washington from July 1863 to May 1864.

Sunday, September 27. . . . The week has past away with the usual monotony. I have been at the President's almost daily, and have seen him twice. On Tuesday I presented a cane to him in behalf of my friend Mr. James Nokes. . . .

Monday, November 2. . . . Ned's Willie and Eddie have diptheria [sic], neither very sick, but may be. She [Mary Ellen] has brought dear little

Mary home with her, for which I am glad, as, I think the disease would go very hard with her, and we must keep her out of the way of it, if possible. . . .

Friday, November 6. We have not had so disagreeable a day by the way of wind and dust for months, as this is. I was down in the city for two or three hours this forenoon and came near being suffocated. Pa. Avenue was one cloud of dust from end to end, and it was nearly as much as one's life was worth to pass up or down 7th St.[,] the wind being N.W. seemed to whirl all through that street in eddies, whirling the dust in thick clouds in every direction.

For the week past the workmen have been putting up the bronze doors made by Randolph Rogers,[1] between the old and new Halls of the Ho. Reps. in the Capitol. The doors are now in place and are magnificent. They embody, in the semicircle over the transom, and in the panels, the history of Columbus. They are a study for a month, and after the brick work is filled in & the entire job finished, I intend to study them at my leisure.

The first iron column of the lanthorn of the Dome was put in its place this morning. The others will follow, and the place for "Freedom"[2] to stand upon will soon be ready. The outside of the Dome will now be completed in a few weeks. It will take at least a year to finish the inner Dome, which is to be very highly ornamented.

When the Capitol is finished, if ever such an event occurs, it will be, in every respect, a noble building, and will contain hundreds of things worthy the study of the connoisseur in the Fine Arts—Mechanics—etc. . . .

Col. Lamon is to be Marshal-in-chief at Gettysburg, on the 19th inst.[,] when the grand inauguration of the Cemetery for soldiers killed, or who died there, takes place, and he has invited me to aid him, which I have agreed to do. This will be a task. But we are all in for doing what we can to show our Patriotism, and I should not think I was doing my duty were I to decline. If alive & well I shall be there. . . .

1. Randolph Rogers (1825–1892), an American-born sculptor who spent most of his career in Italy, executed the "Columbus Doors" that serve as the east entrance to the Rotunda.
2. The figure of "Freedom" atop the Capitol dome was designed by Thomas Crawford (1813–1857) and executed by Clark Mills. Thomas Ustick Walter, as architect of the Capitol extension, referred to the figure as "Liberty."

Saturday, November 14. . . . Thursday morning at ½ past 6, with Col. Lamon and Doct. Stephenson, I started for Gettysburg, Margaret and

Mary Ellen accompanying me as far as Balto. where they went to see Sarita.

We left Balto. at ¼ past 9 with a tremendous train—hundreds of secession prisoners, with a guard, being with us—and, as usual, missed the regular connection at Hanover Junction. We, however[,] made known our business, and a special train was sent on with us, and we arrived at Gettysburg between 3 & 4 and went to the Eagle Hotel, kept by Mr. John Tait. David Wills, Esq., Gov. Curtin's Agent,[1] called on us soon after we arrived, with Mr. Codey of N.J.[,] and we accompanied them to Mr. Wills's office, where we labored till 6 in making out programmes, etc. Then we returned to the hotel and dined—or supped—my first food since 5 A.M. We then returned to the office and finished up all we could for the evening. Doct. Stephenson being sick with a chill could not accompany us. At about 9 Col. L. & I returned to the hotel and went to bed. Instead of sleeping, I composed some rhymes for the celebration. Mr. Wills had told us during the evening that he had endeavoured to get Longfellow,[2] and Bryant, and Whittier, and Boker[3] to write something, who all declined. So my muse volunteered. I arose early yesterday morning and reduced my thoughts of the night to writing and gave a copy to Mr. Wills, and another to Col. Lamon. Perhaps it will be used, perhaps not. I did my best.

At 9 yesterday morning we visited the cemetery. I do not feel like writing now and will defer my account of our visit till I feel better.

I will only say, now, I arrived home at 10 last night after a very pleasant and satisfactory visit.

1. David Wills was a prominent resident of Gettysburg, and chairman of the cemetery board. It was he who extended the invitation to Lincoln to make "a few appropriate remarks" at the dedication of November 19. Andrew G. Curtin (1815–1894), Republican governor of Pennsylvania, 1861–1867.

2. Henry Wadsworth Longfellow (1807–1882), enormously popular American poet.

3. George Henry Boker (1823–1890), dramatist and sonneteer of Philadelphia. He was later U.S. minister to Turkey and Russia.

Sunday, November 22. And now for a full journalization of my visit at Gettysburg. I intended to write a more full account of my first visit . . . but the latter so much involves the former that I shall commence at the preparations for that.

Marshal Lamon called a meeting of all his Aids—some 60 or 70—at the City Hall on Monday evening last. A goodly number attended[,] and the meeting was duly organized with Judge Casey[1] in the Chair. All the information that had been obtained as to the manner, time, etc., of going, the equipment, facilities for being taken care of, etc., was given by the Marshal, and he stated that a car on the Washington R.R. was to be at his disposal at 3 P.M. on Tuesday. I took the liberty to give my friends warning that if they postponed going till that time they would probably be out all night. They disregarded my advice and the sequel will show how correct I was. They voted to leave Washington at 3 P.M. on Tuesday. I announced my determination to leave at ½ past 6 A.M.[,] and with my friend Doct. Stephenson, did so, and after a very pleasant trip, we arrived at Gettysburg at ½ past one P.M. Quite a crowd accompanied us from Baltimore & Hanover junction. Doct. Stephenson had his rooms engaged & had no trouble. Finding that there was no certainty of my being well accommodated at the hotel I went to *Brother* Robert Goodloe Harper's,[2] whose name had been give me by Bro. Creigh,[3] and he at once said that he would take care of me, and to him and his excellent wife and daughters am I indebted for as much comfort and happiness as any man in Gettysburg enjoyed from 2 o'clock on Tuesday until 1 o'clock P.M. on Friday. Mr. Harper is 64 years old & moves about with all the elasticity of a boy. He owns & edits the *Adams Sentinel*, a paper established many years ago by his father. He has had twelve children, 10 by his first wife, who died 20 years ago, & 2 by his present wife[,] to whom he has been married some 8 or 10 years. She is now 32 years old. He has grandchildren who are grown up. The whole family are remarkably hospitable and pleasant. I spent the afternoon and evening in listening to Mrs. Harper's account of the battle, and the many incidents accompanying it which fell under her observation. She remained at her house through the whole of it, and it became a hospital after the battle was over. Mr. Harper was absent from the town. Two bullets came into the house through the windows, one of which struck a crib at the bedside of a wounded officer, the other passed within a few inches of Mrs. Harper. One shell fell in the garden within a few feet of the house, but did not explode. It was picked up, the charge extracted, & now lies on the parlor table, where I saw it. Being much fatigued, and not having slept well the previous night, I retired early to rest. On going to the hotel Wednesday morning I found my Washington friends had not arrived! At ½ past 9 the Marshal and some 15 of his aids arrived, having been on the road from Washington since 11 o'clock the preceding day! It seems that on Tuesday morning the Marshal was informed by the R.R. Co. that they could not accommodate him with a special car at 3 P.M. but could at 11 A.M. He gave notice to all he could reach & they started at 11—the others, and among them Ben & Nathan, took the ½ past 6 train Wednesday morning and arrived about 4 P.M. At 6 P.M. came the President of the U.S.[,] Secretaries Seward & Usher, and P.M. Gen. Blair of the Cabinet.

The French & Italian Ministers and their Secretaries, & Messrs. Nicolay & Hay[,] Private Secretaries to the President, Mr. Seward, Mr. Berchinatti (the Italian Minister) & his Secretary[,] Mr. Cova, stayed at Mr. Harper's, where I did, and the President and the others of his party at Mr. Wills's next door to Mr. Harper's.[4] In the evening the President came into Mr. Harper's and spent an hour. That evening there was a large influx of visitors, and the President & Mr. Seward were serenaded and made brief speeches. The Marshals had a meeting at the Court House, which I, of course, attended. We made all the necessary arrangements for the following day, and contributed $160 to purchase food for our starving prisoners at the Libby prison, Richmond. I gave $20.

[And now while I am writing comes in Mr. Barrett with a piece of cornbread, coarse, unsalted, and like a piece of brickbat, 4¼ inches long[,] 2¾ inches wide, & 2 inches thick, on which is written "One day's ration, issued to Wm. Sanderson(?), Iowa soldier in the Libby prison at Richmond, on the 16th of November, 1863—the day he was discharged, after 7 months imprisonment." I broke off a crumb of it which I intend to keep as a specimen of the food *so generously* contributed to our poor prisoners by the infernal dynasty of the Arch traitor Jeff Davis!][5]

On my return to Mr. Harper's I said to the company that we had raised $160 to purchase food for our prisoners at Richmond. Mr. Seward said that the Rebel government would not permit it to be given them. I told him that they would if it came from *individuals,* but not from the Government. He then handed me $10 saying "put that down from *Marshal* Seward *an individual.*" At this point let me say that I have seldom, if ever, met with a man whose mind is under such perfect discipline, and is so full of original and striking matter as Secretary Seward's. His conversation, no matter on what subject, is worthy of being written down and preserved, and if he had a Boswell to write, as Boswell did of Johnson, one of the most interesting and useful books of the age might be produced from the conversations and sayings of William H. Seward. He is one of the greatest men of this generation.

After I retired to rest, the public square on which Mr. Harper's house fronts seemed to be filled with people. They sang, & hallooed, and cheered. Among other things they sang, in full chorus & admirably, the whole of that well known production whose refrain is—

We are coming Father Abraham, three hundred thousand more.

I went to sleep between 1 & 2 A.M. & arose at daylight. As soon as breakfast was over I sat [sic] about procuring a horse, which I got of the Quartermaster, Capt. Blood.[6] A shaggy, unpromising looking nag he was, but on mounting him & using the spurs pretty freely, I found he was a

spirited & easygoing beast, and he performed all I desired admirably.
The Marshals were all assembled, mounted, in the square, with sashes
on and batons in hand, at 9 o'clock, and by 10 the procession commenced
moving. Never was a procession better formed or more orderly. It was
escorted by nearly 2,000 troops of all arms under command of Major
Gen. Couch.[7] We were all on the ground about 12. The programme was
as follows and was carried out to the letter.[8]

As soon as the dignitaries who occupied the stand, numbering perhaps
250, were seated, Hon. Edward Everett & Rev. Thos. H. Stockton[9] appeared[,] escorted by a Committee of Governors of States, and being
seated, one of the bands struck up and performed a solemn piece of
music in admirable style. That over, Mr. Stockton made one of the most
impressive and eloquent prayers I ever heard. The Band then played,
with great effect, *Old Hundred.* Mr. Everett then arose, and without notes
of any kind, pronounced an oration. He occupied two full hours in the
delivery, and it was one of the greatest, most eloquent, elegant, and
appropriate orations to which I ever listened. I stood at his very side,
through it, and I think the oratory could not be surpassed by mortal
man.

I stood at the side of John Quincy Adams when he delivered his great
Eulogy on Lafayette, in the old Hall of the House of Representatives,
Dec. 31, 1834, and standing there, by Everett's side at Gettysburg, how
the past came back upon me, and I thought if Adams could be alive, &
here today, how his pure and honest heart would swell with the patriotism that has followed his own great efforts to bring about that emancipation of the negro race which is so rapidly approaching. I hope his
immortal spirit could look down upon us all with an approving smile,
on that auspicious day.

Mr. Everett was listened to with breathless silence by all that immense
crowd, and he had his audience in tears many times during his masterly
effort.

When he had finished[,] the following, headed

"Consecration Hymn[,]"

was sung beautifully, & with much effect[,] by a Musical Association from
Baltimore. (See margin.)[10]

I can say *here,* that I never was so flattered at any production of my
own, as in relation to that same Hymn. All who heard it seemed to
consider it most appropriate, and most happily conceived.

As soon as the hymn was sung, Marshal Lamon introduced the President of the United States, who, in a few brief, but most appropriate
words, dedicated the cemetery. Abraham Lincoln is the idol of the American people at this moment. Anyone who saw & heard as I did, the

hurricane of applause that met his every movement at Gettysburg would know that he lived in every heart. It was no cold, faint, shadow of a kind reception—it was a tumultuous outpouring of exultation, from true and loving hearts, at the sight of a man whom everyone knew to be honest and true and sincere in every act of his life, and every pulsation of his heart. It was the spontaneous outburst of heartfelt confidence in *their own* President.

After the President had concluded, the Gettysburg Choir sung a Dirge, accompanied by the Band, in excellent style, and with great effect.

Doct. Baugher,[11] President of the College, then pronounced the Benediction, and the Marshals formed and escorted the President back to his lodgings, where he arrived about 3 P.M. After dinner, the Marshals assembled on foot & escorted the President to the Presbyterian Church where an address was delivered by the Lt. Gov. of Ohio.[12] I should have said that for about an hour after the return of the President to Mr. Wills's, he received all who chose to call on him, and there were thousands who took him by the hand. At ½ past 6 he left in a special train for this City, and arrived home about midnight. That evening, and the succeeding morning[,] a vast multitude left Gettysburg. The Marshals all procured horses about 10 o'clock on Friday and rode out to and over the Battleground in a body. A Mr. Bachelder,[13] a native of Gilmanton, N.H., who is preparing a map of the battleground, & has studied the localities thoroughly, rode out with us & described the battleground from a number of points in a very clear and interesting manner. I had a very hard going horse, & headstrong, and found the labor of riding so severe that when the cavalcade left the Cemetery for more distant points, I trotted down the southern slope of the hill to the house occupied by Gen. Meade[14] as his headquarters, it being a very interesting point to me, as Capt. William H. Paine,[15] an Engineer in the Army, was with Gen. Meade[,] and when the Gen. left for another part of the field, Capt. P. was left in charge of the house and remained in it[,] as he supposed, alone, through all the tremendous cannonade, during which shells & shot passed again and again through the house, and 17 horses were killed all around it. After the firing ceased, several men appeared to Capt. Paine's astonished vision ascending from the cellar where they had been keeping themselves out of harm's way! This same Capt. Paine was born in the same town in which I was, and within ten rods of my father's house. I knew him when a boy, he being many years my junior. He was at my house several times summer before last. Well, I went to the house mentioned. The door was locked, and a little girl was on the piazza, or porch, who told me that the people were at the barn. I looked particularly at the outside of the house & saw where the shot and shell perforated it. On my way to the barn I passed the carcases of two dead horses, which were very offensive. I found a young man at the barn who said his mother occupied the house. He said he was at Fortress Monroe when the battle occurred, as a soldier in the three months service. Since his return he had mended up the barn, which was shattered worse than the house. He showed me many shot holes which still remain. He said he burned the carcases of 15 of the horses that were killed, but the two that remained were so near the outbuildings that he could not burn them without endangering the buildings. After making all the observations I desired[,] I started to return to my horse when I saw two men with a camera down in the field in front of the house. I walked down and found Mr. Gardner[,][16] a Photographist of this City, was the man. At his urgent request I walked back to the house and took a position on the porch where I was, I suppose, photographed with the house. There were, then, two children on the porch with me.[17]

I then mounted my horse and rode leisurely up through the clump of trees on top of the hill every one of which had been hit with some missile, and many of the largest were cut off at from 6 to 10 feet above the ground by shot or shell. I then rode into town along the street where stands a house, the south end of which was torn nearly to pieces by shells fired into it[,] as I was told, by our batteries at the request of its owner, the rebels having taken possession of it. In less than 10 minutes after I passed, a man and boy who were engaged in *unloading* a shell, were blown up by its exploding—the boy killed instantly & the man losing both arms & probably his eyes. The Doct. pronounced his case almost hopeless, and he is probably dead ere this. Mr. Barrett, who went out with me, was opposite the place when the shell exploded[,] and at the request of the screaming women went after a surgeon, whom he found on the street and sent to them. We all returned to town about 12, and at about ½ past one were off for Washington, where we arrived at 10 P.M. The trip to Washington was very pleasant. The Marshals' car was crowded from Gettysburg to Baltimore, but its inmates were joyous. We had conversation, singing & merriment. The Star Spangled Banner and other patriotic songs were sung in full chorus, and even Doct. Watts[,][18] with the sacred tunes to which his Psalms & Hymns are set, swelled their choral notes upward with fine effect.

We arrived in Baltimore at ½ past 5 and all went to the Eutaw House where we partook of an excellent supper. At 8 we took the cars for Washington, where we arrived, as above stated, at 10 P.M.

The whole affair from commencement to close was conducted in the most admirable manner, and without a single accident or baulk. It was most creditable to all concerned, and the memory of it will be forever precious.

1. Joseph Casey (1814–1879), Whig congressman from Pennsylvania, 1849–1851, was appointed to U.S. Court of Claims in 1861 and became chief justice in 1863.

2. Robert Goodloe Harper was the publisher of the *Adams Centinel* in Gettysburg from 1817 to 1867. He also served as the treasurer of Adams County and held a number of other local offices.

3. A Masonic friend of French's.

4. John George Nicolay (1832–1901), private secretary to President Lincoln. He later collaborated with John Hay in writing a ten-volume biography of Lincoln. John Hay (1838–1905), private secretary to President Lincoln and also his biographer. He later had a long and distinguished career as a diplomat, culminating in his service as Secretary of State, 1898–1905. Chevalier Joseph Bertinatti had been the minister from Sardinia since 1855 and then from Italy, following Victor Emmanuel's assumption of the title of King of Italy in 1861. Leon de la Cova later served as vice-consul in Philadelphia for Colombia and Venezuela. The unnamed French minister was Henri Mercier (1816–1886), who served at Washington from 1860 to 1863. He was an early and persistent advocate of recognition of the Confederacy.

5. The brackets are French's.

6. Captain Henry Bloyden Blood, assistant quartermaster, was involved in the issue of supplies during the Gettysburg campaign and in the retrieval of government property after the battle.

7. Darius N. Couch (1822–1897), a major general of volunteers, organized state levies for the defense of Pennsylvania during the Gettysburg campaign. He was in charge of the ceremonies at the dedication of the cemetery at Gettysburg.

8. At this point in his journal French inserted the printed "Order of Procession for the Inauguration of the National Cemetery at Gettysburg, Pa., on the 19th November, 1863." It was issued by Ward H. Lamon.

9. Thomas H. Stockton (1808–1868), Methodist minister, was one of the great pulpit orators of his time. He was chaplain of the Senate at this time.

10. There are no marginalia on this page of French's journal, nor attachment to it. A copy of the hymn, however, is in French's papers.

11. Henry L. Baugher (1804–1868), president of Pennsylvania College (now Gettysburg College).

12. Benjamin Stanton (1809–1872) had been a Whig congressman from Ohio, 1851–1853 and 1855–1861.

13. John B. Bachelder (1825–1894), born in Gilmanton, N.H., prepared a bird's-eye view of the battlefield, as well as a map that is still considered to be one of the best ever done. He later designed one of the deathbed scenes of Abraham Lincoln.

14. George Gordon Meade (1815–1872) commanded Union forces in the Peninsular Campaign, at Second Bull Run, Antietam, and Chancellorsville before taking command of the Army of the Potomac on the eve of Gettysburg.

15. William H. Paine, of Wisconsin, rose to the rank of colonel by the end of the Civil War.

16. Alexander Gardner first worked for Mathew Brady but soon established his own place of business, Gardner's Gallery, at 511 7th St. in Washington. In addition to his famous battlefield pictures, he photographed Lincoln more than any other photographer.

17. This photograph is reproduced in Ill. 12 of the Maps and Illustrations Section.

18. Isaac Watts (1674–1748), English clergyman, composed some 600 hymns, including "O God Our Help in Ages Past."

Sunday, November 29. . . . Friday morning [November 27] a letter came announcing from Frank that they should arrive that evening, and Mary

Ellen went at once to work making preparations, and I think was on her feet about all day. I had an engagement at 4 & had to go down in the City. I returned at ¼ past 6 and found Frank, Ellen, Bessie & little Amos just arrived. It was a most joyful event. Ellen had not been here since she was married, and Frank not since the death of his adored mother. We gave them as hearty a welcome as it was in our power to do. . . .

Wednesday, December 2. Today at 12 o'clock meridian, *they* finished putting the statue of Freedom on the tholus of the dome of the Capitol.[1] Being Commissioner of Public Buildings and, by law, charged with the care of all the Public Buildings, I thought that those having the control of putting up the statue, under John P. Usher, the present Secretary of the Interior, would have done me the trifling honor of notifying me, *officially*, when it was to be done, and have requested my presence on the occasion, but it was not done, and I remained in my office.

Freedom now stands on the Dome of the Capitol of the United States— may she stand there forever, not only in form, but in *spirit*.

I called on the President today—found him in his chamber, sick—just recovering from an attack of varioloid.[2] I had not seen him since I saw him at Gettysburg. He first felt the effects of it while there, and came home sick, as he told me. I did some official business with him and then left, and returned to the Capitol. . . .

The members are coming in pretty rapidly, and next Monday a 6 or 7 months' session of Congress will commence.

1. The crowning feature of the statue—the head and shoulders of the colossal figure— was steam-hoisted from the ground to a height of 300 feet in twenty minutes.
2. A mild form of smallpox.

Saturday, December 5. It is ½ past 3 o'clock P.M. Frank and I left at ½ past 9 this morning in the buggy and rode up to Cabin John Bridge. The Secy. of the Interior[,] Mr. Usher, appointed today to turn on the water from the Potomac River.[1] We have had it heretofore from "Powder mill Branch," about 4 miles above Georgetown, and our Corporation voted to celebrate the occasion, so Frank and I rode up to help them. We met the City cavalcade about two miles this side of Cabin John on our return & we concluded that the operation of the Secretary would not take place till 4 or 5 o'clock, so we came home. At 6 there is to be a Corporation dinner at the National Hotel, which I am invited to attend, and intend to go.

1. The water still flows through this aqueduct.

Monday, December 7. I attended the dinner at the National. It was quite a nice affair. Vice President Hamlin and General Martindale[1] made eloquent speeches, all the rest, while I staid, was milk & water. Secy. John P. Usher spoke in reply to a sentiment complimentary to the President, in a manner that would shame a ten year old school boy. I think I never heard as weak a speech from a grown-up man, nor one more tame in its delivery. . . .

Today Congress has assembled. I have been in my office all day and know but little of what has been done. I know Schuyler Colfax has been elected Speaker of the House, at which I sincerely rejoice, for he is a good and pure man.

I have been immensely vexed lately at the doings of those who controlled placing the statue of Freedom upon the Dome. I regarded the event as one of great moment, particularly at this time, and yet those having the control of it, for reasons that I cannot fathom, *unless they fear the Southern Rebels,* issued written orders to Capt. Thomas,[2] who had intended a small display of patriotism, for *he,* at least, is a true patriot & a true man! ordering him preremptorily [sic], not to suffer *any* demonstration of rejoicing to be made by the men under him, or by himself. Capt. Charles F. Thomas has shown more scientific ability in the raising of that statue than all the rest combined. He *alone* invented the manner of raising it. He erected the scaffolding he had invented. He superintended the rigging of it, & all the hoisting apparatus, and it was *solely* through his skill that it was raised to its position and fastened in its place without accident, and all this skill and efficiency was repaid by closing his mouth, and the mouths of all those under him. It was an unpatriotic, damnable, secession proceeding, and every man who had anything to do with it, if I had my way, should be turned, neck & heels, out of office! and if Congress does not make some little stir regarding it I shall be disappointed. . . .

1. John H. Martindale (1815–1881) was governor of the District of Columbia and a corps commander during the Civil War.
2. Charles F. Thomas, a mechanical engineer, was the superintendent of ironwork on the dome.

Tuesday, December 8. Frank has just said "good-by" to us all & with Ben has gone to the Depot to leave in the ½ past 8 o'clock train for New York, & thence tomorrow night for Boston. His visit has been short but most pleasant, and I feel very sad to have him leave. At my age it *is* hard to be so far separated from my eldest, who, were he with me, would be so great a comfort. . . .

Saturday, December 12. . . . Today went to Gardner's Photographic Gallery in the morning and looked at photographs, and was much interested, particularly with his "Incidents of the War." The carnage at Gettysburg, as shown by views taken by him while the field was strewn with the dead, gave me a most realizing sense of the concomitants of Battle. Oh the blood that has been needlessly shed during this awful war of rebellion! I sat for a *cart[e] de visite* while at Gardner's. Thence I went to Philps & Solomon's[1] gallery & saw a proof of Frank's photograph taken last Monday. It is admirable. Then I came to the Capitol and worked till 2 o'clock, and then came home, dined, & have been fussing over an old picture frame in which I have put a view of Meade's Head Quarters at Gettysburg, honored by my own presence on the porch, I happening, most accidentally, to be there when Mr. Gardner was photographing it on the 20th of November. I succeeded in framing it, but broke the glass. . . .

1. Philp & Solomons was a stationery and book store at 332 Pennsylvania Ave.

Sunday, December 13. . . . Yesterday all Congress went on board the Russian ships lying off Alexandria. I should think, by the account of the visit contained in the *Chronicle* of this morning, that they had a splendid time. We could see from our windows the flashes of the guns which saluted the party when they left, considerably after dark. The Russians were exceedingly polite and, at a time so fearful in our history when we hardly know who are and who are not our friends among the Nations of the world, it is truly gratifying to have a powerful Empire like Russia able, with us, to cope with all the world besides, exhibit for us such marked friendship. I have always regarded the Russians as a noble people, and I trust we shall not permit them to outdo us in courtesy.

Thursday, December 17. . . . Yesterday at 7 o'clock P.M. Ben left us to go to Boston and study awhile with Frank. I felt very sad at his departure, but it is very much better for him than to remain here in idleness. His penchant for spending money is the strongest that I have ever seen. He ought at this moment to have a thousand dollars at least out of the earnings he has received within the past two years, and he has nothing— or comparatively nothing. This desire to squander is the only bad habit that I know of that he has. He has great natural abilities and, I hope, will get over his extravagance & become a man of note, as he can. . . .

Sunday, December 20. . . . A new phase of employment has been forced upon me recently that is taking much of my time. The ladies, who are always doing something for the good of their fellow beings, are striving to inaugurate a splendid fair for the benefit of our soldiers. There were two parties, and it so happened that they thought that a union could be brought about by my influence, so I suffered my name to be used, and, at a meeting of the two, they united and elected me their President, which place I accepted for the sake of harmony, and now they are holding almost daily meetings which I must of course attend. Yesterday we met at Mr. Bowen's[1] at 10 A.M. The meeting was not so harmonious as could be desired, as a sort of a reorganization took place by adding gentlemen to the Committees, making a gentleman Secretary, and electing a gentleman Vice President (H. D. Cooke, Esq.). This rather grated on the feelings of a "Mrs. Lt. Brookfield,"[2] who was truly the *primum mobile* of the whole thing, but who rather disgusted the other ladies by an attempt to monopolize everything. She got angry, used improper language, and I was forced, unpleasant as it was, to call her to order. . . .

At ¼ to 12 I went to the President's where there was to be a reception given to the Russian officers. All Congress, the Supreme Court, the Cabinet, the Army & Navy officers, and many prominent citizens were invited, it being an *invited* reception. *My* two Mrs. French's—Mary Ellen and Ellen—were there. The reception did not commence till after one; it was the most brilliant I ever attended, because it was the only one where the mudstained people did not mingle with the court dresses, epaulettes, shoulder straps, etc. The crowd was quite large. The Russian officers were magnificently uniformed, and exceedingly polite and *stiff* in their manners, as all foreigners appear to be to us free-and-easy "Yankees," as the people in Jeff's Dominions think proper deridingly to call us, & which we delight to be called, considering it an honor instead of a reproach. . . .

1. Sayles J. Bowen (1813–1896), who had been commissioner of metropolitan police in 1861, was at this time postmaster of the City of Washington. He was elected mayor in 1868 and served until 1870.
2. A Lieutenant Alexander Brookfield, U.S.A., is listed in the Washington directories at 371 Pennsylvania Ave. However, no such officer is found in standard military listings, nor is he indexed in the *Records of the War of the Rebellion*.

Friday, December 25. . . . Last evening my good friend William Forsyth, brought a dozen bottles of old South side Madeira, as a present from Mrs. Forsyth to Mrs. French. We drank the health of the giver in it, at dinner, also our remembrance of Frank & his visitors. It is superb wine, such as would cost at least 5 dollars a bottle at any hotel. We enjoyed our Christmas dinner very much. After dinner the household scattered, and, I believe, slept—I did at any rate. . . .

My Christmas presents[:] the 4th Vol. of Pierre Irving's *Life of Wash-ington Irving,* by Mary Ellen—a Latin Dictionary[,] by Willie Russell—and a gold toothpick[,] by Ellen.

I have given away 5 cents to a little apple girl yesterday, who asked for a Christmas gift! That is all. Now, while writing, $50 from a Friend to me.

Sunday, January 3. . . . I left home about 10 A.M. [January 1], the sun shining[,] and wind blowing from the N.W. Went to the President's. At 11 The Diplomatic Corps, Judiciary, & members of the Senate and House came. Mrs. Lincoln not being quite ready, The President appeared without her, and the reception commenced. At ½ past 11 she appeared and did her part of the reception with her usual ease and urbanity. After the above-named dignitaries, the officers of the Army and Navy came, and then *the people en masse.* Mrs. Lincoln remained till ½ past 12 and then, concluding she had done her duty, left, bidding me good morning. Supposing my *duty* over I left. I understand she afterwards returned, and my friend Mr. Stoddard[1] acted in my place.

On leaving the President's I went to P.M. Gen. Blair's & saw him and his agreeable & handsome wife. From there I went to Gov. Seward's, then to V.P. Hamlin's, who had a nice entertainment, and with his amiable wife and daughter made all callers perfectly *at home.* At V.P. H.'s I met my friend, Hon. E. B. French,[2] with whom I went to Secy. Chase's, where we found a crowd, and the elegant Mrs. Senator Sprague doing, in her usual graceful manner, the honors of the Mansion. I think her one of the most lovable women I ever saw, and I wished her many, many, happy years from my very heart. From Secy. Chase's we went to Mayor Wallach's where there was feasting in abundance. . . .

1. William O. Stoddard (1835–1925) served as a secretary to Lincoln, 1861–1864. He wrote over a hundred books, including *Inside the White House in War Times* (1890), and many stories for boys.
2. Ezra B. French, of Maine, second auditor of the Treasury Department.

Thursday, January 14. . . . Tuesday evening there was a reception at the White House and I had to be at it till nearly 11. Mrs. French (my wife) & Mrs. French (my daughter-in-law) went. It was a *sparse* reception—the smallest I ever saw. Why? Can't tell. Mrs. Lincoln seemed disappointed. Abraham was in his usual trim & usual good nature.

Wednesday, January 27. . . . Mr. Tuck came here last Thursday noon, and Doct. Wells about 10 that evening. The latter was on a flying visit of business and left Friday evening. Mr. Tuck remained till this morning when, at ½ past 7, with Ellen and her two babies, he left for home. . . .

Sunday, February 21. . . . The 153d N.Y. Volunteers left their barracks on Thursday last, under orders, it is said, for Texas. That Regiment has been stationed here since Monday, July 20, 1863—7 months—and I will say for it that I never have seen a Regiment so quiet and orderly, or under so good discipline. Col. Davis,[1] its Commander, has been tried by a Court Martial during the past 7 or 8 weeks, for cruelty to his men, but was honorably acquitted. I was summoned 3 times before the Court, but was examined only once. I testified to Col. Davis's good character as an officer and a gentleman, so far as I knew. . . .

The Barracks are now occupied by 4 or 5 companies of the Invalid Corps, who came on the day the others left. . . .

I met Gen. Geo. G. Meade at Mrs. Lincoln's reception yesterday. He looks sick. He has just returned from Philadelphia where he has been quite sick. He says he is recovering. I hope he is, for we want him well when the Spring opens, and we hope and trust he will whip out Jeff and all his legions. . . .

1. Col. Edwin P. Davis (d. 1890) was the commanding officer of the 153d New York Infantry from April 1863 to October 1865. Under him, the regiment had garrison duty in Washington and Alexandria, in the Department of the Gulf, and in the Shenandoah Valley.

Tuesday, February 23. Yesterday was a busy day to me. Immediately after breakfast I went to my office and attended to all my necessary morning business. At 9 went to the Fair room at the Patent Office Building. Then with Mrs. French to Secy. Seward's to procure some articles for exhibition. Then to Mrs. Blanchard's. Then back to the Fair room. Then out on my own responsibility to get a carpet for the stage, etc. Got it & had it put down. Then I went about the room directing, advising and working till past 4 P.M. Then we all came home. . . . The first thing I found was a Telegram from my friend R. G. Harper of Gettysburg, informing me that he should be here with Mrs. Harper in the evening. We dined, I *finished* my poem *once more*, Mary Ellen & the girls went again to the Fair Rooms, & I waited for Mr. & Mrs. Harper who arrived about ½ past 5. Soon after their arrival we all went down to the Fair, & such a crowd as was there I have seldom seen. There must have been 3,000 people at the least. At about ½ past 7 the President & Mrs. Lincoln arrived and the exercises of opening commenced.

Dr. Sunderland[1] opened the exercises with an ardent and very impressive prayer. Mr. Chittenden[2] followed with an eloquent address of perhaps 40 minutes, and having lost his manuscript in coming to the Hall, he had to depend upon his memory and his skill, and they stood by him admirably, for his address was a capital one. I followed with a poem, and the President, after much persuasion, made a few closing remarks, when Doct. Sunderland pronounced the benediction, and "The Great Fair" was opened. We all stayed till about 11 o'clock, and then came home pretty well used up! . . .

1. Byron Sunderland (b. 1819), pastor of Washington's First Presbyterian Church.
2. Lucius E. Chittenden (b. 1824), of Vermont, register of the Treasury, was the author of *Personal Reminiscences* (1893).

Sunday, February 28. . . . Yesterday morning I went early to the Capitol. When the mail came a letter came from Mr. Whiting[1] saying the Secy. wanted to see me. I went down but did not succeed in seeing him till nearly 12. Had a long talk about the course I had pursued in relation to a certain bill now pending before the Senate, transferring the Capitol extension and dome to the Com. of P. B. and making his office independent of the Interior Department. Also about a letter I had written to Mr. Heustis.[2] He reproached me severely, but it did not hit hard, because I was conscious I had done what was right, and I know he has not! I believe him to be a corrupt, unfeeling, unprincipled man, with no soul worth saving. (I am mistaken as to the time I saw the Secy. It was on Friday morning we had the talk.) Yesterday morning I saw Senator Foot and related to him my interview with the Secy. I now record a solemn vow to follow up that Secretary till I drive him from office, or go out myself! He is a contemptible scoundrel! and an insufferable liar, and I believe a traitor to Abraham Lincoln, and he (A. L.) will ere long find it out. There can be no compromise between me & Usher.

I staid at the Fair yesterday till ½ past 12 and then went to the President's and attended Mrs. Lincoln at her reception till 3, then returned to the Fair. . . .

1. Perhaps George C. Whiting, who was in the Interior Department's office for the suppression of the African slave trade.
2. William H. Heustis, superintendent of marble work on the Capitol extension.

Saturday, March 5. . . . Thursday, 3d. All the morning at the President's with Messrs. Starr, Randall, and Radford, members of the Committee on Public Buildings & Grounds of the House of Representatives, examining the premises with a view to appropriations for repairs.[1] . . .

1. John F. Starr (1818–1904), of New Jersey, was a founder of the Camden Iron Works and a Republican congressman, 1863–1867. Samuel J. Randall (1828–1890), of Pennsyl-

vania, served briefly in the Union army and then as Democratic congressman, 1863–1890; he was speaker, 1876–1881. William Radford (1814–1870), Democratic congressman from New York, 1863–1867.

Monday, March 14. . . . Monday 7th, although suffering with a cold I went to the Capitol and was very busily engaged in my office till after 3 P.M. Came home a little after 3 and was soon seized with a severe pain in my stomach which held on with various phases of better and worse till Friday morning. Sometimes I was in agony, sometimes greatly relieved. Doct. Johnston attended me and my dear good wife hardly left me a moment. She did all a mortal could to cure me, and to her untiring care I think I owe it that I recovered so soon. Friday morning the pain left me, and I felt well all day, and have continued well. My cold is not yet well, but better. The Doctor pronounces my disease without doubt the passage of gallstones from the gallbladder into the stomach. It is the same disease I have suffered with so severely, at times, for the past 20 years, be it what it may. I have had perhaps ½ a dozen attacks during that time. I suppose, if I live, I have got to endure more of them. I hope this one is over for a few years. My last attack was at Chester, N.H., in August 1860, and it was far more severe than this, but, although the premonitories had existed for several weeks, the attack itself did not last over 5 hours. This time there was no premonition, but the attack lasted from 70 to 80 hours! . . .

Sunday, March 20. . . . Thursday at 11 A.M. I met the Secretary of the Interior, The Honorable J. P. Usher, before the Committee on Public Buildings and Grounds of the House of Representatives, a bill being before that Committee in relation to the office of C. of P. B. which proposes to place the Capitol Extension and Dome under the Commissioner and to take away the supervision of the Secy. of the Interior over the office. The Hon. Secretary fights this bill as if it were his last hope of salvation to hang on to the power he now exercises so much like a Tyrant, and an unprincipled scoundrel, as he is. He stood up before that Committee and lied like a dog. He is a poor[,] weak critter anyway, and *how* *it* happened that he ever rose above a tenth rate lawyer, and a pothouse politician, is to me an amazing mystery. That such a man as Caleb B. Smith should be deceived into placing a man so small in the Interior Department is passing strange, and that Abraham Lincoln, a man who can read and understand *men* as well as anyone within my knowledge, should permit a man so weak and so universally held in detestation as Usher to remain in his Cabinet is, to me, truly wonderful. But time will develope his ignorance, worthlessness, falsehood and dishonesty. To me the man is despicable.

The Committee did not get through and we are to have another hearing on Thursday next.

Friday I was engaged pretty much all day about Fair matters, and in the evening The President & Mrs. Lincoln, Gen. Sickles & his staff, Commodore Montgomery & Col. Cunningham, Gen. Oglesby & Miss Harris (daughter of the Senator) attended the Fair, and were escorted in by Columbia Commandery of K. T. which turned out in good numbers, and in "high feather."[1] Genls. Sickles and Oglesby made elegant speeches. The President spoke briefly, but earnestly, in praise of the women of America, and I, as President of the Association, did the introducing and made a few closing remarks.

Yesterday I was at my office all the morning, and at noon went to the President's and attended the usual reception. I had the honor to present to the President a pair of woollen socks, knit by Miss Addie Brockway[2] of Newburyport, the secession flag *underneath the foot* of each, the Flag of the Union in front on the top. *Very suggestive*. The President received them most graciously, & with much apparent pleasure. . . .

1. John Berrien Montgomery (1794–1873) served in the Union navy as a commodore on shore duty during the Civil War. Richard James Oglesby (1824–1899), of Illinois, major general of volunteers; he was later governor of Illinois and a U.S. senator, 1873–1879. Miss Harris, daughter of Ira Harris, senator from New York, 1861–1867.

2. Perhaps Miss Harriet Brockway of 53 Lime St., Newburyport, Mass.

Wednesday, March 23. . . . I went to the President's in the toughest snowstorm of the winter. Snow when I started, about 4 inches deep, and it was falling fast. Had to walk through the Capitol & to the west gate, & my feet were perfectly wet when I got into the car, and most frozen when I got to the President's. Fortunately I had a pair of dress boots there, so I borrowed a pair of stockings of Mr. Nicolay, and got through the evening very nicely. The reception was very handsome, though not large. Mrs. Lincoln was as amiable as possible, and Abraham as full of fun and story as ever I saw him. The evening really passed off most pleasantly. . . .

Sunday, March 27. . . . Thursday at 11 o'clock I again went before the House Committee on P. B. & G. and there met the Secy. of the Interior, Mr. Usher. I defended myself against his attack at the meeting before, speaking and reading 1¼ hours. He got excited and angry, and so left. Friday I devoted most of the day to the preparations for the ball, which,

I somehow fear, is to be a failure. . . . Yesterday at one I went to attend Mrs. Lincoln's reception—the girls with me. Although the day was dark, rainy and gloomy, the reception was a very fine one. As I came out from the reception Edward handed me a letter from the President, the contents of which showed what a liar and scoundrel a Secretary of the Interior can be. He may succeed in ruining me with the President, but he cannot injure me with the public or with my own conscience. His turn will come by & by, for he is a wicked, unprincipled, lying wretch. He will, unless Providence interposes, ruin the President. I have this day written a letter to President Lincoln, endeavouring to show him that he has been deceived, but do not know as it will do any good. I have seen Senator Foot & made known to him my exact position, & he will see the President.

Last evening I dined with Senator Morgan.[1] . . . The dinner was magnificent in everything, and the guests enjoyed themselves until 10 o'clock, when we all arose & repaired to the parlor, where coffee was served, & we soon after left. Senator Lane,[2] who sat near me, amused us very much by relating his experience at the first Bull Run battle. He was there as an *amateur,* and during the *flight,* a zouave near him threw down his gun, when the Senator addressed him thus. "Pick up that gun and join your ranks!" "At which[,]" said the Senator, "he very deliberately pulled out a pistol and said[,] 'Look here old man, if you have any brains to spare just say that over again.'" "And[,]" continued the Senator, "having no brains to spare, I said no more." . . .

1. Edwin D. Morgan (1811–1883), Republican senator from New York, 1863–1869.
2. Henry S. Lane (1811–1881), Republican senator from Indiana, 1861–1867.

Wednesday, April 6. . . . Saturday at one I went to the President's in the rain & snow mixed, and attended the reception. Considering the awful weather[,] the reception was a fine one. The President looked well, and seemed happy, and Mrs. Lincoln was uncommonly cheerful. The city councils of Baltimore, who came here to visit the Deaf, Dumb & Blind Institution at Kendall Green, attended the reception with a committee of our own Councils, and Mr. Horner of the Baltimore Councils sang most beautifully "We are coming Father Abraham, five hundred thousand more." All present who could sing joined in the Chorus, and the whole went off grandly.

After the reception was over Mrs. Lincoln took me up into the Library to see a most beautiful arrangement of wax fruit, etc., made by a negro woman and presented to herself and Mr. Lincoln. She seemed to appreciate it very highly & to be exceedingly pleased with it.

She remarked that she had not been in that room until that day since poor little Willie died. It was his favorite resort[,] and she could not bear to visit it, and the tears came into her eyes, & my very soul pitied her. Alas, alas! what are all the honors of this world when offset against such an affliction as that poor woman has undergone! . . .

Thursday, April 14. . . . John C. Rives, one of our best & most valuable citizens, died last Sunday morning and was buried yesterday. I regretted very much that my engagements prevented my attendance at his funeral. He was about 70 years old. How our good citizens are dropping away!

I had a very pleasant and satisfactory interview with the President last Monday, at which I think I convinced him that I had been misrepresented to him. I think he has confidence in me, and certainly I have done nothing to forfeit it. Usher acts like a fool and a knave, not only toward me, but toward everybody else I believe. Let him act on. His race, at all events, is drawing to a close, & he will go out of office with the curses of thousands whom he has wronged, on his head. . . .

Sunday, April 17. . . . I never felt so much like "pulling up stakes" here in Washington and going to Europe as I have for the past month. It seems as if all my friends were deserting me, and that I was to be left to be oppressed by a pitiful scoundrel who happens to be, in some measure, *officially* my superior. If I were clear of my real estate here[,] one month would not find me a citizen of Washington, for I am disgusted with office. Enough for tonight. I am not in a pleasant mood.

Wednesday, May 4. . . . For the week past I have been "cat hauled" by the miserable, contemptible, mean Usher, who disgraces the Interior Department in all the ways he could devise to make me uncomfortable. I hope I shall live to see March 4, 1865! If I can see that jackass out of office, I shall be satisfied. He is no real friend of Abraham, and I wonder that good & discerning man does not see through the transparent friendship of that miserable wretch. That will do for this time! . . .

Thursday, May 12. . . . Yesterday I took Fannie to the Arsenal in the buggy. We went all through the workshops and saw all that was to be seen. She was very much pleased and carried home with her as trophies, a loaded and unloaded fuse, and a minnie bullet, of the sort she saw them making at the rate of 70 to the minute. . . .

Sunday, May 22. . . . We, i.e.[,] Mary Ellen, Hattie & I attended a party at Mrs. Sprague's (Secy. Chase's) on Friday evening. We were invited to hear little Teresa Carreño[1] play on the piano. She played splendidly, and there was some excellent song singing by two gentlemen. The party was very pleasant, & consisted of at least 150 people. We came home at a little before midnight.

The news from the Army does not amount to much lately, and I begin to imagine that Grant[2] is not going to beat Lee so easily as everybody seemed to suppose. Those Rebels fight like a parcel of wildcats, and from the way they seem to recuperate I should think the cats kittened as often as once a day! I do hope we shall overpower the infernal villains soon.

1. Teresa Carreño (1853–1917), of Caracas, Venezuela, was a sensational child pianist at the age of eight. She first appeared in New York City in 1862, then studied with Louis Moreau Gottschalk, and went on to a full musical career in the United States and abroad as pianist, composer, conductor, and singer.

2. Ulysses S. Grant (1822–1885), who had been promoted to lieutenant general on March 9, had just come through the Battle of the Wilderness and the Spotsylvania campaign, and was attempting, unsuccessfully, to flank Lee.

Sunday, May 29. . . . Our garden is a paradise, such a show of roses I scarcely ever saw. The vegetable garden looks well, the strawberries and cherries are ripening fast, the grapes have set elegantly, and all is as promising as we could desire. This is not so miserable a world after all. There is a good deal more sunshine than shadow in it, and I like it very well. Mary Ellen thinks that if she has such a beautiful garden and so many other beautiful things (beautiful husband no doubt included) she shall not be willing to die. . . .

4 P.M. Since writing the foregoing we have dined, smoked our cigars and drank our juleps in the summer house in the garden. Two of Nathan's friends, James Brown of Concord, and a Mr. Brown of Worcester, who is here to look after the wounded of that place, are now here. Nathan has taken them into the garden to see it. They have been telling me about the wounded. The number is immense, and, according to their account, they have not been well cared for. Poor fellows, it is a shame and a sin that those brave men who have perilled their lives for their Country, should not, when disabled in so glorious a cause, be properly taken care of. . . .

Thursday, June 9. . . . At 7 P.M. Tuesday Mr. Barrett came in and told me that he had just seen Arthur Chase at the Armory Square Hospital very badly wounded. That he had Telegraphed his father in my name, in N. York City. I was not very well, and the news operated upon me as exciting news always does, by giving me a severe headache, so that I could hardly sit up. . . . Mary Ellen returned about 8, and with Ben went down and remained till nearly 11. They found poor Arthur with 4 wounds upon him—one through the lungs, one through the neck, one in the shoulder, and a slight one, from a spent ball in the leg. Early yesterday morning I went down and found that the poor fellow was gone. He died at 5 o'clock yesterday morning.

While writing the above[,] Mr. [Samuel L.] Chase, Arthur's father, came. He is much distressed. We have breakfasted. I can write no more now.

Saturday, June 11. This is a cold unpleasant, cloudy morning. Ther. 58°.

Immediately after I had written the foregoing on Thursday, Doct. Chase and I went to Armory Square Hospital. We found that all had been done that could be with Arthur's remains. On Wednesday we sent down the proper clothing in which to dress the body—a coat, shirt, collar and neck tie of Ben's, and a pair of pantaloons of Nathan's. We found him embalmed and dressed and looking very natural, ready to be put into a coffin. He was put into an officer's coffin while we were there, and was sent to the Express Office to be forwarded to Lockport that afternoon. Chase and I then went to the Express office where he paid $27 for freight—thence to the Medical Director's Office at 19th St. on Pa. Av. to ascertain where other wounded men were, but could find out nothing. Then to the Treasury to see Edmund. Then to the President's where delegations to the Baltimore Convention were assembled to call on the President. I introduced Chase to the President—whom he had never before seen—and we remained half an hour, and then returned to the Capitol, and then home and dined. At 5 o'clock Chase left for home.

Sunday, June 26. . . . On Tuesday Nathan came home with the melancholy intelligence of the death of our dear friend Col. Geo. L. Prescott of Concord, Mass., whose name appears often in the pages of my journal for the past 3 years. He was shot through the body in front of Petersburg on Saturday morning the 18th, and died the next day. His remains came up to this city on Wednesday, & Mr. Barrett and James Brown took charge of them & had them properly prepared and coffined and sent on to Concord Thursday. His death was very mournful to us all. He had fought from the 1st Bull Run battle on to the time of his death. He was a brave, honorable, pure-minded unflinching patriot, & Massachusetts never lost a better or a nobler specimen of humanity than she lost when Prescott fell. . . .

Sunday, July 3. . . . Secy. Chase has resigned his office as head of the Treasury. The whole Nation was taken by surprise at the announcement on Thursday morning last. Gov. Tod[1] of Ohio was immediately nominated by the President to take his place, but declined, *as every on[e] said,* and Wm. Pitt Fessenden (the best man in the U.S. & the one I named for the place the moment I heard of Chase's resignation) was nominated and at once confirmed by the Senate. He, at first, declined to accept the place in consequence of his worn out health, but so urgent has been the pressure upon him from all parts of the loyal states that, I believe[,] he has decided, as a patriot and a sterling man as he is, to accept it. I look upon his acceptance as the financial salvation of the Country, for his eminent ability, his untiring industry, his perfect integrity, his high character in every respect, point him out as the man, and I believe the *only man*[,] that can save us in these times, from ruin. . . .

1. David Tod (1805–1868), a coal, iron, and railroad executive, was the Union party governor of Ohio, 1862–1864.

Sunday, July 10. . . . Another invasion of Maryland by the rebels, said to be led by the ingrate J. C. Breckinridge, is now in progress. It commenced a week ago and was so quietly managed by the cunning and wicked men who are striving to overthrow our Government [that] it was hardly known until the "butternut johnnies" were on the soil of Maryland, committing their depredations. At first it was supposed to be only a raid of a small party; now it has assumed the proportions of an army of 20,000 men, and the news of this morning give rather a squally aspect to affairs up about Frederick, Md. No one, of course, can tell what the result is to be: I will not undertake to prophecy again. When, about one year ago, Lee, with his entire army, crossed the Potomac, I did think they would never be permitted to return . . . but, although soundly whipped, they did return and Lee still lives to lead his armies and defy ours! Now, it seems to me as if another golden opportunity is offered to capture an army sent against us, but I fear it will not be done, and it is not impossible, as things seem now to be going, that we may "catch a Tartar!" I will, however, abide the result without flinching or getting frightened.

The 4th of July passed away with a greater amount of squibbing, I think, than I ever before heard. Some societies, schools, etc., celebrated the day, and Congress celebrated it by adjourning! The best thing they could well do. . . .

Tuesday, July 12. . . . There was considerable fighting North & N.W. of the city yesterday, and the rebs doubtless will make a desperate attempt to capture the city, but—"we shall see what we shall see"—which, I think[,] will be such a defeat of the rebel hordes as they have never yet experienced! Ben, whom I have not seen since yesterday afternoon, went off at 5 this morning, and when Mr. Barrett got up he told us that he (Ben) was appointed on Maj. Gen. Thomas's[1] staff to some position with the rank of Major, and had gone to the war. Well, I hope he will do his duty come what may, and distinguish himself. . . .

From the papers of this morning not much satisfactory information can be obtained. Although great damage has doubtless been done by the enemy, I think the prospect is, upon the whole, encouraging all round. A very large number of troops have been gathered in front of Washington, enough, I think, to make victory to our side certain.

1. Charles Thomas (1800?–1878), a veteran of the Mexican War, served in Washington as assistant quartermaster general during much of the Civil War.

Sunday, July 17. "The *raid* it is over and gone"—Tuesday morning when I last wrote herein, nobody knew what the result was to be. Ben had gone, but returned toward noon, having been out as a mere spectator with Capt. C. L. West.[1] He went to Fort Stevens and saw shooting and heard bullets, and, as West said, "stood it pluckily." Tuesday I was at my office till nearly 3, then came home, dined and at 4 went down to the Smithsonian, where the public schools of the 3d District (this) were to assemble and receive their premiums. The room was crammed with a most beautiful display of children. It was one of the hottest afternoons of the season. I delivered the address—less than ½ an hour in length— and the Mayor distributed the premiums. It took till past 7. I came home saturated with perspiration. That evening we heard that the rebs had destroyed the railroad between this place & Baltimore, and, for the first time, I felt really mad. The thought that *we* could not protect our own railroad was humiliating enough, and I felt like going right into the field and helping defend. The first thing I heard Wednesday was that the invaders were retreating with all their booty, and now we know that they *are gone*—all got away safe & with whatsoever they captured. It is humiliating enough, and it seems to me as if it ought not to have been permitted. My friend Abraham has got to do something to retrieve this awful blunder or he is "a goner!"

Last Thursday morning, at the earnest request of a friend who was urged to act by a most respectable gentleman from North Carolina, now in this city, I went to the President and submitted to him the following proposition in writing.

"Let from five to ten thousand men leave here (say 100 days' men from Massachusetts, or other States) as soon and as quietly as possible, for Gen. Peck's[2] command at New Bern, N.C. Let them make a grand raid on Raleigh, seizing everything possible, and not trying to hold the place.

The effect of such a dash, if successful, as a retaliatory measure for their recent raid here[,] would be great, and the effect would be paralyzing.

Something of this kind is imperative for political effect."

The President read it carefully through and remarked that there were two insurmountable objections to the attempt. *First,* it would be hard to raise the troops required. *Second,* nothing could be done without the rebels finding it out immediately.

"Then[,]" said I, "it is in vain to attempt to carry out any such measure?" He replied that he thought it was. Then he told me how the rebels had all escaped with their booty, and I came away low spirited enough. Gen. Millson[3] of Virginia was with the President.

1. Clement L. West, the general superintendent and disbursing agent for the U.S. Capitol extension. He was also disbursing agent for the Washington aqueduct.
2. John J. Peck (1821–1878), a West Point graduate, banker, and railroad executive.
3. Clearly Millson in French's journal, but there is no such officer listed in the indices to the *Records of the War of the Rebellion.*

Sunday, July 31. . . . Another *raid* or *invasion* up in Pennsylvania! We got the first intimation of it yesterday. The rebels have taken Chambersburg and burned it, and their numbers are variously estimated from 800 up to 50,000! Wide awake fellows our men must be to have an enemy come upon them like a thief in the night, and they be utterly ignorant of his numbers! But Pennsylvania seems *now* to be wide awake to her danger, & *perhaps* we may punish the rebel freebooters as they deserve! But the chances are, judging from the past, that they escape, booty and all, scot-free! We shall see in due time. . . .

Sunday, August 7. . . . The Rebs. are still raiding around up in Maryland and Pa. Grant blew up a fortification in front of Petersburg last Saturday (a week) &, but for the bungling way in which it was done, the result might have been glorious. As it was, it was a failure. The engineer had *a powder fuse* which went *out twice,* and delayed the blowing up an hour and a half. Who would have supposed, in these days of galvanic batteries & copper wire, that *anyone* would have been so behind the age as to depend on a powder fuse put in *a wooden box*, when a sure thing could have been made of it at *any instant* with a galvanic battery & wire! I wish I had been down there to advise! But the thing is over—we were defeated, & all I hope is "better luck next time"—or, at least *more science next time!* . . .

Saturday, August 20. . . . I went with Col. Seymour[1] and examined the Navy yard Bridge with a view to deciding as to the kind of draw to have built. From there we went to the Botanic garden to see about a culvert, & then I went to Doct. Humphries,[2] dentist, to see if he could do anything toward extracting the root of a tooth[,] the crown of which Doct. Hayward[3] of the firm of Sigesmond & Hayward broke off in an attempt to extract it last Monday, and after two attempts to extract the root, which half killed me, he gave up. It has pained me constantly ever since. Doct. Humphries examined it and said the only way he could take it out was by drilling a hole on the sound side & getting under it and lifting it out with an instrument he had made purposely for such operations. He began on it & worked nearly ½ an hour I should think, when he hurt me so that I became nervous & faint and could bear it no longer. So I came away with the root still in. As soon as it gets over this effort I shall go again, for I am determined to have it out if possible. . . .

1. Truman Seymour (1824–1891) was promoted to colonel for gallantry at Antietam. He had been captured during the Battle of the Wilderness and was exchanged on August 9, 1864.
2. G. W. Humphreys' dental office was at 12 Market Space.
3. C. D. Hayward was a dental partner of S. B. Sigismund at 260 Pennsylvania Ave.

Sunday, August 21. Toothache all night! Sailors have a habit of "damning their *eyes*"—were I to anathametise [sic] after their fashion I should certainly *damn my teeth*—for they have plagued me enough to deserve damning many times over. I feel, however, much better than I expected to this morning. My teeth are well, and my head, which ached considerable when I first awakened, is also well. If I can only get through this day and night without pain, I think I shall be ready to labor tomorrow. . . .

Friday, September 2. . . . McClellan is nominated by the Democrats to run against Lincoln. I am armed cap-a-pie[1] for the conflict, and if honest old Abraham cannot beat George McClellan, why the country is gone to the dogs—that's all. If our people are bewitched so far as to desire prosperity to Jeff Davis and treason, they will elect Mac; if they are true to the Union & Constitution, Lincoln will be elected by an overwhelming vote. I firmly believe Mac stands no chance, but we shall see. I feel a very great interest in the result, & hope and pray that Lincoln may succeed. . . .

1. From head to foot.

Sunday, September 4. . . . Atlanta has at last fallen[,] and Sherman and his brave army are triumphant. This, with the capture of Fort Morgan in Mobile Bay, will be a bitter pill to the *patriotic* Democrats & the Mac & Pend[leton][1] ticket. Now let us have Mobile, Petersburg & Richmond, Charleston and Wilmington, and *the jig is up* with Treason in the South & subornation of Treason in the North. . . .

1. George H. Pendleton (1825–1889), Democratic congressman from Ohio, 1857–1864, and senator, 1879–1885. In 1864 he was vice-presidential candidate on the Democratic ticket with Gen. George B. McClellan.

Wednesday, September 7. . . . The doctor pronounced, yesterday, sentence of death of my little namesake. There is some organic disarrangement of the heart that he says must be fatal—still the youngster lives on, and sometimes even doctors are mistaken.[1]

Margaret is very poorly—much more so than usual. Mary Ellen staid with her last night and came home at ¼ before 6. She says Margaret did not sleep at all, but suffered dreadfully with headache all night. Poor woman, I pity her, and hope, if she survives this trouble[,] she will not have another of the kind. Eleven children are enough for one woman to give birth to, and, although she has one of the best of constitutions, it cannot stand everything! . . .

1. Benjamin Brown French, recently born son of Edmund and Margaret, died the next April. See April 6, 1865.

Friday, September 9. . . . I have been on my feet nearly all day. At the President's all the morning with some gasfitters, trying to find a leak of gas, which almost suffocated the President in his own office!

Sunday, September 25. . . . I have been several times at the President's and have seen both him and Mrs. Lincoln. One evening—I now forget what one—I went down at 15 minutes' warning and made a speech from the balcony of the "Hotel Gerhardt," upon the raising across Pa. Avenue of a splendid Lincoln & Johnson flag, by the German Association, and talked till I was so hoarse I could scarcely speak in my ordinary tone of voice.

Everything relating to the war betokens a speedy and patriotic issue ere long, and the reelection of Lincoln, which seems, now, to be a foregone conclusion, will result in a glorious victory over the prime movers in the wicked rebellion. . . .

. . . Our cow has not been home since yesterday morning[,] and I much fear we have lost her, as Robert has hunted everywhere where she is accustomed to go and cannot find her. I had rather lose $100 than not find her, for she is a first-rate cow. Her absence troubles me much. . . .

Oh how I wish this war was over, if for nothing else, that this city may once more be *a civil* city, instead of a city of Camps, corrals, and soldiers, and I am sorry to say, a goodly number of whom are continually drunk! Disgusting everybody!

Sunday, October 2. . . . We are all packed up to start for New England tomorrow morning, intending to be away 4 weeks.

Our man, Robert, found the cow Sunday evening. She had doubtless been shut up and milked. We have kept her in the stable all the week. . . .

Reading, Mass., Wednesday, October 5. On Monday last Mary Ellen and I left Washington at ½ past 7 A.M. for this place. . . .

Friday, October 7. Yesterday at ½ past 8 went into Boston with Frank. . . . Called on Col. John S. Keyes at his office. . . . Col. K. & I rode down to Geo. Keyes's place of business. Geo. had gone fishing. The Col. showed us the goods, etc., taken from on board a captured blockade runner, and we went on board the captured vessel. She was a long[,] slender, passenger steamer, built some 5 or 6 years ago at Wilmington, Delaware. She had a powerful engine and must be very fast. . . .

Concord, Mass., Sunday, October 16. Here I am in the same room where, two years ago on the 9th of last month[,] Mary Ellen & I plighted to each other our troth & promised all that the marriage rite requires. . . .

. . . *Friday* morning [went] into Boston at 8:10'[,] arrived before 9. Was escorted by Lowell Commandery to the Common, and then to the Freemason's Hall in Summer St. where I met the G. Master of Templars and hundreds of my Masonic Brethren. Was recd. with all honor by the G. Enc[ampmen]t of Mass. & R.I.[,] & then we moved to the Common and joined the immense procession—two miles long—and after marching an hour, we came back to the place where the cornerstone of the Masonic Temple was to be laid. . . .

Friday, October 21. I left this place on Tuesday last at 8 A.M. & went to Boston. Went from the depot to Geo. Keyes's place of business on Lewis's Wharf and, with Mr. Brown & George, on board the Steamer *Bat,* which had just arrived, a prize to some one of our National vessels I believe. She is a long, narrow, English-built, steel sidewheel steamer, with a very fine and powerful oscillating engine, made expressly for a blockade runner. She had on board an assorted cargo, & is, probably, a valuable prize. . . .

Arose at 6 A.M. Wednesday morning.[1] Frank left at [sic] for Boston, and Lem took me over to Major Ben Perley Poore's at Indian Hill in a chaise that morning, leaving Haverhill at ½ past 7 and arriving at the Major's at ½ past 9. The Major had invited my good friend & Bro. Sir Kt. & M. W. Grand Master Parkman[2] to join us[,] & he arrived from the Depot with the Major a few minutes after we did. The house at Indian Hill farm is one of the greatest curiosities I have ever seen. . . .

Major Poore has travelled the world over, and has not returned from *any place* empty handed. His collection of Autographs is, by far, the best and most extensive one that I have ever seen. It is superb. He showed us all through his house[,] which is very old and very unique. Then he showed us over his farm. When we arrived on the very topmost height of Indian Hill, overlooking all the country about, we found a true *oblong square,* enclosed with two rows of evergreen shrubbery. It is the exact form of a Masonic Lodge, which the Major laid out and planted with his own hands, and which, when the shrubbery is sufficiently grown, he intends to have dedicated in regular Masonic form. When we arrived there we found one of his hired men with a large wooden square & a spade. We measured off a regular distance on the East side, squared it, two holes were dug[,] and Bro. Parkman and I planted, each, an oak tree there, which, if they grow, are to be memorials of our 19th of October visit! The following is a plan of the place, with our trees indicated.[3]

At about 12 we returned to the house, and at one sat down to such a dinner as one seldom eats at a Farmer's house. The table absolutely groaned with delicacies, and the company was such as one seldom meets at a Farmer's table. . . . Wit and wine accompanied that dinner, and it is one that I shall not soon forget. After dinner we sat down in the Major's curious library, smoked and examined hundreds of most curious things, and were highly entertained by the Major with his reminiscences of his travels, most particularly by his Masonic experiences. It was truly "A feast of reason & a flow of soul." . . .

I took the horsecars for Cambridge, spent the night at my Brother Henry's, and came back here at noon.

Found all well here. Willie French is here, and very much out of health so far as regards mind. He is low spirited and melancholy. Runs of a notion that he is very wicked; cannot tell the truth, has no conscience, no affection, etc. Nothing can induce a smile upon his countenance. I have talked with him much and done my best to rouse him, but all in vain. It makes me—and indeed all of us—very sad, for he is a fine and a promising young man, highly educated, and very intellectual, and before this malady came upon him was one of the merriest of the merry. May God remove this shadow from his mind & restore him to us! . . .

1. French had traveled to Haverhill, Mass., on Tuesday afternoon to preside as grand master over an installation of officers of the Haverhill commandery. He spent the night there at the home of Dr. Lemuel Barker.

2. William Parkman, of Boston, was grand master of the grand lodge of Massachusetts.

3. Here French made a drawing of the "oblong square," showing the location of the French and Parkman oaks.

Tuesday, November 1. It is 7 A.M. and while the women are packing up for a start I will make my final New England record for 1864. Well, we have made all our visits and had a most pleasant month of seeing our dear ones.[1] We have been received by *all* as if they were delighted at our advent among them and have been entertained as if we were "Angels unawares." Finally we have had a glorious time, and now that it is over the sooner we get home the better. . . .

1. During the course of his visit to Concord, French visited friends and relatives in Lancaster, Milton, Reading, Cambridge, and Boston. He also performed some Masonic duties in Boston.

Washington, Thursday, November 3. Here I am once more at home. Let us gather up the threads of the past three days. . . . Having arrived at the Depot we *kinder hung round* till the train came when we had a regular shaking hands and kissing bee, when the two Mistresses & the undersigned hopped into the cars and off we buzzed to Boston. Ralph Waldo Emerson[1] happened to be with us on his way to Philadelphia, when I saw him for the first time. Arriving in Boston we found George Keyes at the Depot with a man and wagon to carry the baggage over to the Worcester Depot. . . . We got into the cars where we met Mr. Emerson, & he took a seat beside me and we talked steadily till we arrived at New London at ½ past 10. The boat was crowded, and it took me an hour to get to the Captain's office & secure the keys to our staterooms. . . . We had quite a good night of it, and the boat *City of New York* made a splendid run. We were at the Jersey City wharf at a little after six yesterday morning. . . . There we sat till after 8, when we took our seats in the cars & at ½ past 8 were off for this City, where, after a ride of 10 hours, we arrived safely without any incident worthy of a record at ½ past 6 P.M. We found all right and well. . . .

1. Ralph Waldo Emerson (1803–1882), essayist and poet, had by this time written most of his great works. He was still active on the lecture circuit, however, and made brief mention of this trip in a letter to William Emerson, October 27, 1864. He was to give a speech in New York on November 5 in honor of William Cullen Bryant but first paid a short visit to Philadelphia. Cf. Ralph L. Rusk, ed. *The Letters of Ralph Waldo Emerson* (New York, 1939), vol. 6, pp. 385–386.

Wednesday, November 9. . . . The election is over and Abraham Lincoln is reelected President of the U.S. Thank God it is thus, for it is the salvation of the Country.

God is with us!

Sunday, November 20. . . . Lincoln is reelected by the votes of all the states save Ky., N.J., and Delaware, and the Country is safe for four years, at any rate. . . .

On Thursday I went gunning with Mr. Belshaw[1] in the woods & fields north of the City. We travelled at least 8 miles and got two birds (partridges). I had not been out for years and supposed two or three miles would be the extent of my endurance, but I came home from a tramp of 8 as lively as ever. I felt the fatigue most sensibly after I had been home awhile. I think, now, I could stand a tramp of a dozen miles easily. . . .

1. William Belshaw, a member of the U.S. Capitol police force.

Monday, December 12. . . . I want to make one record here about a table. Soon after my return home last month, I went on the Dome of the Capitol with Mr. Fowler, who furnished the iron castings and had them put up. There was a single baluster left of the balustrade that surrounds the top of the inner dome. I asked if I might have it to make a standard for a table. He said "yes" and also told me I might take any of the pieces that were left over. So I selected an ornament for the legs, and a piece of broken paneling for the top, and a screw bolt to put them together with, and was about to have them brought over here (to my house) that I might put them together, when Mr. Fowler's foreman volunteered to put them together for me. He did so, and Mr. Galway[1] had the table painted and sent it over on the 1st day of this month, and there it now stands in the bay window, a very handsome and very solid table—the admiration of all my visitors, and such an one as, probably[,] the world never saw and will never again see. In the summer I intend to keep it in the garden, and think I shall eventually present it to some Historical society as a memento of the Capitol of the U.S. . . .

Tomorrow we expect Frank, and perhaps the Judge. How glad I shall be to see them! I do love to have my house full, it is so cheerful to have one's friends around one, and, as we are to live this life but once we may as well live it merrily—*dum vivimus vivamus.*

> I'll laugh through the world in defiance of strife
> For laughter's an oil to the salad of life.

1. James Galway, a master painter, had painted the exterior of the old portion of the Capitol, 1861–1862.

Thursday, December 15. . . . Judge French & William, his son, arrived at ½ past 6 Tuesday evening, and Frank arrived a little past 10. We had a house full of company that evening. . . .

Friday, December 23. I wrote last herein last Thursday, since when we have had a house full of company and a good time generally. The Judge, considering his son William's state of mind [melancholia][1][,] has been in good spirits and has kept himself up wonderfully. Frank has as usual been full of fun & glee, and Will has, we all think, improved. The Judge, Will, & Frank left at 6 last evening for home. . . .

. . . [On Thursday] the judge, being very anxious to see Doct. Nichols of our District Insane Asylum, which is about 3 miles from here, I had my horse harnessed into the buggy and we started. Got along very well till we arrived at the Navy Yard Bridge, where we found the ship *Old Dominion*, lying with her stern against the bridge, she having dragged her anchors & drifted up the stream. Just as we got onto the bridge, she made a sort of lurch & her stern came against the railing with force enough to break it, which frightened the horse & he began to back. I thought for a moment that the ship was going stern foremost through the bridge, and did not blame the horse. I turned him round, and the judge got out & enquired whether they expected to carry away the bridge, & upon being assured that [they] should do all they could to prevent it, we turned the horse's head bridge-ward and the judge led him by the ship, when we went on our way rejoicing. We arrived at the Asylum & could not find Doct. N. . . . I sent for Doct. [B. N.] Stevens (Doct. N.'s assistant)[,] and he came and took us into a large[,] cold room where we sat down, my feet tingling with cold. Two hot air registers in the room, both shut, I opened one—cold air instead of hot! The judge began to state Will's case to Doct. Stevens and had about finished when Doct. Nichols came, so he had to state it over again to him. They talked, and I froze, for about ½ an hour, and I was fully repaid for freezing by the encouraging view the Doct. took of Will's case. He expressed the opinion without any doubt, that he would gradually recover. He imputed his state of mind to overexertion while serving as soldier, and at the same time keeping up with his class at Harvard College. . . .

    1. The brackets are French's.

Friday, January 6. . . . *Monday* was celebrated as New Year's day. I went to the President's at about 11 A.M. and attended officially to the introduction of the crowd—such as desired it—to Mrs. Lincoln. At about 2 Mrs. L. withdrew & I left. . . .

Saturday, January 21. . . . I have been much engaged for a week on a committee to make arrangements for the Inauguration Ball.

    Committee met at Mr. L. Clephane's last evening and completed lists, etc., to report this evening.

    I attended Speaker Colfax's reception last evening. It was a jam. Saw many distinguished personages whom I well knew, there.

    I hope Speaker Colfax will be the next President of these United States. He is eminently worthy to be, & I intend to work for it.

    Now I will go to the Capitol.

Sunday, January 22. . . . I went to the office about 9 yesterday and remained there until ¼ past 12, when I started for the President's to attend, *officially*, Mrs. Lincoln's reception. I did not suppose it would be very large, in consequence of the inclement weather, and was much surprised to find how large and brilliant it was. Some of the most fashionable ladies in Washington were there, & it was peculiarly honored by the Military.

Secy. of War Stanton, Gen. Phil. Sheridan,[1] Gen. Burnside, Gen. Butler, Gen. Holt, and ever so many Cols., Majors, Captains, and Lieuts. were present. Gen. Garfield[2] of the House, and other members, with their ladies also graced the Blue Room with their presence. But I do not remember a single Senator! The Blue Room was pretty well filled all through the reception. The President appeared well and in excellent spirits, and Mrs. Lincoln never appeared better. She was dressed in admirable taste—A rich black satin gown high in the neck, with a very rich white lace shawl thrown gracefully over it. Pearl and diamond jewelry— a very graceful lace headdress falling back to her shoulders, etc. I never was much at describing ladies' dresses, but I know that her *toute ensemble* never made a more favorable impression upon me than yesterday, and she greeted every guest with such cheerful good will and kindness as to do infinite credit to her position and her heart. . . .

Mr. Powell, the painter of the *Discovery of the Mississippi,* now in the Rotunda, came yesterday. He has with him a picture of the Battle on Lake Erie—*Perry's Victory*—which he desires to place in the rotunda for exhibition. Ben went to the Depot with him to get it, about noon yesterday[,] and did not get home till 11 last evening. They got it and had it placed in the rotunda, where it is to be put up today, Sunday being the only day on which it can be well put up without interruption.

I have been engaged much of the past week in aiding, as Chairman of a Committee, in making arrangements for the Inauguration Ball on the 6th of March. It is to be in the immense hall of the Patent Office Building, & we hope to make it a grand affair. . . .

1. Philip H. Sheridan (1831–1888), the devastation of the Shenandoah Valley behind him, was about to begin his campaign to cut off Lee's army from the rest of the South.
2. James Abram Garfield (1831–1881), of Ohio, was chief of staff of the Army of the Cumberland in 1863. Elected to the House of Representatives in 1863, he served until 1880, when he was elected to the presidency. He was assassinated in 1881.

Sunday, January 29. . . . Wednesday I was at the Capitol all day. Saw Powell's picture in the Rotunda. It certainly is magnificent—a great improvement on his discovery of the Mississippi. He desires to paint a Naval picture to be placed at the head of one of the main stairways in the Capitol. I hope he will be successful in obtaining the order from Congress.[1] . . .

1. An enlarged replica of Powell's *The Battle of Lake Erie* was acquired eventually and is located in the Senate wing, east staircase.

Friday, February 3. It is ¼ past 7, and Mary Ellen and myself are actually seated in the Library alone, intending to spend the evening *at home*! She is sewing. . . .

Monday at the Capitol all the morning and at Col. Gardner's,[1] where there was a gathering of between 30 & 40, in the evening. It was the 48th wedding day of the Col. & Mrs. Gardner, and they were quite merry on the occasion. There were 4 euchre tables & those who played seemed to enjoy their games. There was music and plenty of conversation. It really seemed as if Capitol Hill had gone back 20 years! Only the heads of those who used to assemble were a little whiter, & some who were children then are men & women now. But it seemed to me like an old Capitol Hill gathering, and certainly it was a most pleasant one. We came home about 12 midnight. . . .

1. Charles K. Gardner (1787–1869) served as an officer in the War of 1812, published several military studies, edited a newspaper in New York City, and had a series of political appointments in Washington, including postmaster, 1845–1849. In 1865 he was a clerk in the Treasury Department.

Sunday, February 19. . . . Arose as usual yesterday morning with a miserable feeling in my head—a feeling that has come upon me several times within the past 5 or 6 years, which is really indescribable, but the nearest I can come to it is to say that it seems as I were two beings. I can go on with my ordinary business and employment as well as ever, and yet my mind seems to be dwelling on something that seems like a dream. It is very curious and very uncomfortable and annoying. It lasts only a few hours. I went to the Capitol after breakfast and before the Com. of W. & M. of the House at 10 o'clock, where I explained the items of appropriation for which I had estimated & asked. Remained in the office till ¼ past 12 & then attended Mrs. Lincoln's reception. The feeling of *duality* gone. Came home at a little before 4, dined, laid down and slept an hour and a half, awoke very much refreshed, and at ¼ before 8 started with Mrs. French & Mr. Barrett for the "1st Art Soiree" of the Metropolitan Club. It was quite a splendid affair. The walls of the front parlor were adorned with some of the rarest pictures that could be procured from the galleries of the Messrs. McGuire and Riggs.[1] The party was very select & genteel, consisting mainly of the wives, daughters, and female friends of the Members of the club. An elegant collation was provided. The ladies had an opportunity to see the gentlemen play billiards, and to join them in a game of euchre. . . . There was a splendid band of music in attendance, and toward the latter part of the evening there was dancing. Mrs. French & I left about ½ past 10 and got home a little after 11.

1. Among the painters represented were Emanuel Leutze (1816–1868), Albert Bierstadt (1830–1902), Elihu Vedder (1836–1923), and John F. Kensett (1816–1872). French placed a printed list of the subjects, artists, and owners in his journal. McGuire was probably

James C. McGuire, whose place of business as an auction and commission merchant was at the corner of 10th Street and Pennsylvania Avenue. Riggs was the prominent Washington banker, George W. Riggs.

Tuesday, February 21. Charleston has fallen! Thank God the hotbed of Treason is humbled. Its own citizens are laying it in ashes. All right. I hope there will not be left one stone upon another of that city where treason was hatched & grew up into a crowing & strutting cock. Thankful am I that its spurs are at last cut off, and it will crow no more! . . .

Thursday, February 23. It took me all day to celebrate the 22d yesterday and I had no time to write. I arose at ½ past 5 A.M. At a few minutes after 6 George Keyes and his wife Mary and Annie Keyes[1] arrived, & were received by us with great joy. After breakfast Keyes and I went to the Capitol. Col. T. P. Shaffner called, and I went with him and Keyes onto the Dome; while there I was sent for and on getting to my office found Vice President Hamlin and Speaker Colfax there. They directed the Capitol to be illuminated in honor of the day. It was after 10 A.M.[,] but I went to work and, employing all the force I could get, got ready at 7 in the evening to light up. The building looked very splendid from the Avenue. I worked personally all day. . . .

1. Anne Keyes, daughter of George and Mary.

Friday, February 24. . . . Col. Shaffner was here, & has just gone. We have spent the evening talking about Freemasonry in Europe and this country. He informs me that the Order there is conducted very differently from the manner it is conducted here. He is very anxious that a Masonic convention should be got up in some way, to meet in Europe and establish a uniformity of recognition, etc.

Shaffner has been away, this time, about six years and has travelled all over Europe, and been engaged, as a Military Engineer, in the wars there. We had a most interesting conversation.

Tomorrow, if I am well, I expect to have a hard day's work. At 1 I must be at the President's to attend the usual reception. At 3 a party at Senator Sprague's commences, to which we all expect to go, as it is to be a very brilliant affair, and within reasonable hours—viz. from 3 to 10 or 11. Really[,] I shall rejoice when Lent begins, for I am tired of gaiety. I expect the Inauguration and the Ball will about use me up. But Congress will be gone, and I can recuperate. . . .

Sunday, March 5. The second inauguration of Abraham Lincoln is safely over, God be thanked. For the week past I have tried to give all the aid in my power to perfecting the arrangements, and yesterday, from early morning, until an hour after the procession left the Capitol, I was on my feet and hard at work. I came home about 2 P.M.[,] dined at 3, and then rested till ¼ past 7[,] when I went to the President's and attended the largest reception I ever saw. From 8 till ¼ past 11 the president shook hands steadily, at the rate of 100 every 4 minutes—with about 5,000 persons! Over, rather than under, for I counted the 100 several times, and when they came the thickest he was not over 3 minutes, never over 5. It was a grand ovation of *the People* to their President, whom they dearly love. Mrs. Lincoln was present through the reception and avowed her intention to remain till morning, rather than have the doors closed on a single visitor. She appeared very gracious and well. She certainly is a woman of endurance, having been all the morning at the Capitol.

The Civil Bill, usually known as the omnibus bill, was lost, with all the appropriations for the Public Buildings & grounds. What I am to do I know not. The President says "We must *pick* along in some way." . . .

Monday, March 13. . . . The past week has been one of dissipation. Monday night we all attended the Grand Inauguration Ball. It was, indeed, a grand affair. I had so much to do as a sort of head manager, in attending to the President of the U.S. and Mrs. Lincoln, the Secretaries, Diplomats, etc., that I wore myself out. We left at about ½ past 2 & were at home and in bed between 3 & 4. . . .

Wednesday evening we had a little party, consisting of the Adams's [sic], Russells, Ned's family, Col. Keyes & Mr. Boynton[1] & Mr. Pollard.[2] We had quite a merry time and our visitors left at midnight. We were in bed before one. Thursday evening we attended the Opera. Bill annexed.[3] Got home about midnight.

Friday evening we went to Ford's Theatre—bill also annexed.[4] Got home a little after midnight.

Saturday evening at a little gathering at Edmund's. Supped between 10 & 11, & soon after supper, came home. . . .

. . . Notwithstanding all this nightly dissipation, I have been attending daily to all my duties, and my health has been perfect. I wonder that I can endure so much, and could not were my Constitution any thing but an iron one. . . .

1. Charles B. Boynton (1806–1883), Presbyterian minister and author, was chaplain of the House of Representatives, 1865–1869.
2. Perhaps Henry M. Pollard, of Ludlow, Vt., a captain in the 8th Vermont Infantry.

He was promoted to major in April 1865 and mustered out in June. He was later a Republican congressman, 1877–1879.

 3. The annexed playbill is for *Der Freischutz*, at Grover's Theatre.

 4. The annexed playbill is for the dramatization by the Irish comedian John Brougham (1810–1880) of *Mystery of Audley Court.*

Sunday, March 26. . . . Col. Shaffner called last evening. He is just up from the front, where he has been exhibiting his Artillery mining apparatus, and has convinced the best Engineers of our Army, and Gen. Grant, that he "can do the state some service." They have given him a most favorable report. Ben and I called on him at Willard's today at 10 o'clock, and he showed us his invention and exploded fuses with his portable battery, which is a most curious and simple, but a most ingenious contrivance. He can explode a mine through light copper wires at any given distance, and can place fuses of his own invention and construction among a large quantity of powder, so as to burn *the whole of it.* Some of his experiments in Europe, of which he has photographs, show how completely he can destroy a vessel with his mine at a distance of 30 feet from her. He thinks he could have exploded the powder vessel in front of Fort Fisher in such a manner as to have destroyed the Fort and all the men within it! He desires a commission[,] and I think will get one. He asks nothing more than that for his invention. He is desirous of returning to Europe a Major General. He has received honors in Europe which give him there a higher rank than that.

 The war goes on, but Rebeldom is fast being "played out." We had a victory at the Front yesterday that must lead to glorious results ere long. The rebs attacked two of our Forts—they succeeded in taking one, but it was recaptured[,] and they were driven out with immense slaughter and were repulsed overwhelmingly from the other. They seem to have checked Sherman[1] a little in his advance, but I think he will not stay checked a great while.

 1. William Tecumseh Sherman (1820–1891), after completing his march to the sea in December 1864, had turned northward through the Carolinas.

Saturday, April 1. Another week ended. It has been somewhat exciting in various ways. The President is at the Front with General Grant and there has been considerable fighting. Things seem to be approximating toward an end, and I now believe that the Fourth of next July will dawn on a re-united and peaceful union. My hope is, I admit, father to my belief. Grant is certainly doing all he can; Sherman is working steadily on toward Richmond, and Sheridan, with his cavalry, is raiding around the enemy and giving him precious little rest. The President telegraphs from the front this evening what Grant is doing, and all seems to be well. Col. Shaffner came up day before yesterday & returned yesterday. He says it will take three months to take Richmond. I hope not quite as long as that, but it may. He knows better than I do. . . .

My own week has passed away without any particular excitement or movement. In consequence of the failure of the Bill containing the appropriations for the Public Buildings and Grounds, I am greatly embarrassed and have but little to do. Besides[,] a new Secretary of the Interior, Mr. Harlan,[1] has been appointed and is to enter into office on the 15th of May. For this I am thankful, for I believe Mr. Harlan to be one of the most honest, upright, reliable men living, and I think he will not undertake, as the present Secretary has, to interfere with everybody, unjustifiably, who is under his supervision. Mr. Secy. Usher is a man easily influenced by designing men, and he has suffered himself to be prejudiced and made a tool of all through his official term. He is totally unfit for the place he occupies, & it will be well for the President, the Country, and all concerned, to get rid of him. I shall rejoice at his departure. . . .

1. James Harlan (1820–1899), of Iowa, was a Whig and Republican senator, 1855–1865, before becoming Secretary of the Interior on May 15, 1865.

Thursday, April 6. The time since last Monday noon has been a perfect whirl to me, and I imagine to most of my fellow citizens. At noon on Monday the news came that Richmond was taken. I was in the Criminal Court, and the judge, Olin,[1] who was holding it, read the news from the Bench and ordered the Court adjourned. The courtroom rang at once with cheers, and all sorts of demonstrations of joy were visible. On getting into the Street I found all the population apparently about half crazy. Women were on balconies waving flags, and at windows waving handkerchiefs. Men were shouting and shaking hands and running to & fro. Speeches were being made, cannons were being fired, bands of music were moving rapidly from place to place playing "Yankee doodle[,]" & I immediately found myself, involuntarily, marching to the music. I came to the Capitol & found a letter from F. W. Seward,[2] Assist. Secy. of State, advising me that the Public Buildings would be illuminated *that evening*. I set all the men I could muster at work preparing to illuminate the Capitol, but had not progressed far when another letter came from Mr. Seward advising a postponement of the illumination until the next (Tuesday) evening. So we had all of Tuesday to prepare, and we did it well. The Capitol made a magnificent display—as did the whole city. After lighting up my own house and seeing the Capitol lighted, I rode up to the upper end of the City and saw the whole display. It was indeed glorious. The newspapers have given all the particulars so I will not. I will only say that *all Washington* was in the streets. I never saw such a crowd out-of-doors in my life, that I remember—and I have seen immense crowds in my day. I will record, here, one incident. I had the 23d verse of the 118th Psalm printed on cloth, in enormous letters, as a transparency, and stretched on a frame the entire length of the top of the western portico, over the Library of Congress—viz., "This is the Lord's doing; it is marvellous in our eyes." It was lighted with gas and made a very brilliant display, and was a marked feature, as it could be read far up the Avenue. Gen. Cameron[3] was on the terrace with me after it was put up and was much pleased at the selection, "For," said he, "I have said from the beginning that this was the Lord's war."

I came home at ten that night completely tired out, & went to bed with a general ache all over me, and, as a matter of course[,] arose on Wednesday morning with a severe headache. I went to the office and labored till noon and then came home and went to bed and slept. At 3 o'clock I arose much refreshed, and was told of the death of my baby nephew[,] Benjamin Brown French, who had been suffering for several days with pneumonia. Poor little fellow. He had a short life, but a happy one. . . .

1. Abram B. Olin (1808–1879), Republican congressman from New York, 1857–1863, and Justice of the Supreme Court of the District of Columbia, 1863–1879.
2. Frederick W. Seward (1830–1915), son and secretary of Secretary of State William H. Seward. He later edited his father's autobiography.
3. Daniel Cameron (d. 1879), of Chicago, a founder of the *Chicago Times* in 1854. A Scotsman, he commanded the 65th Illinois Infantry, a Scottish regiment, until his resignation in July 1864.

Saturday, April 15. "We have supped full with horrors"—Well may every tongue in this city, & almost throughout the land, thus exclaim today.

I arrived home from a visit to Richmond with my wife, and a most pleasant party, at about 8 o'clock last evening, (the particulars of which I shall endeavour to write down in pages following this) feeling most happy. We went to bed about 10, & I slept well till about daylight, when I awoke and saw that the streetlamps had not been extinguished. I lay awake, perhaps ½ an hour, & seeing that they were still burning, I arose and saw a sentry pacing before my house. I thought something wrong had happened, so dressed & went down & opened the front door, & while standing in it a soldier came along and said, "Are not the doings of last night dreadful." I asked what. He replied[,] "Have you not heard?" I answered, of course, in the negative, when he proceeded to inform me that the President had been shot in Ford's Theatre, and Secretary Seward's throat cut at his residence. He told me, hurriedly, all that he knew.

I immediately went & told Mrs. French, & then started to find out all I could. I went first to the Capitol and ordered it closed, then on to 10th Street, and up to the house where the President lay. He was surrounded by the members of his cabinet, physicians, Generals, Members of Congress, etc. I stood at his bedside for a short time. He was breathing very heavily, & I was told, what I could myself see, that there was no hope for him. I then went into a room where Mrs. Lincoln and Robert were, surrounded by ladies, none of whom, except Miss Kinney,[1] were known to me. I took Mrs. Lincoln by the hand, and she made some exclamation indicating the deepest agony of mind. I also shook hands with Robert, who was crying audibly. I sat a few moments, when I left the room, and was asked to get into the President's carriage, then at the door, and go for Mrs. Secy. Welles,[2] & Mrs. Doct. Gurley.[3] I did so. Mrs. Welles was not up, & a lady at the house said she was too unwell to go, so I returned to the carriage, but, before we could get away, someone said from the upper window that Mrs. Welles would go. I returned to the house and waited for her to dress and take a cup of tea & some toast, & then the carriage took us round to the President's House—I, supposing she was to go there and be ready to see Mrs. Lincoln when she should get home. She thought I was mistaken, and that she was to go to 10th Street. So I remained, and she went on. I staid at the President's a short time, directing that the house should be kept closed, etc., and then came home and ate a very light breakfast. At nine, I again started in my own carriage with Ben and we drove up. We entered the gate very soon after the President's remains were taken in, and I went immediately to the room where they were and saw them taken from the temporary coffin in which they had been brought there. I went in, at the request of someone, to see Mrs. Lincoln. She was in bed, Mrs. Welles being alone with her. She was in great distress, and I remained only a moment. I then gave all the directions I could as to the preparations for the funeral, and staid till between 11 & 12, when my head ached so badly that I had to come home. I came through the Capitol, gave directions for clothing it in mourning, saw my friends Sergt. at arms Brown and Ben Perley Poore in the Sergt.'s room, and then came home. Dined at 3 and soon after went to bed with a very severe headache and slept till about 7 when I arose, relieved of my headache, took tea, and have written this.

It has been ascertained, beyond a doubt, that the President was assassinated by J. Wilkes Booth,[4] who has been arrested, it is said, & who is, I presume, confined on board of a Monitor at the Navy Yard. (He had not been.)

The President died at 22 minutes past 7.

The attack on the Secy. of State was an exceedingly desperate one, and not only the Secy. but his two sons and two servants were wounded, F. W. Seward, it is feared, mortally.[5] There is no doubt that it was an organized conspiracy, of no great extent it is to be hoped, to murder the President and Secretary of State. One very singular thing took place at the Capitol at about the hour of the attack, which was the sudden extinguishment of all the lights on the terrace of the Western front. The police discovered it immediately and caused them to be relighted. Nothing further occurred about the Capitol to excite suspicion.

It is now nearly ten o'clock. I have written the foregoing while carrying on a conversation with three ladies, viz., Miss Emma Barrett, Miss Carrie Reed,[6] & Mrs. French. I will postpone my history of the excursion till tomorrow.

1. Mrs. James Dixon, the wife of Senator Dixon of Connecticut, and a friend of Mary Lincoln, was summoned to the William Petersen house at the request of Robert Lincoln. Mrs. Dixon, in turn, sent for her sister, Mrs. Mary Kinney, to join her. Mrs. Kinney did and brought her daughter Constance with her.

2. Mary Jane Hale of Pennsylvania had married Gideon Welles, her first cousin, in 1835.

3. The wife of the Reverend Phineas D. Gurley of the New York Avenue Presbyterian Church.

4. John Wilkes Booth (1838–1865), a Shakespearean actor from a family of actors, was shot to death in Virginia on April 26.

5. Frederick W. Seward recovered.

6. Caroline Reed, a friend of Mrs. French's.

Monday, April 17. I could write nothing herein yesterday, being all the morning engaged in writing letters and attending to company. As soon as I had eaten dinner I went to the White House & saw that all was going on well in regard to preparations for the funeral. I saw the remains of the President, which are growing more and more natural—indeed[,] but for the bloodshot appearance of the cheek directly under the right eye, the face would look perfectly natural. After remaining an hour at the house I went over to Secretary Seward's, where I met Senator Foot. We went in & saw Gen. Seward,[1] Miss Seward and others who were present. Gen. Seward described to me the manner in which the assault was made on his brother & father. Secy. Seward is very much better, and out of danger. There is hardly any hope of the recovery of Frederick. After staying a short time with the Seward's [sic], Mr. Foot accompanied me to the President's, and we stood together at the side of the form of him whom, in life, we both loved so well. I had agreed to meet Assist. Secretary Harrington[2] at the Treasy. Dept. at 5, to aid in making the programme of Arrangements for the funeral, so I remained at the President's until that hour, then went to the Treasury Dept. and remained with Mr. Harrington till 6, and agreed to return at 7 to meet

Several Senators, Members of the House & Military officers. I came home in a horsecar, had my carriage harnessed, took tea, and was back at 5 m. past 7. I met at the Dept. the two Assist. Secretaries, Harrington & Field, Senators Foot & Yates, Representative Arnold, Gov. Oglesby, Maj. Gens. Halleck & Augur, Brig. Gen. Nichols, Admiral Shubrick, Mr. Gobright of the Associated press, and several other gentlemen whose names I did not learn.[3] We spent an hour talking over the Arrangements and agreed to meet at 2 today again. We left at a little past 8, & Senator Foot rode to his boardinghouse (Mrs. Carter's) with me. I came home & at about 10 went to bed. So passed away yesterday.

Trip to Richmond

I will now commence writing an account of our delightful trip to Richmond and back.

We had no idea of going until 9 o'clock A.M. of Monday, April 10, when I was told that my neighbor, Geo. T. Brown, Esq., Sergt. at Arms of the Senate, was making preparations to go to *Charleston* with the Committee of Congress on the conduct of the War. Mrs. French expressed much anxiety to go, as she was told there was a very pleasant party going. I went to the Capitol, saw Mr. Brown, and it was partly arranged that we should go. So I went into my office and arranged my business so as to leave, and came home & told Mrs. French to be getting ready, as I had written a note to Senator Wade, Chairman, asking if I could go, to which I expected an answer. I waited till nearly 11 and then went again to the Capitol to see Mr. Brown, and he had left for my house, which I did not find out for half an hour, when a messenger came and told me that Mr. Brown wanted me immediately at my house, and his carriage was at the door. So I came down & rode immediately home. I found that Mr. Brown had very strongly insisted upon Mrs. French going with him, but she declined unless I could also go. He said he had no authority to invite me, but could invite my wife. I went over to see him, and he invited me to go to the Boat & there we could see the Committee. So Mrs. F. & I packed up & at ½ past 12 rode down to the boat, where we were most kindly received, and the Committee expressed much pleasure that we had come. At 2 o'clock P.M. the boat was cast off & our trip commenced.

The party soon became each acquainted with the other, and a more genial, congruous, and lively party has been seldom, if ever, assembled. It consisted of the following individuals: Hon. B. F. Wade, Hon. Z. Chandler of the U.S. Senate; Hon. Geo. W. Julian, Hon. D. W. Gooch, of the U.S. Ho. of Reps., who composed the Committee. Hon. H. L. Dawes of the Ho. of Reps.; Hon. John Covode, ex Member of the House; Wm. Blair Lord, Esq., Phonographer of the Com.; E. G. Chambers, Clerk of the Com.; George T. Brown, Sergt. at arms of the Senate; A. L. Willis, son-in-law of Mr. Lord; B. B. French; Mrs. Caroline R. Wade; Mrs. Josephine S. Griffing; Mrs. General Custer; Mrs. Cora W. King; Mrs. Sallie S. Barrett; Mrs. Louisa L. Lord; and Mrs. Mary Ellen French.[4] The Boat was Commanded by Capt. Mitchell.[5] She was provisioned & found by Mr. Brown, Sergt. at arms, and all the servants were his employés in the Capitol, which made it very pleasant, as we knew them. We ran straight down to Fortress Monroe without any delay, & without even stopping the engines. The Boat was *The Baltimore*, a large & fine Boat, but somewhat old[,] & her upper works out of repair, but with a splendid engine, & she was, in all respects, most comfortable.

We arrived at the Fortress at 6 A.M. Tuesday [April 11], and were soon told from the flagship of Commodore Ronckendorf[6] that the Steamer *Alabama* would be alongside at 10, ready to take us to Charleston. The Commodore, himself, came on board. Between 8 & 9 an officer came on board & reported that the *Alabama* had come down from City Point with only six hours coal on board, and that it would take all the next day to coal her, but that she would be ready the next (Wednesday) evening. Within ten minutes we were under way for Richmond. At City Point Admiral Porter[7] came on Board and, it being nearly dark, suggested that he had better furnish us a pilot, which he did, and we arrived at the wharf at "Rocketts," about two miles below Richmond, at 9 o'clock, without accident or incident worthy of mention. Mr. Gooch went up to Gen. Weitzell's[8] headquarters in Jeff Davis's house, and the Gen. agreed to send down conveyances early the next morning [April 12] to take the party over Richmond. At 8 o'clock they came—hacks, ambulances, and saddle horses. I mounted a horse and[,] with Mrs. Barrett on another, *and on a cavalry saddle*, away we went, in advance of all the rest. The mounted cavalcade, consisting of Messrs. Chandler, Julian, Dawes, Chambers, and one or two others, overtook us on Maine Street, and on we went to Gen. Devins's[9] headquarters, near Weitzell's, where we all dismounted, and a side-saddle was procured for Mrs. Barrett. Our party had been joined by a few of the others, & we went to Gen. Weitzell's on foot.

He occupied the house of Autocrat Jeff[,] and we were admitted and went through the lower story and found it a splendid mansion elegantly fitted up and furnished. Jeff skedaddled, leaving everything in order. We walked back to Gen. Devens's & there found the rest of our party, who had visited Libby Prison and Castle Thunder. We again mounted and rode to the Capitol, over which we went, and saw the Halls of Legislation occupied as military tribunals of some sort. We went to the top of the building from whence we had a view of the entire city, and then we could fully appreciate the vandalism—the revenge—the wickedness that the flying Chivalry had left behind them. Nearly all the business portion of the city was a heap of smoking ruins! Millions upon millions of property had been cruelly and ruthlessly committed to the flames, and thousands of good citizens had been ruined. Belle Island, that place of torment and starvation to our brave soldiers who had been captured, was before us, a little island not over a quarter of a mile in diameter, as it seems to me, then dressed in living green[,] was the abode for long months of thousands of our prisoners who were turned on to it without shelter, and without any place to lay their heads, except the ground! Oh Treason, Treason, what have you not to answer for! At the Capitol I found that Mrs. French was suffering with a severe headache, so I left my horse and got into the carriage with her. We all went to Jeff Davis's house again, & I had Yankee doodle played on "Lady" Davis's piano.

We then undertook to go out to the defences but, finding the roads exceedingly muddy, and Mrs. F.'s headache increasing, we turned about after having ridden about two miles and returned to the Boat. The remainder of the party came scattering in, Mrs. Barrett with a little black & tan terrier in her arms last, at about 5 o'clock. She had ridden out two miles on horseback after that dog, who was unanimously christened "Richmond" and was petted as never dog was petted before, the remainder of the trip. As soon as Mrs. Barrett came on board we cast off and ran down to City Point, where we arrived at 9 o'clock. We had a capital opportunity to see what the untiring industry of the Rebels had accomplished in defending the river. The banks for miles were crowned with forts and studded with heavy cannon. The channel of the river was filled with all sorts of obstructions and almost sown broadcast with torpedoes. Enough of the obstructions and torpedoes had been removed to allow vessels, properly piloted, to navigate the river in safety, but a great many of the torpedoes still remained, buoyed out, with little red flags flying on the buoys. We saw Butler's famous Dutch Gap canal, which is opened through, and about 200 feet long. It is not of sufficient depth for a steamer to pass through, but small boats can do so & save 7 miles! It can be sufficiently enlarged, at a trifling, comparative expense, to admit the passage of any vessels, and will be a great thing for Richmond.[10] Soon after we arrived at City Point the rain began to fall, & it was as dark as Egypt. So we anchored and laid there until 9 A.M. on Thursday [April 13]. The rain poured all night, and nearly all of Thursday. At 9 we got underway for Fortress Monroe, where we arrived at 2 P.M.[,] finding the *Alabama* all ready to take us to Charleston. But Senator Wade was not well, and declined going. The other members of the Committee would not go unless he did, and after a consultation among them it was concluded that, instead of going to Charleston[,] we should return to Washington. We spent a good portion of the afternoon in visiting the Fortress and were exceedingly interested in all we saw. The big guns—the casemates—the drawbridges—the ditch filled with water—indeed all the contrivances for defence, wherein millions of money had been expended, awakened our admiration and our National pride. At about 6 we were again on board, and the old *Baltimore* was poking her nose up the bay under a full head of steam, at the rate of 10 to 12 knots an hour. The evening was perfectly delightful, and we all staid on deck till a late hour. At ½ past 1 A.M. Friday we anchored off Point Lookout, and early in the morning the boat hauled in to the wharf. Ambulances and saddle horses were furnished as soon as we had taken breakfast, and we all rode up to the camps[,] where about 18,000 rebel prisoners were confined. I was one of the horsebackers, and Mrs. Barrett was of our party. We fairly raced our horses thro the camps and then dismounted and walked through the hospitals. The visit was very interesting, and the rebs expressed much anxiety to be exchanged or released. At 10 A.M. the party were again on board & we got underway for Washington. The day was one of the most perfect imaginable. At the very hour at which the flag was to be raised on Sumter, the gentlemen of the party assembled and drank perpetuity to the Union and the old flag forever! I happened to have a copy of some rhymes in my pocket, which I wrote for Grover,[11] to be rehearsed at his Theatre that night. I submitted them to some of our company, who read them and pronounced them most appropriate. We arrived at the Navy Yard wharf at 7 o'clock P.M. & at home about 8. It was a most delightful trip, and I believe everyone of the party enjoyed every moment of it. Mrs. French, with many others, were [sic] very much disappointed that we did not go to Charleston. I confess to some disappointment myself, but more on my wife's account than on my own. I said to her that I believed Providence had ordered that that party should not go to Charleston for some especial reason that we could not understand. I believed that I was *specially wanted in Washington*—but for what I could not tell. Time would show. Alas, alas! little did I then anticipate that my first awakening after my arrival should be met by the dreadful announcement, "The President has been shot at the Theatre, and Mr. Seward's throat cut in his bed at his own house!"

We left Mrs. Gen. Custer in Richmond where she expected to meet her husband. In Richmond I met my old friend Mr. Trueworthy Dudley, Jr., who has been true to the Old flag from the beginning and has suffered greatly by the war. They have had him in prison, & watched all his movements with suspicious eyes. When Richmod fell an Order was again out for his arrest and imprisonment, which he only escaped by hiding. His daughter Fannie is now in this City, and partially under my care. I saw Col. Brady[12] of Pa. who led the first Regiment into Richmond, and gave him Mr. Dudley's name, with a request that he would look after him.

I place, on the next page, the Autographs of our party, collected on the way up, so that Mrs. Custer's is not among them.[13]

1. William H. Seward, Jr. (1839–1920), son of the Secretary of State, was with the 9th New York Artillery. He had been made a brigadier general in 1864.

2. George Harrington (1815–1892), of Massachusetts, was Assistant Secretary of the Treasury, 1861–1865, and U.S. minister to Switzerland, 1865–1869.

3. Maunsell B. Field (1822–1875) had served at the American legation in Paris and was an assistant to the Secretary of the Treasury, 1861–1865. Richard Yates (1818–1873), of Illinois, was a Whig congressman, 1851–1855; Republican governor, 1861–1865; and senator, 1865–1871. Isaac N. Arnold (1815–1884), Republican congressman from Illinois, 1861–1865. Christopher Columbus Augur (1821–1898), who had been badly wounded at Cedar Mountain, August 9, 1862, was given command of the Department of Washington in October 1863, a position he held until the war's end. George W. Nichols (1831–1885) was with Sherman as aide-de-camp on his march to the sea. Nichols's *The Story of the Great March* (1865) was based on his diary. William B. Shubrick (1790–1874) served in the War of 1812 and the Mexican War. He was chairman of the lighthouse board, 1852–1871. Lawrence A. Gobright (1816–1879) came to Washington as a reporter in 1841 and represented the New York Associated Press there for the next thirty-three years.

4. Zachariah Chandler (1813–1879), Republican senator from Michigan, 1857–1875 and 1879, and Secretary of the Interior, 1875–1877. George W. Julian (1817–1899), Free-Soil and Republican congressman from Indiana, 1849–1851 and 1861–1871. In 1867 he took part in drawing up the articles of impeachment against President Johnson. Daniel W. Gooch (1820–1891), Republican congressman from Massachusetts, 1858–1865 and 1873–1875. Henry L. Dawes (1816–1903), Republican of Massachusetts, congressman, 1857–1875, and senator, 1875–1893. John Covode (1808–1871), of Pennsylvania, was an Anti-Masonic and Republican congressman, 1855–1863 and 1867–1871. William Blair Lord, as phonographer of the committee, took testimony by means of phonetic shorthand. Caroline Rosekrans Wade, the wife of Senator Benjamin F. Wade. Josephine S. W. Griffing (1814–1872), social reformer, worked in Washington for the cause of the freedmen, becoming an assistant commissioner of the Freedmen's Bureau. Mrs. George Custer, née Elizabeth Bacon of Monroe, Mich.; her husband had been in pursuit of Lee's army and was made a major general of volunteers on April 15. Sallie C. Barrett (d. 1905) was wife of Oliver D. Barrett, a prominent Washington lawyer. Louisa L. Lord, the wife of William Blair Lord.

5. The boat, the *Baltimore*, was a side-wheel steamer built in Baltimore in 1848. She was turned over to the navy in 1861 and used as an ordnance vessel and ferry on the Potomac.

6. William Ronckendorf was actually a commander in the U.S. Navy.

7. David D. Porter (1813–1891) took part in the capture of New Orleans and Vicksburg and was superintendent of the U.S. Naval Academy, 1865–1869.

8. Godfrey Weitzell (1835–1884), major general, had taken possession of Richmond after its evacuation.

9. Charles Devens (1820–1891), major general. He was later a justice of the Massachusetts supreme court, 1873–1877 and 1881–1891, and U.S. Attorney General, 1877–1881.

10. Dutch Gap was a narrow neck of land at the base of a very long horseshoe bend in the James River below Richmond. Gen. Benjamin F. Butler, in order to improve and better secure the approach of U.S. war vessels, decided to cut a canal across Dutch Gap. Capt.

Peter S. Mitchie was placed in charge of the engineering work in August 1864, and the canal, 174 yards long and 27 yards wide, was not fully completed until April 1865.

11. Leonard Grover's new theater, fronting on Pennsylvania Avenue, between 13th and 14th streets, had opened in October 1863 with an advertised seating capacity of 2,500.

12. Col. Hugh J. Brady, commander of the 206th Pennsylvania Infantry, was involved in the occupation of Richmond. However, Maj. Atherton H. Stevens, Jr., of the 4th Massachusetts Cavalry, and Maj. E. E. Graves of his staff are generally credited with leading the first Union troops into Richmond on April 3.

13. The autographs were recorded on the facing page of French's journal. Following thereafter are three newspaper columns, consisting of a narrative of the events of April 14–23 written by French for the *National Republican* of April 25, 1865.

Sunday, April 30. I put the above picture of our Martyred President into this book and wrote the quotation below it, last Wednesday morning, intending to write more, but I was interrupted by visitors and then had to go to the Capitol.[1] Had no more time to myself on that day. . . .

1. A small oval portrait of Lincoln is affixed above this entry, and is labeled "Our Beloved and Martyred President." Apparently a Lincoln autograph was also once pasted next to the portrait. French also included, below the portrait, a long quotation about Oliver Cromwell.

Sunday, May 7. Somehow I have no heart to journalize now. The excitement of *4 years of warfare* culminated in the dreadful excitement that followed the assassination of the good President. That is now, in some measure[,] over, & my nerves are not up to writing[,] I believe. Besides, I have nothing special to write about. I am much engaged at the Capitol in moving my office from the attic to the basement. I hope to get moved down this week. . . .

Abbie Thomas is here on a visit. Ben enjoys her company very much.

Sunday, May 14. . . . 10 m. to 10. When I came up from breakfast I went out and got the *Chronicle* and the first thing that met my eyes was "*Capture of Jeff Davis*" in letters two inches long. Thank God we have got the arch traitor at last. I hope he will not be suffered to escape or commit suicide. Hanging will be too good for him, double-dyed Traitor and Murderer that he is.

The trial of the conspirators is now progressing at the Arsenal. I have read the published proceedings which are exceedingly interesting. . . .

Since writing the foregoing this morning[,] news has reached us that death has again entered our family circle. At eleven o'clock came a Telegraphic Despatch from Brother Charles E. Soule announcing the death of his wife—my sister Ariana—this morning. The news came so unexpected that it overcomes us all. We had not heard that Ariana was dangerously sick. Well, a good, earnest, loving, and beloved woman has gone, in the very pride of her womanhood, and she will be missed, oh how much, especially by her bereaved husband and children. . . .

Sunday, May 21. The past week has been a very busy one to me. The new Secretary of the Interior, Hon. James Harlan[,] entered on the duties of his office last Monday, and it so happened that certain matters and things touching the vacating of the White House by Mrs. Lincoln rendered it necessary that I should have almost daily interviews with the Secretary. I have also had to write him a long official letter in answer to one enquiring especially about my office. Besides[,] I have had a great amount of official duty to perform otherwise, so I have no especial record of my private transactions to make. I wrote a letter of 8 pages to Sister Pamela today, and ought to write to Frank. Mrs. Lincoln talks of leaving tomorrow.

Wednesday, May 24. It is one o'clock P.M. and the last of the great review, so far as East Capitol Street is concerned, is over.

Yesterday morning it commenced. The ninth corps[,] numbering 15,000 men, formed on East Capitol Street quite early in the morning. I put out a gilded eagle over the front door and festooned a large American flag along the front of the house, the centre being on the eagle, and above the eagle, in a frame placed in the window, I placed a quotation from the 40th Chapter of Isaiah[,] verse 2d[,] "Speak ye comfortably to Jerusalem, and cry unto her that her warfare is accomplished, that her iniquity is pardoned." . . . This was cheered by the soldiers. About ½ past 9 the troops commenced moving, and there was a constant stream until after 12. Among the troops was Captain Hollis[1] & his company, who gave us three hearty cheers while passing. After the 9th corps had all passed I went to the Capitol with Mrs. Kelsey of Columbus, Ohio, her daughter Minnie and her Niece Sarah, who are visiting us, Marg. Gray and her little brother. We went on the dome, from which we could see troops by the thousands in every direction—I presume there were more than 50,000 in sight at one time, as we could see the entire length of Md. Avenue West, Pa. Avenue East, N.J. Avenue South, and all of Pa. Av. west from the Capitol to the Treasury, and they were all literally filled with troops. It was a grand and a brave sight.

Today, the 17th Army Corps, commanded by Maj. Gen. F. P. Blair, Jr.,[2] formed on East Capitol Street. It was followed by some other troops I think[,] as the last squad (or whatever it can be called) consisting of horses, mules, jacks, cows, goats, poultry, etc., the horses and mules loaded with bags, guns, mining tools, and what seemed to be debris of the whole army, passed about ½ past 12. It was a very queer sight to see this wide street filled for a quarter of a mile with such a motley crowd of *nondescripts*. The horses, mules and jacks were ridden by men and boys of all sizes, colors and complexions, all of whom seemed to be in high glee and enjoying themselves hugely. It was the most laughable sight of the entire review, and I think the President and General Grant must have enjoyed it. A rear guard of about 20 men finished the column.

Mrs. Kelsey & her lady attachés went to the President's to view the procession from one of the stands. Mrs. French, Abbie, Ben and I went to the Capitol, and after viewing the troops from the portico of the North wing for an hour, we concluded we would go to the dome, and did so, from which, as on yesterday, we could see the tens of thousands. It has been one of the grandest displays of military that this Nation has ever exhibited, or this people have ever seen, and it is not probable our successors here will ever see such another. But I should think the poor soldiers would be glad when it is all over, for it must be a weary job to them. God Bless them all. I saw them depart for the war, and my eyes moistened with grief, as I thought how many of them would never return! I have seen many of them come back—brave veterans who have fought and bled to preserve the liberties for which their fathers fought so well, and my eyes moistened with joy to think that they were on their way *home*.

Mrs. Mary Lincoln left the City on Monday evening at 6 o'clock, with her sons Robert & Tad (Thomas). I went up and bade her good-by, and felt really very sad, although she has given me a world of trouble. I think the sudden and awful death of the President somewhat unhinged her mind, for at times she has exhibited all the symptoms of madness. She is a most singular woman, and it is well for the nation that she is no longer in the White House. It is not proper that I should write down, *even here*, all I know! May God have her in his keeping, and make her a better woman. That is my sincere wish. . . .

1. Abijah Hollis was the husband of Henry Flagg French's daughter Harriette.
2. Francis P. Blair, Jr. (1821–1875), of Missouri, Free-Soil and Republican congressman, 1857–1859, 1860, 1861–1862, and 1863–1864. He served under William T. Sherman in the Civil War.

Sunday, June 11. . . . Mail came and I wrote two letters called for by letters received—then a letter to Brother Soule; then came out here in the Summerhouse where I am writing this, and read awhile, then got the hammock, which I had not seen for *more* than 3 years—perhaps 4—

and put it up between two apple trees, and lying down in it looked up and noticed that one of the trees was considerably inhabited by cater-pillers, so I arose, got the stepladder, and went "at them" like Wellington's soldiers at the French at Waterloo, and I exterminated perhaps less than a million, but quite an army. . . .

. . . Thursday the 6th Corps marched through Pa. Avenue and was reviewed by the President. I undertook to go to the President's, but only succeeded in getting to the Interior Department, where I had a long business interview with Secy. Harlan. Returned to my office and was busy till 3 o'clock. Saw nothing of the Review. Friday at the Depts.[,] the Pres-ident's, etc. Made it a day of travel and errand doing over the city. . . . Last evening we were at Edmund's, where we met the Barkers, Wm. N. & wife & John,[1] who went off on the Rebellion spree in 1861, and have returned after a 4 year's absence, sick enough of their bargain. We passed a very pleasant evening. William seemed to be in excellent spirits and ready to take the world as it might come; John was silent & sober. . . .

William talked freely with me about the rebellion—spoke of his hard-ships, and denounced Jeff Davis. He has taken the oath of allegiance, and is a clerk on board the Steamer *Northerner,* now plying between this city and Richmond. John is either in business at Baltimore, or about to go in. I wish them both well with all my heart, but I do hope they will never again be in the official employ of the U.S. Government. They were born in Philadelphia; their father, Major J. N. Barker, was an excellent man and a true patriot. He held office[,] either military or civil, most of his life, and did every duty faithfully. His sons both resigned offices to go South and engage in the Rebellion, and I really mourned over their diriliction [sic] of duty, as it appeared to me, and espousal of the traitor cause. I hope they have seen fully the error of their course and that they will henceforth be good citizens. What could have induced them—North-erners by birth as they were—to go, has been and is, to me[,] a mys-tery. . . .

1. John Barker, brother of William N. Barker.

Sunday, June 18. . . . I cannot go into detail as to my own movements of the week. One day I went with Mrs. French down to the Arsenal to witness the trial of the conspirators. I went into the courtroom and, in the midst of a hot & seething crowd[,] saw all that could be seen. Mrs. Suratt[1] in her usual corner, face closely veiled and a large palm-leaf fan held before it, so that nothing of her face could be seen. Then Herold,[2] with his meaningless face and low, baboon-like forehead, having the ap-pearance of an idiot—partly, I am told[,] assumed. Then Payne (alias

Powell)[,][3] a tall, well-formed sinewy-looking fellow, with a smooth, brazen face, indicating a willingness to do any desperate act, as the brute preponderates in his countenance. Then Adsterodt,[4] a low, dark, round-faced, bad-looking man. Then, O'Laughlin,[5] a handsome, genteel, plain-looking man—the last one, from his appearance, whom one would believe guilty of such a crime as he is now on trial for. Then Spangler[,][6] who, during all the time I was present, sat with his head leaned forward on the railing, so that I could not see his face. Then Doct. Mudd,[7] an ordinary looking man, with red hair & whiskers, and a bald head. Not a very old man, but prematurely bald on the top of his head. And lastly Arnold,[8] another man who does not look, to me, like a criminal. The military tribunal were seated around a table, but so hidden by the immense crowd that I could scarcely see them. Assist. Judge Advocate Burnett,[9] a very handsome man, was reading C. C. Clay's[10] letter to one of the Richmond authorities while I was there. I could catch an occasional glance of General Holt, & Judge Bingham, and those were all I could see who were known to me. I staid, perhaps 15 minutes, and my curiosity was then sufficiently gratified, but Mrs. French desired to remain till the recess (1 P.M.)[,] and I went down and waited in one of the anterooms for her. That was, I think, on Monday. . . .

Wednesday Frank & I visited the Bank and Jay Cooke & Co.'s office, and lunched at the office with Henry D. Cooke. We got home a little past 3. Thursday, I was at my office, very much engaged all day. After dinner Frank & I rode over to Georgetown and spent several hours at H. D. Cooke's house, where we had a very pleasant call. . . .

Friday I was all day in the office, and yesterday at office in the morning, then at Interior Dept. & had a long interview with Secy. Harlan about the bills for the President's funeral expenses, then to the White House, then back to office, and at a little after 3 home. . . .

1. Mary E. Surratt (1820–1865), keeper of the boardinghouse where the conspirators met, was hanged on July 7 for complicity in the assassination of Lincoln.
2. David E. Herold (1846–1865) had been employed as a drugstore clerk in Washington. With John Wilkes Booth when Booth was killed, Herold surrendered and was hanged on July 7.
3. Lewis Thornton Powell, alias Lewis Paine, was a deserter from the Confederate army. The attacker of William H. Seward and Frederick Seward, he was hanged on July 7.
4. George A. Atzerodt (1835–1865) was assigned to kill Vice President Andrew Johnson but lost his nerve and fled. He was hanged on July 7.
5. Michael O'Laughlin (1840–1867), a native of Baltimore, had served in the Confederate army. He was imprisoned at Fort Jefferson, Fla., and died there.
6. Edman Spangler (d. 1871) worked as a stagehand at Ford's Theater. He was imprisoned at Fort Jefferson, Fla., for about four years until pardoned by President Johnson.
7. Samuel A. Mudd (1833–1883) was given life imprisonment at Fort Jefferson, Fla., for setting Booth's broken leg. He was pardoned in 1869.
8. Samuel Arnold (1834–1906), of Baltimore, who had served briefly in the Confed-

erate army, had known Booth since boyhood. He was pardoned after about four years' imprisonment at Fort Jefferson, Fla.

9. Col. Henry L. Burnett (1838–1916) prepared evidence in the trial of the Lincoln conspirators.

10. Clement Claiborne Clay (1816–1882), Democratic senator from Alabama, 1853–1861, and member of the Confederate senate, 1861–1863, also served in Canada as a diplomatic agent of the Confederacy.

Sunday, July 2. . . . I am working all the time, officially, like a drayhorse, and think I am a fool for doing so. The salary of my office just about half supports me, the rest comes out of my income from other sources entirely aside from my office. . . .

My old friend G. A. Schwarzman[1] called on me yesterday and got his pardon which I obtained for him from the President. He went off into rebeldom at the outbreak of the rebellion, but never was a rebel at heart I believe. He was very much affected when he met me, and wept like a child. While he was with me I recd. a letter from Albert Pike enclosing a petition for his pardon, which I immediately sent to the President. I believe it will be best to pardon all but the head devils. I would hang Davis, and a few others, & let the rest go. . . .

1. Gustavus A. Schwarzman, of Germany and North Carolina, had been a clerk in the post office before the war.

Wednesday, July 5. . . . Well, another fourth of July has passed away[,] & it was observed in this city with uncommon noise and display. From very early morning until I went to sleep it was a constant uproar of guns, pistols, crackers, etc. I commenced the day by discharging out of the chamber window the five loads which I put into my revolver on the day that the President died. After that I *was silent.* . . . At one part of the day I took down my journal of July 4th, 1861, and read from that, to after the 1st Bull run battle, to Mary Ellen. That was before dinner, and dinner stopped my reading. How very interesting it is to read those old memoranda of past events! I believe, if ever I can find time to do it, I shall sit down and index my journals from No. 1. up, then I can find out what I have been doing for 40 years! and can find certain events when I desire to do so without looking through hundreds of pages.[1]

1. Unfortunately, French never did this.

Saturday, July 8. . . . Yesterday, at 20 m. past 1 P.M.[,] Mrs. Surratt, David E. Herold, Lewis Paine and Atzerodt, the conspirators, traitors and murderers, were hung at the Arsenal, within the old Penitentiary yard. If ever four criminals met the just deserts of an awful crime, those wretches did. I have not had, from the beginning, the least doubt of their guilt.

I was very busy all day yesterday. I went quite early to the Interior Dept. and spent an hour with Judge Otto, fixing up a contract for the Library Extension, and then went to the War Dept. to try and get the Brevet Brigadier General appointment of my second-cousin[,] Jos. S. Smith[1] of Maine, now a Col.[,] who has done brave service in the war. He is the son of my Cousin[,] Hon. Jacob Smith,[2] of Bath, Maine, who has been my friend, and at times companion, for nearly 50 years. Col. Smith called on me day before yesterday, for the first time, and I promised to obtain his appointment, now made out, but not signed by the Secy. The Dept. was in a perfect turmoil, crowded with persons who were trying to get passes to see the execution! I did not succeed in my purpose, but got a promise from Gen. Hardie[3] that my friend should have his commission in a few days. . . .

1. Joseph Sewall Smith, of Bath, Me., had entered the war as a private. He became a brigadier general within a few days of the writing of this entry. French estimated his age at twenty-seven.

2. Jacob Smith (1803–1876), judge of the municipal court of Bath, Me.

3. James Allen Hardie (1823–1876), staff officer with the Army of the Potomac. He was later the chief of the inspector general's office.

Sunday, July 9. . . . The President has been quite out of sorts for more than a week. I saw him yesterday and was with him some time. He appeared to have entirely recovered, although he said he had not, but felt better than for a long time. I saw Mrs. Johnson[1] and Mrs. Patterson.[2] I like them both very much. Mrs. Patterson is one of the very nicest, and most amiable ladies I have met with for a long, long time. It will be a pleasure to me to attend to her[,] I know.

1. Eliza McCardle Johnson (1810–1876) was sixteen when she married Andrew Johnson. When Johnson became President, Eliza's health prevented her from acting as White House hostess.

2. Martha Johnson Patterson (1828–1901), the President's daughter, had spent holidays with President Polk's family in the White House while attending school in Georgetown. She married David T. Patterson (1818–1891), who was Democratic senator from Tennessee, 1866–1869. Mrs. Patterson assumed the responsibilities of White House hostess, assisted by her sister Mary.

Friday, July 14. . . . I was at the President's yesterday and had a very pleasant interview of half-an-hour with Mrs. Johnson and Mrs. Patterson. I took their instructions to purchase several things for the house, and ordered them. I do not see how the house could have [been] stripped so completely of its furniture. I knew much had disappeared, but had no idea how much! . . .

Monday, July 17. On Saturday Mrs. French and I went down to Harper & Mitchell's to purchase tablecloths for the President's House. From that place I went to the Department of the Interior and saw the Secretary on business, where I was detained an hour, at least. Then came to my office and worked a while bringing up my daily business. . . .

Mr. Cheney,[1] of the Architectural Iron Works, New York, the contractors to enlarge the Library of Cong.[,] commenced work today. I went up on the work and saw them going on with it energetically. I think they will do it & do it well.

1. Nathan Cheney was the vice president and acting treasurer of the Architectural Iron Works.

Sunday, July 23. . . . I was twice on the dome—once with Mr. Cheney and then with Secretary Harlan who came up to examine Brumidi's[1] painting. He is a working Secretary, and is exceedingly particular, so much so as now to embarrass the work under his supervision. But he is new in office & determined to ferret out all peculation and dishonesty, if possible. I hope he may succeed, but doubt, for "the heart is deceitful above all things and desperately wicked," and through this deceit and wickedness, I fear my good friend Harlan will not find out all, sharp as he tries to be! . . .

1. Constantino Brumidi (1805–1880) came to America from Italy in 1852. His artwork appears in many places in the Capitol, most notably in the canopy of the dome, where his fresco, *Apotheosis of Washington,* is the focal point of the Rotunda, and on the Rotunda frieze, where he completed about one-third of the work in fresco. He also painted French's portrait.

Sunday, August 27. . . . My office duties have been pretty laborious, as I am making all my preparation to leave for Ohio next Thursday, to be absent a month. Yesterday I had a long, pleasant, and satisfactory interview with the President, in which he assured me that no one had any right or authority to say that he contemplated any change in the incumbency of my office. That he had not intimated such an intention to anyone, & that he *had* no such intention. That I need give myself no uneasiness, from any rumors, for, if he contemplated any changes I should be the first person to hear of it from him. We then sat down on one of the iron seats, under the shadow of a tree in the grounds, and talked together on the condition of the country, and what ought to be done, for at least an hour.

Monday, August 28. . . . . *Evening.* I have been thoroughly engaged all day. At my office all the morning. Then up to the upper part of the city on business, back to the office where I remained till a few minutes before three & then home. Dined at 3. At 4 rode up to the Ball ground & witnessed a part of the match game of Baseball between the Nationals of this City and the Athletics of Philadelphia, in which the Nationals got tremendously beaten. The last side of the last innings was being played by the Athletics when I left, and the Nationals had scored I think 13, and the Athletics about 60! I never witnessed more elegant batting than that of the Athletics, and therein lay the superiority of their game. . . .

Thursday, August 31. At ½ past 7 this evening we are to leave for Columbus, Ohio. I have been all day engaged in doing such little matters at my office as will enable me to leave all right.

The first column of the collonade of the North side of the Capitol extension was raised today. The Secy. of the Interior (Mr. Harlan) was present and we were all photographed 3 times during the raising.

Saw Secy. Seward & Atty. Gen. Speed at the office of the Secy. of the Senate today. Secy. S. looks better than I ever expected to see him, but he is very much disfigured. He appears well—as well as ever he did. God spare him, for he is our leading Statesman now. Col. Forney has shown up that miserable statesman—or would be statesman—Mr. Montgomery Blair, in the Press of Philadelphia, copied into the *Chronicle* of this morning, in a masterly manner, & is entitled to the praise of all true patriots for it. Blair made a most ridiculous speech abusing Messrs. Seward and Stanton, & he will, I hope[,] get his pay for his folly. I have despised the man for a long time, and wondered that an attempt should be made to make a great man of such small capital. Now he will "squash out."

Columbus, Ohio, Sunday, September 3. . . . . Mrs. French and I left Washington on Thursday evening, Aug. 31 at 7½ P.M. . . . We arrived at the Junction of the Ohio road at about ½ past 8. . . . At 10 & 7 minutes the western train arrived, and we took sleeping cars and were *jolted* on towards Cumberland, where we arrived at ½ past 7 (Sep. 1). . . . Onward among the most magnificent and romantic scenery till 25 m. past 1, when we reached Grafton and all dined. Onward again—the roadway curving among the mountains, and passing through tunnels—it seems wonderful that it should ever have been made. Bold must have been the engineer who surveyed it and bolder the men who had faith enough to contribute the means to build the road. It presents constant food for astonishment all the way onward. At a few minutes past 6 we arrived at Benwood, and got on board the ferryboat for Bellair, on board which it took about ½ an hour to transfer the baggage. We got fairly across about 7, and being too weary to proceed, concluded to spend the night at Bellair. . . . We went to the Belmont House—as nasty, mean, contemptible a hotel as I ever staid at. We managed to survive the dirt & musquitoes, & at 7 A.M. yesterday left for this place, where we arrived at ½ past 1. We rode in the horsecars nearly out to Mr. [William B.] Hubbard's house, & walked the remainder of the distance. The weather *burning hot.* We received a welcome as cordial as possible and were cared for as well as the most attentive hospitality could care for the most beloved of comers. . . .

Saturday, September 9. . . . Tuesday the Grand Encampment met— weather terribly hot. We met in the Representatives Hall in the State House, and I opened the Grand Body. We then repaired to a church, escorted by Columbia Commandery of Washington City, where religious services were performed, and the singing was as good as I ever heard inside of the walls of a church. We returned to the State House, and after doing a little morning business, adjourned over till 8 o'clock that evening at which time we again met and I delivered my triennial address. Wednesday much business was transacted. Thursday the officers were elected. After the first ballot for Grand Master, I withdrew in a short speech, and the *best man we have,* Henry L. Palmer[1] of Wisconsin, was elected in my place, very much to my own satisfaction and pleasure. I feel as if a tremendous burden were off my shoulders, and am very happy that I am relieved. The G. E. adjourned at about 1 o'clock Thursday, and that evening the Grand Bodies of Ohio gave us a splendid Banquet, at which I had to make the first speech. . . .

1. Henry L. Palmer (1819–1909), a life insurance executive, and for many years a national figure in Freemasonry, had been the Democratic candidate for governor of Wisconsin in 1863.

Boston, Saturday, September 16. . . . At 10 Monday morning [September 11], after a most delightful visit, we left the elegant & hospitable mansion of the Hubbards, Mr. Hubbard and George[1] taking us to the Depot in a carriage, and at 20 m. past were steaming towards Cleveland. We arrived at Cleveland at 3 P.M. and went directly on board the propeller *Arctic,* and at 4 were under way for Buffalo. . . .

We reached Buffalo about 7, and at 9 on the 12th (Frank's Birthday) took the cars for Niagara falls, where we arrived at 10, and stopped at the International, intending to dine there. We walked about the Falls, and over Goat Island. . . . We returned to the hotel about noon. . . . and we concluded to leave for Lockport in the first train at ½ past 2, which we did and arrived at Lockport at ¼ to 3. Sister Sarah was very glad to see us. . . .

At 8 Thursday morning we left, and arrived at Albany at nearly nine in the evening[,] being about one hour behind time. The day was terribly hot. About a dozen miles west of Oneida, a gentleman, by the name of Joseph Dodge, died in the car next behind the one I was in. He left Chicago in the last stage of consumption for Boston, but, poor man, was destined never to see his journey's end alive. His death, of course, created quite a sensation in the cars. I went in and looked at him. He appeared to be about 40. It certainly was a ghastly sight to behold. There he sat, his long attenuated fingers stretched at length on his legs, his eyes wide open and clear and glassy, his chin tied up with a white handkerchief, and his feet stretched forward without shoes. His agonized wife stood near him, with a male attendant, & a little child, his daughter I presume, too young to comprehend her loss, was with them, with her father's wrought slippers in her hand. At Oneida, an undertaker was procured who came with his cooling board and a leather strap, and he soon had the corpse laid at length on the tops of the seats, on the board, & then, wrapped in a blanket, it was transferred to a sort of baggage cart & moved off, the widow, daughter, and friend following. The cars moved off, but the sad scene remained in my memory & is there still. . . .

At ½ past 9 [September 15] we crossed the river in the ferry boat, and soon after left for this city. The weather continuing very hot.

We arrived at the Depot here at 5:15′ & found Frank, Ellen & Nathan waiting for us. Mr. Tuck arrived from Europe about the same time, & with his wife were to stay with Frank; so we went to Parker's & spent the night, and came out here this morning.

1. Probably the brother of French's good friend and host, William Hubbard.

Concord, Mass., Friday, September 22. . . . I arose at 5 this morning and George and I went quite a distance up the river fishing. Caught 3 pickerel. Fished with a metallic, artificial bait—which I pronounce a miserable contrivance. With one old-fashioned hook and a good bait, I could have caught a dozen pickerel. After breakfast Harry & I tried our luck, and caught one each. The sun came out blazing hot, & we came home, and at about 11 commenced preparing for a chowder and picnic on egg-rock. All the material was shipped on board the boats and taken over to the rock, a fire kindled and operations there commenced. Mr. Brown presided over the chowder-making, and Mr. Stacy[1] over the frying of the potatoes, and Mrs. Brown & Mary over the coffee, doughnuts, pears, gingerbread & such. George kept *a snake* out in the bushes that we went out to kill once in a while, but he was hard to die, & required pretty constant attendance. We generally took with us some ice water and a tumbler *to suffocate him in*! and, instead of running into his hole when we approached, he *run out*! . . .

After chowder there was a general dispersement of the party. A few left for home. Others went boating, others walking, and others, among whom was this deponent, sat quietly and smoked & talked. We all had a proper good time. Between 3 & 4 Col. Keyes & Harry rowed me down the river to the Col.'s farm, and I went all over the house he is renovating. It is nearly opposite the "Old Manse" where Hawthorne wrote his "Mosses," and was built before the revolution. At the time the British troops marched to Concord, April 19, 1775, they passed that house on their return, & its owner, standing in a door, was fired at, and the bullet passed through the side of the house, about 3 feet from his head. The bullet hole is still there, and Col. Keyes, in clapboarding the house, has had a diamond shaped place left around it so as to show the hole—a mark of patriotism worthy of the patriotic gentleman who has done it. . . .

1. John Stacy (d. 1866) was a bookbinder and operated a bookstore in Concord, Mass. He had been the town's postmaster, 1841–1845.

Chester, Sunday, September 24. Here I am in the old mansion where my childhood and youth were mainly passed, although I was not born here. My father was building this house at the time I was born, and lived in the third house above this on the opposite side of the street, but I was brought here an infant, and here my mother died. I do not believe any mortal, with any feeling in his composition[,] can forget his birthplace. . . . There are those, I presume, who wonder how I see anything in this poor old Chester to love. I confess that it is a dull, dismal, old town, but it is the very first town I ever knew—my associations up, certainly[,] to early manhood, were all with it, and here, in this house, associations of the loved and lost troop about my memory till it almost seems as if I could hear familiar whisperings from the spirit land! I feel that it is good to be here. . . .

Washington, Sunday, October 1. We left Frank's, 158 Concord St., Boston, at 5 o'clock P.M. on Friday, and Worcester Depot at ½ past 5. Edmund and Harry were with us. We "ground on" as Phoenix (Derby)[1] would say, on the *"tip and sifter"* railroad cadence, till we arrived at New London at a little past 10, where we took the good steamer *City of Boston*, & had just about as comfortable and pleasant a run to New York as need be. At about ½ past 5 yesterday morning we reached the wharf in N. York, and a little before 7 crossed over to Jersey City where we eat *a kind* of breakfast at the Depot Restaurant, and at 8 o'clock & 10 m. were off for this City. We had a hot, dusty, uncomfortable ride, but a safe one, and arrived here at 6 P.M. finding all well and everything in good order. I was delighted to be at home once more. . . .

1. The American humorist, George Horatio Derby (1823–1861), who wrote as "John Phoenix." His *Phoenixiana* appeared in 1855 and *The Squibob Papers*, posthumously, in 1865.

Monday, October 9. . . . I think I never was more thoroughly disgusted with this same office of Commissioner of Public Buildings than now. The labor is immense and the salary of $2,000 will not pay more than one-half my ordinary expenses of living. If I had no other income I should be forced to resign. As it is, I succeed in getting just about enough to meet my expenses, while, at my time of life I ought to be accumulating something, for my working days cannot last many years longer. . . .

Thursday, November 2. . . . At ¼ before 7 I started for the Metropolitan clubhouse, it being Annual Meeting night. I took a car on Pa. Avenue, near 1st Street E.; it was perfectly crammed. At the foot of Capitol Hill we entered into the midst of the Workingmen's procession, and I thought we never should get through it. It was a display such is seldom seen. Thousands of people in procession, with colored lanthorns, torches, etc., and immense vehicles on wheels representing all the trades. I had a capital view of the whole thing from the car window. We worried along about a rod at a time till we got to Third Street, when the street became comparatively clear[,] & at about ¼ to 8 I got to the Club House. We had our meeting—election—and a supper, and played euchre till ½ past 10, when Doct. Brodhead, Mr. Thos. M. Smith, Mr. Barrett and I came out, took a Metropolitan car, & came to the Capitol. As we passed the City Hall, the Workingmen's meeting was in full blast, presenting a spectacle of display and grandeur seldom presented at a public meeting. The stand was brilliantly lighted up with gas, and the mottoes were very prominent. All the vehicles representing the Trades were drawn up in front of the stand, and a full-rigged miniature man-of-war, on wheels, manned & illuminated, presented a prominent feature of the pageant. . . .

Today I spent at the Capitol. I went all over the Library extension with Mr. Feelwell of Philadelphia, of the firm of Wood & Co., steamheating furnace builders, to examine the practicability of heating the Library with steam. It took us several hours to make our examination. . . .

Sunday, November 12. . . . In the evening I went down and constituted Columbia Commandery No. 2 as proxy of our new Grand Master, [Henry L.] Palmer. Albert Pike was present, and I saw him for the first time since the close of the war. I was really glad to see him and greeted him most cordially, but I could not help thinking of what he had been, although I have much charity for him, knowing, as I do, that he was against secession, and was *driven* into the rebellion by circumstances, and I firmly believe he is now a true national man. . . .

Monday, November 13. . . . I wish I could know the necessity of keeping this City crammed with troops and munitions of war. Every morning a train of about 100 four-mule waggons comes up East Capitol Street and goes—I know not where, returning again at night—empty both ways. In the course of the day many other waggons pass Eastward, loaded with hay, boards, lumber, etc. There are about 1,500 soldiers in the barracks just East of our house. What all this can be for[,] unless to put money—the money of the people—into the pockets of a parcel of favorites of the War Department, I do not know.

Capt. Wirz[1] was hung on Friday last at ½ past 10, at the Old Capitol Prison, and when he was executed the mob gave three cheers! Not, as I think, in very good taste, although Wirz, doubtless, deserved his fate, for he was a cruel man and murdered hundreds of our soldiers, when prisoners of war, in cold blood. His carcase now lies in the Arsenal grounds alongside of those of the conspirators, Surratt, Paine, Atzerodt, & Herold. There let them rot in evidence that justice lives, and murder and treason cannot go unpunished in this land.

1. Henry Wirz had been commandant of Andersonville Prison in Georgia.

Tuesday, November 21. Yesterday I went early to the office and after doing my morning business rode to the Department of the Interior and had an interview with the Secretary. He intends to bring up all contractors with *a round turn* I should imagine, by his conversation. If he dislikes the terms of a contract he annuls it without mercy, and it is my opinion he will find, ere long, that there are *two parties* to every contract. Mr. Harlan is an honest, upright, excellently well-meaning man, but not a man of enlarged views, or of a comprehensive mind. I like him very much, but God never intended him for a member of the Cabinet of the President of the U.S. He was an admirable Senator, and I hope and trust I may live to see him again representing Iowa in the U.S. Senate. There he will do himself honor, as Secretary of the Interior he will not. . . .

Wednesday, December 13. . . . On Monday morning at ½ past 6, I left this house in my carriage and rode over to Mr. Stevens's—took him in and rode to the steamboat wharf at the foot of 6th Street, where we went on board the steamer *Keyport*, & at 7 precisely she left the wharf for Aquia Creek. Bro. J. B. Donaldson[1] was with us, we being a Committee of our Grand Lodge to visit the Grand Lodge of Va. and endeavour to reconcile any misunderstanding that might exist in consequence of the issuing of a dispensation by the G. L. of the District to Union Lodge in Alexandria, during the war.

We reached the Creek at about ½ past 10. We remained there until the Richmond train arrived, at 5 minutes before 11, and then started for Richmond, where we arrived at ½ past 2. . . . Richmond was hardly the same place that it was when I was there on the 11th of April. Business has revived and they are building up the burnt district quite fast. . . .

My visit at Richmond was pleasant and interesting. I saw many people and was glad to see evidences of a return to the principles of the fathers.

I think those who were the most bitter secessionists are now convinced of their error, and are striving to sustain the Union and Constitution in good faith. So, at least it appeared to me. They avow that they went in fully expecting to win, and regret that they did not, which is natural and to be expected. But they confess themselves beaten, and are now ready to make the best of it.

1. Robert B. Donaldson (1826–1907) was the deputy grand master of Masons in the District of Columbia in 1865. He practiced dentistry in the city for forty-five years.

Wednesday, December 20. . . . Another explosion at the Arsenal Monday, I was sitting in my office with Mr. Geo. Keyes when it occurred. It shook the Capitol; the window in my room rattled as if a gale of wind were blowing. I supposed it to be the discharge of a very large gun, but in a few minutes learned the fact. Nine men were killed & several more wounded. Congress is about to adjourn over the Christmas and New

Year's Hollydays, and I shall have some peace I hope, as the members
will not be here to ask for offices.

Sunday, December 24. . . . Yesterday being Mary Ellen's birthday (34) I
went to Gault's and purchased, with her approbation, a coral set for her.
I should have preferred something more extravagant, but $40 seemed
to be the height of her ambition, and so, as Grant says, we "went in" for
that. . . .

There is only one thing that, in my old age, I envy the young people
in their enjoyment of, and that is skaiting. I remember my supreme
pleasure when in my younger manhood I could buckle on my skaits and
sweep away over the polished surface of some miles square of ice, feeling
like "a bird let loose." From morning till night have I skaited, and from
dusk till past midnight, many's the time and oft, with more real pleasure
than I can now express. In those days ladies did not skait; now they do,
which must be a still stronger inducement for the young men to engage
in that delightful pastime. If I had a good opportunity, I would once
more put on a pair of skaits and try for a broken head or a rush forward!
I fear my old ankles would hardly endure the strain that 195 pounds of
corporation would require of them!

We are all enjoying ourselves[,] I hope, during these days of holly and
mistletoe. We ought to do so as there is no shadow of the present over
us. We have a comfortable house, good food and plenty of it, and all the
means of comfort and happiness, and if we are not comfortable and
happy we ought to be whipped! . . .

Thursday, December 28. . . . I was just the busiest man all this morning
that ever lived. I went to the office at 9. At ½ past 10 to the Potomac
Bridge, a portion of the underwork of which was swept away by the ice
a few days ago. Indeed *all* the piles that supported the span beyond the
southern draw had been washed away, so that the keepers of the draw
& the workmen on the bridge feared to slide the draw off lest the bridge
should break down under its weight, and there was quite a fleet of vessels
detained. There were four or five captains, and Mr. Ray[1] of Georgetown[,] at the Bridge to meet me and see what could be done. After a
thorough examination I concluded that there was no danger of the
breaking down of the bridge by the opening of the draw. We all thought
it might settle some, and perhaps the draw could not be closed after
being opened, but I concluded to run the risk, as it would be better to
stop the travel than to stop the navigation. So I gave the order to open,

and the men went at the windlass, and back went the draw *all right*, and my friends the Captains were delighted and thanked me over & over. But that bridge is an old rattletrap, and must be extensively repaired or it will be down.

From the Bridge I went to the President's, & saw him, & with Col. Moore,[2] we talked over the program for next Monday. From thence I went to the Metropolitan Police office & spoke to the Chief about the squad to be sent Monday to the President's; then I returned to the Capitol where I staid till almost 3 P.M. & then came home and dined, and then took a nap on the sofa. . . .

1. Alexander Ray had a coal shipping business and a coal yard in Georgetown.
2. William G. Moore (1830–1898) had risen from private to colonel in the Union army before becoming Andrew Johnson's private secretary.

NINE

Johnson and Reconstruction

1866–1868

s the United States entered the early years of Reconstruction, French found his political career bound closely to Andrew Johnson's. A Jacksonian like French, Johnson came to Washington in 1843 as congressman from Tennessee and served in the House while French was Clerk. The only Southern senator to support the Union, he was nominated for Vice President on the Union-Republican ticket in 1864, and assumed the presidency on the death of Abraham Lincoln. A long bitter battle over how to deal with the South ensued between the radical Republicans and the more conciliatory Johnson, culminating in the impeachment of the President in 1868. French sided with Johnson and, as this chapter reveals, paid a heavy price.

Unaware of what lay ahead, French started a new volume of his journal cheerfully, describing in loving detail the series of gala receptions with which Andrew Johnson opened the social season. According to French, the President "appeared calm and pleasant, . . . firm in the belief that the people [would] sustain him."[1] As befitted an old man, French seemed more interested in the past than the future as he reviewed Mary Lincoln's behavior, visited Gettysburg, and read with relish Henry J. Raymond's study of Lincoln's administration.

But before long the agony of Reconstruction in Washington began to dominate the journal. On February 21, 1866, French reported the radicals "in a rage"[2] when Johnson vetoed the new Freedmen's Bureau bill, which authorized the use of military tribunals to protect the freed slaves from the black codes in the South. On May 16 French remarked knowingly that the leading radical, Thaddeus Stevens, "was *not* there!"[3] when Johnson held a particularly "grand" reception. French, however, managed to keep on good terms with Stevens, who rode home with him in the same carriage after attending a dinner at the deaf-mute college.

Even on a trip north in the fall French could not escape Reconstruction, for on the train from Boston to Concord one day, he sat with

Congressman George S. Boutwell, who was running for reelection. The election of Boutwell and other radical Republicans later that fall gave the radicals control of the next Congress, and Boutwell himself served as one of the seven Republican managers who conducted the impeachment. French reported that during the train ride Boutwell spoke "in not the most respectful terms"[4] of the President.

When he returned to the Capital, Reconstruction continued to dominate the journal. On February 8, 1867, he had the pleasure of dining with George Peabody, who had just announced his multimillion-dollar grant for education in the South. Following the dinner French went directly to the White House and arranged to have the President call personally on Peabody to thank him for the bequest. Less than a month later Congress passed over Johnson's veto the first of several Reconstruction bills, which established military rule in the South for much of the next decade. Soon afterward the same Congress removed French from his position as commissioner of public buildings, one of the charges being that he had written poetry praising Andrew Johnson.

For French this was a demoralizing episode. With uncharacteristic bitterness he wrote that he wished his enemies "Hell on earth, & everlasting damnation hereafter!"[5] When his efforts to set up a claims agency similar to the one he had operated before the Civil War failed, he was forced to suffer the humiliation of accepting a minor clerkship in the Treasury Department. For once French could not find an escape in his family. He was continually worried about the future of his son Benjamin, who did not seem capable of providing for his wife and child. Mary Ellen's young half-sister Sarita also caused anxiety because she was showing unmistakable signs of deteriorating health. With his own health more and more in doubt, French became depressed and gloomy.

More than anything else the impeachment trial of Andrew Johnson in the winter and spring of 1868 brought direction back to French's life. He was outraged at the flimsy charges brought against the President— that, for example, he had corresponded with John Wilkes Booth—and he was fearful that his friend would be removed from office. Thus, he was much relieved on May 26 when Johnson was acquitted by one vote. The Civil War and Reconstruction were still very much on French's mind four days later when he wrote the last entry for this chapter, discussing the ceremonies for decorating the graves of the Union dead at Arlington Cemetery.

1. Feb. 23, 1866.
2. Feb. 21, 1866.
3. May 16, 1866.

4. Oct. 9, 1866.
5. May 12, 1867.

Journal

Monday, January 1. . . . This day comes off, the first public reception given by Andrew Johnson, President of the United States. I must be there, it being one of the *duties* of the Commissioner of Public Buildings to attend all public receptions, and to introduce people to the presiding lady, who this year is Mrs. Patterson, as nice a woman as ever lived, and one who will, I think[,] do all the duties of the place most admirably. The day is about as unpromising as any New Year's day I ever saw in Washington. Snow lying a foot deep—cold and rainy. . . .

Evening ½ past 8. At 10 [A.M.] I started for the President's, where I arrived in about 20 minutes, and immediately set about all the duty required of me in making preparations for the reception. At about ¼ before 11 I waited on Mrs. Patterson in her chamber, and on the President in his, and at 11 all was ready, & the President accompanied by Marshal Gooding,[1] and Mrs. Patterson and Mrs. Stover[,][2] whom I accompanied, marched down in solemn state[,] and we all took our places in the Blue room, and the Diplomatic Corps, the Judges of the Supreme and other Courts, Members of the Senate and House, and officers of the army, navy and marine corps, with such of their ladies as accompanied them[,] were introduced to the President, Mrs. Patterson and Mrs. Stover. Among the Army officers Gen. Grant was *least conspicuous,* and most gazed upon. There were Major Generals, Brigadiers, Cols., Majors, Capts., & Lieutenants in abundance; and Admirals, Commodores, Captains, etc., of the Navy; indeed it was a most brilliant reception, as far as that part of it went. On account of the miserable weather, the popular reception was not up to many I have seen, although a constant crowd of humanity poured along for two hours, closed up by 15 minutes devoted to "*our colored brethren,*" who seemed delighted at having a chance to take their places among men. The entire reception went off well.

At ¼ past 2 I got into my carriage and went to Secy. Harlan's, Atty. Gen. Speed's, and Secy. Welles's, and then I came home. . . .

1. D. S. Gooding of Indiana was marshal of the District of Columbia under Andrew Johnson.
2. Mary Johnson Stover (1832–1883), Andrew Johnson's daughter, became a widow when her husband Daniel Stover died in 1865. She married William Brown in 1869.

Thursday, January 11. . . . Yesterday I was before the Committee on Appropriations for one hour, and was examined by them as to the furnishing and *unfurnishing* of the White House. The Committee were very inquisitive regarding the number of boxes furnished to Mrs. Lincoln for packing before she left—as to what they contained, *where* they were sent, *how* they were sent, etc. Also as to certain bills that she insisted upon having paid before she left. They directed me to procure certain information & appear before them again on Saturday, and they ordered several witnesses summoned. They seem to be making a pretty severe investigation of the good lady's doings, which, although just and proper, for the sake of the memory of her husband, I greatly regret. I hoped that they would have permitted "bygones to be bygones."

Friday, January 12. It is half past 8. Wife gone to take a bath. I am alone. Today at one P.M. went to the President's to attend, officially, Mrs. Patterson's reception. The afternoon beautiful, and a very large, and brilliant company present. I introduced hundreds to Mrs. Patterson and Mrs. Stover. Oh how different it is to the introductions to Mrs. Lincoln! She (Mrs. L.) sought to put on the airs of an Empress—these ladies are plain, ladylike, republican ladies, their dresses rich but modest and unassuming, their manners such as become an American woman and the daughters of Andrew Johnson. I never see Mrs. Patterson that I do not come away feeling better for my interview; she appears so kind and so entirely unassuming. If there is guile in her heart, I shall mistrust the Angels!

Since about a week ago, we have been removing the scaffolding beneath Brumidi's *great* picture in the dome of the rotunda, and it can now be seen from the floor in all its magnificence.[1] That picture, as a work of art, surpasses any one in the world, of the kind. So says Doct. Walter, and so do I believe. It is a *chef d'oeuvre*, and years hence will be better appreciated than it now is, for it will grow upon those accustomed to look upon it, just as Trumbull's[2] pictures on the walls of the rotunda do. If that picture by Constantine Brumidi be a success, I take the credit of that success—if a failure I am responsible for that failure, for, *but for me*, it never would have been there. It was approved by Secretary Smith, but he declined giving the order for the contract—I went to him at almost the last moment of his incumbency of the Interior, and urged him to authorize me to make the contract. At last he asked me if the picture was in the architectural drawing which was originally submitted. I told him it was. "Then[,]" said he[,] "there is no necessity of an order from me. The dome is to be completed according to that plan, and I advise you to make a contract with Mr. Brumidi, at as reasonable rate as you can, to paint the picture." That was enough. I took the responsibility, & the contract was made. Secy. Usher tried to break it up, and arbitrarily suspended it for a time, but we triumphed over him, *and there the picture is*, probably for all time![3] . . .

1. Brumidi completed his fresco, *The Apotheosis of Washington*, in eleven months. The forms in the inner circle represent the thirteen original states, and Liberty, Victory, and George Washington. The outer groups symbolize arts and sciences, the sea, commerce, mechanics, and agriculture.

2. John Trumbull (1756–1843) painted four of the eight panels in the Rotunda: *The Surrender of Burgoyne, The Surrender of Cornwallis, The Declaration of Independence,* and *The Resignation of Washington*.

3. Caleb Blood Smith was Secretary of the Interior, 1861–1863, followed by John P. Usher, who was Secretary, 1863–1865.

Sunday, January 14. At the Capitol all day yesterday—before the Committee on appropriations of the House for two hours. . . . No evidence was elicited that Mrs. Lincoln carried away anything in the 75 to 100 boxes that she packed and took with her to Illinois. I think the Committee have abandoned further investigation. Thank God I knew nothing as to what she took. All I know is what was left when the house came into President Johnson's possession, and, so far as beds and bedding and table linen & the necessary housekeeping utensils are concerned[,] there was absolutely nothing left. I had to purchase an entire new "set out." But where the things went I do not pretend to know. Rumors say that a great many were sold by Mrs. L.[,] but no evidence of the fact, at all reliable, has ever come to me. I hope no further investigation will be made. If crime has been committed let the consciences of the criminals bear the burden. The U.S. can afford to be magnanimous toward the widow of their murdered President, if any such magnanimity be necessary. That she has been awfully belied I know, & "further your deponent saith not." . . .

Tuesday, January 16. Again at home for the day, indisposed. I was engaged *all day* yesterday at the President's, at the Treasury, and at home, in making an estimate of what it will cost to properly repair and refurnish the President's House. I came home in a snowstorm with my feet wet; another result was the bringing back of my cough and stuffed-up feelings at my lungs. . . .

Wednesday, January 24. . . . Yesterday I did a very hard day's work. Went to my office early and labored there steadily till three P.M. Then, with

Chief Justice Chase, Dr. Sunderland and David A. Hall,[1] Esq., rode out to the Deaf Mute College, of which we are Directors, to attend a meeting of the Directors. Mr. Kendall and Mr. McGuire were not present. We four, Mr. Gallaudet[,] President and Mr. Stickney,[2] Secy.[,] were there. . . .

1. Hall, of Vermont, had served as president of the District of Columbia New England Society.
2. William Stickney was son-in-law of Amos Kendall.

Monday, January 29. It is 4 o'clock P.M.[,] and I have been steadily at work all day at my office. Saturday I labored on a Tabular statement showing the length and breadth of all the Avenues in Washington, the square yards in each, and the cost of paving them in three different styles, and I finished it yesterday and this morning and sent it to the Committee on the Dist. of Columbia of the House. . . .

Friday, February 2. It is evening. Four days have past away since I wrote the foregoing page. Tuesday evening I was at the President's where the largest and most elegant reception I ever witnessed took place. For about three hours the human current rolled along, and the house was absolutely crowded. I stood at the side of Mrs. Patterson and introduced people to her and Mrs. Stover, and think I never felt the task so *wearingly* as I did on that evening. Both the ladies were just about exhausted by the kind attentions of their thousands upon thousands of friends. At about ½ past 10 I left and came home, the reception being over.

. . . Today I have attended Mrs. Patterson's reception. It was a very full and elegant one. I was before the District Committee of the House from 10 to 12, and then came home, dressed and went to the President's. Mrs. French went down to Edmund's before I left, and on my return I went after her in the carriage. Mrs. Patterson and Mrs. Stover receive with great propriety and elegance. They are unassuming, plain matter-of-fact ladies to whom it is a great pleasure to introduce. I like them better and better every time I see them. When I bade Mrs. Patterson good-by she handed me a beautiful bouquet she had held all through the reception, & asked me to present it to Mrs. French, which I did. It was looked upon by me as evidence of her thoughtfulness and kindness, and I appreciated the act most highly. . . .

Saturday, February 3. In less than an hour I must start for the Club where we are to have a social gathering and supper. I suppose they will ring me in for a speech, and so I have been lying on the sofa thinking over what I would say, which is rather an unusual performance for me, as I generally trust to the time and the inspiration for ideas, but as I want now to give some little reminiscences of clubs I thought I would arrange in my mind the outlines of what I would try to say.

. . . Ben has gone to ride horseback. He will be 21 tomorrow. I wish we could invent some way to make him uncommonly happy. . . .

Wednesday, February 7. I went to the club Saturday evening, and I made a short speech about Clubs as I intended, which seemed to be well received. I did not get home till past midnight. Sunday was Ben's birthday, when he was 21. I spent most of the forenoon in writing him a paternal letter. . . .

Monday I was all day at the office, & about the two Houses doing business, except that I went at 1 o'clock with a Committee, consisting of the Mayor (Wallach)[,] Doct. Hall,[1] President of the Board of Health, and Doct. Dove,[2] Secretary, to call on the Secy. of War, Mr. Stanton, to ascertain whether he would place at the disposal of the Com. of P.B. and Board of Health, a hospital in case the cholera came to this city. We were requested by the House Com. on the Dist. of Col. to do this. We were very graciously received by the Secy.[,] who referred us to Gen. Meigs, Qr. M. Gen.[,] & he referred us to Gen. Barnes,[3] Surgeon Gen.[,] and I think we shall have two hospitals assigned to us, although I hope we shall not need *one*.

Monday evening Mrs. French, with Louisa Russell, accompanied me to Secy. Harlan's reception. It was a very pleasant one, and we were warmly greeted by the good Secretary and his cordial & warm-hearted lady. We met numerous friends there and had a very pleasant time. At a little after 10 we left for Lieut. Gen. Grant's, where we found a magnificent party. We paid our respects to the Lt. Gen. and his lady, who received, as they do everything else, with a modesty of demeanour most becoming to persons in their high rank in life. Gen. Grant is, without exception, the most unassuming man, high in public office, whom I ever saw. He is a pattern for great men. We remained at Gen. Grant's till nearly midnight & then came home, and went to bed about ½ past 12. . . .

1. J. C. Hall of 334 Pennsylvania Ave.
2. George M. Dove, 29 4½ St. West.
3. Joseph K. Barnes (1817–1883), surgeon general of the United States, 1864–1882, officiated at the deathbeds of presidents Lincoln and Garfield.

Sunday, February 11. . . . Friday I was at the office all the morning, and at the Reception at the President's in the afternoon. I got there somewhat earlier than usual, and had a most kind invitation to lunch from Mrs. Patterson, which I did with her, Mrs. Stover and Mr. Bancroft, who is now a guest at the White House. . . .

I have read and written letters all the morning. Tomorrow Mr. Bancroft is to deliver his eulogy on Lincoln, and right glad shall I be when it is over.

Wednesday, February 14. According to the programme hereunto annexed, the Capitol was closed till 10 A.M. [February 12] to everybody except the members and officers of Congress and the employees in the Capitol. The morning was rainy and uncomfortable, notwithstanding which long before 10 o'clock the Capitol was surrounded by persons holding tickets, and many who had none, eager to be admitted. At 5 m. before 10 the Eastern portico was perfectly jammed with persons, & when the door was opened there was a rush to get in as severe as if an entrance to Heaven itself depended on the success of the first moment. I was at the door with four policemen to assist me, and no remonstrance that could be made would induce the crowd to hold back; so we had to keep it back by force. I should think that in five minutes we admitted 500 people, each one having to exhibit a card of admission. As soon as the rush was over, I went to other parts of the building, and finally to the centre door in the crypt, which was opened that the carriages might drive beneath the arcade out of the rain, where I stood more than an hour waiting for the President's daughters, Mrs. Patterson and Mrs. Stover. They came at last, accompanied by Mr. Kasson,[1] one of the Committee, and he and I escorted them to the seats reserved for them in the gallery of the House. I afterwards escorted Gen. and Mrs. Grant, and Mrs. Senator Foster, in like manner to the reserved seats, and then busied myself in seeing that the regulations of the Committee were observed. At 20 minutes past 12 all were in and seated, and the Marine band, stationed in the upper vestibule behind the Speaker's chair, played a dirge splendidly. At precisely ½ past 12, Rev. Mr. Boynton,[2] Chaplain of the House, made a prayer. Then Senator Foster,[3] President p.t. of the Senate[,] rose and introduced Mr. Bancroft, the orator of the occasion, with a few eloquent and appropriate remarks. Mr. Bancroft commenced his Eulogy at 10 m. before 1 and closed at exactly 20 minutes after 3, occupying 2 hours and thirty minutes. The eulogy was very eloquent, and was delivered with great effect, and the latter part of it applauded so constantly [as] to interrupt the orator at almost every paragraph. The oration can be read in an ordinary manner in one hour, but Mr. Bancroft was very deliberate, repeating the pointed passages, and with the interruptions by applause, the exact time above named was consumed.

As soon as the Benediction was pronounced, I repaired to the gallery and escorted the President's daughters to the Rotunda, where they took a look at the great picture in the Dome, which was lighted for the occasion, [and] from thence to their carriage, when they left, in company with Mr. Kasson and Judge Patterson,[4] for home. The Capitol was then opened to the public and I came home. . . .

1. John Adam Kasson (1822–1910), Republican congressman from Iowa, 1863–1867, 1873–1877, and 1881–1884.
2. Charles B. Boynton.
3. Lafayette Sabine Foster (1806–1880), Republican senator from Connecticut, 1855–1867, and president pro tempore of the Senate, 1865–1867.
4. David T. Patterson.

Friday, February 16. . . . A negro band came and serenaded me last night at about 11. I was in bed with a wet cloth around my breast, but I arose, went to the window and thanked them. They must have been very desirous to compliment me, or they never would have turned out on such a night! . . .

Sunday, February 18. Weather has moderated. Cloudy and looks like rain. Yesterday all day at office. Nothing special occurred. At the President's at 3 P.M. to see some experiments proposed to be made on the grounds South of the President's House, by Col. Tal. P. Shaffner, in Artillery mining, etc. A formidable array of 24-pounders were on the ground, a lot of barrels, and two wooden structures containing mines, all of which Col. Shaffner proposed to explode by his electrical apparatus. The whole thing had such a formidable appearance, that Gen. Augur, Mil. Gov. of the District, issued orders stopping the performance, and it did not come off. . . .

Wednesday, February 21. The political cauldron is boiling with a vengeance. On Monday the President sent to the Senate his message vetoing the new Freedman's Bureau Bill, and yesterday the Senate refused to pass it by the Constitutional majority of two thirds and ultradom is in a rage. I have the honor of agreeing with the President. I read the bill carefully through as soon as I could obtain a printed copy, some two weeks ago, and then pronounced it an outrageous bill. It carried upon its very face extravagance of expenditure, executive patronage beyond anything I had ever seen in a single measure, partiality for a race beyond reason, and a direct conflict with the Constitution. I hoped it would not pass, and predicted its veto if it did. I rejoice that it has been killed. But it vexes me beyond measure to see the copperheads, who have opposed the President & his war policy throughout, endeavouring now to seize upon him and drag him by main strength into their ranks. I hope and I *think* they cannot do it. I believe the President to be true, at heart, to the principles he has advocated for the past four or five years, and that he will sustain the Republican party in every act in which they deserve to be sustained. He means, conscientiously, to *do right*, and he will do right, let what will be the result, and the people will sustain him!

I was at the President's yesterday morning & wanted to see him, but there was such a crowd waiting upon him, and copperheads at that, that I did not attempt to obtain an interview. I saw Mrs. Patterson and Mrs. Stover, and had a talk with them. . . .

Friday, February 23. When I was writing the foregoing Wednesday evening, my brother Henry and his wife Pamela arrived, so of course I stopped writing and have not found a moment since to renew my record. Now all the family who are at home have retired, and I thought I would take the occasion to write a few words.

Yesterday, the 22d[,] was set apart by Congress for the memorial services, in the Hall of the House of Representatives, in respect to the memory of Hon. Henry Winter Davis.[1] The Judge and I went over in good season, and at ½ past 11 went to [the] Hall and got good seats on the floor of the House where we could see and hear all that was said. . . . I knew Henry Winter Davis well but not intimately. I knew his character, have listened to his surpassing eloquence, & appreciated his very uncommon scholastic attainments, his unshrinking boldness, and his great tenacity of purpose; and, while I regarded all his good qualities, he was *to me* a haughty, unapproachable, coldhearted being, who had no charms, except in his wonderfully handsome face and perfect physical form, for me. I undertook once or twice to hold communion with him, but he did not seem to regard my approaches with cordiality, and I never press myself on those who do not treat me kindly. Still[,] I held his character as a man and a statesman in high respect, & felt, when his death was announced, that the Country had lost one of her most able and most promising men. Mr. Creswell[2] did ample honor to his memory.

In the evening Judge French & I attended Mr. Speaker Colfax's reception. The house was crammed. There I met and was introduced to Mr. Samuel Bowles,[3] of Mass.[,] the author of *Across the Continent*. He is a fine looking, genial man, and made a good impression on me in the very few minutes I had to speak with him.

Today I attended Mrs. Patterson's & Mrs. Stover's reception from 1 to 3 P.M. It was very crowded and very brilliant. I saw the President and talked with him. Notwithstanding the violent feeling which prevails among the ultras against him, he appeared calm and pleasant, and is firm in the belief that the people will sustain him. I think he is right.

1. Henry Winter Davis (1817–1865), Maryland congressman, represented the American party, 1855–1857, the Republican party, 1857–1861, and the Union party, 1863–1865.
2. John Andrew Jackson Creswell (1828–1891), Republican senator from Maryland, 1865–1867.
3. Samuel Bowles (1826–1878), influential editor of the *Springfield Republican*.

Monday, February 26. . . . In the course of the day I wrote a letter to Miss Mary A. Dodge—*alias* Abigail Dodge, *alias* Gail Hamilton, copying into it what I wrote about that same lady in my journal of Feby. 13, 1859. . . . Having therein pronounced her homely, I had to smooth that over in the best possible way—*so* smooth that Pamela & Mary Ellen called me a hypocrite! "Oh the folly of sinners!" I first took her signature to the Judge's letter to be MAB, which reminding me of the Queen of the Fairies[,] I suggested that perhaps I should take it into my head to out-Spenser Spenser,[1] and write a poem to her as my "Fairie Queen." So I gave her this specimen of it.

> The muses nine incline me to indite
> A poem to some ladies of the land;
> Of whom can I with greater fancy write
> Than she, the fairie of the facile hand,
> Whose pen is sharper than a Scottish brand;
> Who mid the hosts of genius holdeth place;
> Who on the mount of Science takes her stand;
> A brave, bright mind among the human race,
> By whatsoever *name* she holds her regal place.

Also wrote to Frank, although I did not think he deserved a letter. *This day* nothing!

1. Edmund Spenser (1552–1599) published his allegorical poem *Faerie Queene*, vindicating Puritanism in England, in 1590 and 1596.

Friday, March 2. . . . Today we—i.e. the Judge & his wife, Mary Ellen and I—started from the Capitol about 1 P.M. and went to the Navy yard, where we saw the big trip hammer forging sheet anchors, and many other things going on by machinery, such as rolling copper, marking nails, cutting off bolts 2 inches in diameter, etc. Then we went on board the monitor *Miantonomoh*, & were shown all over her by the most gentlemanly man I have met for many a day—Engineer Borden, who not only showed us that vessel but four or five more moored all along the stream.[1] We were all delighted.

1. The ironclad *Miantonomoh* was modeled on the *Monitor* and named for a sachem of the Narragansett Indians.

Monday, March 11. Have been sick a week, vertigo commencing very suddenly a week ago this morning. Could hardly raise my head from the pillow for five days, and then began to get better. Came downstairs for the first time yesterday. This is my first attempt at writing with a pen. My head is inclined to *whirl* now at the least exertion.

The Judge & his wife left this morning.

Wife *commands* me to stop writing. I obey!

Friday, April 13. At ten minutes before 6 A.M. on Thursday, Apl. 5th, Mrs. French and I left this house to take the cars for Gettysburg, Pa. . . . At Gettysburg we went directly to Mr. David Wills's where we were received and entertained with all possible hospitality. . . .

. . . Monday morning [April 9] clear & cold. . . .

. . . I read in Raymond's life of Lincoln[1] till ½ past 11, and then walked out and over the National Cemetery and was much gratified at seeing how elegantly and *permanently* it is arranged. The segments of circles where our brave boys "sleep their last sleep," are admirably laid out, and the granite on which are the inscriptions, is laid exactly like the best of granite curbing, the inscriptions being cut upon the top. It looks as if it would last *forever.* Returned at ½ past 12 & dined. Read again. Slept a while, and then took another walk. The folks returned about ½ past 6.

Tuesday the 10th. Mr. Wills absent at York on business. Before dinner, Mrs. Wills, Mrs. Cooper,[2] Mrs. Harper,[3] Mrs. French, myself and little Annie Wills walked over to the Cemetery, & all over the battleground in that vicinity. We saw the turrets, where our cannon were planted on Cemetery Hill, in an admirable position, by Gen. O. O. Howard,[4] commanding all the approaches from the North & East. The selection of this position, and the working of the guns there, are said to have saved the day to our forces! From there we went to Culp's Hill, where the battle raged the fiercest, and where the gallant Gen. Geary[5] poured his deadly fire into the rebel ranks so hot and heavy that they could not stand before it. Every tree bears the marks of the fierce encounter, being scarred with musket bullets & cut with cannon shot & shell. We walked about 5 miles and got home in time for dinner. After the fatigue of the morning I was glad to rest through the afternoon. In the evening Mrs. Harper came in, and we played euchre for a while, Mr. Wills having returned, and then Miss Annie Cooper[6] & I undertook to teach Mr. Wills and Mrs. Harper how to play bizique [sic].

Wednesday, immediately after breakfast, Mr. & Mrs. Wills, Mrs. Harper, Mrs. French, myself & little Annie started on foot for the mineral spring beyond Seminary Ridge, on which the great Battle commenced. We walked out on the turnpike, about a mile, and then got over a fence and passed along a cross fence, where, in a sort of wet ditch[,] we saw the remains of a number of rebel soldiers. Skulls, leg bones, ribs, shoes, with the foot and stocking in them, etc. I traced at least two bodies, with the point of my cane, from head to feet as the remains lay. The skull of one was broken, apparently by a cannonball, as it lay in fragments. I poked some of the bones of a foot out of a shoe, wherein the foot had decayed. Rather disgusting, upon the whole.

From thence we walked on to where Gen. Reynolds[7] fell. His orderly was with him and marked the spot[,] and the tree against the root of which his head struck as he fell forward from his horse is labeled with a piece of wood, on which is written, "The tree where Gen. Reynolds fell." He was shot through the neck by a sharpshooter, while passing from one Corps to the other. No one was with him except his orderly. From this place we passed on, around the woods, to the place where the "Iron Brigade" under my old friend Gen. Sol. Meredith fought, and where Archer's[8] Brigade was captured, and thence on to the spring, the water in which is clear as crystal, but I could perceive no taste different from other pure water. I tried it *plain* & with a dash of *whiskey*. We next passed out to the turnpike at a house and barn, in the latter of which Mr. Wills told us he saw two hundred wounded and dead men, all mixed together, the Sunday after the battle. Through all our walk we saw all about us marks of the deadly contest & the debris of battle—trees shattered, scattered bones, human and animal, torn and decaying cloth that once was soldiers' clothing, pieces of knapsacks, haversacks, hats, caps, belts, marks of shot & shell through the roofs of buildings, etc. Our thoughts could not be anything but sad, especially when we thought that it was war where Brother fought against Brother. May God in his mercy forbid that such another should ever occur. We traveled not far from 5 miles, and returned home in time for dinner. . . .

1. Henry Jarvis Raymond, *A History of the Administration of President Lincoln* (1864).
2. Mrs. James Cooper, aunt of David Wills's wife.

3. Mrs. Robert Goodloe Harper.
4. Brigadier General Oliver Otis Howard (1830–1909).
5. Major General John White Geary (1819–1873).
6. Daughter of Mrs. James Cooper.
7. Major General John Fulton Reynolds (1820–1863).
8. Brigadier General James J. Archer was the head of a Confederate brigade. He and many of his men were captured at Gettysburg.

Sunday, April 15. One year ago this morning, Abraham Lincoln, the good President, and the best man I ever knew, died. How my memory goes back to that awful morning, and all the little circumstances connected with it that fell under my observation. How I stood by the bed of death—how my hand was wrung by Mrs. Lincoln as she sat on the sofa in an adjoining room—the overwhelming distress of Capt. Robert Lincoln, who sat in the room with his mother—how, at the request of the family, I got into the President's carriage and rode to Secy. Welles's after Mrs. Welles—how I waited there until she could rise from her sickbed, dress, and take a little refreshment—how we rode to the White House, where I remained to take charge of it & see that it was placed in proper care, while the carriage bore Mrs. Welles to Mr. Peterson's[1] in 10th St. where the President lay—how I returned to my house & breakfasted—how, just as I had finished, the bells commenced tolling—how I returned to the President's house in time to accompany the remains in & to the guestchamber where they were deposited—how I saw them taken from the box in which they were enclosed, all limp and warm, and laid upon the floor, and then stretched upon the cooling board. All this and a hundred things more that occurred that day, are indelibly impressed upon my memory, and death alone will erase them. Indeed, all of the events of the ensuing terrible week are there burned in, as it were, with a heated branding iron! Of one single circumstance that occurred on *Sunday* the 16th, one year ago this day, as the days run, I am now reminded with an interest very much deeper than it would otherwise be, by the recent death of my dear friend Senator Foot. After being at the President's on Sunday afternoon for a time, I walked over to Secretary Seward's to enquire for the victims who had so miraculously escaped death there. I met Senator Foot, and we went into Mr. Seward's together. After staying there for a time, Mr. Foot walked with me to the President's and we went up to the room where the body lay, together. Senator Foot looked upon the dead form of the noble martyr for a few moments in silence, and then spoke in those deep full tones of voice which no one who ever heard them can forget. The following are very nearly, if not exactly, his words, spoken so solemnly and emphatically that they made a very deep impression upon me.

"Our murdered president! A good man struck down by the hands of an Assassin for doing his duty—the result of Treason—God will not suffer this great crime to go unpunished! 'Vengeance is mine, I will repay it[,] saith the Lord!'"

We stood a while by the body, and then the Senator left. At 7 that evening there was a meeting at Assistant Secy. Harrington's office to make arrangements for the funeral, and Senator Foot was there. I brought him home in my carriage. He aided with his usual zeal in making all the arrangements for the funeral.

One little year has passed, and the beloved and noble senator stands, with his martyred friend and beloved President in the presence of his Maker. "Blessed are the pure in heart, for they shall see God."

1. William Petersen, a tailor.

Sunday, May 6. Frank, Ellen & Bessie arrived at ¼ past 6 last evening, and were received with all the honors and all the joys. Ellen came for her health, she having been very sick last winter, & now troubled with a cold.

Yesterday I arose in the morning with a severe headache. Still I went early to my office and then to the President's, where I had a long talk with him about the refurnishing of the White House. He wanted information about the old debts, etc., & as to the balance that would remain after their payment, and advised that unless I could fit up the public portion of the house in a manner creditable to the Nation, that I should not do it at all. I told him the funds were in my opinion sufficient, with proper economy, to do all that necessity required to the public rooms. He expressed a desire that the public part of the House should be handsomely furnished, but said that he cared nothing about the private part occupied by himself. It was good enough for him, he said. . . .

Monday, May 7. . . . Twenty minutes ago Ben left for Chester, Pa., to be married to Miss Abbie M. Thomas on Wednesday next. May God bless him and his bride.

Frank & Ellen rode down to the R.R. Depot with him to see him off.

Friday, May 11. First writing of the season in the Summerhouse. Recd. a letter from Ben this morning written at the Continental hotel, Philadelphia, on Wednesday evening, announcing his marriage to Miss Abbie M. Thomas that morning.

I hope this grave change in Ben's life will result in a great good to him. He has never yet learned to prize, as he ought, the happiness and prosperity that has attended his life thus far. He will now, I trust[,] fully appreciate them and will learn particularly the value of money. He has been a good boy, although given to extravagance, and I sincerely wish him and Abbie all the happiness earth can give them. . . .

Wednesday, May 16. . . . Yesterday, after considerable office work in the morning, I went to the President's to ascertain whether all proper arrangements had been made for the reception advertised for last evening. Found everything arranged as well as it could be under the circumstances—we having commenced dismantling the house in view of repairing and refurnishing. . . .

Last evening there was a grand reception at the President's. I was there officially, and Mrs. Wills & Mrs. French accompanied me. The company was large and brilliant, & we enjoyed it. We got home at 12′ past 10. I officiated in introducing about an hour, & then my head began to be affected & I got Mr. Barrett to *finish up* the introducing.

Gen. Grant & Lady were there.

Thaddeus Stevens[1] was *not* there! . . .

1. Thaddeus Stevens (1792–1868) of Pennsylvania, Whig congressman, 1849–1853, and Republican congressman, 1859–1868, was chairman of the managers to conduct the impeachment proceedings against Andrew Johnson in 1868.

Sunday, June 3. . . . [June 2] Returned about 3, dined, took a nap, played croquet till dark, and Maggie[1] and I played euchre against Fannie & Mary Ellen, and we were beaten! Mary Ellen did her best to convince them that I was a cross old critter when playing euchre, but my amiability put all her efforts out of joint. I do suppose that I really am the most amiable of mortals!

At a few minutes before ten Ben and Abbie came, and we were all precious glad to see them. Abbie is our new daughter, Ben's wife, and of course when she walked into our house she walked into our hearts. I believe her to be a dear[,] good woman, and intend to love her. . . .

1. Margaret Brady French.

Sunday, June 10. . . . [Last Wednesday] Mrs. Carlisle,[1] Secy. of the Fair, sent up a note requesting me to go to the President's & try to persuade him to be present at the grand opening in the evening. About 5 Doct.

Brodhead called & sat in the garden with me. Mrs. French came out with other ladies, and we played croquet till past 7. Then I went to the President's[,] and he agreed to be at the Fair between 8 & 9. I was requested to join the Committee to receive him, and did so. He came at 9, & the Committee escorted him to the stand. By request, at the moment most unexpectedly made, I called the meeting to order & introduced Senator Wilson to the immense audience, and he opened the ceremonies with a few most appropriate remarks. He was followed by Gen. Banks, Gen. O. O. Howard, Representative McKee,[2] Senator Lane of Ia. [Indiana][,] and the President, who was received with rapturous applause. All the speeches were good and appropriate, and were well received. At about 10 the President left. I accompanied him to his carriage and then came home. . . . Friday I had engagements at my office, at the President's[,] and elsewhere all the morning. Dr. & Mrs. Bliss[3] went to the Capitol with me and went all over it. I went to sit for a portrait for "the deathbed of Prest. Lincoln" picture, which Bachelder[4] is getting up, then to the President's. . . . Yesterday we went to Mount Vernon—Dr. & Mrs. Bliss, Mary Ellen, Abbie[,] and I. . . . We walked over the grounds and through the house, and I talked with Mr. Herbert,[5] who has charge of the premises. The only fund available to carry on the concern is the income from passengers—30¢ each, I think, as a landing fee. Small enough, when we consider that the place is only visited during a few months of the year. The whole Country ought to take hold, *in earnest*, once more, & put the preservation and good care of the place beyond a contingency. . . .

1. Mrs. James M. Carlisle.
2. Samuel McKee (1833–1898), Republican congressman from Kentucky, 1865–1867 and 1868–1869.
3. D. W. Bliss, 407 New York Ave.
4. The same Bachelder whom French saw making a map of the battlefield at Gettysburg in 1863.
5. Upton H. Herbert (1819–1906), the first superintendent of the Mount Vernon Ladies Association.

Thursday, June 14. . . . *Monday* I went early to my office where I staid an hour, then went to the President's and saw Mrs. Patterson and arranged as to the work we would have done on the four lower rooms, exclusive of the East Room. Had the bust of John Bright,[1] which was presented to the U.S. by somebody in England, brought over from the State Department to the President's and placed in one [of] the niches in the lower hall. . . .

1. John Bright (1811–1889), member of Parliament almost continuously, 1843–1889, supported the North during the Civil War.

Thursday, June 21. . . . I came home from the Capitol at 1 A.M. Monday so dizzy that I could hardly walk home, and went directly to bed, so I was prevented from attending the funeral of my old and valued friend Col. Seaton, whose remains were buried on that day, with all the honors of Freemasonry. Since then, although I have been busy at home, I have not been at my office. Tuesday I rode out to the Deaf-mute college and dined with the Committee on Appropriations of the House, at Mr. Gallaudet's by his invitation. We had a very pleasant time & the members of Congress seemed delighted. I rode home in a carriage with Mr. Thaddeus Stevens, who was almost enthusiastic in praise of the Institution and its management. Speaking of Mr. Gallaudet[,] he said[,] "That man could not be dishonest if [he] were to attempt it; one can see that from his face and from all his acts." The only Directors present were Chief Justice Chase and myself. . . .

Monday, July 2. . . . On Wednesday last at 5 P.M. we (Mrs. F., Harry & I) left home for Baltimore to attend the exercises on the next day at Mount de Sales, where *our* Sister Sarita graduated with all the honors. . . .

On Thursday we went out to Mount de Sales and attended the Annual exercises. We spent about an hour on our first arrival in examining the work of the pupils exhibited in the playroom. It consisted of drawing, painting, embroidery, crochet work, and many kinds of needlework, and was all most creditable to the young ladies. Sarita's name appeared as often, and [was] attached to as creditable productions, as that of any young lady. . . .

Tuesday, July 17. . . . I do not like the political throwings out. Gen. Sherman has been making a speech to the boys somewhere, in which he predicts a war where the fighting will be such that his, in comparison, will appear like mere boy's play![1]

Secretary Seward is reported to have said at a social party recently, that if Congress adjourned without admitting the members-elect of the eleven states which were in rebellion, that the second session of the 39th Congress will never meet![2] I do not like to hear of such givings out; it seems ominous of evil! That the loyal men of the eleven states should be represented in Congress no good patriot can doubt, but I would see the Government overthrown before I would admit a man on the floor of either House who had ever wielded a weapon against the soldiers of the Union, and if I understand President Johnson, he stands exactly there. There are too many in Congress with whom party is paramount to everything and official life is a sweet morsel that they are determined not to give up if possible, & so things have to be warped to suit them. Time will determine what is to be. . . .

1. Sherman was referring to the fighting in Mexico between Emperor Maximilian and Juarez.
2. Johnson had restored governments in the southern states by December 1865, but Congress refused to seat the newly elected members from those states.

Wednesday, August 1. . . . At about 4 o'clock P.M. . . . [July 26] I went down to the boat. I found General Holt there[,] and we went on board & sat and talked a while, when my guests began to arrive.[1] Mrs. French and her ambulance load did not get there until ½ past 5, and, as I had agreed to wait for Huntington and his wife till 6, if they did not come sooner, it was 6 o'clock when we cast off from the wharf, Mr. H. having arrived a few minutes previous. The evening was just as beautiful as an evening could well be, and the party was just large enough to be comfortable. We had a fine band of music on board, and soon after the boat got under way the forward deck was cleared and dancing commenced. It was kept up by the young folks until we arrived at the pavilion at Glymont. The run down was beautiful & everybody seemed happy. . . .

1. French is describing a party that he held at Glymont, twenty miles down the Potomac.

Thursday, August 2. . . . I did not have time to finish up my record of the excursion. To proceed, we arrived at Glymont about 8 P.M. and all immediately went on shore to the pavilion, which is very finely arranged for dancing. The young folks immediately went at it and danced till supper was ready about 9 o'clock. The table was set for 150, and the food and drink were plentiful, and everybody ate and drank to their hearts content. We had cold chicken, ham, tongue, bread & butter, watermelon, cake, ice cream, milk in abundance, nuts, raisins, champagne, claret punch, etc. The supper was finished about 10, and at ½ past 10 the steamer was off for Washington. . . .

[Yesterday] went to the City Hall, and at 1 o'clock, with Secy. Harlan, Mayor Wallach, and Mr. Brown,[1] warden of the jail, went in a hack searching for a site for the new jail. The law requires the Secy. of the Interior to select the site, and I think he is favorably inclined to select the square once known as a public enclosure for condemned stone down N.J. Avenue, opposite Carroll's place. It is the best location, take it all in all, that can be selected. . . .

1. Thomas B. Brown.

Sunday, August 12. . . . I do not really think that any other of my doings of the week are worthy of a notice here. I did some duties outside of my regular office duties, such as attending a meeting of the Directors of the Fireman's Insurance Co. on Tuesday P.M. and going from there to the foot of 17th street where my fellow citizens were celebrating the completion of a dam and tide gates across the arm of the river to drive the water through the canal, which is held within the dam after having flowed in by the rise of the tide. At the beginning of the ebb the gates shut by the action of the water, & as the tide falls the water caught must run out through the entire length of the canal, thus keeping it clean & pure. . . .

Friday I was all over the city with Angus, seeing to my out of door improvements. First to the President's, then to Smith's spring, then to Benning's Bridge, then to Lincoln Square, and up East Capitol St. home. Yesterday at the office all day. After dinner M.E.[,][1] Sarita & I rode to the Cong. Burying ground, & roamed over that. I saw, for the first time, the elegant monument erected to the memory of the female victims of the explosion at the Arsenal three or four years ago. . . .

1. Mary Ellen French.

Sunday, August 19. It is ¼ past 12 P.M. I have read the *Chronicle,* written several letters, arranged some books in the library[,] and read, for the first time, all the proceedings as published by the Senate on the death of Senator Foot. . . . Reading the eulogies pronounced by Senators and Representatives brings back freshly to my mind all I knew of that good man, and perhaps few except those with whom he was associated in Congress and his own family knew more of him than I did. . . . Of the eulogies pronounced in the Senate, Mr. Fessenden's is the best and Mr. Sumner's the worst. Every word of Mr. Fessenden's is true and touching, and I felt the gathering tears beneath my eyelids many times as I read on. Mr. Sumner's allusions were in bad taste & the entire eulogy anything but what a eulogy should be. All the others were good and just and true. No one could say too much of the illustrious Senator.

During the week past I have been so so in health, but working like a horse at my office. Nothing very wonderful has occurred.

On Wednesday I had the honor to accompany Emma,[1] Queen dowager of the Sandwich Islands, all over the Capitol. . . . I received her in the Rotunda, where she was introduced to me by Mr. Chilton.[2] I welcomed her, & we shook hands. I presented her with a bouquet, and then we started. Went first to the very top of the dome, as far as anyone can ascend by steps. On our return we went through the Supreme Court room and its offices, then to the Senate Chamber, and through all the rooms attached; then through the library of Congress; then to the Hall of the House, through the old Hall, and to the Speaker's Room; then down into the cellar to see the heating apparatus, etc.; then across the cellar and up on the opposite side; then to the bathrooms; and finally to the crypt, whence the Queen and her attendants passed out the East door; & I handed her into her carriage under the archway, when she thanked me very kindly for my attention, shook hands and bade me good-by.

Queen Emma is, they say, 27 years old. She is a well-formed and graceful lady, doubtless well-educated. Her complexion is dark copper color, well-formed features, mouth rather large, splendid teeth, prominent black eyes, and jet black hair. Her smile is uncommonly pleasant, and her manner kind, ladylike, and entirely without affectation. Of the hundreds whom I have accompanied through the building, I never accompanied one who manifested so much interest in everything she saw, as did Queen Emma. I was very much pleased with her. . . .

1. Emma was queen of the Hawaiian Islands during the reign of King Kamehameha IV, 1854–1863.
2. Robert S. Chilton, clerk in the State Department.

Tuesday, September 4. Consequently I am sixty-six years old this day. Pretty well along in life! Well I have *lived it all,* and although it has been a very pleasant life, I would not, if I could, live it over again. "Vanity of vanities[,]" saith the preacher, "all is vanity."

I arose this morning at 5 o'clock and finished boxing an iron table, which I had made several years ago of 3 pieces of iron left from the iron of the Dome of the Capitol given me by Mr. Fowler, the contractor. The leaf, about 2 feet square, cut from a piece of a broken panel; the standard[,] one of the balustres, and the only one left of the balustrade[1] around the opening through which the picture on the concave surface of the Dome is seen; the feet[,] one of the ornaments of the inner surface of the Dome. This table I had carried to the Capitol on the morning of March 4, 1865, and placed on the platform erected for the second inauguration of Abraham Lincoln, *the good,* as President of the United States; and it stood before him, with a tumbler of water upon it for his use, when he delivered his inaugural.

Afterwards I told President Lincoln that when his Presidential term was over, I would make him a present of that table to take to Illinois with him as a memento of the Capitol. Alas, the hand of the assassin prevented the consummation of this promise. After the dear old President had departed, I made the same promise to Hon. Solomon Foot,

Senator in Congress, at the close of his Senatorial career. The inscrutable decree of a wise Providence prevented the consummation of this promise. So, on Sunday, the 26th of August, I wrote to Hon. Robert C. Winthrop[2] of Boston, proposing to present the table to the Massachusetts Historical Society, and yesterday I received a letter from him accepting the same, which letter I preserve between these pages.[3] Yesterday afternoon, hot as it was, I commenced boxing that table, but a thundergust interrupted my operations, and this morning, as above stated, I finished the job, commencing at 5 o'clock and finishing about 9. Oh how the perspiration rolled off me, but it did me no harm. . . .

1. The railing around the dome's upper balcony.
2. Robert C. Winthrop (1809–1894), Whig congressman and senator from Massachusetts, 1840–1851, and later chairman of the board of the Peabody Education Fund.
3. In the letter Winthrop asked that the table arrive in time for the meeting of the society on September 13.

Amherst, Mass., Sunday, September 16. At half past 3 o'clock yesterday afternoon, Mary Ellen, Sarita, and this humble individual arrived in the *car* (singular number) in this town of Amherst. My brother Henry, the President of *this College*,[1] met us with his horse and carriage at the depot, and "*fotch*" us to this ancient and honorable residence, somewhat dilapidated, it is true, and *slightly* out of plumb and not *perfectly* level, with windows of 24 lights, of 6 & 8 glass, each, where we met with "a more than Highland welcome." Here we found Mrs. Pamela, Sister Kate (Wells), Sally, William, and Daniel, and in the evening arrived Doct. Wells. . . .

1. The Agricultural College, now the University of Massachusetts, founded in 1863.

Monday, September 17. . . . Yesterday was spent in a most devotional manner. A portion of the family attended meeting morning and evening. In the afternoon, the two Mrs. Frenches (Pamela & Mary Ellen)[,] the Judge, Sarita, Dan, and I went out exploring. The weather was delightful, and we went first to the site where the Judge commenced laying the foundation for the College buildings when he was stopped by a vote of the trustees, a majority of whom want the buildings down on the flatland west of where the first location was decided upon, which is certainly by far the most preferable, and anyone with half an ounce of sense in his head, and any taste for propriety[,] would decide in a moment on the site first selected. I could arrive at no other possible conclusion than, that those who voted to change the location are jackasses, and it is to be hoped that Providence, who seems to have arranged the locality precisely right for the location of the College Buildings where the selection was first made, will so interfere as to prevent the consummation of the plans of the malcontents.

We walked to the top of the hill and there saw the belt of pines ¼ of a mile long, at least, which the Judge caused to set out two years ago (about 800 of them) all of them alive and growing finely. Thence we passed along to the well he has dug on the summit of the hill, 10 feet deep & some 8 or 10 feet in diameter, now filled with water, and overflowing, whence the water for the buildings is to be supplied. We then took a sweep around the summit of the hill northward and westward and descended into the valley. Crossed the glen across which a dam is to be built for a roadway and to create a pond, which will form a beauteous feature in the landscape. Then we gathered apples and came home, having had a very pleasant walk. . . .

Wednesday, September 19. . . . We had a jolly time last evening. Will got up an exhibition of a most amusing character. About 8 o'clock a Mr. Carmichael,[1] a student, with two Misses Newman, came, and Mr. C. was one of the performers. The long dining room was divided about midway with a white curtain, one portion of the room being the stage, the other the auditorium. At ½ past 8, notice was duly given that the curtain was about to rise. The audience, consisting of the Judge & wife, Doct. Wells and wife, the two Misses Newman, Sarita, Mary Ellen and myself, and Hannah (the serving maid) all took their places, and the curtain rose on about the funniest scene I ever beheld. Mr. C. & Dan were the rollers of a panoramic belt formed of shawls or blankets on which were fastened devices cut from white paper by Will in the most artistic manner, which he, dressed in Oriental costume, explained in the most grotesque language. While he was explaining the scene in view, Sallie, behind the belt, was pinning on another scene; then the order was given by the manager[,] "The Panorama will move[,]" at which the living rollers would commence revolving, and a new scene would be presented. In this way about a dozen scenes were presented and explained in a manner that made me laugh till I thought I should suffocate. The next scene was a display of shadows on the curtain which were managed in such a way as to make the most grotesque appearance possible. One scene was, a great pair of hands appeared coming up from the floor, followed by the body and legs, then the hands would go up, apparently through the ceiling, & the legs, as if climbing over the top of the curtains, would disappear. Then the whole person would *come down* head foremost, with a sound as of falling, upon the stage, and after a half dozen jumps up and down, going higher at each jump, it would finally jump *up out of sight*—apparently going up through the ceiling! It was exceedingly funny, and we all "laughed fit to split." Then was exhibited "wax work," the figures being represented by various persons. Then a fight, over a wall or fence formed by a sheet, between two soldiers, the soldiers being the arms of Mr. Carmichael, who lay on his back under the sheet, with his arms dressed, a hat on each hand. It made quite a spirited fight. The exhibition of the elephant, formed after the usual manner of stage elephants[,] closed the exhibition at about ½ past 10. I never laughed heartier, or was more amused at a real theatrical exhibition. . . .

1. Henry Carmichael, of Brooklyn, N.Y., was a senior at Amherst College.

Thursday, September 20. . . . It is ½ past 9 A.M. and raining! We must all be housed up today. Well, we will make the best of it. The Judge will return this evening, probably disgusted with his Agricultural Presidency, if what the party goers heard at Prof. Tyler's[1] last evening be true, as it was currently reported there that "Col. Clark"[2]—the Judge's main opponent here—had been successful. I hope the Judge will resign forthwith. . . .

1. William S. Tyler (1810—1897), professor of Greek at Amherst College, 1836—1893, was the author of the *History of Amherst College* (1873).
2. William S. Clark, Colonel, 21st Massachusetts Infantry, promoted the establishment of the agricultural college while representing Amherst in the state legislature, 1864—1865.

Saturday, September 22. Still at Amherst. Frank came at ¼ to 8 last evening, looking well and hearty, so we are here to remain till Monday morning.

Yesterday it cleared off about noon and the afternoon was decidedly hot. I took Mary Ellen, Sallie and Sarita in the Judge's carriage and rode about the town. Then we went to the college gymnasium and saw the College boys exercise with poles and dumbbells, and jump & climb, & perform all sorts of *gymnastiums* for an hour. Then we came home. . . .

Sunday, September 23. Yesterday afternoon, the Judge, his wife Pamela, Mrs. Wells, Frank, Sarita, Daniel, Mary Ellen and I went to Mount Holyoke. . . . We passed through the ancient town of Hadley. . . .

From Hadley village we proceeded on to Mount Holyoke. We all had to leave the carriage soon after entering what, on a large signboard[,] was denominated "Holyoke Avenue." We were green enough to take our carriage up to the foot of the inclined plane with us, while the Judge, with superior sense or knowledge, left his at the aforesaid signboard. We, being considerably ahead, had not the benefit of the Judge's experience. We all arrived safely (though some of us were rather *blown*) at the foot of the inclined plane, up which, in a car drawn by a large rope attached to a stationary steam engine at the summit, we were to be hoisted, 4 at a time, very nearly perpendicularly, to the Mount Holyoke House. Frank, Sarita, Dan and I made the first load, the Judge, Mrs. Wells, Mary Ellen and Pamela, the second. It certainly is a somewhat *pokerish* matter to be hoisted 363 feet perpendicular over a road 600 feet long, with the idea uppermost in your mind that "*if the rope should break you would be smashed into something like a jelly in about a quarter of a minute!*" But we all went up safely, and the scene that presented itself was well worth the "*excelsior*" that we determined upon (some of us rather reluctantly) at the foot of the precipice. . . .

Concord, Mass., Tuesday, September 25. . . . We arrived here at 2 P.M., ½ an hour behind time. We found George Keyes at the Depot with a carriage for us and a wagon for our baggage, and were brought to this elegant and hospitable mansion forthwith, and were right glad to get here, where we were received by Sister Ann and Mary & the children with a welcome that was a welcome. Frank left us at Worcester for Boston. . . .

Sunday, September 30. Yesterday was a sort of miscellaneous day. Wrote the foregoing before breakfast. Soon afterwards Tom and I went in the boat, down to the monument, where we landed and walked up to Col. Keyes's.[1] The Col. showed us all over his house. It is really a curiosity, and shows what a comfortable, pleasant, and elegant dwelling can be made of an old, low-posted, dilapidated building. It is really one of the most comfortable houses to live in that I know of. In the two parlors are two mantlepieces of marble, one of which, and a great portion of the other[,] came from the Capitol at Washington, and were in the old Hall of the House of Representatives. . . . The first time I ever saw Hugh S. Legaré, he was standing before the mantle now in the front parlor of Col. Keyes's house. I remember the circumstance and the facts attending it as well as if it were yesterday. It was only a few days after Mr. Legaré had taken his seat in the House. Col. Burch, the Chief Clerk in the office, came into the Hall before the meeting of the House, and as we were standing together before the fire, Mr. L. came in and stood near us.

Burch said to me, "There is a member who I have not before seen, who is it?" I told him it was Legaré. "What," said he, "that little ducklegged fellow[,] Legaré!" "Well, he has come here with a great reputation and his *head* looks as if he might sustain it, although his *legs* are short." He was really a great man, and died in Boston very suddenly while on an excursion with President Tyler, whose Attorney General he then was. I knew him well.

After going all over the Col.'s house, I agreed with Ann that I would come up early in the afternoon and play croquet with her, the family being invited up to take tea and spend the evening. Tom and I returned about 10, and I read the *Atlantic Monthly* for October till dinner time. I read the article entitled "The Usurpation."[2] It is, in my opinion, false in its statements and its conclusions, and where it represents facts, it so distorts them as to make them mean anything but what was intended. It is in fact an article intended to lead public opinion astray in regard to President Johnson's position, opinions, and intentions, and does the President infinite injustice and wrong. Were I in Washington where I could get at all the necessary historical facts[,] I would answer it. I cannot do it here. I hope it will not be left unanswered.

I also read the extracts from Hawthorne's diary—or, rather, Journal.[3] Having been personally acquainted with Hawthorne, and the Journal having been written at the "Old Manse" in this town, and opposite Col. Keyes's, I felt an interest in reading that it would not otherwise possess, for it is, in quality, mere twaddle, written, doubtless, to while away a leisure hour, with no thought of its ever meeting the public eye, and in my judgment a wrong is being done to the memory of Mr. Hawthorne, who, when he wrote for the public, wrote carefully and beautifully, in publishing such careless writing about *raising peas, sawing wood, cleaning up avenues,* etc. Hawthorne was a genuine good fellow, with as chaste and really romantic a mind as any American ever possessed.

After dinner half a dozen of the family, myself among them, walked up to the rock over which the grapes are trained and gathered grapes, corn, melons, etc. I noticed for the first time what very much amused and interested me, the manner in which Mr. Brown *mended* his apple trees after the mice had knawed around them just above the ground. He turned back the bark above and below the girdle and inserted twigs, cut from the upper limbs, perpendicularly, under the bark, which conducted the sap from the roots and saved the trees. Of 60 trees thus girdled & thus treated, not one was lost. And now, several years thereafter, the twigs inserted have become portions of the trees, showing each twig in a fluted form of the size of from one to two inches in diameter. They appear to me as if they improved the tree by making it firmer and stronger, and it seems impossible that the mice should again perform the same operation on the trees thus treated. . . .

1. John S. Keyes, the father of George Keyes.

2. George S. Boutwell, "The Usurpation," *The Atlantic Monthly*, 18(1866), 506–513.

3. "Passages from Hawthorne's Note-Books," *The Atlantic Monthly*, 17–18(1866). This was the first publication of the notebooks after Hawthorne's death in 1864.

Chester, October 4. Here I am, in the front parlor of the old mansion which my father built more than sixty years ago. . . .

We spent most of yesterday afternoon before a rousing & cheerful wood fire in the back parlor. I read "Snow Bound"[1] aloud to the Governor and Mary Ellen. It is the 3d or 4th time I have read it, & it presents new beauties each time. . . .

1. Published by Whittier in 1866.

Concord, Mass., Sunday, October 7. Yesterday George & Mary, Mary Ellen & myself[,] and Sarita & Tom Wells went to Boston in the Express train, arriving there at ½ past 8. I went with the rest shopping on our arrival, and did all my shopping to the amount of two pairs of merino drawers & a pair of stockings, and went down to Frank's bank and put them on. . . .

Tuesday, October 9. . . . Between 1 & 2 Mr. Brown read to me a narrative of the moving of their family from Newburyport to Chester in 1814. . . . Soon after Mr. Brown moved to Chester—I think it was the same winter—he purchased an old building, once occupied by my Grandfather as a store, which stood perhaps a hundred rods below—or East—of Mr. Brown's house, with a view of moving it near the house and converting it into a workshop for good old "Uncle Sleeper," a brother of Mrs. Brown, who was a carpenter's toolmaker, and the best workman in that line I ever knew—so good that the best English tools were sometimes brought to him to be altered before they would work well.[1] This building was duly prepared for removal that winter, and, according to the custom of the time and place, all the farmers about were invited to be present with their oxen on a certain day when the snow lay deep and level, to haul the old building from its old site to its intended future locality, and *also*, according to the custom of the time and place—a custom *now* "more honored in the breach than in the observance"—the hospitable Mr. Brown furnished plenty of the *ardent* to inspire the men, whose *voices* were expected to inspire the beasts; and on that particular occasion it was the best of gin, dealt out, as I *most emphatically* remember, through the medium of a *copper teakettle*. It seems as if I could see the clear white liquid at this very moment delivering itself into the glass tumbler presented by the thirsty driver of oxen, to be swallowed at a gulp, as the poor beasts, under the torture of the goad, accompanied by the yelling of a hundred throats, strained at their heavy burden, which, amid the cracking of timbers, the snapping of chains, the pounding of axes, the heaving of levers, and the universal din always concomitant to "a hauling," moved toward its destination. The *boys* of those days, aping their seniors, were allowed to join in *all* the ceremonies and were not backward on that occasion in "sucking that monkey" of a teakettle, and I believe did full credit to their seniors in getting as gloriously drunk as the best of them. I can answer for one that no "lord" in his best estate ever went home from a revel more gloriously fuddled than I did. I remember of trying to hit some of my companions with snowballs, & that they went anywhere but in the intended direction; that I pitched head foremost into a snowbank, as I then thought[,] "just for fun," but that I found it a matter of some *earnest* to get out again; that I got home and into the barn, where I cut up *shindies* that induced the hired man to get me into the house and to bed. And it is yet in my memory how dreadful sick I was in the night, and how I sneaked off the next morning with my head snapping, ashamed to be seen by anyone! . . .

Yesterday morning at 10 m. before 8, I started with Frank and Geo. Keyes for Boston, where, from ½ past 8 to 11, I did errands, saw friends, & ran round. . . . Called at the Rooms of the Massachusetts Historical Society in Tremont Street, where I saw the iron table that I presented to that Society last month, formed of 3 pieces of the iron of the Dome of the capitol. . . . Then started to the depot, and on my way saw Mr. [Amos] Tuck for a moment. At 11, started in the cars for this place and had the pleasure of occupying a seat with Gov. Boutwell[2] all the way to Concord. We talked a good deal about the President, he abusing his policy and speaking in not the most respectful terms of himself, and I defending him. Our talk was good-natured, but he was very firm and decided in his opposition, and I was equally so in my defense. It would be a useless waste of time and ink to detail our conversation, as it would cover pages of this book. The President must expect the bitterest and most cruel opposition and denunciation next winter. . . .

1. French's brother-in-law, Simon Brown, was the reader. Simon's father, Nathaniel Brown, was the one moving to Chester; he purchased the old building from French's grandfather, Benjamin Brown, Mercy Brown French's father (not related to Simon Brown). Uncle Sleeper was Simon's uncle. Mrs. Brown was Simon's mother, Mary Sleeper Brown.

2. George S. Boutwell (1818–1905), governor of Massachusetts, 1851–1852, Republican congressman, 1863–1869, was later Secretary of the Treasury, 1869–1873, and senator, 1873–1877.

Thursday, October 11. . . . Found Gov. Boutwell here, & he and Brown and the Judge exulted awhile over the result of the late elections—just as if they really regarded what everybody knew must be the result, as a triumph! *We* don't care how the elections go *now* if we can only elect Seward President in 1868! And unless some unpardonable folly prevents, *we* can do it.

A convention, held here yesterday, renominated Boutwell for Congress, at which I am well pleased, as I like *the man* very much, although I think him by far too radical in his political notions. He goes the "whole hog" and a small pig over! I believe him as honest a man as lives, and *I know him to be* a most amiable gentleman. He is a member of *our* Metropolitan club at Washington. . . .

I have been reading the *Boston Journal* and regret exceedingly to see that the President has, by a series of questions addressed to the Attorney General, indicated an intention of questioning the authority of the present Congress. Whatever the Atty. Gen. may say, the President cannot stand a moment on that issue. He cannot, if I do not very much mistake the temper of the times, find a corporal's guard, out of the Southern States, who will sustain him. On that issue I am decidedly opposed to him, and, if made in earnest, shall resign my office, as I will not hold office under a President to whom I am opposed, especially in so radical a matter as that would be. . . .

Washington, Sunday, October 14. *Home again*! And, although my visit to my kinfolk has been very pleasant, as the foregoing pages indicate, still it is pleasant to be once more at home. . . .

Wednesday, October 17. . . . Yesterday the first message I received at my office was that the President wanted to see me. I worked on till past 11, and went up to see the President. The Cabinet were just assembling when I got there, but I saw the President for a few moments and was never received by him in a more kind and cordial manner. I had only a few words of conversation with him, but they were such as encouraged me to hope that I might hereafter say something that he would listen to, and that would aid in relieving him from the unfortunate position in which he at present stands. . . .

Sunday, November 4. . . . This afternoon I read in the *Life of Horace Mann,*[1] a very interesting book. Mr. Mann was one of the best of men. I knew him well and respected him most highly. His erect spare form, with his *peculiar hat,* as I used to see him when he was a member of Congress, taking his accustomed walk around the Capitol square, are as palpably before my mind's eye at this moment as they were actually at the time; and well do I remember how much I felt honored at seeing him among the audience when I delivered the annual address before the pupils of the Public schools of Washington, at the Smithsonian Institution about fourteen years ago. My first knowledge of Mr. Mann came from my reading his admirable reports as Secretary of the Massachusetts Board of Education, and [I] entertained a very high opinion of him, which was very much increased by a personal acquaintance with him. Hence I take a deep interest in reading his life. . . .

1. Mary Tyler Peabody, ed., *Life and Works of Horace Mann* (3 vols., 1865–1868).

Friday, November 9. . . . After our company[1] had gone I picked up my gunning things and prepared to go with Mr. Nokes & his son James, up to Mr. N.'s farm in Prince William County, Va., about 40 miles from Washington, gunning. . . . From Alexandria to "Nokesville station," 35 miles, the desolation that war brings with it, and the remnants of the doings of the contending hosts to sustain themselves, were constantly visible. In & out of the City of Alexandria I saw the soldiers' cemetery, where hundreds of neat[,] white headboards mark where as many brave fellows who sacrificed their lives for their country "sleep that sleep that knows no waking." The cemetery occupies perhaps two or three acres, is beautifully laid out and kept, at the expense of the United States. A flagstaff occupies the centre of the ground on which is kept floating the dear old stripes and stars that the sleepers beneath it loved so well in life.

Blockhouses, built of hewn timber and rough logs, partially burned, circular or square enclosures, formed of oak piles driven into the ground endwise, say 10 or 12 feet in height, with loopholes for musketry, stockades of considerable length, etc., were very frequent before we reached Manassas; there we saw the embankments which once constituted the impregnable defenses of the rebels, stretched in all directions and still of formidable appearance. The two houses where were the headquarters of Lee and Beauregard, were pointed out to me. In passing through a cut between Manassas and Nokesville, Mr. Nokes told me that in that cut were concealed a large number of our troops under Gen. Hooker [and] that a large rebel force was advancing to attack a battery east of the railroad which Hooker had been placed there to defend. When the rebels had advanced within fair musket range, Hooker's men rose and delivered their fire with most terrible effect, killing seven hundred of the enemy and wounding two or three times as many more. They retreated in a hurry. The entire distance from Alexandria to Nokesville was marked by the ruins of houses, some of them, I was told, the elegant & expensive dwellings of men of fortune. Chimneys crumbling gradually away marked the spot where some of them stood. The cellars and foundation stones marked the sites of others, while of others hardly a vestige remained. It will take many years to restore that portion of Old Virginia to what it was before the accursed rebellion burst upon the land. On our way we passed the famous "Bull Run," a small and sluggish stream, appearing generally as we passed along it in the cars very much like the Delaware Canal at Princeton & along that route. . . .

We arrived at Mr. Nokes's farm about 9—"Nokesville Station" it is called—and were soon in the field with our guns and dogs. The sun was blazing down with July intenseness, & there was no breath of air stirring. After walking some miles through briers, marshes, thick underbrush, & all such sorts of hiding places as partridges like to stay in, without seeing a single bird, & shooting one poor little rabbit, I concluded I had roasted long enough; so I struck a beeline for Mr. Nokes's house. . . . Mr. Nokes said, on coming in, "Major[,] there are no birds about here, what say you to returning this evening?" I replied, "If you desire to go[,] I am ready," & so we went to packing up, and at 3 o'clock took the train for home, where we arrived at about ½ past 5. . . .

On my return home I found my beloved wife just ready to go to Georgetown with Fannie[2] & Louise[3] on a visit to Ben & Abbie. They left, and I took my tea and went to writing. . . .

1. Neighbors who came in to play cards during the evening.
2. Fannie Gilbert.
3. Either Louisa Russell, French's sister-in-law, or her daughter Louise, who was now twenty-one.

Tuesday, November 13. . . . [Yesterday] went to bed about ten, and got up twice in the night to look after the shooting stars, which are expected to show off about these days—or nights—but they disappointed us last night. We shall expect them tonight, it being precisely 33 years since they made such a magnificent display all over the United States, at which some people were almost frightened to death! I turned back last evening to the account of it written by myself for the *N.H. Spectator,* which I then edited. I did not see it, but an eye witness described it to me on the morning of the 14th, 1833. . . .

Friday, November 23. . . . At ¼ before 3 on Monday, the 19th, Mrs. French and myself left here for Baltimore to attend the laying of the cornerstone of the new Masonic Hall on the 20th. . . .

. . . At about 10 we were all in line, at least 1,000 Templars, from all parts of the Union. The procession was very large, as many, and I think more, Templars than in Boston when we laid the cornerstone of the Hall there in 1864, but not as many Craft Masons. After a long and fatiguing march, in the course of which the entire procession passed around the Washington Monument with uncovered heads, we arrived at the site of the new Temple, where, on the platform, I met Bro. Andrew Johnson, President of the United States, clothed in Masonic regalia, being the first President I ever saw so clothed. . . .

Sunday, December 23. . . . On Friday I went to Baltimore and brought Sarita home with me, and she now adds her cheerfulness to our dwelling. She is a happy little body, and her disposition is all sunshine, and her affection is, to me, beyond price. Were she my own daughter I could not love her better—dear little lady. . . .

I finished reading the Life of Horace Mann on Thursday evening. I have been reading it, at odd times, for several weeks, and have read it carefully, and there are very few written lives that I have read that were more interesting and satisfactory. He possessed the purest and most lovely character of any man I ever knew or read of *save one,* and he was crucified. Horace Mann gave *his* life for the benefit of the rising generation of his day. His labors in the cause of education were arduous and incessant; for that cause he sacrificed comfort, position, high political elevation, property and life! Massachusetts has honored his memory by placing a fine bronze statue of him in front of her Capitol, and I revere it more than I do the noble building which it *more* than adorns! I had the great honor and pleasure of knowing Horace Mann in life and ranking myself among his personal friends. I remember how very highly I felt honored at seeing him among the audience upon an occasion when I addressed the schoolchildren of Washington, at the Smithsonian Lecture Room in August 1852. After I had concluded he shook me cordially by the hand and thanked me for what he was pleased to call my excellent address. Oh that he could have lived longer to benefit his race!

Sunday, December 30. . . . Yesterday I was at my office and about the city. I attended the opening of the Skating Park, where I was invited about 2 hours before I went, to make the opening address. I found the ice covered with skaters and the rooms crammed with lookers-on, and, seeing no chance to get the crowd together to listen to an address, I advised the officers not to have one. They insisted that I *must* make one, so I compromised by gathering a few about me in the room, & giving them an outline of what I intended to say, and promising to write it out, which I have this day done. I put on a pair of skates, and believe I could have, in a few minutes, got back some of my old facility of using them, when one of my bootheels ripped almost entirely off, and I had to give up. . . .

Saturday, January 5. Got a suite of new chamber furniture, cost $550. It consists of a bedstead, springs, and thick and elegant mattress, bolster, and pillows, and a silk patchwork quilt. A very large wardrobe with a glass 5 or 6 feet long in the centre door, a bureau, with a large mirror over it, and little brackets at the sides, champagne glasses, toilet glasses, and other little ornaments came with it. A washstand with heavy marble top. A chamber set, full, china and gold—very elegant. An *etegère,*[1] closed lower part, marble slab and bookshelves, for a corner, which we have put in the front parlor—the other pieces in our own chamber. This furniture was exhibited at our Masonic Fair and valued at $1,500, & raffled at that price. The "Fair" had 100 tickets of the 300, and won it. Someone offered $500 for it. I authorized a friend to purchase it for me at $550. He was told that it had been sold for $600, and there the matter was supposed to end, and just as I was felicitating myself with the idea that I had escaped the purchase, up it came to my door about 12 o'clock on Thursday. Mrs. French sent to the Capitol for me, and over I came. Such *a time* as we had! There was all this heavy, magnificent furniture to put up in a house already fully furnished. I brought 6 men with me, and we went to taking down first. One bedstead and bureau we put in the garden, and I sold them on the spot to two of the men. The furniture in our own room we had removed into the back chamber, and then we set up the new furniture[,] and about 7 o'clock P.M. the house was once more in order. Mary Ellen did not seem to appreciate my purchase at first, but I think she is becoming reconciled. She thinks the roof of the house ought to be raised to accommodate the new furniture! This is an episode in our housekeeping that I thought ought by all means to be noticed in my journal. . . .

1. French meant étagère, a small piece of furniture with shelves.

Friday, January 11. The ladies came down and I agreed with Sarita, for they did look magnificent.

We went to Gen. Grant's . . . in the Capitol Extension carriage, driven by Edward. We had a grand time amid that tremendous crowd who honored the great General, and who was, really, the most modest, unassuming gentleman there. . . .

Friday, January 18. . . . This morning, at ¼ before 8, it was discovered that the conservatory at the President's was on fire. It caught from the bursting of a flue. I did not hear of it till past 9, when on my way from the City Hall, where I had been on business, to the Capitol. As soon as I was told of it, at the horse R.R. Depot, I ran after a Navy Yard car that was passing, and caught it at the foot of Capitol hill—got in and rode to the President's, found the Fire Department hard at work and two steam fire engines in full play. The fire had been nearly got under, but was still burning beneath [the] floor of the conservatory, between that and the roof of the line of outhouses over which it was built. I went all around the building, and into it where I could, going half a leg deep in water at some places. After spending half an hour in overlooking the exertions of the firemen, who worked well, and getting pretty much wet and very cold, I went into the house, pulled off my boots and dried my feet, put on a pair of Wm. Slade's[1] shoes, & *again went out*. Found the fire pretty much out. Went through the greenhouses and found the plants in the main conservatory nearly all destroyed. Those in the small greenhouse, running South, were saved. I gave all necessary directions for saving all that were left, and at a little before 12 left for my office, where, after two hours labor[,] I became so completely exhausted that I could hardly stand. I came home and laid down. Went to sleep and awoke at 3 much refreshed. Eat my dinner and wrote this. . . .

1. William Slade, steward of the White House, died before Johnson left office.

Sunday, January 27. It is nearly noon. I have been all the morning writing letters, and am tired. But how much better I feel than I did when I last wrote. A cloud seemed to be over me and all looked dark and gloomy; today all is bright and cheery. There is one thing that annoys me some. I dare to speak well of the President of the United States. I dare to think that he is at heart a patriot, and means well for his country. I *dare* do this, and I am denounced by those to whom I have done nothing but kindness. Let them go on and abuse me & threaten me. I care not. . . .

Wednesday, February 6. Mrs. French and Sarita are getting ready to go with me to General Grant's reception. I am all ready except changing my dressing gown for my coat. . . .

As the close of the session approaches[,] my duties become more troublesome and vexatious, as I have a great deal to do in urging the proper appropriations to carry on my office and the various works under my charge, and I am *poked at* on all sides because I happen to [be] a personal friend of Andrew Johnson's. *Let 'em poke!* My turn will come again by-and-by, if I live. . . .

Yesterday I saw Gen. Phil Sheridan introduced by the Speaker to the House of Representatives. He, accompanied by General Grant, [was] escorted to the Speaker's stand, where they stood at the left of the Speaker, who in a few remarks, very handsomely and eloquently spoken, introduced Gen. Sheridan. He bowed his acknowledgements, & expressed, in about three words, his thanks, and then all the members who could do so shook hands with him. Such exhibitions of patriotism in these unpropitious times are really refreshing. I looked on that scene with admiration, and thought better of the safety of my country for it.

I am amazed when I see the length to which the hatred of men can carry them. . . . I was the friend of Andrew Johnson long years ago. The Republicans thought fit to select him as their candidate for Vice President. I regretted it, because I was a true & zealous friend of Hannibal Hamlin and advocated his renomination. But Mr. Johnson was nominated and elected, and on the lamented death of Lincoln became President. His views, in some things, did not correspond with those of a majority of Congress—nor with my own. Still I believed him honest and a patriot, and daring to say so, an attempt is making to ostracise me. . . .

Saturday, February 9. It is 8 A.M. Last evening Mrs. French and I dined with Mr. George Peabody[1] at Willard's. It was an occasion never to be forgotten[,] more in consequence of the announcement there of the munificent bequest made to the South by Mr. Peabody of $2,100,000! Mr. Winthrop informed me of it on my arrival at the house, and while at the dinner table printed slips were brought in, of Mr. Peabody's letter, and distributed to the guests. . . .

Evening. Immediately after writing the foregoing I went to the Capitol where I remained only a short time and then went to the President's, saw the President and suggested to him the idea of calling personally on Mr. Peabody and thanking him for his munificent gift to the South. The President instantly agreed to call at 12 o'clock. . . . A short time after 12, accompanied by Col. Wm. G. Moore, his confidential Secretary, he came. I introduced him to Mr. Peabody in the passage, and he took the President by the arm and very gracefully handed him into the parlor and introduced him to the few persons there assembled. The President shook hands with all and was cordially welcomed by Mr. Peabody, when he (the President) went on to say to Mr. Peabody that he had called to thank him in person, and on behalf of the nation, for the magnificent bequest he had just made. The President then went on and spoke most eloquently and appropriately for from three to five minutes, and Mr. Peabody responded in the handsomest manner, closing by saying how much he felt honored by this kind attention of the President, etc. The President then grasped Mr. Peabody by the hand and said that the honor was all on his (Mr. P.'s)[2] side, for that *he* felt honored in having the opportunity of rendering to him his thanks for his noble generosity, and, although he (Mr. P.)[3] had lived to be advanced in years, he hoped and prayed that Almighty God would so prolong his life that he might live to see the great benefits that were sure to flow from his unprecedented munificence.

I believe there was hardly a dry eye in the room at this little scene. A few cordial words passed between the President & Mr. P. when the former took leave, and retired. Everyone present was delighted.

1. George Peabody (1795–1869) was a wealthy American financier who lived in London and gave millions of dollars to many charities, including this grant (eventually $3,500,000) for education in the South.
2. French meant "Mr. President."
3. Mr. President.

Sunday, February 10. . . . Thursday.[1] At office all the morning. At the President's reception in the evening. Mrs. Johnson present for the 1st time, and everybody delighted to see her. Mrs. F., Sarita & Abbie were there early. Ben came after a while, and relieved me in introducing. It was the largest jam I ever saw at *any* reception. Mr. Geo. Peabody and Mr. R. C. Winthrop were there, and invited Mrs. French and myself to dinner on Friday, which dinner we attended. . . .

1. This is a retrospective account of events on Thursday evening, February 7, the day before French dined with Peabody.

Sunday, February 17. . . . At Mr. Peabody's dinner the conversation between Mr. Russell and myself was, at one time, about Prof. S. G. Brown of Dartmouth College, and his life and writings of Rufus Choate was mentioned.[1] Mr. Russell spoke of it in very high terms of praise, and Prof. Brown being my own Cousin, I had a curiosity to read it. Enquiring at the Bookstores I found the book was out of print, and could not be purchased. I procured a copy from the Library of Congress and am reading it. It interests me exceedingly, inasmuch as I well knew Mr. Choate, he being one of the Regents of the Smithsonian Institution, while I was acting as its first Secretary. This life of Choate shows that he possessed a mind absolutely *crammed* with classical literature and almost everything else. As he says of Cicero and Burke, "they knew everything," so this book shows of him, that *he knew everything.* He was a wonderful man, and I never felt so much like a literary pigmy as I have since I commenced reading that book! If I could live my life over again, would not I be a scholar! That I would. How my attempts at learning, in my youth, were frittered away! Uncle Edmund Flagg, while a student at law in my father's office, did his whole duty toward me in grounding me in English and the rudiments of Latin, but, when he left, I was bandied about from the *common district school* in Chester to the *commoner,* if possible, Academy there, taught by a numbskull named Johnson, who put me from *Corderius*[2] straight into *Virgil*! and hence I took a distaste to Latin—as what *child* would not. At 11 I was sent to North Yarmouth, Maine, where, for one year, I was under the instruction of my uncle, Rev. Francis Brown—Prof. Brown's father—who really tried to do his duty toward me, but having his pulpit, his family, and his parishioners to look after, I was left mostly alone in his study to work my way along as I best could. He, however, put me into Arithmetic and Mathematics mostly, and in them I made good progress. On my return to my father's I was again put under the instruction of an office student who[m] I could have taught, & so three years were frittered away. Then I went again to North Yarmouth with my Grandfather Brown, and from Jany. 1815, about 2 years, I attended the Academy at that place—in those days taught by *anybody* that could be picked up. I think in the time I was there we had at least a dozen preceptors, not one of whom had a capacity for teaching, and I studied just what I pleased—mostly *deviltry,* I believe, and, of course, made more progress in that than in anything else! As an evidence of the way we were permitted to go on, I remember that, while I was *supposed* to be reading Cicero's *Orations,* I read *Rollin's Ancient History*[3] through, and even now, though I do not remember ever to have opened it since, I know more about it than I ever knew about Cicero! The masterly "retreat of the ten thousand" is as clearly in my mind to this day as if I read it yesterday!

My *classical* education was abruptly finished at North Yarmouth by my undergoing a punishment that I did not deserve at the hands of a drunken tyrant, who taught the school for a few weeks and was then dismissed, and for whom I had the greatest possible contempt. I submitted to his unjust punishment, and then[,] telling him exactly what I thought of him, I marched out of the Academy, never again to enter it, or any other school, except as a Teacher! I returned to my father's[,] entered upon the study of the law at 19, and was in 1825 admitted to practice. Thus, was I educated. I spent time enough—for I began my Latin at about 9—to have been made, with proper instruction, an elegant scholar! Although it is said that we are "never too old to learn," I think a dive, at my age, into "the humanities" would hardly do me any good, so I will try to plod on, with what I *do* know, and add all I can to it, along the common road of acquisition.

There is a digression! Well, I shall finish the Life of Choate, & perhaps pick up some food for my mind from it. If I do not[,] set me down a blockhead!

I understand the Senate, after an entire night session, passed the bill to take military possession of the Southern States. I make no comments, but as "the old man eloquent"[4] once said, "We shall see what we *shall* see!" I fear our Country is in a bad way, but I hope that *He* who has watched over and sustained us through so many fierce trials will not desert us in this hour of peril. I have full Faith still that *He* will permit only what is best to be done, and that, in *His* own good time, *He* will find *a Moses* who will lead this people to permanent happiness and prosperity. The Nation has sinned & *must be punished*!

1. George Peabody Russell, nephew of George Peabody. Rufus Choate (1799–1859), famous lawyer and orator, who represented Massachusetts as congressman, 1831–1834, and senator, 1841–1845. Samuel G. Brown, ed., *Works of Rufus Choate with a Memoir of His Life* (2 vols., 1862).
2. Mathurin Cordier (Latin, Corderius) (1479–1564) was the French author of a beginner's Latin manual, translated into English as *The Colloquies of Corderius* (1563).
3. Charles Rollin (1661–1741), *Ancient History* (Paris, 1730–1738).
4. John Quincy Adams.

Sunday, February 24. I have been in an excited state all day. The *Chronicle* of this morning contained the Congressional proceedings of yesterday, and among those of the House I found that my humble self had been prominent. The Honorable Mr. Schenck[1] sent some poetry I wrote in praise of President Johnson last summer to the Clerk's table & caused it to be read, and the House, I should think[,] had a jollification over it, and immediately proceeded to abolish, so far as they could, the office of Commissioner of Public Buildings, and to create a Superintendent, to be elected by the Senate! Dignified work for the House of Representatives of a great Nation! To snub poor modest me, just because I dared speak well of Andrew Johnson. It looks delightfully consistent to see Congress pitching into the President for turning out men who do not agree with him, and then, I must say, *meanly* resorting to a roundabout way of removing me because I would not abuse the President! Whether the

Senate will concur or not in such small business remains to be seen. They all seem to forget my untiring devotion to Abraham Lincoln, my unceasing patriotism, and all I have done to sustain the Union, because I have dared to be a friend of the President. . . .

. . . I have besought President Johnson to approve the "reconstruction" bill, & I do hope he will do it, but fear he will not. I believe it would do more to calm the present excitement than anything else that could possibly happen. On considering my own position, I have about concluded that the best thing that could possibly happen to me would be to be out of office. But I *will not resign at present.*

Friday evening, Mrs. French, Louisa, and myself went to the President's. Such a crowd I think I never beheld. From 8 to 11 the house was crammed. Mrs. Johnson was present at the reception. She is a very amiable, unassuming woman, and acts her part so modestly and so well as to win the affections of all who see her. She is as good as she can be. . . .

This afternoon Mr. Carpenter,[2] the artist who painted *The First Reading of the Emancipation Proclamation*, was here with his friend Benson.[3] We talked a good deal about President Lincoln, whom I so well loved and whose memory I most deeply reverence. Among other things he told me of the love of Mr. Lincoln for Ann Rutledge,[4] and recalled to my memory what I sometime since read from the pen of Mr. Herndon.[5] In connection with this he told me that Mr. Herndon had sent to him Mr. Lincoln's copy of Byron just as Mr. Lincoln left it when he came to this city. In it he found a leaf turned down at the two stanzas written by Byron at Athens, Jany. 16, 1810.[6] I handed him my Byron, when he immediately turned to the page, turned down a leaf to show me how the one in Mr. L.'s was turned down, and read the stanzas, remarking that, when read, with the circumstances attending that love, and Miss Rutledge's death, and Mr. Lincoln's almost frenzy after it, they possessed a deep interest. I subjoin them.

> The spell is broke, the charm is flown!
> Thus is it with life's fitful fever!
> We madly smile when we should groan;
> Delirium is our best deceiver.
> Each lucid interval of thought
> Recalls the woes of Nature's charter,
> And he that acts as wise men ought,
> But lives, as saints have died, a martyr.

In my Byron, which Mr. Carpenter thinks is the same edition as Mr. Lincoln's, the stanzas are on page 523, and I intend to leave the leaf turned down in memory of Mr. Lincoln and his admirable limner, Mr. Carpenter, whom I very much admire.

1. Robert C. Schenck (1809–1890), Republican congressman from Ohio, 1863–1871.
2. Francis B. Carpenter (1830–1900) was the author of *The Inner Life of Abraham Lincoln: Six Months at the White House* (1866). The painting hangs in the Capitol.
3. Eugene Benson (1839–1908) was a painter who, like Carpenter, came from New York.
4. Ann Rutledge (1816–1835) was supposedly engaged to Lincoln when she died. Their relationship has been overromanticized.
5. William H. Herndon (1818–1891) became Lincoln's law partner in 1844 and was author of *Herndon's Lincoln* (1889).
6. Byron spent ten weeks in Athens that winter.

Sunday, March 3. I freely admit that the past week has been one of excitement to me. Still I have kept on "the even tenor of my way." The Senate struck out the clause in the House Bill abolishing the office of Commissioner, and inserted another abolishing the office & providing for the appointment of an Engineer by the President, by and with the advice and consent of the Senate, & giving the appointment of the Police to the Prest. p.t. of the Senate and Speaker of the House. To this amendment the House yesterday disagreed, and there the matter stood when I left the Capitol last evening. Whatever is to be done (if not done last night) must be done *today,* as both Houses are in session!

Mr. Robert C. Schenck has made another attack on me, calling me *dishonest.* All I have to say in reply is that he is a liar and a miserable, sneaking poltroon, & if he were not protected by his Congressional privilege, he should smart for thus accusing me. As Uncle Toby[1] said about the *fly, "Go miserable devil,* go. The world is big enough for thee and me.". . . .

1. Uncle Toby, the uncle of Tristram Shandy in the novel of that name by Laurence Sterne.

Monday, March 11. . . . Well, Congress *abolished* the office of Commissioner of Public Buildings & directed the Chief Engineer of the Army, Gen. A. A. Humphreys,[1] to perform the duties heretofore performed by the Commissioner. The act was approved last Monday morning, March 4th, although it bears date Mar. 2, Congress having held a continuous session from the 2nd to the 4th. . . .

1. Andrew A. Humphreys (1810–1883), chief of the Corps of Engineers, U.S. Army, 1866–1879.

Thursday, March 14. At last, thank God, I am a *free man.* This day Brig. Gen. N. Michler[1] appeared with the proper credentials and entered on duty as Engineer in Charge of the Public Buildings, etc. I handed over everything of public property in my charge, gave him all the information I could, went to the Interior Department with him and introduced him to the Secy.[,] and then we returned to the Capitol[,] and after staying there a short time, I bade the Gen. good morning & left, feeling as if a monstrous load was taken off my shoulders. . . .

> 1. Nathaniel Michler (1827–1881) was a topographer for the U.S. Army.

Sunday, March 17. . . . The longer I am out of office the better I feel about it. I have accepted propositions from my friend Hon. K. V. Whaley,[1] late a Member of Congress from West Virginia, to enter into a business partnership with him and our mutual friend E. L. Stevens, Esq., and I spent much of yesterday in drawing up the articles of agreement, and expected to see one of them, but did not. . . .

> 1. Kellian Van Renssalaer Whaley (1821–1876) was born in New York, settled in what was later West Virginia, and served as Republican congressman, 1861–1867.

Saturday, March 23. A week, lacking one day and no record. And what of the six days gone? I hardly know, and yet I have not been idle. My contract of Partnership with Whaley and Stevens was signed on Monday, and on Tuesday we went office hunting together, and engaged the only room that we could find that would in any wise suit us, and a miserable one it is, No. 10, 3d story, Washington Building, on Pa. Ave. It was all out of order, and Mr. Simmes,[1] who rents it to us at $12.50 per month[,] has agreed to have it repaired and whitewashed, we having the walls papered at our own expense. We expect to have it ready by Monday, when we hope to commence business.

. . . I went out to a meeting of the Directors of the Deaf Mute College at ½ past 4 P.M.[,] taking out Mr. Hall in my carriage and bringing in Chief Justice Chase. . . .

> 1. Probably John W. Simms, wood and coal dealer.

Thursday, March 28. . . . I have not got settled down in our new Firm yet. Whaley has been sick & Stevens gone to New York, and our rooms opposite Willard's not ready. We hope to *set in* next Monday.

Congress is still dragging its slow length along, doing all a set of unprincipled demagogues can to ruin the Country. Happening to be in company with Chief Justice Chase a few days ago, I remarked, in relation to a matter of which the Judge did not fully approve, "Congress has authorized it." "True[,]" said he, "but Congress do not know what they are about!" He spoke the truth, and nobody knows it better than I do! . . .

Sunday, March 31. . . . Tomorrow our new Firm of "French, Whaley and Stevens" is to start into existence, and *we* hope to do a reasonable amount of business. We shall try at least, as I do not consider myself exactly dead yet, although not feeding on the *pap* furnished by our Uncle Samuel. He has done feeding me, unless he gives me *more than half rations* as heretofore, whatever that delectable,[1] unprincipled wretch John W. Forney may say about my "bread and butter." *He,* a man who has waded waist-deep into the Treasury and has fleeced everybody he possibly could for the past 10 years, who has been time-server and lickspittle to all who have tolerated his iniquities, and has deserted & betrayed all who would not do so, he to talk about other people's "bread and butter"! with his own throat crammed with the spoils of office! . . .

1. French meant "detestable."

Tuesday, April 2. Yesterday the Firm of "French, Whaley & Stevens" started in earnest. Instead of taking Room No. 10, "Washington Build-ing[,]" which we at one time had engaged, . . . we have taken rooms at No. 217 Pa. Avenue, opposite Willard's Hotel. Very eligible and pleasant, and where we hope to do ever so much business. Most of my day's work yesterday was the starting of the Firm. . . .

Tuesday, April 9. . . . I got up yesterday morning and worked hard till 10 o'clock, fixing things about the premises. I ought to devote at least a week to the garden, for everything is out of shape, and our colored individual, "Harris," although very industrious, is very numb, & not very swift, and he is now our sole dependence for out-of-door work. I sold "Lindenburger cottage" and its *elegant* surroundings to Mr. C. P. Russell, on the 1st inst. for $4,000. I was sorry to sell it, although it takes much trouble and expense off my mind.[1] . . .

1. This was the house next to French, which he had rented to the Russells for years.

Sunday, April 14. . . . Friday evening Frank and I rode over to George-town to visit H. D. Cooke, *Esq.* He was out, but Mrs. Cooke received and entertained us in a manner to win all our affections. She is a dear good little lady. She showed us all through their magnificent house, to which a large and beautiful addition has recently been made. The house abounds in evidences of the excellent taste of its generous and kind-hearted owner. The paintings, the engravings, the magnificent editions of Milton, Dante, & other old writers, and the Library generally we looked upon and admired. . . .

Sunday, April 28. . . . Went to see the President relative to two cases, and to the Departments about four others. I spent from 10 A.M. to ½ past 1 P.M. in this vexatious business, and now *I am done.*

I never saw the President appearing better, and he was so cheerful and kind, and listened to all I had to say so pleasantly and patiently, that, had I not liked him so well before, I should have loved him for his kindness yesterday, and for the deep interest he manifested in the matters about which I went to see him. . . .

Yesterday, at 4 o'clock & 10 m. P.M. died Avariah Darnold, familiarly known as "Maria," "Aunt Maria," or "Aunt Ava." She was of colored skin, but with as white a soul as was ever placed in a mortal bosom, and with a natural intellect that only needed cultivation to have shone out as clear as that of any white woman. She was, I think, not far from sixty years of age.

On Tuesday, Oct. 30, 1838, my sainted wife and myself commenced housekeeping on almost the identical spot where I now write—not in the same building, that was torn down years ago—and Avaria—or, as we always called her[,] "Maria,"—was our only "help," our hired servant, and she remained with us, according to my present recollection, about *fourteen* years! and left us only on account of ill health. . . . My former wife ministered constantly to all her wants, and when leaving with me on her deathbed her last wishes, the *first* thought was of Maria. "I want you[,]" said she, "to give Maria two dollars a month as long as she lives." I have done it, and added largely to it in the necessaries of life to make her comfortable, and my beloved and largehearted wife, who now blesses my being, has carried out *all* that my Betsy could have done had she lived.

As soon as we heard of poor Maria's death last evening, we walked down to her humble residence & directed all to be done that can be to have her respectably buried. We found her lying in death, but looking like life in calm repose. Her colored friends, who have been indefatigable in their care of her while sick, had laid her out, not only decently but handsomely[,] and I never saw her look better in life. I shed more than one tear to her memory—I could not help it, although unused to weep.

She is this day, I trust, with her old mistress, whose death she so sincerely mourned, in Heaven. Farewell, faithful Maria! . . .

Monday, April 29. . . . Came in, dressed, went to the office, where I remained about an hour, then came home, lunched, and at 2 P.M. with Mrs. French, went to Maria's funeral. The house was filled with colored people, and the religious exercises were conducted by a colored clergyman, who performed all the duties appropriately and well in the manner following. First a hymn was read and sung. Then a prayer made with great fervency and in very good language in which the minister quoted—

> The year rolls round and steals away
> The breath that first it gave.
> Whate'er we do, wher'er we stay
> We're travelling to the grave.

Next he read from the scriptures, then delivered an extemporaneous address, then another hymn, which was sung, and the services were closed with a benediction.

Mrs. French and I did not go to the burying ground, but let our carriage go to carry the clergyman, while we walked home. . . .

Sunday, May 5. . . . About 6, at the invitation of Mr. Brown, who has purchased the "old Capitol," we all, viz. Mrs. M.E. & Mrs. Ellen French, Fannie, Louise[1] and I, went over to see the famous building, now being demolished. We visited the different rooms, & the one in which Wirz was confined was specially pointed out to us, & from it we brought home several pieces of wood as relics. I brought a piece of one of the washboards made of the best North Carolina pine, doubtless used in the original structure of the building, of which I yesterday made a rule— quite a handsome one too—and gave it, duly labelled, to Ellen. I also brought home quite a large piece of washboard taken from the room used as the Hall of the House of Representatives, when the building was occupied as the Capitol, after the British destroyed, as far as they could, the Capitol itself.

We roamed, in the cold, all through the building, & some of the ladies even went out upon the roof. We then came home about half frozen.

How many reminiscences are connected with that ancient building— not very ancient either as it must have been built about 52 years ago. It was built by either citizens of Washington generally, or by a Company, expressly for the accommodation of Congress while the Capitol was undergoing repairs. It was erected in times when they did such things *well*, and it is now an evidence of the faithfulness with which work was done in those days.

Congress held its sessions in it for a number of years.

It was afterwards occupied for sundry governmental purposes, and then fitted up for a Congressional boardinghouse. When I first knew anything about it, it was occupied by Mrs. Lindenburger and afterwards by Mr. Henry Hill,[2] and was greatly patronized by Southern Members of Congress. In that building died Peter E. Bossier,[3] a Member of the House of Representatives from Louisiana, and John C. Calhoun, a Senator from South Carolina.

It ceased to be used as a boardinghouse sometime before the war of the Rebellion, and was occupied for various purposes, among others as a schoolhouse.

When the war commenced it was fitted up by the U.S. as a prison. When I became Commissioner of Public Buildings in Sept. 1861, I was surprised to find that the civil control of the building was under that officer, and for some time I exercised that control, disbursing all money for repairs, etc., and partially supervising all work there. It was not long, however, before, at my own earnest desire, I was relieved from that duty by the Secretary of War.

All through the war that building swarmed with prisoners—not only soldiers of the rebel army, but our own citizens, arrested on suspicion of giving aid and comfort to the enemy, or for the commission of some petty crime, or interference with military discipline. It was a sort of American Bastille, and it is well that its walls cannot tell the story of official outrage which they concealed from the public eye!

Within the spacious yard of that prison stood the gallows whereon Wirz and at least one other paid the tribute of life to crime—and I have the impression that one criminal was shot within that yard.[4]

The premises were surrendered to their owners (a Company of individuals) within the past year, who recently sold them to Geo. T. Brown, Esq., Sergt. at arms of the U.S. Senate, for, as it is understood, $18,000, not more than half their real value. Mr. Brown is now causing all except the main building to be demolished, and is tearing out the inside of that, with a view of ascertaining what he had better do with it. His present idea seems to be to convert it into one or more dwelling houses. My wish is that a handsome hotel could be erected on the site. A large, elegant, well-kept hotel in that place would be well patronized. . . .

1. Louise Russell, daughter of Louisa.
2. Henry C. Hill, clerk in the Treasury Department.

3. Pierre E. J. Bossier (1797–1844), Democratic congressman from Louisiana, 1843–1844.

4. In April 1862 one prisoner was shot dead by a guard for refusing to go away from a window.

Sunday, May 12. . . . I think I have had enough of public office, and although Congress abolished the office I held for the purpose of punishing me for writing poetry in praise of Andrew Johnson, they really conferred upon me the greatest favor possible. Nevertheless, for the *animus* which induced Schenck, Sloan,[1] & Kelley[2] to lead off in what they meant to be my persecution[,] I sincerely wish them Hell on earth, & everlasting damnation hereafter! And I hope, should it ever be in the power of my children to pay either of those mean, contemptible wretches for their intended injuries to me, that they will not fail to do it, with interest several times compounded. Possibly I may live to repay a portion of the debt myself. Should that be the case, they shall be paid with a bitterness of heart that can feel no mercy. Oh how I despise and hate them. I hope none of them are Freemasons! But, even Freemasons joined in that crusade against me, who, in their hatred for Andrew Johnson, forgot all their vows and obligations, while good old Thaddeus Stevens, an antimason to the backbone, stood firmly by me and defended me. May God bless him for a noblehearted, honest, and honorable man as he is! . . .

1. Ithamar C. Sloan (1822–1898), Republican congressman from Wisconsin, 1863–1867.

2. William D. Kelley (1814–1890), Republican congressman from Pennsylvania, 1861–1890.

Sunday, May 26. . . . I neither take, nor care to take[,] any part in politics, being neither a Radical nor a Copperhead. I am vexed that Jeff Davis, who I think deserves to be hung, has been let off so easily. I am vexed that the Radicals have undertaken to enslave the white people of the South. . . .

Tuesday, June 4. . . . I am getting to be about tired of my business connection. I find the burden both of *purse* and labor is on *me*, & I cannot stand it much longer. Both my partners are absent and I have all the work to do. As soon as they return we must turn over a new leaf if they intend to have me remain in the firm.

Wednesday, July 10. . . . *Templar trip to Boston.*[1] At 20 m. before 8 o'clock on the morning of [Friday,] June 21st, the Templars were all in line, nearly 200 strong, at the Depot. At a few minutes before the hour fixed for starting[,] the President of the U.S. & Secy. Seward arrived, were saluted, and passed into the cars, followed by the escort, and were off for Boston. The morning was glorious and all appeared happy, so our start was propitious.

At Baltimore we were joined by a few Templars of that City. Nothing of special interest occurred until we arrived at New York, where our escort was received by the Templars of that City in full ranks. The President was waited upon by Admiral Farragut,[2] who conducted him immediately to the wharf and on board a tug, by which he was conveyed on board the U.S. Ship *Franklin,* lying off the Battery. The tug returned and took all the Templars, in two trips, to the Battery, where the President had already arrived. The column was formed, military in front, Templars next, and then the President & suite in carriages, and we marched to the 5th Avenue Hotel, where we arrived shortly after sunset. A carriage was procured for me, but I preferred to march with the Templars, and did so. Having escorted the President into the Hotel, our rooms were assigned to us, and about 10 P.M. we sat down to dinner, the President being with us—he having declined a private dining room, *saying he preferred to dine with his escort.*

I did not go to bed till past 12, and was up at ½ past 4. We breakfasted at 6, formed our lines at ½ past 7, and escorted the President to the New Haven Depot. We left New York about 8, and after a very pleasant ride, during which all attention was paid to the President at the various depots of the cities passed through, we arrived at Longwood, about 5 miles from Boston, between 4 & 5 P.M.[,] where the President was received by the authorities, Military & Civil. . . .

Sunday morning the 23d I arose early, wrote a long letter to my dear one at home before breakfast.

As soon as breakfast was over, [William] Taylor took me in his carriage, with Frank & Freddy,[3] and carried me to Quincy, where I had agreed to meet Secy. Seward and attend church with him and the Adams family. Arriving at Mr. John Quincy Adams's[4] (son of Charles Francis Adams)[,] who resides in his father's house, I found only Mrs. Adams at home, Mr. A. having gone into Boston after Mr. Seward. I walked to church with Mrs. Adams, and as the services were about commencing, Mr. Adams with Mr. Seward came in. So I had the honor and the pleasure of occupying with Mr. & Mrs. Adams, and Mr. Seward, the pew in which Presidents John and John Quincy Adams had worshipped for years.[5] On either side of the pulpit are the marble tablets, placed there to commemorate the two Presidents. My memory wandered back to my old, honored, and venerated friend John Quincy Adams, and I fear I thought more about him than I did about the sermon, which was not, to me, strikingly eloquent.

At the close of the services we walked back to the house, accompanied by Josiah Quincy.[6] We sat on the portico and talked, Mr. Seward being, as he always is in conversation, exceedingly interesting and happy. Taylor, Frank, & Freddy came after me, but the Adamses insisted on our staying to lunch with them, which we did, and I hardly remember ever to have spent a more pleasant hour. Mr. Seward's & Mr. Quincy's reminiscences were exceedingly interesting and rich, and there was more discussed in that hour than I ever heard in a single hour of my life. I wish I could recall it, but I cannot. I only know Daniel Webster, Edward Everett, John Randolph,[7] John Quincy Adams, and many other of our departed statesmen were talked over, and anecdotes respecting them were told, and the peculiarities of their characters discussed. In the course of the conversation Mr. Seward remarked that no man ever made a speech without some previous preparation. Mr. Quincy related a youthful experience of his own when in Washington with his father. He said that John Randolph seemed to take quite a fancy to him. That at one time, when he was in Mr. Randolph's room, that eccentric statesman commenced making remarks to him, and went on for about two hours. That a few days afterwards he arose in Congress and made the same speech, it being the one which led to the duel between him and Henry Clay, wherein "Blifil & Black George"[8] were introduced.

I instanced President Johnson as a man who spoke without much preparation. Mr. Seward said I was mistaken, & that he had often been surprised at finding how much President Johnson relied on his previous reading and study for what appeared to be extemporaneous speaking, etc.

At about 2, the lunch being over, we bid the Adamses, Mr. Seward & Mr. Quincy good-by and returned to Milton.

Early Monday morning [June 24] I started in full Templar *tog* with Wm. Taylor in his buggy for Boston. We were about ½ an hour driving in. I went to the American House, & our Washington Templars were soon in line, & at a little past 8 were escorted to the Common by the De Molays. I left the column on the Common and went to the new Hall and attended the Dedication ceremonies, which were very imposing. There I saw, and shook hands with[,] the President and a large number of old and esteemed friends, and was assigned to a carriage, in which I started in the procession. The carriages were all halted in Boylston Street (the President's among them) that the procession on foot might pass, which took nearly two hours.

. . . It was well towards night before the entire procession had marched by and to the Music Hall where the address was to be. . . .

Tuesday morning [June 25] opened cold, windy & rainy, so I gave up the idea of joining the excursion down the harbor, and did not go into the city until the 8 o'clock steam train. Arrived at the Judge's [Henry Flagg French's] office at about 9, went round the city some, dined at Parker's with the Judge[,] and at ¼ past 2 started in the train for Concord with him. . . .

[Saturday, June 29] we got up and breakfasted and were at Keyes's a few minutes past 6, ready to start—the Judge, Pamela, Brown & I—in Keyes's carriage drawn by his two horses, for Chester. At ½ past 6 we were off, and if we did not have a merry time going that 34 miles[,] then I never had one. We talked & laughed, and sang, & repeated poetry[,] & *picnicked,* and did all that was agreeable. The horses went beautifully, Brown drove beautifully, the dinner in the woods was beautiful, the world generally was beautiful, and *we* were certainly beautiful. We bought lobster, strawberries & confectionery at Lowell & had with us, leftover of Pamela's dinner, no small quantity, so we were fullhanded.

We arrived at Chester at ½ past 2, and, *as usual,* the letter the Judge wrote several days before announcing our intended visit had not arrived, so we took Mother & Helen by surprise. Chester is about the same at all times. The days were hot, the nights cold. Saturday evening we walked down to Greenough's store & purchased eggs. Sunday morning [June 30]—as a work of *Mercy* if not *Necessity*—I mended the pump, and then went to meeting and heard Mr. Armsby[9] of Candia preach from the text, "He that believeth and is baptized, shall be saved, but he that believeth not shall be damned." The sermon was good *in its kind.* I put in no demurrer, but "pleaded the statute of limitations," and then, for the first time in 40 years in church, went to sleep! The Judge, however, was wide awake, and doubtless attended to the *case* sharp enough! . . .

1. This is a retrospective account of French's trip to Boston.
2. David G. Farragut (1801–1870) was the hero of the Battle of Mobile Bay, 1864, and Commander of the European Squadron of the U.S. Navy, 1867–1868.
3. Son of William O. Taylor.
4. John Quincy Adams (1833–1894), who served in the Massachusetts legislature, ran unsuccessfully for governor.
5. The two former Presidents and their wives are buried in a crypt in the basement of the same church.
6. Josiah Quincy, Jr. (1802–1882), son of Josiah Quincy, president of Harvard, was mayor of Boston, 1845–1849.
7. John Randolph (1773–1833) of Roanoke, Va., extreme state-rights Republican congressman, 1799–1813, 1815–1817, 1819–1825, and 1827–1829, and senator, 1825–1827. Noted for his caustic wit and oratory.
8. Two characters from Henry Fielding's novel *Tom Jones.* Randolph compared President

John Quincy Adams to the prig Blifil and Henry Clay to the scoundrel Black George. In the ensuing duel neither Clay nor Randolph was hit.

9. Lauren Armsby, Congregational minister in Chester, 1846–1856, went west and served in the army before returning to preach in Candia, N.H.

Saturday, July 13. . . . . Fannie Gilbert, one of the sunny rays of our household, left for New Hampshire last evening to be gone a month. We shall miss her cheerful voice and never-ending good nature. I went over for a few moments to call on my friend Hon. Thaddeus Stevens, and presented to him a bouquet that I cut in my own garden after dinner, expecting to be back to bid Fannie good-by, and when I got back, lo she was gone! I was disappointed at not seeing her again. . . .

Friday, August 2. . . . . I feel nowadays as if I were spending my life to little or no account. We get nothing at our office for all we do, and I am quite discouraged. We have been in business four months[,] and Stevens has not been in the city one month of that time. Whaley does not stay in the office much, as he does most of the out-of-door work. He has been absent from 4 to 6 weeks, and nearly all the real business devolves on me, and I cannot and will not stand it much longer. We have considerable business before the Departments, but it drags along as if it never would be ended. As yet we have not received one dollar on account of business before any of the Departments! . . .

Monday, August 12. . . . . The revelations now going on in the newspapers, involving Representative Ashley[1] in a conspiracy to suborn evidence to impeach the President, seems to me to be somewhat damaging to the character of that *pure Knight Templar,* for whom I did nothing but kindness while I was Commissioner, but who *broke his Templar vows* in voting to ostracise me without any reason. Knowing him, therefore, to be a perjured Templar, it is no stretch of belief on my part to become convinced that he would stoop to any crime to carry out his vile purposes. I have hardly a doubt that all that is published of his infamy is true. May God deal with him accordingly! . . .

1. James M. Ashley (1824–1896), Republican congressman from Ohio, 1859–1869.

Tuesday, August 27. . . . . At about 9 I started for my office. Did business at the Pension and Patent Offices on my way. Remained at the office until about 12, then came home, lunched, and at 2 started with Doct. Ford[1] for the Ball ground on 14th street. Such a jam of humanity as occupied the 14th Street cars I have seldom seen, and not being very well, I was almost exhausted when I got to the grounds. We had excellent, airy seats—thanks to Dr. Ford—and I soon became so interested in the game as to forget sickness and all else. The Mutuals played splendidly. The Nationals caught and ran well, but in batting were *nowhere* compared with the Mutuals. The game lasted from a little before 3 to 6, and the score stood at the end of the 9th inning, Mutuals 40 Nationals 16. It was rather a dimming of the laurels won by the Nationals in their western trip. But it was very evident that the Mutuals had been through a practical training that it will take the Nationals a year or two of constant practice to arrive at. The President honored the game with his presence, and I was rejoiced to see him there. . . .

. . . Capt. Washburne[2] came and spent the evening and entertained us very much by relating his frontier experiences. He is a remarkable man, and one who understands the world and especially the Indians, as well as any man I know of. He is exceedingly modest and unassuming, & had not Peter, who knew him *well* in Arizona, written us to draw him out, we should never have heard of his hairbreadth escapes and exciting adventures. He staid till nearly ten, and then we went to bed.

This is a cool, pleasant morning. Wife has gone to market and I will go to my office.

I wonder how much longer I am to be made the working man of the office, while both my partners are away. I rather think *not much longer,* for I cannot stand it, and *will* not.

1. C. M. Ford, 582 New Jersey Ave.
2. Charles Washburne, clerk in the Treasury Department.

Monday, September 16. Sarita returned Saturday evening looking well[,] and we were glad enough to see her. I saw the President Saturday. He looked well and was very cheerful. I told him what untiring efforts were being made to hunt up testimony against him, and cautioned him to be on his guard against the machinations of the evil spirits that were seeking his downfall. He said he knew they were doing all that they possibly could by forgery, falsehood, & subornation of perjury to make testimony against him. I told him what I had specially heard and that I *knew* that an individual who was his warm friend had accidentally fallen upon a clue which I thought he would follow up to some purpose, and that his discoveries would result much to his (the President's) advantage, and I made an appointment with him to see that individual today. He went to see him, but whether he succeeded I have not learned. I have been told that the would-be impeachers have said that the President wrote letters to Booth, & I have been assured that they have offered $50,000 for one of them! I asked the President the plain question, "Did you ever write a letter to Booth?" "Never!" replied he most emphatically. "I never saw the man, to my knowledge." The President treated me most kindly, and, by a most unexpected question, showed his deep interest in my welfare, which I shall never forget. I sincerely believe him to be the most unjustly persecuted man I ever knew, and have an abiding faith that he will come out of the furnace pure gold, undefiled by the wicked and malicious attempts that demagogues and villains are making to ruin him!

This day I have notified Col. Whaley, my partner, that I withdraw from the firm, which dissolves it, and from this day whatever I may do I do *on my own hook*. I hope I may get enough out of the concern to pay the debts. I have neither seen or heard from either of my partners for about 4 weeks and hardly care if I never see or hear from them again, for they have treated me outrageously. I think it is my last partnership! . . .

Thursday, October 17. . . . About an hour ago (it is ¼ to 1) Ben and Abbie arrived here with their little daughter [Abbie]. They came from New York yesterday. I was very glad to see them. Oh if Ben will only do as well as he can[,] how my heart will rejoice. And now, with a wife and child dependent upon him, I cannot but think that he will. . . .

Mrs. French, Sarita and I went to the Theatre last Friday evening the 11th & saw Mr. Chanfrau[1] in *Solon Shingle*, and *The Widow's Victim*. I think he entirely overdid Solon, and was not all pleased with him in that part, but his imitations of Actors in *The Victim* were most admirable. Burton[2] was as palpably before me as he ever was in life. Forrest[3] was exact, the elder Booth[4] Capital. These, I believe[,] were all whom he imitated that I had ever seen. The play being over, Doct. Ford, who was at the Theatre with his wife, invited us all down to Harvey's[5] where we supped. It was my first visit to Harvey's splendid establishment, which has very recently been opened, and there was such a rush that night as to overwhelm them, and the consequence was that it took forever to get waited upon. Everything we had, except the fried oysters, was excellent— those were miserable. I called the next day, and Mr. Harvey most politely showed me all over his establishment. It is very large & admirably arranged. He apologized for our being so neglected the evening before, and told me that he had hardly got the machine into working order, and that the crowd was so large and unexpected that he could not possibly serve them as he desired to do, but when I came again I should find all shipshape. I intend to go again soon and repay Doct. Ford for his kindness by taking him & his wife with us. . . .

1. Francis S. Chanfrau (1824–1884) was well known for his mimicry.
2. William Evans Burton (1804–1860), English comic actor, who moved to America in 1834.
3. Edwin Forrest (1806–1872), American actor famous for his roles as Lear, Coriolanus, and Richard III.
4. Junius Brutus Booth (1796–1852), leading American actor, father of actors Junius Brutus Booth II, Edwin T. Booth, and John Wilkes Booth.
5. Oyster house of T. M. Harvey, 281 C St. North.

Sunday, October 20. . . . I was engaged constantly, yesterday, in *something*. In the morning, as soon as breakfast was over, I went to my workshop and mended the handle of Sarita's parasol. It had been broken short off. In working it down to receive the brass ferule with which I mended it, I discovered the cheatery of parasol makers. As soon as the covering coat of varnish, or enamel, or whatever the handle is covered with, was removed, I found the handle had been broken, probably in putting in the wire spring that catches the brass tube to hold up the parasol when spread, and had been glued together, so that it really had very little strength. I am pretty well convinced that all citizens are arrant knaves and cheats when it is more profitable to cheat than to be honest. I mended the handle *well*, and without covering any of my own cheatery! . . .

After dinner I sat down and read Greeley's history of the Rebellion[1] a while. Doct. Ford invited us to go down to Calvary Baptist Church with himself and Mrs. Ford at ½ past 7 to witness the reception to be given to Amos Kendall by the congregation, he (Mr. Kendall) having built the Church edifice, and having just returned from a long visit to Europe. We went down and enjoyed the reception very much. The house was well filled, with well-dressed and good-looking people. . . .

I never was more happy in paying my own respect to merit than on that occasion. I have known the Hon. Amos Kendall for 34 years. I knew him *well* by reputation ten years at least before I made his personal acquaintance, he having studied law with Chief Justice Richardson, my first wife's father, and his name being of course a household word in the Judge's family. On my arrival in Washington in 1833 almost the first person I called on was Mr. Kendall—then 4th Auditor. From that day to this I have been, I may say, intimately acquainted with him. We were for many years associated as Directors of Telegraph Companies, and for some years past have held the same attitude towards each other as Directors of the Deaf & Dumb Institution at Kendall Green, of which he is the Father.

Mr. Kendall commenced life in poverty. He has accumulated an independent fortune, principally by being the Agent of Prof. Morse in taking care of his Telegraphic Interests. He is spending the income of that fortune in a manner worthy of his strong mind and excellent & generous heart. His movements are all controlled, as it seems to me, by the spirit of philanthropy, and God and Man will bless him. . . .

1. Horace Greeley, *The American Conflict* (2 vols., 1864–1866).

Sunday, October 27. . . . [Thursday] Walked down to Philadelphia Row on 11th St. where Ben had taken a house & moved a part of his furniture. Found Abbie and the baby there, with the servant, without any fire, waiting patiently for Ben. I helped the servant make a fire in the furnace and waited till near sunset, but Ben came not, so, with Abbie and the baby, we came up here. Ben came about dark, and about 8 they all left for Willard's, where they were staying. After they had left[,] Mrs. French told me they had concluded not to keep house!

Although opposed to their keeping house, the sudden determination, after hiring the house, purchasing fuel, moving their furniture, and getting nearly ready, to give up, really distressed me. It showed such a lack of determination, such apparent childishness, such evidence of all want of forethought, that I went to bed perfectly wretched, and worried myself almost sick, & arose Friday morning so dizzy I could scarcely stand. Friday evening, Abbie came here with her baby, and Ben was to procure a boarding place yesterday. She, poor thing, staid all day, but no Ben, and he did not make his appearance until after dark last evening! They spent the night here, and Ben promises to get a boarding place tomorrow morning.

Ben is the first man I ever saw that I could not comprehend at all. He, although my own son, and brought up in my own house, is an utter enigma to me, and God only knows what is to become of him. With natural abilities sufficient to be anything he chooses, he has thus far frittered away his life and his property. No young man has had better advantages. I have assisted him till I am tired. If he was like anybody else on earth[,] it would be a satisfaction to have him here with me; now it is distressing to me, because I have lost confidence in him. He can reform if he will, and when I find that he has[,] I am willing to do all in my power to aid him. I pity his wife and child, and love them, and they are most welcome to my house. May God bless them. . . .

During the week past I have gone $10,000 into a stone quarry at Seneca, by advice of Henry D. Cooke.

Our Bank Directors met last Tuesday, declared a dividend of 5 per cent, and lunched at the Club House. In the evening Mr. Cooke, Mr. Huntington, and Mr. Evans,[1] V.P. of the Safe Deposit Company, visited us, and we had a very pleasant evening.

1. George O. Evans, corner of 15th Street and New York Avenue.

Sunday, November 10. The Grand Lodge met . . . and among other things, elected me Grand Master. Under all the circumstances I accepted it as a very high honor. When my dear deceased Bro. Whiting was last elected—I mean when he was elected the first year for his last series of terms—I was very much pressed to suffer my name to be used, but peremptorily declined. I had been Grand Master for 6 successive years, Dec. 1847 to Dec. 1853, and never again intended to hold the office, but now I shall accept it as a mark of the confidence of my Masonic Brethren, after the unprincipled scoundrels in Congress, & some of my Masonic Brethren among them, have tried to put me down! They cannot do it! The Grand Lodge sat Tuesday evening till 12 o'clock and then called off till Wednesday evening at 7, when it met and finished its annual session. . . .

Abbie and her baby came up here Friday evening & are here now. The cause of their coming is sickening to my heart, Ben behaving so outrageously that they could not remain with him. After all his solemn promises to me, it is really awful. I can do no more. My patience is exhausted! Let him throw himself away now as soon as he pleases. I can and shall do no more, & if I can help it, fret no more. . . .

Monday, November 18. . . . On Monday morning last Ben came over and saw Abbie, and made most solemn promises of reformation. So Abbie went back to their boardinghouse with him, and I have heard of no trouble since. I *hope* and that is all I can do.

To sum up last week's doings in short metre, I mended the cellar stairs, which had rotted almost down. I purchased 200 shares in the Seneca Quarry Company—paid $10,000 for them. . . .

Thursday, December 5. When I had written thus much yesterday morning I was interrupted, and found no more time during the day to add to my journalizing.[1]

Well I *had* just finished reading the President's message, and was about to say of it that I very much regretted that the President had seen fit to rehash the veto messages of the past two years and again serve it up to

Congress. Admitting that his views are right, what is the use of reiter-
ating them over and over again with no further obvious intention than
that of creating excitement, when everybody is earnestly praying for harmony. It reminds me of the saying of a rough laborer that, in years long
gone by, worked on my father's farm. When working on an out lot, a
mile or more from the "Old homestead," he took his dinner with him in
a tin pail. It[,] the pail[,] was generally pretty well filled, and upon one
occasion he invited a companion to partake of his meal. They sat down
on the ground with the provend-pail between them. My friend helped
his companion and then himself. The visitor took the pail & began to
search the contents quite inquisitorially. The laborer eyed him quietly
for a time, until he had turned the contents to the very bottom over two
or three times. Then he, the proprietor of the dinner, losing all patience,
burst out as follows—"Look 'er here my Christian friend, I've stood that
long enough. I am willing that you should turn them things in that 'are
pail *over and over,* but as for turning them over, and over, *and over again,*
I'll be d—ned if you shall!"

My impression is that the President has turned over the contents of
the legislative pail presented to him by Congress often enough, and I
am sorry that he has undertaken it again. . . .

1. On the previous day French had started to write about Johnson's message.

Sunday, December 8. . . . Last evening I accompanied Sarita to the
Theatre to see Hackett[1] play Falstaff in *Henry IV.* He played it admirably,
as he always does. Hackett and Tyrone Power[2] are the only persons who,
in my day, have played the fat knight well. I have seen them both in it,
but cannot now remember sufficiently about Power's acting to say which
I considered best. Poor Power was lost with my old friend Rev. Mr. Cookman in the Steamer *President.*[3] . . .

Yesterday the House of Representatives of the United States voted
against impeaching the President by a direct vote of 57 Ayes to 108 Noes!
God bless the House of Representatives for that act of Patriotism and
justice. Among those who voted in the affirmative I was pained to find
the names of my friends and esteemed Brethren Bromwell[4] and Orth.[5]
I wish they could have found it in accordance with their views of Right
to vote the other way, as did my Republican friends & Brethren, Banks,
Dawes, Garfield, Spalding,[6] and Welker.[7] . . . On the 1st day of Jany.
1866, *I wrote a poem.* The writing thereof was the cause of my official
death, and, as I firmly believe, of my physical life, this day! In that poem,
which so exasperated the *Honorable* Robert C. Schenck, I wrote—

The end approaches—that sublime event,
The People rallying to their President,
Ere long the world shall see, etc.

That is now becoming prophecy, and it would not be any more wonderful than many political events that I have witnessed if the mad efforts
of the ultra radicals to criminate Andrew Johnson should make him
President for another term! Just such an onslaught upon Martin Van
Buren made *him* President of the U.S.[,] and the American People have
a way of rebuking those who undertake to persecute a man they respect
and honor, in that way. So let the bitter enemies of honest Andrew Johnson beware! . . .

1. James H. Hackett (1800–1871), American comedian.
2. Tyrone Power (1797–1841), Irish comedian, grandfather and great-grandfather of
American actors Frederick Tyrone Power and Tyrone Edmond Power.
3. See May 16, 1841.
4. Henry P. H. Bromwell (1823–1903), Republican congressman from Illinois, 1865–
1869.
5. Godlove S. Orth (1817–1882), Republican congressman from Indiana, 1863–1871,
1873–1875, and 1879–1882.
6. Rufus P. Spalding (1798–1886), Democratic congressman from Ohio, 1863–1869.
7. Martin Welker (1819–1902), Republican congressman from Ohio, 1865–1871.

Wednesday, December 25. Christmas day. 4¼ P.M. Well, I have got so
far through Christmas day. At 4 A.M. Mary Ellen, Sarita, Annie Rainsford, Fannie & Louise all rose and walked to St. Aloysius' Church and
paid their morning orisons *and heard the music!* which they pronounced
"splendid."[1] I arose at ¼ before 7, like a Christian, shaved, dressed and
read the papers. A little before 8 the party came home and we had
breakfast. Annie went home to spend the day soon after breakfast, and
the lady of the house and Sarita took naps. I wrote a while, and then,
having taken my armchair up twice in the pockets of my elegant new
dressing gown—a present from my precious wife, made by her own
hands—I went out [to] the shop and got out two pieces of black walnut
and nailed them over the scrolls of the arms, so that the[y] cannot get
into my pockets! Then I read till 2, and then we all went into Mr. Russell's
and dined. . . . Last evening our parlor was like a Fair room with Christmas presents. I never saw such a display. I should think they would count
by hundreds, both in presents and dollars. My presents were:

An elegant merino dressing gown	from Mrs. French	
Queens of American Society	"	Fannie and Louise
Half Hours with the Best Letter Writers	"	Sarita
Ruined Castles of the Border	"	Little Mary

Confectionery	"	Frank & Ellen
Two gallons of whiskey	"	W. Forsyth, Esq.
Two Boxes cigars	"	W. Forsyth, Esq.
Elegant china coffee cup & saucer	"	Harry.

I believe that is all. The dressing gown & *whiskey* were not less acceptable than the other things! . . .

1. Anne Rainsford French and Fannie Gilbert.

Thursday, January 9. . . . The 8th was duly celebrated by the Democrats at the Metropolitan Hotel, last evening. The *Intelligencer* is filled with the speeches this morning. I wanted to attend, as I have always attended the celebrations of that day, but my political *status* is such that I could not consistently do so. The men who got it up were opposed to the war and I fought them bitterly all through it. The Republicans, with whom I went most heartily during the War, have acted so much like fools since it was over that I was driven on principle from the support of their Vandal policy, and in feeling have been with those who support the *Constitution & the Union,* be they whom they may, but I cannot consistently unite with either party in celebrations. So, I satisfied myself in recurring to the oldentime when, in 1835, I united in a celebration of the 8th at the *same place*—then the "Indian Queen Hotel," when Thomas H. Benton presided, assisted by Silas Wright, James M. Wayne,[1] Isaac Hill, James K. Polk, & a host of other eminent democrats of that day as Vice Presidents, where speeches were made by men whereof we shall hardly see the like again.

I remember that Benton, Wayne, Polk, Forsyth, King,[2] Woodbury, Hugh L. White, R. M. Johnson, P.M. Gen. Barry[,][3] and many others made eloquent speeches on that occasion. A letter from "the Old Hero," *par excellence,* was read & received with shouts of applause. At that celebration, in addition to some of the most prominent civilians that this or any other Country ever saw, there were present glorious representatives of the Army and Navy—Maj. Gen. Macomb, then Commander in Chief of the Army, Gen. Jesup and Gen. Wool, Commodore Rodgers[4] of the Navy[,] and other officers both of the Army & Navy. It was really a glorious celebration. When I think of these great men and patriots, *now all passed away,* and read the record of those who were at the head of affairs last evening, it makes me almost sick.

Jeremiah S. Black[5] filling the place of Thomas H. Benton!! Jonah D. Hoover, in the place of Henry Hubbard! Thomas B. Florence[6] in the place of James M. Wayne! And so on. Giants and Pigmies! Oh my Country to what have you descended in the *genus Homo!*

It was announced as the celebration of the anniversary of the Battle of New Orleans. But one would hardly know from the speeches or toasts that there ever was such a battle! But enough. It was a farce, & will ever be looked upon as one.

1. James M. Wayne (1790–1867), in his third term as congressman from Georgia at the time, was appointed to the U.S. Supreme Court on the very next day and served until his death.
2. John P. King (1799–1888), Democratic senator from Georgia, 1833–1837.
3. William T. Barry (1785–1835), of Kentucky, was Postmaster General, 1829–1835.
4. John Rodgers (1773–1838) served in the War of 1812 and was Secretary of the Navy briefly in 1823.
5. Jeremiah S. Black (1810–1883), of Pennsylvania, served on the state supreme court, 1851–1857, before being appointed U.S. Attorney General by President Buchanan.
6. Thomas B. Florence (1812–1875), Democratic congressman from Pennsylvania, 1851–1861.

Thursday, January 16. On Monday, I do not think I did anything worthy of note. If I did I have forgotten it. On Tuesday it commenced snowing in the morning and snowed all day. I went to the 1st National Bank about noon, and we held our annual meeting of Stockholders and elected the old Board of Directors, Cooke, Wills, Fahnestock, Huntington & French. The Directors held a meeting and elected Cooke President, & then declared a dividend of 5 per cent. Adjourned and went up to the old Club House and lunched. Mr. Cooke being detained by company, did not go. We discussed political matters—Wills, Huntington and I—at the table pretty considerably. Wills radical, Huntington and I friends of the President, thought Congress were moving towards the absorption of the entire government pretty fast. Wills stated some evidence of Johnson's inconsistencies which I did not believe, and so said, but not intending to impeach Mr. Wills's statement, but my belief in the falsity of the evidence he relied on—being statements made by Southern radicals to Judge Kelly[1] of what Johnson said to them when he first assumed the Executive power. Wills read from Kelly's speech at Cincinnati. The information given to Kelly I believed false, and I still believe so. We had just got the news of Stanton's reentry on his duties as Secy. of War, and of Grant's abdication, and I believe we all concurred in expressing the opinion that Stanton could not, as a decent man, possessed of one spark of honor or one atom of dignity, remain any time at the head of the War Department. He is still there. If he remains "shame fa' him," is all I have to say about it. . . .

1. Joseph L. Kelly.

Sunday, January 26. . . . At 3 yesterday afternoon, Sarita and I set off for our calls in the carriage, Harris driving us. We went first to Chief

Justice Chase's where the lovely and accomplished Mrs. Senator Sprague was receiving in her usual graceful manner, causing everyone to feel that she was really glad to see them. Miss Nettie[1] was at her side as cordial and kind as her captivating sister. Neither the Chief Justice nor Senator were present. The attendance was not large while we were there. I introduced Sarita to those whom I knew, took a cup of hot chocolate, and left for Mayor Wallach's. There we found quite a gathering, and dancing in progress. . . .

1. Janette Chase, daughter of Salmon P. Chase and his third wife, Sarah Bella Chase (d. 1852).

Friday, January 31. . . . Political matters are in a very strange state just at this time, and I am rejoiced that I am not mixed up with them in any way. As the woman said when her husband and the bear were fighting, so say I, "Fight on[,] devils. I don't care which licks." I was a warm Grant man two months ago, but circumstances have somewhat cooled my ardor. I have been longing for years to see Salmon P. Chase placed regularly on the Presidential course. He is a good, conscientious, learned and reliable man, and as much of a statesman as we have living. *He* would make an excellent President, and I could heartily and conscientiously advocate his election. But it now looks to me as if *Military glory* was to eclipse all civil excellence, and the fight is to be between Grant and Hancock![1] Last August I wrote some rhymes applauding Grant. I *shall not publish them now.* A single copy is in other hands, & they may possibly see the light, but I hope not at present.

1. Major General Winfield Scott Hancock (1824–1886) repulsed Lee's attack on the Union center at Gettysburg on July 3, 1863. He was later Democratic candidate for President in 1880.

Sunday, February 2. . . . I was in the upper part of the city yesterday and saw a gentleman who professes to be well posted in political matters, who informed me that *he knew* that there was an awful conspiracy among the leading men of the President's Cabinet and others to betray the President and the Country. He mentioned Secy. McCulloch, Atty. Gen. Stanbery, Secy. Stanton, P.M. Gen. Randall, Gen. Grant, Gen. Sherman, Senator Sherman, Ben. Wade & a few others, as the leaders, and told me especially what they intended to do.[1] He avowed his intention of informing the President all about it. I think it very likely there is truth in what he told me, but I much doubt whether it is *all* true, for I cannot believe that McCulloch, Randall and Stanbery can ever throw themselves into the arms of the Radicals. If they do I despair of ever finding an honest man. As *the greatest man of all this world* once said, and I heard him say it, "We shall see what we shall see!" I do wish the President would stand more strongly than he does, by his true friends, of whom I claim to be one—*strong and hearty*!

Charles Dickens arrived in the city last evening, I understand, and made Welker's on 15th St. his headquarters. Yesterday's *Intelligencer* contains some extracts from my reminiscences of 1842 concerning him.

1. Hugh McCulloch (1808–1895), Secretary of the Treasury, 1865–1869. Henry Stanbery (1803–1881), U.S. Attorney General, 1866–1868, who acted as President Johnson's chief counsel during his impeachment trial. Alexander W. Randall (1819–1872), U.S. Postmaster General, 1866–1869. John Sherman (1823–1900), Republican congressman from Ohio, 1855–1861, and senator, 1861–1877; he was brother of Gen. William T. Sherman.

Monday, February 3. . . . Mrs. French, Mrs. Wills and the children have gone out to enjoy the beautiful day—for it *is* beautiful although cold. Sarita has gone skating. I think, considering Sister Ambrosine's ideas of her health, when in her care—that she had *curvature of the spine, incipient consumption,* and "all the ills that flesh is heir to," and doctored and petted her accordingly—that the little witch exhibits a toughness and endurance that few girls in perfect health exhibit.[1] I would pit her against any boy of her age, within my knowledge, to go through a series of exposures and hardships, that the world calls *pleasures,* and bet largely on her being the winner. She is full of life, animation, and endurance. . . .

1. Sister Ambrosine (Mrs. Campbell). The sister was correct; Sarita died at the early age of forty-six.

Wednesday, February 5. . . . After dinner went down and attended a meeting of the Directors of the Masonic Hall Association, then went to hear Mr. Charles Dickens. Met Mrs. French, Mrs. Wills and Sarita there. My seat was as far back as it could be, but Judge Holman[1] of the Ho. Reps. insisted on my taking his seat, so as to be next to Mrs. Wills, who was two benches nearer Mr. Dickens. I felt under very great obligations to him, and accepted his courtesy.

Dickens read from *David Copperfield* that portion describing Mr. Peggotty's dwelling in the old boat—the engagement between Ham and Emily, Steerforth's rascality, Copperfield's supper to Mr. & Mrs. Micawber, his courtship of Dora, and the awful storm wherein Steerforth and Ham were drowned. He then read "Bob Sawyer's Party." He occupied just about two hours. I was generally pleased with his reading, but disliked his continual raising of his voice as if he had the hiccoughs. His reading of Mr. Peggotty's decision to go after his niece through the *wureld* was a masterly piece of acting, and pleased *me* better than any other portion of his reading. He read the description of the Micawber supper with great effect, and much to the amusement of the audience. I came away, on the whole, well satisfied, & Mary Ellen & Sarita were delighted. . . .

1. William S. Holman (1822–1897), Democratic congressman from Indiana, 1859–1865, 1867–1877, and 1881–1895.

Friday, February 7. . . . I was at the Capitol a few days ago, and having some business in the Committee Room on Appropriations, I went in and there met my old friend Thaddeus Stevens. He took me most cordially by the hand and seemed really glad to see me. He looked as pale and deathlike as he ever can look, but seemed in as good spirits as I ever saw him. I asked him how he was, to which he replied that he was about as bad as he could be. He then asked me *if I was teaching a singing school.* I replied that I had hardly come [to] that yet. "What are you doing?" said he. I answered[,] "Trying to practice law a little." "Ah[,]" said he[,] "you have got *down to that have you,* you can't get much lower!" We talked and laughed for a few minutes and I left. Thaddeus Stevens is a most remarkable man, and now, on the brink of the grave, as he doubtless is, he is as full of wit and humor as ever he was, and will die game to the last.[1] There is here a gentleman by the name of Simon Stevens,[2] a man of middle age, who studied law with Thaddeus, and is[,] I believe[,] a relative—perhaps a nephew. Capt. Williams, not knowing that Thaddeus has always been a bachelor, has always supposed Simon to be a son of Thaddeus. Not long since Simon called on the Capt. and told him that Thaddeus desired to see him a moment in the Committee Room. The Capt. went up and said to Mr. Thaddeus, "Your son has just been in and asked me to come up as you desired to see me."

"*My* son!"—"*My* son!" said Mr. Thaddeus—"you say[,] *My* son!" "Well I should like to know how the devil he found out that *I* was his father!"

The Capt. was taken somewhat aback, and explained that he had always supposed that Simon Stevens was his son, when Thaddeus assured him that, never having been married, he had no children *to speak of!* An[d] so the *contretemps* ended. I had this story from Capt. Williams the day the interview occurred, happening in at the Commissioner's office, where he is employed, shortly after he came down. He related to me another characteristic anecdote, of the time. Mr. Stevens sent for him to take the acknowledgement of a deed, he being a Magistrate. When he had done it[,] Mr. Stevens asked what was to pay? "Nothing[,]" replied the Capt. "Nothing!" said Mr. Stevens—"Nothing!" "Well, if you do business for nothing, you never can do any more for me. I always pay for everything that is done for me." The Capt. replied that if he took that view of it, his fee was fifty cents. "Very well," said Mr. S. handing him the money, "now if I have any more business in your line I shall send for you."

A gentleman of my acquaintance told me that Mr. Stevens on being asked if Simon was related to him, replied, "We do not raise *calves* in our family!"

1. Stevens died in Washington on August 11 that year.
2. Simon Stevens, who was for a time Thaddeus Stevens's law partner, was not a relative. He helped attend to Thaddeus in his dying days.

Monday, February 10. I sit down to write this evening sick in body, and sicker in mind. My head has been out of order all day. I asked for an office at the Treasury which I supposed vacant, the salary of which is $2,000. The President gave me a note to the Secy. favoring strongly my application. On calling at the Dept. I found that the *disbursing* clerkship I supposed vacant was not, but that an $1,800 clerkship was, which I could probably have by applying for. By advice of some of my friends I applied for it[,] and Col. Cooper,[1] the Assistant Secy.[,] at once ordered the appointment, provided there was a vacancy. I went to the appointing Clerk, Mr. Creecy,[2] and he said he must see the Secy. and if I would call tomorrow he presumed all would be right. I left, feeling as humble as a whipped spaniel to think that after holding the offices I have, I should humiliate myself so much as to accept a 4th class Clerkship! But, my experience is that *money* is very uncertain, even if a person can get business, and I *need* the $1,800 per ann. *to live*. So I shall descend to do it with as much grace as possible. But it makes me sick in mind to think of it. . . .

1. Henry C. Cooper.
2. C. Eaton Creecy of Mississippi.

Thursday, February 13. I went to the Treasury Dept. Tuesday morning and was told my appointment was all arranged, and an order was handed to me to go to Mr. West[,][1] Chief Clerk[,] and be examined. I went, *and passed all the examination he required*, when he endorsed the paper "OK" and I returned it to Mr. Creecy, the Appointment Clerk, who requested me to report the next morning, and the regular appointment would be ready. So, yesterday at 10 A.M. I called, received the appointment and was sworn in. After considerable consultation it was concluded that I should report to Hon. J. M. Brodhead,[2] Second Comptroller[,] which I did, and today he has assigned me to duty, and given leave of absence for one week, firstly because the room is repairing, secondly, to enable me to arrange my business matters. . . .

1. William H. West of Maryland.
2. French's friend Dr. John M. Brodhead.

Thursday, February 20. Yesterday I started out as soon as I had eaten breakfast and did a few errands and attended to the getting some of my old business off my hands, then went to the office to which I have been assigned in the Second Comptroller's Bureau and arranged my desk for business. Saw a crowd of Indians, conducted, as someone told me, by Kit Carson.[1] I should think about half the Clerks in the Treasury were following them through the building. I got into the midst of the crowd, & was thoroughly surrounded by Indians, but was neither scalped nor tomahawked! . . .

This morning at 9 I rode to the office, Will French accompanying me to drive the horse home, to commence my official duties. Having no special work assigned to me, I labored hard on some briefs I am making until nearly two, and then went down to the Theatre, and heard The Riching Opera Troupe sing, and saw the Japanese perform for the benefit of the Poor. . . .

1. Christopher ("Kit") Carson (1809–1868), Indian agent, guide, and soldier, was in the East, seeking to improve his failing health. He died soon after returning to the West.

Saturday, February 22. . . . Congress has walked over and trodden down the Constitution, while the President has endeavoured to maintain and defend it. But he is a determined man, and has listened to bad advisers, and his act of yesterday in removing Edwin M. Stanton from the office of Secretary of War, where the Senate have unconstitutionally and illegally placed him, although right itself, was, in my opinion, injudicious, and will bring on a fearful state of things! I must stop now.

Evening. I had to stop writing at the bottom of the preceding page, business calling me away. I will now continue. I think the President's action was injudicious, because it *must* result in impeachment, and probably in conviction; but, whether the latter event takes place or not, the whole country is to be thrown into a state of fearful excitement, and I cannot help feeling that there is, at this moment, more danger threatening the Republic than there has ever been before. . . .

Sunday, February 23. I have read the Sunday morning *Chronicle* which is filled with "*Impeachment.*" The House worked on till eleven o'clock, and eloquent speeches were made. Brooks[1] and Bingham spoke like Statesmen and Patriots, I judge, not only from the meagre report contained in the *Chronicle,* but from what a gentleman told me last evening, who heard them. Farnsworth's speech, of which I judge only from what I have read in the paper, was a rigmarole of abuse and misrepresentation. I can see that he misrepresented Brooks very much. His speech goes to show, when compared with Bingham's, the great difference between a learned and eloquent man, and a mere dabbler in commonplace. . . .

I have but one hope, and that is that the question of the Constitutionality of the "tenure of office law" will soon get before the Supreme Court, where, I cannot doubt, it will be decided to be unconstitutional. My own private life dwindles into a nothing before this great matter of the life of the Nation!

1. James Brooks (1810–1873), congressman from New York, 1849–1853, 1863–1866, and 1867–1873.

Monday, February, 24. . . . 5 P.M. William Russell comes from the Capitol. "President impeached." Vote 126 to 47. The President has, it is understood, caused Gen. Grant to be arrested, and the rumor is that he has called out the Maryland Militia. The state of affairs is becoming frightful, and I think I foresee more civil war. If all this ends without the shedding of blood, the people may render up thanks to a merciful Providence. . . .

Tuesday, February 25. . . . *Sarita's Party.*
The house having been put in as perfect party trim as possible, and everything prepared, at 8 o'clock I lighted the gas and the mirror and mantle lamps. The parlors never looked better, and the Library looked well enough. Doct. Brodhead was the first visitor to arrive, and he and I talked over the occurrences of the day for ½ an hour, and agreed that the President had made a tremendous blunder in his action regarding the removal of Stanton. He had the right bower and ace in his own hand and lost the game! He agreed perfectly.

The company began to flock in by 9 o'clock, notwithstanding the steady fall of snow, and by 10 we had as gay, goodlooking, and merry a party as I ever saw anywhere. Dancing commenced and was kept up steadily until supper was served at a few minutes past 1. Doct. Brodhead, Capt. Washburne, Willie French and I made up a game of euchre about 10, and with some occasional changes at the table, kept it up till supper was ready, and, even then, we waited till the younger people were through, and then went down and partook. . . .

After supper the dancing re-commenced and was kept up till ½ past 4 A.M. I, as above stated, retired to a bed in the attic, so as to be as far away from the noise as possible, at about ¼ past 2. There were in the neighborhood of a hundred at the party, and it was an entire success. . . .

The snow lay six inches deep at 5 this morning, when the party broke up, and was still falling. It fell steadily all night. . . .

Saturday, February 29. Thursday morning at 10 I again went to the President's with Capt. Daniels.[1] A crowd was there, and at 12 I told the Capt. I could wait no longer, but would return at 1. So I went to my office and at 1 returned to the Prest. and at about 2 [we] were admitted to see him. Our interview was satisfactory. I never saw the President in better apparent spirits. Not a word was said about Impeachment, nor was the subject alluded to. Now it is time for me to go to Doct. Ford's, where I am invited to a Euchre party.

1. Daniels was seeking a position in the registry of deeds.

Sunday, March 1. . . . In the evening [Friday, February 28] Mrs. French and I went [to] the State dinner at the President's in accordance with the subjoined invitation. The dinner party was very brilliant, although the *Chronicle* of yesterday seeks to belittle it by saying there were *about a dozen* present. The large table in the State dining room, at which at least 40 can be seated, was full, except 2 seats.[1] . . . Mrs. Johnson did not appear. Her health is miserable this winter, and I do not think she will live long.[2] The President and his amiable daughters appeared well, and by no means troubled at the impending trial. I have this morning read the articles of impeachment as presented in the House yesterday, and if the Senate can convict the President on those flimsy charges[,] I shall, I confess, be astonished. I do not believe they can, or will. . . .

1. French lists about half of the guests, including six members of the Supreme Court.
2. She died in 1876.

Wednesday, March 4. . . . Two years ago this day I was stricken down with vertigo, and from that day to this have not been a *well* man, although my head is not affected unless I undertake to look up for some length of time, or to do work that requires reaching up. Occasionally my head is giddy for a day[,] which seems to be in place of my old nervous head-aches[,] which I do not now have. But I am an old man!

Thursday, March 5. . . . Mrs. French and William were at the Capitol to see the Impeachment begin. They swore the Senators down to Wade, and objection being made to his being sworn, the *Body*—a mongrel between a Senate and a Court—went to debating whether he ought, or ought not, to be sworn, and the question was under debate when they left to come home to dinner. . . .

Sunday, March 8. . . . Although I *am* a personal friend of Andrew Johnson, I have no cause to love him—or even respect him—*officially*, for he has not treated me with any sort of consideration. He has promised me twenty times within the past year, *voluntarily*, that he would place me in some official position suitable to my social standing, &, although opportunity after opportunity has presented, he has not kept his promise, and he has come very near speaking to me, as the Indians would say, "*with a forked tongue.*" At any rate such has been his *duplicity* toward me that I shall not trouble myself to visit him *very* often in future. Still, every humble effort I am capable of will be made to bring about his triumphant defence, for I believe him to be a true patriot, and honest in his intentions, though very unfortunate in his actions.

Thursday, March 12. . . . Monday[,] Willie & I concluded we would *Theatricalize* the back parlor and give an exhibition. So Tuesday morning at 8 o'clock we began, and[,] by dint of hard labor, about 4 P.M. we had a most respectable proscenium erected from the north projection of the chimneys to the south side of the door into the passage, with wings extended diagonally to the sides of the arch, giving an "exit & an entrance" into the passage on the East side, & leaving a place for "traps" on the west. . . .

The opening to the stage was covered by a pair of yellow curtains looping up by drawing the cords at the sides, and when all was finished *we* pronounced it "well done," and fixed Wednesday evening for the *exhibition*. Wednesday was the day of busy preparation, and, although there were no "armorers closing rivets up," there were ladies sewing damask up, and gentlemen manufacturing Elephants, Lions, Tigers, & all sorts of terrestrial and aquatic *beasts*, arranging programs, and fixing things generally, not forgetting the *machinery to wind up the waxwork!* About 40 were invited to behold the performance, to commence at 8 P.M.[,] and all but 3 came, and two who were not invited called to pay their respects, and of course staid. At 8, precisely[,] the audience were all seated in chairs in the front parlor, and the *curtain rose*. A charade was enacted to the satisfaction of all, it is believed. The performance went on till about ten, when an intermission took place for the audience to refresh with chicken salad, crackers, cake and lemonade, all prepared in abundance by our *better half*. The entertainment concluded with an exhibition of "The Elephant[,]" who performed all his wonderful feats to the admiration of all, and at ½ past eleven all had departed professing themselves highly gratified with all that had been done. . . .

Monday, March 23. . . . I saw Mrs. Patterson at the Executive Mansion on Saturday. She seemed in good spirits, and spoke of the impeachment of her father calmly, admitting, as gracefully as possible, the probability that the family would not remain much longer in the white house. She remarked, in speaking of some of the attempts of the Committee to worm something out of the employees of the President detrimental to him, "Let them find out all they can—we have no secrets here!" She doubtless spoke the living truth, and I honored her for her calmness & propriety.

Sunday, March 29. . . . We have eaten dinner and at ½ past 2 Mr. Brown and I are going to Georgetown on Masonic business touching the A∴ & A∴ Rite.[1] I begin to feel as if I ought to give up active operations in that Rite; it is pressing too hard upon me. Indeed all my Freemasonry is taking too much of my time, and having for 20 years been a devotee to the cause, I feel as if I had done my share and ought to be let honorably off, and with the expiration of my Grand Mastership, in Dec. next, I intend to try & be relieved, if I live to see that time. . . .

1. The Ancient and Accepted Scottish rite, an advanced order of Freemasonry.

Friday, April 17. A record of the last 4 days, if properly and fully written, would finish this volume! But I cannot spend time to write it. I will, however[,] briefly notice the events. . . .

Wednesday, 15th—being the day of the dedication of the Lincoln Statue—I went down to the City Hall about 11, and remained there until nearly 1, when I went to the Masonic Hall, and the Grand Lodge being assembled[,] our arrangements were soon made to proceed to the statue. We left the Hall at 1:40′ &, marching through several streets, arrived at the base of the statue promptly at 2—the hour fixed—where we had to stand in the mud, and a slightly drizzling rain, for half an hour at least, during which all the arrangements were made on the platform, and the Rev. Wm. Hamilton[1] prayed. The Masonic services were then performed, and I went on to the platform and delivered the address, which was about ¾ of an hour in length, and well received.[2] All the ceremonies being over, I returned with the Grand Lodge to the Hall, and closed it, and then came home. . . .

1. William Hamilton of the Methodist Episcopal Church was also a clerk in the patent office.
2. A copy of French's address is inserted in the journal. Benjamin B. French, *Address: Dedication of the Statue of Abraham Lincoln, Erected in Front of the City Hall, Washington, D.C.* (Washington City, 1868).

Wednesday, May 6. . . . I have been daily working away at my Clerkship in the 2d Comptroller's office, and trying to give Uncle Sam a *quid pro quo* for the $150 per month (Internal Revenue off!) which the kind old gentleman allows me for such labor as I can give him! . . .

Monday, May 11. . . . I called at Mr. Brown's *palace* as I came to the office and found him and Miss Hyde[1] reading the morning papers. We talked over the programme for tomorrow, & he told me what precautions he should take to prevent any outburst of applause in the Senate galleries on the rendering of the impeachment verdict. We also talked about getting a good supply of water for our part of the city—now very meagre, but easily to [be] made sufficient.

I believe now there is nothing thought of in Washington but the result of the Impeachment. There are about as many minds as there are men, and bets are being freely made. I have been told, from excellent authority, that the President himself feels certain of an acquittal, and Col. Rives,[2] his private Secy.[,] assured me on Friday that there was not a doubt that the President would be acquitted, & that he thought there would be 24 votes in his favor—nineteen only being necessary to acquit. I do not pretend to have any opinion on the subject; I only know that, having read all the testimony[,] I see no ground for a conviction. . . .

1. Margaret Hyde, the companion of George T. Brown.
2. Lieutenant Colonel Wright Rives.

Thursday, May 14. I think I have never seen people in this city so excited as they have been since last Tuesday. Monday evening it was pretty generally understood that a sufficient number of radical Senators would vote for the acquittal of the President to insure it. Tuesday morning opened with all sorts of rumors, and every person who could obtain a ticket of admission to the gallery of the Senate was on the *qui vive*. "The Court was op'ed with three oyesses"—as McFingal[1] has it—at 11½ o'clock, and Senator Chandler arose and announced the sickness of his colleague, Senator Howard,[2] and moved the adjournment of the court, and it did adjourn till Saturday! From that time to this everybody has been speculating on the result. Those radical Senators who have avowed themselves for acquittal have been abused and berated worse than if they had been known malefactors of the deepest die. The newspapers have denounced them in unmeasured terms of abuse, and they have been attacked on all sides as if they were guilty of some dreadful crime in acting in conformity with the dictates of their own consciences, under the solemnity of the oath they have taken!

I now predict that no vote will be taken on Saturday, & probably not until after the Chicago Convention is over, and not even then, unless the certainty of conviction is apparent! Evil times—oh, evil times—have we fallen upon. . . .

1. An allusion to the poem "McFingal" by John Trumbull.
2. Jacob M. Howard (1805–1871), Republican senator from Michigan, 1862–1871, was strongly opposed to Johnson.

Saturday, May 16. . . . Thursday evening Mrs. French, Mrs. Whitman and Luly, Fannie, Louise and Sarita, Mr. Whitman and I walked out to the Deaf and Dumb Institution, where the Council (formed by a representation from the principal Institutions in the U.S.) was assembled.[1] We witnessed the reading of several essays by the College students—they delivering them in the Deaf & mute alphabet & signs while one of the professors read them. They were admirable productions, and one of them, by a Mr. Logan,[2] would have done credit to an accomplished and thoroughly educated scholar. Gen. Garfield, who was present by invitation, made a most admirable speech of some 15 or 20 minutes long, expressing his pleasure at what he had witnessed, and applauding in terms admirably suited to the occasion the system of Deaf & mute education. Prof. Peet,[3] the President of the Council, also spoke. . . .

Yesterday morning at 9 I had the horse harnessed into the carryall, and Harris drove Mr. T. [Tomlinson][4] & myself out to the Institution, where the day was to be spent by the Council in the reading of papers, discussion, etc. . . . At 2 we sat down to an admirable dinner, after which we went to the Baseball ground and saw the deaf-mutes play, and then I came home, pretty well used up. . . .

This morning, being the day on which the High Court of Impeachment was to resume its session, all Washington was wild with excitement, & *everybody wanted a ticket*—except me—and I had one & did not want it, for I went not. It was generally supposed that no vote would be taken, and I certainly so supposed until 10 o'clock, when I heard that all the sick Senators were to be at the Chamber, & then I changed my mind. The Senate met and a vote was taken on the 11th article—supposed to be the one, if any, on which a conviction would be had—but thanks to *nineteen* Senators, whose names shall hereafter be immortal, the President was acquitted on that article! and the *majority* immediately adjourned the High Court over to the 26th inst.[5] It is a glorious triumph of honesty and patriotism over hatred, malice, and an unholy desire to grasp the reins of government for party aggrandizement, and a hellish grasping after Rule! . . .

1. The widow Rowena Whitman and her children Charles ("Mr. Whitman") and Lucia soon after this moved to East Capitol Street.
2. James H. Logan.
3. Harvey P. Peet (1794–1873), director of the New York Institution for the Instruction of the Deaf and Dumb, 1831–1867.
4. J. Logan Tomlinson became minister of the Chester Congregational Church in 1863.
5. The eleventh and last of the articles of impeachment was called the omnibus article because it summarized the earlier accusations concerning the removal of Secretary of War Edwin Stanton and other charges. The vote was 35 for conviction and 19 for acquittal, one vote short of the two-thirds vote needed to remove the President from office.

Monday, May 18. . . . I have finished the papers—*Intelligencer* and *Chronicle*—and am ready to spend the day. The *Intelligencer* is calm and dignified; the *Chronicle* bitter, but by no means as raving as it was yesterday. . . .

The abuse of that best of men and greatest of living Statesmen, Chief Justice Chase, is wicked & malicious in the extreme, and how Senator Sprague, whose lovely and beloved wife—deservedly beloved by all who know her—is Chief Justice Chase's daughter, can permit such abuse from such a source to pass without censure or interposition, is to me a mystery. Had Sprague voted "not guilty," as many prophecied he would, there would have been no stint to the abuse that would have been heaped upon his head! . . .

I pray most fervently and sincerely that Salmon P. Chase may be the next President of these United States, and I will do all in my power to aid in such a result. . . .

Sunday, May 24. . . . Wednesday; the day fixed for laying the cornerstone of our new Masonic Temple. . . . The procession having been formed in the street, at 3 the G. L. was formed and marched down. At the door President Johnson joined us and took his place in the procession at my right. The procession immediately moved, and after marching about 3 miles— in about 1 1/4 hours—we arrived at the foundation of the Temple, and all the ceremonies incident to the laying of a cornerstone, *in ample form,* were performed, when the Hon. Bro. Bromwell, a member of the House of Representatives and Past Grand Master of Illinois, delivered a most able and interesting address. The ceremonies closed at about 6, and we returned to the Hall. . . . The President walked the entire route and remained with us until the Benediction was pronounced. I used the Washington gavel, owned by Potomac Lodge, and a silver trowel made of Nevada silver and used in laying the cornerstone of the Branch Mint in that State. . . .

Grant and Colfax are nominated as the radical candidates for President and Vice President. I like them both, and esteem them as good men and true. Six months ago I preferred Grant to any living man as a candidate for the Presidency, but I thought his desertion of the President when Stanton was thrust back into office by the Senate was a breach of faith, and from that day I have not thought him a proper man for President, and do not now think he is. Still, unless the old Democrats & recalcitrant Radicals unite on a good and popular candidate, I regard Grant's election as certain. *He* is no politician, and I doubt whether he has his mind firmly made up as to *any policy,* and I now predict that, as likely as not, if elected, he will entirely disappoint those who have placed him in the field, and I should not be at all surprised to find them cursing him before the first year of his Presidential term expires!

As for Colfax, everybody knows exactly where to find him. He is an honest, conscientious man, and a man in whose intention to do exactly right I have the utmost confidence. He is, however, an extreme Radical, and a *politician,* and his party may place in him the utmost confidence. He will do his best for them. . . .

Wednesday, May 27. . . . Yesterday I came home from the office about 2. Mrs. French and Sarita were at the Senate attending the Impeachment. Soon after I came home Sarita came in, beaming with joy, and exclaimed[,] "Major, the President is acquitted, and the High Court has adjourned without day."!! Right glad was I to hear the announcement, and my heart rejoiced, for, as I have seen the trial in print, the President was no more guilty of an impeachable offence than the best patriot living. . . .

Saturday, May 30. It is 1 o'clock P.M. I expected to be at Arlington at this time, to witness the ceremonies at the decorating of the "graves of the Union dead," and with that view left home at a little past 9, with a basket of flowers. I went to Foundry Church and there deposited my flowers. Thence I went to the Treasury and staid till after 11, & then left with the intention of going to Arlington, but remembering some business I had with Mr. Cooke[,] I called at his Banking House, and was detained much longer than I anticipated. Coming out at about 12, I found the weather scorching hot, with very strong indications of a thunder gust during the afternoon, in addition to which I saw the evidence of a great crowd, and so, instead of going to Arlington I came home. Found that my wife, who had most decidedly determined, before I left home, *not to go to Arlington, had gone there!* Had I supposed any persuasion could have induced her to go, I should most certainly have gone. But, when I got home it was too late. . . .

TEN

The Final Years

1868–1870

ndrew Johnson's acquittal and the celebration of the first Decoration Day in both the North and the South, which ended the last chapter, symbolized the beginning of reconciliation. The readmission of seven of the Confederate states a month later pushed the process a step further. As the nation turned away from the painful memories of the Civil War, so did French. At Christmas 1868 he "rejoiced" to learn of Johnson's amnesty proclamation and hoped that finally there would be *"peace* in earnest."[1] When he went back to Gettysburg for another visit in February, it was to give a lecture, not to glory again in the Union victory, and he refused to accompany his sister Helen on a tour of the battlefield.

As he put the war behind him, French succeeded also in pulling himself out of his depression. The appointment of Elizabeth's nephew William A. Richardson as Assistant Secretary of the Treasury gave him an influential ally and led him to remark smugly that the pendulum was "settling down honest & right" for himself.[2] He began to look ahead hopefully for the future of the young people in his family. In April 1869 Henry Flagg French's son William treated the family to a show consisting of panoramas and waxworks, and then left for Chicago to launch a career as art critic and director of the Art Institute of Chicago. When visiting Henry that summer, Benjamin was much impressed by William's brother. "*Dan is a sculptor,*" he wrote, "a natural born sculptor."[3] French was correct. Within four years his nephew was commissioned to sculpt a statue for the centennial of the Battle of Concord, and when the Minute Man statue was unveiled, Daniel Chester French won instant fame.

It was even more gratifying for French to see his own sons starting careers. Frank first became a partner in the Boston banking firm of Foote and French and then moved to New York to join Jay Cooke and Company. And with obvious relief French wrote in September 1869 that Ben had become an engineer on the Portland & Oxford Central Railroad

in Maine. The job had been arranged by the son of French's old friend
F. O. J. Smith.

As the end approached French spent more and more time in his journal reminiscing. After straightening up his workshop one day he spent
two pages describing how he had cleaned up a much messier schoolroom
at North Yarmouth when he was sixteen. Several more pages were devoted to an evening at Horatio King's. As French rose to read a poem
before the large gathering, his host reminded him of an occasion twenty-
six years before when King had encouraged French to go on writing
poetry. More than once he considered writing his reminiscences of Abraham Lincoln, but decided against it because he would have had to include
stories about Mary Lincoln.

He was also conscious of the passing of his generation. Born in 1800,
French was part of the generation that included Stephen A. Douglas,
Abraham Lincoln, Thaddeus Stevens, Franklin Pierce, Robert J. Walker,
Amos Kendall, and George Peabody. Douglas and Lincoln had died dur-
ing the Civil War, but the rest were still living as this chapter begins. In
August 1868 French noted sadly that his friend Stevens had died and
described the procession that escorted his body to the Capitol building.
That same month French saw Pierce for the last time before his death
in 1869. When Peabody, Walker, and Kendall all died in November 1869,
French wrote that the month would be "remembered as having marked
the gathering in of a harvest of great men."[4]

For French there was time for just one more trip to New England to
see Frank and his family. While there he made a short visit to Concord
and a brief stop at Chester. He drove thirty-six miles through the rain
to reach Chester, stayed over long enough to attend church, and then
drove back through the rain to Lowell, where he took the train for Boston. Back in Washington the last months went quickly as he read, worked
around the house, attended parties, gave speeches, and wrote in his
journal. He died on August 12, 1870, just one month after the last southern state, Georgia, had been readmitted to the Union. Both he and the
Union were at peace.

1. Dec. 25, 1868.   3. June 17, 1869.
2. Mar. 20, 1869.   4. Nov. 14, 1869.

Journal

Wednesday, June 3. The clock is striking 8 A.M. I have read the *Intelligencer* and eaten breakfast, and am now ready for business. The examination of the election returns at the City Hall yesterday showed the election of Mr. Bowen by 83 majority.[1] Although I voted for Mr. Given,[2] I am perfectly satisfied to have Mr. Bowen for Mayor, for we have been warm personal friends for years, & he is, in my opinion, as honest, upright and reliable [a] man as lives, and will perform every duty devolving upon him conscientiously. . . .

Brother Wm. H. Faulkner's[3] son was killed by a negro with a razor on Pa. Avenue last evening. It seems to have been a deliberate murder, from all that I have heard today about it. The negroes last night acted as if the Devil had possessed them, and if such doings are to go on with impunity, the white people will soon rise in their majesty and expel the colored race from the city. I am almost convinced that giving them freedom has given them so exalted an estimate of themselves that it will be hard to keep them in their proper places.

As Mr. [James] Buchanan, who died on Monday, is to be buried tomorrow, the Departments are to be closed, by order of the President, in honor of his memory. So I shall not have to go to the office.

1. Sayles J. Bowen, Republican, formerly president of the Freedmen's Aid Society, was supported by blacks, who had received the vote in the District of Columbia in 1867.
2. John T. Given, Democratic businessman.
3. William H. Faulkner, a shirt manufacturer, was master of the Washington Centennial Lodge #14.

Monday, June 15. . . . I ate my lunch—4 slices of Graham bread and butter—at the office, and took some whiskey toddy, *as a medicine*, after I got home. Mr. Rufus Clark[1] (R.L.B.)[,] who is in the same room that I am at the Treasury, introduced me today to his sister, Mrs. Lippincott of Philadelphia—the accomplished lady who writes under the *nom de plume* of "Grace Greenwood."[2] I only saw her for a moment, but she made a most favorable impression upon me. I hope to make her more perfect acquaintance while she remains in Washington.

1. Rufus Clarke, one of eleven children of Thaddeus and Deborah Clarke of New York State.
2. Sara Jane Clarke Lippincott (1823–1904)—pseudonym, Grace Greenwood—author of *Greenwood Leaves* and other works.

Friday, June 19. Yesterday and today have been hot. I called yesterday morning to see my Friend Geo. T. Brown about our wretched supply of aqueduct water. I addressed a letter to Admiral Radford[1] telling him how the constant use of the water at the Navy Yard for mechanical purposes deprived us on Capitol Hill of it, and asking him, if possible, to cause it to be used more sparingly, in which letter Mr. Brown joined. I also wrote a letter to Senator Lot Morrill on the same subject, at Mr. Brown's suggestion. That done I rode to the Treasury and staid till between 3 & 4. Then came home[,] and Sarita told me all about the review which came off near the Lincoln Barracks in honor of the Chinese Embassy, now here with my old friend Hon. Anson Burlingame[2] at their head. She described it as "perfectly splendid." The President and Gen. Grant were there. . . .

1. William Radford (1809–1890), who commanded Union ironclads in the Civil War, was promoted to rear admiral in 1866.
2. Anson Burlingame (1820–1870), Republican congressman from Massachusetts, 1855–1861, was minister to China, 1861–1867. As head of the first Chinese diplomatic mission abroad, 1867–1870, he negotiated the Burlingame Treaty with the United States in 1868.

Friday, June 26. . . . Monday evening I read a notice that the Stockholders of the Seneca quarry Co. were to visit the quarry on Wednesday, and were to go to Great Falls in their own conveyances, & be there at 8 A.M. I determined to go.

Tuesday I was at the office all morning. While at dinner was told that two bolts going through the axeltrees of the carryall were broken—one in each axeltree. They being the main bolts that secured the eliptic springs to the axels, I saw that it would not do to go with it without putting in new bolts. It was after 5 P.M.[,] and I was to leave at 5 A.M. the next morning, and there being no time to send to mechanics, I, with the assistance of William, who was to drive me, and Harris, took off the body, separated the upper bar to which the springs were attached, from the springs, made two new bolts of ¼-inch wire, cut screws on them, fitted nuts to them and put them in, having the vehicle all ready for travel before sunset. . . .

Saturday, June 27. . . . At ½ past 4 [Wednesday], breakfast being ready, I ate it, and at 5 William and I started for Seneca. . . . The morning was glorious, and we pressed along over the fine road made by the U.S. along the line of the aqueduct, at the rate of about 6 miles an hour. We overtook Mr. Dodge[1] & Mr. Hayden[2] (our President and Secy.) within about 3 miles of the Falls. A heavy shower was gathering, & we had not proceeded ½ a mile in their company when it burst upon us, and the rain poured. The lightning flashed and the thunder bellowed. The reverberation among the hills was grand. We arrived at the Falls at 10 m. before 8, having driven at least 18 miles. The rain ceased soon after our arrival, and the sun came out warm and bright. Our party (small to what we expected) had all arrived at 9 o'clock. The *provend* was taken on board the boat, and at 9½ the horses were put to and we moved off for the quarries, 8 miles distance. . . . The boat is a small one, having been a pontoon boat, with a cabin built upon it by Mr. Dodge. It was light and fast, the horses trotting all the way. We had six or eight locks to go through, and were continually meeting and passing other boats. We arrived at the quarries at a little past 11. Things there looked brisk and businesslike. The quarries run nearly a mile along the canal, directly on its banks. They are opened only a short distance, but anyone can see the immense quantity of stone they are capable of producing—millions upon millions of perches.[3] We have a large mill running by water, in which are several gangs of saws and large circular stones for smoothing the stone after it is sawed, and preparations are now making to erect another and larger mill, as we cannot supply the demand upon us. There are now about 80 men at work. I feel satisfied that, with proper management, the Company has fortunes for each of its members at its command. Mr. H. D. Cooke told me he expected, when the thing got into full work, that we should get dividends of 30 perct. on our capital, which would give me an income of $6,000! Well, I would compromise on the assurance of $3,000! . . .

We attended the Theatre last evening with Mr. Geo. T. Brown and Miss Hyde. Occupied one of the stage boxes. The play—if play it could be called—was an exhibition of Leon's Minstrels. About a dozen first appeared as negroes and performed many pieces of music admirably. He of the bones was truly an astonishing performer. I never saw or heard anything like it. We then had dancing, singing, a burlesque court of justice, with speeches, decisions, etc., and to conclude, a burlesque of the Grand Duchess, capitally performed. I never was more amused. The Theatre (National) was crammed. The President & his family, with Secretary Seward, occupied the box opposite ours. I think it was the first time President Johnson has attended the Theatre since he became President. . . .

1. Edward Dodge of Jay Cooke and Company.
2. Charles W. Hayden.

3. A perch is a measure of stonework, usually 1 rod (16.5 feet) by 1 foot by 1½ feet, or 24.75 cubic feet.

Saturday, July 4. . . . I would be awfully patriotic today were I not overcome by the heat! It is really a day for one who cares for his Country to be patriotic, for our good and patriotic President has issued his proclamation of Amnesty today, and all generous hearts must thereat rejoice. Also the Democratic Convention for the nomination of a candidate for the Presidency is this day in session in the City of New York, and, if it does its duty, the results of this day's work there will be almost as glorious as have been those of the 4th of July, 1776!

I have read, in today's *Intelligencer,* Gen. Frank P. Blair's view of the Duty of the Conservative element. It is bold, decided, uncompromising. It has the ring of the old Hero of the Hermitage about it, and if necessity calls for the action it recommends, and such action takes place, let the timid "stand from under," while the brave will rejoice. I am delighted with Gen. Blair's bold & striking views, and, if alive, will be one to aid in carrying them out when the occasion demands it. . . .

Thursday, July 9. . . . I went to the Capitol about 10 and saw Mr. Thaddeus Stevens in his Committee room looking more like a dead than a living man. It is really surprising to see how he holds up, and his cheerfulness of mind and love of fun, in a body so worn down by disease and old age, are wonderful. Speaker Colfax came in to see him while I was there, as good-natured & smiling as ever. I remained only a short time at the Capitol, and then came home and *lazed* round till 5, when I went down and attended a meeting of the Board of Directors of the Firemen's Insurance Co. We made a semi-annual dividend of 15 per cent, drank champagne and ate crackers & cheese and sardines for an hour, when I went to my friend John Purdy's and took tea. At 7 we (Mr. P. & I) went to a meeting of the Directors of the Masonic Hall Association. That being over, we returned to Mr. Purdy's house, and soon after, Mrs. French and Fannie came[,] and we spent the evening, getting home about 10. We passed a very pleasant evening.

Yesterday I went in good season to the office and worked till ½ past 11, when I had business at the Bank. At 12 our Board of Directors had their Quarterly meeting. We declared our usual dividend of 5 per cent & then went to the old Club House and partook of our usual quarterly lunch. Gen. Cushing happening in, we invited him to join us, which he did, and I listened for an hour to his "table talk," with as much interest and delight as I ever listened an hour to anything. He excels any man I ever met in conversation on such an occasion. His ideas are brilliant, original and striking, and he has the faculty of setting "the table in a roar" and keeping it so at his pleasure. Caleb Cushing is a wonderful man! . . .

Saturday, July 11. . . . Arose before 6 this morning & read the *Intelligencer.* The nominations of Horatio Seymour[1] & Francis P. Blair, junior, for President and Vice President seem to be hailed all over the Union with much enthusiasm. I have never known a presidential nomination to be as coldly received by the politicians here as Seymour's, and I have heard more than one Conservative predict the certain election of Grant in consequence of it; but no one can yet tell what the result is to be. Time alone can unravel *that* future. I think the conservative party are ready to unite in order to put down the Radicals, & if they are, and do so, Seymour and Blair will be elected. If there should be any split, they will not. As for me, being utterly disgusted at the infamous rule of Radicalism, I shall do all that one humble individual can to elect Seymour & Blair, although I neither ask nor expect any favors from them, or any party in power. My *political life* is ended!

1. Horatio Seymour (1810–1886) had been Democratic governor of New York, 1853–1855 and 1863–1865.

Wednesday, July 22. . . . On Saturday evening last at 9 o'clock died very suddenly of apoplexy Emanuel Leutze[1] (pronounced Litzie)[,] the artist, who painted the picture at the head of the marble staircase on the west side of the Hall of Representatives in the Capitol[,] *Westward the Star of Empire Takes Its Way.* I was well acquainted with Leutze. He was a genial, kindhearted gentleman, generous to a fault, and exceedingly companionable. It is only a few days since I met him near Willard's, and he invited me to go into Witzleben's with him and look at a portrait he had just finished of General Sutter.[2] He pressed me to call at his studio, which I promised soon to do. On Monday morning I was exceedingly surprised to see an account of his death in the *Intelligencer,* and at 7 o'clock in the evening of Monday I attended his funeral at Glenwood and performed the Masonic burial service over his remains. So we go, and but for the assurance of the soul's immortality, what would life be? The merest shadow of a shade! . . .

1. Emanuel Leutze (1816–1868) studied painting in Europe before returning to the United States in 1859, where he continued his career in historical painting. Perhaps his most famous work is *Washington Crossing the Delaware,* in the Metropolitan Museum of Art, New York.

2. John A. Sutter (1803–1880), on whose California estate gold was discovered in 1848. In 1871, Arthur de Witzleben was living at 38 Pennsylvania Ave.

Saturday, July 25. . . . Bridget Hannan, our servant maid, is sick with cholera morbus, and Mrs. French & Fannie have done all the housework for two days. My negro man, Harris, got into a fight yesterday about his lumber, which the rain was floating away, and which he was attempting to recover, in which he knocked a white man, by name Edward Edwards, down and hurt him considerably, for which he was arrested this morning, examined before Justice Lynch, who bound him over to answer, and I became his bondsman.[1] I knew nothing of the fight until I was sent for between 10 & 11 at the Treasury Dept. to give bonds, doing which, in consequence of the absence of the Magistrate, took till after 2 o'clock. So I did not return to my office, but staid at home and read. Harris insists that the man picked up a stone and struck him in the breast with it before he struck, and that all he did was in self defence; and having known Harris for a year or two, and knowing him to be a peaceable, truthful, honest man, I believe him, although the principal part of the evidence was the other way. It is a fact, however, not to be disguised, that the absurd legislation of Congress in regard to the negroes in this District has so inflated their consequence that it is hard to get along with them, and they will have to learn by bitter experience that they are *no better* than white people! I have seen, for months past, that Harris, though perfectly respectful and obedient, has, as they say of horses, "felt his oats." He is almost as ignorant as a horse anyway.

I am invited by my old friend Hon. Anson Burlingame and his Chinese Associates . . . (Chi-Kang) and . . . (Sun Chia-Ku) to visit the Embassy at 9 this evening at the Metropolitan and intend to go and see their High Mightinesses.[2]

How little occurrences trouble us! Bridget's sickness, Harris's fight, and not finding the cow last evening! (we found her this morning) have been a worry to me ever since sunset last evening, and have made my head ache!

1. Edward Edwards, a carpenter, lived at 373 West 15th St. James Lynch was a police magistrate.
2. In typical fashion the Ch'ing (Manchu) government of China sent one Manchu, Chih-kang, and one Chinese, Sun Chia-ku, both officials of the second rank, as Burlingame's associates. Someone had drawn Chinese characters in the spaces before each name.

Sunday, July 26. I went to see Mr. Burlingame and his Chinese companions, forming the Embassy. I arrived early, sacrificing gentility to curiosity, knowing by old experience that the *regulars,* who think it a degradation to be less than an hour behind the appointed time, would not *envelop* the Embassy till 10. The hour fixed was 9, & I was there about ¼ past. Only a few visitors had arrived. I had not seen Mr. Burlingame for five or six years—not since he left for China. He looked as young and handsome as ever, and received me with great cordiality & introduced me to his fine-looking wife, to Chih-kang and Sun Chia-ku, with others of the Celestials, and to Mr. Brown,[1] also of the Embassy. I presented Mrs. Burlingame with a little bouquet, which I cut in our garden just before leaving, & which she honored me by holding in her hand all though the reception. There were some ten or fifteen Chinese present, all dressed in their long, tight-fitting gowns, with head coverings cone-shaped—like old-fashioned dish-covers, surmounted with round knobs of glass or metal, from which fell, all around the hat, rich red plumes. There were, of the Embassy proper, three or four. The others, as Mr. Brown explained to me, are students, some of whom speak English perfectly, some French, some Russian, and, I believe[,] other living languages. They all appeared happy, and looked pleased, and shook hands with a cordiality that bespoke a hearty welcome to all comers. Mr. Burlingame appeared perfectly at home and at his ease, and seemed to strive to make all who came welcome. I was particularly pleased with Mr. Brown, with whom I had considerable conversation.

By ten the large parlors of the hotel were crowded with guests—the very *elite* of the City and the Country, and all seemed delighted. I was surprised to find how many I knew personally among the crowd. . . .

The citizens were handsomely represented, and there were ladies in abundance, in superb costumes. The foreign legations were there in full force, of whom I recognized Barons Stoeckl[2] and Gerolt. Two persons I met there with more pleasure than I can well express—one was my venerable friend of more than 20 years, Hon. Moses H. Grinnell[3] of New York. He is on a visit to the city, and our meeting was most cordial and pleasant. The other was my young friend Robert Lincoln (son of President Lincoln)[,] who also greeted me as if he were heartily glad to see me.

The press was represented largely. I saw my always friends Ben Perley Poore and L. A. Gobright. Snow[4] of the *Intelligencer* was there, but the immaculate Forney was nowhere to be seen! The tall good-looking editor of the *Republican*, whose name is out of my mind now, was there. (Peck)[5] . . .

1. J. McLeavy Brown was at the time acting Chinese secretary of the British legation in China.
2. Baron Edouard de Stoeckl, Russian minister, had recently completed the sale of Alaska to the United States.

3. Moses H. Grinnell (1803–1877), formerly Whig congressman from New York, 1839—1841, may have been in Washington seeking a political position, because he was appointed collector for the port of New York in 1869.

4. Chauncey H. Snow and John F. Coyle took over the *Intelligencer* after the death of W. W. Seaton in 1865. Publication ceased in 1869.

5. Benjamin D. Peck.

Sunday, August 2. I went down and attended Harris's trial, and, although the witnesses against him swore pretty hard, those in his favor preponderated with the jury and they acquitted him. The case was, to my mind, a perfectly clear one in his favor. I was almost sick all the morning and the heat of the Courtroom overcame me so much that I could hardly keep up, and as soon as I got home, between 12 & 1, I went to bed and laid most of the afternoon. I have felt very well today, have written a long letter to Henry and one to Reverdy Johnson,[1] who I intended to go to Baltimore and see off yesterday, had not my presence in court as a witness been necessary. Mr. Johnson is a man whom I hold in the very highest respect & esteem, and I very much wanted to aid what little I could in paying honor to him as he left, but, as I could not, I wrote my good wishes to England. He is a true patriot, a perfect gentleman, and a good man, besides being a sterling statesman. . . .

1. Reverdy Johnson (1796–1876), Democratic senator from Maryland, 1863–1868, resigned July 10, 1868, to become U.S. minister to England (1868–1869).

Wednesday, August 12. I have just read, in the *Intelligencer,* a notice of the death of Hon. Thaddeus Stevens. He died at his residence in this City, No. 279 North B street, Capitol Hill, at midnight last night. With all his political peculiarities, he was a generous, noblehearted man. He was bold and outspoken as to his beliefs, and the world always knew exactly where to find him. He was my warm personal friend, staid firmly by me in the political raid that legislated me out of office. Take him all in all, he was a good man. . . .

Milton, Mass., Saturday, August 15. . . . Thursday morning I went to the office where I remained till noon. As I passed through the Capitol grounds on my return home, I saw the remains of Thaddeus Stevens borne to the Capitol, escorted by a company of colored Zouaves. The procession was headed by Gen. Eakin[1] and Sergt. at arms Brown. There was a very small attendance. They entered the ground on the railroad track south, moved "slowly and sadly" to opposite the main entrance to the rotunda, there "filed left," and moved into the Capitol. It was then my intention to return and look once more on that old familiar face, but there were preparations to be made that I had not thought of, for our journey, which occupied every moment of my time till the starting hour came, and I saw my good old friend no more. . . .

At a little past 6 P.M. Thursday a gathering was seen at the front of our home consisting of the six travellers, and a goodly number of good-byers. . . . I had secured my berth in the sleeping car, so I took the Baltimore car with the ladies and rode with them till we arrived there and then bade them all good-by and sought my sleeping berth. I went to bed about 9 and had a very tolerable night's rest. We arrived in New York about ½ past 5, and at Doct. Wells's at 6. The Dr., Mary, and Tom & Henry comprised the family. Charley Soule[2] had recently arrived from China, and was there as a visitor. After breakfast Charles Russell (who had called to see me)[,] Tom and I went over to New York[,] and I took a car and went up to Pier No. 40, where the steamer *Bristol* lay, and paid for my stateroom ($4.00) and secured a berth for Bridget. Then I went to Mr. Thomas's, No. 205 West 11th street[,] and found Ben and Abbie. Remained there an hour, when, accompanied by Ben, I walked to Stewart's "uptown" store, and saw Capt. Thomas and from thence, we went to Doct. Wells's, by way of Fulton Ferry.[3] We dined at the Doctor's[,] and at 3 Bridget and I went to New York, and to the steamer. At 5 we left for Boston. . . .

1. Constantin Eakin commanded a brigade of Pennsylvania volunteers in the Civil War.
2. Son of Charles Soule.
3. Allen E. Thomas, a passenger agent, and John J. Thomas, a broker, lived on West 11th St. They were relations of Ben's wife, Abbie.

Sunday, August 16. I wrote up my journal as above yesterday. On my arrival here I found Ellen and little Amos ready to welcome us—Bess was with us, having ridden in with her father. Frank resides very pleasantly here in Milton in a hired house, but is preparing to build one of his own near here. I examined his plans yesterday, which, if carried out, will give him an elegant and comfortable residence here in one of the most delightful spots on the face of the globe. . . .

Monday, August 17. . . . After dinner, Frank, Ellen, Bridget, the children and I rode in a carryall down to Hough's neck. The tide was out, and it was dead low water, and about as unpromising of seaside enjoyment as anything I ever saw, so, without getting out of the carriage, we turned about and rode towards home. At another place, looking a little more promising for ducks and wading children, we all alighted and walked down to the water, and finding that there were plenty of clams, each grown person, armed with as flat and sharp a stone as could be found, commenced digging, and the fruits of our labor for perhaps ½ an hour were about a peck of as fine, though rather small, clams, as I ever desire to see. We emptied the lunch basket (a large one) and nearly filled it with clams, and on our return, we boiled them and had a most satisfactory clam supper. They were really delicious—better than oysters! Our ride was very pleasant. We passed the old Adams mansion in Quincy, about which cluster a thousand memories of the past, awakening in the mind of the patriot reflections as to what this Nation *was* and what it *is*, more brain engrossing than can be awakened by almost any other place in the Union. . . .

Friday, August 21. The doings of yesterday afternoon are worthy of a special record. Frank arrived with two one-horse carriages, at a few minutes after ½ past 1, and dinner was ready in a jiffey. We sat down, and, while eating it[,] the rain began to pour. It slacked some in say 10 or 15 minutes after we had finished dinner, and being bent on clams & bathing, & there being a tolerable prospect of its clearing off, we buttoned down all the curtains and stowed ourselves, with our baskets, blankets, waterproofs, old clo' for bathing, spades for digging, etc. The three girls, Ann, Julia, and Bridget occupied one carriage, Frank, Ellen, Bess, Amos, & myself the other, and so, in high glee, we emerged from the umbrageous surroundings of this beautiful place into the highway and shot off toward Quincy, the rain falling pretty briskly. . . .

Just as we arrived opposite a long and well-appointed barn, the doors of which stood invitingly open, with a couple of men standing in them, the storm burst upon us, and, without saying "by your leave," into the barn floor we drove. We were received, however, with a cordial welcome, and expressed our thanks accordingly.

That barn was one of two belonging to John Quincy Adams, the son of Charles Francis Adams, and the grandson of my old and honored friend John Quincy Adams, "the old man eloquent," who, as a scholar and statesman, surpassed any man this country has ever produced. It was, to me, worth a journey from Washington to see—for I had never seen anything like it. It was, I should judge, at least a hundred feet long. The lower part of the entire west side was devoted to stanchions for cows, wherein were confined the necks of 34 as fine cows as one could desire to look upon, and, at the head of them a patriarchal-looking bull. One feature of the economy of keeping stock, which I never saw or heard of before, struck me with special favor. There was a trough for water running in front of the entire array, standing at such a height from the floor as not to interfere with convenient feeding, and from which the animals could drink at pleasure. This trough was kept filled with water by an iron pump at the upper end. Opposite the cow stalls, at the upper end of the barn, were horse stalls, filled with horses. I did not particularly notice the number. The entire barn not occupied by the animals was crammed with hay, and in a small enclosure near it were a number of immense stacks of hay. The man in charge told me there was another barn of the same size filled in the same way. The farm is a very large one with a handsome dwelling house upon it, and, as the man told me, was given to the present owner by his grandfather, whose name he bears.

The rain poured in torrents, as we remained in that barn. We all got out of the carriages & the grown people walked and looked, while the children ran and romped from one end of the floor to the other. We staid about an hour, and there being a lull in the rain, but no prospect of clearing off, we again put our faces toward the beach. The road was in some places nearly knee deep with water, and again the deluge commenced, but we persevered, and actually went to the beach, where we found numerous carriages, a barn full of horses, every tent occupied, and no chance either to bathe or dig clams! So we turned about and faced the storm toward home. It rained steadily all the way. . . .

Chester, Sunday, August 23. At ½ past 7 yesterday morning George Keyes took me to the Depot in Concord at the fastest kind of a trot, with his mare of the span, and at 8 the Judge and I took the Express train for Boston. . . . At 12 noon we took the cars for Derry, where we arrived at 2 P.M. and where the compactest kind of a driver crammed *fourteen* living *immortals* and one *mortal,* in the form of a puppy, into a stagecoach capable of carrying just *nine* comfortably! Of course, to use Sairy Gamp's[1] favorite word, we were "squeeged" in. The Judge and I had, besides our valises, a half-bushel basket containing groceries, a cantelope, half a peck of tomatoes and two lobsters, weighing severally 8 & 3½ pounds, filling it (the basket) heaping full, also a gallon demijohn, full of—something, perhaps vinegar, *more* perhaps not, at all events a liquid which we desired to have handled with especial care. The basket I had to endure between my knees, and the wh—tut-tut-tut—I mean the demijohn, I had to have *in my eye* for its especial safety! All the grownup ones had valises, and one man had a gun. There were on the rack behind[,] five or six trunks and two large bags of oats. And all this load was hauled by two, not very large horses. . . .

We found Chester very much as it was 20 years ago, only the trees have the natural growth of that time, a few houses have been built, and a few removed. Still it *is* Chester—good old Chester—and there are few towns in these United States that can show such a half a mile of street, shaded on either side by noble trees. Elms, maples, ashes, and I think other varieties of forest trees, green and luxuriant, adorn the wayside over which my ancestors moved in all the glare of the summer sun! For the most of that grand avenue of trees, Chester is indebted to my brother, Judge French, who in his earliest manhood planted many of them with his own hands.

We found Mother and Helen well and glad to see us; and in about ½ an hour they had a dinner on the table fit for a king to eat. . . . At 9¼ I went to bed, and slept in the same chamber, and the same place in the chamber, where I remember to have slept with my father at least sixty-four years ago! The world has changed considerable since then, and this Mansion, then *new,* is now *old*! . . .

1. Sairey Gamp, an old nurse in Dickens's *Martin Chuzzlewitt.*

Concord, Mass., Wednesday, August 26. The Judge and I left Chester at 7½ Monday morning. Luther Fitz[1] of Chester took us to Raymond Depot, from which at 9 A.M. we took the cars to New Market. We remained at New Market till ¼ to 12—one hour over the regular schedule time, consequent on either accidents or *camp meetings,* we could not find out exactly which. We arrived in Exeter at 12 noon. . . .

. . . At ¼ past 3 we started in a buggy, with a boy to drive us, for Hampton Beach [where Frank joined them].[2] . . . [Tuesday morning] the Judge [left] at 9. I hired a horse and buggy[,] and Frank and I rode over to Little Boar's Head and made a call on Ex-President Pierce at his house there. We found him in bed suffering with neuralgia in his left shoulder and arm. As soon as it was made known to him that we were there, he sent for us to come to his chamber, which we did, and were most kindly & cordially welcomed. I have not seen him before since he left Washington, and was surprised to see how well he bears his age. He does not look a day older than when he left the Presidential chair. After a most pleasant ½ hour spent with him, we walked over to where he told us Senator Grimes was staying, & had a very pleasant interview with him, finding him far batter than I ever expected to see him when he last left Washington.

From Little Boar's Head we rode up to Hampton Depot & took the first train that came along for Boston, where we arrived at ¼ before 2, and I took the ¼ past 2 train for this place, arriving here (at the Browns' & Keyes' mansion, "River Cottage," the most homelike place except my own home, to me, on earth) at ½ past 3, hungry, dirty, tired, *used up.* I washed, changed my clothes, and Sister Ann gave me some dinner, and I was a new man! . . .

1. Luther Fitz, farmer and blacksmith, was the youngest brother of French's friend Benjamin Fitz.
2. Frank had come up from Boston.

Milton, Mass., Saturday, September 5. . . . Since I left Washington another of my faithful employees, who was with me through all my service as Commissioner, and had been in the office between 20 & 30 years when he died, has passed away. Poor old faithful Hannibal Graham has gone to his long home. Colored though his skin was, he had as white and pure a heart and as keen an intellect as many and many a man who boasts his Caucasian descent. He was messenger and laborer in the office and never shirked a duty or committed a wrong to my knowledge. I respected him as highly as any man I ever had under me, and the Office, without "the Captain" and "Hannibal," will seem to me lonely and sad, should I ever again enter it! . . .

Concord, Mass., Thursday, September 24. Since I last wrote in this journal I have visited St. Louis, Mo., travelling, in going and returning, nearly 3,000 miles. I got back here at 12 o'clock noon today, finding my wife and all the dear ones well. I am writing this at George Keyes's library table, and shall content myself with this memorandum of my return, and begin to write up a history of my journey tomorrow.

Friday, September 25. At ½ past 7 last evening, Mary Ellen, Mary Keyes, Sarita, Bessie, Thomas Wells, and I, all in one small carriage, drawn by "Calico" (that's the old mare)[,] I being driver, rode down to Judge French's, where about as gay a family party, with two Bartletts[1] thrown in, were assembled, as turns up in a September evening. Will had arranged some of his peculiar entertainments—panoramas, tableaux, shadows, etc., and we were all entertained to our hearts' content for two hours, in which there was more laughing and applause than I ever witnessed at a regular theatre for the same length of time; after which we partook of just about the best watermelon I ever tasted, and between 10 & 11 we rode home in the rain, and I, who was driver, got my new coat pretty well soaked about the sleeves and breast. Nothing but a visit to my Brother & the capital entertainment could possibly have kept me awake so late, after three days' and nights' consecutive journeying from St. Louis to this place. . . .

1. Lizzie Bartlett and probably her father, Josiah Bartlett II.

Saturday, September 26. . . . *A Chapter on Trunks.*

I believe that all the trunk makers in the United States are in league with all the porters and baggage men. I believe that no trunk that can be made will last through 6,000 miles of travelling without being used pretty much up. Our daddies and mamies used to travel all their lives— even to three score years and ten—with one or two, not very strong, wooden trunks, to each family, which descended generation after generation. Now, the best made sole-leather trunk, for which one pays 40 to 50 dollars, returns from its first journey of any considerable length— lock broken, straps torn off, handles gone, and perhaps other serious injuries. Damages repaired, you start again, and probably, at the end of your first stage, you find your duds protruding from a hole in one corner, where the *careful* baggage man has managed to stave a hole! . . .

Now all this staving and ruining of trunks is by the most careless and rough handling possible. I have seen a mountain of trunks on a depot platform, with three or four stout men tossing them, end over end, from six to ten feet—"lickity split and hellity clue," as an individual of my acquaintance used to express it somewhat graphically and originally— and I have seen, more than once, a trunk burst open by the operation, and all the domestic paraphernalia of a travelling lady exposed to the gaze of a gaping, laughing crowd, as if it were the best joke that could possibly happen! This careless, unpardonable, indecent, ruinous, rascally, damnable, smashing up, *on purpose,* of trunks, ought, in some way, to be stopped. . . .

5 *P.M.* Now for the history.

On Thursday, Sept. 10th, at 7¼ A.M. I took the cars at the Concord Depot for New York, *via* Worcester. . . . The next day, *Friday,* was one of the hottest days of all the hot summer. Thermometer about 90. I went first to Simon's, 30 Catharine Street, & procured my *Excursion* tickets for St. Louis & back to N.Y. . . . At 5¼ the train left the J.C. [Jersey City] Depot and we were on our way to St. Louis. The first night in the cars was not particularly pleasant, as among our party there were, as usual, a few who did not wish to sleep themselves, nor would they allow any sleep to others. They were full of fun and *slightly* noisy. However, without accident or delay we duly arrived at Pittsburgh on Saturday and at St. Louis at about 2 o'clock on Sunday [September 13]. . . .

As all our proceedings are to be published it would be folly in me to attempt to write an account of them here. It is sufficient for me to say that, from Tuesday to Saturday night, we were all engaged either in Masonic duties, attending banquets, excursions, etc. . . .

Sunday morning [September 20] we of Bro. Collins's[1] household all rested. After dinner, our good & kind Brother took Mrs. Collins, Mr. Buist[2] & myself in his carriage out to Henry Shaw's[3] Garden, one of the most elegant and extensive gardens I ever saw, extending over 600 acres of ground, and on which is cultivated all the most valuable and rare plants of the world. Hothouses, Greenhouses, pagodas, labyrinths, & all the garden appliances to make a garden interesting are liberally scattered over the grounds. An elegant dwelling house ornaments a portion of it, into which we were invited by the owner, who accompanied us over as much of the premises as our time would permit us to see. Among other things, Mr. Shaw has erected a Botanical Museum, being a large and elegant building with cases arranged for such curiosities as he can collect, and an Agricultural and Horticultural Library. He has just commenced making his collections. It seems to me as if a million of money must have been expended on that garden as it now is. It puts entirely in the shade all other gardens, both *public* and private, that I have ever seen. I left, feeling very grateful to the *Bachelor* owner[,] whose good taste was exhibited in everything but his failure to select a wife to enjoy with him all the beauties of his delightful residence. Uncle Sam at Washington ought to cast his eyes over his own domain in that National City and blush and be ashamed of the miserable parsimony that prevents him from coming within cannon shot of rivalling this munificent private gentleman of St. Louis! . . .

Monday morning Mr. Collins, Mr. Buist and I walked down to Market & thence to Mr. Collins's business place. . . .

I returned to Mr. Collins's before noon, and Mr. Collins & Mr. Buist came soon after & we dined luxuriously about ½ past 12. At 1:20 the omnibus came for us, & bidding our dear good hostess good-by, Mr. Buist and I, accompanied by Mr. Collins, rode to the Planter's Hotel, where we shook our excellent & beloved Bro. by the hand and bade him farewell. We were then whirled down on board the ferry boat, crossed the river, and took the cars, and at about ½ past 2 left glorious St. Louis behind us, to live, as it always will, indissolubly connected in my mind with kindness and unbounded hospitality!

. . . We arrived at Pittsburgh about 4 [P.M. Tuesday, September 22], dined or supped—they call it "supper"—and then deposited ourselves in our sleeping cars, and, something after 5, were off for New York, via,

Harrisburg, etc. . . . It was exactly 3 minutes past 11 [Wednesday, A.M.] when we left Easton, and at 20 minutes after 1 [P.M.] we were in the depot at J. City—75 miles. . . .

. . . Arrived in Boston at 6½ [Thursday, September 24], took breakfast at Parker's, tried to find some of my relatives. None in the city. They arrived late. At 11 I took the train for this place, and . . . arrived here at 12 noon.

And so ends the history of my trip to St. Louis & back.

1. Martin Collins (b. 1826), a prominent Mason, was the St. Louis register of water rates.
2. James M. Buist, florist, 807 Broadway, New York City.
3. Henry Shaw (1800–1889) was a successful merchant who established a garden in St. Louis for the study of plants.

Dorchester, Mass., Tuesday, September 29. The hour is ½ past 12 P.M. The place is Frank's house, corner of Ashmont and Adams Streets. . . . At ¼ before 8 A.M. yesterday morning we left "Hospitality's Home" in Concord, took the 8 o'clock express train and were in Boston at ½ past 8. . . . Ellen & Mary Ellen met me with a carriage & brought me here. . . .

Washington, Friday, October 2. It is ¼ past 8 A.M. We arrived *home*— Mrs. French, Sarita & I—at 5 last evening. Our journey on was rather quiet and pleasant. . . .

Sunday, November 8. . . . Tuesday came the Presidential election, and perhaps as quiet an election as was ever held. Grant and Colfax were elected, as I was satisfied they would be from the start; although in consequence of the infernal treatment I underwent from the last Radical Congress[,] I confess I desired the defeat of the party in power. I took no active part in the election, and like General Grant personally very much indeed, and do not doubt that he will make a good President. If he will show a little of his well established firmness in keeping his radical partizans within reasonable bounds, the Country will be safe. In my very soul I wish him success. I ask no political favors from him or anybody else. My political life is over. . . .

Tuesday, November 10. . . . Last evening attended the annual meeting of the Grand Chapter of the Dist. of Columbia and was, most unexpectedly, and without the least intimation, elected Grand H. Priest. I was taken *all aback,* and hardly knew whether to accept or decline, but, at the earnest solicitation of those about me, I concluded to accept for the year, and did so. . . .

Friday, November 27. . . . Mrs. French came home about dark, and after reading a capital story to her—"A stroke of business"—from *Harper,* we started out to spend the evening *somewhere.* First we went to Doct. Brodhead's, Doct. and wife *out*—they always are. Then we went to Mr. Clarke's, *only to make a call.* Mrs. Lippincott (Grace Greenwood)[,] Mr. Clarke's sister, is there, and we were so pleasantly entertained that our call lasted till ½ past 9. We got home a little before 10 and went to bed. Now breakfast is ready. And *now* it is eaten. . . .

Friday, December 25. Christmas day does not seem to be *much.* We had a grand Christmas eve here last evening. Our parlor was the general rendezvous for the family Christmas presents, and it was literally filled. I never saw so many together. Edmund's family, the Russells, Whitmans and Doct. Ford were all present—& all had presents. Mine were abundant—a pair of pictures from M.E. & Sarita; a handsome match-safe[1] from Edmund; a beautiful hemstitched handkerchief from Fanny; a kind of a protuberant soldier, with a belly full of confectionery from Louise; a set of plated nut pickers from Harry; a deer from Ill. Bro.[2] Collins of St. Louis; *five gallons of whiskey from Mr. Forsyth*; a pincushion from Sister Blandina. I believe this is all. We had quite a parlor full of people, and all were merry. This day, up to this time, 3 P.M., has been about as dull a day need to be. Up to 11 A.M. I was engaged in various things, such as seeing that the fires were in order, putting away my whiskey in demijohns, sawing open a 100 lb. keg of butter, mending a Masonic jewel & fussing about generally. . . .

I rejoiced to read in the papers of this morning the President's Amnesty Proclamation. Although it pardons Jeff Davis, who ought to be hung, still I am glad it has been issued! I hope now we shall have *peace* in earnest.

1. A matchbox.
2. Illustrious Brother (Masonic term).

Saturday, January 16. I have about concluded that I *will* make my journal *a diary*, even if I only write a single line daily.

Last evening I read Tennyson's Idyl "Elaine" aloud to Helen and Mary Ellen. I thought I had read all Tennyson's *Idyls of the King*, but if I ever did read "Elaine" before I had entirely forgotten it.[1] It is a beautiful little myth, beautifully told. . . .

1. Alfred, Lord Tennyson (1809–1892), had been appointed poet laureate in 1850. He first published *Idylls of the King* in 1859 and added to it in 1869, 1872, and 1885.

Monday, January 18. I arose at 7 A.M. this day. As soon as breakfast was eaten went to the office and worked steadily, neither eating nor drinking, till 4¼ P.M. Then came home and dined, and here I am. We heard this morning, through the newspapers, that the Bank of Commerce of Havana had suspended. This being "Fesser's[1] Bank," in which all Sarita has is invested, the information comes upon us somewhat harshly, and appears to have considerable effect upon Sarita. I hope she has been protected, as she should have been if the Fessers are the honorable gentlemen they have always been represented to be. Her funds have always been in their hands, & she has ever had such full confidence in their honor and generosity that she would not listen for a moment to any transfer of her funds. But she need not worry much, as she will always have a home and all its happinesses with me as long as I have one of my own. . . .

1. Sarita's mother had left Sarita money, which was in the care of Edward Fesser of New York and his brother in Havana.

Thursday, February 11. It is 7 P.M. Gen. Albert Pike invited me to attend some kind of a gander party at Cornelius Wendell's[1] this evening, but a severe toothache and a cold prevent. The New England Society, also, have a "Reunion," and I cannot be there. So I shall stay at home.

I spent all the morning at the Government Printing office, & started them correctly in making up the first form of the Digest. Then I came home and went to work covering my old rocking chair. Did all I could on that, and then grunted an hour with toothache. Put some laudanum on it and it is better.

I read in the morning papers an account of the disgusting proceedings in the Convention of the Senate and House yesterday, when met to witness the counting of the votes for President and Vice President. Wade raised himself very much in my estimation by the firm and manly course he pursued, and Colfax's dignified and noble bearing and manner will live in history forever.[2] He is [as] noble [a] gentleman as ever lived, and I always loved & honored him.

Oh how different such things are conducted now from what they formerly were.

I witnessed the counting of the votes for nearly 20 years, and never witnessed such a scene as occurred yesterday.

This has been a delightful day, and I begin to think we shall have no more winter.

1. Cornelius Wendell lived at 423 F St. North.

2. After a joint session of Congress passed a resolution avoiding the question of whether the electoral votes of Georgia should be counted (an academic question because Grant had won the election by a wide margin), the Senate voted to accept the votes and the House concurred. President pro tempore Benjamin F. Wade of the Senate presided with dignity over the tumultuous debates in the joint session.

Friday, February 12. Met "old Ben Wade" on the pavement near our house this morning, and congratulated him on the firm stand he took while presiding over the Convention of the two Houses on Wednesday. Met Gen. Frémont on the sidewalk between 1st and 2d Streets W. almost at the place where I used to meet him 34 or 35 years ago when he was [a] spruce young Lieutenant and had just married Jessie Benton, and the marriage was the theme of Washington gossip. I well remember that a lady told me that Jessie pointed out to her the very spot where she stood when the marriage ceremony was performed. The Gen. did not recognize me today, although we used to be quite well acquainted.

He has been, in my opinion, the most overestimated man that ever this country produced. . . .

Wednesday, February 17. I went to Dentist Howland[1] yestermorning, to have a tooth extracted. I was kept waiting an hour, and then attempted to take "laughing gas," which came so near suffocating me, before I lost any consciousness, that I was forced to desist, and then found myself in such a nervous condition that I could not have the tooth out. So there it remains! Was at the office and hard at work all day. Am going to Gettysburg today, and as I am to leave at 9½ must get ready. . . .

1. Edwin P. Howland, 27 4½ St.

Saturday, February 20. I went to Gettysburg last Wednesday. My sister Helen accompanied me. We arrived at Mr. Wills's at about ½ past 4 and were received and entertained in the most hospitable manner. Mr. Wills met us at the cars. The Committee of students—Mr. Brinkerhoff[1] and Mr. List[2]—called on me in the evening and invited us to visit the College the next morning, which we did[,] accompanied by Mr. Wills, and were most kindly shown all there was to see—such as the Society Halls, the

Libraries and the Museum. We were then introduced to Doct. Valentine,[3] the President of the College; and in coming away we met Prof. Stoever[4] (pronounced Staver) whom I well knew, having formed his acquaintance at Gettysburg several years ago. We returned to Mr. Wills's and dined sumptuously, and at ½ past 1, the Committee sent a carriage to take Helen over the battleground. She went accompanied by Mr. & Mrs. Wills, and they returned about 4. At ½ past 4 Mr. Wills and I went to the Depot, and awaited the arrival of the cars, in which came my brother (Judge French) and Doct. Ford.

At 7¼ we all went to "Agricultural Hall" where I delivered my lecture on "Lecturers and Language" to an audience of four or five hundred. They seemed to receive it well, and applauded considerable, and after I had concluded, the President, Professors, and others came upon the stage and complimented and thanked me. I occupied an hour and six minutes in the delivery. We were all at home at a little past 9, and passed two or three very pleasant hours before retiring.

On rising yesterday morning our eyes were saluted with a fierce snow-storm, and the ground was white. Fortunately, about 9 A.M. the weather cleared up and the Judge, Doct. Ford and Helen went off to visit the Battleground, armed with a hatchet to cut out bullets from the trees. I, having visited all the interesting points several times, did not care to accompany them. At a little past 12 they returned with the trophies of battle, consisting of 4 minnie balls cut from trees, the bone of a man's heel, dug up by Doct. Ford & *Helen*! and a piece of other bone from the same *corpus,* bits of leather, etc., all to be kept, I suppose, as memorials of the greatest battle ever fought in America—and perhaps on earth. . . .

1. John J. Brinckerhoff (1848–1919), valedictorian for the class of 1869 of Pennsylvania College (now Gettysburg College).
2. William A. List (1849–1908), valedictorian for the class of 1870, was later a banker in Wheeling, W.Va.
3. Milton Valentine (1825–1906) was president of Pennsylvania College, 1868–1884.
4. Martin Luther Stoever (1820–1870), professor of history and Latin at Pennsylvania College and editor of the *Evangelical Review,* 1857–1870.

Thursday, February 25. . . . On my way home called at Miss Vinnie Ream's[1] studio in the Capitol and saw her statue of Lincoln. The likeness is wonderfully perfect, and the position the exact one I have seen Mr. Lincoln in many and many a time. I was delighted at her complete success. I only remained a few minutes & then came home. Found Carrie Reed here, also Mamie and Jamie,[2] Ned's children. They all dined with us. This evening five gentlemen have called on business, and have just gone. Sarita has a Reading Society in the parlor. Mrs. French has gone somewhere, and Fannie has just come in and it is my duty to entertain her, so I will close up.

1. Vinnie Ream (1847–1914) studied under Clark Mills, and at the age of eighteen was the first woman to receive a Congressional commission for a statue in the Capitol Rotunda. When French saw her statue of Lincoln, it was not completed; it was unveiled in January 1871.
2. James French (b. 1865).

Monday, March 1. . . . At ½ past 8 I went to Willard's and saw Senator Henderson,[1] who has just returned from Havana, about the Bank of Commerce there, in which Sarita's capital is invested, and was rejoiced to learn that the Bank stood well. Thence I went to the office, read proof till between 1 & 2, and then walked to the Govt. Printing Office & attended to some business there, and then came home. . . .

1. John B. Henderson (1826–1913), Democratic senator from Missouri, 1862–1869.

Wednesday, March 3. . . . Yesterday, after working at the office till near 1 P.M.[,] I went down to the National Theatre to witness the ceremonies attending the graduation of the Medical class of Georgetown College. Being honored with a seat on the stage, I had an excellent opportunity to see and hear everything. . . .

Thursday, March 4. It is ½ past 12. Morning dawned with rain falling. Prospect gloomy. About 10 more promising. Now blue sky to be seen, and a tremendous crowd about the Capitol.

Cannon firing, and, doubtless, Ulysses S. Grant President of the United States. Well, once more, God bless him. . . .

All I have seen of the Inauguration was what I could see from our bay window, and that was precious little. Everybody left the house except me, and I had to stay at home to see that no robbers intruded.

The sun has been shining out bright. . . .

Evening. How well I remember 4 years ago tonight when we had the great Ball at the Patent Office building, at which I was among the principal managers, and had President & Mrs. Lincoln especially in charge during all the time they remained. "That was a Ball as was a Ball." Tonight I am here alone, with no desire for Balls, nor anything else but quiet. I expect the Ball tonight will be a grand affair. Sarita is going, and will probably tell us tomorrow that it was "*perfectly splendid!*"

Wednesday, March 10. . . . Mr. A. T. Stewart has declined the Secretaryship of the Treasury, & President Grant is relieved—doubtless against his will—of that difficulty. It is better for both that it should be so, as New York would have been in a perfect political ferment had Stewart been Secy. A gentleman from N.Y. told me yesterday, that a more unpopular appointment could not be made. That the merchants of N. York hated Stewart, and wished that he was dead! He said[,] "Stewart grinds everybody to powder who comes into competition with him, and, in consequence of his vast wealth & ability to do as he pleases, he possesses the power to do it. I shall regard his going into the Treasury Dept. as a great misfortune to the Country."[1]

That was the opinion of a gentleman of high character & standing, who knows Stewart well, and is his personal friend and a warm supporter of President Grant. . . .

1. Alexander T. Stewart (1803–1876) was appointed and confirmed but was barred from the position because he was engaged in business. He was disliked because of his shrewd trading practices and his harsh methods of dealing with his employees.

Sunday, March 14. . . . President Grant does not move at all in the direction of making arbitrary official changes, and, I am informed by authority undoubted, has avowed that he will not as long as the *tenure of office law* remains unrepealed! Good for the stubborn old General. I glory in his spunk! It is a damnable law and a disgrace to the statute book, and the House have almost unanimously repealed it, but inasmuch as its repeal will deprive our regal Senate of some of its usurped power, they delight too well to roll the sweet morsel under their tongue to be governed by that plebeian set, the Representatives of the Sovereign People! They will squirm awhile and then surrender. They will find Grant too popular to be trifled with!

Tuesday, March 16. . . . I have heard many find fault with Grant's "obstinacy[,]" as they term it, in taking his own way and consulting nobody. "If he goes on in this way," say they, "he will soon find himself high and dry." That Grant is a Patriot and an honest man who means to do his duty, and to do it right, I have no doubt, but he never can run this immense governmental machine *alone,* any more than a first-rate Ship Captain could run the *Great Eastern* safely across the Atlantic with no one but himself to navigate her! That he will find out ere he is 6 months older! . . .

Wednesday, March 17. It is 9 o'clock P.M. and, considering that it has been the Anniversary of Ireland's Patron Saint, it has been a right pleasant day. I went, as in duty bound, to my office in good season and labored steadily and faithfully till ¼ past 3, when I felt worn out and came home. Found a Telegram from Frank informing me that Judge Wm. A. Richardson, who is offered the First Assistant Secretaryship of the Treasury, would arrive in this evening's train. He being an intimate friend and kinsman of mine, at 5 o'clock I walked down to the depot and met him when the train arrived at 5:20', and invited him to our house. He came up with me, dressed and supped and then went out to visit his friends, and will not, probably[,] return much before midnight. He is in a perfect quandary whether or not to accept the proffered office. Left entirely to himself I have no doubt he would decline; but his friends are urging him very strongly to accept. I, governed as we all are, more or less by selfish motives, should be delighted to have him accept. But were I in his exact position, I do not believe I would do it. And, from his conversation, I think the chances are that he will decline.

Saturday, March 20. For the past 3 days I have not found a moment which I could devote to this journal. Judge Richardson has been with us all the time since I wrote on Wednesday evening. He concluded to accept the office of Assist. Secy.[,] was nominated yesterday and confirmed by the Senate at 4 o'clock P.M. today. . . .

Nothing that I can now think of has taken place within my personal observation for the two past days worthy of being written down. I have been about with Judge R. considerable, and have seen a good many public men, and have found, I imagine, that I am not considered quite that political ogre that some of my old political friends have thought me.

There are compensations in everything touching worldly movements, and the pendulum is settling down honest & right as regards me. "*I bide my time.*"

The Senate are fighting desperately over the *unconstitutional* and ungodly tenure of office statute, and it seems to me as if repeal was gaining ground. Once off the statute book it will never again get on! I met Mr. Caleb Cushing and Mr. Evarts[1] (two ex-Atty. Generals of the U.S.) in the Supreme Court yesterday. Cushing said, "Mr. Evarts, the enemy will surrender within forty-eight hours—the tenure of office law will be repealed!" They then went on to speak of it as it deserves to be spoken of, as a disgrace to the statute book. I, being in conversation with them, took the liberty to remark that I thought if it should be repealed, the House of Representatives would never be again guilty of the folly of clothing the Senate with such powers.

I do not now know whether Gen. Cushing's prediction has turned out to be prophesy or not, as I do not know the result of the doings of the Senate today.

I have this day finished reading *The Moonstone*, a novel by Wilkie Collins.[2] It is exceedingly interesting and the story is just as improbable as a story can well be. . . .

1. William M. Evarts (1818–1901), Attorney General, 1868–1869, later served as Secretary of State and senator.
2. Wilkie Collins published *The Moonstone* in 1868.

Saturday, March 27. . . . Judge Richardson returned last evening, and we have concluded to keep him as an inmate of our house for the present. He entered on his duties as Assistant Secretary of the Treasury today. . . .

Saturday, April 3. . . . Today at the office till 3. Then home and witnessed the rehearsal of *The Spirit of '76*, a burlesque comedy exhibiting the *manly* triumph of a woman!, which the young folks are getting up to be performed at Carroll Hall, on Monday evening next, for the benefit of some charitable association. The rehearsal was good and promises a rich treat to the audience. We dined at ½ past 5. At 7½ Mrs. French, Helen, Sarita, and the Fords went to the Theatre to see *Rip Van Winkle,* by Jefferson.[1]

Mr. Greenleaf[2] came in soon after they left, and has just gone. He was exceedingly interesting and I enjoyed his visit much. Judge Richardson retired about 9, leaving Mr. G. & myself sole occupants & we talked steadily about many things. He gave me a most entertaining account of a journey he had in 1861, I think, from this city to N.Y. with Henry Ward Beecher,[3] during the whole of which they discussed (pleasantly) the status of the negro and slavery. . . .

1. Joseph Jefferson (1829–1905), American comedian, beloved for this role.
2. William C. Greenleaf, treasurer of the Washington & Georgetown Railroad.
3. Henry Ward Beecher (1813–1887), famous antislavery clergyman at Plymouth Church, Brooklyn, was in 1870 accused of having an affair with a parishioner's wife. In a trial (1874–1875) Beecher was acquitted.

Sunday, April 11. . . . Tuesday evening at 5½ o'clock my brother Henry arrived and has been with us all the week. Thursday William French[1] and I fitted up the back parlor into a Theatre, and Friday night we had a grand performance of the *Spirit of '76*, together with Will's peculiar panoramas, *waxwork, a la Jarley*!,[2] etc. About 2 hours passed away very pleasantly, there being present an audience of more than 50, all of whom seemed very much gratified. The Theatricals being over, the company partook of a collation of ice cream, water ice and cake, & then *the young folks*—including myself—went to dancing, and it was one o'clock before we retired. . . .

1. Henry's son William, 25, had graduated from Harvard and served in the Civil War. Now he was on his way to Chicago for a career as art critic and director of the Art Institute.
2. Mrs. Jarley, the owner and exhibitor of waxworks in Dickens's *Old Curiosity Shop*.

Tuesday, April 13. . . . Will French *started* for Chicago at 4 P.M. yesterday, & missing his through ticket he went to Annapolis junction & then returned here to look for it. But it cannot be found. He had it Sunday, & Judge Richardson and I saw it & read it. How he lost it is unexplainable. He will take another departure today. . . .

Thursday, April 15. . . . At 5½ yesterday morning I started in the carry-all, with the old horse "Jim" and William Taliaferro to drive, for the Great Falls. At 10½ past 6 we were at Henry D. Cooke's in Georgetown, where about 20 gentlemen assembled, and at about ½ past 6[,] 9 carriages left Cooke's for the G.F.

We all drove like Jehu, and arrived at the Falls at 7:50', doing the 15 miles in 1 hour & 45 minutes. The morning was charmingly clear and exceedingly cold, so that on my arrival I was next to frozen. We found a small fire in a forsaken room, & by hovering around it, and drinking *a drop* of whiskey and eating a sandwich[,] I managed to get comfortable.

At a little past 8 our company, increased to over 30, got on board the little propeller *Minnesota*, "well found" and *admirably provisioned*, and were speedily under way for the Seneca Quarries. At 10 m. before 9 we sat down to as good a breakfast as need be eaten. Before 11 we were at Seneca admiring the magnificent arrangements for quarrying and preparing stone for the market. The mills, two in number, were doing all the work they could & everything looked lively and businesslike. The entire party walked about the premises and we had pointed out to us the proper site on the bluff that overlooks the river for a town which is to be *planted* there. No more beautiful place for one can be imagined. . . .

Wednesday, May 19. For the past month I have suffered considerably with the toothache. Two teeth troubled me, the last of my wisdom teeth and a molar. The former has ached for the month nearly all the time, and was so painful night before last that I determined that it must come out. So, at two o'clock P.M. yesterday, I went to Dentist Smithe[1] and told him to put me under the operation of the gas, and, if possible, extract both teeth. He and Dr. Hills[2] proceeded to work. I took the gas, and when I awoke[,] lo only the molar out, and the blood flowing copiously. For half an hour they applied styptics to the gum, but no diminution of the flow of blood followed. On a minute examination Dr. Hills concluded that the blood did not come from the gum, and after carefully looking my mouth over he at last found that my tongue had been cut by the sharp edge of the tooth (for it was like a lancet)[,] and from thence the blood came. Every means those two Doctors could think of they applied, and still I bled on. At length, without my knowledge, they sent for Doct. Hall. In the meantime some pounded ice was procured, and there being some whiskey in the room, I, of my own accord, mixed ice with the whiskey and held it in my mouth, and before Dr. Hall arrived, the flowing stopped. I felt faint and dizzy, and came home a little past 4, with my aching tooth still in, where it now is! . . .

We expect General Benj. F. Butler to dine with us today. . . .

1. J. C. Smith, 366 C St. North.
2. T. O. Hills, 306 Pennsylvania Ave.

Thursday, May 20. We had a very pleasant dinner party. Gen. Butler was pleasant & agreeable. He conversed with the ladies about household matters; said he always had lobsters fresh from the ocean on his breakfast table in the season of them. . . .

. . . At 3 I went to the Dentist's, and on carefully examining my aching tooth, he said that he was almost certain that it would break off if he attempted to extract it, and advised me to let it remain & have an application made to destroy the nerve, which I did, and for an hour after I got home I endured the most excruciating pain. Then it ceased and the tooth now is as free from ache as any tooth in my head. But the under part of my tongue is sore and very uncomfortable, and almost makes me sick. . . .

Sunday, May 30. . . . Yesterday was decoration day. All the Departments were closed, and nearly all Washington went over to Arlington to hear the oration and witness the doings. I sent flowers and a letter enclosing $5, but remained at home myself. . . .

Sunday, June 6. In the garden—Arbor-time, 12½ P.M. Weather clear and cool. Thermometer 68, wind N.E., my dress a thick winter coat. This is my first writing *out here* this summer. . . . It is an everlasting shame that a man, within 27 months of his three score years and ten, who has devoted 26 years of that time to the public service, and tried faithfully to perform every official duty, should now be obliged to perform the duty of an 18 hundred dollar clerkship to enable him to live! . . . People think I am rich. They think a man who has held office and disbursed public money, as I have, *must be rich*! They reason from analogy, I suppose. I own, thank God[,] the soil whereon I live. I bought it for almost nothing. I built upon it, and improved it, and it is mine! I have, by industry and economy, added something to it, but not enough to afford me and mine ½ a support, & so I work, work, work on, and live! . . .

. . . I am sorry to say that Sunday does not exhibit much of that kind of thing the World calls piety in my own life. My wife is a conscientious Catholic and lives square up to her professions, & I hope she has enough religion over and above that necessary for her own salvation to save me! *But,* I do not believe in an outward show of piety, and I mistrust anyone's *honesty* who makes any great display of piety! I never yet undertook to accommodate a professedly ultra religious man pecuniarily that I did not get "sucked in." I believe in *worldly honesty,* but do not believe in *worldly piety.* It is a cheat & a humbug! . . .

Wednesday, June 9. . . . Since my last writing we have passed through a Municipal election. In this ward a Sunday could not have been more quiet; in other parts of the city there was riot and bloodshed. We Radicals had it all in our own way, and carried everything before us. Of Copperheadism there is scarcely a grease spot left.

Dorchester, Mass., Thursday, June 17. ½ past 2 P.M. At 9 A.M. yesterday Frank and I left for Boston.[1] We went in a train at least ¼ of a mile long, as all creation, *and a good many soldiers,* were on their way to the Jubilee and General Grant. Every inch of standing room on every platform was occupied. We walked from the Depot to the Bank, where we found Judge French and Dan, who were down to see the show. At 11 A.M. I took the cars for Concord and arrived at George Keyes's at ¼ past 12. Found them all well there. In the evening Mr. & Mrs. Brown, Bessie and I rode down to Henry's where we spent the evening. Henry, Brown, Dan and I walked over the farm. I have seen no place so large, in such perfect order. Strawberries and asparagus, almost by the acre. The land as rich and mellow as possible, the strawberry beds all mulched with straw, and the vines covered with fruit. The barn full of cows, yielding now 90 quarts of milk daily. I do not see why, in a very few years, that farm will not produce an income of four or five thousand dollars a year, and it is carried on by the Judge and Dan, with the help of a single man. It really gave me the first impression I ever had *of profitable farming.* I do not know but what, when George Keyes gets his farm fairly under way, that may be profitable too, but at present it is costing a lot of money to get things in order. It will be a magnificent place one of these days.

Dan is a sculptor. I mean it—a natural born sculptor—and his works show it: He has a bust of his father nearly finished, and the most perfect likeness, in a bust, that I ever saw. He has moulded—or, rather, wrought out—figures of dogs, frogs, etc., which give evidence of superior skill in the art. He has also a head of a young girl, said to be as good a likeness as that of his father. Never having seen the original I could not judge; I only know that it is an excellent piece of art. I prophecy that the name of Daniel French will hereafter stand by the side of the best sculptors in America & aye, in the World! . . .

Now I will fill up the gap between the time when I left Washington, and when I arrived here.

. . . At about 6 [Monday, June 14] we arrived at Jersey City, and immediately proceeded to N. York. The rain was falling in torrents, so we procured a hack and went to "the Metropolitan" where we break-fasted. Ben called soon after breakfast, and we went together to Brooklyn to visit the Wells's. We arrived there between 9 & 10 intending to stay till about 11, but, the rain continuing to pour, I stayed and lunched. Ben went over to New York, where I met him at Fulton Ferry, and we went together to Mr. Thomas's and saw Abbie and the baby, who is a beautiful, bright little girl. I then returned to the Metropolitan, found Mrs. Rich-ardson, and at 20 minutes to 5 took a hack and drove to the *Bristol* steamer. We had a full boat, but a beautiful run through the Sound, and arrived at the wharf at Fall River about 4½ A.M. It took till after 6 to get the passengers and baggage transferred to the cars. The train was im-mense and we did not arrive in Boston till 8¼. . . .

1. In this and the next two entries French describes his final trip to New England. The chronology was as follows.

Sunday, June 13	Left Washington
Monday, June 14	Arrived New York
Tuesday, June 15	Arrived at Frank's house in Dorchester, Mass.
Wednesday, June 16	To Concord for overnight visit
Tuesday, June 22	To Newbury, Mass., for three-day visit with Ben Perley Poore
Friday, June 25	To Concord for overnight visit
Saturday, June 26	To Chester
Monday, June 28	Back in Dorchester
Tuesday, June 29	Visited in Cambridge
Wednesday, June 30	Left Dorchester
Thursday, July 1	Arrived New York
Friday, July 2	Arrived Washington

Tuesday, June 29. I left this place [Dorchester] on Tuesday last [June 22] at 2 P.M. and returned at 3 P.M. yesterday, and will now try to dot down[1] the main points of that week's experience in my own life.

Left Boston for Newbury, Byfield station, at 3½ P.M. on Tuesday. Major Poore met me at the station with his "Beach Waggon" and took me to his house at "Indian Hill Farm," where I met every attention, to use a phrase of an old friend, "that heart could wish or fancy could invent." The Major took me all over his "curiosity house," for it is that not only as *a house,* but as to its contents. Since I was there a few years ago, he has added what he calls "the Continental parlor, kitchen, sink room, and chamber." In the hall leading to the parlor are the stairs brought from the old "Stacy House" of Newburyport, in which Washington, Lafayette, & Louis Philip[2] were guests. The parlor is entered between two columns that have Revolutionary history which has escaped my mind. The parlor itself is the selfsame one of the old Province House, built by the Provincial Governor of Massachusetts. The marble mantlepiece at its end is from the Old Stuyvesant House, N.Y. Directly over it a carved wooden mantlepiece from the old Hancock House, Boston, and over that a mahogany panel from the house of Edward Everett. The kitchen is in fact an old-time kitchen with its big fireplace, crane, pothooks and trammels, pots, kettles, etc., and all the paraphernalia of a kitchen of a hundred years ago, pewter platters & all! The sink room is ditto, & in it hangs a linen *roller,* the flax of which it was made, raised, rotted, broken, swingled,[3] spun, woven & bleached on Indian Hill Farm! The chamber corresponds with the kitchen & sink room. . . .

Afternoon, 2 o'clock. While I was writing the foregoing page, breakfast was announced. After breakfast Frank and I went to Cambridge. We saw many of his old friends and classmates. He voted for overseers; we lunched with Judge Richardson at his splendid residence on Kirkland Street, with others of the Alumni of Harvard. Mrs. George Richardson[4] came in while we were at the table. Mrs. Judge was at the Church witnessing the exercises, and Isabel[5] not sufficiently recovered from her poisoning[6] to be visible. We had an elegant lunch, & returned to Boston and took the 1 o'clock train for this place.

To proceed with my regular history, which must be as brief as I can make it.

Wednesday, 23d. Major Poore took me to Newburyport. Called on my 2d Cousin Anthony S. Jones[,][7] who enlightened me much as to my maternal ancestors, who were old Newbury people. My grandfather moved from Newbury to Chester, long before I was born. . . .

Thursday, 24th. The great day. We all went into Newburyport early, and the doings of the day, are they not recorded fully in the public newspapers, particularly in the *Boston Journal* and *Newburyport Herald?* . . .

Friday, 25th. Major Poore, with his usual hospitality, had invited all Freemasons who chose to come, to breakfast with him at Indian Hill at 6 A.M. on this day, and the mansion in all its parts abounded with good things to eat and drink. I never saw such a glorious display in all my life. Eatables by the acre & drinkables by the ocean! Washtubs of punch of all kinds, and everything to match. At least 140 people took breakfast, and it was all glorious. . . .

Saturday morning at ½ past 6 the Judge took me up to Keyes's & I breakfasted there. Took a look at Mary & the twins,[8] & at 7 Brown & I started for Chester with a horse of Keyes's who, before we had got a ¼ of a mile, kicked and reared & plunged as if he were possessed by a devil. I jumped out, got him by the head, & we succeeded in quieting him so that Brown drove him back to the house, where we took the reliable old mare, "Calico," and started again at ½ past 7. We rode to Chester, 36 miles, in about as pouring a rain as I ever rode in. Arrived there between 3 & 4, staid over Sunday, and heard Mr. Tomlinson preach an excellent sermon, and at 4½ yesterday morning left—I for Lowell, Brown for Concord. It rained all the first 15 miles of our journey. At Lowell I took the cars for Boston and arrived here[,] as heretofore written down, at 3 o'clock yesterday. And *so* one week has gone. . . .

1. Colloquial for "jot down."
2. Louis Philippe, King of France, 1830–1848.
3. Meaning to beat and clean flax.
4. Wife of George Richardson (b. 1829), son of Daniel Richardson, elder.
5. Isabel Richardson (b. 1850), daughter of Judge William A. Richardson.
6. From poison ivy.
7. Anthony S. Jones, son of Mercy Brown French's cousin.
8. Twins of Mary and George Keyes, born 1869.

Washington, Sunday, July 4. As I write this, St. Aloysius' clock is striking 11—evidence that the sun is right!

Soon after writing the foregoing at Frank's on Tuesday afternoon last, I packed my trunk, putting this book therein, that Frank might take it to Boston Wednesday morning and have it checked for this city, which he did. . . . Frank returned from Boston at 3½; we dined[,] and at 4, he, Ellen & the children accompanied me to the cars in the *old rain carriage,* and at 4:20 the train came and I bid the dear ones good-by and began my journey homeward. . . . We arrived at the wharf at N.Y. about 6 [A.M. Thursday, July 1], and before 7 were safe at Doct. Wells's, where we were joyfully received. . . .

I remained till ½ past 8 [P.M.], when, accompanied by Ben, who had been with me at Doct. Wells's nearly all the day, I started for Jersey City Ferry. Got to the cars for this City in good season, bundled into my sleeping berth, and slept quite well all night. We arrived here at 6½ [A.M., Friday, July 2] and I came home, finding all well and glad to see me. . . .

Tuesday, July 6. A glorious but somewhat cool morning. Thermometer 64.

Yesterday was treated as the 4th, and Independence went off in cannons, guns, pistols, firecrackers, rockets, etc., notwithstanding Mayor Bowen's proclamation forbidding the firing of them, and ordering the Police to arrest all who should do so! There was not, however, a tenth part of such displays of *patriotic* noise as there used to be under former Mayors. There was very little celebration in this city. The colored element turned out largely and marched in procession to the President's and sang to him, as I have been told by one who was present, very well. As for me, I sat in the house all day—wrote letters and read Mrs. Stowe's[1] *Old Town Folks.* . . .

1. Harriet Beecher Stowe (1811–1896), after *Uncle Tom's Cabin* (1852), turned to New England for her subject matter. *Oldtown Folks* (1869) was one of the results.

Sunday, July 11. . . . During the past week I have read Mrs. Stowe's recent novel, *Old Town Folks.* I confess to much disappointment. It is not what I expected. All the religious creeds that were dinned into my ears from the time I could comprehend anything, up to my 17th or 18th year, are discussed in Mrs. Stowe's book *ad nauseam.* Calvinism, Arminianism,[1] Hopkensianism,[2], Romanism, Episcopalianism, etc., to the end of all the *isms*, are set forth and commented upon, and, if the witch of Endor[3] is not introduced, other witches are, and visions are perfectly abundant. Some of the characters have that age that the book described, strongly marked upon them, and the dullness, to me, of the constant religious discussion that goes through the volume was relieved by finding characters described that I could individualise as well as if the writer had had before her the very persons the descriptions brought *in propria persona* before my mind. But they are gone now—all gone—and I hope the "tough old jade," who was the "Miss Asphyxia" of my boyhood, and the apparently most unfeeling woman I ever knew, and whom I saw in her schoolmarm capacity thrash a little girl with a tough switch till the blood ran down her back, has found a more lenient judge in the other world

than she ever was in this. The scouring out of poor little "Tina's" mouth
with soap and sand was exactly in keeping with the way and manner that
hated of all about her, used to punish *us* her scholars!

The book, take it all in all, is a pretty good one. . . .

1. Arminianism, the religious doctrine of the Dutch Reformed theologian Jacobus Ar-
minius (1560–1609), who held a less strict view of redemption than Calvin.
2. Hopkinsianism, the doctrine of Samuel Hopkins (1721–1803), who called on everyone to take his or her place in the divine plan.
3. A witch consulted by King Saul.

Thursday, August 5. . . . Yesterday went to the office in good season.
Worked till nearly one P.M. Then got into a car, and rode to 7th street,
and thence to the "Shutzen Verein" Park, where the "Fest" is now in
progress. Met Admiral Goldsborough[1] at the 7th st. intersection and he
went with me. He is a noble gentleman, and exhibited his generosity by
paying for the entrance into the Park of half a dozen poor boys, because,
as he said, "Poor little fellows, it will afford them so much pleasure."
How I honored him for that touching little exhibition of his kindness.
"Verily I say unto you, inasmuch as ye have done it unto one of these
little ones, ye have done it unto me."

I always liked the good old Admiral; I like him still better now!

We went all over the Park together; saw the shooting and bowling,
heard the music, which was not great; saw the hobbyhorses go round,
and the spring guns for children, *grown* or otherwise, to shoot at artificial
birds with. The rifle shooting was a regular fusilade. There were, say, 8
or 10 targets 200 yards from the place of shooting, and a shooter at each
target, who shot as fast as he could load, aim, and fire. All shot from
rests, and the charges fired were quite heavy. The rifles were regular
"turkey shooters[,]" as we used to call such in my young days, as distinguished from "sporting rifles." They had globe sights and curious fixtures under the stocks to aid in steadying them. Every shot was
registered, and men were at the targets, out of sight, to attend to the
shots there. How the thing was arranged so that each could tell his exact
shots, was to me a mystery, and nobody could tell, at the house, as I could
see, how exact the shooting was. I was told that there was a telegraph
from the targets to the stand, but I did not see it. I was invited to shoot,
and a very gentlemanly German offered me the use of his rifle and
ammunition, but I declined, although I think I could have made some
good shots. . . .

1. Rear Admiral Louis M. Goldsborough (1805–1877) commanded the North Atlantic
Blockading Squadron in the Civil War.

Sunday, August 8. We had the Eclipse yesterday in all its glory. Our house is so situated that the pathway of the declining sun is visible from it even to the very setting. The ladies, with William Russell, went to the Capitol in sufficient season to get to the Dome before the eclipse began. Judge Richardson and I sat on our front door steps and saw the beginning. We could see the first touch of the moon's shadow on the sun at 5 m. past 5—the sun being entirely away from clouds. Mr. Bartlett[1] came over soon after[,] & Judge Richardson & he went to the Capitol, leaving me alone. Soon after Mrs. Bartlett came, & she and I watched the obscuration until the sun appeared like a very young moon indeed. At a few minutes past 6 we could perceive that the shadow was going off, and then, both of us complaining of being dizzy, we came into the house and took only an occasional look till the eclipse was over. During its continuance the sun was occasionally beclouded for two or three minutes—in all perhaps 10 minutes. I looked at it through my spyglass about 5 minutes before the greatest obscuration, shielding my eye with a piece of smoked glass. The view was grand, as the sun was magnified many times I should judge. The sunset & twilight following the eclipse was as gorgeous as any one I ever saw. The reflection from the West could be seen on the tops of the trees in our garden for nearly an hour after the sun had set, and the Northwestern heaven was in a blaze of light.

I have witnessed two total eclipses in my life—one in 1806, when I stood at my Grandfather Brown's side in the street in front of his house in Chester, N.H., at the moment of the sun's total obscuration. The other must have been in 1842, as I was in Chester on a visit at the time, and witnessed the total obscuration from the very spot from which I saw that of 1806—taking especial pains to go and stand on the very spot of ground, which I perfectly remembered. To my regret, I can find no record of it in my journal, and am not certain whether that was the time. I only judge from the fact that a total eclipse occurred in 1842, and I was at Chester that summer.[2] . . .

1. William B. Bartlett, bookseller, 86 East Capitol St.
2. French included in the journal a newspaper clipping, which gave the following dates for total eclipses between 1806 and 1867: 1806, 1842, 1850, 1851, 1856, 1860, 1861, and 1867.

Monday, August 16. We went to the Camp meeting, Judge Richardson, Mrs. French, Sarita and myself, in Judge R.'s carriage & new span of horses (belonging to the Treasury Department). Such a dusty ride as we had! but then we heard the colored clergyman, who spoke remarkably well and showed a mouthful of the whitest ivory, as he emphasised his periods and held aloft a large bible. He spake himself almost breathless, gesticulated accordingly, and walked from one end of the stand to the other, as I have seen a caged wild beast move from side to side of his cage. The women were getting religion at a devil of a rate, & the crowd bawling and groaning. I have no doubt that such a gathering of ignorant odds and ends of humanity tends to very far more crime and sin than all the negro preaching of a century can counteract! We staid perhaps an hour, & then came home by way of the Navy yard. . . .

Sunday, August 29. . . . I wrote to Judge French on the morning of the 27th and in my letter bet a nickle cent the Harvards would beat. But they did not, so, being an honorable man, and desiring promptly to pay my bet, I this day wrote as follows to him, enclosing the cent.

> Once, in a spurt of patriotic heat,
> I bet *one cent* the Harvard crew would beat.
> The sequel proved my bet was somewhat rash,
> The Oxfords beat—I lost—and here's the cash!
> But, though the Harvards lost the well-earned bays,[1]
> They won a dearer boon—*All England's praise*![2] . . .

1. Garlands made of laurel.
2. The first Oxford-Cambridge crew race took place in 1829; the first intercollegiate crew race in the United States, between Harvard and Yale, took place on Lake Winnipesaukee in New Hampshire in 1852.

Friday, September 3. . . . Ben has, at last, got something to do, as Engineer on the "Portland & Oxford Central R.R." After a year or two of idleness—perhaps I should not say *idleness,* for I believe he has studied and labored to improve his mind—but after being out of regular employ ever since he left Washington, he has been engaged by Frank B. Smith, son of my old friend F. O. J. Smith, as above, and, from his letters, I judge, is well pleased with his situation, and is doing well. I think I know Ben's natural capacities well enough to be of opinion that he can, *if he will,* stand at the very head of his profession. He has a chance now, and I hope and trust he will improve it. His position, for the past two or three years[,] has been a great trouble to me—indeed, almost my only trouble. If he does well now I shall be amply repaid for all I have endured. . . .

Saturday, September 4. . . . Judge Richardson talked to me . . . about the troubles he has regarding the appointment of ladies to office. There is a constant pressure upon him, and under the rule that there shall not be two of any one family, there is constant reference to those in office ever so distantly related to each other, with pressure for removal that the applicant may get the place.

I think the manner of removal and appointment of subordinates is becoming a curse and a disgrace to our Government. Instead of Jefferson's question—"Is he capable? Is he honest?" the test now is "Has he—or she—any relative, this side of Adam & Eve, in office?" . . .

Thursday, September 9. . . . Secretary of War Rawlins,[1] having died of Tuesday, is to be buried today—or, rather, his body is to be entombed at the Congressional Cemetery, and a most imposing funeral pageant is in preparation. . . .

11½ A.M. The procession is coming. I hear the music. I will go to the top of the house.

12 o'clock. I went, spy and opera glass in hand, and saw all of the procession until perhaps 20 carriages following the hearse had passed. I went up, like a ninny, with nothing on my head, and as soon as my brains *began to boil* I came down.

The Military procession was just nothing compared with those I have seen—such as Harrison's, Taylor's, and Lincoln's.

But after the grand two-days parade following the close of the War, *all* military processions must necessarily be tame enough!

1. John A. Rawlins (1831–1869), of Illinois, a member of General Grant's staff in the Civil War, was promoted to chief of staff of the army in 1865 and named Secretary of War in 1869.

Sunday, September 12. 50 years ago this day I received my honorable discharge as a Sergeant from the Army of the United States, having provided a substitute, having enlisted for 5 years on the 10th of the preceding May. *Served my Country 4 months!* . . .

Friday, September 24. . . . *The Morning News,* a little 7 by 9 penny paper just established in this city, seems to have started on a mission of abuse of my friend Judge Richardson. Let them abuse on. His armor of honesty and upright purpose is far too thick to be penetrated by their puny shafts. I think I have never known a man in public life who manifested a purer intention of performing every duty devolving upon him with an eye single to the public interests than does Wm. A. Richardson, and abuse of such a man will only recoil on those who manufacture it. We shall, ere long, see "the Engineer hoist with his own petard."

Fanny and Mary Ellen are talking and I cannot write and listen to their interesting conversation, so I will close my journal.

Sunday, October 10. . . . On Friday we heard of the death of Franklin Pierce, President of the United States from 1853 to 1857.

Franklin Pierce and myself were intimate friends from about 1825 to the time he took his seat as President. I was a member of the Baltimore convention that nominated him for the Presidency and did as much as any one man to secure his nomination, and certainly expected much more from him than I received while he was an incumbent of the Presidential chair. But I have written in my journal of that time all that need to be said as to his treatment of me, and I need write no more.

The last time I saw President Pierce was at his house at Little Boar's Head, at Hampton Beach, on the 25th of August, 1868. . . . I am now exceedingly glad I went to see him then. . . .

No living man knew Franklin Pierce, from his young manhood to the day when he left Washington the last time, better than I did. He had many of the best qualities that adorn human nature. "*De mortuis nil nisi bonum.*"[1]

1. Of the dead say nothing but good.

Sunday, October 17. . . . My brother Henry argued his case before the Supreme Court (which he came on here to argue) on Wednesday and Thursday, and left for home at 9 o'clock Thursday evening.

Judge Richardson returned at 10 P.M. Wednesday. We were all delighted to see him. He came with a fixed determination not to stay beyond next Saturday, but at the earnest solicitation of Secy. Boutwell has concluded, I believe, to remain until the 1st of Jany. . . .

. . . Wednesday, Harris & I erected a coal bin in the furnace room of sufficient capacity to hold 8 to 10 tons of coal. We have always kept our coal in the wood house, and lugged it in hods. . . .

Sunday, October 24. . . . [Saturday] I was constantly employed cleaning up and rearranging my shop. The floor was two inches thick with sawdust, other dust, shavings, and the *debris* of several years of carpenter & tinker work; the lumber and old stuff were scattered in corners, under the workbench, and around generally, and I had 5 hours of about as dirty, dusty, suffocating work as I ever attempted. I remember only one job of my life that compared with it, and that was the cleaning of North

Yarmouth Academy, when I was about 16 years old. We had a preceptor who had no idea of cleanliness, and so the Academy went on month after month without being swept or cleaned in any way. At last the Trustees ascertained the awful state of filth it was in, a day was assigned for cleansing, and volunteers among the scholars were called for to aid in the work. I was one, and on the day designated I was there bright & early[,] and we began with brooms, shovels, and baskets, and such a *smudder* of dust as we raised in that old building I never saw before. There was a broad aisle from the door to the rear of the building, on each side of which, ascending and facing the aisle, were the seats—one side being appropriated to the girls, the other to the boys. Beneath these seats the dirt had so accumulated that, unless "Royal's River"[1] had been diverted from its course nearby and run through it, nothing could have been devised to prevent the dust; so there we worked, sweeping and shoveling, until our lungs, our noses, and our ears were absolutely filled with dust; but we cleaned the old thing up before night, and General Edward Russell,[2] the Trustee who undertook to oversee the Herculean labor, equal almost to the cleansing of the Augean Stable, thanked us formally for the work. I went home, the perfect picture of a meal bag just emptied by being turned inside out, and I spit dust for a week!

So, yesterday, after my shop cleaning, I was a sight to behold, and taking advantage of my condition[,] I went into the "manhole" of the furnace and, with Harris to help me, put in the drums that go behind the furnace and have to be taken out every spring to preserve them from rust. . . .

Mary Ellen recd. a group of Rogers's[3] statuary, *Taking the Oath,* as a present from Judge French, day before yesterday, which was very thankfully received. I must either make or purchase a bracket for it, and put it up.

1. Royal River flows into Casco Bay near Yarmouth, Me.
2. General Edward Russell was secretary of the original board of trustees of the academy.
3. John Rogers (1829–1904) reproduced clay groups in plaster, depicting popular subjects, such as *Checkers Up at the Farm.*

Saturday, November 13. I was looking over my old journal of more than 30 years ago, last evening, and finding how carelessly I kept it and how many lapses of time when I neglected to journalize there are, I became more convinced than ever that it is the duty of every man who is in any wise mixed up with the great rush of national affairs, and with national men, as I have been, to keep a constant and faithful journal of what he sees and how he hears; and I deeply regret my own negligence in not keeping a continuous journal of passing events. . . .

Sunday, November 14. . . . Hon. Robert J. Walker, a gentleman to me well known, and who has filled a large space in the public eye for years past, died in this city on Thursday last, at the age of 68, and was buried on Saturday. Mr. Walker was formerly Secretary of the Treasury, Senator in Congress, Governor of Kansas, and a great financier, statesman, and scholar. In honor of his memory the Treasury Department was closed yesterday.

Hon. Amos Kendall died on Friday morning last, at the ripe age of 80 years. He is to be buried at 2 o'clock this afternoon from Calvary Church, which was erected mainly by his generosity. I am honored with an invitation to officiate as one of the pall bearers, which I shall do.

It is now nearly 40 years since I first became acquainted with Mr. Kendall, and I have known him well since 1833, and intimately since 1840. We were associated for years in the Magnetic Telegraph, having, both of us[,] been Presidents of the first Company—"The Magnetic"— ever formed. We were prominent in forming the "Washington & N.O. Company" and aided in its management for several years.

We have been Directors together of the Columbia Institution for the Deaf & Dumb for several years, and we have been good friends during all the years we have known each other. Amos Kendall was emphatically a great and a good man. For a portion of his life a warm partizan, and so uncompromising in his political notions and opinions as to render him exceedingly obnoxious to some men who sought to use him but found they could not. During the latter portion of his life, after fortune had smiled upon him, he was a true and noble philanthropist. His name will stand upon the record as a good, an honest, a generous, an accomplished man, of uncommon foresight, great shrewdness, and brilliant abilities as a statesman and a scholar.

November 1869 will be remembered as having marked the gathering in of a harvest of great men. George Peabody, Robert J. Walker, and Amos Kendall!! Names that shall live, as long as history is written. I may well add to these that of Col. Charles K. Gardner, who, though not as widely known, was as good and as true a patriot as either; and the venerable Admiral Charles Stewart[1] and not much less venerable Major General John E. Wool have also been victims to this sad month, which is not yet half gone!

Sunday evening, 7 o'clock. At a few minutes past 12 I left home to attend Mr. Kendall's funeral. . . .

We (the pall bearers) went across the street to Mr. King's house and remained till a few minutes before 2, when we returned to the church, and bore the coffin, followed by the mourners, into the body of the building, and deposited it in front of the pulpit, when the funeral services were eloquently performed. . . .

1. Charles Stewart (1778–1869) served as a naval officer in the Barbary War and the War of 1812.

Sunday, December 19. Tuesday, 14th, I attended the annual meeting of the "New England Society." We elected officers. Mr. Fessenden having declined to be a candidate, Hon. E. B. French was elected President. I was reelected Vice President from New Hampshire. We agreed to celebrate the anniversary of the Landing of the Pilgrims on the 22d by a dinner at the Masonic Hall, and expect to have a good time. I remember nothing further about Tuesday other than I was all day at the office. . . .

Thursday, 16th. All day at the office. Preparing most of the early evening to go to the Levee of Washington Commandery at Willard's Hotel. At 8, with Mrs. French and Fanny, I went to Willard's in a hack, and, being chairman of the committee on reception, I at once had my hands full in seeing that the ladies were escorted to their rooms. At ¼ before 9 President Grant & Vice President Colfax arrived, & I escorted them to a parlor, and afterwards Sir Kt. Will[1] and I escorted them to the dancing hall, where I introduced to them all the ladies. The lines were formed by the Templars at a few minutes past 9 and the *grand entrée* took place. After a short drill in presence of the distinguished guests, the commandery broke ranks, and the President and Vice President intimating that they had another engagement and must leave, I attended them to their parlor & thence to the door. At the door I prepared to call up the President's carriage, but before I could do so, he ran down the steps and said in a loud voice, "Alfred! Drive up!" Alfred drove up from the opposite side of the street, the distinguished guests took their seats, I bade them good night, and away they went.

Gen. Grant is a man after my own heart. He has not a particle of false pride in his disposition, in which he very much resembles President Lincoln. He seems glad to make everybody at ease about him, and to make as little parade and show as possible. The manner in which he ran down the long flight of steps and ordered up his carriage is a fair specimen of the man. Although well acquainted with General Grant before he was elected President, I have not seen him, to speak to him, since his inauguration, till Thursday evening. . . .

1. J. B. Will, clerk in the office of the sixth auditor, Treasury Department, was deputy grand master of the District of Columbia Masonic Lodge.

Saturday, December 25. . . . Edwin M. Stanton died at 3 o'clock A.M. yesterday. He was emphatically a great man, and this Union owes as much to his determined and energetic action, while Secy. of War during the Rebellion, for its preservation, as to any one man. I did not like him because he did not treat me well personally and in many things was a Tyrant, but I always . . . avowed my belief in his patriotism. . . . His brother, Doctor Darwin E. Stanton,[1] who was my Assistant at the Clerk's table while I was Clerk of the House of Representatives, was my intimate personal friend. . . .

Christmas day is, as usual here, desecrated by the constant discharge of firearms. They have been banging since midnight. If I had the power I would either stop it or discharge every police officer in the city.

1. Darwin E. Stanton committed suicide in 1846.

Sunday, December 26. . . . Judge Richardson advised me to write a book of reminiscences of Abraham Lincoln. Were it not impossible for me to do it without mingling Mrs. Abraham in the narrative in an unpleasant way, I am not certain that I would not attempt such a work. The conversation touching this matter was induced by an allusion to some reminiscences published by Col. J. W. Forney, of Mr. Lincoln, in this morning's *Chronicle*. . . .

Sunday, January 2. . . . Took a car for Washington. Went to the President's. Such a crowd that there was no prospect of getting in for an hour. Left in disgust, and went to Vice President Colfax's. Found him and his elegant lady all smiles and attention to those who called, and they were many, for our Vice President is very popular. Thence to Secy. Fish's where I had a delightful call. The Secy., whom I had not seen since he was a Senator, was exceedingly cordial and pleasant, and said it seemed like old times to see me. He was a member of the House when I was Clerk, and I was quite intimate with him. I partook of a few oysters, and left. My next call was on Secretary Boutwell. A very pleasant one. Then to Noble D. Larner's.[1] The Masonic Choir were leaving his door as I arrived; they were in an Omnibus, & he was with them. Mrs. Larner received me most kindly, & I partook sparingly of nogg. I then went to General Sherman's, and the noble and gentlemanly old soldier received me, as he did all, with that hearty welcome that characterises the man. He is the very soul of chivalry. Then to Ex-Mayor Wallach's, where I had a most pleasant call, & was kindly received by Mr. W.[,] his excellent wife, & Mr. & Mrs. Marshall Brown. From there I walked to Capitol Hill, called on Gen. Dunn,[2] Senator Trumbull, Mrs. Dr. Ford, Judge Sargent, and so ended *my* New Year's calls. I got home about 2, pretty well tired out. Found Mrs. French, assisted by Sarita, Fannie, Miss Spalding,[3] and Annie receiving. We had upwards of 140 callers during the day, among them the Masonic Choir, who sang several pieces splendidly. . . .

Evening. 9:20. At 8:30' Judge Richardson left us for home—it being what he believes and we all suppose is his final departure from Washington, he having resigned the office of Assistant Secretary of the Treasury. . . .

1. Noble D. Larner was secretary of the National Union Insurance Co. and grand secretary of the District of Columbia Masonic Lodge.
2. William M. Dunn (1814–1887), Republican congressman from Indiana, 1859–1863, was named assistant judge advocate general of the army in 1864 and judge advocate general in 1875.
3. A friend of Sarita's.

Wednesday, January 12. . . . .I want to write down here what Mr. Cooke said yesterday at our lunch. We were discussing the characters of eminent men. Mr. Cooke said he did not desire to pluck a single laurel from the grave of E. M. Stanton, but *he knew* that the man was still walking the earth who was the mainstay of the country during the early and trying years of the war. That man was Salmon P. Chase! He did more than all the rest. He formed the plans and wrote them out, and the country was more indebted to him for its salvation than to any other man—that, had it not been for the wonderful resources of the Country, the cause would have been lost to us, even after Grant was ordered to the front. That his policy was to conquer at any risk, and if men could not have been found to fill the depleted ranks we must have gone under. But when money could be raised to obtain recruits at $1,800 bounty, each, the country could not be conquered! He told us he was in a position to see and know *all* the inside workings, and Chase was the great man of the war.

I was glad to know this from Mr. Cooke, for I have heard the same from others in whom I did not place half the confidence. I have *always* been a very ardent admirer of Judge Chase, and while it suits the envy of certain politicians to abuse him, it gives me the utmost pleasure to hear him characterised as *the* great man of the war. . . .

Wednesday, January 19. . . . . [Captain Whitney][1] said Capt. Grant told him that he had been offered two dollars a foot for that part of his square below here fronting on East Capitol street, and asked me if I believed it. I told him I would sell my land and all that was on it at that price—that all I asked for the place was $50,000, and at 2 Dollars per foot it would come to just about that.

1. George H. Whitney, hotelkeeper.

Thursday, January 27. Frank came just as I had finished writing the foregoing on Sunday morning.[1] He remained until last evening, and we had a delightful visit from him.

We concluded to take Prof. Cook[2] and his wife. He came Tuesday evening, but his wife did not. He commenced his lectures last evening; is to deliver five. Frank, who was one of his scholars in College, says he [is] the most scientific man in the world. . . .

1. French is referring to his brief entry of January 23.
2. Josiah P. Cooke (1827–1894), professor of chemistry at Harvard (1850 ff.), led the way in classifying elements by their atomic weights.

Friday, February 4. It is 5½ P.M. Nothing worthy of being writ down has occurred in my beat. I went into the 1st National Bank today and saw Gen. J. C. Frémont. It is a long time since I have seen him to speak to him. I believe not since the summer when he was a candidate for the Presidency when I visited him at his house in New York. He is, now, a very handsome old gentleman.

Last evening Mrs. Mary Ellen, Miss Fannie, Miss Deane,[1] Will Russell, Dan French, and this individual, went to the President's reception. There was an immense crowd in attendance, and it was through much tribulation and tremendous squeezing that we succeeded in getting to the Red room, & through that to the Blue room where the President and Mrs. Grant received. The President stood as erect and stiff as if here on the parade ground at West Point, doing his best to be military. He was pleasant, but has not the *suaviter in modo* that even good, awkward President Lincoln had.

From the Blue room we passed on, after paying our respects to Mrs. Grant, who looked as well as a lady "with one eye in the pot and the other up chimny"[2] could look, to the East room, where an assemblage of all that is brilliant of Washington Society, and much that is not brilliant, were assembled. We threaded the crowd, bowed to some of our friends, shook hands with others, and walked and gabbled till ten, when Mrs. F. and I found ourselves sufficiently tired to leave. We got home a little before 11 and soon after went to bed.

So passed the first Presidential reception that I have attended since the winter of 1866–7 when I appeared in the role of Lord Chamberlain to Mrs. Johnson, Patterson & Stover. . . .

1. Mary Dean, clerk in the internal revenue bureau.
2. Julia Grant was slightly walleyed.

Monday, February 7. . . . A few minutes past 8, Gov. McCormick (now delegate in Cong. from Arizona)[,] Gov. Safford, now Governor of the Territory, & Mr. Plumb, late Consul to Havana, came to see us, and remained till about 10.[1] Mr. Plumb told us all about Havana and the Cuban insurrection, and advised Sarita as to her Havana Bank stock, which looks rather shaky. I am afraid she will never realize much for the $15,000. Mr. Plumb's account of the "Banco del Commercio" is not by any means encouraging. We will hope for the best. . . .

1. Richard C. McCormick (1832–1901) was war correspondent before being appointed secretary and then governor of the Arizona Territory. He was delegate to Congress, 1869–1875. Anson P. K. Safford was governor of the Arizona Territory, 1869–1877. Known as the "Little Governor," he was remembered for his educational program. Edward Lee Plumb, formerly chargé d'affaires to Mexico, 1867–1868.

Friday, February 11. . . . I have had, all this day, a confused sensation in my head, such as I have often had before. It is a something that makes realities like dreams, and dreams like realities. It is a troublesome and most unpleasant accompaniment to life, but does not affect my capacity to do business in the least, and, unless I speak of it, no one knows it is upon me. Today I have mentioned it to no one.

Mrs. French has gone to bed with a headache.

Dan has just come in.

Sunday, February 13. . . . Dan has just made me a present of a paper cutter, with an ornamented handle, carved by him, of black walnut. It is beautifully done, and I shall prize it much.

Monday, February 28. . . . Friday evening we had a nice little party of 50 to see *The Spirit of Seventy-Six* enacted. It was well done by Mr. Brackett as Carberry, Mr. Whelpley[1] as Wigfall, Luly Whitman as Judge Wigfall, Lou. Russell as Victorine, Sarita as Miss Griffin, & Anna French as Mrs. Badger. Mrs. Lippincott (Grace Greenwood) gave us a recitation, personifying an old man and woman disputing about the Revolutionary War, etc., which was excellently done. Mrs. French got up a collation of oysters, lobster salad, ice cream, oranges, coffee, etc. The company seemed to enjoy everything, and left between 12 & 1. . . .

1. James W. Whelpley, a clerk in the Treasury Department, married Louise Russell in 1871.

Sunday, March 13. . . . Last evening Sarita, Lou. Russell and I went, through all the storm, to Mr. King's reunion, where we found a houseful, and were interested and delighted by the reading of a paper on Joan of Arc, by Mrs. Lippincott (Grace Greenwood). It was an exceedingly well-written sketch of that most remarkable of women, and beautifully read. It occupied precisely one hour. We got home at 10.

The *days* of the week have passed as usual. I have done a good deal of work, *pro bono publico,* and have spent all the fixed official hours at the office.

My literature has been the reading of "Mark Twain's" (Mr. Clement's) [sic] *Innocents Abroad.*[1] It is one of the best written books I have ever read, and I have had many a hearty laugh over [it]. It is, doubtless, true history, illustrated in that funny way that no one but "Mark Twain" could illustrate it. Commend me to him for fun. Ever since I read his sketch of Horace Greeley I have read everything I have seen from his pen. . . .

1. Samuel Langhorne Clemens (Mark Twain) (1835–1910) published his first book in 1867, and *Innocents Abroad* (1869) established his reputation. *The Adventures of Tom Sawyer* (1876) and *The Adventures of Huckleberry Finn* (1884) were to follow.

Sunday, March 27. This is a stormy, ugly day. The wind was from the North all day yesterday, and it was cold and raw, and the clouds looked hard and brassy. I had engaged to read a poem at Hon. Horatio King's "Reunion" last evening, and at ¼ past 7, accompanied by the following nine, I went down—viz. Doct. and Mrs. Ford, Fannie, Louise, Lucia & Charles Whitman, Miss Deane[,] Sarita & Mrs. French. The weather was somewhat threatening, but not bad. There was quite a large and most respectable audience present. At 8 o'clock Mr. King arose and said that 26 years ago there were in this city two young men, one of whom wrote a poem, the first Canto of which he was printing for private distribution, and he requested the other young man to read it in the proof sheets, & submit to the writer his opinion as to whether he should continue writing. That the writer's friend replied in a poetical letter, which he, Mr. King[,] would read. Mr. K. then proceeded to read the letter, the burden of which was *"write on, write on."* The whole thing was most gracefully done, and most complimentary. I felt it so, and acknowledged it.

The two young men were *Mr. King & myself,* who were then neighbors, and who, as we have ever since been, were intimate friends. I submitted the poem to him, and he returned to me the poetical reply, a copy of which he must have kept, as I had not the most distant idea of his intention of making known, as he did, the little episode of so many years ago! The poem he read was the 1st Canto of "Fitz Clarence," and I read last evening the second Canto of the same, which, as I informed the audience, was, in conformity with my friend's advice to "write on," written and completed 10 or 12 years ago, and now, for the first time, presented to the public in any way, except that three of the short poems embraced in the main poem, had been printed in the newspapers.

Well, I read the poem, and it appeared to be well received. . . .

Tuesday, Wednesday, Thursday and Friday of the past week I was required to attend the Supreme Court of the Dist. of Columbia as a witness in a suit pending between Eslin[1] & the Corporation of Washington. It gave me an opportunity to listen to the trial of a case wherein Catharine Brown, a colored lady, had sued the Alexandria, Washington & Georgetown R.R. Company for ejecting her from a car intended for white people (there being a special car in the train for colored) and injuring her person. She laid her damages at $20,000. Cook and Bond[2] for Plff.[,] Merrick & Phillips[3] for defendants. So far as I heard, the case was ably tried. Merrick's closing argument was a brilliant effort of forensic eloquence. He is a splendid Lawyer, & I consider him at the head of our Bar here.

The case was submitted to the jury, after a five days trial, on Friday morning; and about 11½ o'clock, they returned a verdict for the Plff. of $1,500. From what I heard of the case I would not have given a verdict for over $100—because it seemed to me to be a purposely got up case for the sake of a judicial row between the colors. . . .

1. Charles Eslin, contractor, or Columbus Eslin, brickmaker.
2. William A. Cook and S. R. Bond.
3. Richard T. Merrick and Philip Phillips. Phillips (1807–1884) was a former congressman from Alabama, 1853–1855.

Sunday, April 3. It is 7 A.M. I arose at ½ past 5 that I might have a respectable bath, the hot water in our Bathing room declining to run after six. I am sorry to say that the water from the aqueduct is now, on this part of Capitol Hill, a d—nd humbug, and nothing shorter. Wednesdays the Navy Yard *steals* it all away from us, and Sundays, of course, every bathing tub is in use all over the city, at our expense, and so we have to pay for what we cannot get; although Congress promised us "a bountiful supply of pure water," we really get only a very meagre supply of, at present, the muddiest, dirtiest water that ever went down the throats of human beings! and I much fear it will be worse rather than better! . . .

Last evening I was at Mr. Horatio King's "Reunion," where Mrs. Lippincott (Grace Greenwood) read a lively sketch, the subject of which was the spending of a summer at Maplewood—but principally about cats and kittens. It was, doubtless, written for a Magazine article. It was racy, witty, and exceedingly well read. She followed it by reading, in true yankee style and voice, one of the "Biglow Papers," commencing

> Thrash away, you'll *hev* to rattle
> On them kittle drums o'yourn.[1]

She read it well, emphatically well, but I was a little doubtful of the propriety of reading it before *that audience*, and I heard more than one remark that it was not exactly in good taste. I have seldom seen a more select and appreciative audience assembled in a private dwelling than the one which honored the pleasant dwelling of my friend King last evening. President Grant, Vice President Colfax, Gen. Sherman, Gen. Holt, Gen. Dunn, Senator Sherman, Doct. Cox,[2] several other Senators, and quite a number of members of the House; Comptroller Brodhead, Auditor French,[3] and a delightful assemblage of female beauty graced the occasion. The three parlors were well filled—there being, I should think, 150 present. . . .

1. James Russell Lowell (1819–1891) satirized the U.S. government's conduct of the Mexican War in *The Biglow Papers* (1848) and published a similar series on the Civil War.
2. Jacob Dolson Cox, Jr. (1828–1900), Secretary of the Interior, 1869–1870.
3. Ezra B. French.

Sunday, April 17. . . . Within the past week I have given away, as follows. Washington Commandery $20. B.B. French Lodge $5. Baseball club $5. Masonic Ball $3—$33 dollars in one week, which added to *our* wedding present to Lucia—cost $10—is pretty liberal. Must be stingy now!

Sunday, April 24. *The Wedding* of Mr. Charles Pinkney Russell of New York City to Miss Lucia Whitman of Washington was solemnized in our parlor at half past 6 o'clock last evening; Rev. Dr. Boynton officiating as clergyman. There were nearly one hundred wedding guests present, and all seemed happy. The Bride and the Bridegroom occupied the exact position in the room, during the ceremony, that Frank and Ellen did when they were married on the evening of March 5, 1861.

The wedding ceremony over, and the kisses and congratulations duly given, at 7¼ the company repaired to the Library (where I now write), and where a bountiful wedding collation, furnished by the Bride's brother, was arranged, and of which all partook. At 8 the guests, excepting the families especially interested, left, and at ½ past 8 the newly constructed family—Mr. and Mrs. C. P. Russell—happy, I hope, as a couple of "clams at high water," left for the Depot, on their way to Baltimore, whence, tomorrow morning, they start for New York. Mary Wells threw one of my old shoes after them for luck, and all our good wishes, prayers, and blessings went with them. So the wedding was over, and we all pronounced it a success. May the wedded life of the happy couple be a success for long years to come, and may their children rise up and call them blessed.

Mary Wells came Wednesday evening, as an *avant courier* of the bridegroom, who was detained by his business engagements till Friday evening, and only arrived yesterday morning—thus devoting *one day,* and that his thirtieth birthday, to his beautiful and accomplished bride! Oh the practical utilitarianism of this "workiday" American world! I often think it is wonderful that any man of business can find time to die! Now this young Bridegroom will rush back to New York tomorrow and will be found, bright and early on Tuesday morning, at his place of business, working like a dray horse in his gears! "Work, work, work," is our American motto, but, thank God, the remainder of poor Hood's[1] lugubrious line—"in poverty, hunger and dirt"—seldom, if ever, applies to the workers on the *little area* between the Atlantic and Pacific Oceans, over which U.S. (in more senses than *one,* or even two, *at this present time*) Presides. . . .

1. Thomas Hood (1799–1845), English poet, published comic poems and essays.

Thursday, April 28. It is 5 o'clock P.M. and a hot afternoon, with indications of rain. Since Sunday, when I last wrote herein[,] some little matters have occurred of which I desire to make a record.

Monday evening Mr. Sergeant at arms French[1] of the Senate of the U.S. came over and summoned me to appear at 10½ the next morning, before the Senate Committee on Pensions, to testify in the matter of granting a pension to Mary Lincoln, widow of President Lincoln. I at once imagined that the old White House matters were all to be raked open again, and made up my mind to answer truly whatever questions I might be asked and volunteer nothing. I appeared before the Committee. Senator Edmunds,[2] and four other members, being present. . . .

Senator Edmunds, the Chairman, put all the questions but two or three which Senator Pratt[3] put. I was before the Committee about an hour, and gave them all the information I could relative to the *doings* at the White House while I was Commissioner. Whether the furniture disappeared—where it went—what was packed in the boxes that Mrs. Lincoln *had* made after her husband's death—how much it cost to replace the things taken away—how the Prince's dinner was paid for—how much the first appropriation for furnishing was overrun—the incidents attending it, etc. Some I could readily answer, some I could not. Some dates I could not give without referring to my journal. So, after I came home, I referred to it, found the dates, and wrote a letter to Senator Edmunds. Tuesday was pretty much used up by this call on my time. . . .

1. John R. French, French's second cousin, was sergeant at arms between 1869 and 1879.
2. George F. Edmunds (1828–1919), Republican senator from Vermont, 1866–1891.
3. Daniel D. Pratt (1818–1877), Republican senator from New York, 1869–1875.

Sunday, May 15. . . . *We*—my darling wife[,] Mrs. Russell and I—went down to the Potomac yesterday according to the program. The President & Mrs. Grant, Secretaries Cox and Belknap, Attorney General Hoar, a hundred or two Members of Congress, and five or six hundred of our best citizens, nearly all accompanied by ladies, were of the Company.[1] The day was splendid, the evening was splendid, the boat was splendid, the eatering was *about middling splendid,* until it *gave out entirely* at about 6 P.M.[,] notwithstanding which everybody had a splendid time and was *splendidly* happy! We steamed down to within about 8 miles of Piney Point—then "came about" and steamed home. . . .

I met hundreds whom I knew, and rejoiced in meeting them.

Of one person whom I met for the first time, I must make a brief record; and could I record my exact feelings and impressions, it would be a glowing one. It was Mrs. Kimball of Cincinnati. She is a sister of Hon. J. R. French's wife, now dead. After I had talked with her ½ an hour, and discovered that she was a portion "of the salt of the earth," and about as bright! and well informed as any woman who has recently crossed my path, she up and told me that she was a daughter of my old friend Nathaniel P. Rogers[2]—author of *The Old Man of the Mountain,* formerly of Plymouth, N.H., afterwards of Concord, where he edited *The Herald of Freedom.* This knowledge of her origin interested me many fold in her favor, for her father was one of the best and most talented of men, and one whom I esteemed most highly, and I found we knew numberless old N.H. citizens in common. So I sat and conversed with her the two or three last hours of our pilgrimage, and fully experienced the truth of the line—"How softly falls the foot of Time that only treads on flowers." I did not fall in love with her, but *fell into admiration of her,* and hope to see much more of her while she remains in Washington. . . .

1. William W. Belknap (1829–1890) of New York, Secretary of War, 1869–1876. Ebenezer R. Hoar (1816–1895), Massachusetts Supreme Court justice, served as Attorney General, 1869–1870.

2. Rogers, an abolitionist, took over the *Herald of Freedom* in 1838.

Sunday, June 5. It is 5 o'clock P.M. I have been most of the day putting my papers in order and cleaning up my desk, having, day before yesterday, resigned my clerkship in the Treasury. It is well enough for me to state the facts as they are, inasmuch as the newspapers give me the credit of having voluntarily resigned, which is not exactly the truth.

On Thursday Mr. Vanderbilt,[1] the Appointments Clerk, was sent down by the Secretary to Comptroller Brodhead to request him to request me to resign. The Comptroller sent for me and informed me of the wish of the Secretary, at the same time expressing to me his deep regret to have me leave the office, doing me the honor to speak of my usefulness in the office and saying how much he should miss my services. I proposed to send in my resignation at once, but he expressed a desire to see the Secretary before I did so. He saw him, and informed me immediately that he had never seen the Secretary exhibit so much feeling. That he spoke of me in the kindest manner and expressed his regret that, in consequence of the continual annoyance he experienced from office seekers, who invariably held me up as a *democrat!* and a rich man, he was driven to ask my resignation, to take effect on the 30th June with leave of absence to that time. . . .

1. Henry S. Vanderbilt, of Pennsylvania, chief of appointments division, Treasury Department.

Saturday, June 18. I went to Williamsport with the Templars. At a little before 9 Tuesday morning I wended my way to the R.R. Depot. At a few minutes after 9 both Commanderies, about 80 strong, in full uniform, preceded by the full Marine Band, arrived at the Depot and took the cars assigned to them, and at 9:25′ the train started. The first incident that occurred was within two miles of the city. A man, whom I have learned was Mr. John Cameron,[1] was walking from Clark Mills's, where he had been on business, to the city on the track on which our train was proceeding; seeing it, he changed to the other track on which the Baltimore train was on its way to Washington, just in time to be in front of the latter train, with his back towards the engine. The Engineer whistled "down brakes" just as the Engine was passing the window at which I sat, and it almost stunned me. I had just time to say, "That was the shrillest whistle I ever heard," when a Sir Knight behind me said excitedly,

"There's a man killed!" The trains were stopped as soon as possible. The man was pronounced to be dead, and our train moved on. The person behind me saw the engine strike the man, and told me it knocked him high into the air, the blood spouted from him, and he fell, apparently dead. On our return, I learned at Baltimore that it was Mr. Cameron, a most respectable and worthy citizen. At the moment when the train struck him, one of our party, Sir Knight Poindexter,[2] put his head out of the car window and was struck in the forehead and quite badly cut. He bled profusely, and our first thought was that he was severely hurt, but on examination it was found that his wound was only skin deep. . . .

1. John Cameron was a member of Lafayette Masonic Lodge #19.
2. William M. Poindexter sang first bass in the Masonic choir of the District of Columbia.

Sunday, June 26. I think it was on last Tuesday that I spent some hours in mending my fountain skimmer, which had got very badly broken at the place where the socket for the handle was attached. I had to get out a piece of copper, fit it to the skimmer, and rivet it on. Then fit the handle to it. It was well done, and, I think, one of the best jobs of work in that line that I ever did! . . .

On Thursday morning we concluded that the old oil cloth on the floor of our dining room must be renewed, and that the wainscotting across the south side, having become very much decayed, must be taken down and replaced by new material. We went to market and then to Dodson's, where we invested $36 in oil cloth. From thence I went to Linnvill's and purchased 72 feet of tongued and grooved flooring and came home. . . .

Friday I arose at 4½, went to my shop and sharpened two saws—then reduced the clothes-hanging platform about 8 inches, it having been made too high. As soon as breakfast was over we cleared the dining room and went to work in earnest. Took up the oil cloth which, across the North end of the room, was totally destroyed by dampness. Then tore down the wainscotting across the South side and found that the inside of the boards was like rotten punk—the painted front being a mere skin from which the back, black, damp, and decayed, peeled like— to use Byron's striking simile—a ripe fresh fig from its skin. The fixtures to which the boards were originally nailed were a mass of rottenness, and the wall was covered with mould and moisture. Having disposed of that mass of decay, I went at the floor, about two feet of which, across the North side, was laid anew five or six years ago. On taking it up, I found most of the material *then* used for flooring of so absorbent a character that it was completely water soaked so that the moisture, in the form of water, absolutely spurted up as I drove an iron wedge under to pry up the boards, while the cypress sleepers were as sound as they were on the day they were laid down, in June 1842—twenty-eight years ago! and so was the old N.C. [North Carolina] flooring over the rest of the room, which was laid down at the same time, proving that the material last used was unfit for the use it was put to. A few pieces of N.C. pine, side by side with the decayed pieces, were as sound and dry as possible.

I removed all of the two feet of floor across the North side of the room, and replaced it with the best stuff I could get, and finished that day's work at 3½, having worked 11 hours as hard as I ever worked in my life, and I left off as tired as, it seemed to me, any mortal could well be.

Yesterday morning I arose at 4½, went to my shop and dressed over with a smoothing plane and beaded all the stuff for my wainscot. Put up the inside strips to nail to, and then put up the stuff. Then made a new carpet strip and put [it] down around the hearth, and finished at 1½. . . .

Saturday, July 2. . . . Judge Hoar, who has just resigned the Attorney Generalship of the U.S.[,] called on us last evening to bid us good-by. How different has been his conduct toward me & mine from that of Gov. Boutwell. There was no special reason why Judge H. should treat us with marked attention; still he has done so ever since he came to Washington. There were strong reasons why Gov. B. should have shown us at least a small particle of kindness—he having been my brother's partner in business, and the *apparent* friend of my brother-in-law, Gov. Brown—but if he had been cased in ice, he could not have been colder towards us than he has. Judge Hoar has *a heart,* Gov. Boutwell was born with a lump of ice where his heart should have been, & never can feel for anybody, and is not a gentleman. If he ever should be President, God save the United States. . . .

Monday, July 4. Independence day has come again, and the resounding of guns, pistols, crackers, and all sorts of bedevilments composed of explosive material has been going on since daybreak.

My Colt's revolver, which was loaded by Harry French in August 1865 while I was off visiting, and has hung in our chamber ever since, untouched, required, as I thought, discharging; so, to add to the jubilee of the morning, I took it down to the back door and let it off. Every barrel went as readily as if it had been loaded yesterday, at which I was surprised. I must clean it and load it up again today, so as to be ready for burglars or any other unlawful intruders. . . .

Today "The oldest Inhabitants" celebrate by presenting a block of mar-

ble, properly inscribed, to the "Washington National Monument Society"
to be placed in the Monument, and I am to be orator of the day. . . .

Tuesday, July 5. It is 7 A.M.[,] thermometer 73, cloudy and cool.

Our celebration yesterday was a good one. Mrs. French and I left at
11 in a horse car. She got out at 4½ street to accompany any of the
Adams's to the grounds. I went on and found them there. She came soon
after. The oldest Inhabitants and the Washington Monument Society
turned out strong, and there was a very respectable audience present.
There was a stand erected for the Societies against the East face of the
monument and seats arranged for the audience in front. The stand and
the seats were well filled, and there was quite a crowd, in carriages and
on foot, beyond the seats. The full Marine Band occupied the rear of
the stand and discoursed such music as no other Band in these U.S. can
discourse. The block of marble to be presented was placed on skids
between the stand and the audience. . . . Mr. Goddard[1] of Georgetown
then read in the best possible style and manner (without any spread eagle
about it) the immortal "*Declaration.*" "The Orator of the Day" (that was
I) then stepped forward and *Orated* for about 25 minutes, and it may not
be improper, in this private journal, to say that his remarks were received
with much manifestation of pleasure, and he was congratulated by nearly
every member of the Society and numerous others on his successful
effort, as soon as he had concluded. . . .

At a little before 2 we took a car and came home. The Capitol grounds,
East, were literally crammed with our colored population, who had, I
believe, a gathering of the colored schools there. They were quiet and
orderly and seemed to be enjoying the day very much. Is there a living
soul who could envy them their pleasure and hilarity? My heart rejoiced
with them.

Arriving home we dined, and I was quite out of sorts all the afternoon
with an excruciating nervous pain, by spasms, in the left side of my left
foot. I have had it slightly, for a moment at a time, for months, but yesterday it was almost continuous for hours, and seemed to deprive me of
all my strength. Were it not that there is no soreness of the foot, and as
soon as the spasm of a single instant is gone, the foot is perfectly well, I
should think it was gout. Now, I think it is a derangement of a nerve.

1. M. R. Goddard, grocer.

Sunday, July 10. . . . Last evening Mrs. French and I went up to 17th
Street and visited the Parris's;[1] had a most pleasant call. "Sam" gave me

the best glass of whiskey I have drunken for a long-long while. *Mem.* Visit him often!

From the Parris's we went to "Demonet's" Ice cream saloon, on Pa. Av. bet. 18th & 19th Streets, and ate some superb ice cream—frozen as stiff "as a mitten." (I wonder where that figure of speech came from.) I know, by youthful experience, that a wet mitten, when frozen, is a very stiff thing; and I suppose *a cold* refusal on the part of a young lady to a lover, called "giving him the *mitten*," means *a frozen reply*! We ate our ice cream, took an Avenue car, and got home at 10:15'. I will not journalize any more today.

1. Samuel B. Parris, a clerk in the second comptroller's office.

Sunday, July 17. . . . We were all surprised—I may almost say shocked— at hearing on Tuesday of the death of Admiral John A. Dahlgren on the morning of that day. He died very suddenly. I have known him for years and esteemed him very highly. He was an honorable, honest, upright and brave man, and, *as I well know,* was highly esteemed by President Lincoln, who exemplified his appreciation of him by making him a Rear Admiral[,] somewhat, I believe, out of the ordinary course of promotion. . . .

Yesterday Mr. Henry D. Cooke—that prince of a man—gave to the "*Press* gang," an excursion down the Potomac on the Steamer *City of Alexandria.* I was one of the invited guests. There were, as Mr. Cooke told me, 115 present. We went down as far as Glymont. After taking a run up the Eastern Branch as far as the Navy Yard Bridge—passing the *shot-indented* iron "Monitors," moored in the stream, the iron blockade runner, *Virgin.,* long, narrow and sharp, as if she would cut through the water at a tremendous rate, and many other "naval relics" of the late war, and being interested with a panoramic view of "Uniontown," "Giesboro Point"—famous as the *horse* depot during the Rebellion—the "Navy Yard" and its *surroundings,* "The Insane Asylum" with its spacious and lovely grounds—we returned to the wharf and took on board a goodly quantity of *creature comforts,* which Mr. Cooke's provider had neglected to have at the wharf in season, and at 3 m. before 5 took our final departure for Glymont. We had a beautiful, pleasant, and most agreeable run down—everyone seeming happy. We arrived at Glymont at about sunset, and at 8 o'clock the company sat down to as elegant a dinner as need be. "The mirth and fun grew fast and furious," and after eating, drinking, toasting, speech making and singing, at a little past 10 the jolly company reembarked, & our good steamer poked her nose toward Washington. . . .

Saturday, July 23. It is 5½ P.M. I have just finished reading a book entitled *The Life of George Peabody,* by Phebe A. Hanaford.[1] A small volume of 308 pages. Just as if a book of such size could contain anything like a history of such a man as George Peabody! It is well enough as a book of reference as to some of his prominent charitable acts, but as a history of *his life,* it is about as unsatisfactory to me as it can well be. I had the pleasure of forming an acquaintance with George Peabody about 1822— it might have been a year or two earlier or later. It was while I was a student at Law in my father's office in Chester, N.H., and while I boarded at Reverend Joel R. Arnold's,[2] where Miss Judith Peabody,[3] who was then teaching school in Chester, also boarded. She was a beautiful and accomplished girl, and a great favorite not only of mine but of everyone who knew her. Her brother George, who was making a visit to his old home in Danvers, came to Chester to visit his sister, and I became acquainted with him and was very much pleased with him. . . .

    1. Phoebe A. C. Hanaford, *The Life of George Peabody* (1870).
    2. Joel R. Arnold (b. 1794) was Congregational minister in Chester, 1820–1830.
    3. Judith Peabody's brother George, then twenty-seven, was already partner in the firm of Riggs and Peabody, Baltimore, and on his way to wealth.

Sunday, July 31. It is 6 A.M. I am sick. Suffering with shortness of breath and pain in my breast. Under Doct. Ford's care. I can not exert myself at all now, and, unless I get better[,] must soon give up. This is a cool, pleasant morning. Have had splendid showers during the past week.

Judge Richardson came Wednesday evening, and now, in the absence of Secy. Boutwell, is acting Secy. of the Treasury.

Sarita and Fannie left for N.E. on their Summer vacation at 9 P.M. Friday.

Yesterday was the first cool day we have had for weeks. It was really reviving.

I feel better than when I began to write, but much oppressed.

Monday, August 8. I am sitting alone in my sick chamber, Mrs. French, who is devoted to me and seldom leaves my side, having gone down with Judge Richardson to dinner.

I have had a hard week of it, having been confined to this room and under the Doctor's care ever since I last wrote in this book, one week ago yesterday. My disease is congestion of the lungs, and at times I am almost suffocated[,] my breathing is so labored. My nights are dreadful, as I can sleep but little. This has been the best day I have had since I was first taken. My breathing has been easy and natural, and I have had some refreshing sleep.

We have had Doct. W. P. Johnston (my old family Physician) to consult with Doct. Ford. He was here yesterday and today and is to come again on Wednesday. They have placed me on a very spare diet & pronounce me better.

The weather has been excessively hot during the week during the daytime. The nights are tolerably cool.

Mrs. French has come up and says I must not write any more.

I obey.[1]

1. Marginalia by French's grandson, Amos Tuck French: Last Entry . . . The Major died August 12, 1870, 4 days later.

Epilogue

Benjamin Brown French's death was announced in a lengthy column in the Washington *Evening Star* of August 12, 1870, and the *New York Times* reported it on the front page of its issue of August 14. The *Evening Star* again devoted a full column on August 15 to the funeral, Masonic observances, and the procession to the burial site in the Congressional Cemetery. The whole long route of the procession had been "lined with spectators."

Beyond the generalized and formal mourning of his fellow citizens and Masonic brethren, however, were the special thoughts of some of those who knew him best. His half-brother, Henry Flagg French, wrote in his diary on August 13:

> My dear brother B. B. died the evening of the 11th at his home in Washington[.] 70 in Sept.—a good man—a good brother—the head of our clan—a man of perpetual youth—healthy, happy, simple hearted. It is well with him.[1]

Sarita Brady who had lived with the Frenches during Benjamin's last years, and whose liveliness and high spirits had meant so much to him, put her thoughts in a letter of August 15:

> Everything is over. The sunlight and warmth look into the rooms, more desolate in their confusion than they ever could be in order, and the day arouses us to the desolation of heart which no words can picture. . . . I cannot describe to you the house. The clock at the head of the stairs that he took so much care of, stopped a few hours after his death, and will probably never be touched again. The grass is tall in the garden, and the flowers are all dried and withered: Then the Library, where everything bears his imprint—his blotting paper, the thermometer that he will never look at again—his books and his Journal and his pens,—Oh Nannie, these dumb things are so eloquent.[2] . . .

625

1. Henry Flagg French, Diary, Aug. 13, 1870. Daniel Chester French Papers, Manuscript Division, Library of Congress.

2. Sarita Brady to Anne Rainsford French, Aug. 15, 1870, typescript copy. Benjamin Brown French Papers, Manuscript Division, Library of Congress.

Bibliography

In seeking to understand French and his world we have found help in a variety of places. For example, in identifying the names in the journal, we have used standard reference works such as the *Dictionary of American Biography, Appleton's Cyclopaedia of American Biography, The National Cyclopaedia of American Biography, The Biographical Directory of the American Congress, Register of All Officers and Agents of the United States Government, Register of the Department of State, The Records of the War of the Rebellion, Historical Register and Dictionary of the United States Army,* and *List of Officers of the Navy of the United States and of the Marine Corps.* We have also searched through registers, directories, gazetteers, atlases, and genealogies, as well as family, town, county, state, and regimental histories for New Hampshire, Washington, and points between. We have read obituaries and taken notes from gravestones. We have benefited greatly from the resources of the New Hampshire Historical Society and from those of the Manuscript, Geography and Map, Music, Rare Book, and Prints and Photographs divisions of the Library of Congress. The following is a brief list of other useful sources.

Auker, Ralph H. G. *History of the Scottish Rite Bodies in the District of Columbia.* Washington, D.C., 1970.

Bell, Charles H. *The Bench and Bar of New Hampshire.* Boston: Houghton Mifflin, 1893.

———. *History of the Town of Exeter, New Hampshire.* rev. ed. Exeter, N.H.: Heritage Books, 1979.

Boatner, Maxine T. *Voice of the Deaf.* Washington, D.C.: Public Affairs Press, 1959.

Brown, Joseph T. *Eulogy on the Life and Character of Benjamin Brown French.* Washington, D.C.: J. L. Pearson, 1870.

Bryan, Wilhelmus B. *A History of the National Capital.* 2 vols. New York: Macmillan, 1914, 1916.

Carter, Nathan F. *The Native Ministry of New Hampshire.* Concord, N.H.: Rumford Printing Co., 1906.

Chase, John Carroll. *History of Old Chester.* rev. ed. Derry, N.H.: Record Publishing Co., 1926.

Cresson, Margaret French. *Journey into Fame: The Life of Daniel Chester French.* Cambridge, Mass.: Harvard University Press, 1947.

Denslow, William R. *10,000 Famous Freemasons.* 4 vols. Trenton, Mo., 1957.

Documentary History of the Construction and Development of the United States Capitol Building and Grounds. Washington, D.C.: Government Printing Office, 1904.

Dyer, Frederick H. *A Compendium of the War of the Rebellion.* 3 vols. New York: Thomas Yoseloff, 1959.

Fairman, Charles E. *Art and Artists of the Capitol of the United States of America.* Washington, D.C.: Government Printing Office, 1927.

Foss, Gerald D. *Three Centuries of Freemasonry in New Hampshire.* Concord, N.H.: Grand Lodge of New Hampshire, 1972.

French, Amos Tuck, ed. *Exeter and Harvard Eighty Years Ago: Journals and Letters of F. O. French, '57.* Chester, N.H.: Privately printed, 1932.

————. *From the Diary and Correspondence of Benjamin Brown French.* New York: Privately printed, 1904.

French, Benjamin Brown. Papers, Manuscript Division, Library of Congress.

French, Daniel Chester. Papers, Manuscript Division, Library of Congress.

French Family Association. *Edward French of Salisbury, Mass.* 5th rev. ed. Sanford, Me.: Privately printed, 1986.

French, Mary. *Memories of a Sculptor's Wife.* Boston: Houghton Mifflin, 1928.

"Funeral of the Late Major B. B. French," *Washington Evening Star,* August 15, 1870.

Gobright, Lawrence A. *Recollections of Men and Things at Washington.* rev. ed. Philadelphia: Claxton, Remsen & Haffelfinger, 1869.

Green, Constance M. *Washington: Village and Capital, 1800–1878.* Princeton, N.J.: Princeton University Press, 1962.

Harper, Kenton. *History of the Grand Lodge and of Freemasonry in the District of Columbia.* Washington, D.C.: R. Beresford, 1911.

Klement, Frank L. "Benjamin B. French, the Lincolns, and the Dedication of the Soldiers' Cemetery at Gettysburg," *Historical New Hampshire,* 42(1987), 36–63.

"The Late Major B. B. French," *Washington Evening Star,* August 12, 1870.

Leech, Margaret. *Reveille in Washington, 1860–1865.* New York: Harper, 1941.

McDonough, John J. "The Journals of Benjamin Brown French," *The Quarterly Journal of the Library of Congress,* 28(1971), 287–289.

McGiffen, S. P. "A Temperate Course. The Correspondence of Benjamin and Henry French," *Historical New Hampshire,* 38(1983), 141–160.

Miers, Earl Schenck, editor-in-chief. *Lincoln Day By Day.* 3 vols. Washington, D.C.: Lincoln Sesquicentennial Commission, 1960.

Monkman, Betty Claire. "Benjamin Brown French. Commissioner of Public Buildings 1853–1855, 1861–1867," Master's thesis, George Washington University, 1980.

National Archives. Record Group 42. Records of the Office of Public Buildings and Grounds of the City of Washington and the District of Columbia. Letter Books, 1853–1855, 1861–1867.

Neely, Mark E., Jr. *The Abraham Lincoln Encyclopedia*. New York: McGraw-Hill, 1982.

Nichols, Roy F. *Franklin Pierce: Young Hickory of the Granite State*. rev. ed. Philadelphia: University of Pennsylvania Press, 1958.

Poore, Ben: Perley. *Perley's Reminiscences of Sixty Years in the National Metropolis*. 2 vols. Philadelphia: Hubbard Brothers, 1886.

Potter, Chandler E. *The Military History of the State of New Hampshire*. rev. ed. Baltimore: Genealogical Publishing Co., 1972.

Randall, James G. *Lincoln the President*. 4 vols. New York: Dodd, Mead, 1945–1955.

———. *The Civil War and Reconstruction*. New York: D. C. Heath, 1937.

Reid, James D. *The Telegraph in America*. Reprint. New York: Arno Press, 1974.

Seale, William. *The President's House: A History*. 2 vols. Washington, D.C.: White House Historical Association, 1986.

Scudder, Townsend. *Concord: American Town*. Boston: Little, Brown, 1947.

Turner, Justin G. and Linda Levitt, eds. *Mary Todd Lincoln, Her Life and Letters*. New York: Knopf, 1972.

Vinton, John Adams. *The Richardson Memorial*. Portland, Me.: B. Thurston, 1876.

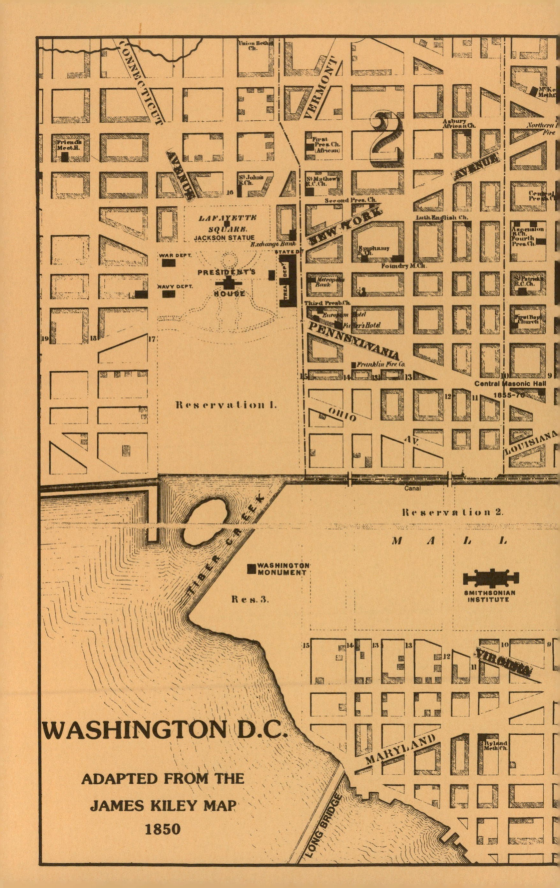

Calendar of the Complete
Journal of Benjamin Brown French

Manuscript Division, Library of Congress

CHAPTER ONE (1828–1835)

1828—Aug. 13, 21–23, 28–Sept. 1, 4, 6, 10, 15, 26, 28, Oct. 4–5, 18, 21, 28, Nov. 12, 23
1829—Jan. 5, 11, 13, 20, Feb. 9, 13, May 8, Sept. 18, Nov. 2
1830—May 8, June 7, July 7, Oct. 20, Nov. 15
1831—May 1, June 2–3, 7–8, 10, 15, 18, 21
1832—July 18, Aug. 14
1833—Mar. 3, Apr. 6, June 2, 4–6, 10, 17, July 20–21, 25, Dec. 21, 30
1834—Jan. 4, 14, Feb. 17, Mar. 21, May 23, July 24
1835—Sept. 10–12, 14, 16–20, 22–25, 27, 29, Oct. 1, 4, 5, 7–9, 11, 13–14, 16, 18, 21, 23–25, 27–28, 30–Nov. 2

CHAPTER TWO (1835–1841)

1835—Nov. 4–6, 8–10, 12, 15–17, 19, 21, 23–24, 26, 28, 30, Dec. 2–3, 5, 9, 15
1836—Mar. 20, Apr. 10, Nov. 27–29, Dec. 2, 5, 7, 9, 13, 15
1837—Jan. 1, 8, Apr. 2, May 1, Sept. 19, Dec. 26
1838—Jan. 7, 9, 22–23, 26, 29, Feb. 6, 17, 21, 28, Mar. 10, 12, 29, Apr. 4, 18, 26–28, May 7, 10–25, 27, 30, June 3, 6, 10–14, 17–23, 26, July 1, 8, 11–12, 14, 24, 28–29, 31, Aug. 3, 12, 15, 18, 20, 22, 24–26, Sept. 1, 3–4, 7–8, 12, 19, 22–23, 26, Oct. 1, 7, Nov. 4, Dec. 6, 9, 18, 29
1839—Jan. 1, Feb. 3, May 19, 21, 24, June 2, 9–10, 16, July 14, 29, Aug. 9, 14, 29, Sept. 17, 21, 29–30, Oct. 20
1840—Jan. 19, Feb. 3, June 19–20, 23, Aug. 3, 9, Sept. 6, 27, Oct. 1, 9, 14, 25, Nov. 10–11, 16, 20, Dec. 1, 18
1841—Jan. 3, Feb. 1, 7, 13

CHAPTER THREE (1841–1844)

1841—Mar. 6, 14, 28, Apr. 1, 4–7, 18, 25, May 16, 30, June 1, 6, 13, 27, July 4, 18, 25, Aug. 8, 12, 15, 23, 29, Sept. 1, 3–5, 9, 13–15, 24, 26, 28, Oct. 5, 7, 24, 31–Nov. 1, 6, 18–19, 24, 30–Dec. 1, 3, 12, 15, 29
1842—Jan. 10, 13, 22, Feb. 6, 25, 27, Mar. 6, 10, 13, 18, Apr. 10, May 1, July 24, 28, Aug. 12–13, 21, Sept. 4, 13, 24, Oct. 2, 21, Dec. 21

1843—Jan. 1, 6, 8, 10, 22, Mar. 4, Apr. 2, 9, 23, June 1, 11, 19–21, 23, 25,
     July 2–3, 5, 8, 12, 14, 16, 19, 30–31, Aug. 10, 12–13, 18, 20–21,
     Sept. 13, 16, Oct. 1, Nov. 18, 26, Dec. 18

1844—Jan. 9, Feb. 24, Mar. 3, Apr. 21, July 26, Aug. 24, Sept. 6, Oct. 20–21,
     23, 28, Dec. 5

CHAPTER FOUR (1845–1853)

1845—Apr. 19, May 18, June 16, 20, July 13, 15, 20–21, Aug. 24, Sept. 4–5,
     9–11, 14, Oct. 4, 19, Dec. 17

1846—Jan. 2, Feb. 15, Mar. 1, Apr. 21, 26, May 25–26, 28–29, June 1, 3, 8,
     July 4, Aug. 21, 23, Oct. 2–4, 11, Nov. 6, 17, Dec. 11

1847—Jan. 3, 10, Feb. 14, Apr. 11, June 24, Aug. 8, Sept. 4, 7, 19, Dec. 16

1848—Feb. 6, 11, 22, 24, 27, Mar. 2, Apr. 9, May 23, June 4, 25, July 30,
     Aug. 27

1849—Jan. 7, 21, Mar. 11, Sept. 11, Nov. 18, 27, Dec. 25, 30–31

1850—Jan. 1, 6, Mar. 3, Dec. 21

1851—Jan. 4–6, 16, Mar. 9, Apr. 6, June 1, 22, July 20, 25, 27, Sept. 4, 28,
     Nov. 23, Dec. 25

1852—Jan. 1, 3, 10, 25

1853—Jan. 2, 7, 16, 23, Feb. 6

CHAPTER FIVE (1853–1857)

1853—Mar. 27, Apr. 3, 10, 17, 24, May 29, July 31, Aug. 21

1854—Jan. 1, 4, 8, 15, 29, Feb. 10, 13, 26, Mar. 5, 13, Apr. 2, 30, May 7,
     July 4, 9, Aug. 8, 20, Sept. 3–4, 10, Dec. 24

1855—Jan. 1–2, 14, 21, 28, Feb. 4, 12, 18, Mar. 4, 13, 25, June 3, 7, 10, 12,
     24, July 1–2, 8, 15, 22, 29, Aug. 1–2, 5, 16, 19, 21, 25–26, 31, Sept. 2,
     11, 28, Oct. 2, Nov. 4, Dec. 10–11, 16

1856—Jan. 1–2, 13, 21, 26, Feb. 8–9, 17, 24, 27, Mar 2, 8, 29, Apr. 13,
     May 25, June 3, 6–7, 15, 22, July 21, Sept. 4–5, Nov. 4, 20, 23

1857—Jan. 2, 19, Feb. 1

CHAPTER SIX (1857–1861)

1857—Mar. 8, 19, Apr. 5, 25, May 4, June 9, 28, July 26, Aug. 6, Sept. 16–17,
     Oct. 5, 14, Dec. 6, 20, 27

1858—Jan. 2, 10, 17, 23–24, 31, Feb. 7, 15, 28, Mar. 1, 7–8, Apr. 11, 25,
     May 2, 9, June 13, 20, July 4, 12, 29–30, Aug. 1, 3–6, 17, 19, 23–25,
     28–29, Sept. 4–5, 7–8, 10, 13, 15, 19, 26, Oct. 3, 11, 17, Nov. 1, 8, 21,
     29, Dec. 12–13

1859—Jan. 1, 4–5, 27, Feb. 3, 11, 13, 25–26, 28, Mar. 11, Apr. 3, 11, 22, 24,
     May 15, 29, 31, July 10, Aug. 11, 14, 21, 29, Sept. 4, Oct. 9, Dec. 4, 13,
     23

1860—Jan. 1, 22, 29, Feb. 5, 9–10, 16, 18, Mar. 4, 18, Apr. 22–26, 28–29,

May 4, 6, 13, 20, 28, June 17, July 8, 15, 25, Aug. 3, 12, 17, 21, 26, 28,
Sept. 4, 6, 23, Oct. 2, 9–10, 21, Nov. 4, 11, 16, 27, Dec. 1, 9, 19, 25, 30
1861—Jan. 1, 9, 20, 24–25, 30, Feb. 3, 10, 12, 24, 26, Mar. 1–3

CHAPTER SEVEN (1861–1862)

1861—Mar. 6, 19, Apr. 5, 14, 19, 21, 23, 25, 28, 30, May 3–4, 6–10, 12, 14,
18–19, 21–26, May 28–June 7, 9, 11–12, 15, 19, 22, 26, 30, July 4, 7, 9,
11, 13, 17, 19–23, 26–30, Aug. 2–3, 8, 10–11, 17–18, 20, 22–23, 26,
29, 31, Sept. 4, 7–8, 12–15, 17, 22, 26, 28–29, Oct. 5, 8–9, 18, 27, 31,
Nov. 2–3, 6, 8, 10, 20, 23–24, 26, 28–29, Dec. 2, 6–8, 12, 16–18, 22–
23, 25–26
1862—Jan. 1, 8, 10, 12, 17, 19, 24, 28, Feb. 2, 8, 10, 15, 23, Mar. 2, 9–10, 16,
23, 29–30, Apr. 6, 11, 13, 20, 25, 27, 29–30, May 2, 4, 7–8, 10–11, 18,
21, 26–27, June 1, 8–9, 16, 22, 30, July 4, 7, 10, 12–16, 19, 21, 23, 28,
Aug. 3, 10, 17, 24, Sept. 4, 7, 13, 18, 25–26

CHAPTER EIGHT (1862–1865)

1862—Oct. 6, 10, 19, 26, 29, Nov. 2, 7, 9–10, 23, 25, Dec. 3, 8, 21, 26
1863—Jan. 2, 7, 11, 22, 31, Feb. 3, 8, 13, 15, 18, 22, 28, Mar. 3, 7, 15, 19, 22,
28, Apr. 1, 5, 12, 20, 26, 30, May 3, 6, 10, 17, 24, June 8–10, 12, 16,
18–19, 22, 26, July 5, 8, 10, 12, 17, 22, 26, 31, Aug. 2, 8, 14, 16, 23,
30, Sept. 2, 4, 7, 9, 13, 22, 27, Oct. 3, 18, 23, Nov. 2, 6–7, 14–15, 22–
23, 29, Dec. 2, 5, 7–9, 12–13, 17, 20, 25
1864—Jan. 1, 3, 10, 14, 17, 27–28, Feb. 2, 16–17, 21, 23, 25, 28, Mar. 5, 14,
20, 22–24, 27–28, 31, Apr. 6, 14, 17, 25, May 4, 6, 12, 14, 16, 22, 29–
30, June 6, 9, 11, 19, 26, 28–29, July 3–4, 10, 12, 17, 26, 31, Aug. 7,
14, 20–21, 28, Sept. 2, 4, 7, 9, 11, 18, 25, Oct. 2, 5, 7, 9–10, 16, 18, 21,
24, 26–27, 30–Nov. 1, 3, 9, 20, 24, 28, Dec. 7, 12, 15, 23, 25
1865—Jan. 1, 6–8, 12, 21–22, 24, 29, Feb. 3, 12, 15, 19, 21, 23–24, Mar. 2, 5–
6, 13, 20, 26, Apr. 1, 6, 15, 17, 30, May 6–7, 14, 21, 24, June 1, 4, 11,
18, 26, 29–30, July 2, 5, 7–9, 14, 17, 23, Aug. 6, 20, 27–29, 31,
Sept. 3–4, 9, 16, 18–22, 24, 27, 29, Oct. 1, 9, 16, 19, 21, 30–Nov. 2, 4,
9, 12–13, 17–19, 21, 26–27, 29, Dec. 3, 8, 13, 17, 20, 24–26, 28, 30–31

CHAPTER NINE (1866–1868)

1866—Jan. 1–2, 4–5, 7, 11–12, 14, 16, 18, 20, 24, 26, 29, Feb. 2–3, 7, 11, 13–
14, 16, 18, 21, 23, 26, Mar. 2, 11, 17, 19–20, 22, 24, 26, 28, 31,
Apr. 3–4, 13, 15, 21, 25, 30, May 2, 5–7, 11, 13, 16, 19, 24, 30, June 1,
3, 5, 10, 14, 21, 24, 27, July 2, 4, 7–8, 14, 17, 21–22, 26, Aug. 1–2, 5,
12, 19, 26, 29, Sept. 1, 3–4, 7, 9, 16–23, 25–26, 28–30, Oct. 1–5, 7, 9,
11, 14, 17, 19, 28, Nov. 2, 4–5, 9, 13, 23, 26, 29, Dec. 1, 7, 10, 16, 23,
25, 27, 30–31
1867—Jan. 2, 5, 9, 11, 13, 18, 23–25, 27, Feb. 1, 6, 9–10, 14, 17, 21–22, 24,
Mar. 3, 11, 13–14, 17, 23, 27–28, 30–31, Apr. 2, 9, 11, 14–16, 24, 28–

29, May 1, 5–6, 12, 19, 25–26, June 2–4, 15, 19, 21, July 4, 8, 10, 13–
14, 19–20, 25, Aug. 2, 5, 9–10, 12, 15, 19, 23, 25, 27, 29, Sept. 1, 3–4,
8–9, 13, 16, 23, 28, 30, Oct. 4, 10, 15, 17, 20, 27, 30, Nov. 3, 5, 10, 18,
21, 23, 28–29, Dec. 4–5, 8, 12, 18, 24–26, 29

1868—Jan. 1, 7, 9–10, 12, 16, 19–21, 25–26, 28–31, Feb. 1–3, 5, 7–11, 13–14,
16, 18, 20, 22–25, 27, 29, Mar. 1, 4–5, 8, 12, 15, 17, 22–23, 27–29, 31,
Apr. 1, 7, 12, 17, 19, 26, May 6–7, 11, 14, 16, 18, 24–27, 29–30

CHAPTER TEN (1868–1870)

1868—May 30–June 4, 6–7, 9–10, 12–13, 15, 17, 19, 22, 26–27, 30, July 2, 4,
6, 9, 11, 15, 17, 22, 25–27, 30, Aug. 1–2, 5, 7, 9, 12, 15–17, 19–23, 26,
29, Sept. 1, 3–6, 9, 24–29, Oct. 2, 4, 11, 13, 18, 26, 30–31, Nov. 8, 10,
13, 22, 27, Dec. 2–3, 6, 9, 12, 17, 22, 25

1869—Jan. 1–2, 6, 8–9, 16–Feb. 17, 20–21, 23–26, 28–Mar. 1, 3–6, 9–10, 13–
17, 20–21, 23, 27, 30, Apr. 1, 3, 5–6, 11–15, 19, 23, May 2, 6–7, 14,
19–20, 27, 30, June 3–4, 6, 9, 12, 16–17, 19–20, 22, 29, July 4, 6, 9,
11, 17–18, 25, 28, Aug. 1–2, 5–8, 12, 15–18, 21–22, 27, 29, 31,
Sept. 3–5, 9, 11–12, 14, 18–19, 22, 24, Oct. 2–3, 10, 17, 24, 31–Nov. 4,
7, 9, 13–15, 17–19, 21, 26–27, Dec. 5–10, 12, 14, 19, 21, 25–26, 28

1870—Jan. 1–2, 9, 12–13, 19, 21, 23, 27, 30, Feb. 3–4, 7, 11, 13, 17–18, 21,
23–24, 28–Mar. 1, 6, 13, 16, 20, 27, 29, Apr. 3, 10, 17, 24, 28, May 8,
14–15, 22, 29, June 5, 10, 14, 18, 20, 26, July 2, 4–5, 10, 17, 23–24,
31, Aug. 8

Index

Numbers set in bold-face type indicate pages where individuals are identified. The following abbreviation is used: BBF, Benjamin Brown French. Sub-entries are most often in chronological order.